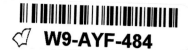

Highway A1A

Florida A&M University, Tallahassee
Florida Atlantic University, Boca Raton
Florida Gulf Coast University, Ft. Myers
Florida International University, Miami
Florida State University, Tallahassee
University of Central Florida, Orlando
University of Florida, Gainesville
University of North Florida, Jacksonville
University of South Florida, Tampa
University of West Florida, Pensacola

Herbert L. Hiller

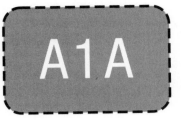

HIGHWAY A1A

FLORIDA AT THE EDGE

University Press of Florida
GAINESVILLE
TALLAHASSEE
TAMPA
BOCA RATON
PENSACOLA
ORLANDO
MIAMI
JACKSONVILLE
FT. MYERS

10 09 08 07 06 05 6 5 4 3 2 1

Library of Congress Cataloging-in-Publication Data
Hiller, Herbert L., 1931–
Highway A1A: Florida at the edge / Herbert L. Hiller.
p. cm.
ISBN 0-8130-2833-7 (acid-free paper)
1. Atlantic Coast (Fla.)—Description and travel. 2. Florida State Highway A1A (Fla.)—Description and travel. 3. Florida—Description and travel. 4. Atlantic Coast (Fla.)—History, Local. 5. Florida—History, Local. 6. Tourism—Florida. 7. Florida—Guidebooks. I. Title.
F317.A74H55 2005
917.5904'64—dc22 2005046522

The University Press of Florida is the scholarly publishing agency for the State University System of Florida, comprising Florida A&M University, Florida Atlantic University, Florida Gulf Coast University, Florida International University, Florida State University, University of Central Florida, University of Florida, University of North Florida, University of South Florida, and University of West Florida.

University Press of Florida
15 Northwest 15th Street
Gainesville, FL 32611-2079
http://www.upf.com

For Mary Lee, without whom nothing happens

CONTENTS

PREFACE

This book is divided into chapters that correspond to the thirteen east coast counties of Florida traversed by State Highway A1A. It is divided into two parts: the main narrative section followed by detailed lists that might be useful to travelers.

The book is a public affairs review that examines tourism, development, and the emergence of year-round residential Florida downtowns. Tourism and development have shaped Florida for more than a century. The book argues that the emergence of year-round Florida downtowns marks a new phenomenon that indicates the growing influence of nature, heritage, and culture on tourism and development and suggests that especially tourism could become a less perverse influence on Florida in the years to come than in years gone by. Development, following tourism downtown, might also become less perverse.

The book is also a guidebook. In the first instance, it's meant to introduce travelers, whether outsiders or Floridians moving around within their own state, to what the place is about. County by county, I have tried to show how tourism and development drive the way people live and reveal the dynamics of place. Throughout, I have attempted to answer the questions for travelers: "When I'm here, where am I? What's going on? What makes the place different?" This information almost invariably gets left out of conventional guidebooks or gets quickly brushed over. Disproportionate attention gets paid to sights and sites and to where to eat, sleep, and shop. This book reverses that pattern. The listings are subordinate to the narrative. In almost all cases, I have personally experienced my choices in the listings; occasionally I am following the recommendations of others I trust.

Florida has long been my beat. I first traveled to the state with my parents in 1938. I returned to stay in 1958. For thirty-seven years I lived in different parts of metropolitan Miami. Since 1994, my home has been the rural northeast. I have traveled the state some 30,000 miles by bicycle and more conventionally 20,000 miles a year by car, bus, train, boat, and plane. Like almost anyone conscious about where they live in Florida, I have a love-hate relationship with the state. I work that out by seeking to influence change. Over the years, I have initiated the state bicycling movement and the state bed-and-breakfast movement, and I have played a role in state trails. By my writing and in other ways, I have tried to influence tourism to respond better to conservation and preservation. This book stems from these various efforts.

So many people have helped me in researching the book that I dare not mention any for the risk of leaving so many others unmentioned. Let me simply acknowledge that without the assistance of these many, the book could never have been done. I trust that their assistance combined with my own efforts will reward those who take the time to read what follows.

INTRODUCTION

For the first time since tourism became vital to Florida's economy 130 years ago, state promoters in 2005 launched an initiative that aligns the selling of Florida to tourists with environmental policy, even if adventitiously. For the first time, this engages tourism in rethinking Florida's future. The state promotional board, known as Visit Florida, began a campaign to attract visitors to Florida's cities where, also for the first time, year-round residential downtowns with their compelling cultural arts and entertainments have been fashioning a newly sophisticated urban American tropic.

Though most of Florida's big cities were already in place by the turn of the twentieth century, they remained seasonal, busy at the onset of winter that drove northerners down, then closing up when hot summer reared. After World War II, when air conditioning became widespread, government incentives favored cars and suburbs instead of mass transit and downtown. Populations that might have hastened city growth settled elsewhere, leaving the cities unfulfilled.

One result was the environmental degradation of inland Florida with its collateral impacts on coastal resources. Most of Florida is a low-lying, narrow peninsula, but even its puny rivers discharge polluting runoff that affects coastal life in every way. Floridians depend on these rivers and the aquifer beneath the land's porous subsurface for drinking water. Yet the suburbs trouble the supply by drainage that prepares land for housing and by paving over critical water recharge areas. Wells sour from the intrusion of salt water sucked inland as rising demand pumps out the retreat of fresh. Ironically, to protect homeowners now living in floodplains, highly engineered flood-control systems discharge precipitous bursts of freshwater into brackish estuaries just often enough to overwhelm corals and fisheries and limit their recovery.

The consequence is a complex and contradictory condition that Florida policy has never adequately addressed because, as we shall see, the economy sustained by tourism has relied from the outset on land sales to these visitors and others they influence. One after another, every state administration has aggressively promoted the tourism–land sale connection, shaping an unsustainable economy by limitless in-migration at the expense of resource protection. A swollen commitment to property rights further worsens the balance. Left to operate only at the fringe of the problem, land planners have been ineffective at controlling the rush away from the cities, only weakly able to redress the environmental fallout that shortsighted policy generates. This hasn't kept planners from imagining that if the cities could only get a handle on crime and if they could only acquire fresh infusions of capital, the cities could bloom with urban culture and compete with the suburbs, diminishing their prepossession and at last strengthening a commitment to conserve and protect.

Nevertheless, signs of turnaround mounted by the turn of the twenty-first century. Factors that couldn't easily have been modeled—economic, social, global, artistic, intellectual—created a push-me-pull-you force that began redirecting where Floridians chose to live. In one important shift, government began awarding incentives for people to return to the coasts, where Florida's big cities first formed. The gospel prevailed that increased densities allowed local governments to provide services more affordably, while downtown reinvestment yielded higher property tax returns. Respected developers began shifting their investments downtown as they measured trends that showed the driving force of Florida's population growth had diversified from a mainstream of well-off northerners retiring to the suburbs to newly include wealthy Latins and Europeans, who preferred city life. Eastward Ho! became the rallying cry for renewing Florida's Atlantic coast. City streets that had exploded with race riots and the shootouts of cocaine cowboys two generations before had passed through the mellowing life-as-art stage of *Miami Vice*, emerging less scary and cloaked in edgy cachet. Urban forms in music and dance, in building design, in landscaping, in mounting credibility for the "new urbanism," and in sidewalk dining as its own new social form all remodeled the future that became synonymous with downtown.

Even as sprawl continued to out-distance Florida's best efforts at containment—developers everywhere still hinge gates around suburbs in the retro ghettos of retirement escape—the young, the gay, and party-prone by their energy and their command of hip media began turning the national debate over sprawl versus downtown into a generational no-brainer. Disney's new urbanist project at Celebration and Robert Davis's earlier trend-setting Seaside in the Panhandle showed more in common with the sexy, harlequin style driving the revival of Florida downtowns than their buttoned-down planners might care to acknowledge.

The pull of Florida's east coast playgrounds has become more than their promise of urban style. It's urban style plus the beach. There's nothing else like this in mainland America. Where else can you throw off the business suit and jog to the beach, returning refreshed to restaurant rows and jazz clubs along landscaped boulevards with their leisure parks? Rich in the mix also is almost effortless access to nature, whether to reefs where the water deepens beyond the beach, to the Everglades and marshes of the upper St. Johns River just inland from the coast, or to myriad less celebrated sites. This urban scene that flared without precedent in South Beach quickly followed all the way up coastal Highway A1A to Jacksonville and crossed the peninsula, seizing command in St. Petersburg, Sarasota, and Fort Myers on the Gulf coast and along the way arousing sleepy Orlando, earlier put to rest by theme parks, which themselves, albeit neutering the bacchanal edge of South Beach, adapted its look to their own pseudo downtowns. Now newly into the urban mix have poured empty-nest suburbanites who, first drawn by the arts, entertainment, and shopping, have returned for the lifestyle to stay.

How this shift has played out is largely what this book is about. It's the somewhat optimistic story about how tourism may be realigning itself away from the great anti-city dynamic of 130 years toward something more hopeful. At least tourism shows the potential for something like this. Yet anyone who pays attention knows that it's way late in the cycle of Florida's degradation. Even as you want to believe, you have to wonder whether tourism really can help advance green values taking hold. If it can, it will be by becoming the voice and image of big-city Florida, influencing media to think less about promoting the burbs. Developers will follow tourism as they always have and, at least the farthest-thinking among them, will add to their downtown portfolios. For tourism, connecting with these trends has become its own no-brainer. Visit Florida sees that conservation, culture, and the arts have taken hold. Why ignore this any longer? There's more to it.

Also significant among the trends, small towns are reviving by positioning themselves as hubs for Florida's newly acquired vast conservation tracts. Trails are lengthening and beginning to connect cities to towns, affording city dwellers, as well as suburbanites and tourists, new ways to enjoy lifestyles that combine conservation and fitness. You can love city life, but you can also get out. Visit Florida calls its new initiative "Downtowns and Small Towns," positioning the move as an extension of a program launched earlier in the new century called "Culturally Florida," which for the first time drew attention to the range of cultural facilities that had developed largely unnoticed in the brainless phase of promotion that for decades had characterized the state. As part of this awakening, Visit Florida posted a new website that at last made it easy for Sunshine State travelers to find out about "the other Florida"—about outdoors Florida and the state's historical and cultural gifts.

Log on to Florida's official travel website and you can learn about the state's 160 state parks—the system in 1999 named the nation's best by professional park peers around America. You can learn about the state's 1,000-mile Florida National Scenic Trail, about its unmatched Florida Reef, its animal rescue sites, its aquariums, aquatic preserves, bat caves and bat tower, birding festivals and birding trail, carillon recitals, environmental education centers, equestrian and paddling outfitters, ethnic corridors, folklife center, forts, halls of fame, literary shrines, museums, national forests, national parks, National Register districts, national wildlife refuges, national seashores, performing arts centers, planetariums, rail-trails, scenic roads, science centers, springs, street festivals, tropical gardens, waterfalls, wild and scenic rivers, zoos.

These riches have helped make Florida, long the world's playground, home to 18 million people. For better—not for worse—they have overcome the bewitchments of Paradise to make their places real for themselves. From the Tennessee Williams Theater and the White Heron National Wildlife Refuge in the Florida Keys across almost 800 miles to Pensacola's doll house–like Spanish Quarter in the far western Panhandle, where that city's arts council and the Gulf Islands National Seashore command national respect, the state is richly and alternatively displayed, more colorfully than its sunsets, more diverse than its beaches and theme parks, more universally alluring than at any time since Florida began attracting visitors.

This push to attract visitors to the cerebral and soulful side of Florida tracks where the market has been trending for decades, even as tourism's historic embrace of development has left Florida still gripped by anti-environmental policy. We have to go back before these trends to evaluate the changing face of Florida and Florida tourism. Even though the Florida of our time begins in 1880 after Reconstruction, it's important to quickly review how Florida before 1880 found itself broke, barely unified, and underpopulated.

Sources of Florida Exploitation

Until 1821, when Florida became U.S. territory, only meager development had taken place. Florida in Spanish times (and during the British interregnum of 1763–83) had been East Florida and West Florida, two distinct territories divided by the Apalachicola River. Before 1821, the Panhandle extended all the way west to the Mississippi River, with its administrative seat in Pensacola. To the east lay the northern peninsula with its seat at St. Augustine, founded in 1565 and America's oldest permanent city. Between lay a trace of Spanish missions tenuously linked by barely improved Indian trail.

Spain began colonizing Florida in 1513 when Ponce de Leon arrived as the first of a band of explorer-warriors who began stripping the land from native tribes by battle, bribe, enslavement, miscegenation, and by the capture of souls and transfer of communicable disease. But neither gold nor silver materialized in Florida, and so *La Florida* remained an outpost, barely settled inland of the coasts. St. Augustine became important as a military post mainly to fight off British attacks on treasure ships heavy with booty from Peru and

Mexico propelled swiftly northward up the Straits of Florida toward the mother country.

Spain built no cities in Florida, imparted no glory. Far removed from the plenipotentiary capitals of Lima and Mexico City, Florida remained a daub and wattle frontier. Florida was a burden, a cross to bear. Its value lay ulterior to the place itself. Missionaries, in league with the military, were meant to bind Indians to the Spanish cause and so prevent their alliance with English colonists to the north that might—and often did— attack by way of land.

Below its missionary trace, Florida lay largely underwater. The land formed in vast shallow pools among jungle hammocks, where majestic waterbirds flew thickly obscuring the sun, where bear and panther roamed equal in the contest with bow-and-arrow hunters, and gators surveyed wetlands as lords of prey. Where the land gained some little elevation, longleaf pine forests reached beyond horizons. Summer rains replenished wetlands, deepening pools and trickling rivulets into streams that became the myriad runt rivers that everywhere drained the interior and made canoes indispensable for getting around.

It was a place, as seen during travels by the eighteenth-century botanist William Bartram, where "all appeared wild and savage; yet in that uncultivated state it possessed an almost inexpressible air of grandeur."

The peninsula's gaudy elevations, reaching to 298–foot-high Iron Mountain in Lake County, resulted from epic cycles of ebb and flow during the Ice Age. When the continent froze, the icy littoral extended, the long peninsula spread. When glaciers receded, the sea slowly reclaimed the land, immersing all but the highest of the collected moraine that became a stationary ark of species protected atop a north-south ridge. Today that ridge remains clearly visible through Highlands, Polk, and Lake counties, containing biota unmatched in the American Southeast and constituting the first national wildlife refuge chiefly devoted to plants (though reduced by development to only 10 percent of its original mass).

Notably, Calusas, Tequestas, and Timucuans lived from the bounty of the sea, while Apalachees and tribes elsewhere inland relied more on farming and hunting. Spain refused to farm, co-opting the natives while corrupting their civilization.

Soon after being ousted from South America by revolution, Spain gave up Florida. American settlers poured in, hot on the tracks of Creeks from Alabama and Georgia already once displaced by settler predations. General Andrew Jackson's success against these Creeks—newly named Seminoles and intermingled with runaway slaves—opened northern Florida to plantation economies, the first railroads, and American control of commerce. The American urge to control unhampered by accommodation or the niceties of treaty provoked a series of settler wars against the Indians that were finally resolved only in the mid-1850s after the longest period of conflict in American history. Attempts at settling the frontier peninsula south of the ancient Spanish realm largely halted until after the Civil War and the decade and a half of Reconstruction.

At last by 1880, with the close of Reconstruction and with the election of Governor William D. Bloxham, began the moves that would transform Florida from beguiling wasteland into a modern domain. It was a time when enterprise and technology would ditch a canal across the sands of Egypt, light the world's cities with electricity, speed commercial transactions by automating cash registers, and, in Florida, produce an automatic ice-making machine. The instruments of Florida's transformation would be the dredge and the railroad; a later addition would be air conditioning, which evolved from that Apalachicola icemaker.

Essentially the task in Florida was to get rid of the water. Flooded land was the chief resource signed over on the last day of his presidency by John Tyler following Florida statehood in 1845. But when peace overcame Civil War, that land was encumbered by Florida's unpaid debts. Before the land could be drained and developed, Florida had to pay off its bonded railroad obligations incurred just prior to what most Floridians called the War between the States.

Florida engaged a Philadelphia industrialist, Hamilton Disston, for the task. Disston agreed to pay $1 million for 4 million acres and otherwise accept as compensation half of all the acreage he would drain. Was 25 cents an acre a ridiculous bargain? Of course it was! Even 120 years ago, bondholders knew it and complained. But at the time the land as it lay was worthless. Spain never could make anything of it. In time America would. Florida would realize the cash for redeeming its bonds. Disston would develop his land. Property values would rise with corresponding revenues.

And so the dredges cranked up, channelizing the vast interior and forming land bridges that connected rivers and lakes in a transportation system that linked the St. Johns River in the north to the Caloosahatchee in the south. Disston's dredges gave rise to modern Fort Myers and St. Petersburg, to Kissimmee and St. Cloud, and ushered in the rebirth of Florida's sugar economy wasted during the Indian wars.

Disston's legacy had still greater impact in how it shaped the pattern of profligate grants to outsiders who would transform Florida.

That pattern achieved pinnacle success with Florida's turn-of-the-last-century railroaders but persists today in value dispensed by the wink and blind eye turned to transgressions against land management scruples that would otherwise raise the cost of exploitation. In Florida, the agents of development would become lords of the realm. Not only railroads would abet their reign. Even more so would tourism, outlasting the railroads and burrowing like a tick deep into the groin of Florida culture. As railroads tracked the way for tourism, so tourism would become the handmaiden of development and the auspice of retirement, the tripartite regime that would grow unrivaled in its political grip over Florida. Henry Morrison Flagler came to Florida the same as Disston, the same as Edison, the same as countless millions of others who first vacationed here and then returned to live, either seasonally or, for much of the twentieth century, to enjoy their last air-conditioned years. Flagler patterned the sequence into consummate business form.

He first arrived in 1878 while sharing the top echelon with John D. Rockefeller at Standard Oil. He came to succor an ailing wife in Jacksonville, then in 1883–84 wintered with his second wife in Jacksonville and St. Augustine. He found a realm of unimagined winter attraction and unequaled investment opportunity but unserved by civilized standards of hospitality.

And so it fell to Flagler to build the railroad that would sweep away the rabble settlements sparsely strung along east coast Florida and everywhere he touched transform wilderness into fabled resorts. Most impressively, in St. Augustine, Ormond Beach, Palm Beach, Miami, and Key West he dreamed up greatly expanded monumental hotels served by his railroad that became the outposts of conquest that Spain across more than three centuries never realized.

Florida's political directorate had cast the die with Disston that would endow Flagler and his fellow railroaders across the length and breadth of the state with gifts no mere Disney, Huizenga, or less famous entertainment and sports moguls could equal a century later. For laying track, Flagler and his cohort received every alternate mile of land to either side of rail bed often to a distance of more than the mile squared. For Flagler alone, the largesse amounted to more than 2 million acres. So in the name of development was the pattern of giveaway enshrined in Florida policy. Flagler used his railroad to bring the big spenders who bought rooms in his hotels. Through his publicity machine, the world learned of investment opportunity that Flagler satisfied by selling land. The farmers and town-builders that followed southward shipped their supplies and carried their families to Florida on Flagler's trains. They shipped their produce back north the same way. Florida with its pattern of development was getting up steam.

"With One Superb Gesture"

By the 1920s, Florida enjoyed unprecedented boom. Its sources of prosperity were many: wealth unleashed by war, tribute from the American imperium, liberation achieved from Victorian constraints, strategic skills honed by defying Prohibition, mass-produced cars ready to roll down nation-spanning highways. The stuffy resorts of Flagler were giving way to airy realms of fantasy designed first in Palm Beach and then Boca Raton by the libertine Addison Mizner. Comparable liberties in style saw the raking of northern newspapers with the first systematic assaults of resort-world press agentry.

The possibility of escaping winter cold in a realm of bathing beauties stirred enormous appeal. Visitors poured down on lengthening railroads and in their newly affordable cars along the highways that became U.S. 1 and coastal A1A. The millions of drained acres (with plenty millions more still underwater) lay waiting for the spark to ignite get-rich-quick dreaming.

Florida was ready to exploit the moment. Florida, which only a few years before had changed its divorce laws specifically to gratify Flagler's libido, now began a frenzied rush to indulge the intemperance of all America. Florida turned itself into the state of dreams when, in the twenties, it gave constitutional sanction to the connection between tourists, their fantasies, and land sales.

As reported by T. H. Weigall in *Boom in Paradise,* swept away by twenties euphoria, "the state legislature, in abolishing with one superb gesture the state income and inheritance taxes and in abandoning any attempt whatever to enforce the [P]rohibition and anti-gambling laws, joined in the chorus and definitely adopted the policy of making the wealthy and pleasure-seeking visitor its primary consideration, and practically its only one."

An early tax exemption of $500 for personal property was followed by a $25,000 homestead exemption. That gift eventually induced legions of retired newcomers in doublewides, free of property tax yet with full claim on government services—fuller claims when tornadoes and hurricanes reduced their tax-free shelters to flinders. The Mob checked into Miami Beach hotels, brazenly running Miami charity drives, while the Ashley Gang rained terror along the coast to the north, the Ma Barker Gang holed up in North Central Florida, and corrupt sheriffs and the KKK set dubious standards for malfeasance and racism that much of the state would supersede in measure and notoriety through the rest of the century.

When the boom collapsed and America soon thereafter plunged into Depression, tourism helped Florida toward recovery.

Government financed the replacement of Flagler's Overseas Extension to Key West, blown away by a 1935 hurricane, with a motor highway and successfully promoted Key West as an artists' colony. Grand hotels like the Don CeSar in Pass-a-Grille were offering rooms with meals at $30 for the week while more thrifty visitors motored down newly paved roads. "Tin can tourists," they were called, in their precursor RVs, arriving, as critics complained, with a $20 bill and the shirt on their backs and changing neither during their winter stays. New stadiums hosted baseball spring training, the Roosevelt administration financed construction of Florida's first state parks, and *The WPA Guide to Florida* in 1939 noted "a Manhattanish touch to the gleaming white and buff skyscrapers" of recovering Miami.

By midcentury, wartime prosperity had Florida booming again, and land hucksters were promoting free Florida trips to former GIs first dazzled while training along beaches in the Florida sun and now ready to begin living their lives in the near-tropics they had imagined. They sat through obligatory sales pitches, often buying lots sold by hucksters situated miles from anywhere. True scam artists sold land still underwater. State regulators looked the other way.

In the 1960s, Florida lawmakers, themselves dazzled by the land-boom success of Long Island's Levittown and tract developments elsewhere, authorized unprecedented political and economic control for Walt Disney over his mid-Florida domain after the master showman explicitly linked tourism with plans for moving people down—gusher flows of tourists tied to an "experimental prototypical community of tomorrow" that, according to one report, would "dump 50,000 tourists a day into this community along with 50,000 new jobs and build 40,000 new homes."

Sanctioned Ruin

Meanwhile, in the effort to lure every visitor with Florida's accessible beauty, the natural systems that underlay that beauty were everywhere turned into the currency of trinkets and schlock. As metaphor for the half millennium of ignorance that would follow to our own time, Columbus made his epic New World voyage of 1492 unaccompanied by any man of science among his crews. Spain in Florida would treat the land as simply not worth knowing about. America would know more but behave with scarcely greater enlightenment. Under American suzerainty, there followed the shooting out of wildlife by "sportsmen" from the decks of narrow river boats, the decimation of egrets by plume hunters to exploit the millinery trade, the dredging and filling of the landscape everywhere.

In Miami, Flagler laid sewer pipes that emptied their untreated effluent into the once-pristine Miami River, the same as he filled the openings between islands while extending his rail line to Key West, disturbing the cleansing flow of waters from Florida Bay across the Florida Reef—the same as Flagler princelings of our own time have poured into the Keys, extending pipes from their toilets into the porous foundation of their lifestyles and so turning their waterfronts into stagnant scum and complaining angrily about affronts to their almighty property rights and the unfair limits to the rewards of their cupidity.

Across the state in St. Petersburg, early lauded by a medical practitioner as Florida's unique "health city," the great fishery of Boca Ciega Bay was turned into a cesspool by unregulated development, its shellfish beds wiped out, its once superabundant catches of food fish reduced to the fewest pitiful strikes. Blind eyes were turned to chemical spills, and runoff overloaded with nutrients degraded Lake Apopka—once the second-largest lake in Florida and a legendary fishing hole of crystalline waters—to a pea-green soup of algal scum, its shores filled with pesticide-laden farms, its fish camps by the dozen bankrupted.

On Key Marco, the site of stunning archaeological finds at the turn of the last century, developers in the mid-twentieth monstrously scraped the entire island bare in Florida's environmental crime of the century. All across South Florida the Everglades was doubly dis-served by the plumbing system that delivered flood control to coastal cities encroaching upon the great marsh that flood control left high and dry and open to calamitous fires.

Repeating an unforgivable retreat from enlightened prospect decades ago when the Florida Keys were dropped from the plan to create Everglades National Park and so sacrificed to ravaging development, in our own time sugar plantations that thwart the flow of water crucial to restoring the Everglades have been accorded imperial prepotency. As a consequence, despite massive billions now to be raised for Everglades restoration, the best hopes for a floodway through sugar lands have already been given up. Meanwhile, the Everglades will never amount to more than half its original size, while its wildlife has diminished by more than 90 percent.

Waters that would naturally flow in the "river of grass" south from Lake Okeechobee across today's barrier sugar plantations instead pile up behind the high flood-control dike surrounding the big lake. Whenever their volume threatens the fabric of the great circumferential wall, the waters are released instead in catastrophic flood down the St. Lucie and the Caloosahatchee rivers, which, as already acknowledged, spike brackish estuaries with intolerable bursts of freshwater that devastate marine life and the businesses that depend on its abundance.

Dairies relocated from the north shore of Lake Okeechobee to relieve the moribund lake of their unacceptably high nutrient discharge have relocated to the Suwannee River basin, where that famed stream and its valley's legendary springs newly show alarming rise in phosphorous, precursor to cloudy waters and stifling algae blooms.

In Florida's Big Bend—ironically, a region pitched as the "Nature Coast"—the problem of the Fenholloway River, vastly degraded by pulp mill waste, was neatly solved by classifying that stream as an "industrial river." End of problem.

South along that coast, the springs of Crystal River and Homosassa, famed as winter habitat for Florida manatees, suffer algal turbidity as newcomers in their retirement subdivisions refuse to tax themselves for sewer hook-ups, sacrificing public welfare (and tourism) for maintaining lifestyles still ahead of the curve of trouble because wastewater, like all water, runs downhill.

Urban Pinellas County has so degraded its own environment that, decades ago, its wells were wasted by saltwater intrusion. To maintain its real estate boom, Pinellas acquired wells in Pasco County neighboring to the north, sucking portions of that county dry so that residents there, who believed they had bought lakefront property, instead found drained trash pits outside their doors, and sand instead of water spurting from hoses and showers. Nearby, north of Tampa, a prominent landowner who may well have usurped public authority by closing recreational access to the spring that supplies the headwaters of the Hillsborough River, seeks to divert up to a quarter of its flow to benefit the bottling operations of Perrier (and himself).

Sarasota, to fuel its growth, is draining water from the Peace River, which threatens the saline balance of the vast Charlotte Harbor Estuary, while inland DeSoto and Hardee counties, long left behind in Florida's prosperity gush, invite the violation of their countryside by phosphate mining that no one doubts will worsen the water quality of the Peace River even as its flows diminish.

Everywhere in Florida the public realm has been diminished for private gain. Classically, in the beautiful Harris Chain of Lakes, famed for its bass fishing, shortsighted newcomers diminish Florida's Edenic state to the confines of their private lots. Along the still-picturesque shores of Lake County, citizens voice outrage over ordinances proposed to restrict the clearing of lakefront bush from their properties. That bush serves as the surest way to trap and filter pollutants from entering the lakes. Meanwhile, sport fishing has collapsed and the waters foul with untreated runoff. County administrators call for federal and state dollars to ease the woes of pollution caused by subdivision roads that they permit to proliferate without limits. Estimates to cure the problem run to $100 million. Nimby and chutzpah joined.

Floridians, who might reasonably expect government to undo the despoliation, often find government the culprit. In 1999, antiquated pipes in St. Lucie County, burst by pressures from successive hurricanes, spilled 7.1 million gallons of sewage into the Indian River Lagoon, decimating one of the most fecund inland fisheries in America. A spokesman for the utilities authority declared the damage amounted to no more than "spitting in the ocean."

In Collier County, voters urge better environmental safeguards while county commissioners endlessly permit more golf courses that inundate waterways with fertilizer runoff. A charter boat captain reports that the water is "a lot browner than it used to be. It's not as clear; there's more foam and slime on the top than there used to be." Early in 2001, soon after two county commissioners were indicted on palsy-walsy corruption with a major developer (himself indicted), the sewer system bearing the load of Collier's most intense development blew its capacity, spilling raw sewage into waterways and resulting—in a situation that not even Florida's flaccid Department of Environmental Protection could ignore—in a de facto moratorium (the dreaded "M" word) on new so-called "wet" sewer hook-ups. In this CEO retirement paradise—among a population of a quarter million with a median income of more than $65,000 (Florida's highest), though only 40 percent of its residents earn a weekly paycheck—the excrement had hit the flabellum.

In Key West, the new century arrived with beaches closed by pollution and a growing popular Keys-wide rebellion against government's relentless push for more tourists. Residents demand that promotional dollars be used instead to repair the damage caused by 3 million visitors a year in a fragile island chain inhabited by only some 80,000 permanent dwellers. Already a virtual moratorium on commercial construction is in place. Native "Conchs," outpriced in their homes, have exiled themselves to the far reaches of Ocala. Against county government's wish, visitors driving down could find a two- to three-dollar toll imposed by the state just to cross the Overseas Highway as one way to fund critical habitat restoration.

Elsewhere, the state permits cement factories close by still-pristine rivers. It's quick to authorize cleanup of toxic creeks by rerouting outfalls into larger rivers in an approach to environmental protection known as "solution to pollution by dilution." In 1999, the state's feckless environmental protection agency sought to satisfy a federal call for scheduling the cleansing of dozens of environmentally substandard waterways by "discovering" that half its noncompliant list had been mistakenly categorized. And although Florida's coast provides the essential beach resource for Florida's dominant economic sector, despite more than two hundred occasions when beaches have had to be closed or posted because of contamination since 1998, the state has yet to propose a monitoring standard.

Not a Community but a Crowd

It is the curse of Florida that no binding myth defines what it means to be Floridian. Once, long ago, the state's meager population was unified by the manifest destiny land grab from Native Americans whom they viewed as savages. But in the century and a half since, Florida has become overwhelmingly populated by newcomers. They neither know Florida history nor have they lived here long enough to care. Increasing numbers are recruited from out of state for tourism jobs that pay six and seven dollars an hour—what David R. Colburn, director of the Askew Institute at the University of Florida, calls "dead-end jobs. . . crucial to this industry [but] not conducive to the long-term economic prosperity of the state's citizens."

Ever more transplants, as we all know, come not to begin careers but to collect their retirement reward for careers achieved elsewhere. Florida's fastest-growing population cohort is sixty-five years of age and older, forecast to constitute a quarter of the state's population within twenty-five years. According to *Florida Trend*, newcomers will make up at least half this rank and, in the words of a respected state observer, will constitute “an enormous burden on Florida.” In Collier County, one of the hubs of fast-growing Southwest Florida, more than half the population has lived there less than a decade, and more than two-thirds of all have come from outside the state.

Along with the aged has come a massive influx of Latinos concentrated in the lower peninsula. Already 16 percent of the population, by 2025 their numbers are forecast to reach almost one in four. Most arrive poor and eager to get ahead, the same as Florida’s yeoman migrants from the North a century ago for whom conservation in the land of opportunity constituted the antithesis of their purpose. Florida, as former lieutenant governor Buddy MacKay says, isn’t a community. It’s a crowd.

And yet, despite the worst forecasts—likely because of them—some combination of sentiment, self-interest, and civic awareness also combines to make a difference. How else to explain the great constituency that mounts in favor of conservation?

A Will to Redeem

Perhaps a century of gain corresponding to the century of loss can be measured between founding of the Florida Audubon Society in 1900 and passage in 1999 of the act known as Florida Forever. Florida Forever extends into 2010 Florida’s landmark conservation policy that, in 1990 under the title Preservation 2000, began earmarking $300 million a year for buying up the state’s most critically endangered conservation lands.

In the bracketed century, a conservation policy early began taking hold. In 1903, President Theodore Roosevelt designated America’s first national wildlife refuge at Pelican Island, located in the Indian River Lagoon offshore from the fishing village of Sebastian. In 1947, even as the great flood-control dike was being completed around Lake Okeechobee with its imminent threat to the health of the Everglades, President Harry S. Truman dedicated Everglades National Park.

Even as the Kissimmee River was being ditched and straightened at a cost of $30 million in the 1960s, with its devastating consequences to Central Florida habitat, the clarion voice of ecologist Arthur R. Marshall was heard decrying the loss and correctly forecasting impacts so unsustainable that the ruin would have to be undone. And so by the mid-1990s the undoing began in the greatest attempt at environmental restoration ever attempted, a monumental undertaking at a cost of $490 million to rekink 22 miles of the river as a way to relieve big Lake Okeechobee, the river’s mouth, of a main source of pollution while restoring wildlife habitat across a vast floodplain. A $100 million project of like intent has now largely restored the headwaters of the St. Johns River—at 310 miles, Florida’s longest—with palpable improvement in water quality and the renewal of habitat and fisheries.

In 1986, Volusia County initiated a public land conservation program. More than $20 million has been invested there, which has led to the acquisition of some 75,000 acres. This initiative has since been widely followed. Florida counties elsewhere, typically backed by popular vote, have, for example, committed sums of $400 million in Broward County, $100 million in Palm Beach County, approximately $77 million in Lee County (Fort Myers), $55 million in Brevard County (Cape Canaveral); and in Duval County (Jacksonville), led by a highly popular recent mayor committed to conservation and acting without benefit of ballot support, $312 million. Volusia in 2000 renewed its commitment, voters agreeing by 60 to 40 margins to tax themselves another $160 million to acquire not only conservation lands but to fund new cultural and heritage resources as well. In 2004, Miami-Dade voters passed eight bond questions, most concerning conservation matters, totaling $2.9 billion. Another six counties and an additional city committed themselves to $436 million for parks and conservation, although three counties narrowly defeated initiatives but none by greater than 52 percent to 48 percent.

In 1972, in landmark legislation to protect its water systems, Florida authorized the creation of five water management districts, granting appointive bodies the power to tax while insulating them from routine politics. These districts have now become the managing agents for most of the land acquired under P-2000, Florida Forever, and related acts of the state, operating almost without hint of corruption let alone the malfeasance that so troubles so much of Florida politics otherwise. Regrettably, the districts are bound by public policy to raise no question about how limitless in-migration troubles the state's water supplies and, in their shackled policy formulations, turn instead to drawing down rivers, relying on expedients instead of wise planning.

Yet Florida gave the nation the wise and legendary Marjory Stoneman Douglas, whose epic work, *The Everglades: River of Grass,* contributed so largely to the cause of Everglades preservation and environmentalism throughout the state. Florida gave Nat Reed to America, the environmental chief under Richard M. Nixon, whose unsullied legacy as undersecretary of the Department of the Interior included launch of the Environmental Protection Agency. It was also Reed and Nixon who ended the boondoggle known as the Cross-Florida Barge Canal, which had threatened the entire underground water supply of much of the state. More recently, Florida gave Carol Browner to Washington as the most effective director in the history of the EPA. Apart from the giants have been the ground troops, the legions of Floridians—many newcomers and retirees among them—who have staffed the state's large and growing number of environmental education centers and who volunteer as monitors of everything from bird counts to water salinity to the encroachment of alien legions of exotic vegetation.

A consensus forms that Florida's economy needs to shift from dependence on ever-expanding population to something more focused on a quality of life based on environmental restoration. Indeed, that the time has come at least to debate whether Florida can continue as a low-tax state that, while allowing for limitless population growth, increasingly burdens the treasury with out-of-control expenditures to repair private-sector impacts. In this different scheme of things, Florida visitors would increasingly be wooed for the state's environmental and heritage values and less for escapism—something possibly presaged by the 2005 initiative of Visit Florida.

The shift in sentiment has yet to capture the attention of Florida's legislature. In 1998, Florida voters overwhelmingly backed a constitutional amendment that calls for a policy that polluters pay to clean up their own pollution. Regrettably, "polluter pays" has gone without implementing action by a legislature still in cahoots with the state's power elite.

Yet if Disney World represents the apex of real-world avoidance, its newest theme park, the Animal Kingdom, extols wildlife, the integrity of habitat and of humans living in harmony with wildlife. Disney's other new Florida enterprise, the new town of Celebration, suggests a model for containing sprawl that preoccupies Florida government virtually at all levels. One by one, slowly, painfully, election by election, county commissions change their philosophical outlook, closing their pockets to payoffs, tightening rules against lobbyist influence, taking on the toughest job of all, jawboning voters about alternative futures. Setbacks notwithstanding, as these new officeholders move into state positions, the balance may shift more decisively in Florida's legislature.

The myth that might yet bind Floridians together would form from the shared conviction that, regardless of the tourist-developer-retirement syndrome that so largely accounts for their presence, they are less invested in its politics than enlightened by its impacts, and that if not they, than who shall redeem Florida's promise of Eden?

This is a state in great flux where the best and the worst collide, carom off each other, and day by day contest the future. It's a wrestling ring, a mosh pit, a politically seedy and yet, for all of that, peculiarly exalted realm. What happens in the Florida Keys foretells what will happen throughout Florida; what happens in Florida foretells what will happen around America. Together, conservation, ethnicity, and tourism may become major determinants of Florida's more promising future.

For the entire twentieth century, Florida lured visitors with false promises of paradise. If anything, the lures have become more sophisticated in the new century. In mid-2004, *Florida Trend* published an advertising section called "Residential Resort Living." "Whether you're seeking a primary residence, a vacation home or condominium," it said, "top builders and developers are creating resort living communities to suit your lifestyle. At these resort living communities, your vacation memories can be year round reality." Tourism and development openly declared their fusion. Vacation slogans became land sale slogans. "Remember your dreams. Fulfill your promises," declared one.

Yet the impacts of new urban tourism were also apparent. Among the advertisers was a thirty-one-story condominium tower rising in downtown Orlando, part of the rapid transformation of that city from an adjunct of suburbanizing theme parks to one of Florida's newest and most quickly emerging tourism-driven downtowns.

Change continues today no differently from the decades before, nowhere faster than along the Atlantic, this halcyon Highway A1A shore—Florida at the edge.

1

NASSAU COUNTY

Where Highway A1A Begins—or Ends?

Figure 1.1. An information station on the roadside in Yulee, Nassau County, circa 1949. Courtesy of the Florida State Archives.

Figure 1.2. Downtown Fernandina Beach, Nassau County. The Palace Saloon on the left is the oldest bar in Florida. Courtesy of Amelia Island Convention Bureau.

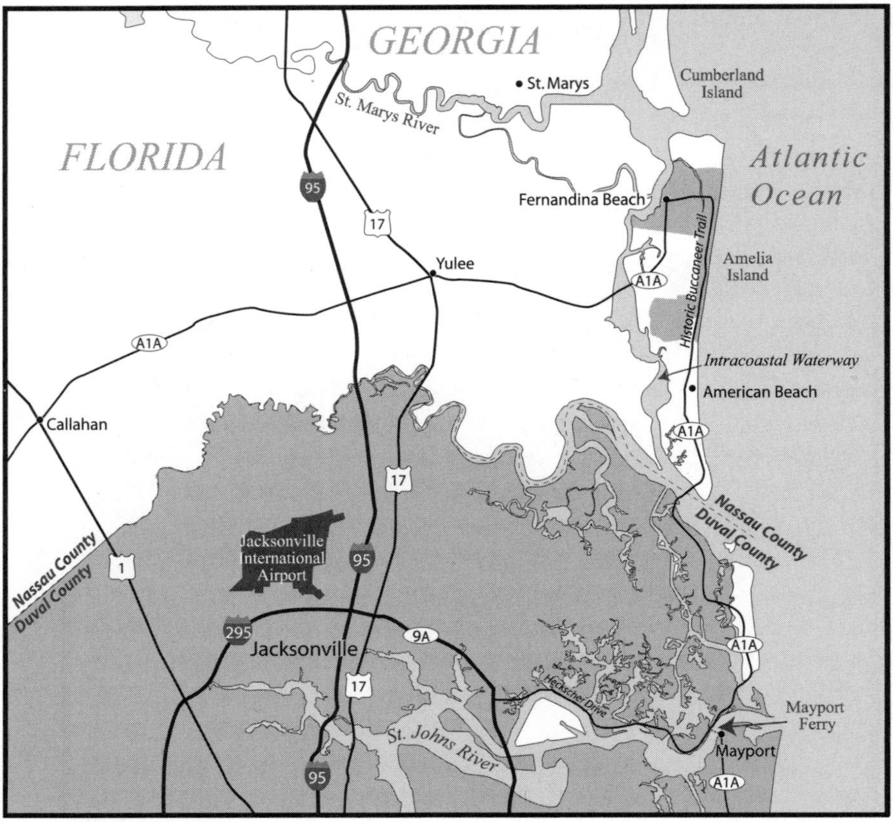

Map 1. Nassau County

Almost the same week that a vacant lot at Amelia Island Plantation sold for $2.3 million, the chairwoman of the Nassau County Commission, worried about growth, declared: "We need to do something now before we have a problem. We're already behind the eight ball. I just don't want us to be run over by it." She might as well have been standing mid-metaphor in front of an 18–wheeler crashing through her living room.

Plans call for 20,500 new houses north of the unincorporated crossroads at Yulee. A county retailing hub has already erupted on a dry spot along the one road between the crossroads and the county seat at Fernandina Beach. A stadium-sized Lowe's home supply center and a Super Wal-Mart have gone up. Together, the giant retailers have thrust development west into a county where the two mainland cities combined contain only 4,000 people. Altogether, the county numbers just 60,000, 40 percent of whom live along the coast. By comparison, more than a million people live in Jacksonville, bordering Nassau to the south, where more than half of Nassau's people work. Florida's Department of Transportation, which in the 1970s four-laned the road from Fernandina Beach to Yulee and continued the widening west another 3 miles to I-95, already plans to six-lane it. At the same time, calls issue for a new east-west road that parallels A1A to the south. Others call for light rail. What's going on?

Jacksonville projects its future growth north toward Yulee and toward Nassau's next westward crossroads at Callahan. From downtown Jacksonville, it's only 25 miles to Yulee; from Jacksonville International Airport, a magnet for the city's new growth, only 15. But almost all the new housing already planned for Nassau lies to the county's northeast, where important regional planning has begun. Little planning prepares the county where Jacksonville's growth aims between Yulee and Callahan, and where the four-laning of A1A now continues west from the interstate. Where Jacksonville has already grown in the opposite direction southeast into St. Johns County, single developments entirely by themselves include half as many houses as Nassau plans for altogether. Nassau is the county where motorists on I-95 enter Florida. They don't have to drive beyond if they want to understand what's driving the Sunshine State.

Yes, Florida boasts fun in the sun, but it virtually flaunts itself as out of control, by dint of developer-driven mismanagement unwilling to curb relentless, transforming growth. Floridians may be conflicted about this, but government's ongoing preference is to promote more tourists who become more residents who invariably require more houses, more shopping centers, and more and bigger roads. Natural assets are steadily stressed, calling for massive remedial expenditures, in effect subsidizing the building industry, which lobbies effectively against paying its own way. That's a double-dip subsidy for developers. The state and counties already spend a quarter-billion tax dollars to promote the tourists who become the new house-buyers.

Although elsewhere Nassau County residents fight to keep Highway A1A two lanes and the roads that run off A1A rustically unpaved, developers are whipping change down a homestretch where big bucks invariably rank as the horse to beat. The shopworn attitude prevails that you can't fight progress. Development is the Florida thing if not the American way. Now former county commission chairwoman Vickie Samus sees a "big challenge in front of us. It's a give-and-take to be good neighbors. We're all about to have a lot of new neighbors." And although retired state representative George Crady has pushed for the steady upgrading of east-west Highway A1A, now retired after twenty-three years in the Florida House of Representatives, Crady admits privately that he would like to see Yulee remain the way it is. "I don't want to see it spoiled and I'm afraid it might be."

This passivity in the face of overwhelm takes on a tainted aw-shucks character to the west in Callahan, where Highway A1A begins at the crossroads of north-south U.S. 1, 23, and 301 and east-west S.R. 200. S.R. 200 to the east of Callahan is the first designated section of Florida A1A. Callahan lies 12

Figure 1.3. Aerial view of Amelia Island. At 13 miles long and 2 miles wide, this barrier island sits on the northeast tip of Florida. Courtesy of Amelia Island Convention Bureau.

miles west of the A1A exchange with I-95 through a region of creeks and wetlands cut through by logging roads. Part of the two-lane road now more than doubling in width rises on embankments. Here and there a house goes up. Otherwise, doublewides strew the bush, rusting pick-ups beside single-wides. A Jim Walter housing center in a new clearing showcases pre-fab homes. Billboards urge folks to spay and neuter animals and admonish that Love Shouldn't Hurt, urging guys not to beat up their wives. Alongside A1A just outside of town there's an un-grassed-over mountain of trash. The Winn-Dixie shopping plaza has both a Dollar General and a Family Dollar. From the overpass where U.S. 301 heads south, you look down to a chain-link fence topped with coiled barbed wire that surrounds a group of institutional buildings. Looks like a prison. It's a school. There's Christy's Wings-N-Things and a New and Used This N That. The four downtown corners boast a Shell gas station, a Flash Foods gas station, a Clark's Rainbow Tires Services, and a Castrol Quik Lube. Callahan is a town for passing through. Few folks pay it much attention.

Inattention has proved a problem. In 2004, a three-year investigation still continued into a hornet's nest of official malfeasance you wouldn't think a city of fewer than 2,000 could pull off. Already cited have been the pilfering of petty cash, nepotism, fraud in the handling of grants, criminal manipulation of town records and arrogant self-advantaging. Attitudinally summing the town up, the proprietor at the natural foods store explains that she doesn't carry any food to speak of, mostly supplements. "We're not very sophisticated up here," she says. There's a bookstore attached, mostly Christian things, a lot of Civil War stuff, Eugenia Price titles, and a 1978 copy of *Writers Market.*

About Highway A1A, she concludes, "Well, we're either the beginning or the end. I guess we're the end."

Elsewhere to the east, venality adopts a more polished style, and people more image-conscious suggest Nassau is the beginning, not the end, of A1A.

A Piratical State of Affairs

The beginnings of Nassau are less debatable. Boasted history goes back to early in the New World, when settlement occurred in 1567, only two years after St. Augustine. Florida always surprises northerners brought up on the sacred memory of Jamestown and Plymouth Rock. St. Augustine, Pensacola, and Fernandina shock by their Renaissance origins. Two years before settlement, the island that became Amelia was remarked upon by an English sailor, John Sparke, who observed, that "In ranging this coast along, the captaine found it to be all an island. . . the countrey was marvelously sweet, with both marish and meadow ground, and goodly woods among." Even though Spain had long claimed all Florida, driving out brief French claimants, it was the marauding Governor James Oglethorpe of Georgia who, on an expedition in 1735, gave the island its enduring name of Amelia, for the daughter of England's George II.

Little changed before the Treaty of Paris in 1763 ended Europe's Seven Years War, ceding all Florida to England. The English remained for only twenty years, departing after a second Treaty of Paris that ended the American Revolution. Under one of the treaty's provisions, Spain regained Florida. But weakened after a century of military defeats by England, Governor Vincente M. de Cespedes allowed those English and Americans that remained to retain their lands by pledging allegiance to Spain. Many who pledged would later trouble the Spanish crown. This second Spanish period, which lasted fewer than forty years before Florida's transfer to the United States, saw Fernandina engulfed by skullduggery, piracy, and turmoil. This period, too, bestowed its own legacy. With the purging of time, local businesses began adopting the names "buccaneer" and "pirate." A peg-legged blackguard stands in front of a popular downtown restaurant, and Fernandina's schools have adopted pirate caricatures as their symbols. Until recently, county interests promoted Highway A1A through Nassau as the Buccaneer Trail, and in neighboring Duval County one of the ferries that carries visitors to Amelia Island across the St. Johns bears the name Jean Lafitte for one of the corsairs who terrorized southern Gulf coast shipping.

One impetus for the piratical state of affairs was Thomas Jefferson's Embargo Act of 1807, which closed American ports to shipping. Florida, across a porous Georgia border from the United States, boomed with contraband. The most vicious smuggling abused Africans. Although slavery flourished in America, the importation of African slaves had been outlawed in 1808. But

Florida was Spanish, and Spanish Florida was too weak to resist takeover of its port by smugglers. Too much revenue was at stake. Spain tolerated (and profited from) the contraband fleet captains, who—in a practice even more horrific than slavery itself—often threw their chained Africans overboard when American patrols approached to enforce the embargo. That notorious practice hardly ended two centuries ago. Still today, the smugglers of Haitians into Florida ports jettison their unfortunate human cargo when threatened by Coast Guard patrols. Fernandina's reputation grew and remains among African Americans as an "evil place."

Boosted by the riches that poured into its port and that spurred renewed growth, Spain in 1811 replatted Fernandina, making this the last Spanish attempt at town building in the New World. The town took the name of King Ferdinand VII.

If a fledgling America acted nobly at sea, it showed different motives ashore. Georgians and other like-minded southerners allied with rebellious planters ostensibly loyal to Spain in repeated attempts to capture Northeast Florida. The United States played a cagey game, outwardly condemning the insurgents but clandestinely supporting them with money, munitions, and "good offices." Incursions followed by land and sea. One assault led by Sir Gregor MacGregor, a Scottish soldier of fortune, hoisted a flag of his own invention, the Green Cross of Florida, over Fernandina. Another brought the rogue Luis Aury, a French pirate who had been first governor of Texas under Mexican rule and who, exploiting that still-dubious connection, hoisted the flag of Mexico. By 1821, the island and all of East and West Florida were acquired from Spain by the United States. The slogan of Eight Flags over Fernandina was gestating.

The town's importance grew for most of the century following its designation in 1824 as seat of newly formed Nassau County. Plans for coastal Fort Clinch began in 1842. A turning point occurred in 1853 when a favorite son launched a railroad from Fernandina to the Cedar Keys on Florida's Gulf coast. This was David I. Levy. Levy was born in St. Thomas in the West Indies. He was a visionary of Florida development and an early advocate of statehood. During his lifetime, he operated sugar plantations, brought northern capital to Florida, operated his railroad, and became an important political figure, one of Florida's first U.S. senators and the Senate's first Jew. Levy legally changed his name to Yulee on assuming office, yet both his surnames became Florida place names: Yulee in Nassau County and Levy, the name of the county where his trains reached the Gulf. When he laid out his railroad, Levy relocated the town of Fernandina from its original Spanish location to its present site on more solid ground, endowing the original town site with the informal name Old Fernandina, which—along with the designation Old Town—is still in popular use.

Skirmishes mainly affected Northeast Florida during the Civil War. However, the port and the new fort, named for U.S. General Duncan L. Clinch, who was active in Florida's Seminole Wars, largely remained in Union hands. Although the war devastated the town, and Levy's railroad was lost to northern interests, the town quickly recovered. The first of its tourist heydays followed construction of the elegant seventy-five-room Egmont Hotel. Steamships brought vacationing northerners. Fernandina in the north and Key West in the south became east coast Florida's leading resort cities. However, yellow fever epidemics twice set the town back. War with Spain in 1898 gave the town a boost, but a hurricane late in the year ended that.

Perhaps the historical event of greatest significance to Fernandina was a nonevent: that Henry Flagler never delivered his modern-day railroad to the town. Flagler, of course, was the great developer of Atlantic Coast Florida. His Florida East Coast Railroad opened the long and largely empty shore to hotels for the rich, to land speculators, and to farmers. But by the time Flagler began laying track from Jacksonville south, Fernandina was again feeling prosperous enough that it refused to welcome the great robber baron. Fernandina had its own railroad. But commerce suffered after railroader Henry Plant was denied a port terminal at Cedar Keys. Plant relocated his Gulf coast ambitions to Tampa, vowing to bring Cedar Keys to its knees and doing so, to the detriment of Fernandina. Flagler's influence would pall the town more enduringly a hundred years later. Meanwhile, north-south rail lines destined to Jacksonville of necessity passed through Nassau. Callahan developed as an important rail yard.

If Fernandina suffered by Flagler's investments in the cities he developed—Jacksonville soon far surpassed Fernandina in shipping, and St. Augustine far surpassed Fernandina in tourism—many resident businessmen were already wealthy from timbering. Before the turn of the century, they had built beautiful Queen Anne homes around the town center. Shrimping developed in Fernandina, where a Sicilian invented a kind of trawl that made harvesting the sea creatures easier. Later, during the Depression, pulp mills opened—Container Corporation of America in 1936 and Rayonier Corporation a year later—just when needed for jobs. Within hours after the first mill opened, "everything smelled like rotten cabbage," said retired harbormaster George Davis, a fifth-generation native. "Every house looked like somebody had spit tobacco juice over it." But the mills no longer blacken the town, and, as Davis pointed out, "at least to millworkers the stench smelled like money."

Accordingly, Fernandina enjoyed a rare Florida economy through the entire twentieth century, only minimally dependent on tourism and relatively unaffected by outside events. Because its port and its mills did business far and wide, the town suffered no sustained period of inactivity. No "rediscovery" occurred, no outsiders swept in with new ideas that might have radically changed the town and its look. Townspeople remained inwardly focused and, if the economy slackened and the town's distinct Victorian look lost its sheen, no force swept it away.

During this long period, there were actually three towns: Old Fernandina, new Fernandina on the mainland, and Fernandina Beach on Amelia Island. It wasn't until the 1950s that the three became one, adopting the name of the island town even though most everybody still refers to the off-beach town simply as Fernandina.

If all three Fernandinas became one in name, a new naming matter newly divided at least downtown Fernandina Beach and Amelia Island.

Amelia Island Plantation

Because the county was so long bypassed by the development that turned Florida into a satrapy of northern affluence, when Nassau's turn came only a few decades ago, people more alert to opportunity wound up affronting those who liked things the way they were. Typical of the wrangle was an episode related by David Caples. Caples and his wife, Susan, operate a small property on the island. Few people have done more to advance the cause of small hotels in Florida. The Caples' twenty-five-room seaside inn, the Elizabeth Pointe Lodge, looks like it has been around for a hundred years, a cross between Cape Cod design and a great humped Alice-in-Wonderland kind of creature. It's a bare fifteen years old. Caples explains how back in the early eighties he decided to identify the location of an earlier lodge he and his wife operated as "Amelia Island" instead of "Fernandina Beach."

"There are hundreds of 'Beaches' in Florida," explains Caples about the marketing advantage of his move, "but very few 'Islands.'" Amelia Island seemed to have more cachet than did Fernandina Beach, not that Fernandina Beach didn't have a wonderful name and tradition (though, as Caples points out, some people find the name hard to spell and pronounce). He made the change on his letterhead and envelopes. Before this, the prominent resort-residential development known as Amelia Island Plantation had already specified its location as Amelia Island both by its choice of name and because it sits outside the city limits of Fernandina Beach. But Caples' bed-and-breakfast was inside the city limits. No problem at first. Mail came as it always had. But one day the postmaster told Caples he would have to change the name back to Fernandina Beach. Caples went down and talked to the postmaster. He brought up the matter of zip codes and explained that it shouldn't make any difference whether he told the world he was in Fernandina Beach or Amelia Island—it's the zip code that counted. The mail was getting through. Those arguments didn't placate the postmaster, who said that unless Caples changed the name back, he would stop delivering his mail. Whereupon Caples told him that the first time he heard that his mail wasn't arriving, the postmaster's job would be at risk. The mail has come through ever since.

Caples's newcomer insistence on effecting change was only a trace of how Amelia Island would soon overshadow Fernandina in influence and change county destiny. Precisely the island's remoteness in December 1970 drew the attention of a developer who would change the island forever. That was Charles Fraser. Fraser became the Flagler that the island had never experienced. Fraser wasn't turned down.

Fraser was a developer who understood that by preserving environment he could attract buyers willing to pay a premium to live in a place that valued its immediate surroundings. Before Fraser, the general pattern of large-scale Florida development was to wipe sites bare, replace diverse native vegetation with palm trees and ornamental plants, and put up either grand hotels in the style of Flagler and Plant or house rows behind gates around a golf course. Most still operate like this, even on Amelia Island. But Fraser's approach instead responded to new environmental awareness. Significantly, Fraser served on President Lyndon Johnson's Citizens Advisory Committee on Recreation and Natural Beauty, a twelve-member commission established in 1966 and headed by Laurance Rockefeller, whose resort properties in the U.S. and British Virgin Islands were setting new environmental and aesthetic standards.

Fraser had already successfully developed Hilton Head Island in South Carolina according to his new environmental playbook. The land he acquired toward the south end of Amelia Island existed as primeval maritime hammock, dense and junglelike mainly with tall oaks, magnolias, and palmetto scrub behind the beach and dunes. Portions had been cut to accommodate small settlements in the early nineteenth century, but these settlements were long grown over. Otherwise, the chief use of the land had been for mining minerals mixed in the beach sand. But Union Carbide Corporation, which owned the land in midcentury, had already abandoned the site after discovery of better grade ores elsewhere and in 1970 sold to Fraser.

Fraser acquired more than 3,000 acres for $4.65 million, or about $1,500 an acre. The property, which was (and remains) divided by Highway A1A, extended from near the foot of Amelia Island where the island lies bordered to the south by Nassau Sound, to the west by the Amelia River, to the east for 4 miles by the Atlantic Ocean, and to the north by American Beach, a once-segregated vacation area owned by an African American Jacksonville insurance company and later by private beach dwellers. In time, Fraser acquired additional acreage north of American Beach. Upon his acquisition of the Union Carbide site, the *Fernandina Beach News-Leader* (Florida's oldest weekly newspaper) declared that, "Not since the Spanish slogged ashore in the 1500s and the paper industry moved here in the late 1930s has any one announcement meant more to ultimate progress than the purchase of the south end of the island this week." Fraser would "put Fernandina Beach on the map in such a way that countless years from now people will still be taking [*sic*] about that great day in December 1970." Six hundred would be employed at a time when the entire county numbered barely 20,000.

Fraser called the project Amelia Island Plantation. He retained the firm of Wallace, McHarg, Roberts, and Todd as ecological and land use planners together with a team of scientific consultants to master plan the large property.

Wallace McHarg was acclaimed for including ecological values in land planning. His firm worked for more than six months before any construction began. At a time when Florida placed few limits on what developers could and couldn't do, Fraser set aside 25 percent of the entire site in conservation lands. He created an ecological inventory of where not to develop. He used gray water for golf courses and laid out golf fairways behind the fore dune in an area subject to flooding from hurricanes instead of converting more environmentally sensitive land. Construction was set back of that. Altogether, Fraser and his successors have preserved some 70 to 80 percent of the tree canopy that existed at the site before development.

Fraser set up strong land use covenants that couldn't be broken. The Plantation controls the community's architectural review board and literally owns all the trees, so that residents need permission to remove any.

Another of Fraser's early moves was to donate $10,000 to help restore downtown Fernandina's Centre Street. This is the historic main street of the town, which, despite its preservation by long years of inaction, needed upgrading. Brick pavers, landscaping, and street lighting went in. Fraser saw that the old town would be an asset to his resort and property buyers. To Fraser, Fernandina and its working history was part of the real Florida that he wanted to protect. For him, development was a way to generate the funds he needed to carry out ambitions of conservation and beautification. The notion was that if development was sweeping across America, his way was preferable. Although his developments would house mainly the rich, Fraser saw his projects becoming models that would improve the aesthetics of all America.

Yet there were downsides to Fraser and the Plantation too. Fraser set in motion a model of resort and residential development that no other developer was able or cared to duplicate. Hardly anyone could acquire so great a single parcel of sensitive land for development. Here and there in Florida's Panhandle at Bluewater Bay and along the Gulf coast at South Seas Plantation and at one or two other inland golf resorts, the resort-residential style was developed at similar grand scale. But none of the others left anywhere near equal portions of land in conservation. That didn't prevent claims that proliferated everywhere about pristine waters and unspoiled lands. A great wave of greenwashing swept across Florida like some hurricane-driven surge of tidal hype. Florida, too, began to proclaim itself an eco-destination, even as millions of wetlands acres were filled in and, even when mitigated, were rarely effective as viable ecosystems.

The Plantation's Amelia Island legacy was even more troubling in the way that it perpetuated resort development as the concomitant of residential and, more recently, retirement living. This was nothing new in Florida. Henry Flagler's pall would prove more enduring than Fraser's vision and impel its course.

So enshrined had the connection become between tourism and residential-retirement living that by the time Fraser arrived in Florida, with all his good intentions about conservation and aesthetics, there was never doubt that he would base his enterprise on the same dynamic connection. Florida would fill at the cost of its natural resources in the name of improving American quality of life.

One of those who grew up in Fraser's organization, calling himself privy to Fraser's vision though he came up through the accounting side, now serves as president of Amelia Island Plantation. Jack Healan says that Fraser "set the standard for resort-residential development since followed by people in Vail and elsewhere." He tells how Fraser, traveling to resorts as a young man, saw resorts as "beautiful places with beautiful trees in unique areas. Wouldn't it be wonderful," Healan says, speaking as Fraser might have, "to live within a resort the rest of your life and enjoy beautiful natural scenery and the amenities of a first-class resort? The resort was a tool to attract real estate buyers. At Sea Pines, when real estate sales went in the tank, the resort side could be developed more fully." And vice versa. Though speaking during the aftereffect of 9/11, when the resort business was down, Healan could point to the lot "sold on the beach for $2,350,000. Charles had bought the entire thing for twice that thirty-three years ago."

Only a few months before Healan spoke, the *Orlando Sentinel* led its Sunday paper with a report on the mammoth Central Florida retirement development called The Villages. The paper wrote: "Cheryl Skinner feels as if she has died and gone to Disney World.

"There's the old-fashioned downtown with false storefronts and fictitious histories. There's the town-square statue of 'Founding Father' Harold C. Schwartz that bears a resemblance to Uncle Walt minus Mickey. There is the uniformly manicured landscaping, exceptionally clean streets, the relentlessly cheerful residents.

"But most of all, there is the everyday lifestyle of a permanent vacation—16 golf courses, 12 swimming pools, 18 tennis courts, 400-plus clubs.

"'It's like an adult Disney World,' said Skinner, 50. 'I feel like I'm living in a resort.'"

Now Florida governor Jeb Bush pressures to have real estate information distributed at the state's five welcome centers, traditionally meant to satisfy visitor interests in last-minute accommodations and other vacation needs. Until now, only tourist literature has filled the racks of these gateways to the state where visitors can drink free orange juice and otherwise relieve themselves after hours in the car. Though tourism feeds into development, until now no real estate information has been allowed.

"We see this as a problem," said Tom Waits, recently retired longtime chief of the Florida Hotel and Motel Association. By limiting the distribution of lodging information to licensed hotels and motels, Florida's welcome stations ensure regulated levels of security and safety. But long-term rentals aren't regulated nearly as stringently. Waits cites condominiums and residences that people can rent where they only pick up the key. There is no quality assurance. "Until we have an enforcement program over these types of lodgings," he says, "we ought not to be the vehicle through which more visitors can access these types of facilities."

Meanwhile, the governor had also appointed a "destination commission" to look anew at the retirement market. Florida has been losing market share of retirees. Head of the commission is a vice president for Disney. Said recently retired executive director of Visit Florida Austin Mott: "People in favor of posting real estate information at Welcome Centers will use the argument that most retirees are tourists before retirement. But we say, once they become a resident, we lose them as tourists. Another argument says we need to be careful in opposing something the governor wants." Especially a governor who is a developer.

Fraser and Amelia Island Plantation failed in a more direct way too. As Healan points out: "Charles was a great visionary and not such a great businessman. He wound up losing control." Everything he amassed north of American Beach wound up in other hands. It's there that an ordinary beachfront condominium project called Summer Beach got built in more typical slash-and-burn Florida style. (The same developer is now building in Nassau west of I-95.) It's there, too, where the Ritz-Carlton built one of its most successful projects but at the cost of the great tree cover. The developers of Summer Beach are now building condominiums sandwiched between Highway A1A and the marsh, directly across from the Plantation on land Fraser once owned. The tree cover has been stripped away, the bulky condos built directly to the road edge and overlooking the marsh. More are coming.

Continue south through the Talbot Islands and you learn what Amelia Island lately looked like. Outside the Plantation, the natural look is gone and otherwise going. Yet even owners in the Plantation grow dismayed. It's one thing to hang out on the Plantation's still considerable grounds, golfing, dining, shopping all beneath the canopy. It's another to feel yourself increasingly isolated on some island of green surrounded by built-to-the-lot-line condos. "Amelia is being destroyed," they say. Bring the matter up to Healan and he gets a sour look on his face. "We never like to talk against other developers."

Reform Finally Arrives

Others outside the Plantation have more courage. True to the vacation-retirement syndrome, Phil and Jane Scanlan were vacationing at the Caples' Elizabeth Pointe Lodge a few years ago. After five days, they put a deposit down on a house in Summer Beach. The Scanlans had lived in New Jersey where both worked for AT&T, retiring to Amelia Island at the turn of the century. It didn't take long before they became engaged in environmental issues. Scanlan had seen what environmental advocacy could accomplish. In New Jersey, nearshore sewage pollution had killed off half the bottle-nosed dolphins that migrated through the coastal waters. Beaches were frequently closed. Scanlan began a ten-year campaign that not only reduced pollution by some 90 percent but turned the declining shore economy around, making it the fastest growing section in the state. His secret was to develop a system of awards, not just fines, in dealing with polluters. "We looked for the root cause and set goals. This hadn't been done before. People need to see results in their own activities. You have to help make things work where people live." As a result of his leadership, Scanlan was appointed to the board of the Ocean Conservancy, which is now applying his systems approach nationally.

In their fifties when they retired, the Scanlans figured they could continue making a difference. They joined the Sierra Club. He right away became conservation chair and introduced himself to Nassau County environmental issues. He saw that people had to become pro-active instead of trying to take on developers at the end of the process, when they inevitably have their way.

"Most people," says Scanlan, "see things after they're done and go, 'Oh, my God!' People think government looks after things. You can't trust government without citizen input. Citizen involvement gives you checks and balances." Some people aren't anxious to become engaged in volunteer work in their retirement. "But guess what? Other people are engaged, and they're developers and realtors and they have influence. The one thing you can count on is that traffic will be up and trees will be down. We're trying to slow the degradation. Otherwise it would get worse faster. This whole area is ten years behind in dealing with overdevelopment," Scanlan says. "There was no protection. What's happening now is that on smaller lots, people have been building on every square inch."

It took a year, but a tree ordinance is finally in place that so far applies only to Amelia Island but could be applied elsewhere in the future. In another battle, the water services company was going to sell out to a town in the Panhandle more than 300 miles away fronting for a water resource grab. That one got stopped when Scanlan and fellow homeowners convinced the county commission that it didn't want an unregulated monopoly determining county water policy in return for franchise fees without homeowner representation.

In still another battle, Amelia Island Parkway and AIA that it parallels through the posh developments were both to have been four-laned. That would have removed all roadside trees. A traffic study already called for the four-laning. By revisiting the question, Scanlan and an association he initiated succeeded in keeping the residential section of the parkway two lanes, though a section near the county airport will go to four and so may A1A in time.

If you wonder why Scanlan and his fellow homeowners can achieve this influence when Amelia Island represents only 3 percent of the county landmass, consider that it pays 70 percent of the taxes and, at the time Scanlan spoke, contained 40 percent of the people. Says Scanlan: "Protect the value. People want to believe they live in a wonderful place. This benefits the county. In New Jersey we showed that for every dollar they spent to clean the shore, they got back ten dollars more from the improved economy. Money wins and environment loses unless you can show both benefit."

One problem, says Scanlan, is that you have commissioners who are real estate people. They appoint developers to the planning board. "These people benefit from each others' business, but that's not legally seen as a conflict of interest. It only becomes illegal where you benefit directly on every project. We have to sensitize commissioners where we can. Others will have to be voted out of office."

Scanlan found that the commissioners were not listening to Sierra because they represented only environmentalists, not taxpayers. "So, we were dismissed. But taxpayers care as much about this, too." Scanlan's move was to start an association of homeowner associations. "They had all been focused inside their gates. We got them starting to look outside the gates, talking to the city, the county, the state, the water management district. We started on this a year and a half ago. Now, out of seventy-three associations, we have thirty-four members." Each association volunteers one representative. Together, the group looks at traffic, growth, trees, water, drainage, and so on. With Sierra, Scanlan had only four or five members working. Now he has twelve committees with two or three members each. The Amelia Island Association (the association of associations) lately represented 2,496 Amelia Island homeowners and, combined with the affiliated Amelia Island Plantation Homeowners Association, 41 percent of all Amelia Island homeowners. By its second year, the association saw twelve of its first fourteen positions supported even if sometimes on close votes.

Now the mayor of Fernandina Beach, the commissioner for the south end of the island, the state representative, Scanlan, Healan, and a few others have set up an informal Amelia Island Council that meets quarterly and addresses islandwide issues. No little elitism is at work here. But the council represents who lives on the island these days, and their influence is growing.

That influence has begun to reach countywide. Shortly after the county commission revealed in mid-2004 that it couldn't afford a comprehensive traffic study of the A1A corridor and that it was approaching nonprofit groups to help fund a new library, the Amelia Island Council called for a sweeping overhaul of county management. Under relentless development pressure, the government staffing in five years had increased from 449 to 728—more than 60 percent in four years—expenses had risen 49 percent and debt had more than doubled. More than 10,000 homes were built or approved with zero impact fee for schools. The Amelia Island Council proposed an agenda for reform that quickly gained attention.

Talk of a countywide tree ordinance suggests that environmental issues might also get newly reexamined. This need became newly apparent in 2003, when the developer-dominated county planning and zoning board gutted a proposed ordinance to keep Highway A1A tree-lined through the Yulee corridor. Instead of the proposal's call to preserve 65 percent of the existing trees, the planning and zoning board called for nothing and otherwise proposed a road that looks like it does today in front of the recent scarring by Wal-Mart and Lowe's. The Amelia Island Association position paper described the planning and zoning board's changes as "driven by short-term, cost-based considerations of developers." Also up for reexamination is a decision influenced by rural timber and farm interests that in 2000 led the county commission to resist incorporating the county's riverine system into the Timucuan Ecological and Historic Preserve, a move sought by both Duval County and the National Park Service. Nassau's participation would more than double the size of the preserve, adding 66,000 acres (90 percent open water) to the existing 46,000 in Duval and provide protective oversight and recreational support for the area. As described in more detail below, the promise of more to come occurred in 2004 when the Timucuan Preserve did incorporate a revered site in the Amelia Island American Beach Community.

Historic Fernandina Beach

If the seesaw of political action increasingly tilts between Amelia Island and unincorporated Nassau to the west, historic Fernandina Beach continues to balance itself between conservation and overdevelopment and between residential and tourist interests, though that balance is increasingly at risk. Residents lately fought off plans that would have greatly increased the size of the port and widened the road that leads from Centre Street to it. An as-yet unresolved battle raged early in the new century over plans to develop Crane Island, which lies in the flight path of the airport. The city successfully imposed a moratorium on new construction while it tried to update its land use management plans that allowed developers to have their way long after public sentiment had changed. On the mainland, a proposed moratorium failed, even though most new development along Highway A1A was stalled by overcapacity on the road, which triggered a temporary halt in construction permits.

Downtown Fernandina long continued aloof from contention. To either side of winding Centre Street, fifty mostly residential blocks constitute a National Register Historic District, virtually sacrosanct and glorying in its pageant of grand facades. Although they don't front everyday commerce anymore—the day-to-day has largely moved to shopping centers south of town—Centre Street never became irrelevant and merely quaint. Locals still patronize a vicinity market and nonboutique clothing stores. Nassau County's restored courthouse remains where it has since 1891. For almost 150 years, the town has remained a rail freight terminal and seaport, though Standard Marine Supply, a world-source for hand-tied and hand-dyed nets, closed its doors early in the new century.

Change rarely upsets the district's historical character. A welcome center occupies an 1899 passenger rail station, but the caboose *David Yulee* that long stood outside is gone. An old town jail has become the Amelia Island Museum of History. Mansions have become bed-and-breakfasts. Modest houses have become restaurants, aromas from worldly kitchens newly scenting the Fernandina night rich with garlic-roasted lamb, rosemary pork tenderloin, feta-topped shrimp provencale. Facades remain with inscribed crown moldings, with brick arches and brows, and with second-story plaster bays. Notable is the Palace Saloon—oldest in Florida, where du Ponts and Pulitzers once cut loose from their wives—which still attracts locals and visitors. Nearby is Southern Traveler, in 1877 the Three Star Saloon; operating today under the condition that it never dispense liquor again, it dispenses marionettes and crewel rugs instead. Locals walk on errands. Breakfast and lunch they pack the Marina Restaurant, leaving work early for a midday table. Owner Pat Toundas says she can't remember names but does remember "who's steak and gravy, who's sausage and biscuits." She seats willing visitors who don't know each other with her. They leave the wiser about town.

Houses are board and batten, pastel clapboard and shingle. Outbuildings add character, some as much shed as garage, adapted, you suspect, from carriage barns. Their tin roofs rust beneath red bud, magnolias, and oaks with maybe a marmalade cat atop. Young women who work at Amelia Island Coffee know the names and mixed breeds of patrons' dogs. There's the lumber company right downtown and the hardware store. The Antique Warehouse was an auto repair shop and still opens with its old garage door onto its original brick floor. A marina welcome station once had a lighthouselike rig atop with an observation walk, dedicated at a time when Confederate flags still flew at official occasions and blacks weren't meant to be seen unless they were collecting trash. All that's gone. New, floating docks now provide more stable footing for those taking a sightseeing cruise or heading offshore in search of dolphin, grouper, king mackerel, sailfish, and snapper.

The whole of downtown has become site of an annual Amelia Island Chamber Music Festival that places world-class artists in the town's familiar venues like the Palace Saloon, the courthouse and churches—performers like Gil and Orli Shaham and Ruth Laredo—whose programs from Bach to modern masters accentuate the town's intimate scale and augment its appeal to visitors in search of such places.

Yet recent plans for the waterfront trouble vicinity homeowners who fear that the city may exercise eminent domain powers to convert their properties to tourist-driven commercial redevelopment. A newly formed Concerned Friends of Fernandina is also troubled by plans to build higher and wider along the town's beachfront where larger chain motels are already replacing mom-and-pop places, the kind that were already losing out in John Sayles's wry 2002 Fernandina-based movie *Sunshine State.*

You wonder how long some recent comments of retired harbormaster George Davis will hold up. Before he moved into a retirement home, Davis observed: "I still feel like the whole damn town belongs to me, even though nobody who used to live and work here is left. People used to live upstairs and have their businesses downstairs. Now, even though most of the businesses are new, the buildings are old. It's wonderful that people want to come and reuse these places." Troubling signs came with gutting of the county's planning staff in 2003–4, some taking jobs with developers and a conservation-minded member of the city's planning advisory board being sacked after complaints by a prodevelopment commissioner—moves seen by some as a collusive effort to further weaken opposition to developer designs.

Largely unnoticed by visitors is the year-round community of some 9,000 Amelia residents. They work at the resorts, at the paper mills, at the port; go shrimping at sea; and commute to Jacksonville, some crossing on the Mayport Ferry. They come downtown on county business and use the beach for year-round recreation same as visitors. Sunday evenings, young couples get together to play softball. Boys and girls throw sticks for dogs to chase, while others ride bicycles and still others pedal out to play volleyball on the beach.

Beach and town get along better here than anywhere in Florida. The place feels in sync with itself. There's the long, broad ocean beach so far for miles unblocked by build-up. There's the river port with its historic district. With only the little Egans Creek waterway separating the two, the 2 miles between get filled in by town. For some families, "town" is the new 100-acre virtual downtown of Amelia Park, a Celebration-like community that opened in 2000 that takes its architectural cue from traditional Fernandina, a contrast with hodgepodge strip shopping that over recent years has mushroomed mid-island.

Fort Clinch State Park occupies a 1,100-acre preserve northeast of town. The approach is a full 3 miles alongside algal ponds and high white dunes that contrast with deep green forest. The fort itself stands beside the Amelia River with formidable masonry walls built before the Civil War but never tested in battle. Rangers dress in 1864 Union uniforms and act out life of that time, talking with visitors as if the big news were still Sherman's victory at the Battle of Atlanta. Union reenactors perform full garrison reenactments each May, Confederates each October.

American Beach ran down after integration lessened its attraction for vacationing African Americans. Amelia Island Plantation began plucking its land for expansion but backed off after scourged by critical media and awareness that the once-vibrant community had now gained historical cachet that would appeal to its tourists and residents. About half of the hamlet has been identified as a national historic district. Pressured by longtime resident MaVynee Betsch, granddaughter of founder A. L. Lewis, Amelia Island Plantation has given 8 acres of exceptionally high dunes that now buffer AIP from the community to the National Park Service. The site represents the first land in Nassau County administered as part of the Timucuan Preserve. AIP is now working with others to build an American Beach community center with space for a small museum. Betsch, once a highly praised black operatic performer on the European stage who in her recent efforts to save American Beach became outlandish in floor-reaching dreadlocks, has become a charismatic figure. Russ Rymer made her the focus of his 1998 nonfictional account *American Beach.* In 2005, the seventieth anniversary of the community's founding, Betsch was to star in a film scheduled for showing at the Sundance Film Festival. The film will be the second to tell the American Beach story. The first was director John Sayles's barely fictional 2002 film, which captured the tourism-development-retirement syndrome.

Historic as Fernandina is, there's also remnant Old Fernandina, or Old Town. Here are the beautiful Bosque Bello Cemetery and the site of historic skirmishing when rebels in 1817 briefly captured the island during those four years before Spain ceded Florida to the United States. A group of preservationists was hoping for a 2005 start for a small inn, two houses and additional cottages, a bakery and limited cultural facilities at the original entrance to Old Town. Old and "new" Fernandina are both old today but newly colorful again. Yet the place is less frontally touristy than, say, Key West, which it resembles architecturally. Nobody comes to Fernandina to make a statement. There's no Conch Tour Train with its loudspeakers on public streets. The town wouldn't allow that. This place hasn't gone notoriously commercial the way of Key West's Duval Street, but that's another story at the end of the road.

2

DUVAL COUNTY

"God's Own Natural Highway"

Figure 2.1. Main Street in Jacksonville near the ferry landing. Date unknown. Courtesy of the Florida State Archives.

Figure 2.2. Southbank Riverwalk in Jacksonville. Courtesy of Jacksonville & the Beaches Convention and Visitors Bureau.

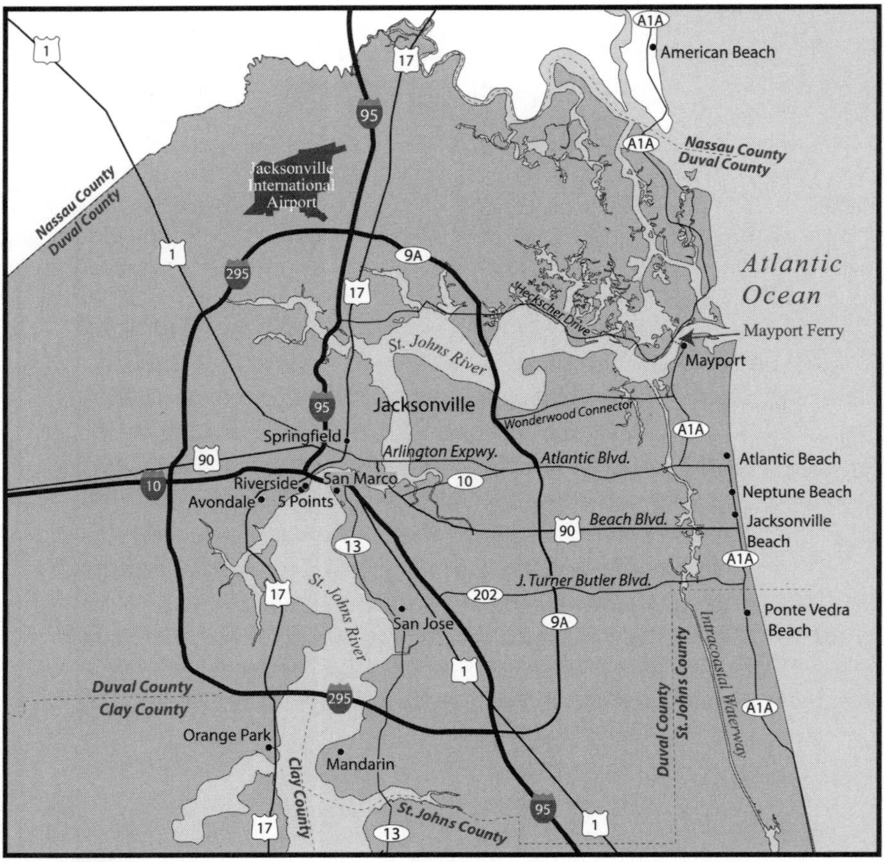

Map 2. Duval County

Visitors don't shun Jacksonville beaches. They just don't know about them. No mystery why not. Jacksonville does business, not tourism. Jacksonville is Florida with its nose to the grindstone, the state's commercial and industrial powerhouse, dominant in military affairs, communications, insurance, pulp manufacture, and transportation. Instead of tourism, it's the daily rush hour that drives traffic to the beach. Almost seven out of ten beach area residents work in the city. End of the day, they're going home or relaxing for the weekend. They drive east-west along Atlantic, Beach, Butler Boulevards, and a new fourth soon-to-be-finished east-west Wonderwood Connector. Jacksonville beaches are more for living than vacationing. The tourists who do find their way here have only the one north-south road, Highway A1A. They're fewer than the commuters, and by the time they reach the beach, they're more sorted out by discretionary income than wherever they set off from.

Driving north, the rich among them have pulled off the road beneath the *porte cocheres* of Ponte Vedra Beach in neighboring St. Johns County, a collection of estatelike subdivisions that, with their golf and boating facilities, were among the first in Florida to blur the lines between upscale tourism, gated retirement, and semiretirement. Jacksonville esteems the blur. This is what the good life is all about, the vacation that never ends. The executive class constitutes a signature constituency of the city even if many live just over the county line. Jacksonville built the county line–hugging J. Turner Butler Boulevard to serve them. Their wealth and energy power Jacksonville's economy.

Less well served are Jacksonville's poor. While corporate high rollers like the NFL Jacksonville Jaguars got multimillion-dollar breaks preparing for the '05 Super Bowl, improving black neighborhoods like Springfield went begging just north of downtown. Hoi polloi Jacksonville hardly fares better as upscaling condos replace RV parks, starting to price out low-end workers from the beach towns. Their counterpart tourists rank equally low coming north of Ponte Vedra to vacation in Jacksonville Beach or arriving there from Nassau County where the rich proceed no farther south than Amelia Island. Tourists who drive the beach road, Highway A1A, find mostly ordinary motels where their stays may contribute to beach town economies but cheapen Jacksonville's image.

Almost from its start, beach tourism conflicted Duval County. It conflicts the consolidated city-county still. In its clearest demonstration of what counts and what doesn't, the county never thought twice about the military takeover of one of its historic beach towns. For the last half century, the Mayport Naval Station has been the tail that wags the dog of what remains of little Mayport, its vicinity discovered before St. Augustine. The mammoth naval installation sits just beyond where Highway A1A comes north through Atlantic Beach and continues west around the base into Mayport village. More than 70,000 military personnel, their dependents, and civilian workers make up the navy family that lives, works, and sets sail from here. The station's combined ship and air facilities occupy the entire site of the city's discovery, a cape at the mouth of the St. Johns River first described in 1562 by Capt. Jean Ribault of France as "the fairest fruitfullest and pleasantest of all the worlde . . . a sight not able to be expressed with tongue."

The base and nearby Jacksonville seaport supply the muscle that leaves tourism the 97-pound weakling along this Northeast Florida shore.

In 1948, the navy base swallowed East Mayport (as the cape was known), paving over almost 3,500 acres, including nearly a full mile of beach and 4½ miles of riverfront. Third-largest naval installation after San Diego and Norfolk, the base today registers more than a $1.35 billion peacetime economic impact—let alone what it spins off even in a regional war. Just upriver at Blount Island, big Jaxport—the second-largest vehicle-handling port in America—powers an almost equal $1.3 billion wage-tax contribution to the local economy. Jaxport generates 45,000 jobs, while the navy base drives 45,000 cars a day through the intersection where Mayport Road splits from Highway A1A and continues north into the base.

Military, industry, business. Hard bucks. No Mickey Mouse. Those hard bucks support estimable beach living and dependable property tax collections not subject to the whining of motel operators who face the only predictable aspect of tourism: unpredictable up and down seasons. Tourists? They pinch pennies. Orlando threatens a plague of kitsch, while Daytona Beach—with its dependence on spring break, Black College Reunion, and boozy Speed Weeks—repels Jacksonville. Jacksonville business leaders are control freaks.

When Jacksonville Loved Tourists

Yet, before the holocaust of 1901 swept downtown away, Jacksonville itself was big into tourism. It claimed to be "the winter city in summer land." Writers extolled its comforts that awaited travelers who arrived by steamship or steam train. Abbie M. Brooks, under the pseudonym Silvia Sunshine, in 1880 wrote, in *Petals Plucked from Sunny Climes,* that "This city has fine accommodations [that] can furnish more than one hundred good places of entertainment, among which may be found several colossal hotels." Jacksonville's tourist appeals were many. Brooks described "beauties of landscape gardening [and] artistically-arranged . . . pleasure promenades." She wrote of a river that "appears overspread with a kind of semi-transparent mist, through which the sun shines with a nimbus of golden sheen. . . . How smoothly we glide on its peaceful bosom."

But tourism was soon heading south to more assured winter warmth, rolling on Henry Flagler's rails that bridged the St. Johns in 1890. Automobile bridges followed. Winter in Florida soon meant winter in *South* Florida. Jacksonville, 25 degrees colder than Miami, had a snowball's chance in hell of competing, while nobody ever thought spring, summer, and fall were much worth promoting. Those times of year, folks from Georgia drove to Jax beaches, a clientele hardly esteemed for gliding on the St. Johns' "peaceful bosom."

Apart from tourism, Jax did stay big-time. The city's relative warmth briefly made it the movie capital of America. The timbered interior of Florida flowed through the big port that developed. American military valued the St. Johns from a time before Florida statehood when irregulars harassed the Spanish. Later a fort went up to fight the Seminoles. Bases provisioned troops for fighting Confederates, depot commandants intrigued with profiteers in actions against Spain in Cuba, then finally the navy established its forceful presence not just at Mayport but upstream, marching the city to its drum. Instead of the in-and-out tide of tourists, big business flowed in. Banking and insurance-company towers rose on both shores of the river, laced together by girders of steel that gave Jacksonville alone, of all Florida cities, that metropolitan look that thrust it separate from its Cracker region and Sunshine State parodies. Dominant in South Georgia and North Florida, Jacksonville preferred the image of Chicago, Carl Sandburg's "city of the big shoulders."

Yet precisely its bigness and success left Jacksonville vulnerable to the narrow boardroom and church pulpit views of ossified gentry at a time when Florida elsewhere was experimenting with socialist communities and religious communes, exploring Everglades frontiers and liberal education. Together with its braided, hob-knobbing military and its fortuned developers who controlled land in much of the state elsewhere, manipulating Florida's growth to the city's agenda, Jacksonville's perspective puckered to the dollar and gentrified pursuits. As if to "save" the bare-skinned sinners who clung to the beaches with tourism, the early oceanfront hotels all burned. Religious leaders didn't like the uninhibited lifestyles of the film crowd any better. After World War I, when California captured the flicks, Jax said good riddance.

Jacksonville, though industrially a city of the New South, was racist and suspicious. Outsiders didn't fit in the way they did so quickly in Miami and tourist cities elsewhere. When the sixties rolled their thunder across America, Jacksonville took to the barricades against a pair of different assaults. Exposure of massive corruption shook the city. Blacks, so long locked in inner-city precincts as whites moved to the suburbs, had become a majority and were poised to take over city hall.

Whereupon, in 1968, in a move to strengthen conservative monied interests against conservative Bubbas and to shut down the troughs of municipal corruption, Jacksonville leaders pushed through consolidation. The move effectively disenfranchised the city's blacks as all of Duval, except for the beaches and a rail hub to the west, became the City of Jacksonville. Now the entire county voted in municipal elections along with those locked in the core city itself. All of Duval County newly claimed Jacksonville's wealth. White flight continued, and downtown fell into depression. The beaches retained their municipal independence, but Jax controlled the promotional purse. Only moths shook loose.

Consolidation did little for the average job holder, black or white. Despite incentives to business, in the twenty years between 1980 and 2000, per-capita income moved, then slid back; it was 93 percent of the national average to start and 93 percent two decades later. Cities like Birmingham and Charlotte raced ahead. Even after eight recent years of dynamic mayoral initiatives in downtown redevelopment and conservation, the city left the beach towns tethered to its preexisting stale outlook, ignoring their capacity for anything but bedroom communities. Accordingly, the city as well as the towns collectively failed to imaginatively reconsider the assets that were in place at the turn of the century and available to reconfigure the beach anew. Almost

Figure 2.3. Jacksonville Landing and port. Courtesy of Jacksonville & the Beaches Convention and Visitors Bureau.

wholly unrealized, here were 17 miles of oceanfront as potentially appealing as anyplace along Florida's coast. In a state where tourism, for all of its economic benefits, relentlessly exploited resources and otherwise lent truth to a caricatured view of Florida, an archetype was emerging that Jacksonville could pridefully claim as its own, could help develop and promote in a way that would newly and advantageously help maintain the city's urge to remain apart. Jacksonville Beach was finally breaking out of the pack, but there is a lot of history to overcome.

Once-Emerging Beaches

First beach settlers lived simply in board-bottomed tents. They ran a general store and post office in a place they called Ruby. Supplies and mail came from Jacksonville by boat. Then change sped up beginning in 1886, when the 16½-mile, narrow-gauge Jacksonville and Atlantic Railway Company linked city and beach. In forty-five minutes, town connected to the "finest [beach] in the world." Ruby became Pablo Beach, named for the marsh that set the beach apart. Access led to the subdividing of beach lots and construction of hotels. Up went the magnificent Murray Hall, an exuberance of towers and turrets embellished with pennants like a racetrack pavilion by the sea. Though fire consumed the hotel only four years later, visitors were already riding excursion boats to the Fort George Hotel on its namesake island north across the St. Johns near the river's mouth. By 1899, Henry Flagler was buying up beachfront, preparing to acquire the Jacksonville and Atlantic, converting the rail to standard gauge, extending the line north from Pablo up the beach to Mayport, and erecting his stupendous, 1,100-foot-long Continental Hotel directly facing the Atlantic. At a time when fire was wiping out downtown, the Continental boomed the beach. By 1910, Atlantic Boulevard opened from town and swells from the city began building homes north along the beach from Flagler's hotel. Pablo Beach, its heyday already passed, became their worker town.

After fire swept away every one of the grand new hotels, others less grand continued to satisfy the demand for beach vacationing promoted by beach business interests. The towns took on the names they bear today. Mayport never incorporated. No town formed on the river's north shore.

By 1927, S.R. 78—which became A1A—newly connected the beach towns south to St. Augustine and from there, eventually almost straight along the coast to Miami Beach. Only a year after mule teams had graded the beach dune, the road was locally complete. A beach town promoter ecstatically declared: "The prosperity of Jacksonville Beach is now assured . . . when thousands and thousands of cars will pass through this City . . . when tourists will get their first glimpse of the majestic Atlantic Ocean in Florida and see the first stretch of God's own natural highway."

"God's own natural highway" stayed in place, but the Depression smote business meant to thrive along it. The beach became chiefly summer homes where families came to vacation and husbands began the daily commute to town and back. By 1949, a second bridge crossed the marsh, connecting Jacksonville Beach to town along Beach Boulevard, so that beachites no longer had to drive up to Atlantic Boulevard to reach work. Others traveled to the beach because they could buy legal alcohol there. The city itself was dry. As the beach towns developed residentially, only a few hundred guest rooms remained. Mom-and-pops mainly looked after the tourists, who had already long stopped coming in winter. Highway U.S. 1, which ran inland from the coast, made it easy for visitors to drive directly south from the city and bypass the beach towns.

At a time when winter resorts were gilding the beaches of South Florida, Jacksonville beach towns lapsed hopelessly hick. Dwight Wilson's family ran a small Jacksonville Beach property. He remembers trying to sell rooms in winter for eight dollars a night when guys would come bargain for five dollars. In Miami, they paid a hundred. Of course, they got more for their money. Wilson would lock up and check the competition. The competition locked up and checked him. The few tourists who came, came because this was the first place they could see the ocean. "Tourists would park the car, jump out, and run to the seawall," recalls Wilson. "Over and over you'd have to push them out of the sea edge because they would drive right in. One wrecker had a ramp running out to the beach. You'd go out his ramp, get stuck and he'd charge five dollars to pull you out."

Nothing could bring the business back. Everything conspired against it. The navy base turned all but beachside Atlantic Beach into a hub of debauchery. In the late fifties, tourism throughout Northeast Florida was hit by race riots in Jacksonville and confrontation in St. Augustine. Conflict with Cuba put the region on war alert. Warships sat offshore as convoys headed for South Florida. Rocket trailers rolled down the road. People feared the atomic bomb. Then in 1964, Hurricane Dora blew out the back wall of the Atlantic Beach Hotel, a small property that had gone up at the site of Flagler's Continental. "That was '64," says Wilson, "and ever since everything along the beaches has been dated before or after Dora. Dora tore up the oceanfront and broke down the seawall. The hotel got taken down." Compounding the woe, Disney World soon opened, drastically curtailing even summer bookings.

"We used to get people staying a week or two," recalls Wilson. "We could stay busy for ninety days in summer. But now so many people went straight to Orlando and straight back home. They'd come for a night, just so they could get to the beach."

Convinced that the beach was *the beach* and that tourists would inevitably come back, the chains moved in. They put up boxy big buildings the size of hotels but kept them drab and understaffed like motels so nobody would confuse them with expensive places to stay. Quality Inn, Howard Johnson, Holiday Inn, Ramada Inn—all tried. All failed. A Days Inn became a condo. Only the Sea Turtle Inn, an eight-story property on the strand at the end of Atlantic Boulevard survived. Neptune Beach became almost entirely residential. City families rented there for the summer. Otherwise, the town's few transient rooms sit close by the Sea Turtle Inn where Neptune Beach butts up against Atlantic Beach on the south side of Atlantic Boulevard.

Jacksonville Beach, which became the commercial hub of the beaches, spent two decades mired waiting for urban renewal that never happened. While one plan after another got talked up, landowners did nothing to improve their properties, uncertain about how renewal might affect them. The town remained blue collar, a work in progress without luxury resorts or trendy shops. Uncaring property owners unwilling to fix up houses boarded them up with planks they left sloppily untrimmed at their ends. Yet nimby aversion to everyday retailing elsewhere along the beach road left Jax Beach the default choice for ample lodgings, including a few bed-and-breakfasts, restaurants, and shops.

Renewal of the Beaches

Even as new forces stir to redeem the beach towns, it's hard to think of the strip from Jacksonville Beach north as east coast Florida's fresh new place. Hard to imagine if you come looking for the manicured swales of Amelia Island north or Ponte Vedra south. The mushrooming of residential towers directly on the beach doesn't suggest much different. The towers are as architecturally dull as the steroidal motels they replaced, the newer crop of motels less egregious but in no way suggesting anything heritage. A1A doesn't show off the place any better. Through Jax Beach and Neptune Beach to where the road swings west onto Atlantic Boulevard, it's named plain old Third Street and carries six lanes of asphalt that start off where J. Turner Butler Boulevard ends alongside a hodgepodge of shopping centers that Ponte Vedra doesn't want south of the county line. A1A's mile or two west along Atlantic Boulevard anticipates the look where it turns north again to become Mayport Road, the sailor strip of body shops, tattoo parlors, plumbing supply houses, self-storage places—of the psychic Mrs. Ann and the upholsterer Mr. Bill.

Third Street is too wide for the height of what's built alongside, and what's alongside is nondescript. It's a road waiting for *charrette*-driven citizen input on what it ought to look like. The coastal forest is long gone, but the reminiscence of an old-timer sticks in the mind about how only two generations ago the teenage daughters of a couple that relocated from town "freaked because they were being moved into the woods." If no longer in the woods, the place still feels tentative, waiting for definite form, long past what it once was yet equally distant, if not in time, then in dream. The biggest buildings along Third are Duncan U. Fletcher High School (named for a turn-of-the-nineteenth-century senator) and the Beaches Library, community buildings likely to remain for decades and help keep community character rooted.

You grasp this regard for community and how it begins to drive change when you visit the shops. People who work in Jax Beach love the place. Especially young adults and families extol the hometown feeling. A mortgage banker comes in to Cycle Spectrum for a beach cruiser and wants a "Cantainer" mounted on the handlebars, good for carrying a beer. She says people who live here would rather change jobs than move. Freddie Urrutia, who manages the shop, calls Jax Beach "real small-town but with a lot of people. It's all about friends." Seven years ago, when he came up from Miami and Orlando, he hated the place. "Different from [Miami] Beach, they encourage skateboarding and surfing here. Other places these same activities might be illegal. Old movies? It's the coolest thing. Who doesn't want to hang out on the grass and watch a free movie?"

Urrutia is talking about Friday nights in summer when the new amphitheater beside a section of renewed beachfront shows old films, and everybody comes with their blankets and picnic baskets. Thanks to the city's live-and-let-live style, you can bring a beer or a bottle of wine as you watch *Breakfast at Tiffany's, Arsenic and Old Lace, Grease.* A woman walks into the bike shop and calls Friday nights "pixie dust." At *My Fair Lady,* the audience claps after every song. For *The Wizard of Oz,* they come dressed as Dorothy and the Tin Woodman. Kids come in jammies. Sunday evenings they do Cool Sounds of Hot Summer Nights.

The amphitheater sits just off newly redesigned Latham Plaza, a square that leads from city hall to the beach. Laid out with paver tiles and decorative bollards, lined by Canary Island palms, the two-block plaza seems impractically broad and open. It wasn't long ago that if you hung out here you might get accosted. This wasn't a family area. Beach festivals were all about how much beer you could drink.

Thousands still come for the events that take place between March and December, starting with a seafood bash and the annual Springing the Blues Festival and ending with a December holidays concert. Now, though, events are well patrolled and the bars that used to booze up the crowds have shaped up to stay in business. At the beach end of the square stands the American Red Cross Volunteer Lifesaving Corps Station, a landmark since 1914, replaced with the current white deco-style building in 1947. A new boardwalk with shops runs six blocks along the dune. A new 1,350-foot fishing pier called the Sea Walk has opened at Fourth Avenue North, replacing an older pier ten blocks south destroyed in 1999 by Hurricane Floyd. That's now Oceanfront Park with its sculpture of a young boy riding a dolphin.

Stores line the north side of the square and extend up First Street. Some fronts are designed cowboy-style with second-story picket porches and canopies over the sidewalks. The look isn't kitsch; it goes back to the town's early days. There's Campeche Bay Mexican Restaurant and a small fixed-up motel with a South Beach–style patio entrance. Next door, Freebird Café feels like it belongs in Arcadia, in the heart of Florida cow country. The place is owned by the widow of Ronnie Van Zant of Lynyrd Skynyrd fame. Leon Russell and Willie Nelson gigged here a while back. The beach is a popular music scene. Bands play across the street at Bukkets Oceanfront Grille in a block of shops that cater to the surf and skate crowd. Up the block, restaurants have opened. Bands play weekends at Nancy Hundemann's Nancy's Too, known for breakfasts that feature ten varieties of pancakes but also stays open late. Hundemann remembers that where condos now rise, the beach was once blighted. What's driving the change? "Yeah, sure, money greed, but you know, life, too. Some people can't adjust to how you now need to make $100,000 a year to live on this side of Third Street. But we keep getting the regulars, locals—and the 'coupon people,' you know, the ones who want a free meal. They drink water, they don't tip and they run your ass." Hundemann plays 96.9 FM, beach music, because her girlfriend was a DJ on the station and died from an overdose of legal drugs. "I keep it on for her."

Up First, Magellan's Restaurant adds to better dining introduced by First Street Grille, one of Northeast Florida's best, just behind the beach dune where a patio with live music stays packed summer nights. The Casa Marina Hotel, a place that looks like Bogart and Bacall might be sipping gin and tonics on the porch that fronts the boardwalk, seems good for the long haul. Mediterranean style and one of the oldest standing beach properties, the Casa struggled for years. One night in a room during one of the hotel's many makeovers, the AC wasn't working and a guest had the first-floor window open. Early in the morning a shot rang out and a cat flew through the opening. These days, cats snooze in the middle of streets that lead to the beach.

When City Hall began programming the renewal of town, they continued—even as they policed—the loud, beer-drinking festivals that Jax Beach was known for. "The idea was to get people back downtown," says Marilyn Matejcek, events and public relations coordinator. "But we right away switched and started aiming at the community instead of bringing outsiders in. We might still get 200,000 for a major event. The Naval Air Station will send its bands over, its big band and its rock 'n' roll groups. You see, we're a big retired military community. Even with the crowds, we make sure that early next morning the tractor comes by and the beach is clean for when people start showing up again."

Jacksonville native Krista Weller, who moved to the beach and bought The Daily Grind coffee shop where she first came as a customer, shut down after a Starbucks opened on Third Street. Her place was hidden away on First Street across from one of the town's B&Bs, the Fig Tree Inn, which is still here in an old shingle house. Nearby on Third Street, florist Tiffany Whiteley, who has designed flowers at Floriade for twenty-two years, figures that "Jax Beach will never lose its small-town appeal. I go shopping at Publix and I see five people I know. As a town, this place is the difference between art and commerce." Still, Jax Beach housing prices have begun steadily outpacing Jax Beach incomes, threatening its down-home style.

The art scene improved measurably with the opening of an exceptionally attractive gallery off Third on Fourth Avenue North. It's the J. Johnson Gallery in a bold Mizner-style building painted desert tan. The space is magnificently high ceilinged, exquisitely lit. A side gallery is antithetically ornate. Sculptures and antique décor evoke a Moroccan mood. Main gallery shows are rigorously modern.

Jennifer Johnson of the Johnson & Johnson pharmaceutical family built the gallery. She was schooled in art in Boston. New York's Metropolitan Museum of Art displays her photography in its permanent collection. Johnson is a contemporary art maven. She had never been in Jacksonville Beach before the navy reassigned her husband to Mayport. They lived in Jacksonville Beach and fell in love with the town (even though they've since moved to the city). Johnson's gallery would be right at home in Palm Beach, Winter Park, or Sarasota.

"Jennifer could afford to do what she likes to do. She could have done this anyplace. She could have done it in Ponte Vedra," says gallery director Bruce Dempsey. "She wanted to make a statement. She thought the Beach was like Chelsea, at the beginning of a turnaround architecturally and culturally, a place in waiting."

The building occupies an entire city block that had lain empty until the gallery opened late in 2002. "We realized that Jacksonville had many venues for local and regional art," says Dempsey, former director of the Jacksonville Art Museum. Today the gallery showcases established American painters and sculptors, though with occasional shows that include young and upcoming artists and with the occasional Picasso and Matisse. "Most of our work isn't easily embraceable by the general public. It's much more expensive. It's art as borderline investment," says Dempsey.

This explains why on a Friday in February you might find parking directly in front of the gallery and yourself the only visitor. The Johnson is a gallery, after all, not a museum. Most sales are done by phone. Yet museums like the Cummer in Jacksonville's Riverside district and the Jacksonville Museum of Modern Art book the gallery for their own fund-raising events, and five opening nights a year might each draw 1,000 guests. Matrons arrive chauffeur driven. Groups show up during the PGA Tournament in Ponte Vedra and at any time from Marriott's Sawgrass Resort there, from the Ponte Vedra Club and the Ritz-Carlton on Amelia Island. But so, too, do art students from Fletcher High. "The only rule," says Dempsey, "is they leave their skateboards and Rollerblades outside."

What might the Johnson influence? For one thing, the Beaches Art Center, a showcase for local work in 2004 facing financial woe, decided to stay on the beach. But Dempsey feels the gallery sets the groundwork for future building in the area; it sets a direction to follow. Certainly, its architecture challenges whatever anyone might build next. Worthwhile would be some sensitive prodding toward more uplifting design. Art, as Johnson and Dempsey conceive it, has transforming power. Still, ordinary buildings keep going up, though an ordinance limiting their height gained new advocates when a Beaches Watch Group formed in 2004, successfully passing thirty-five-foot height limits in Jax Beach and Neptune Beach. At any rate, public sculpture requirements may soon compensate for the disappointing aesthetics of towers already risen.

Neptune Beach and Atlantic Beach shun commerce by the sea except at the Town Center shared by both municipalities across Atlantic Boulevard. Town Center is an attractive low-rise section of shops handy and fun for locals and visitors, its tidy streets done with brick pavers, its shops with tin roofs, much of what's here reworked into rescued board houses. The scale is exactly right, another model for Jax Beach redevelopment. That town is only a mile and a half away. Locals along the beach of both towns can walk or cycle to the Town Center's coffee shops and restaurants, its boutiques and few professional offices. The natural foods store and bookstore are the only ones along the beaches. Ragtime is yuppie heaven, a hangout for shrimp and brew in a setting of woody banquettes and ferns, the buzz stirred by paddle fans. Weekends, crowds mill on sidewalks, looking through picture windows at the envied already at tables. Across the street, the crowd hangs at Sun Dog Diner in a burnished deco setting.

Town Center was a civic initiative. Prodded by residents, government made it happen but with private dollars. The end of Atlantic Avenue had been the neighboring beach towns' main street. This was the old commercial section. As shopping centers developed west of Third, supermarkets opened and the old groceries shut down. The neighborhood pharmacies, the hardware store, and the five-and-ten closed. Sun Dog was an old army-navy store.

The road ends at the beach. Sea Turtle Inn occupies the north corner. Its exterior is big-box shaped, though at least its couple hundred rooms have been newly redone in nonflashy Caribbean decor. From the inn, the beach extends 2 miles north backed by houses that have gone up over a century. Dawn comes up like lamb's wool, silver rose against blue. Gulls flap, pelicans fly by in formation. Bow lights twinkle red and green at sea where ships wait to clear entry to the St. Johns. It's so easy for inland Floridians to forget the big river extends all the way here, with no great town directly at its mouth, no delta. Mayport Light rotates its beam.

There is no Florida beach like this that's public and so easy to get onto. The look of the houses west along the beach is organic, some slow but steady accumulation that defies the fits and starts that have otherwise accompanied beach town tourism. The look is beautifully board and shingle. However large the houses have grown—there are no McMansions that once-small beach towns from Captiva to Seaside have succumbed to—they remain for the most part modest in effect, mostly single-family. The row stands orderly but not uniform. It's the individual differences that make the long row so appealing. Uniformity is martial, stressful. Design controls, like Disney's at Celebration, feel contrived. Here, instead, you sense civic consensus at play. Intuitively, everyone respects how each benefits the whole.

First light dimples shingled bays and gables, chimney bricks, porch pickets. Sash windows glow. Here and there sit an A-frame, a modern house, these friendly with the traditional forms, mostly shingled and derived from Cape Cod, though here, too, Prairie impressions and a western style with the ends of its rafters extending beyond the slight overhang. Native-born Val Bostwick explains that to start, these were all second homes of town people. They built these places smaller with 10-by-10-feet and 10-by-12-feet rooms, small closets, single beds, and a bureau. People came to spend the three months of summer. Then they closed the house up and moved back to town for the rest of the year. "This had nothing to do with tourism and still doesn't," Bostwick says. "You either live out here or you're a house guest." Rentals can be had, but not for the night.

Before Hurricane Dora, each house would have had a concrete bulkhead and patio just above the high-water mark where the barbecue was installed. But Dora's tides sucked out the sand beneath and behind the bulkheads. The patios buckled, though their collapse tossed up protection barriers that helped save the houses themselves from destruction. Later, people just threw sand over the collapsed concrete and the dune grasses grew atop. Private boardwalks cross the dune, though here and there a public walk also cuts through. These public walks accommodate locals who live on the inland streets where, if anything—especially in the Selva Marina section—homes tend to be grander. Though Jacksonville Beach allows parking at street ends, Neptune Beach and Atlantic Beach don't, thereby discouraging day-trippers. Overnight visitors of course park at their motels and walk or ride bikes. North at the end of the house row is Hanna Park, a large Jacksonville city park of dunes and mountain bike trails, of fishing ponds unfortunately no longer clean enough for swimming. Winters, house trailers park here for under $450 a month. Beyond the park, the navy base takes over.

Atlantic Beach and Neptune Beach are each two towns in one, each with its favored residential beach district and, to the west, with less costly housing and the desultory Atlantic Avenue business strip. The navy base drives commerce here. Though many live on the base, many rent in the neighborhoods. Cost of living remains low, and where A1A turns north, housing west along Mayport Road remains substandard. People still live in 700 feet of space depending on kerosene heaters in winter. Trailer parks here leave a lot to be desired. The navy is cooperating with improvements. People have high regard for the navy. Without them, there would be no Little League teams or Boy Scout troops and few active churches or civic volunteers. When one of the base ships that were deployed in the Mediterranean took a missile from the Israelis and lost twenty-seven lives, the town rallied round. Within a day, additional phone lines were installed and free calls were authorized anywhere in the world. When the aircraft carrier *John F. Kennedy* recently came in for overhaul, a back gate for contractors would have created a monster shutdown of A1A leading to Mayport village. As a preventive move, Atlantic Beach mayor John Meserve got Florida DOT in five months to install a stacking lane directly into the base, paid for by the City of Jacksonville.

"Mayport Road is still the worst blight in Atlantic Beach," says Mayor Meserve, himself retired navy and, in his civilian job, executive director of a navy retirement community. "It's the most dangerous road to the beaches. We want to clean it up." He sees the road becoming an attractive route between the ferry and the beach towns with tree-planted medians and reduced traffic lanes now that the Wonderwood Connector will soon open from downtown directly to the Base. Meserve wants a bike path to replace closed traffic lanes and extend all the way from Amelia Island through the beach towns, a distance of 80 miles. "We need to get going on this," he says, "before development takes over and shapes it. Let's shape it ourselves. We need a joint vision of what we want the change to become." He points to $400,000 houses that have already gone up along the Intracoastal marsh. Condos and marinas are going up, and one developer, undeterred by the conservation zoning for 7-acre Johnson Island in the waterway, wants it rezoned for his profit. Arrogance notwithstanding, the move further indicates overcoming of the blight.

"We still have to go through light industrial areas with some warehouses in bad shape, trucks parked around, but we're getting a handle on this over time," says Meserve. "The natural attractiveness of the area will bring it around. In the end, the economy will take over the road. We've already had a lot of bad bars go away."

The mayor observes another important change. "Most sailors are married now. They marry young, and they're not carousing. The world's changing. We need to keep changing with it."

Mayport and the Timucuan Preserve

Mayport is hard up against one more round of change. The navy amputated the town from its historic beachfront neighborhoods. Families here for generations watched as the navy bulldozed churches and, denying residents the timbers of their houses, poured gasoline on them and set them afire. Better off kids at Fletcher High called Mayport kids "those shrimper trash." Then came the Florida constitutional net ban, and the shrimp boats that once lined up three and four abreast quit operating. Maybe twenty remain. Like so much that has happened along the beach towns, shrimping enjoyed a brief heyday. Everything had been finfish until trawl technology came south out of Fernandina in the 1930s. Sixty years, and largely gone. Mayport Shrimp Co-op is the Coast Guard base today. Mullet Beach, where 100,000 pounds of mullet could be seined in a day, is just a name now.

In this community, where everyone was on septic tanks, tougher environmental regulations have closed down one business after another, including restaurants. A couple remain, notably Singleton's, where the vegetable of the day is always collards, and where, from the screened deck, you can time when you ask for the check to catch the *Jean Lafitte* for its next north crossing. The oldest remaining restaurant, Strickland's, has been taken over by a casino ship. Two of these ships now operate, threatening what remains of Mayport's character.

"The big loss," says Mayport native and Fletcher High teacher Larry King, "is that the whole culture has died. This was one of the richest, most historical, most fun subcultures, and it doesn't exist anymore. People couldn't live here anymore." King, from a family where both his grandfathers worked for the old Jacksonville Mayport & Pablo line, himself has moved to the city, though he remains related to most everybody in town and can tell you the real-life characters on whom G. W. Reynolds III based his ribald *Jetty Man*, soon to be a movie.

King recalls that as a young man he would row over to Fort George Island to court Vivian Elizabeth Broward, granddaughter of former Florida governor Napoleon Bonaparte Broward, who lived in her grandfather's old house. "I wore out two sets of good ash Coast Guard oars courting Beth Broward," King says. He remembers that her family kept a wheel in the big living room.

That was from *The Three Friends*, the boat that Broward as a young river navigator used to smuggle supplies to Jose Martí's revolutionary forces in Cuba.

Drive around the remaining town with King and everything has a story. Without taking a breath, he can talk for two weeks. The former working lighthouse, in place since 1848, was a problem for Confederates who wanted to keep Yankee gunboats from coming ashore. A great-great uncle (or was it a cousin? King never remembers) couldn't race up the stairs fast enough to switch the light off, so he shot out the light with his shotgun.

Frank and Genevieve Ponce ran the whorehouse and the boarding house. Frank fed black families during the Depression. Genevieve was known to everyone as Aunt Babe, "except that the blacks called her Miss Aunt Babe." The madam was Rosa White, and of course mothers wouldn't let their daughters walk on the sidewalk when she came by, King says. One day, when his Aunt Isabel was a young woman, Miss Rosa called over and gave her a vial of perfume. "Don't tell your mother," Miss Rosa said. King conjectures that "Isabel probably had that the day she died."

Women in these parts used to gripe when stray dogs showed up in their yards, King says. "They'd complain that the dogs caught the ferry to shit in their yards. There isn't a day that hasn't been salty in Mayport."

What's next? Singleton's has a collection of wood boats carved by the restaurant's founder. The fellow who operates La Cruz Casino has bought up much of the town and will control a lot of what happens. "People not in the casino business seem to like him," says King, who's afraid the village could turn out like the worst kitsch of St. Augustine. The La Cruz entrepreneur will undoubtedly influence what happens with the Mayport Partnership. That's a group of state agency representatives, regional parks administrators, civic leaders, and more. They're meant to chart what comes next. So far they've installed decorative streetlights, but there's still not enough to do to attract a hotel. The village is still just a jumping-off place. Cars thread their way off the ferry heading south. They collect to board heading north. Maybe one day they'll stay awhile.

The ferry is the last big boat still operating in Florida. When state government threatened its shutdown after years of financial losses, citizens and business interests of Amelia Island and the beach towns rallied to save it, arranging for its operation by a company that now runs the service profitably, competently, and stylishly. Tourists and even locals go out of their way to enjoy the ten-minute river crossing. The ferry is a fanfare introduction to vast riverfront conservation lands assembled and innovatively managed by government at all levels.

North across the river where King courted Beth Broward on Fort George Island, the Ribault Club has been rebuilt and newly reopened. The hotel that burned and later the club, during the 1920s, lodged Jacksonville's elite and their visitors. They golfed and sailed in the beautiful, but increasingly silted creeks and bays that spill into the mouth of the St. Johns. Depression closed the club. The golf course returned to bush. Now the club has become one of a series of interpretive sites that link together the big, 46,000-acre Timucuan Ecological and Historic Preserve. The club concentrates on the story of Fort George Island, from its archaeological Timucuan Indian past to the present. The site was crucial in Spanish missionizing and the demise of Timucuan culture. Separate exhibits detail the natural history and cultural history beginning with European settlement and including the times of French, Spanish, African, English, and American dwellers.

At the north end of a narrow, unpaved 4½mile loop road, marked by wayside exhibits, sits Kingsley Plantation, oldest plantation in Florida and legendary. Zephaniah Kingsley figures importantly in the history of the region that he helped cultivate as far south as Drayton Island in Lake George and Orange Park, where his plantation gave rise to the town. Kingsley was conflicted about slavery, depending on African laborers housed in hovels that still surround the site today, yet marrying one of his slaves and carefully planning for her freedom and their family's in Haiti, after his death.

At the time of the hotel's opening in 1928, visitors were still coming to downtown Jacksonville by steamship, connecting to the island by excursion boat. Later, the Army-Navy Club that occupied the old Kingsley house rekindled recreation on the island. The idea was that the island would combine the luxury that people were accustomed to at places like Jekyll Island and at South Florida resorts. The moving force was a Ret. Adm. Victor Blue, who resisted construction of what became Heckscher Drive along the north shore of the river because he didn't want the isolation of his club or his guests' privacy reduced. The island still occupies 17,000 acres virtually on the ocean. Heckscher was built anyway, linking the club to the city without need for ferry. The Army-Navy Club became the Ribault Club.

From the north end of the island, the islet-studded waterscape lays out distinctively as the Caribbean. Sandbars, marsh grasses, occasional docks and hammocks array. Anyone who looks upon this realm has to respect that the site's preservation qualifies as the highest achievement of government and public interaction. It's a source of singular inspiration. It makes as much sense to bring business students out here as train them in computerized systems. To learn production skills is relatively easy. To be inspired about what to produce and about how to benefit lives of those at work requires a vision that sights like this inspire. You look in awe and realize what a great place this is *not* to build a condominium.

The site will remain, and more may be added or at least integrated with the Timucuan Preserve as it exists. For this is one of the most dynamic preservation projects in America with a potential to satisfy Jacksonville interests now that the city's downtown is reemerging as a residential district and, even if still lagging, as a center of commerce. The development owes much to the recent two-term administration of Mayor John Delaney, who—as a Democrat turned Republican for political expediency—barely compromised his regard for the outdoors, in particular the St. Johns, and his insistence that downtown, with whatever subsidies, bring people back to live.

"The next wave downtown has to be residential," says Delaney, now president of the University of North Florida. "Experts would say Bohemians move in first, then art circles, then the gay community—a cycle of those who tend to come first. Then yuppies. We're trying to jump-start that process." He attacked crime with police on bikes and horses and in golf carts. He began bringing downtown back to where he could credibly assert, "The risk of being a victim of crime is higher in any shopping mall than in the entire downtown." He called for synergy between the hotels and residential, sure that retail follows residential. Then would come the markets, bookstores, movie theaters. "We want to take land out of development and squeeze growth into clusters where it will work," he said. "If we package our great outdoors and market it right, people will come from all over the world." Under Delaney, Jacksonville developed the largest urban park system of any American city.

Delaney moved City Hall from a river site better used for redevelopment to an abandoned department store across the street from a downtown park. Though widely criticized for awarding financial incentives to bring developers to the river—something that developers elsewhere in Florida fight for—by the end of his second term in office, his goal of bringing between 5,000 and 10,000 new residents downtown by 2005 was in sight. Apartment houses newly stack alongside the river and back off it where older buildings, including the historic Roosevelt Hotel, have been turned into loft apartments. An Adam's Mark Hotel opened with 900 rooms. New 750-foot residential towers could edge the south bank before 2010. New pedestrian walkways will tie front doors to the Riverwalk. On the north bank, a big children's park has opened, and the Riverwalk, now underway, will extend almost 2 miles from this park all the way into Riverside Park at Five Points. Water taxis link the river banks. Though it didn't happen during Delaney's term, new downtown residents and visitors will soon be able to ride water taxis into the Timucuan Ecological and Historic Preserve and rent canoes and kayaks there to tour the watery realm. Additional amenities will outlast Jacksonville's hosting of the 2005 Super Bowl.

Headquarters of the great preserve is Fort Caroline atop the bluffs on the south shore of the river, midway between downtown and the beaches. The fort occupies the site of the ill-fated French settlement that followed Ribault's entry into the St. Johns—what he called, for the date of his arrival, the River of May. In 1988, late U.S. representative Charles Bennett sponsored legislation that expanded the small site into the vast preserve, five times the size of New York's Central Park. Bennett, a published historian with political savvy, included in the boundary not only federal land but state and city and, boldly in addition, private lands. Bennett's vision imagined that the park service would figure a way to get all these entities to cooperate because without that cooperation, the ecology of the realm would be compromised and its integrity lost. Bennett's vision and how the superintendent of the preserve has carried it out is of course another source of inspiration for transforming the beach towns.

Superintendent Barbara Goodman recalls that "it took me a while to get my brain around what this place was. A great park with wonderful resources but little control." She had spent sixteen years with the park service at more traditional sites. Here she had such untraditional "partners" as the navy, Jacksonville Electric Authority, and more than 300 private owners of lands and homes. "That our boundary overlay all this meant nothing to these other people. We had—and have—no regulatory authority other than influence. We had to work with those people because they had boundaries inside our boundaries."

She concentrated first on her fellow park managers. She took them to Golden Gate National Park in San Francisco where a similar multijurisdictional management plan had been worked out. Until then, the three park managers had never sat at the table together. "We spent ten days at Golden Gate Park. We bonded as individuals. We formed a common vision about Florida. We decided to start with just the three of us." The timing was propitious. As they began working together, Delaney was invited to fish in the preserve. It was the first time he had penetrated the preserve in his life. Though he lived in Neptune Beach, he said he had had no idea the preserve was as grand as he found it. He is famously remembered to have said: "They're gonna build condos here? We can't let that happen!" That started his Preservation Project, which since has committed the expenditure of 312.8 million dollars to protect the best conservation lands that remained within the city. The city has committed a dollar-for-dollar match with the federal government. "Although we don't intend to buy everything," says Goodman, "we have set some targets. So, for example, Black Hammock Island on the north side of the river already has too much private ownership. No attempt has been made to acquire that. Yet, because conservation land completely surrounds it, the trailers are likely to go in time and the private homeowners may become willing to sell in return for keeping life estates. On the other hand, the city has acquired all of Pumpkin Hill, a vast marsh that was slated for development. Early in 2003, a prime marsh site, once a virtual dump west of Mayport Road, was opened as a recreational park.

Barbara and Kitty Ratcliffe arrived in Jacksonville the same year. Ratcliffe until late 2004 was executive director of the Jacksonville and the Beaches Convention and Visitors Bureau. They quickly got together. Goodman, Bob Joseph—who manages state parks in the Timucuan partnership—and the head of the city's Preservation Project all sat on the CVB marketing committee. "We have this rich natural and historic environment," says Goodman. "We believe this is what Jacksonville needs to market. It may be a niche, but we would best fit in by distinguishing ourselves from the rest of Florida. Yes, we have beaches and golf and all these other things. We need to capitalize on what we have that people don't have."

Bob Joseph looks after Big Talbot and Little Talbot Island State Parks, a gorgeous piece of coast from the Atlantic west through the marshes to Pumpkin Creek and Cedar Point. It's the last section of Jacksonville adjacent to Amelia Island. Joseph says that ten years ago the parks might have drawn 180,000 people a year. Today, the expanded state parks draw more than a half million. The numbers keep rising. A lot more groups come for birding. Kayak Amelia, an eco-sensitive concessioner, has been installed on Long Island. Joseph grew up in Atlantic Beach before leaving to work up and down east coast Florida. Now back, he sees "the city coming of age. There's new respect for natural heritage. This has always been a place of significant edge effects," says Joseph. "Timucua met Guale here. It's the geological boundary between ocean and land. Twenty thousand years ago the coast would have been 80 miles offshore. The ocean is still rising. We're in a very dynamic pattern. The French and Spanish edged together here. Those cultures interacted with natives. The African Americans brought in another edge and this was all edge to the English."

Once ferries were poled across the inlets that causeways span today. Old bridges are fishing piers. Horses, once used to cross the islands, today carry visitors across Little Talbot for rides along the beach. Roseate spoonbills, wood storks, and other waders stalk prey in the marsh. Driftwood lines beaches, in some places reached by trails that tunnel beneath oaken canopies. A portal opens onto the beach thick with boat-sized driftwood; entire trees lay out. These have eroded from the bluffs, becoming sculptures weathered by wind and salt. "Salt-pruned shapes," Joseph says. Roots entangle Medusa-like, like elk, their antlers hopelessly entangled in battle, beasts left to starve. Shoals constantly move south, leaving the creeks restless about change. Thousands of birds nest in summer on Bird and Little Bird Islands. Nassau Sound scours the shoreline, revealing ancient ship keels.

Joseph says that we can only protect these resources if people love them. "People have to come here for that. The feeling is contagious."

3

ST. JOHNS COUNTY

Ancient History and Modern Affronts

Figure 3.1. A wooden bridge crossing the Matanzas River in Saint Augustine to Anastasia Island, 1896. Courtesy of the Florida State Archives.

Figure 3.2. The Bridge of Lions in St. Augustine. Courtesy of the St. Augustine, Ponte Vedra, & the Beaches Visitor and Convention Bureau.

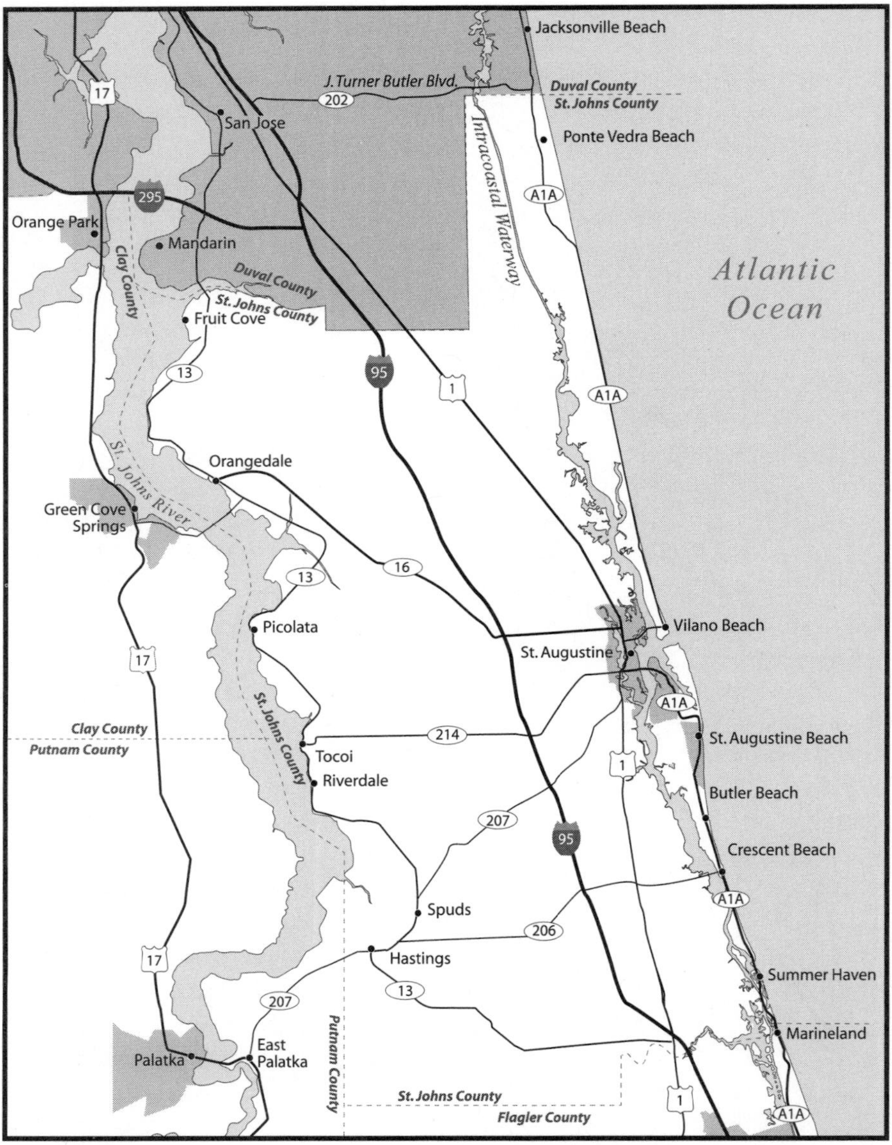

Map 3. St. Johns County

Pressed by nature and pressured by man, sections of Highway A1A from one end of St. Johns County to the other keep retreating from the shore, shoved around as if impermanent as a line on a map. For early residents, who otherwise could only travel the coast by horse or sail, completion of the road proved as satisfying as indoor plumbing after long outhouse use. Although in places laid atop the fore dune and subject to erosion and collapse, the road moved people in cars faster than by the old ways. When A1A was built between 1926 and 1968, the county outside of St. Augustine was thinly populated and rural. Apart from distinct enclaves of sophistication, it drifted in time. In some parts, it still does.

But the road was also meant to be scenic, to entice visitors who might admire the sea and—like those already having risked new lives in Florida—choose to relocate where they vacationed and stake a claim in the local economy. A 1917 county plan that described the value of tourism beyond the mere sale of overnight rooms explained that "An immense purchasing power is represented by those [visitors] who would doubtless prove a most stable and valuable acquisition could they be encouraged to invest and especially to settle here."

Implicit in the wish was a view of St. Johns County as frontier, strangely unsettled again after its late-nineteenth-century boom, again a resource in waiting that, without some critical mass of people and capital, could not resume its advance beyond the conditions that satisfied Minorcan refugees a century and a half before. Harvesting fish and game, farming, ranching, and otherwise perpetuating the inheritance of Spanish lethargy weren't good enough. More outsiders with more money would help throw off limits.

Arguably more American than elsewhere, Florida perpetuates the American dream that the good life ever lies beyond the metaphorical Alleghenies, that being rooted in place means being rooted in time, stuck in the Rust Belt encased in brick. But to those who dream, Florida offers another possibility: a world where French doors open from within walls of glass and air conditioning onto sunshine-filled patios to swimming pools, a world whose self-image is fueled by the escapist conviction that "The rules are different here."

It's not just the road. Nothing stays put in Florida. Hurricanes threaten everything created by God or man. Jetties shift the flow of sand from one beach to another to the gain of some, the ruin of others—and to the everlasting benefit of lawyers. Rivers that meander get straightened and, sometimes, remeandered again depending upon science, which advances slowly, and politics, which advances fast. Laws aggrandize the folly that lets people build in swamp by steadily diminishing access to the courts to challenge such folly. The state's five water management districts dare not question whether a policy of stimulating unlimited growth might unwisely stress the state's limited water supplies. Government is so ensnared by its disposition to promise newcomers virtual tax-free living that it can't provide minimal education for Florida's children or transportation choices for its adults that might keep them from wasting weeks each year trapped in their cars. When the citizenry rebels and votes constitutional change to meet its needs, the governor declares the people mistaken and challenges them to vote again, while the House of Representatives more expeditiously proposes to ignore the Constitution straight out.

The shifting of Highway A1A from place to place is the merest suggestion of the short-term outlook and unsettled lives from which Floridians suffer. Florida still depends on the sales tax that tourists pay on everything they buy from hotel rooms to lottery tickets and on the fortunes new residents are meant to transfer to guarantee paradise. Highway A1A's impermanence flashes the neon and gilt of F*L*O*R*I*D*A in all our lives.

If the road shifts laterally, the fortunes of St. Johns' coastal communities have risen and fallen like the calliope bursts driven by hot air. These shore towns distinctly juxtapose Floridians at their various styles of leisure. Inexorably, rich prevails.

Ancient and Rural

St. Augustine has been the county's lodestar. Why wouldn't it be? It's the oldest continuously occupied European settlement in America. That should supply some organizing rule. In a state where the mantra is "more," possessing "the oldest" should assert any county's claims. Yet, because the town was so quickly exploited once rediscovered in modern times—then so rudely cast aside as Florida promoters kept questing south for more assured winter warmth—St. Augustine has only weakly influenced the county elsewhere. Revered by some, others disdain it as a tourist trap, as Florida's first theme park. For many, its physical form is hopelessly archaic, hopelessly foiling traffic. Critics argue that theme park St. Augustine might better be reduced to its ancient quarter while the rest of the city gets on with its modern intentions. Yet for others, the town is too quickly dismissed and remains the signature place without which St. Johns becomes one more coastal platitude.

For newcomers drawn to the gated precincts of new luxury developments on the county's north side, the town exists strangely apart. In one of the fastest-growing counties in America, St. Augustine's population barely changes from year to year, now reaching about 14,000. Inherently, this place of narrow streets with its horse-drawn carriages exalts "slow" in all its forms. In 2002, for the first time in memory, the city dared elect a new four-to-one majority to its governing council that takes preservation to heart. Even so, the county commission flogs growth merely requiring high residential impact fees (in 2005 up from an average $2,650 to as high as $9,300), while the city lacks untold millions to preserve everything on its priority lists. County numbers have risen in twenty years from 51,000 to 123,000 while St. Augustine more suggests the rest of St. Johns than do the new growth-driven precincts of affluence.

Visitors who don't experience the county beyond the coast don't realize how rural sections remain distinctly unbuilt-up. Along sections of S.R. 13 to the west, the St. Johns River remains more open than the sea from the coast road. Oak hammocks align the way. Spanish moss blows loose, curling like tumbleweed and rolling across the road to catch beneath board fencing around rural yards. Up in Fruit Cove, lately at the edge of development rampaging south, lives octogenarian Stetson Kennedy in a rustic lakeside compound. Kennedy's crusading journalism in the thirties exposed the Ku Klux Klan in Florida and hallowed the state's folk traditions. He was an intimate of Zora Neale Hurston and Woody Guthrie, who spent peripatetic years living in an abandoned bus at the Kennedy compound. Back south where S.R. 207 connects East Palatka and St. Augustine are the farm towns of Spuds and Hastings and unusual country stores. Hastings, with some 700 mostly poor people, calls itself Potato Capital of the World. It's home to County Line Produce, the best vegetable stand in the region, and to Bulls Hit Farms, regionally famous for thick and crunchy Bull's Chips, unqualifiedly the best potato chips in America. At Molasses Junction—where folks still talk about the "great spill" more than a hundred years ago when barrels of goo tipped from a train—cuke pickers flood in at lunchtime for gizzards, wings, and goulash.

Along C.R. 208, which shows little more than one pine power-line post for every 100,000 pines, a historical marker describes the site where on a May Saturday in 1840, Coacoochee and a band of marauding Seminoles ambushed a theatrical troupe on its way to St. Augustine. One performer and four others died. While search parties tracked the elusive Indians in vain, the undaunted actors fulfilled a two-week engagement in the Ancient City. Months later, the Indians appeared wearing Shakespearean costumes from the plundered baggage wagon.

Mineral City to Fictional Realm

Nonetheless, if St. Augustine compels by history, the driving force of St. Johns County is its far north, which compels by its safe harbor for wealth and its lifestyle. Ponte Vedra Beach has become the luxurious first choice among Jacksonville's bedroom communities. Here, more than anywhere in Florida, the resort way of life and CEO lifestyle merge. Resorts like the Ponte Vedra Inn and Club and Sawgrass, with its grand Marriott and its nationally ranked golf and tennis tournaments, exist surrounded by real estate projects promoted by generations of high-placed Jacksonville developers, all promising life as endless vacation. Building lots at the county's coastal retirement resorts routinely sell for a half-million dollars.

The beach along Ponte Vedra was valuable in a different way when the area first drew national attention. Here, the same as at Amelia Island Plantation in Nassau County, a mining company held the long beachfront. In Ponte Vedra, it was the National Lead Company, which mined the sand for titanium during

Figure 3.3. Flagler College in downtown St. Augustine. Courtesy of the St. Augustine, Ponte Vedra, & the Beaches Visitor and Convention Bureau.

World War I but thereafter left the beach largely undisturbed. By the late twenties, a prominent area real estate firm, Telfair Stockton and Company, first managed and then acquired the property. Telfair Stockton changed the place-name from Mineral City to Ponte Vedra, a name without historical significance that was chosen because Spain had become the image of choice for Florida developments. More significantly, the firm convinced the state to connect Ponte Vedra to St. Augustine by a road along the shore. St. Augustine at least had been real Spain, and the connection was bankable. There things remained through the Depression and World War II, but the resort took off in the boom that followed.

Developers of the new Ponte Vedra Inn and Club boldly reconfigured the landscape. First, they hired Robert Trent Jones to redesign an existing nine-hole golf course to twenty-seven holes. Then they took on the roads. In 1966, A1A was rerouted inland. This left Ponte Vedra Boulevard a limited two lanes effectively reserved for residents of the growing beach community. Stop signs installed at corners further discouraged through traffic, while county commissioners have indulged wealthy landowners by shutting down street parking wherever they ask, resulting in 2004 in a suit by the nonprofit Surfrider Foundation Florida.

By rerouting A1A west, developers also opened up the marsh that extended to the Intracoastal Waterway. By fill and by pumps, new land arose. David Stockton and his partners developed the marsh as Sawgrass. Marriott lent its name to a luxurious hotel. In 1978, the developers scored an eagle by pulling in the Professional Golf Association. PGA was given 415 acres for a token one dollar in exchange for relocating its world headquarters to Sawgrass and establishing the Players Championship Tournament here. By the mid-eighties, Stockton's successors convinced the City of Jacksonville to build J. Turner Butler Boulevard from the city's south side to the beach. Ponte Vedra and Sawgrass became one in the public eye. They formed the *ne plus ultra* of residential-resort living, extending a glow that gave industrial, blue-collar Jacksonville new rosy cachet. By 1990, Ponte Vedra's population of almost 15,000 already outranked St. Augustine's. The numbers today stand at 26,000. Golf holes number 150. Hopelessly overcrowded, A1A rates "F" from state highway officials.

Spurred by renown of its coastal region, the rest of northern St. Johns has developed fast. A state legislator recently promoted the groundbreaking for 31,000 luxury houses, calling the $1.5 billion golf-themed development the "biggest economic baby to hit Northeast Florida in quite some time." On its heels have come announcements for still more projects—one of 4,000 houses, another of 7,500, and another of 14,000. Even before these "babies" come on line, overdevelopment in the county has steadily dropped the water table, causing cypress trees, with their roots dried, to topple. Inexplicably, the St. Johns River Water Management District continues to mismanage public resources for developer gain. Early in 2005 widespread protests followed staff recommendations to permit development of 640 acres that will destroy the headwaters of two of Jacksonville's most important waterways, Pottsburg and Julington Creeks. In an equally egregious case, the district had already permitted withdrawals for more than 2 billion gallons of freshwater over five years to top off recreational ponds and lakes on the ranch of the politically powerful Davis family, owners of the Winn-Dixie supermarket chain. The same land lords are promoting the largest development of all: 12,579 dwelling units, 2.8 million square feet of office space, almost a million of retail, a quarter million of light industrial, and 485 hotel rooms over the next twenty-five years at a forest-felling site called Nocatee. In *Places in the Sun,* Bertha E. Bloodworth and Alton C. Morris say the Seminole-Creek "nocatee" means "What is it?" Runaway development isn't new to St. Johns County. But the start was slow.

Flagler Re-imagines Ancient Glory

For the roughly three hundred years that Spain controlled Florida, its influence was chiefly military and Christianizing. Florida otherwise sat on the back burner. Its strategic location along the route of treasure fleets from Mexico and Peru made Florida worth defending. But Florida itself supplied no gold. The Spanish never worked the soil. They depended on native Timucuans, later on runaway slaves who, between 1738 and 1763, lived at the fort of Gracia Real de Santa Teresa de Mose 2 miles north of the town. This was the first sanctioned town of free blacks in what today constitutes the United States. It resulted from the Spanish policy to subvert slavery among the British in Georgia and South Carolina.

In 1763, in the peace settlement at the end of Europe's Seven Years War, Spain traded Florida to England for the return of Havana. The blacks of Fort Mose and most Spanish loyalists exiled themselves to Cuba. Twenty years later, after the American Revolution, the English swapped Loyalist Florida with Spain for Gibraltar. But Spain, demoralized at the end of empire, hung on for fewer than forty years more before dealing Florida to the United States for a pittance.

During the twenty years of English rule, mutinous farmers had fled the Turnbull colony down the coast in New Smyrna for protection in St. Augustine, establishing a large Minorcan colony that remains influential in city affairs, real estate, seafaring, food, and crafts traditions. Others from up and down the St. Johns River escaped to the city during the Second Seminole War when sugar and cattle plantations were torched. A resort community slowly emerged. Tubercular invalids came seeking relief from northern winters.

Everything began changing in 1883 with completion of a narrow-gauge railroad between Jacksonville and St. Augustine and Henry Flagler's decision to build a hotel. In St. Augustine, Flagler found a city at the cornerstone of America still shamefully unequal to the great nation built upon it. Flagler was a commanding figure. In St. Augustine, he would create a monument to American capitalism and transform himself from robber baron to hero.

For $2.5 million, Flagler built the Ponce de Leon Hotel, a pastiche of Spanish Revival style inspired by Newport grandeur. At a time when St. Augustine had a population of barely 2,000 and Florida still remained largely wilderness, the Ponce outrivaled every hotel in America. The hotel made the careers of its architects, Carrere and Hastings (who went on to design the New York Public Library and the U.S. Senate office building), and of Louis Comfort Tiffany, who arranged the hotel interiors. The hotel introduced the use of poured concrete for the construction of major buildings.

When the Ponce opened in January 1888, it signaled the end of tourism on the St. Johns River. The action moved from riverboats and river hotels to coastal resorts. For Flagler, the Ponce began his transforming impact on Florida. He built a second and acquired a third hotel in the city. He tore down a crumbling Methodist church for its site and replaced it at a cost of almost $100,000. He memorialized his lost daughter, Jennie, and granddaughter Margery with the monumental Memorial Presbyterian Church. He diverted creeks and filled others while amassing a third of a mile of land for a new downtown residential district. He Americanized St. Augustine while preserving its antiquities and thereby transformed the preexisting city into its own tourist attraction. Instead of a resort for consumptives, St. Augustine became America's resort choice for the consuming rich.

To transport his guests from Jacksonville, Flagler acquired the existing railroad and replaced it with standard gauge. With his trains and hotels, he opened up the rest of east coast Florida. His awesome drive and wealth commanded newspapers, the market for land, and state government. Flagler set the pattern that made tourism the master of Florida affairs. His influence patterned the privileges that Walt Disney would claim from Florida's legislature eighty years later, privileges that nevertheless never equaled Flagler's own.

Ambitious and visionary as Flagler proved to be about St. Augustine, eminence waned as the great railroader's own ambition fueled development of empire south through Ormond Beach, Palm Beach, Miami, and ultimately Key West. Each city was either born or reborn by its link to rail, the construction or improvement of monumental hotels, and a barrage of northern publicity. As trains rolled south, Flagler's society rolled with them. The Golden Age of St. Augustine lapsed within a decade. Major fires in 1887 and 1914, minor fires, and thoughtless demolition swept away the Magnolia Hotel (built in 1847) and Kirkside, the Flagler estate, which was taken down when the city in 1950 decided it wasn't worth $20,000 to restore. *Sic transit gloria mundi.*

St. Augustine never died, of course. The treasure is too lofty. Here are the Castillo de San Marcos National Monument—the centuries-old Spanish fortress in the heart of the city—and the Spanish Quarter, an eighteenth-century Spanish colonial village. Here the oldest house in America, the oldest wooden schoolhouse, the oldest store, the ostensive site of Ponce de Leon's landing in 1513, the Government House Museum, the magnificent waterfront. Here too Potter's Wax Museum and the Old Jail. And here, too, the elegant Lightner Museum with its collection of American Brilliant–period cut crystal (the museum built into Flagler's Alcazar Hotel), Ripley's Believe It or Not!—everywhere faded Spain and the faded resort glory of America, culture and kitsch scrambled together and irresistible to schoolchildren whose parents never entirely stopped coming with them, clip-clopping around cobblestone streets in horse-drawn carriages.

When Mickey Mouse began eating St. Augustine's cheese, artists and hippies found the town like ripe Camembert. Bed-and-breakfasts opened. The place quickly gained more restaurants and bars for its population than anywhere in Florida. Pub-crawls began from the White Lion to Scarletts to Tradewinds to St. George Tavern to Mill Top. Even locals ride the tourist trams when they entertain out-of-towners, and everybody else parks on the benches along St. George Street since it became a pedestrian mall with buskers (variously hassling and hassled, removed and tentatively welcomed back).

Many who return to settle remember the place from a sixth-grade trip. Some come because the city lies just below the thirtieth parallel, a powerful lay line that connects with the pyramids of Egypt. Vietnam vets found the place live-and-let-live. Corporate dropouts traveling up and down the Florida coasts see the crenellated towers and the Bridge of Lions and get blown away by the history and figure some new way to make a living. It's a place where some residents only recently began locking doors and where the town lately came together to build a municipal playground—and then to resist a dunce administration that tried to charge the volunteers' kids to use it.

Thanks to tourists, this town of 12,000 boasts a thriving art center, a concert association, a little theater group, more than twenty art galleries, thirty antique shops, an exceptional historical library, a four-year liberal arts college with 1,400 enrolled students. Yet historian and preservation advocate David Nolan thoughtfully observes that the bed-and-breakfasts were once all "single-family homes occupied by widows. When you turn them into five or ten or fifteen units and pave the yard for parking and gussy up the architecture and seek out ghost stories to go with them and speculate in the buying and selling of them, then you do crowd the town and degrade its history and add to the general atmosphere of greed—in addition to any positives they bring."

Regrettably, a first-rate bookstore lately closed, and in 2003, the Monson Motor Lodge was torn down for replacement by a chain franchise. It wasn't its age that made the Monson a local landmark; rather, it marked a turning point in the American Civil Rights movement. In early June 1964, the Rev. Martin Luther King Jr. came to St. Augustine and took part in a sit-in at the Monson. He called this the "oldest racist city in America." The same month, Jackie Robinson addressed a civil rights rally in Lincolnville, the historic black district. The publicity surrounding these two events hastened congressional passage of the Civil Rights Act later the same month. However, local segregationists refused to comply with the new law. Sheriffs' dogs attacked blacks. When the Monson's manager observed blacks in the motel swimming pool, he threw acid into the water, then drained the pool and stationed guards around it. Angry white mobs beat wade-in demonstrators at local beaches. Vigilantes shot up the beach house where a white sympathizer offered to put up the Reverend King. St. Augustine was controlled not only by Bubbas but also by John Birchers. Its reputation took decades to overcome. Even today, African Americans amount to only 11 percent of the county population. Even today, the Monson was torn down to make way for the first franchised hotel in the colonial district because, as some say, "Sure we honor history in St. Augustine, but not *their* history."

History, of course, can't climb out of its past and contains many strands. Not to be despised is its atmospheric dimension. St. Augustine is an easy place to walk around with its functioning downtown, beaches, and supermarkets you can bike to. If pedestrian St. George Street and its surrounding streets north of the Plaza de la Constitucion thrive on kitsch, worthwhile shops appear among the dross. Give thanks for St. George Street anyhow for how it sops up people. Some say it's like one of those blue electronic lights that attract bugs and zaps them. The rest of the colonial district stays remarkably residential. South of the Plaza, the streets are almost empty of people (albeit crowded by any two or three moving cars). One-of-a-kind shops occupy the ground floors of ancient houses along Charlotte and Aviles Streets. But the streets themselves are the attraction. Walk along St. Francis and you have the presentiment of the Caribbean, an old colonial downtown that could be anywhere in Santo Domingo, Pointe-a-Pitre, or St. Kitts. Flowers flaunt themselves everywhere over walls of cut coquina. Birds twitter in trees among tropical foliage, palms, wisteria, and azaleas; old shutters on fanciful buildings fade in need of paint. Clapboard houses with screen porches show furniture less for style, more for comfort. Gates open on stout hinges, trees stricken by lightning stand like veterans of ancient battles with their clefts. Sidewalks come and go. In front of galleries, paintings of the city appear on easels. A parked car in an overgrown yard pours out the sounds of rap-style reggae—so Jamaican. History smites you with a kiss.

No less so in Lincolnville, the suburb that after the Civil War became home to former slaves who years later found work when the great hotels were built. The district was once an Indian village, later site of colonial plantations and orange groves. Segregation turned the district into a vibrant residential and business center and, by 1930, an established part of the city. Its fifty-block National Register neighborhood retains the city's largest concentration of late-Victorian buildings. Ironically, the end of segregation, here as elsewhere, sapped community institutions. But because Lincolnville is located in the midst of the historic city, where everyone wants to live, renewal happens quickly now. Relative African American prosperity has kept the district middle class, though increasingly whitening and with artists newly in the worker mix.

So much is architecturally and graphically striking. Grand houses remain with leaded windows beneath elaborate molding and ornamental bays. Wash flaps on lines in small yards. A historical marker at 81 Kings Ferry Road shows the street as it appeared in 1894. In colonial times, this was the road to the King's Ferry across the Matanzas River (where a 13-acre mixed-use development is underway today that will create a new western gateway to the historic district). The house at 81, in shades of pink with tin gabled roof and more than a century old, belonged to Idella Parker, who rose from maid to Marjorie Kinnan Rawlings to author herself. A mural of black history fronts a house on narrow Washington Street. From here, a slivered view north reveals the architectural extravagance of Flagler's Ponce de Leon Hotel (today's Flagler College), as view-impressive as Oz. Where Pomar and Moore Streets divide stands Spanish-style Excelsior High School, with a sign for the National African American Archives and Museum, a project awaiting realization. It's easy to conclude that you might rather walk anywhere in historic St. Augustine than ride anywhere else in a Rolls Royce.

People enter the ornate Catholic Cathedral across from the Plaza, some to pray, some to avoid the sun or the rain, some because the organist is rehearsing Bach. They walk the bayfront in moonlight after dinner. They hang out in the Plaza, maybe hip to tavern performers who pick up a local gig and never leave—performers like Don Oja-Dunaway with his twenty years at the Mill Top or like troubadour Gamble Rogers, who—when he died attempting to rescue a drowning swimmer—had a state park named for him.

The Bridge of Lions was lately threatened with demolition and replacement so cars could move faster between beach and town and barge traffic could move more safely beneath it. An outraged citizenry and preservationists from around the state convinced the Department of Transportation to back down and go for Plan B: substructure modifications. Saved are ramps of graceful arches and ornamental lights that lead to the bridge draw, flanked by four belvedere towers and marble lions on pedestals gazing into the Plaza. The bridge dates from 1927—a youthful landmark from when this city was already 362 years old but nonetheless cherished. From the bridge, daylight shows the colors of houses along the Avenida. In the distance, a train whistles (a compound at the edge of downtown still serves as headquarters for Flagler's Florida East Coast Railroad). Morning vaults an amphitheater of blue over the city. Rising light shows ochre, pink, dark red, and white. Gray floods the Castillo. Shapes emerge: bollards, sloping bulkheads, picket porches on the fronts of colonial buildings, slanty roofs. Flocks of birds dapple the western sky in wondrous formation. They soar above the spires, they skim the bay. Flapping wings mimic the flutter of wind on water. The city is a stage. Frocks in shop windows appear behind stout stucco walls that make it easy to imagine they were meant to repel cannonballs. Scaffolding for a façade improvement seems designed by people who wear knee britches and jerkins. In the damp, Druids dance. Stained glass windows of St. Luke, St. John, St. Matthew, and St. Mark in this town suggest a time five hundred years nearer theirs.

Conservation Losses and Gains

Along Highway A1A south of town, "big history" vanishes. The look becomes mid-twentieth century, much of the way without trees because the land was filled. The Alligator Farm and Zoological Park endures from 1893 (relocated here in 1922). Behind lies Davis Shores, the subdivision of a twenties developer who worked both coasts of Florida. (His name also attaches to a small island community alongside downtown Tampa.) Nearby is the former estate of August Heckscher, once parks commissioner of New York City, who developed one of two sections of St. Johns County here and whose name attaches to the road along the north shore of the St. Johns leading to the river's mouth.

Across the road, St. Augustine Lighthouse, built in 1876, still stands open to the public. An original light built into a Spanish watchtower in 1824 but decommissioned in 1874, six years later crashed into the sea. However, its restored keeper's quarters, once threatened with destruction, were saved by the Junior Service League and now house a historical museum and an impressive new visitors center. The site has become the second-most-visited after the

Castillo. A recent historical exhibition at the museum revealed more about Florida's racial history. One display explained that at MacDill Field in Tampa, German POWs refused to work if blacks were allowed to dine with whites. When blacks were segregated to separate mess halls, they rioted. When Harlem Renaissance painter Jacob Lawrence was drafted into the Coast Guard, he briefly served at the Ponce de Leon Hotel before he was transferred to an Alaska weather patrol ship manned by an intentionally integrated crew. Lawrence was already established, having exhibited at New York's Museum of Modern Art, but the ship's captain at least helped Lawrence pursue his art. He became a leading twentieth-century painter and the first African American represented in the permanent collection of New York's MOMA.

Back of the lighthouse is the residential section called Lighthouse Park, once meant as the start of a city called Anastasia, but where roads today remain dirt and the houses unusually nonconforming. They are octagonal, brick, board, shingle. Two connect by a wooden bridge. This was one of the county's first residential summer sites and dates from the Flagler boom. In fact, Flagler was given the first lot but never built. One who did was Flagler's second in command throughout his railroad years, James Ingraham. Others who lived or still live here include Andrew Carnegie II, Boss Tweed of New York City, a retired art editor of the *Boston Post,* Ring Lardner's educator grandson, and Gamble Rogers. Residents still speak about Rogers's performance when the lighthouse was saved and reopened after the long preservation struggle.

Beaches line the shore where a long section back to Salt Run marsh is set aside as Anastasia State Park. The site was a military reservation during the Spanish-American War. Park ranger Rick Cain reflects on Spain three centuries before that, when Sir Francis Drake walked this shore in 1586, two years before he defeated the Spanish Armada. For years, that early Spanish history was dramatically recalled in *The Cross and Sword,* an official state play about St. Augustine's founding. But people stopped coming. The amphitheater sits empty except for events like the annual Gamble Rogers Folk Festival.

A Melodrama of Misplaced Meddling

A1A runs everywhere through the resort town of St. Augustine Beach. It ran through the park before a nor'easter in the winter of 1985–86 blew the road out along the beach. A section of that original road, partly dirt, remains signed as Old A1A. Coquina rock quarries mined for building the Castillo de San Marcos and much of the town remain alongside, filling with water and becoming ponds in rainy season. The old road now empties into A1A Beach Boulevard, which exalts the original name as it curves east and south to St. Augustine Beach. A1A without modifiers has become a new road cut through bush to the west that opened new development sites along that side of Anastasia Island, reducing the flow of longer-distance traffic through St. Augustine Beach, where pedestrians absorbed by vacation bliss do better with fewer rushing cars.

Built on Flagler land, St. Augustine Beach became the vicinity's first splashy summer resort after winter resort goers began continuing south. Hotels opened before World War I. An annual Chautauqua developed, but radio killed that, and then the land boom collapsed. The WPA built a fishing pier and twin hotels of coquina. One that remained became St. Augustine Beach City Hall.

A melodrama of misplaced meddling plays out here. The historic sea channel to St. Augustine occupied the Salt Run. Then the Army Corps of Engineers cut a new inlet, the "finest thing in the world." Except that hydraulic effects tore away the beach. Now the resort beach relies on pumped-in sand. But in 2002, the sand was so coarse (from dredging the mouth of the St. Johns River) that the project was discontinued. An alternative plan to pump sand from nearby ocean bottom failed when the late start of the project threatened turtle nesting season. Now nothing will happen until 2005 or 2006. No one seems to get it right. Below the state park in the beach town, so much sand was earlier deposited between the parking lot and sea that the fishing pier barely reaches the water.

The great town planner John Nolen made St. Augustine Beach one of his projects in Florida. But little trace of his work remains. Today, hotels, motels, and subdivisions go up willy-nilly, though residents lately forced through a 35-foot height limit on new buildings. History lives among the scatter. One beach house belonged to the former husband of Flagler's niece and heiress, Louise Wise (some say she was his daughter born by Mary Lilly Kenan before their marriage). At La Fiesta, up the block at the corner, a motel tower shows the decorative tile of Alfons Bernhard, an eccentric who contributed similar tile work downtown, all of which has been destroyed by unsympathetic developers. Farther along the road is the development called Sea Colony. As recently as the turn of the century, this was the last remaining shore of undisturbed maritime hammock outside the state park. Then, developer David Fleeman, accused by many of cynically toying for years with conservationists who tried to acquire the site, cleared it for housing.

Development lessens but hardly stops nearing Crescent Beach where the shore road drops to two lanes. The narrowing was a preservation victory led by real estate broker Pat Hamilton, whose family has lived in Crescent Beach since 1959 (and who in 2004 donated nearby land for an office of the Florida Wildlife Federation that works to protect local marsh). Brad Miller rents kayaks and runs fishing charters from an old shack and board house where Cubbedge Road comes up from the Matanzas River. A bridge once came to ground here. The place was a goner ten years ago when the fish camp owner died till Hamilton and a buddy risked a pile of money to save it. Lots that ran from the beach a mile to the Intracoastal Waterway once sold for $1,000. African Americans bought here starting in 1928. The vicinity was called Butler's Beach for the black businessman who developed it. The fact that development took place after the boom reflects the countercyclical nature of black resorts, typically built at times when whites were out of the market. American Beach on Amelia Island developed in the mid-thirties, and Bethune Volusia Beach in Daytona Beach just before World War II. A few African American owners remain at Butler Beach, as does a public beach on the waterway. Otherwise, low condominiums have replaced the original houses, though on the beach dune, original dwellings lackadaisically maintained appear next to steroidal houses on manicured lots. A road marker merely identifies Butler Beach; no one would know that Gloria, Mary, Minnie, and Rudolf Streets are named for Butler's children. No sign marks the house where Martin Luther King Jr. fled after the attack in St. Augustine Beach.

South atop the dune is the former beach house of Marjorie Kinnan Rawlings and her second husband, Norton Baskin. (Rawlings's maid Idella Parker, before her own authorship, also lived on the grounds but without the view.) Rawlings's house was another of those saved from teardown by developers after a long struggle. You wonder why money means so much to them and memory so little! For privacy, Rawlings paid $1,000 for an extra lot. The would-be developer had eyes for the lot alone that had risen in value to $200,000. But it wasn't only developers that threatened the house. The structure itself was falling down and had to be stabilized and substantially rebuilt. Rooms of the house are imaginatively offset from each other, extending into an addition that the house's savior, Mary Elizabeth Streeter of Indianapolis, built onto the extra lot. The house is delightfully beachy; with board interiors and open beams, it is brightly painted and full of cotton throw rugs. The rooms are filled with Rawlings's books, a photo of her Cross Creek house, a collection of pottery from a Cross Creek maker, art, and memorabilia. The big kitchen with its own fireplace invites conversation. The house is available for weekly and longer rentals.

Rawlings wasn't alone attracted to this almost wilderness beachfront. Former Florida governor Haydon Burns of Jacksonville and former U.S. congressman Sid Herlong had houses overlooking the sea. Pat Hamilton prefers living to the west along the Matanzas River where the wind blows less forcefully over old board and batten houses along dirt lanes tucked into cypress and oak hammock. A bridge crosses from Crescent Beach to U.S. 1, I-95, and a four-lane section of Florida's "Intrastate Highway" to Palatka. The road has spurred new scabby growth along the beach.

Six miles farther south along A1A, a free ferry carries visitors to Fort Matanzas National Monument with its watchtower on Rattlesnake Island. This was a 1742 Spanish fortification against invaders who might have threatened St. Augustine up Matanzas Inlet. The stone tower replaced hurriedly thrown-up wood and thatch.

Summer Haven lies just across the inlet bridge. The colony of pastel houses feels languorous, like some Bahamian out-island. Shell lanes wind through. You reach to the windward section from a gas stop that cuts along a section of old A1A that hugs the shore. Even before the storms of 2004, the road ran narrow and crumbling at its sea edge before it ran out altogether. A barrier guards drivers from the beach where the road has collapsed. The view is wild, bleached by sand and salt with its sunlight-absorbing spray. Tracks run just behind the dune to some last few houses up on stilts—though doomed to wipeout when some hurricane comes bashing through, at least saved for awhile after the storms of 2004, when state funds for beach protection promised to help repair shoreline here.

A Love of Simplicity

Summer Haven evokes the thirties, a time when Tom Schmidt's grandmother would entertain Rawlings and Princess Angela Scherbatow, a Flagler County heiress, at tea. The family was a branch of the Pittsburgh Mellons who settled in Palatka soon after Flagler's railroad arrived in St. Augustine, choosing this place for their summers by the sea. A lodging or two opened, but everything except for the side-by-side houses Schmidt and his wife, Susan, are restoring was destroyed by fire and hurricane. The Hut dates from 1882, the Lodge from 1895, the rest of Summer Haven from 1915. Schmidt's mother tells stories of arriving at the Monson from Pittsburgh to wait for the tide that would float a boat up the river. Mail and groceries came once a week. Rainwater was collected in cisterns; kerosene fueled light. "Off the grid," she says, now eighty-eight, remembering herself as a tomboy who fished and shot a gun. She later learned to fly.

Schmidt for years was chief counsel and vice president of the Nature Conservancy in western Pennsylvania. He doubled as curator for Fallingwater, the Frank Lloyd Wright house donated to the Nature Conservancy by an art patron. The neighborhood holds cachet for environmentalists. John Hankinson, a favorite Florida son lately in charge of the EPA district office in Atlanta and fabled for his rock 'n' roll harmonica, has moved his family here.

A while ago, the county tax assessor suggested that the Schmidts tear their houses down because they weren't worth anything. Memory is. There's a picture of Schmidt at age two being bathed in the sink of the Hut. That's where he and his wife live. They rent out the Lodge, now popular, the same as Summer Haven altogether, summers and winters alike. Schmidt calls the place "a constant in my life. We like that it's not fashionable and not busy." The Hut is a bedroom, a bathroom, a small kitchen and a long woody living room heated by propane without central air-conditioning. Schmidt works at a "desk" made of packing board on a valise propped on a daybed. He cites Freud on the fulfillment of childhood dreams.

"We love the simplicity," says his wife. "It's our doublewide." It's also the repository for historic art. One photo shows people boating along Pellicer

Creek in hats, coats, and full dresses. Another, popular black oysterman Gene Johnson, who long fed locals at his bare-floor oyster shack. Early flicker film in the hands of a friend, Mike Greenberg, retired director of the Whitney Laboratory over the Flagler County line in Marineland, shows cars moving jerkily down A1A soon after the road was built.

Near North of St. Augustine

The Bridge of Lions and the Matanzas River that set Anastasia Island apart from the mainland south of St. Augustine are matched north of the city by the Usina Bridge and a 36-mile peninsular A1A that extends through Ponte Vedra Beach into Duval County to the mouth of the St. Johns River.

Heading north out of the city are the Mission of Nombre de Dios and Shrine of Our Lady of La Leche, America's first mission and the site of the founding of the La Leche League Against Cancer. Along the water, a grove of trees marks the graveyard where the first Catholic nuns on the continent lie buried beside by a 208-foot stainless steel cross. Many feel the good energy of this town emanates from this park. Just north is an attraction that houses the so-called Fountain of Youth.

On a clear morning in St. Augustine, everything hangs out crisply, history etched against blue sky. Everything feels sane. The road is a lovely two lanes leaving the mainland through an early postboom suburb with big trees that embower bungalows. A causeway launches across marsh before reaching the bridge. A road cuts off to the Florida School for the Deaf and the Blind, a little beach park to the other side. The new bridge carries A1A just north of Vilano Beach.

The first Vilano Bridge was built in 1926 to connect a subdivision left from Flagler days. A developer inspired by the boom had linked the beach and mainland by narrow-gauge railroad. But everything burned, and the Flagler momentum was moving downstate, so nothing more happened. After the bridge opened, Heckscher platted a new subdivision, but his timing was bad again. Up to World War II, houses got put up only one or two at a time. A fishing camp went in, some motels and mobile homes, a few restaurants, a pool hall and bar. Not until the 1980s did a large new subdivision called Porpoise Point get developed. That land could have been bought for conservation for less than a million dollars. A purchase opportunity by ballot was voted down. Strangely, comparable acreage has collected in the public domain by a windfall—at least by a tidal shift.

The inlet into St. Augustine had kept moving south, depositing sand along the south side of Vilano Beach, eventually reaching out more than a mile. But the sand was eroding from Anastasia Island, threatening houses along the beach. The new inlet was cut through the built-up sand, which still left more than a quarter mile attached to Vilano. This attached to Porpoise Point. Grass has grown on the fledgling dunes and the site has now become a favorite picnic and recreation area but without facilities of any sort. It floods in heavy rain. Presumably the accreted land belongs to the county. No one is sure what will happen. That might depend on a redevelopment program for the town.

Something had to happen when the new Usina Bridge opened in 1995 and reached the peninsula a few hundred yards north of the beach town. People feared Vilano would die without the traffic that used to come through. But the new bridge hasn't at all dampened prospects. A new fishing pier has succeeded at the foot of the old bridge, as have a marina and charter business. Neon bunnies still hop out of a magician's hat atop the Magic Beach Motel. Gentrification has seen the Lazy Sands Bar turn from a favorite watering hole to a hot dog place. A new Hampton Inn has gone up. The idea is to replace the hardscrabble look of the village with a town center at the foot of the bridge. So far a large gazebo has gone in there. Another is planned for the beach end of the street. Not much is sure beyond that.

The beach all the way up the coast is less crowded than along Anastasia Island, though many of its 20-foot-high dunes were flattened in 1999 by Hurricane Floyd, and much of the way houses sit atop or behind the dunes. The road passes a landmark in the form of an early Irish church. Some call it a castle—four stories without windows, without plumbing, built by a stonemason and carpenter in a grove of oaks gnarled by salt breeze. It's open for devotion and visits the third Sunday each month. A midwife and her husband own it.

Up A1A past the castle, the road was built in the early thirties, finished in 1932. There's nothing but sand beneath the roadbed. It keeps settling and getting repaved. You can feel the ups and downs as you drive. It was paved of Alabama pea rock set in asphalt—"Great for slingshots," says Frank Usina, who grew up here, third generation of a Minorcan family, now with two generations beyond his own also in residence. Usina's father, Francis, was born on the peninsula in 1900. Usina remembers his father saying it was easier to go to Pablo than to St. Augustine. He could ride his motorcycle up there, but St. Augustine had to be done by water. Even with the bridge and road, the south end of the peninsula long remained empty but for Vilano and Surfside, the next settlement north.

Most everyone drives straight through, but the place has its history. Surfside began as a summer-home community reached by that narrow-gauge railway from town, but the horse-drawn service was already gone by 1890. After that, people came by boat. The community is now year-round, still beautiful toward the river where the old oaks grow. Roads of asphalt and lime rock run from the river to sea, so everyone has easy beach access. The Usinas have lived here since 1900. The first family house, from around 1890, is still back on a site that lately held Oscar's Old Florida Grill. Only the sign remains from a recent fire. A little "plant house" in the compound supplied electricity at the end of World War II, powered by a 32-volt generator run on wet cell batteries. Still here, too, is a brick fire pit used to cook oysters over hardware mesh. Lights were strung through the oaks for oyster fries. People ate outdoors at tables. Oscar's came later and wasn't all that technologically advanced. Usina owned it and talks of rebuilding.

The family business is an RV park just north by the river along an old railroad grade. Horse-drawn cars brought people to a bathhouse on the beach in the 1890s. The RV park feels as if it would be congenial to wood nymphs. The roads are shell beneath the maritime hammock. An area is set aside for tents. There's a fire site. The place suffers in the ratings because Usina and his wife, Betty, won't pave the roads. "Pave them and the character goes," Usina argues. Archaeologists digging here have found a superficial level of poor foodstuffs. They surmise that Timucuan women lived here alone with children when the Spanish carried their men away to work elsewhere and women were left unable to gather adequate food.

From North Beach Camp, the narrow way between sea and marsh extends straight-shot north through the section known as South Ponte Vedra. Before the fence law in 1949, hogs and cattle ranged free here. Hogs would dig up turtle eggs on the beach—"Grade-A razorbacks," Usina calls them. At fourteen and fifteen, he would slop the hog garbage. People still remember stories about hogs getting drunk from slop out of moonshine stills.

The dunes have always blocked views of the beach from the road, though every once in a while a gap opens. Vacationing drivers suddenly glimpse the sea, hit the brakes, and get rear-ended. Instead of the dunes, today post–Hurricane Hugo houses block the view. This area was part of Stockton, Whatley, Davin property and was all platted. Few houses were built in the forties and fifties. Now they're almost solid on the ocean for 10 miles. People put up mailboxes shaped like anhingas, dolphins, manatees, mermaids, pelicans, and sailfish because they're happy to be here—though maybe less happy since Serenata Beach has been built. About 1,000 units of beach- and marshfront condos of Spanish Colonial mish mash have gone up, pushing the shore road west, convenient as a driveway for those living here.

It's a blessing that developer Herb Peyton (father of Jacksonville's current mayor), who came to control Ponte Vedra, had some trouble financing his acquisitions at a time when he owned much of the marshy peninsula west across the Guana River, once used by the Spanish and British for rice cultivation. He sold 12,000 acres to the state, which formed a large part of today's Guana Tolomato Matanzas National Estuarine Research Reserve, one of the great gifts of Florida east coast conservation. This section of the reserve runs along the sea, west across the shore road fronting the river and through the farther peninsula. There's a section here that old-timers call "the neck" where the state refused to permit Stockton, Whatley, Davin to build a bridge. Next anybody knew there was a dredge at work and a dam constructed across the neck. The state had not only built the dam but laid a road atop that connected to the far side! There was something about the dam getting built to incubate fish in the northern portion of the river. For sure, everybody knew there was something fishy going on. There still is. The same folks of Ponte Vedra who have turned the river into a septic pit and who aggressively defend property rights and family values keep trying to get a piece of the Guana public wilderness for a school and for ball fields that they're unwilling to provide from their private holdings. Their persistent efforts to close beaches as a way to keep nonresidents out has spurred efforts to pass a Florida Open Beaches Act.

The dam could never be built today, but you likely can't get rid of it either. Too much fertilizer runoff has drained from Ponte Vedra lawns into the dammed section that wouldn't be allowed to flow into the working estuary. Not to say the fishing's bad. The river was always a nursery for shrimp, fish, crab, and oysters. You can still fish here, though the dammed section of the river has turned shallow from sedimentation and on hot summer days big fish will die from lack of oxygen. Still, on moon tides, the dam road is loaded with people fishing and crabbing, though oysters are off limits.

There used to be a Coast Guard station where the road to the dam drops from the shore road. During World War II, there were horse stables and kennels used for patrolling the beach. German saboteurs successfully landed from submarines along the beach at Ponte Vedra. They were caught when another landing party was captured up north and revealed their presence in Florida. In 2005, the research reserve opened a splendid environmental education center at the site.

Pockets of another Florida remain sandwiched in time along stretches of S.R. 210, a conduit for Sawgrass traffic. Where the road ends at the sea, surf washes the site of a pier built atop palm pilings. The place is locally remembered as Mickler's Landing. Until the early 1940s, the pier was a popular fishing place. Nearby west along the Intracoastal Waterway in Palm Valley, Sid Mickler recalls how his dad used to give him leftover tire strips from the Model A Ford for his slingshot. He remembers the day his dad grabbed that slingshot and with a rock popped a rattlesnake dead in the yard.

"To show you how desolate this country was," says Mickler, "I was in the seventh grade when I flushed my first toilet. When the water started rushing in I ran out afraid I'd ruined something. That same year we stopped making moonshine." Mickler lives in the same house he and his wife of seventy-five years have occupied since around 1960, a half mile from where they lived twenty-four years before that. There wasn't anybody within a half mile when Mickler was a kid. Today houses line the roads of Palm Valley. Everywhere, big houses put up along the waterway only a few years ago get bulldozed for mansions two and three times the size. In 2002, the old drawbridge was pulled down for a soulless piece of concrete. A Ponte Vedra developer bought the old Palm Valley Crossing restaurant. He wants to put up an immense boat storage vault. People are up in arms.

4 FLAGLER COUNTY

Spuds, Thunder, and the Authority of Florida

Figure 4.1. A street scene from Flagler Beach in the 1950s. Courtesy of the Florida State Archives.

Figure 4.2. The Flagler Beach Pier and beaches. Courtesy of the Flagler County Convention and Tourist Bureau.

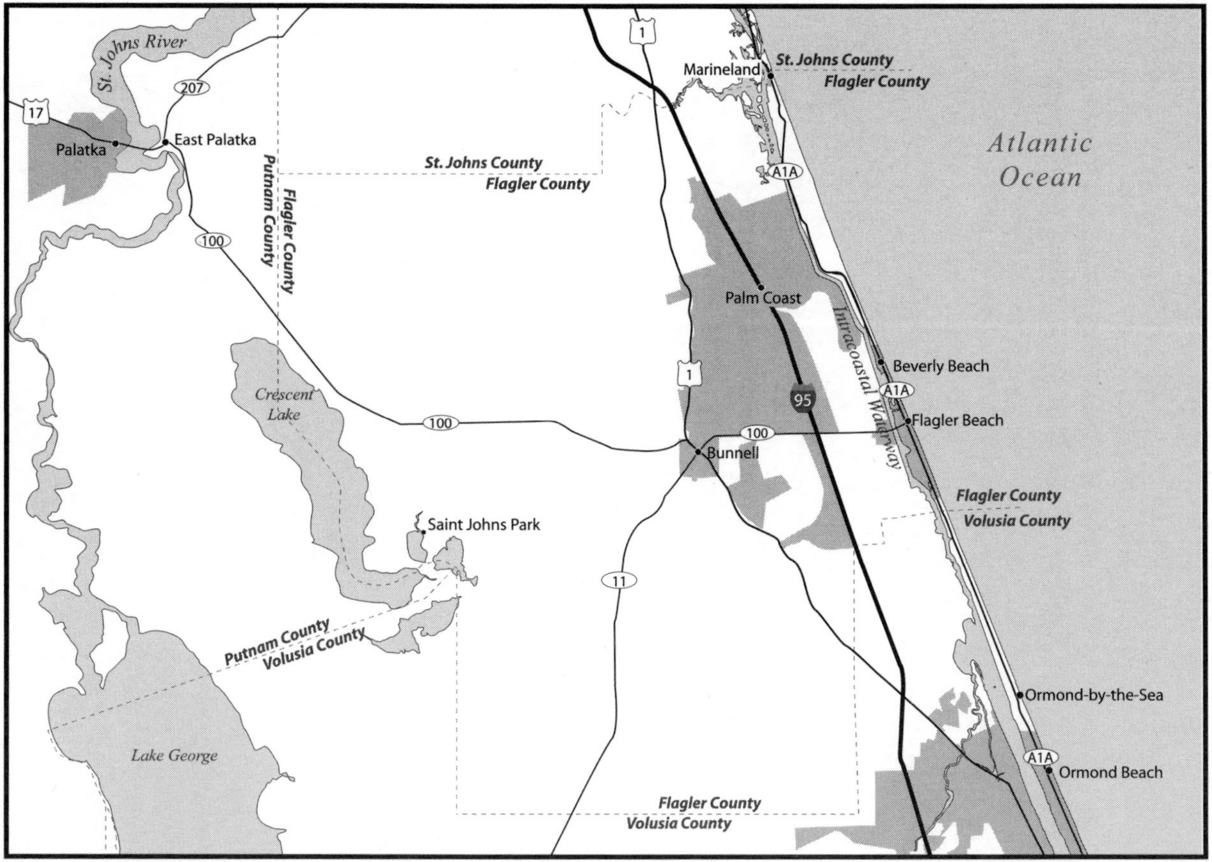

Map 4. Flagler County

When the legislature chose Flagler County for the site of Florida's agricultural museum, contenders elsewhere shook their heads. Flagler? They grow what? Flagler's dirt farmers not only outbid powerful cattle interests that make Florida the number-three cow state east of the Mississippi. They also beat out orange and grapefruit growers that rank Florida among global citrus powers. Flagler stood tall among the tubers. Got spuds? Yeah, but no milk-on-the-upper-lip chic, scant "Real Food for Real People" beef-promoting swagger, few esteemed packing-crate labels to tantalize collectors of grove memorabilia. No claim even on Spuds, the wide spot in the road over the county line. However sore losers might disparage Flagler's win, this anomalous coastal county savors its prize. No small potatoes. Check out the spud on the county seal and on the doors of county trucks. Potato pride—though not much sizzle selling that steak. Where's any market-tempting sour cream and chives or bronzed and saliva-inducing fries?

You have to wonder, too, what contribution potatoes make to logo-loving Florida, which gave the world bikinied beach babes, Flipper, Shamu, and Mickey to the mth degree. You might also ask yourself whether Flagler exists significantly out of touch, and if so, is this altogether a bad thing?

Bruce Piatek will tell you that solid credentials won Flagler its museum prize. The site is close by an interstate highway and near established popular attractions, two of the selection criteria. Piatek's domain is only 3 miles from a fast route to Orlando and only thirty minutes from St. Augustine. It's also in Flagler's favor that its site is far enough from any subdivision so that "we won't have to throw baseballs and Frisbees back over the fence," says Piatek, the museum director.

Though assuredly not part of the selection criteria, Flagler County nonetheless reflects agriculture's precarious transit through twentieth-century Florida. It supplies a bigger-than-IMAX-sized show-and-tell across its 504–square-mile entirety. Flagler hardly stands alone in the fading of Florida's farming tradition, but in the juxtaposition of its distinct places, Flagler stands apart and worthy of telling the state story. Here is the last farming county seat hanging on in Northeast Florida, the last rural-influenced oceanfront tourist town left anywhere in the state, and a freakishly fast-growing developer town almost certain to be the last that reaches from cattle pens to coastal concierge and that steadily drives Flagler as the fastest-growing county in Florida, lately seventh-fastest in America. In their still-separate proximity, the three towns keep the county—a microcosm of the state—off balance and with familiar ways of life subject to tectonic displacement. Summing up two centuries of Florida history, Flagler remains both rooted and flooded by newcomers, caught in the conflict between what its people value and forces of promotional change that defy easy adjustment. High-category hurricanes only rarely blow through, but gales of real estate hype have wrought category-five havoc. Until recently known as "the county that time forgot," Flagler in the next fifteen years is forecast to double its numbers to 120,000.

If Flagler promises some quick overview of Florida, it's additionally attractive because it's so little known. The county claims the appeal of first impression. After you've been to the more famous coastal places, what might Flagler be like? Who outside of Florida has ever even heard of it? The name of Flagler the man—this titan in state memory who was John D. Rockefeller's partner in the creation of Standard Oil, America's greatest monopoly—attaches to little otherwise significant today. Apart from his Palm Beach mansion that is now a much-visited museum of the Gilded Age, there's no Flagler bank, no big league ball team named for him, no Flagler cruise line, no Flagler limo, moustache style, or soft drink. As for anything else that might have made the county famous, does anybody remember Marineland? It's the granddaddy of all SeaWorlds, begun in 1938 as the first marine park in America. An early sponsor of the University of Florida Whitney Laboratory for marine research, for years Marineland was an important source of county revenue. But a decade ago, Orlando's theme parks competitively delivered Marineland a knockout blow, and only lately has a new owner attempted the attraction's revival. Along with revival is coming significant expansion of the Whitney Lab. Flagler also claims big Palm Coast—or, more accurately, big Palm Coast claims Flagler. Fast-growing and now topping 50,000 people, the recently incorporated city has quickly become the county's dominant political influence, starting as a nonplace in the early seventies and forecast to reach 250,000 at build-out. Yet probably few households outside Flagler and its neighboring counties would recognize the name of this sprawling ITT-spawned city. For years it was known as that "Garfield the Cat place" for a rash of billboards along I-95 featuring the in-your-face cartoon character that announced the town's location.

A Curious and Compelling Place

Even the attachment of Flagler's name to the county reveals a history both curious and compelling. Flagler, who became Florida's preeminent railroader and hotelier, never sought to attach his name to anything. After all, public utterance of his name had become a slur when reformers bent on curbing the growth of monopoly power at the turn of the twentieth century attacked him as chief lobbyist for Standard. Nonetheless he wound up on the map when citizens here—hopeful as a cargo cult invoking the Great Spirit—in 1917 split away from St. Johns and Volusia counties. They named their new in-between place for the mogul who ushered Florida into the national economy. Flagler had died five years earlier, but not before his railroad had boomed the coast everywhere between Jacksonville and Key West—everywhere but here. Flagler ran his line inland from St. Augustine to tap then-bustling Palatka before angling back to the coast at Ormond Beach. That left a 29–mile hypotenuse of the great railroader's triangle untracked. It was simple proof that in Flagler, like everywhere else in the state, transportation has been destiny.

Whether as divine reward or something else, the railroad finally came through in the mid-twenties, but it was too late in the Florida boom to pay off. Flagler, the county, languished for almost fifty years.

Ag origins were well rooted. For a time, they bestowed pioneer prosperity on the west side of the county-to-be. The warm Florida climate and western waterways successfully drew settlers late in the nineteenth century. Midwest promoters wholesaled farm sites. The one-lane, bricked Dixie Highway of Carl Fisher that linked Chicago with Miami Beach came through the new county, putting Bunnell, the county seat, on the map. Poles from Wisconsin settled Korona. St. Johns Park grew as the region's economic and social center, at one time boasting a hotel, a rooming house, and a dance hall. Farmers stayed busy year-round from turpentining and timbering, from cattle and chicken raising, wild hog capture, citrus, and notably potatoes and cabbage among row crops. For a time they shipped their produce through Crescent Lake and down the north-flowing St. Johns to Jacksonville. Their economy quickened when Flagler laid his track through East Palatka, bypassing the coast and giving western growers a quicker way to northern markets. But in the absence of east side rail, nothing drew attention to the coast, even after crop disease, regional displacement, and freeze over time shut down many farms. Potatoes and cabbage stayed viable. Cattle still grazed western ag lands, but St. Johns Park disappeared, recalled today only by a fish camp, a couple of boat launches, and a boardwalk through the marsh at Haw Creek Preserve. Once notable Espanola disappeared like most of the Dixie Highway it sat beside, only 7 bricked miles remaining, more weedy than prized.

Because the railroad never opened the coast, land sales in Flagler, different from anywhere else, occurred largely apart from tourism. Only now might that be changing. It is different, too, along the coast, where there never has been any style-setting outpost of northern influence. St. Augustine first, then Ormond Beach and Daytona Beach, all boomed by the railroad, were too powerful for any hard-to-reach beach town to establish itself in between. The Intracoastal Waterway had been dug through what became Flagler County in 1890 without any bridge across it. No road ran along the beach. It wasn't until the war years that a two-car ferry spanned the canal and a recreational casino made beach visits inviting. Two early landowners, George Moody and D. F. Fuqua, opened subdivisions in what pretentiously became Ocean City. Then in 1920, Moody completed the first bridge, a turnstile operation at the site of today's high bridge. Many of the early buyers were successful farmers from the west side. The shore was their families' summer place. Tourists visited Fernandina, Jacksonville, and St. Augustine—city places, cosmopolitan. When a hotel finally opened in 1925, that was local, too, built by Moody and Fuqua. Though the hotel was popular, its clientele ranked far below the social class that favored Palm Beach and Miami. When a beach road took form, for years it was accessible south to Ormond and Daytona only at low tide. Even when relocated atop the dune, becoming the "inside" road, improvements

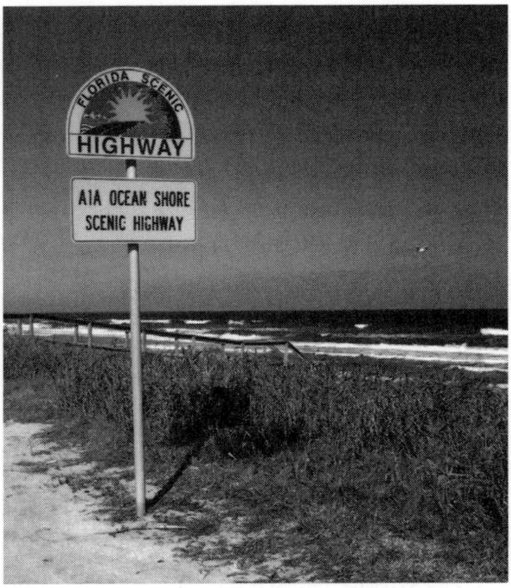

Figure 4.3. Highway A1A in Flagler County has been designated a Florida Scenic Highway. Courtesy of the Flagler County Convention and Tourist Bureau.

were limited to shell and rock surfacing subject to ruts. Development was slow. Even landmark achievements that would have boomed places elsewhere had little impact along the Flagler coast.

Things might have been different in 1927 but for the Florida bust and the Depression that quickly followed. In late winter that year, a prominent Flagler citizen, Claude G. Varn, completed a wooden toll bridge across the Matanzas Inlet north of the Flagler line. Varn was responsible for a significant change in the course of what became Highway A1A through the county. Florida's highway builders had avoided any bridge across Matanzas Inlet because of tricky channel currents. At the time, there was no U.S. 1. The only north-south road through the county was still Carl Fisher's brick road down from St. Augustine and Hastings through Bunnell and then alongside Florida East Coast tracks to Ormond. Varn's bridge changed all that. It cut the 70-mile drive to 48 miles and improved the way with an asphalt surface. For the first time, cars could operate "from Jacksonville Beach to the Halifax Inlet a total of 92 miles," comprising "a combined ocean driveway . . . the like of which cannot be advertised by any other part of the world," boasted the *St. Augustine Evening Record.* A year earlier, the *New York Times* already had announced a 522-mile "marine automobile drive" meant for completion between Jacksonville and Key West. Promoters through northeastern counties were proclaiming what they called Ocean Shore Boulevard, "delightful, dustless, direct," the shortest possible route between St. Augustine and Daytona Beach, "in sight of the ocean practically all the way, as beautiful as can be found in the tropics, as direct as the crow flies [with] dashing waves [and] jumping fish."

Despite the promise of the bridge and the road, the effort just about ruined Varn. He was land-rich and influential. His daughter, Helen Varn Holton, widowed in Flagler Beach today, recalls her father at one time having amassed ownership of more oceanfront property than anyone else in Florida. For a while Varn was a law partner of David Scholtz of Daytona Beach, who later became governor. Varn was ahead of his times, says Holton, in 1911 convinced that segregation was unlawful even though his own father had been a courier in the Confederate army. Holton remembers her father explaining how important the inlet bridge was to raising the value of his Flagler holdings and how, hoping to find willing financiers, "he spent days walking Wall Street trying to get up the nerve to walk in. You see, Daddy was going to build this bridge even though he didn't even know how to use a screwdriver." He formed the St. Johns County Bridge Company and floated bonds the tolls were meant to repay. But soon after, when Florida completed U.S. Highway 1 through Northeast Florida, Varn had to abandon collections.

He began selling off land. One sale completely changed shorefront land use patterns. Ocean Shore Boulevard had run straight north from Flagler Beach (the former Ocean City) to a few miles along the coast shy of the bridge. The state road department had wanted to move the road inland to avoid the threat of erosion. Varn did the deal that put big bends into the road south and north, for 5 1/2 miles running the road through a heavily wooded section called Hammock close by the Intracoastal Waterway. When the highway people relocated the road, they dredged a wetland to form a lake they stocked with fish for Varn's pleasure—part of the deal. Years later, when ITT made its moves on the county, Palm Coast and DOT built a toll bridge spanning the Intracoastal Waterway that helped turn the seafront enclave between the two big curves into the county's most exclusive housing, site of a recently finished condominium-hotel wholly out of scale with anything else—an affront to local sensibilities—replacing Varn's fishing pond with an eighth new east side golf course and in 2003 hinting at the big league tourism that might inevitably follow.

Flagler Beach: Un-themed and Slow Changing

Yet if Flagler exists somehow behind the times, that also suggests that, obversely, it might be ahead of the times. There's no longer any surprise about how this works.

Looking back, twentieth-century Florida stands out as aberrant in its land use. No place like Palm Coast could clear-cut tens of thousands of acres today and dig miles of bulkheaded waterways. Everywhere, sprawl faces challenge. In Florida, the most remarkable land use change in a hundred years sees the emergence of year-round residential downtowns, in part induced by redevelopment incentives but so long resisted and now so quickly occurring that spontaneity seems the driving force. That appearance of spontaneity is compelling. Locals are creating downtowns as cosmopolitan as those long familiar up north—exciting at night, notable for dining, for shops that stay open late, and for innovative ways of getting around, from water taxis to elevated rail and trackless trolleys. Florida downtowns are mild in winter, casual at night, different from anything anyone is accustomed to almost anywhere else. They've become hugely popular and draw the eagerly curious. For the first time, Visit Florida, the state's tourism marketing agency, by promoting the emergence of Florida downtowns has aligned itself with a corrective force in state life. Especially lower down the coast in cities like West Palm Beach, Fort Lauderdale, and Miami, a sense grows that among the players in competitive high-volume tourism, Florida has to offer more than just golf and a beach.

Flagler may claim no trend-reversing downtowns, but little Flagler Beach satisfies in comparable resident-driven ways by its regard for what's genuinely local. It's that local character—big-city style or small town—that makes the difference. With only 5,000 people, Flagler Beach never has changed except slowly. It hasn't given up its character that now leaves it searching for some new identity. It always has remained un-themed with a high consensus that if the place ain't broken, there's no need to fix it. Small-scale works better and keeps the beachfront town the place locals know and like. They figure that outsiders will like it too, with its bed-and-breakfasts, its mom-and-pop restaurants, its walkability. It's this cachet more than Palm Coast or Bunnell that at this point draws worldly newcomers. They've come mainly from down the coast to escape congestion and sameness there for what makes Flagler Beach its own place. It's mostly northerners who relocate to Palm Coast, seemingly unaware before they come that the congestion and sameness they flee in New Jersey and Connecticut have followed them here. Nor does anyone yet seem aware of the genuine attributes of Bunnell that, like Flagler Beach, make it appealing—in the case of Bunnell, as a diamond in the rough. Bunnell's hope would be to remain unredeemed piecemeal.

S.R. 100, also known as Moody Boulevard, has connected Bunnell with Flagler Beach since 1920. It may be newly four-laned, but look down upon Flagler Beach from the high bridge to the sea and the small town slivered in between appears more like a question mark than an exclamation point, more "How come?" than "Gee whiz!" Elsewhere, Florida insists on skyscrapers and logo-topped hotels, but this remains a bathing shore town of still-rural shapes, of nostalgic effect. Ironic, says Helen Holton, because before, when the bridge crossed the Intracoastal at grade, while you could smell the salt marsh, you couldn't see the town. "Only now," she says, "can you see what a small town this is."

Look north and a single tower back of the beach got built. Who's surprised it came with a Hawaiian name? Developers delight in imported pretense. The building could have been called Flagler Towers, though that would have been its own affront, utterly devoid of mogul style as the intrusion is. A couple of mid-rise apartment buildings went up at the town's southern edge. Everyone regrets that these few buildings intruded before the town decided that nothing else would rise taller than 35 feet. Locals take these restrictions seriously. Fridays, a farmers market sets up on the lot where the Flagler Beach Hotel was torn down in 1972. Between that now-vacant lot and Ocean Shore Boulevard sits block-square Veterans Park. The park has a height limitation of 2 feet. When a 3-foot-high shuffleboard storage box got put up, it was protested and removed. That 2-foot height limitation protects the site to the west so that if a replacement hotel ever gets built, people rocking on its porch (the assumption is that people will always want to rock on its porch) won't face anything in the park that blocks their view of the sea.

Public interest lawyer Al Hadeed describes Flagler Beach as a place with a "rural beach town look, not Celebration conformity. It's a celebration of the vernacular, anti–big box and franchise, against corporate standardization, anti-garish—Flagler County Prozac. You know that when you enter the place. Any strategic-thinking businessman knows that what's scarce is worth far more. So the place isn't just intrinsically pleasing but has huge economic value."

Ocean Shore Boulevard still runs atop the dune. Indeed, storm tides still wash the road out. Talk of relocating the A1A designation surfaced a few years ago after University of Florida students presented ideas for reducing the impact of heavy seas. They suggested reassigning the designation a block west to Central Avenue and turning the existing road into a pedestrian way. Not likely. People here resist change. Open to the east with nothing between the town and West Africa, every day is a bad hair day in the little town. The sea blows a salty breeze that nothing blocks. No hotels, no condos. Maybe some days only a breeze blows, and some blessedly blue sky days when pelicans glide uniformly by as if strung together and the sea flattens like a picnic blanket, for an hour or two not even breeze. The open beach, the two-lane shore road, and the low little buildings make the town a tinted postcard, and visitors find themselves in it.

Surfing makes the scene. Surfing is what folks do when the wind blows big. Former national women's surfing champion Frieda Zamba is a Flagler Beach native. Lawyer Dennis Bayer with his office on the shore road has been known to drop his law books and grab his board. Others drive from Tampa and Atlanta to ride the swells that tropical storms crash against the dune. Surf fishing attracts leisurely anglers to the Flagler Beach Pier that, though badly damaged in 2004 by Hurricane Frances (twice before in the 1990s by Hurricane Floyd and Tropical Storm Irene), soon will again extend 854 feet from the little downtown. In the late nineties, a whale herd beaching itself made news.

Bucks run most places. Here, business guys talk funny. Tony Marlowe at the Golden Lion Café says "People tell me I could make a million bucks running a place like this in Miami." Marlowe is describing his restaurant across from the beach, schmoozing while raking the sand around open-air tables beneath slow-circling ceiling fans. "But this is where I want to be." Cara Merz, who runs her namesake sandwich and coffee shop on Central Avenue, says she and her husband first came to nearby Palm Coast. Her homemade macadamia nut cookies for 50 cents and Starbucks-quality coffee at $1.25 for a 12-ounce mug would have packed 'em in there. "Instead we moved to Flagler Beach," she says, watching a lone customer slowly spoon down a couple of scoops of ice cream while watching a TV financial report. "Here you can actually see the ocean."

The same sentiments brought restaurateurs Bob and Karen Iaccarino from the Hamptons to set up the swish White Orchid Inn and Spa, and Pittsburgh hoteliers Margaret and Tom Sheehan to open the ten-suite Plaza Caribe hotel. After he sold his successful boat works north of town, yachtsman Mark Tryworgy and his artist wife, Toni, opened the luxurious, all-suites Cottage by the Sea across from the beach, lately adding a restaurant. Except for gas stations, so far the only chain businesses in town are a couple of convenience stores, the Bank of America branch, an H & R Block office, an auto parts place, and a Dollar General store. A Pizza Hut folded. People prefer La Bella's. It's local.

Because the beach is open and places to stay are small-scaled, visitors don't hang out in lobbies or balconied rooms but instead walk the little downtown. You can walk your dog on the beach and drink a beer. Driving is banned (though not elsewhere in the county, where conservationists and advocates for the handicapped lately squared off about removing cars from the beach). Elsewhere, people meet easily at the historical museum newly opened in the old fire station and at mom-and-pop places like Pegasus. That's the mural-fronted, garage-filling used bookstore with some 60,000 titles run by single mom Bonnie Scott, who brought her then eight-year-old son here eleven years ago precisely because the place was (and is) virtually crime free. Two dogs and burning incense in the shop might seem almost unbelievably casual, but Zoee Forehand at Z Wave Surf Shop, president of the Flagler Beach Chamber of Commerce (different from the county chamber), says, "We want Flagler Beach to remain charming yet have enough tourism to keep our local business owners in business." It helps that most shopkeepers live in town. Like everybody here, they tend to live in bungalows and modest clapboard and shingle houses, even though expensive homes and garden condos are going up south of town. They're inflating land values, and still more posh places are getting built.

Businesspeople are known to leave their doors unlocked when they walk to the post office. The FedEx man hands letters to people when he sees them on sidewalks. At the local meat market, deputy county sheriff Harry Kuleski takes the pressure off busy Bug and Holly by fixing his own sandwiches. The pier has a restaurant that tourists try at least once, though the food's better at the rustic High Tides Snack Jack that sits on the beach a few miles south. Also worth a meal or two are a couple of places across the road: Blue in the old

Topaz Motel (the house that Fuqua built) and Starfire near Gamble Rogers Memorial State Recreation Area just north of the Volusia County line.

Bunnell: Rural and Laid to Rest

Bunnell is only 7 miles west of Flagler Beach. It's half the size of the beach town with only 2,500 people, but it's down and out. Palm Coast is capturing the road between, which in 2005 was newly four-laned all the way west to the county seat. Not that anybody much bothers making the trip except for unavoidable county business. The four-laning makes it easier and safer for truck traffic to travel between U.S. 1 and the interstate. Flagler is the only county along Florida's east coast where I-95 runs east of the county seat. Every kind of business and community activity that might appeal to residents of Palm Coast moved east out of Bunnell to either side of where I-95 crosses Moody. The big new hospital is here, the big new high school, the big new Flagler Auditorium, the main chamber of commerce office, the chain supermarkets. New roads pour into Moody from the most populous section of Palm Coast to the north. New Colbert Lane runs more than 7 miles from the heart of Palm Coast to Moody, where it ends east of the interstate. The entire way that hasn't been bought up for conservation (the Graham Swamp lately acquired) will be developed. Given the location of I-95 east of Bunnell, only piddling traffic comes through on its way from county seats like DeLand and Palatka to the beach.

Until the mid-sixties, when I-95 cut through the county, Bunnell still held its own. It was part of a rural world that former county commissioner Raymon Tucker, who died in 1998 at the age of eighty-four, grew up in. His place was Haw Creek Ranch down in Codys Corner southwest in the county. Tucker raised cattle and horses. It's a place where hay wagons pass by. Cars crunch across rumble strips at the few intersections. Wind shows its path through the moss that sways in oaks. Crows are audible; bees are audible. Enter Flagler the back way east out of Volusia and the already narrow road narrows some more. In winter, barns sit out in sere fields, roads carry four-number designations, as if afterthoughts. Florida evolved like this over a long time.

Tucker's family came from Orange County early in the Depression when he was seventeen. His father ran an outpost and sold everything from groceries to petticoats to ploughshares. "He grubstaked these old hunters. We would get gator skins in the summertime and furs in the wintertime. They'd go for a week before they'd pay for their groceries. There just wasn't any money. Dad would bring supplies 13 miles from the railhead with a team of oxen. It took from before daylight till after dark to make that trip. He bought one of the first Model T Fords that came out. He drove it home, next day got in and headed out, a little excited. We had a gate going out by the store. He came by and waved at us. We started hollering and he hit the gate and went right through it. My mother all those years after if she wanted to get his goat just said, 'Whoa Tom!' because that's what he hollered at the car while coming fast on the gate."

The family moved up to Flagler because an outbreak of Texas tick fever was killing cattle. They added potatoes. When they came, there wasn't any power or phone service. Tucker and his wife petitioned for both to be installed. He had to clear the 10-mile right of way from Bunnell to Haw Creek, renting a tractor to Florida Power and Light to pull the line. "The company had nothing," he recalled. "No equipment. It's hard to visualize. My wife flipped the switch when they turned on the phones so people could talk. That was back in the early fifties."

Tucker recalled how "my brother and I and a neighbor ran this county for ten years. We started out wanting to keep them all isolated at Palm Coast. We had a rule that if you didn't have paved streets, you could only build one house to ten acres. We figured that people might get a long-term deal on a doublewide trailer. But people kept moving in and they kept paving streets. We gave up on the rule. Still, those Palm Coast people didn't find their power for a while, and then a new board got elected. Bunnell and Palm Coast became two different worlds.

"For a long time, Bunnell used to be a gasoline alley for people coming through to Miami. Then some folks routed I-95 away from Bunnell to benefit some landholders. Bunnell became a ghost town. Downtown got to looking real bad. The best they come up with was to decorate some trashcans with psychedelic flowers. That was about it: one fellow laid Bunnell to rest and another fellow decorated the grave.

"Yet we've gotten better hospitals, doctors, and food supplies with Winn-Dixie, Wal-Mart, and the others. Along with the bad there's a lot of good. I've never been to New York City, and I don't want to go any more than I want to go to Palm Coast. But you know, too, I don't have any great love for Bunnell. We go in to church and to do our banking and still get our groceries there, but the next generation of the family all shops at Palm Coast."

In a county of almost 70,000 with five incorporated places, Bunnell rates in the middle above Marineland's 6 folks (down from 31 in 1980) and the 550 of Beverly Beach, a town of oceanfront RV parks just north of Flagler Beach. Founded in 1880, Bunnell lies along U.S. 1 and the FEC tracks, these days a soil-dusty place of commerce in guns, knives, septic tank supplies, and tractors. Town shows off long johns strung on a wash line, yards full of barely redeemable trash sold and traded with neighbors, and a Department of Corrections office. Grandmas in jeans ride their motorcycles up to the Jiffy Way. For entertainment, Bunnell has its annual Cracker Day Rodeo, the Fourth of July Parade, and the City of Lights Hay Ride, apart from the Masonic Lodge, the Shrine Club, and saloons. Palm Coast, incorporated more than a century later, with twenty times the people, now surrounds town on three sides. Residents here have their poodles groomed, check the Nasdaq and Dow averages while kibitzing with fellow retirees, and, at least in season, attend performances of the Russ Morgan Orchestra and the Irish Rovers at the 1,000-seat Flagler Auditorium. Restaurants serve "cuisine," and tennis gets played at the racquet club.

Joann King is a fourth-generation Floridian on her father's side and fifth on her mother's. She has served on the Bunnell Board of City Commissioners since 1990 and as mayor since 1993. She presides in a coquina city hall finished in 1934 by the WPA. The tops of the doors were cut into cross, duck, flower, and heart forms by hatchet. The commission meets at a folding table, and the public sits on folding chairs. Apart from official meetings, King wears blue jeans, sneakers, and a tee shirt that says GRITS for "Girls Raised in the South." Her father was born in St. Johns Park and ran the Flagler Beach Pier with her mother. For a while they ran a motel on Ocean Shore Boulevard. While her family worked at the pier, she met a boy she later married. They settled in Bunnell when the main north-south road still went through.

"This was a fantastic place to raise children. Everybody looked after every child. You knew everybody at the grocery and the post office. If anybody got sick, folks would put on a shrimp boil. There's still a bit of that. That's the way we want to keep things." But the mayor doesn't have a lot of control about what happens. She would like everybody to get together on how their buildings look but, she explains: "We can't go to Main Street because we've got too many people who can't afford it. You see, we used to make all kinds of money in Bunnell, but the minute I-95 went in, people had to leave. They couldn't make a living. We had dry cleaners, we had a movie theater. We lost a lot of gas stations, one or two restaurants and the Dixieana Motel with its restaurant.

"I do not like Palm Coast," she says, not that she can do anything about it. Between construction of I-95 and incorporation of the new city, Bunnell saw its revenues decline from every kind of tax. "We're always putting out little fires and we can't get the big things done," King says. "The city needs a third well, and one of the two is working at about 70 percent. The change could cost into six figures that the city doesn't have." King says the city needs streets redone and curbs, sidewalks, and storm-water systems put in. She lately got a second stoplight she wanted from DOT, and she stood up to them when they wanted to raise the speed limit from 35 to 45 through town, "which people already do. But DOT told me, in so many words, that in ten or fifteen years they're going to do what they want anyway."

Even when town gets its way, who can say it's for the best? In 2005, the state Department of Environmental Protection issued Bunnell a five-year permit to discharge 300,000 gallons of wastewater a day into a canal that drains into formerly healthy Haw Creek.

Ironically, King used to run the office of Lewis E. Wadsworth Jr., the big timberland owner who bought the Princess Place from Princess Angela Scherbatow and later sold his lands to ITT to start Palm Coast. Like Disney,

ITT used front men so sellers wouldn't know that a global company was behind the moves. King says Wadsworth would never have sold if he had known what was going to happen. "This was a beautiful county. My [second] husband would go out to Palm Coast to see what was happening and would say that they just totally raped the land. They scraped the most beautiful oak trees to bare earth. He would cry."

Palm Coast: New Jersey in Paradise

Palm Coast developed suddenly in the history of Flagler County, but it didn't emerge conceptually full-blown. It was part of an old thing in Florida. It was as old as land sold seasonally underwater or land offered as paradise that becomes the place you were looking to escape to paradise from. If no one else knew what ITT was doing, neither did ITT. They knew they wanted to sell tracts to northern buyers. Their buyers would be the same who bought from the Mackle Brothers and the Rosen Brothers, notorious swamp peddlers farther down the peninsula. The "brother pairs" were the Florida models, of course, selling land cheap to people who couldn't afford homes in the established resorts but who—glossy-eyed from Florida images and the idea that they, too, could live warm in winter—were ready to buy down on time. The first people who bought in 1965 and 1970 were people born early in the century, says Jerry Full, who became director of community affairs for Palm Coast, later vice president. He still lives in the city. About those early residents, Full remembers that "Some of these guys might have served in World War I. They had gone through the Depression, and these were the golden years. The houses had two or three bedrooms, a bath or a bath and a half. They didn't need a garage because a carport worked. They didn't have IRAs or 401(k)s; they had meager pensions at best, meager social security. The very nice family homes came along later."

Before ITT, nobody had tried to sell lots this way in these parts of Florida where it gets cold in winter. But this was the sixties. The cities were restless. People wanted out not just for the newness of the suburbs but also for safety. At Palm Coast, they were buying from ITT, the gold standard of corporate America.

ITT had turned to mass marketing lots because deregulation was in the air. Powerful as the company was, the future was uncertain. The company needed big bets to hedge what government had in mind. The company acquired Sheraton to sell hotel rooms. It acquired Avis to rent cars. These were can't-fail mainstream businesses. With Disney in Florida, what could beat retirement lots? All ITT had to do was plat the land, sell, and walk away. But it didn't work out that way. As a public company, ITT was subject to regulation by the Federal Trade Commission, which determined that selling lots in the middle of no place denied buyers adequate disclosure. ITT soon entered into a consent decree that called for the company to provide every lot with streets, sewers, and power and phone lines. When the company found itself in the community development business, it put lot salesmen in charge. Notions of new urbanism were still decades in the future. Suburbs ruled. People had cars; salesmen had quotas.

Nobody could imagine this kind of hustle in Flagler County. As Tucker said, they were all farmers. County population was about 6,000. Nobody had moved here for a long time. "This was a relatively poor county," says lawyer Hadeed. "Flagler did not have the skills to protect itself by planning. ITT had been buying surreptitiously. People thought they were buying for the timber. That's how people sold it to them. They had no idea that ITT would eventually wind up building expensive homes. There wasn't a clue that this was even possible. The scale is what blew them away. They couldn't think beyond their property rights beliefs—who were they to tell someone else like ITT what couldn't be done to its private property? In twenty years, the population multiplied by five and political power shifted to Palm Coast. ITT's people in effect became the county planning department."

Cut east off the I-95 exit that opens directly into Palm Coast and you're into any northern suburb. You're on Palm Coast Parkway instead of Birch Shore Parkway, and the supermarkets are Publix and Winn-Dixie instead of Safeway and Kroger. A Wal-Mart distribution center is going in the size of the Vehicle Assembly Building at Kennedy Space Center. Traffic clogs morning and evening and stays busy round the clock. There's no way to get anywhere except by car—no bus system, no place you can walk to. You can drive miles for a bottle of milk or a bottle of Chardonnay. If the macro-matters go ignored, micro-matters fare no better. An architectural committee is concerned about avoiding housing eyesores, but it doesn't advise about orienting houses for energy efficiency. "There'd be hell to pay," says Jerry Full. "That would be treason. It's not the way we do things. We don't design to use natural light until sundown, we don't require landscaping with native plants. People of our generation are used to traveling around by car. We don't design the city so a household might need only one."

Anybody looking for a house address someplace among the roads that lead off roads that end in circles gets the full impact. You're driving through 40,000–some acres of New Jersey. Get lost in the maze, stop to ask the way, and you might come across a fellow sitting on a beach chair in front of an open garage. The houses on the street will differ in detail but not in basic design group, one alongside the next on recently sodded lots. On a pleasant evening, the new homeowner may be staring at the houses on their lots across the street. Sunset nears as he sits in his shorts and tee shirt. He has a moustache and is in his early fifties. Your eyes pop and your head pulls back because once, while waiting in the condo apartment of an art collector, you started speaking to a cleaning lady who turned out to be a Duane Hanson sculpture.

Here you've found another, sitting in his plain existence beside two cars. You were just starting to ask him a question, hesitated—and then he said something back to you. Yes, he knows that the person you're looking for lives on the next block—more than you expected—and points the way.

Hundreds of building permits get pulled a month in Palm Coast. They've long gone beyond pensioner retirement homes. The new places go up in subdivisions affiliated with sports stars and sell for a half million and more. Each gets its own grand entry fronting state-of-the-stylebook mansion designs. Landscaping replaces bush. Wildlife disappears. Who's to say it isn't pretty and that the sidewalks and bike paths aren't convenient? Who can complain about endless fountain features? A new section of beachfront lots lately went on the market for $650,000 apiece. Flagler County Chamber of Commerce president Dick Morris calls it "controlled growth," though he also calls Palm Coast the "tiger of Flagler County." Morris continues: "The county and Palm Coast have been very environmentally conscious. We've got three state parks and we're a very small county. We do what we can to make sure we don't totally ravage, but we can't stop growth. Absolute growth is driving what happens. It's a good thing, though it brings the things you sometimes don't want." Case in point: the new Intracoastal Waterway development by a fellow named Bobby Ginn in the section called Hammock, long valued for its dense vegetation. Ginn, too, has scraped the land bare, as if ready for a Jersey freight terminal. Pretty houses will undoubtedly go up, but locals refer to Ginn as the Darth Vader of development and make the sign of the cross when they speak his name.

In 2004, Palm Coast scared the county to its no-tax-increase policy roots. Palm Coast wants to convert nearly 3,000 acres along Highway 100 into a CRA—a Community Redevelopment Area—where it can upgrade what little business exists into the city's first new urbanism district, where people would live more densely and rely less on cars. Once set up, CRAs benefit from tax increment financing, which allows the gain in property value to go directly into further upgrades. County administrators see the potentially biggest rise in property values remaining off county tax rolls even though improvements at least in roads will incrementally burden the county. "You have to be concerned," said county administrator David Haas about 3,000 acres off-limits.

If the chamber's Dick Morris is a bit conflicted about new development, lawyer Bayer isn't conflicted at all. Together with Hadeed—a battler to preserve the county's natural systems and its look—Bayer years ago moved up to Flagler Beach from Fort Lauderdale. He remembers camping on the beach where golf courses, condos, and the immense grandfathered-in condo-hotel have since gone up. "It physically pains me now to drive down Sixteenth Road," he says, describing one of the public ways to the beach. Bayer is fighting current efforts to gut height restrictions, the wetlands ordinance, the tree protection ordinance. "Yes, there's an urban services boundary," says Bayer, "but the county has started allowing subdivisions in 5-acre sites without urban services required. They don't even have to have a paved road, no central sewer or central water."

"It really is a race," says Ken Berk, who heads the bi-county Guana Matanzas Tolomato National Estuarine Research Reserve in Marineland. "Almost daily you see the conversion of natural areas into development. It's only what's in public ownership that's going to be preserved. It's not enough if Florida winds up with the best damned park system in a built-out state." Berk works to preserve some of the most productive estuaries in Florida, resources that food businesses, charter fishing boats, bait and tackle shops, and recreational fishers enjoy. He's concerned about storm-water treatment through retention ponds that developers typically fight. People who move to Florida, he says, need information for day-to-day ways to lessen their impacts on the resource. Everything flows into the waterways. People need to know how to minimize fertilizer use. "Homeowners are crucial decision makers," Berk says. "We educate agency people and laypeople across a broad community that uses this as their coast. It's a cultural community, a cultural neighborhood that people need to see themselves part of."

Marineland sits just east of where Pellicer Creek empties into the Matanzas River. The attraction's new owner at the turn of the century promised he would limit development at the site to something "sustainable" built of recycled materials. What's coming instead to the town of 6 will be at least $60 million worth of new buildings, converting 40 acres of the 140-acre town to apartments and condominiums with a marina for eighty-five boats. In the never-ending race Berk describes, Florida loses once more.

Back on the creek is Princess Place Preserve, a stunning acquisition by the state and county public land programs. Flagler was the smallest county to pass a land acquisition referendum when voters backed the measure by almost two-to-one in 1988. The site covers 435 acres, though it dates as a unit to 1791 as part of the Francisco Pellicer land grant. One of the state's first orange groves was planted here early in the eighteenth century. In time, one Henry Cutting built a hunting lodge here in the Adirondack Camp style—probably the only such architectural example in Florida—but instead of northern stones he used pink coquina from nearby beaches and supported a wraparound porch with cedar and palm trunks. All this remains, as does the freshwater pool fed by a continuous flowing artesian well. Cherokee Lodge entertained royalty and the socially prominent from around the world. Cutting's young wife, Angela, was widowed in 1892. When she remarried a Russian prince, she became the princess for whom the lodge was renamed. The site is darkly gothic, draped beneath Spanish moss, dripping in saltwater marsh, freshwater wetlands, oak hammocks, rising to scrub, joined by the restless sheet of water where Pellicer Creek empties into the Matanzas. Visitors enjoy four and a half miles of trails. Adjacent to Princess Place is the site of the agriculture museum Piatek is organizing. Both lie just off the Old King's Highway, one of Florida's first roads, put through in the late eighteenth century connecting southern Georgia with New Smyrna to the south.

The creek fronts Faver-Dykes State Park on the north bank (in St. Johns County), 572 forested acres and tidal marsh that appear much as during sixteenth-century Spanish times. The creek attracts wading birds, gators, otters, and raccoon; the upland, bobcats, deer, foxes, turkey, hawks, and owls. The canoe concession and launch here afford a few hours' of good paddling. The way can be challenging, especially in offshore winds when the creek's open banks provide little shelter and the wind, as you paddle back downstream, will wrestle even the best paddler for control of a high bow. About a mile upstream from the launch, a small community of houses opens suddenly around a bend; you might imagine Thoreau coming in just such a way upon an early Massachusetts settlement during his week paddling the Concord and the Merrimack rivers.

Recreational opportunities are widening as Flagler County's Coastal Greenway develops. The greenway already covers a narrow stretch of the entire county south from the Pellicer Creek Aquatic Preserve to Bulow Creek and the Tomoka Marsh Aquatic Preserve. On the north, the preserve will tie in with Faver Dykes. Highway A1A alongside is already a Flagler–St. Johns designated bi-county National Scenic Byway.

Bulow Creek, south in the county off S.R. 100, is the site of the Bulow Plantation Ruins. A sugar plantation briefly thrived here soon after 1821, when Maj. Charles Wilhelm Bulow acquired 4,675 acres of wilderness. During the short life of his son John, John James Audubon visited and spoke of young Bulow as a rich planter at whose plantation he received most hospitable treatment. But the plantation was lost to attack by Seminoles who, ironically, had received sympathetic support by young Bulow against demands by the United States for their removal to reservations west of the Mississippi. For his defiance, the state militia took Bulow prisoner. When the plantation was nonetheless burned upon outbreak of the Second Seminole War, Bulow abandoned Florida for Paris, where he died at age twenty-six.

The dirt road into the ruins is long, one-car wide, and so densely canopied it urges hope for light at the end of tunnels. The ruins appear like a shrine, a cathedral. On rainy days, the light is bathed in yellow as if hallowing the site. The ruins stand in obelisk pattern where there were chimneys. Oaks rise above all, covered with green resurrection fern. Moss seeps across the stones and the bases of cabbage palms. No attraction in Florida prevails with the authenticity and the emotional excitement of these ruins. When thunder blasts, you feel the authority of Florida.

5

VOLUSIA COUNTY

The Fast Cars and Slow Comeback of Daytona Beach

Figure 5.1. Crowds watch cars racing on the 1956 beach race course in Daytona Beach. Francis Johnson, photographer. Courtesy of the Florida State Archives.

Figure 5.2. "The World's Most Famous Beach." Daytona Beach and its hotels line Highway A1A. Courtesy of the Daytona Beach Area Convention and Visitors Bureau.

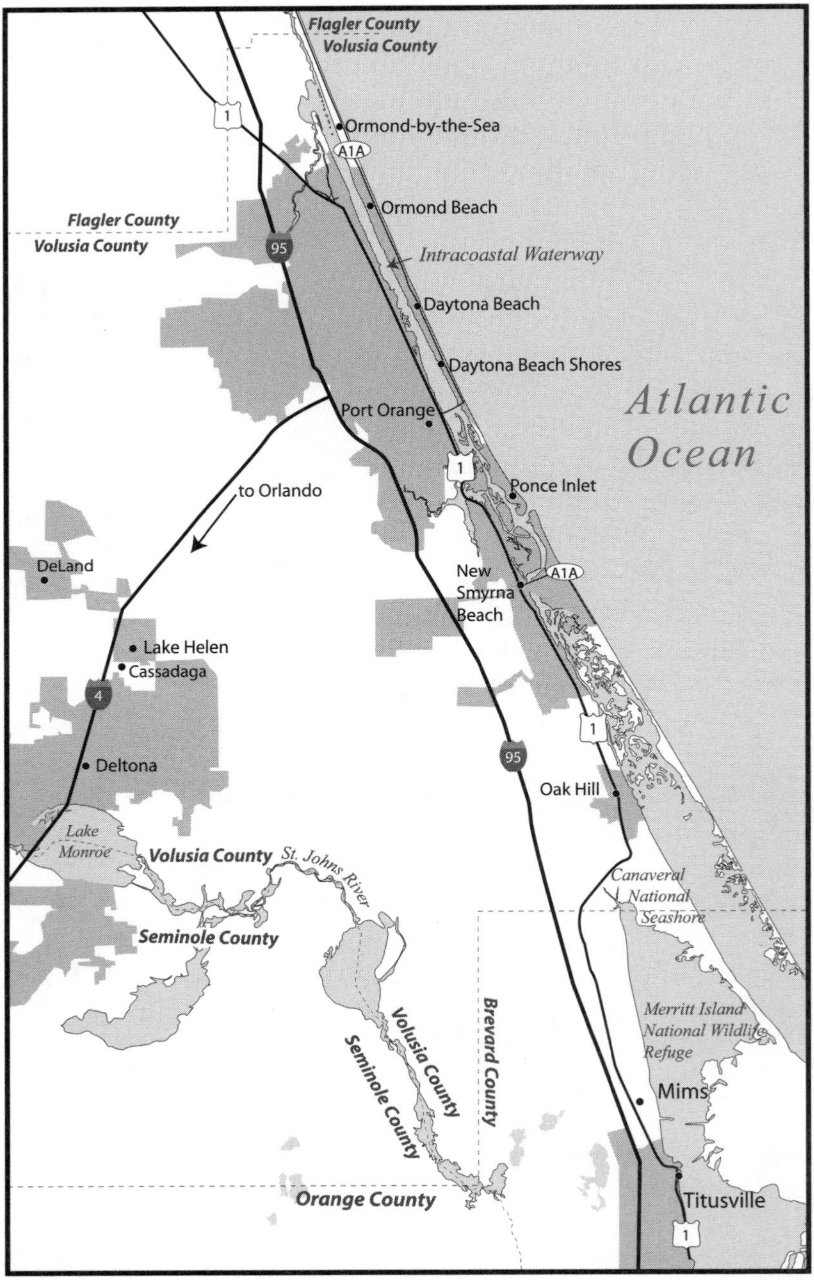

Map 5. Volusia County

Tourism and development bulge the midsection of Highway A1A through Volusia County like a toad passing down the gullet of a snake. It's different north and south at the county lines, where big oceanfront parks border the road. Here and there, people still occupy private homes along the beach. But like most coastal counties, Volusia has been wasteful about its seashore, driven by a history that subordinates resident interests. Late in the last century, when conservation-minded reform began challenging developer priorities, the horse had bolted the barn. Residents have had to fight to safeguard the shore that tourism and development eye as prey.

Long in place, the east Volusia bulge that spans three municipalities is generically known as Daytona Beach, the Daytona Beaches, or simply the Beaches or Daytona. Whatever, the bulge looms dispiriting, a great mess of dated hotels and motels, of newer condominiums and time-shares, of ordinary restaurants, surf shops, body piercing parlors, and saloons. The shore corridor has lapsed from something exceptional to something irredeemably humdrum that's at last trying to turn itself around again. The beach is still there, reduced from the storms of '04 but still hard-packed at surf's edge and appealing. But laws notwithstanding, the beach today belongs to those who put up the buildings that block it from easy access and to those who buy or rent rooms from them. The beach has become more concessionlike than a free good, for nonhotel guests more easily accessible by car than on foot. Walking between the road and beach in many places requires passing between formidable structures that feel like the walls that surround attractions. Swimsuit shopkeeper Stamie Kypreos, in her eighties, recalls: "We used to have parties and picnics on the beach. People get tired of big concrete things."

Daytona promotes itself as "The World's Most Famous Beach" because of its history of car racing along the ocean edge and the elegant resorts like the Clarendon and Princess Issena that catered to the sport's early champagne-set patrons. Fine homes rose along the peninsula between the shore and the Halifax River to the west. Mainland Beach Street claimed its own splendor, above all the mansion of philanthropist Charles Grover Burgoyne. An artifact at the Halifax Historical Museum captures Burgoyne's times in style and technology in the invitation to a musicale at the mansion: "A symphony, one of Bethoven's [*sic*], is stuck fast in Mr. Burgoyne's organ. Won't you come down to his residence, thirty-nine North Beach Street at seven o'clock, Monday evening, December second, nineteen hundred and twelve, and help him pull the 'dam' thing out?"

Different from lower down the coast where mainland cities such as West Palm Beach sheltered chiefly a service class for wealthy tourists on the barrier island, Daytona's cultured denizens populated both sides of the Halifax River as well as the shore. The city was a rare winter and summer resort where residents and visitors were of the same class and mixed freely.

But today, except for three county parks in the 10 miles of the bulge and a small new city park at Daytona's Main Street among too few others, the shore has become alien to locals. No signs welcome locals to the beach. Few bicycle racks exist, and no historical murals or logo-distinct signs that identify adjacent neighborhoods. The WPA Bandshell built during the Depression has been appropriated as a feature of newly built condo-resorts, less accessible to residents than before. But as a convenience to car drivers who come from out of town, signs lately installed on the beach mark the street names of access ramps.

As if with vision impaired from staring at the sun, city officials too long focused on tourism and development stand blind to the claims of year-round residents whose access ought to be paramount. That claim goes barely acknowledged. Resident activism along the bulge is mainly defensive, reacting to the traffic and noise of "binge events." No new vision of who residents are in this place has been awakened for years.

Yet residents influence this county in unusually progressive ways. Volusia was blessed in the last decades of the twentieth century by an exceptional group of conservation-minded leaders who variously chaired the elected county council, served as appointed county manager, and otherwise included newspaper, business, educational, and arts figures. Under their combined influence, Volusia residents in 1986 were among the first in Florida to tax themselves to acquire conservation lands. That bond issue amassed $20 million. Volusia bonded itself a second and third time, in 2000 passing twin $80 million issues, one for additional conservation lands and a second to support ECHO—environmental, cultural, heritage, and outdoors—projects. In 1991, Volusia was the first county in Florida to engage in widespread visioning that called for casting its future in terms of a metaphorical park. By caring for its green and open space, so the thinking went, "Volusia Park" would attract others of like mind, including quality corporations, and remake its brand of tourism. Says longtime public relations figure John Evans: "There's not a lot of counties where the conservation people have been in politics and have clout. Volusia has had that."

Beyond the vision's short-term beneficial impacts on the urban landscape, its longer influence has been in nurturing the notion of the county as a park worthy of conservation. The major measure resulting from this vision has been the creation of a midcounty north-south Volusia Conservation Corridor, a project well advanced yet still incomplete. Recently threatened by municipal annexations and by a county council that in an election year backed away from its promise to effect urban growth boundaries, Volusia Countians again rose up by petition to force the council's hand. They were driven by eastward annexations of the City of Deltona that dented the corridor, together with westward annexations of Port Orange and New Smyrna Beach that threatened the rural communities of Osteen and Samsula. "Volusia County citizens have always been ahead of their elected officials," says the county's guiding spirit of environmental reform, attorney Clay Henderson of New Smyrna Beach. "If this gets on the ballot, it passes." In fact it doubly did but was invalidated by a court on a technicality and now again faces a decision by a newly elected county council whose vote is again uncertain.

Meanwhile, great north and south oceanfront parks have been protected and environmentally devastating state transportation actions now nearly overcome at Rose Bay. The university town of DeLand became a charter Florida participant in the downtown-renewing national Main Street program. New Smyrna Beach converted its dingy mainland downtown to a crisp model of what small city downtowns ought to look like. Soon after, renewal began in Daytona's historic downtown on the west shore of the Halifax River.

The county richly attends to the arts and preservation with museums and archaeological sites among Volusia's most frequently visited places. Daytona may have more buildings on the National Register than any other Florida city. The city is a musical performance and educational center and benefits from the fiercely independent voice of one of Florida's few remaining large family-run newspapers, the *Daytona Beach News-Journal* (its president a Juilliard-trained violinist).

The most closely watched renewal attempt occurs in the midst of the Daytona strip, which covers the few blocks between the Main Street Pier and Seabreeze Avenue. Two sections of a new Ocean Walk condominium-hotel have gone up with street-level shops, and the older adjacent Adam's Mark Hotel (once a Marriott) has been refurbished and enlarged. A parking garage built by the city has allowed the banning of cars from the beach in front of these two properties. Funds have been earmarked to expand the Ocean Center for conventions, and the developer upscaling this section of the strip has committed to re-opening a water-slide amusement attraction that was meant to attract families but that closed soon after opening. First-time visitors who come unburdened by the city's recent history cross Atlantic Avenue (Highway A1A) on the new colorful overpass that connects the garage and beachfront and admire the new art deco look of Ocean Walk and the neon-garish shops below its floors of vacation rooms. They see new multimillion-dollar landscaping improvements along more than a mile of the avenue between Seabreeze and International Speedway Boulevard. To these newcomers, the scene looks as modern and typical of fun-loving Florida beachfronts as any place in the Sunshine State. That look will spread as thousands of new condominium units rise along the ocean shore, replacing tired motels, many damaged by the storms of 2004.

From Glory to Vainglory

To residents, the strip is a sour Tourist Land. They question how far turnaround will get and, more provocatively, whether the tourist beachfront and the special events that seasonally surge through the place—more toads moving through the snake's gullet—will ever redeem the place. Daytona moved through the twentieth century from glory to vainglory, from well-earned pride to leaderless-sanctioned sleaze.

Cars and motorcycles drive and park on most of the beach continuing a tradition begun a century ago when buggies, bicycles, and cars already took advantage of the hard-packed beach sands to roll their wheels. Advocates wrap themselves in the outsized cloak of Daytona history that dates from 1903, when Alexander Winton and Ransom Olds tested each other in the first timed race car trials and earned Ormond Beach the nickname "Birthplace of Speed." Racing took off along the beach, steadily moving south to Daytona and then to a 3.2-mile course just north of the lighthouse at Ponce Inlet. Although racing in 1959 officially relocated off the beach to the oval that became today's Daytona International Speedway, the legend of cars on the beach became sacrosanct. Some call it "Daytona's unique niche" and compare its local significance with Yankee Stadium in New York and Yosemite National Park in California.

But cars on recreational beaches, by their size, their lethal power, and the way they can obscure their occupants' intentions, appear wholly out of place in an otherwise open setting. They menace beachgoers with anxieties about speed and require caution from those who come to relax, often as families. Cars driving here have killed visitors and maimed others—some eighty car-beachgoer accidents in a recent five-year period, enough so that the scandal adds to a defining image of Daytona. "[It's] one of the things we're known for," says attorney Henderson, a former chairman of the Volusia County Council who led the Volusia Park visioning. "It's a lot to overcome, a branding of cars and the beach, the hardest thing to get beyond."

Despite the image, the strip along Atlantic Avenue can eerily turn almost empty between the waves of seasonal visitors drawn by Daytona's special events. Main Street, despite its name, comes to life only during biker events. The bar scene cranks up almost round-the-clock, and the city allows otherwise vacant lots to sprout with the tents of traveling salesmen, who can take in more dollars during a few weeks of boozy, lascivious spending than legitimate merchants could year-round. Daytona's special events—notably Speed Week, Bike Week, Spring Break, and Black College Reunion—occur with singular impact through the towns of the bulge. They're part of the strip's defining fast car and outlaw image. Nor is it only special-event vacationers or conventional tourists who set the beach tone. It's also day-trippers and weekenders. Working off Daytona's macho car-bike connection, these short-term visitors act out honky-tonk swagger as they cruise the road and the beach for pick-ups. Their behavior offends some tourists, who have little choice but to tolerate their shenanigans, while residents who live west of the strip in the peninsula beach towns and on the mainland side of the Halifax River have to drive

Figure 5.3. A scenic drive through Tomoka State Park. Courtesy of the Daytona Beach Area Convention and Visitors Bureau.

themselves to beaches north and south beyond the bulge to enjoy the attraction that brought most of them to live here.

Developer-tourism has its way. Long before 9/11, the strip had been selling at rock-bottom prices. Hotels continue to sell cheap. Motels sell cheaper. Impelled by long-standing common distress, they compete against each other with roadside signs that tout rooms at $24 and $25, $30 directly on the beach. The unkindest sign of all lately was one that read, "Not happy? Why not check out?" The message spoke to a situation where some mornings, guests at some motels demand their money back because of shabby rooms and look to salvage their vacations by checking in elsewhere.

Daytona's challenge is more than having to overcome its bum image. It must overcome a widespread perception that incompetence and poor discipline drive interests that long ago stopped caring. The scene has descended to a free-for-all in which short-term interests drive hotel and motel owners, while what passes as collective action merely covers for collective opportunism and deepens dismay. The name of the game is to hang in, however shabbily, until better times or hurricanes come and then cash out. Although more than just city boosters now believe that the current attempt at renewal will successfully lift the strip out of blight, residents fear endless developer subsidies to keep the new construction going. They fear expansion of the Ocean Center as the wedge of a new phalanx of development along the west side of Atlantic Avenue borne by escalating property taxes that could start a wave of home-selling to seasonal residents and steady erosion of the year-round residential community. Even though promoters claim that the new construction will help ease the property tax burden on residents, rates rose an astonishing

27 percent in 2003. Resident-repudiating tourism stands hotly at odds from what residents want from their towns.

For Daytona, the new beachfront developments represent a now-or-never moment for those who flog tourism to overcome the effects of too much tourism. Elsewhere around Florida the resort world awakens to dynamic new downtowns where residents define their core city character and tourists pour in (see chapters 10–12). Daytona still remains Florida's most troubled resort area. One prominent travel writer a decade ago called it a "dump." Too little has changed since then. Ormond, Daytona, and the Shores get up every morning putting a smiley face on a misshapen beachfront legacy.

Under the diktat of tourism, Volusia is not Volusia Park but rather three counties in one, largely the divisive result of how tourism has played out. At 1,207 square miles, the county is as large as Rhode Island. But more than mere miles divide the three sections. People refer to a Palmetto Curtain that divides the east and west, a politically charged reference to the Volusia Conservation Corridor that's either a godsend or a transgression against property rights, depending on which side of the argument they're on. Growth-hungry municipalities keep trying to pave it over. Visitors are surprised to learn that the county seat isn't well-known Daytona Beach but the college town of DeLand, a city of fewer than 25,000 and center of eco-heritage tourism close by the St. Johns River on the opposite side of the county, a second of its three divisions. Daytona itself numbers a scant 70,000 and was surpassed at the turn of the century by the fast-growing western developer city of Deltona that now claims nearly 5,000 more. Far to the southwest, Deltona and neighboring DeBary connect primarily with the economy of metro Orlando, which in 2003 became more accessible when a pair of new bridges with six lanes of traffic opened across the St. Johns. To the northeast, the expressway connects with Daytona.

The third of the county's divisions centers to the southeast at New Smyrna Beach. If Daytona represents binge-event tourism and West Volusia eco-heritage tourism, then New Smyrna Beach reflects a more residentially branded form, a beach town that effectively promotes itself as both non-Disney and non-Daytona. Several miles of beach remain low-rise residential. Otherwise, condominiums more than hotels front the beach, to which access is plentiful. And although the long shore is eroded in sections, New Smyrna claims two recreational crown jewels. These are the Canaveral National Seashore and the Merritt Island National Wildlife Refuge, both shared to the south with neighboring Brevard County (where both are headquartered). New Smyrna prides itself on its arts and its two small, renewed downtowns, one on the mainland, the other on the beach, though New Smyrna also insists on keeping its beach open to cars.

How the three-way Volusia division plays out became apparent in 2003 when Daytona interests launched a final, successful push to add a sixth cent to the county bed tax to pay for expanding the Ocean Center. The hall fronts Atlantic Avenue in the midst of Daytona's redevelopment district. It has long been too small to compete for conventions that draw more than 10,000. Increase of the tourist tax required approval by the Volusia County Council. West Volusia and New Smyrna interests fought the increase, arguing that they receive no benefit from Daytona conventions. Conventiongoers don't book rooms outside the immediate area. Benefits go to the large number of bulge hotels, which, with their 14,000 units, can easily absorb any convention's entire room demand. The argument against the added tax claimed that guests at hotels elsewhere would be burdened with roughly an extra dollar on their nightly bills that would erode their edge in a terrifically competitive Florida market. Yet, of course, Florida is Florida. People come, people play. A dollar here, a dollar there isn't the issue so much as it is New Smyrna and West Volusia having to pay to prop up their embarrassing rival. As executive director of the Southeast Volusia Chamber of Commerce Steve Dennis said, "If we have consolidation, we don't want that consolidation to reflect Daytona Beach."

Dennis refers to a still bigger problem the county faces. He refers to how Volusia alone, of all Florida's sixty-seven counties, supports three separate tourist promotion agencies. Even in highly contentious Miami-Dade County, Miami Beach, Miami, and most of that county's other municipalities consolidated their tourism promotion efforts more than a decade ago. Not in Volusia, though, where each office maintains its own staff and expends its own budgets to promote its own version of Volusia vacationing. The result isn't just some activity of no concern to visitors, some fief building and ego-tripping. Tourism is far and away the heart of the county economy. Yet tourism pulls the county apart three ways with results that especially burden Daytona's turnaround and leave it the place that disappoints so many visitors today—especially visitors with ample spending power.

Yes, the West Volusia Tourism Advertising Authority mentions beaches that are easily accessible to the east, but it also promotes Disney and Universal Studios just an hour or so in the other direction. Daytona's Halifax Area Advertising Authority mentions river tours on the St. Johns, but it too promotes Orlando-area theme parks. The Southeast Volusia Tourism Advertising Authority mentions Daytona-area museums and Daytona International Speedway but again promotes Orlando-area attractions. As three separate entities, each for its own competitive reasons has to acknowledge the compelling appeal of the theme parks only an hour or so away. All three hope that vacationers from their target markets will choose to stay in their Volusia hotels and make day-trips to the theme parks, instead of the other way around. Yet if the three agencies combined as one, they could concentrate better on Volusia's own distinct offerings. These are many and compelling.

Each of the three agencies is funded with its own bed tax. Each was set up soon after Disney began sucking the family tourist market out of Daytona. The Halifax Authority was set up first. It largely ignored the rest of the county. New Smyrna and DeLand were soon authorized to promote their own interests. Yet different from anywhere else in Florida, instigating private interests had the three competing authorities enshrined by state law. No other county suffers this constraint. Even if the county council should want to change the arrangement, it can't. Only the legislature can. Although in 2003 the three agencies began producing a single countywide promotional booklet, combining the well-entrenched three into one would require a strong wrench from the status quo. The overriding problem is that motels and hotels, so many in flux and ruled by special events, continue to dominate Daytona tourism, leaving it without vision. Its retro ways threaten to subordinate West Volusia and New Smyrna with their environmental and family appeals more attuned even to the markets that developers hope will occupy their new beachfront condominiums. The county also exists divided among three separate hospital taxing districts, although in 2003 a unified water authority was set up for the first time, replacing separate municipal agencies.

This division of tourism interests impacts more than the recent Ocean Center tax controversy. It works to the disadvantage of Daytona residents and to the disadvantage of renewal along beachfront Daytona; it leads to Daytona's disadvantageous overdependence on special events, and, consequently, it negatively impacts how visitors experience the city. At bottom, everything has to do with the inability of Daytona's promotion agency and its chamber of commerce to imagine any course for the future of the bulge except the hotel-dominated beach and special events regime that for years has ruled city affairs. For so long the stepchild of coastal Florida tourism, yet forever unwilling to make the future of tourism a subject that residents might have a stake in, the Beach remains self-absorbed, a captive of its own state of mind. Miami Beach and Fort Lauderdale have overcome the impacts of Disney. New destinations like West Palm Beach and Lee County have emerged successfully. Jacksonville Beach reawakens as a family vacation place. While Daytona squints from its bunker, the new condos will replace hotels and motels, reducing the importance of tourism-as-usual and finally restoring quality to a beach scene long in need.

Fast Cars and Fast Politics

A fourth division hugely influences what happens in Volusia. This is the ring of motorsport interests controlled by the family of the late William "Big Bill" France under the umbrella International Speedway Corporation. It was France's vision and political skills that turned Daytona into the center of car racing in America. It was he who built Daytona International Speedway in 1959 and who was a crucial instigator of the National Association of Stock

Car Auto Racing—NASCAR, headquartered in Daytona and also controlled by France family interests. Other family holdings include additional speedways around America; the Daytona USA attraction; the Americrown Service Corporation, which supplies fans with food, drink, and souvenirs; and Motor Racing Network, which produces syndicated race and race-related radio shows.

To grasp the magnitude of ISC Corp., it helps to appreciate that stock car racing has become one of the great spectator and TV viewing sports of North America. Speedway itself can accommodate more than 200,000 spectators for the annual Race Week in February. (Even after expansion, the Ocean Center will accommodate only 20,000.) Speedway's Bike Week and Biketoberfest exalt Daytona's everlasting biker image. Speedway dwarfs Daytona International Airport, which sits alongside it. From the grandstand, jets that take off and land on airport runways appear miniaturized like the model cars sold at event concession stands.

Speedway and its associated activities employ 700 on site, which makes it the second-largest private employer in the county (after the News-Journal Corporation's 874). Incredibly, however, Speedway pays no property taxes. That was the result of a deal cut by the county with Big Bill when he proposed the track as a way to further promote the city as a world-class destination. Unfortunately for Volusia, nobody at the time thought to "sunset" the tax break. It would go on forever, even though Speedway and its associated interests occupy hundreds of acres that now, thanks to Speedway, lie in the heart of Daytona's retail district. Retailing relocated from downtown to be close to Speedway and the broad boulevard of U.S. Highway 92 that passes its many entrances. That road became International Speedway Boulevard from Daytona to DeLand. When Speedway interests acquired most of the site across the boulevard once occupied by General Electric—GE's departure in the early nineties with the loss of more than 500 mostly high-paying jobs was a devastating blow to the county economy—they got the state to pay some $3 million for an artistically embellished pedestrian crosswalk that links its two properties. Speedway lobbyists never miss a Daytona City Commission meeting or a Volusia County Council meeting.

"What's good for Speedway is good for Daytona," would hardly misstate how Speedway interests view themselves in the city. It's a view shared by many Daytona and county officeholders whose elections increasingly depend on Speedway campaign support. In the Daytona mayoral race of 2003, a seventy-six-year-old retired schoolteacher candidate who, as a city commissioner, long served the city's Speedway-backed special events regime, won office in a tight race thanks to an almost $200,000 war chest compared with the less than $45,000 of her runoff opponent. The job pays $19,500. "No one controls me," said incoming mayor Yvonne Scarlett-Golden. Maybe not, but even that pretense was laughably exposed when ISC apointed its own community affairs director, the mayor's aide-in-chief. As the *News-Journal*'s political columnist Pamela Hasterok asked, "What would you think if the Orlando mayor's companion was Disney World's public affairs chief?"

Hubristically emboldened, France-controlled NASCAR in 2005 invited Daytona to bid on a new hall of fame with six financially stronger venues. Daytona residents had to hold their nose when hall-of-fame supporters floated the idea of the state passing $75 million in sales-tax rebates. Typically Daytona, when it came time to ante up the city's costs for drafting a proposal, took the $20,000 from a developer. The state said no anyway.

Speedway and hotels of the bulge make common cause in behalf of special events. Speedway needs the hotel rooms; the hotels need Speedway crowds. The crowds pour in several times a year. The largest numbers come for Bike Week and Speed Week, in recent years an average of 500,000 and 400,000 respectively. Biketoberfest draws another 100,000. In addition, Daytona each year welcomes a two-month crush of 250,000 divided between Spring Break and Black College Reunion. Rooms at the cheapest motels command $150 for major events, six times their normal rate. That income surge lets them hang on the rest of the year, repairing damage and waiting for that big buyout that they believe, sooner or later, will come.

It's a mistake to think the special events don't benefit the city and county. The events deliver crucial revenues. In a study for the Daytona Beach Halifax Chamber of Commerce, economist Mark D. Soskin has calculated that the combined economic benefit of Daytona's special events amounts to $1.3 billion. As Soskin points out, that's after calculating the "visitor displacement effect" (visitors who stay away because of the special events) and after allowing for the capture of local sales by itinerant vendors and figuring up to about $20 million worth of inconvenience to residents.

Soskin calculates that special events generate the equivalent of 36,500 full-time jobs, and that they represent more than 20 percent of county employment and 15 percent of the county economy. These contributions are critical to government operations. It's no wonder that Speedway and the hotels get their way. It's no wonder that the shabby lodging inventory of the strip can afford to avoid improvements. Yet, it's clear that improvement of that inventory will only augment the hold of tourism and Speedway on Volusia. Years ago, the City of Daytona Beach turned management of Bike Week over to the Halifax Chamber. That made the chamber, more than any of its counterparts elsewhere in Florida, a virtual arm of government and greatly augmented Speedway's shadow role. It's no surprise that even though the resort product may improve, government will remain more than ever a partner with enterprise that seems destined to drift further from hometown influence.

Residents are left to form a fifth division of the county. They may not remain weak, though their current weakness is apparent in the increasingly bold willingness of government to subsidize its partners. Current gifts to Speedway and tourism continue apace with past gifts. Yet many resist the private sector's long dependence on giveaways and question whether these subsidies even motivate the right initiatives.

The strategy behind expanding the Ocean Center is that the added space will bring large numbers of presumably high-spending business travelers to town during otherwise slow periods and smooth out hotel occupancies. This approach has notably worked in places like Miami Beach, Orlando, and Fort Walton Beach. Conventions in those cities help fill rooms during off-seasons. Interestingly, special events already partly satisfy this need. Rates don't have to be discounted the way they sometimes must to attract conventions. Just the opposite. Nor, of course, do the special events require new construction. Big Bill built the Speedway with $3 million of his own money (albeit with his everlasting tax break). Biketoberfest helps fill rooms with high-paying guests in fall, but there's no question that hotels go hungry until February rolls around. Winter is simply too cold for Daytona vacationing.

Nor is it just expansion of the Ocean Center that stands to improve hotel fortunes. Road beautification now underway will extend landscaping to more than 3 miles. Also coming are more new hotel rooms, more condominiums and attractions in the midst of the strip. One next piece calls for $115 million for two more hotels, one sold as condominiums, the other as time-shares, with restaurants and shops adjacent to the redevelopment already in place. Another could be an even bigger deal to build three 600–unit, twenty-five-story condominiums south of the Main Street Pier. The proponent of this project—it would be the biggest single deal in city history—also proposes to relocate the International Swimming Hall of Fame from Fort Lauderdale to Daytona's beachfront. Questions abound. It's not clear that the developer controls the Hall of Fame, and his proposal to link the attraction with new condos was rejected by two South Florida cities, Fort Lauderdale and Pompano Beach, where he first attempted the package deal. A major suit over the matter now pends between Pompano Beach and the developer. That didn't keep Daytona city officials from accepting his hospitality on a recent so-called fact-finding mission to Miami Beach.

The new projects require the county to buy out the last of the Coney Island–style amusement stalls, shops, and rides that have been in place on the beach for more than seventy years, dating from the resort town's heyday. A second phase of the project calls for buying out the private owner of the Main Street Pier and joining with properties to the south that include the new small oceanfront park. By 2005, at least some of the owners in question seemed reconciled to either selling or accepting demolition of their properties in return for newly rebuilt space. All had previously threatened court action if the county moved toward condemnation. Delays could have cost renewal three to five years.

Getting new hotels built along the strip hasn't been cheap for government. Expansion of the Adam's Mark and construction of the Ocean Walk complex have required subsidies from the city totaling $38 million in cash and commitment of another $35 million in interest over thirty years. The parking garage was subsidized with another $11.65 million from multiple governments. City streets and a city park were permanently closed for buildings, and a 22-foot-wide swath of beach was paved over for a walk that connects the length of the hotels. Without these gifts, the developers argued, they could never afford their projects, and beachfront renewal could not go forward. What the latest inducements will cost hasn't yet been revealed, though the county has so far committed some $12 million in tax-exempt bonds to help finance public portions of the new construction, and the city was asked for at least $1 million toward development of the new oceanfront park to replace the one given away. The proponent of the separate Hall of Fame–condo proposition offered only $17 million of his own money, leaving the city to come up with at least ten times that amount. No developer comes into Daytona unaware that voters resist their deals. Commissioners unable to figure out alternative futures for their city pay dearly for the only fix they conceive available to them, then rely on Speedway and its supporters to keep them in office. Recent subsidies and those currently on the table top a quarter billion dollars, overwhelmingly for low-paying hotel jobs. Where's the vision? Alienation grows.

Further cost stems from the wild card of recent Daytona history. A dark side bedevils the Atlantic Avenue strip that is finally going away. As recently as the mid-nineties, the strip was the hangout for large numbers of homeless and adults preying on runaway boys. Media coverage was devastating. Nor has the behavioral problem altogether disappeared. Beachgoers still get knocked down by cars driving on the beach. Each year, too, Bike Week, Spring Break, and Black College Reunion generate national headlines about licentious behavior and about alcohol-related deaths, shootings, and helmetless bikers. Backers of Daytona's mayor claim that she and the new African American majority on the city commission have at last begun calming the misbehavior that accompanies Black College Reunion each spring. But the combination of lewd and rowdy carrying on and the absence of beach nightlife that might appeal to more affluent visitors (an absence long commented on by travel agents) slow Daytona's turnaround. Too much of the same thing has gone on too long. The entire enterprise feels immaterial because transient at its root, and dozens of new condominiums with uncertain numbers of year-round residents in their private towers may not be all the answer.

New Smyrna Beach and East Volusia's Impressive Past

New Smyrna Beach owes its name and its prominence to one of the largest English settlements in the New World, which was attempted here. The venture drew on widely disparate populations for its realization yet—in part because of the cultural Babel—lasted only a brief ten years before failure, rebellion, and ruin. Settlement was the inspiration of Dr. Andrew Turnbull, a widely traveled Scottish physician who, during Florida's twenty-year British interregnum that began in 1763, foresaw that Mediterranean peoples could easily adjust to Florida's climate. During travels through Asia Minor, Turnbull in Turkey married the daughter of a wealthy Smyrna merchant. His settlers came from Corsica, Greece, Italy, and Minorca. During travels through Egypt, Turnbull had studied irrigation systems along the Nile. In 1768, he became the first European in Florida to develop agricultural lands by a Nile-like system of draining and irrigation, a system for land development that grew widely during more than two hundred years before its ruinous environmental impacts led to its ban.

Turnbull's colony began with 1,255 settlers, who at one time worked more than 100,000 acres. The settlers came indentured and were promised 50 acres per household of their own following seven or eight years of service. But by the end of their indentured obligation, settler numbers reduced by hellish treatment and disease had dwindled to 600. Turnbull and his partners suffered financial reversals. Revolution against England in its American colonies (Florida didn't join the American community until 1821) interfered with supplies and commerce. Uncertainty fostered rebellion. By 1777, the colony was finished. Turnbull and his family removed themselves to Charleston. Most of the remaining colonists in desperation trekked overland to St. Augustine, where they were released from indenture and where over time their descendants became leaders in that community.

Remains of Turnbull's colony can be seen today at what's called Turnbull's Palace along North Riverside Drive and Julia Street. The coquina block foundation was set into an Ais Indian shell mound. The site was abandoned with collapse of the colony. A later settler during the second Spanish period did better, completing a two-story house at the site. But this house was destroyed during the Patriots War of 1812, as was a later plantation on the site during the Second Seminole War. An old stone wharf that was the center of town in the 1770s can still be seen at low tide on South Riverside Drive at Clinch Street. And the old sugar mill, built during the 1830s on a site believed to have sheltered an early Spanish mission, now a municipal historic site, sits just south off West Canal Street (S.R. 44) and Mission Drive. Into the 1960s, the town remained an important rail center because Flagler had made it the base of operations for the push to Palm Beach.

Examples of New Smyrna's mixed regard for town history abound beyond the Turnbull sites. Notable among mainland buildings are the Connor Library across from city hall, which dates from 1901 and was relocated to its present site, and the once-luxurious Alba Court from 1905–6 on Washington Street, which still boasts its handsome atrium lobby but with its resort-era accommodations now occupied by long-stay residents grateful for cheap sleep. Several bed-and-breakfasts occupy old family homes on Riverside Drive overlooking the Indian River Lagoon. However, the Indian River Inn and Conference Center, famous in the twenties as the Rio Vista Hotel, was unfortunately allowed to be torn down in 1995.

An arts community claims significant presence. Signature institution is the Atlantic Center for the Arts (ACA), a world-class facility for its programs and architecture on the north side of town along Spruce Creek. ACA chiefly conducts master classes in the arts, drawing to its faculty such luminaries as Edward Albee, Milton Babbitt, the late Allen Ginsberg, and William Wegman. ACA founder and sculptor Doris Leeper in 1999 was inducted into the Florida Arts Hall of Fame only months before she passed away. Harris House is a downtown affiliate of ACA, a 1915 Florida home that is now a gallery and cultural meeting place. Arts on Douglas is the leading gallery among several in town and is another project begun by Leeper and colleagues. It's housed in a 1924 house and displays rotating exhibitions of contemporary art.

New Smyrna also claims quirky distinction. For years it had almost twice as many dwelling units as people because of the many outsiders who bought winter homes here. Town also has two main streets, one on the mainland and the other across the waterway in the section once known as Coronado Beach. Mainland merchants today open their doors to wide sidewalks, handsome street furniture, and re-created period lamps. Beach shops are more laid-back, occupying only a few short blocks from the nineteenth-century pink Riverview Inn alongside the Intracoastal Waterway to the Atlantic, their frocks, tee shirts, art, and souvenirs often displayed outside with informal flea market effect. At Beach Variety you can get any tacky Florida souvenir you want.

Environment, no less than history and arts, figures large in southeast Volusia today. South of New Smyrna, Oak Hill on the Mosquito Lagoon is a small but long lived-in fishing community around a fertile Ais site. One of two large mounds remains, the other dug out and carried away early in the last century when its shells were said to have filled 2,000 railroad cars for roadwork. A house built atop the second mound explains its survival. This is Seminole Rest, a big-porched and dormered two-story house under restoration as part of a 25-acre mainland section of the Canaveral National Seashore. The 1995 constitutional net ban devastated Oak Hill. Displaced fishing families have slowly adapted to clam leases, renewed cultivation of oyster beds, and guided sportfishing. The 1,500 or so who remain here live mainly along a loop road to the east off U.S. 1. The long-resident Goodrich family operates a waterfront restaurant. It features a hole in every table for disposing of shells. There used to be holes in the floor, too, because the restaurant is built over the water. October through April, scores of white pelicans flock here. Yachts, skiffs, kayaks all pass by.

East across the Mosquito Lagoon was Eldora, a fishing village with a hotel from the late nineteenth century. Village and hotel are long gone. Among what remains are the restored Eldora House, home to many families from Reconstruction onward, and the former house of Doris Leeper, both now owned by the Canaveral National Seashore. Both houses speak to the comfort, dignity, charm, and seclusion of life here, experienced in its prime during the 1920s. Leeper's time was the 1960s and 1970s, when the village was already finished. She fought successfully against encroachments by RV park developers and a garbage dump. She kept the road to her place from getting paved. She remained almost alone, well aware that Eldora was doomed. Yet if the entire seashore could be preserved, remnant Eldora might be saved with that. Leeper's conservation instincts matched the Space Center's need for big buffers. One result was the Merritt Island National Wildlife Refuge. The other was the national seashore.

Well worth visiting in this northern section of the seashore is Turtle Mound, accessible by one of many sectional trails. It's the largest remaining shell mound along Florida's Atlantic coast, favored by birders for watching hawk migrations and recalled fondly by adults as the place where, as kids, they would slide down the mound's oyster shells on split cardboard boxes, ending in the river. The park is more than just a boundary area for adults and their youthful memory. It's a significant meeting of temperate and subtropical edge. Philadelphia botanist William Bartram had already noticed this edge effect in 1776, and it was later commented on by his French colleague André Michaux, a friend of Franklin and Washington. The more northern spartina grass gives way here to more southern mangroves. The lagoon system that today divides Volusia and Brevard Counties in pre-Contact times also divided more northern Timucuan and more southern Ais tribes.

Along Turtlemound Road is remnant Bethune Beach. Like American Beach on Amelia Island and Butler Beach in south St. Johns County, this was a well-known African American recreation area of segregation times. Educator Mary McLeod Bethune was among its founders because she wanted students at Bethune-Cookman College, the school she helped found, to have a beach place of their own. Whites with beach houses along A1A weren't happy with blacks traveling "their" road and so had a separate road built from New Smyrna down to the beach for blacks. That was named Saxon Drive for the commissioner who saw the project through. For three decades, mostly Florida blacks owned land at Bethune Beach and stayed at the Welricha Motel along 2½ miles of oceanfront and waterway land where they, like whites north along the beach, also raced cars. Integration ended the ethnic enclave, whereupon real estate operators cajoled black owners into selling out for pathetically small sums. Lots virtually given away for $5,000 have lately resold for fifty times that. Resident blacks have dwindled to a handful. Saxon Drive has become built up with white middle-class homes.

The vicinity north of New Smyrna centers two tenacious struggles to keep important waterways from development and ultimate ruin. One is Spruce

Creek, which forms well west of I-95 and which flows 12 miles between New Smyrna and Port Orange to the Halifax River. Leeper and Clay Henderson (a former president of Florida Audubon) were involved in both fights. The fight to save the creek from development has largely succeeded through public acquisition of its shoreline. More than 2,000 acres of the creek shore were safely in conservation by the start of 2004, this portion now officially the Doris Leeper Spruce Creek Preserve. Protection is ultimately sought for half that much again. In the course of a few hours, paddlers can follow the creek from its pristine blackwater origins through a section between unusually high bluffs. Up here the creek passes the rural turn-of-the-last-century hunting and fishing retreat of James Gamble, the soap manufacturer, whose son-in-law added a replica of the Snow White House from the 1940 Walt Disney movie for the enjoyment of Gamble's grandchildren. The entire site is now maintained by Daytona's Museum of Arts and Sciences and, after closing for several years, is open again to visitors. A ramp to the creek allows paddlers to work their way downstream beneath tropical canopy, reaching salt marsh and the Halifax River, which ultimately flows through dangerous Ponce de Leon Inlet to the sea. Sightings along the way typically include osprey, wood storks, and wading birds as well as manatees in winter. The eastern indigo snake uses the creek corridor, as do black bear and also—as evidenced recently by a sighting by the curator of the Gamble Place—a Florida panther.

North of New Smyrna, Rose Bay, near Port Orange, is an estuary of national significance that was devastated by sewage and storm-water outflows and by the U.S. 1 causeway that blocked the natural water flow, salting the naturally brackish water and upsetting its habitat. Construction of sewer and storm-water management facilities on the north side of the bay and replacement of the causeway with a new, longer shore-to-shore bridge will soon restore water flow and allow regeneration of the bay's natural ecosystem to begin.

North across Ponce Inlet is the town of that name, widely referred to as PI. No place more sharply shows the split between East Volusia residents and their developer-crony governance. For years, PI sat quietly as a fishing village no more developed than Oak Hill, protected by dunes from the sea and marked by Ponce Inlet Light, a National Historic Landmark. The light centered a historical compound that included the lightkeeper's residence and housing for maintenance personnel, much of it now converted to shops and offices. Suzanne Heddy, a former Juilliard dancer who manages the Halifax Historical Museum in downtown Daytona, was the last child born at the lighthouse site. Back when cars still raced along what was called the Beach-Road Course, Heddy's father was hired to keep people off the property inside the end of the loop, which belonged to Dick Pope, who became famous as the developer of Cypress Gardens. Bill France put up signs that read "Warning! Rattlesnake Area!" as a way to keep people from trying to watch the races free.

Highway A1A was the inside leg of the course. At Daytona USA, the attraction connected to Speedway, you can see a slab of asphalt inlaid into the floor that's a piece of the old road from between 1936 and 1958 when it carried the A1A designation. Today's road still ends at the inlet—there's no bridge across—but A1A has cut west across the Intracoastal Waterway on the last bridge, just below Daytona Beach Shores.

Restaurants along the inlet give way to dirt lanes with names like Sailfish and Bounty beneath moss-topped oak limbs that canopy the way. Nearby is the Green Mound State Archaeological Site. But then, beyond canopied old PI, rises an egregious new and unimaginable assault of towers and low-rise condos that have stripped the hammock away to bare ground. It happened in a flash. Though the town charter had limited the height of buildings to 35 feet, a town council in the eighties ruled that it could waive that provision. In came the favored developers. Up went the condos, towering above the landmark light. When a new council tried to retake control of their town, the developers brought suits—$65 million worth! Bill Hoak, a financial officer for several Shores hotels, had moved to PI only in 1997 and right away got elected mayor. "I saw that no one was running the place. These were pretty testy times. I had to get rid of the town attorney, the town manager. You gotta start someplace." Ultimately, he settled all the suits. Unfortunately, permitted condos are still getting built.

One redeeming feature of the development assault? With the increased tax revenues, the town is buying up all its remaining wetlands. But popular as the town quickly became, turning from end-of-the-road-remote to high-end sanctuary, acquisition hasn't been cheap. One 13-acre parcel recently cost $1.2 million, and a quarter-acre for storm-water retention cost $155,000. Even though population has doubled to about 5,000, almost everyone backs Hoak's effort to lock down growth. So fierce is the determination that the town has eliminated its T-1 zoning, which accommodated tourism. "We don't want overnight tourists," says Hoak. Somebody wanted to open a B&B. That led to an uproar. "We're even changing the ordinance on short-term rentals to one month minimum. Residents don't want PI to look like the Shores." Some want the road into town four-laned for hurricane evacuation, but that would mean four-laning through Wilbur-by-the-Sea, the hamlet next north. That's unincorporated county, and the county isn't about to oblige. Hoak's not pushing it. There's no supermarket in town and not likely to be one. A few shops may go in among the boatyards and waterfront restaurants. "Wal-Mart-by-the-Sea? I don't think so," said Pete Grigas, the town's community services director. A county-built Marine Science Center draws on the natural legacy. It sits in maritime hammock and reaches to the inlet. It's all about native habitat. Most of the fish in the reef tanks have been caught in local waters.

Wilbur-by-the-Sea remains the kind of place PI was, though without the lush foliage. Its landmark site among the old shingle and clapboard bungalows is the restored boathouse along the inlet, white clapboard and flat shingled with a picket walkway and a sign atop that's lettered and framed in old train station style.

Daytona Beach Shores shuns the debauching style of Daytona but remains satisfied to shadow its beaches. After permitting condominiums as tall as thirty stories, a city commission majority in the nineties tried to drastically cut building heights. The attempt failed and today the Shores continues building twelve stories high. "We welcome growth but of a residential kind," says Daytona Beach Shores mayor Greg Northrup, who runs a beach concession at the Daytona Beach Hilton. "This is more of a residential area. We don't want the rowdy kids." Different from Daytona, the Shores prohibits outdoor displays of merchandise and itinerant vendors. "We add a little bit more class to the highway," says Northrup. The city has amassed funds for landscaping the A1A median about a quarter of the way through town.

Daytona's arts scene ranks it far and away best among the small cities of the A1A coast. Important institutions include the Daytona Beach Museum of Arts and Sciences, the Halifax Historical Museum, and the Museum of Photography at Daytona Beach Community College. A new performing arts center has opened at Bethune-Cookman College, located between Speedway and the Halifax River, where the home of college founder Mary McLeod Bethune is now a museum. A second performing arts center is coming along the river, sponsored by the News-Journal Corporation. Mainland Beach Street along the Halifax is a handsome attempt at renewing the faded old commercial downtown. It's a comfortable stroll along broad sidewalks with street furniture surrounded by decorative themed arches and kiosks that interact with the waterway. But commerce hasn't fully come back. The problem is equally a failure to plan beyond aesthetic improvements and partly the perceived separation of interests between Beach Street and the beach.

Beach Street is residential to the south before becoming low-rise urban waterfront. A large marina begins the urban section where residential briefly continues. It's a charming segue. Stores line the west side of the street, which looping metal arches, tropical-colored fixtures, and decorative street tiles set apart. But ten years after the improvements, old-time merchants have bailed out and vacancies abound. Restaurants keep turning over, waiting for business. The neighboring residential community lacks density. In part, that's because renewal never carried over farther to the west, where depressed neighborhoods spawn crime and bedevil the entire area. The event-driven economy in this city that lavishes funds on would-be condo-hotel saviors leaves the vicinity among Daytona's many postponed projects.

Also troubling Beach Street is that oceanfront commercial interests have resisted incorporating this authentic downtown as part of the beach appeal. The beach is simply too grabby and the chamber and city haven't shown the leadership. No rubber-wheeled trolley loops across the bridges and back. There is no water taxi. So many excuses! Beach interests assume that tourists can be whisked from the airport across the Halifax without seeing Beach Street—whisked directly to the still extant strip of tee shirt and tattoo parlors. At least lately, none of these have shown up in the restored downtown.

The Natural Glory of Northeast Volusia

Most attractive vacation town in the Bulge is Ormond Beach, north of Daytona almost to the Flagler County line. Like one of those multiple-identity types of pop psychology, Ormond splits its personality four ways. It's the beach town. It's suburbia encroaching west into forest. It's an old downtown divided by a high bridge across the Halifax River, and it's the natural glory of northeast Volusia. The four-way split tests local reconciliation but hardly diminishes the town's appeal to visitors.

The main street is Granada Boulevard, S.R. 40, east of I-95 rolling through near-in suburbs and leafy malls into the old downtown, where it's about three lanes too wide. East across the bridge to A1A is the MacDonald House, home to the Ormond Beach Historical Trust. You can tell someone's in when rocking chairs are on the porch. Here's Billy's Tap Room, opened in 1922 with walls of photos from when Ormond was the Birthplace of Speed—as checkered pole banners proclaim along Granada. Here's Angell and Phelps with free chocolate samples; Granada Gourmet with coffee on the house; and lately two or three natural foods stores, one with a dish of free chips. Is this largesse the legacy of John D. Rockefeller, who, while in retirement here at The Casements, having mellowed from his rascally years at Standard Oil, handed Ormond kids shiny new dimes?

Parks are Ormond's pride. Parks edge each of the four points along Granada where the high bridge comes to ground. Waterfall gardens behind the Ormond Museum of Art cool any summer day by five degrees. At the beach end of Granada is raised Birthplace of Speed Park, an artistic tribute to the one-hundredth anniversary of fast-car racing along the packed sands. Sculpted replicas stand of the Olds' black Pirate and the Winton red Bullet, which won the famous race by a fifth of a second. A pocket park installed by the Main Street program dimples Granada across the street from Frappes North, one of Ormond's two top restaurants; the other, La Crepe en Haut in Fountain Square.

The replacement for Flagler's old Ormond Hotel is a mournfully bad apartment house. Locals call it "the Penitentiary." The hotel had been a great rambling board thing, acquired by Flagler as his first hotel coming south of St. Augustine and greatly added onto. The Ormond's last owners had promised its restoration. Instead they stripped it of its remaining treasures, then sold it for the land. Yet behind the Pen remains a historical section long connected with the old Ormond. The hotel manager's house survives, with its brown log construction and white-painted trim, windows fitted into log cutouts. Ferns, hibiscus, and firecracker bush dress up porches that surround three sides beneath shady oaks. Others remain of shingle and board, some partially or altogether log-built with porches and protective overhangs. Patches of bamboo run through the section interspersed with mighty oaks. Woods remain in patches, some places transitioning with dense shrubbery and grassy yards.

The crown jewels of Ormond area parks lie to the north. One access is north of Granada where A1A remains called Ocean Shore Boulevard, as it was in Flagler County. The road passes sections of still single-family beachfront homes followed by more desultory motels, mid-rise apartment houses, and trailer parks. The last 2 miles emerge into North Peninsula State Recreation Area, where the way proceeds altogether open. Alternately along the west shore of the Halifax, a scenic loop of some 20 miles begins up the riverbank. Along Beach Street, the elegant mansion-and-ranch-house row gives way to awesome canopy as the drive enters into Tomoka State Park. One park after another follows, marked by historic plantation ruins, by a historic tomb, by the huge 800-year-old Fairchild Oak, by the bijou museum of the late Fred Dana Marsh, a deco-era artist whose mural idealizing industrial America of the twenties rings with worker hope. (Marsh lived on the beach north of Granada in a house lately owned by a tanning lotion magnate.)

Yet the virgin hammock surrounding Tomoka Park sounds with the hammer blows of unhopeful new construction. Too much of the woods has been permitted for development. Emotional campaigns to "Save the Loop" have largely been lost because of a county council too long leaderless in the conservation cause. Thin compromise has achieved landscaped buffers of native vegetation, but even so, this seems regrettably patchy from along the numinous road. Preserved more fully are park trails that end spectacularly in quiet river marsh scenes. Breeze paints this landscape, the fronds of cabbage palms dancing to ticklish rhythms. At Bulow Creek State Park, marvel at the Fairchild Oak. Its limbs reach to ground where sections have virtually buried themselves. Resurrection fern bushes the limbs as lichens redden them. The tree is so vast it seems more a feature of geology than of mere botany. A trail leads to Bulow Plantation State Historic Site 6 miles north in Flagler County.

Boardman Road threads a palm-lined way across the marshes of Halifax Creek before crossing the Halifax River over one of the county's last remaining drawbridges. The sand is red and gray. On a drizzly afternoon, a fellow stands in the water with a brown lab, pelicans skimming the sea, waves mere creases. He lives in Daytona, he tells a visitor, explaining that he comes up because he doesn't like beaches along the bulge. "They're dirty all the time with cars," he says, "or grim with buildings."

6 BREVARD COUNTY

Powered by Space, Still Searching for Vision

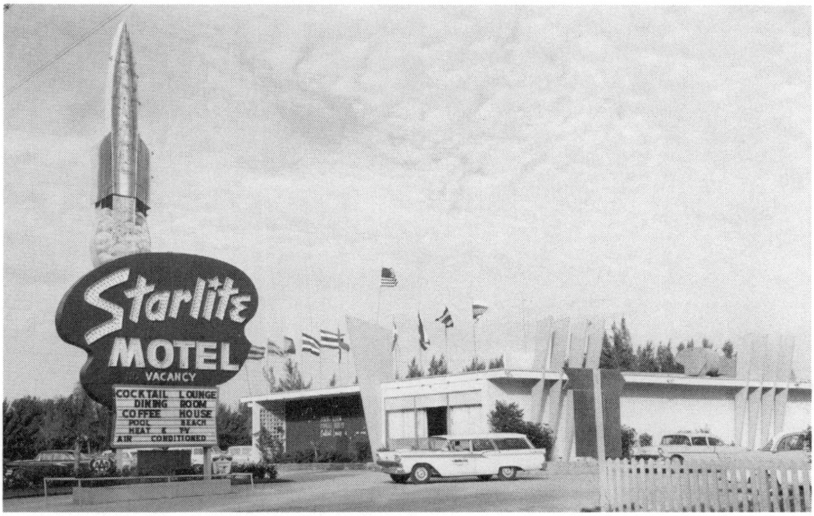

Figure 6.1. The Starlite Motel in 1958 Cocoa Beach. Charles Barron, photographer. Courtesy of the Florida State Archives.

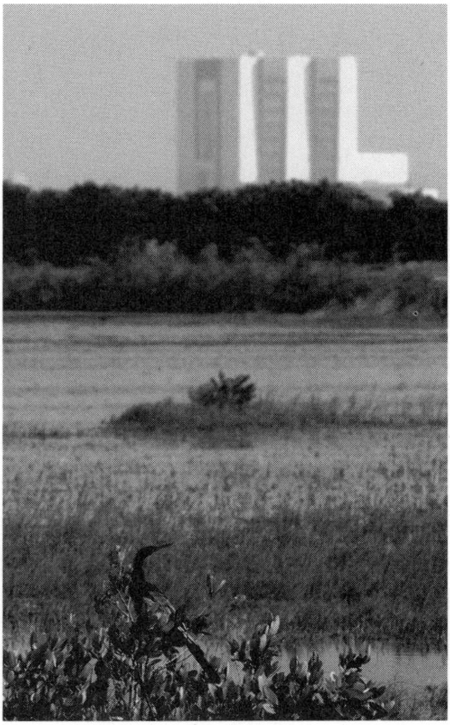

Figure 6.2. Merritt Island and the Vehicle Assembly Building at Kennedy Space Center. Courtesy of NASA.

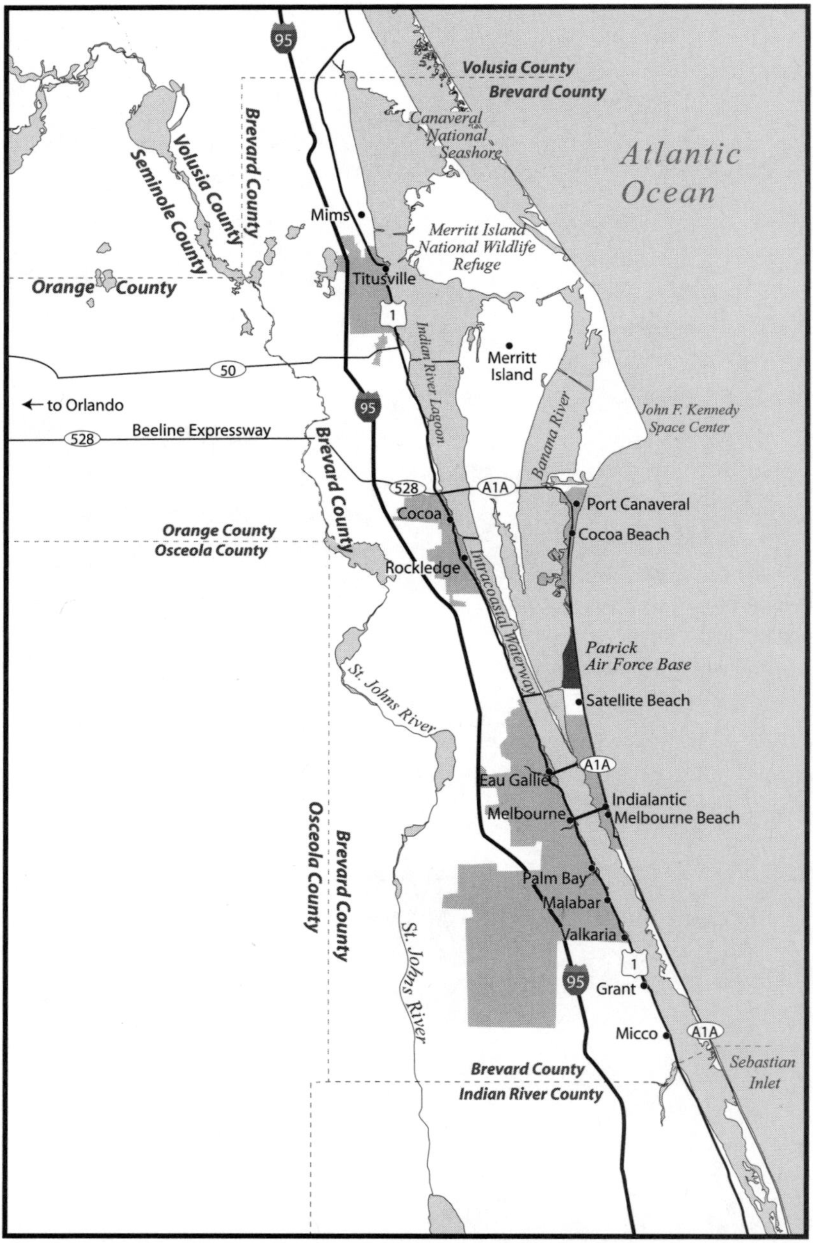

Map 6. Brevard County

Brevard County extends like a missile, long and tapered atop the launch pad of its south county line. To the north, it reaches 72 miles, longer than any other Florida county. It's also narrower than any other, much of the way less than 15 miles across its mainland. The county's two main waterways hem in the land, to the west the St. Johns River and to the east the Indian River Lagoon, part of a vast aquatic system. The system fronts a row of Atlantic barrier islands that encompass Kennedy Space Center and its great buffering nature preserves. Like the umbilicals that attach to physical missiles, those that attach to Brevard's missilelike length occur in the form of roads that reach east from Orlando. People who live or work in Brevard rack up miles on these roads to reach Orlando-area sophistications barely in place locally. When out from behind the wheel, Brevard people turn for enjoyment to their county's rich aquatic resource.

Kennedy Space Center together with Brevard's roadway system and nature preserves reveal the county as much different from anywhere else along Florida's east coast. That difference shapes up plus and minus. Although people drive everywhere for everything and despite enormous recent population growth—which has done little to improve county finances while worsening already painful traffic—some people who already live here still think of Brevard as their vacation place, as "the best of all worlds," as they'll tell you. But it's mainly retireds in the beach towns, close by shopping, who say this.

Any quick look around otherwise shows an ordinary place without the added value that we associate with exceptional vacationing or authentic character. People are spread around too many places. Order is missing in the realm. Apart from parks—essentially what's been saved from development—demand doesn't concentrate leisure facilities. Too much is needed in too many places. There's a zoo and a pair of performing arts centers in Melbourne, here and there small museums, but meager concentration of the arts. Historic districts are few, small, or rundown. The largest city, Palm Bay with 85,000 people far south in the county, is a developer's town hatched to generate lot sales. There are no compelling ethnic quarters. The county is drab. Roads off I-95 to the lagoon towns—notably to Melbourne, Cocoa, and Titusville—line up with every kind of chain store or tiresome franchise. Virtually no public display exists along the way, no monuments, fewest public sculptures or commemorative arches. The towns feel like they're meant to be rushed through. One-way streets or bypass roads speed traffic along, even through Cocoa Beach, the heart of the resort area. Apart from special events and along the beach, nobody is celebrating. Drive major causeways to Brevard's beach towns and they look like what they are: roads endlessly widened, lanes added one after the other for an everlasting and growing stream of cars.

As planners try to figure how to slow growth, watching as 5,000 additional cars squeeze into traffic each year and another 1,000 kids crowd schools, commuters call for more roads. "It's a mess," says one. "It'd be less packed if they

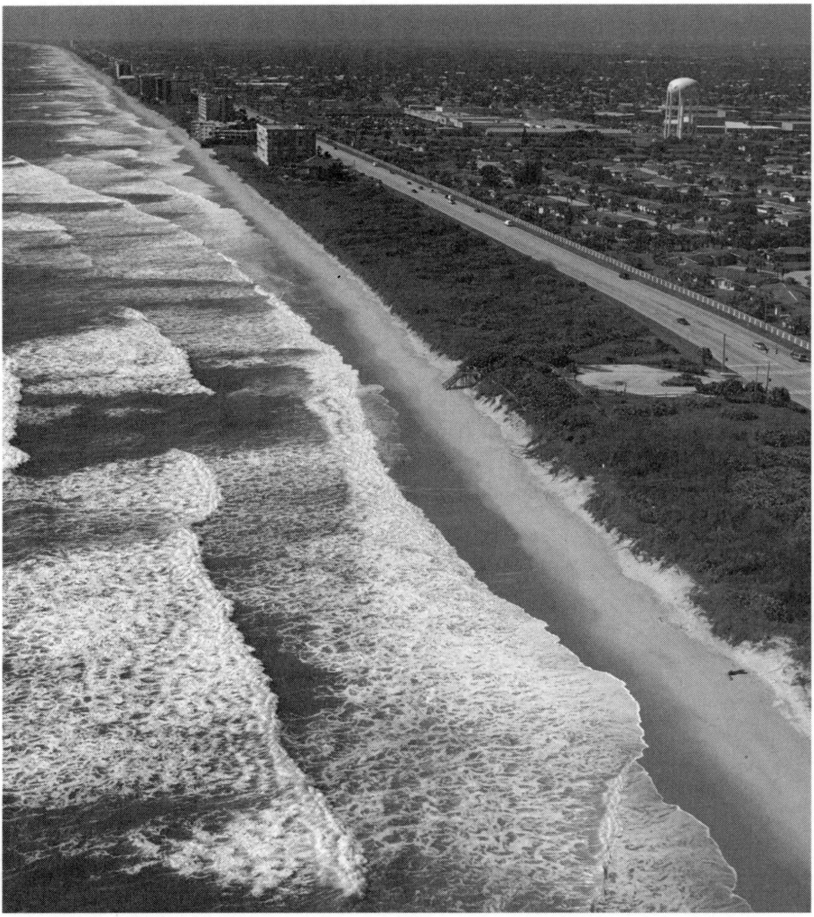

Figure 6.3. Highway A1A in Melbourne Beach. Courtesy of the Space Coast Office of Tourism.

made another lane going straight over U.S. 1." While the nonprofit Brevard Tomorrow plans for pedestrian-oriented places to live, builders putting up the same old same old say they never noticed the economic slump they were supposed to be coming out of in 2004. Construction can't keep up with demand. Says Realtor Betty McCluskey, quoted in *Florida Today,* "We've never had a market like this in 20 years." Nor did the storms of 2004 slow Brevard building, leaving only the beaches badly eroded, with restoration uncertain. In 1998, when voters were ready to buy up almost 10,000 acres of scrub that would have widened a natural corridor from one end of the county to the other, a majority of commissioners (later put out of office but now coalescing again) gave in to developers and never scheduled the ballot.

S.R. 520, across Merritt Island, a once beautiful region of groves between two waterways, has become straitjacketed with big-box retailers and ordinary malls. North-south, the county feels stitched together only by its name and the Space Coast slogan. Where any sense of dignity, of proportion, of excitement? In a state where planning has had to overcome a culture of development at any cost, Brevard seems destined to come around last. There hasn't been time for long views. Everything seems subject to catch-up.

America's Race to Space is largely to blame. If Brevard is remarkably transient both in its population and in the need to drive everywhere, that's because between 1950 and 2000 under the impact of Space, Brevard grew from 24,000 people to an astonishing 476,000 (506,000 in 2004). People flocked in from everywhere for high-paying work. Ever since, Brevard has ranked economically second only to Orange County (metro Orlando) in a seven-county Central Florida statistical area. But space has been an uncertain promise, with funding cutbacks after every disaster until Columbia and workers unsure about whether to stay or leave. People in these situations hold back on civic commitments. Those sure about staying—those most likely to think of the place as the best of all worlds—tend to be retired, relieved from work, living the ultimate vacation. They're happy in their niche and least likely to change things or invest in the catching up. They keep their foot on the brakes. But tourism, too, has been more transient in Brevard than elsewhere, with almost two-thirds of beach town visitors coming only for the day or booking rooms for only a night or weekend, while snowbirds flock to trailer parks. Brevard feels temporary, and every improvement like piggybacking one make-do fix on the last.

One way this shows is in how the highways of Brevard's narrow north-south corridor do double and triple duty. Maybe they do in all places, but the situation seems worse here. I-95 carries long-distance traffic through the county but also more work-hour traffic than it had to because the interstate became the service road for a western pastureland where county government unwisely relocated. That compound—where more than 2,000 work and greater numbers otherwise come calling—could have brought urban character and payrolls more productively elsewhere; to downtown Cocoa, for example, concentrating population to the east and spurring new designs on living all along the coastal ridge. Commuter rail might have become feasible along Florida East Coast tracks. Instead, I-95 became subject to stop-start traffic, while U.S. Highway 1, which runs alongside the tracks, remains an underused local and town-connecting road, its way varying from open Indian River shore with scenic Old Florida postcard views to shabby, barely viable towns.

Highway A1A, often scenic elsewhere along the coast, also passes through sections of Brevard where only the beach and the surf separate cars from where dolphins play and right whales seasonally migrate. But everywhere, A1A also serves as an unlikely commuter road between Brevard beach towns and the big employment hubs at Kennedy Space Center, Port Canaveral, and Patrick Air Force Base, all developed along the barrier islands. One in seven of

Brevard's almost half million year-round residents lives along the shore in the 18 miles between Melbourne Beach and Cocoa Beach. Resort districts spill over where people live. Traffic pours through. There's a constant push to keep moving, a race, however slow, without relief. Where the road remains two-lane, development outstrips efforts to preserve sections of how the county was. Where four-lane through the heart of the tourist zone, height and density restraints insisted on by angry residents ameliorate the worst features of all-out development. One feels the constant political fight like dust under the skin.

Like other coastal counties, Brevard courts its tourists, but more than elsewhere, Brevard tourists compound transportation problems throughout the county and especially along A1A. Visitors include an unusually large portion of day-trippers. They come taking a break from Orlando and its theme parks to relax at the beach or to tour the spaceport. Orlando-area residents looking for a day of fun in the sun also drive over, the same way that thousands of Orlandoans drive back and forth daily to work at the Cape and others from Brevard commute to theme park jobs. Brevard is endlessly in motion. Cocoa Beach supplies the resort world's nearest getaway. Day-tripping tourists and locals alike come over on the toll-road Bee Line Expressway or on toll-free S.R. 50, S.R. 520, and U.S. 192 and head to their beaches of choice. In 2002, when some 1.24 million visitors stayed at least one night in Cocoa Beach, almost twice their number—2.37 million—came just for the day. Many who come for the beach use A1A to cruise the sights.

Although tourists are no more inconvenienced here by traffic than in most coastal resort areas (they're generally not awake during morning rush hour anyway), for residents the tourist traffic represents a loss of control. It's not exactly the tourists that residents don't like. The traffic is only part of the developer effort to capture the beachfront residential communities, cash in on building more densely, and benefit hoteliers (often themselves developers) who reap the nightly receipts of the transient trade. It's the promoters of "big time" who insist on turning Cocoa Beach and neighboring beach towns into rows of hotels and noisy come-ons. Developers get the go-ahead to wall off the beaches right down to the view. They allege that it's not their actions that rile locals up but rather the inconvenience caused by the commuters and day-trippers. These dueling perceptions have contentiously decided a half dozen recent city elections, which early in the new century saw a residents' advocacy group prevail on critical issues that briefly earned Cocoa Beach a reputation as the first city in Florida opposed to tourism.

Brevard before Space

The conflict between these priorities is so new that it's hard to imagine for how long and until how recently Brevard merely poked along. For most of a hundred years, Brevard's beaches were simply too hard to reach for tourism or development to matter one way or another.

After the Civil War, adventurous visitors found their way to Brevard County along a circuitous route that discouraged all but the most determined. There was little to come for unless you wanted to be around the few settlers who grew citrus and raised cattle. Visitors came by steamboat from Jacksonville up the north-flowing river to Enterprise and Sanford on big Lake Monroe, transferring there to narrow and shallow-bottomed boats that could navigate upper stretches of the river to Lake Poinsett. From there, they crossed the 4-mile land bridge to Rockledge on the Indian River by mule-drawn train. In time, stylish small hotels rose in Rockledge, and the town became a popular resort for well-to-do hunters and fishermen. They've been attracted to Brevard places ever since. Rockledge remains one of Florida's most attractive small towns alongside a shore drive through the still-lush maritime hammock. It's here and elsewhere among these preserved areas of the county that Brevard remains not ordinary but exceptional.

But that was mainland tourism. Beach tourism hardly developed even during the land boom of the twenties. A few hotels went up south along Melbourne Beach and Indialantic. But to reach these, you crossed from the mainland on a rickety two-lane bridge and arrived at the beach on shells. It wasn't until 1924 that the first eight houses were built to the north in Cocoa Beach. A year later, the town incorporated. But nothing begun during the boom impressed anyone sufficiently to remain compelling through the Depression, the way, for example, Boca Raton and Coral Gables did in South Florida. Even up to World War II, the only way to Cocoa Beach was by bridge over the Indian River, across a rough 12-foot-wide road that angled northeast to the other side of Merritt Island. After passing over Sikes Creek, motorists dropped several miles south before crossing a wooden bridge that spanned the Banana River (the easternmost lagoon) to the beach where they found only a small section of paved road. The rest remained shell and sand. At the dawn of the space age, only 250 residents called Cocoa Beach home. Two small two-story hotels looked after the few visitors.

Although the war revived a dormant airfield that became Patrick Air Force Base, it wasn't until the start of midcentury rocket experiments and the Race to Space that development struck the barrier islands. Then, it struck full blast.

Local Community Swept Away

America's space program bolted into competition with the Soviet Union. During the fifties and sixties, an entire spaceport had to be built and the workforce assembled in a community that would have to accommodate its technology, transport its hardware, and supply its personnel. Brevard, which in 1950 had those few 25,000 who mostly fished, farmed, and ranched, was quickly flooded with 20,000 workers from outside the area. By 1960, almost 80 percent of the people living in Brevard—now 110,000— had been there for less than ten years. Without plans or normal community process, housing, schools, markets, and everything else had to be organized for people in a place they had never been before—some with families uprooted from home, most uprooted from the stability of home. Until 1958, Brevard hadn't even had a zoning ordinance. Merritt Island, the place chosen for the spaceport, was laid out in citrus and otherwise home of hunt clubs for northern elites. The great cape called Canaveral was a prominent land feature discovered by the Spanish in 1513 (though un-named, it was drawn on maps as early as 1502). By the turn of the twentieth century, the science fiction writer Jules Verne already imagined the cape as the ideal site for launching rockets. When space came calling, Canaveral consisted of coastal scrub and hammock with only a 165-foot-tall lighthouse otherwise. Land had to be cleared and configured for launch pads and runways. Bay-bottom had to be dredged, land filled, causeways built, and roads widened.

Subdivisions and shopping centers erupted out of barrier island and mainland farms and groves. In a burst of explosive growth Florida hadn't seen since the 1920s, every measure of local community was swept away by outsiders who arrived with unrivaled authority. The beach mushroomed and became sheathed in schlock. The motels that went up—meant to augment cheap housing for long-term workers—supplied cheap housing for transients. Everything was built quick and short-term. Motels in Cocoa Beach and Titusville flashed neon rockets and dancing girls. Inside, sequined cuties danced and did more. Motel row became Sin Strip. Forget tourist resort. More important than the beach was the bar. Saturnalia topped Saturn. For a while it seemed that everything took off but the rockets, which too often exploded on their pads or soon after takeoff. Failure got quenched in booze. Delays left waiting newsmen to the same solace.

Much of the cape became closed to civilian access. Hamlets along one of the most desolate remaining Florida coasts were swallowed up. Fishing holes and marinas got wasted. Attempts begun in 1963 to eliminate mosquito breeding in the marsh adjacent to Kennedy Space Center wiped out habitat essential to the dusky seaside sparrow, which, by 1987, became the most recently documented extinction of a vertebrate in the United States.

New causeways went up across the Indian River and the Banana River to rush traffic to the cape. An entire new town called Satellite Beach got built where the old causeway from Melbourne reached the beach. A1A got four-laned up to the missile grounds. Life got swept off its moorings by big ideas untested for reality. Titusville, Brevard's longtime rural county seat, declared itself the City of Tomorrow, the City of Chrome and Steel. Down came its old buildings, but the chrome and steel never went up. Instead, the town got wasted. Thirty years after its heyday, Titusville remained home to a vestige of county offices, while the entire administration had been relocated to a suburb called Viera, a cattle-grazing wetland west of I-95. Whereas only decades before, the cape had boomed the beach towns, populations now swung west as government's grab for the bait of free land for its headquarters hooked success for the immense surrounding development. For the sake of a cheap solution, the county committed itself to sharp westward sprawl. I-95 became a local road. Titusville decayed to ruin. What Space didn't physically swallow could easily slip away in the rush of a wrong move.

The coast began pulling day-trippers almost as soon as space activity began. Although early launches were secretive, PR demand soon forced schedules to go public. Hundreds got swept up by rocket fever. They parked up and down A1A and crowded the new causeways across the Indian River. Many who stayed overnight camped in RVs and tents. As Jerrell H. Shofner writes in his *History of Brevard County*: "Every time a new missile was launched a new motel or restaurant was shortly opened with the same name. The 'snarkburger' was a popular sandwich and the local bars treated tourists and residents alike to such exotic drinks as 'Satellite Cocktail,' 'Snark,' or 'Flaming Matador.'" Hundreds became thousands when, early in 1962, close to 100,000 watched the launch of astronaut John H. Glenn in America's first earth orbit. By 1981, more than 250,000 watched the first space shuttle flight carrying astronauts John Young and Robert Crippen on Mission STS-1. A NASA press officer recalls that it took eight hours to drive from Cocoa Beach to the press site at KSC. When the first launch was scrubbed, she slept on the NASA weather plane so she didn't have to fight the traffic back home.

But space flapped uncontrollable ups and downs through the Brevard economy. First came the fifties and sixties and the rush to build. Then, when the Apollo/Saturn V Moon program ended in 1972, a workforce that had reached 41,000 in 1968 in three years dropped to near 17,000. A slow economic rebuild reversed again in 1973–75, when NASA and the Department of Defense laid off another 6,500. Rapid expansion in the early eighties reversed once more after the destruction in early 1986 of the Space Shuttle Challenger with the death of seven astronauts shortly after liftoff. A two-year delay in launch activity followed, depressing everything from microwave communications orders at big Harris Corporation in Melbourne to tolls on the Bee Line Expressway and Titusville restaurant tips. Says Space Coast economic development director Walt Johnson, "Challenger just about shut down the area for three years."

One result of the outflow of people after the shutdown of Apollo/Saturn—there was no other local work—was the boom of a buyers' market for widely affordable housing that the evacuees left behind. Newcomers showed up who had nothing to do with space. Many retirees from the North came with their pensions and savings. The opening of Disney World in 1972 attracted new attention to Central Florida and to the proximity of Brevard beaches. Tourism began to develop in beach towns as the first of a new wave of motels and then hotels went up catering to the respectable family trade. In 1980, the notorious migration of refugees from Mariel, Cuba, to Miami occurred with its soaring criminal activity that drove widespread "American flight." With Brevard beach towns newly reputable for vacationing and good buys for available homes, an older population that matched retirees from the North began moving up from South Florida. One result was political. The county, which was always conservative, turned Republican in 1988.

Abetting this political shift was an emerging general hostility to government at all levels. For a century before space, Brevard had been rural and conservative. When space took over, authorities in their rush to build put dozens of families off the land with often skimpy compensation. Roads that led to launch sites were overloaded, and at first Washington refused to pay for their repair or capacity expansion. Workers at the spaceport, stressed and frustrated by enormous traffic jams, complained of discrimination by police who stopped them for speeding and driving under the influence. Tensions ran high between military and civilian officials. Locals were angry about in-your-face morals and often peremptory decisions that shut down roads. High-handed behavior by outsiders bred hostility to the government that sponsored the programs that brought them, if not to the economic benefits of the programs themselves.

Under rapid assault from real estate developers, Brevard in 1990 passed its EELs—environmentally endangered lands—program, a bond referendum that provided $55 million to preserve a portion of the county's dwindling natural lands. The St. Johns River Water Management District worked with state and federal agencies to augment funding and conserve regional water supplies. But preserved land means fewer commissionable real estate transactions. It means higher taxes on private property to offset taxes from land no longer on the rolls. Conserving and cleaning water to preserve a regional fishing economy means balancing a limitless right to pollute with regard for civic priorities.

Stewing in their resistance, Brevard Countians began electing staunch property rights candidates to county office. If "anything goes" ruled behavior in the coast towns, a perverse form of the same enlisted citizen hotheads. In 1995, B. B. Nelson, a prominent real estate trader who was upset over a wetlands rule of the water management district, threw a stink bomb into district offices. The building was evacuated and workers complained of mental anguish at a time when terrorists were attacking Americans abroad. Nelson and his gape-headed cohorts dismissed the incident as exuberant exercise of free speech. To others familiar with Florida's murderous attacks on women's doctors, blacks, and overseas tourists at the same time, Nelson's act further roared defiance of civil order. An offense that elsewhere would have resulted in a jail term, in Brevard produced a slap on the wrist. Nelson soon had a billboard up along I-95, ostensibly promoting his real estate business, that read, "B. B. Nelson. Man of Action." Nelson passed away in 2003.

Despite the vigilantism, county policies haven't followed any knee-jerk path. In 2000, liberal Bill Nelson of Cocoa was voted Florida's junior U.S. senator. Voters ousted an anti-environment commission majority by electing three replacements who strongly support conservation. By 2002, the EELs program had already acquired almost 19,000 acres. Although this represented less than 3 percent of the county landmass, the acquisition nonetheless offset some of the worst features of Brevard's too-fast transformation. In 2004, in the same election that seems to have reestablished a conservation-dubious county commission, the electorate by an almost 70 percent majority also extended the EELs program by authorizing another $60 million in acquisition bonds.

A Mixed Bag of Mainland and Beachfront Towns

Turnaround of commission attitudes on environment was long past due. The model for abuse was set by Palm Bay. It got underway in 1959 as a sheer exploitation of the space program. Old-timers remember that at the time, water in the Indian River was gin clear. As part of its pitch to homebuyers, General Development Corporation agreed to install sewers when sales in each section of its project exceeded 60 percent of available lots. In one of Florida's most notorious developer schemes, after each section sold its 60 percent, the company began developing a next section. Leaving land unbuilt-on cost General Development less than putting in sewers. Palm Bay government backed homeowners who refused to connect to sewers at a cost estimated between $6,000 and $10,000 per household. In a county that long put off sewering its residential areas, Palm Bay contributed more than 20 percent of all the lagoon's septic runoff. Under the cumulative impact, this section of the lagoon in particular has turned muddy and often sour. The lagoon is unable to clean itself because the system is tidal only near its few inlets. Otherwise, winds drive the lagoon's 155 linear miles. Turbulence constantly resuspends outfall deposits, which prevent light from reaching the lagoon floor, inhibiting sea-grass growth, disrupting habitat, fisheries, and the traditional economy while emitting sudden palls of toiletlike smells suffered by those living nearby. Under the rules of Palm Bay's incorporation, the city can't install sewers without a vote of the people. Votes are proceeding section by section through the city with small success.

At least for awhile, dolphins still arc through the lagoon and osprey perch atop snags, easily seen where U.S. 1 runs open much of the way alongside. The old fishing towns of Micco, Grant, Valkyria, and Malabar follow close along one another. In a section of the lagoon marked off by clamming leases sits the largest of several spoil islands, unbridged Grant Farm Island, a choice speck for some few dozen who live here with their own boats. Back on the mainland, a house from 1916, presently home of the Grant Historical Society, sits beside the water. Relocated next to it is the old Grant train station painted in Flagler yellow. A scrub ridge just west of the track marks the ancient sand dune of 100,000 years ago. Nearby north, upstream of where Turkey Creek drains into the lagoon, Turkey Creek Sanctuary, with its Margaret Hames Nature Center that memorializes a Brevard environmentalist, occupies 113 acres set aside in 1994. Boardwalks provide access to the sandy-bottom clear stream, best viewed from a pair of overlooks. One occupies a 30-foot-high bluff above a hairpin curve that cuts through a temple of trees. Gators, manatees, and otters are possible year-round sightings. The entire creek extends 4 miles and can be paddled to where it empties into the Indian River below Melbourne.

A handful of sites helps preserve Melbourne's character (population almost 75,000). Five oak-planted blocks along East New Haven Avenue just west of the railroad tracks concentrate the historic downtown. Alleys run back of the stores; up front, cypress-made boxes contain historical markers. The Henegar Center with a performance stage occupies a 1919 school. Restaurants serve at sidewalk tables. A block south off Melbourne Avenue a manatee observation area rises above Crane Creek.

Old downtown Eau Gallie (in 1969 merged with Melbourne) remains a Brevard treasure under assault. Lining Highland Street are the Children's Science Museum, the modest Brevard Museum of Arts and Science, offices of the Brevard Symphony, a few art and antique galleries, and Community Harvest, a natural foods store with a food service counter. Houses date from the turn of the nineteenth century. A portion of the two-story, wood-frame Rossetter House was built around 1860 and remodeled and added to in 1904 by James W. Rossetter. His two unmarried daughters in 1992 donated the house to the Florida Historical Society for use as a historical museum. Newly incorporated into what's now called the Rossetter House Museum is the nearby Roesch House, built around 1901, and marked by distinctive shiplap siding and fish-scale shingles. The complex opened to the public in 2004, and the society, which had occupied the Roesch House since 1992, has relocated its headquarters to Historic Cocoa Village.

Wooded Rossetter Park is one of two recreational sites in the neighborhood. The other occupies the end of Highland Street where benches overlook little Eau Gallie River Harbor. The setting is awesome in its Old Florida aspect. A handful of harbor buildings evokes the essence of nautical architecture. Antiquated Y-beams hold up bay windows, everything resembling a sailing captain's quarters. The old Eau Gallie Yacht Club, formed in 1907 and whose last charter member died in 1934, has been done up as a house with robin's-egg-blue clapboard exterior. Monster apartment houses have intruded into this sanctuary. Though the Melbourne City Council in 2003 voted to limit the height of new buildings to 35 feet and to expand the limits of the Eau Gallie historic area, by the following year developers had the council reconsidering the height cap and ready to repeal it.

Three miles west of downtown in the awesome burbs is Melbourne Village, a half-mile-square intentional community formed in the late forties. From the start a community rather than mere subdivision, there are no streetlights or sidewalks. Instead, turtle crossings, historical markers, trails through meadows, and a place of homes in the woods dispersed enough so that residents believe septic tanks remain viable. Named for a county preservation hero, the 52-acre Erna Nixon Park with a ¾-mile nature trail backs up to the village. Residents played a part in the founding of today's Florida Tech, 2 miles to the southeast. The school began in 1958 as an engineering college linked to development of space. Campus includes a botanical garden and a section known as "the Jungle" where a hundred years ago African Americans occupied Crane Creek wilderness. Melbourne's first schoolhouse, from 1883, has been relocated here. A brochure titled *The Founders' Trail* describes an interpretive walking tour.

Between Melbourne and Eau Gallie is the county's regional airport, which in 2004 took the name Orlando-Melbourne International Terminal. The addition of Orlando to the name follows a move made several years ago by the airport in Seminole County. That facility, located between Daytona and Orlando airports, became Sanford-Orlando International in the hope of attracting international tourists (space-related traffic almost all flies in and out of Orlando International, a quick 40-toll-road-miles from the Cape). Only Delta lately served the Melbourne airport, and its international flights all pass through Atlanta. As a Delta spokeswoman said at the time of the renaming, the company isn't planning any Europe-to-Melbourne flights any time soon.

North of Eau Gallie sits Riverside Park, a slice of hardwood hammock threaded by boardwalk about a quarter of a mile to the lagoon. A ramp slopes to a dark sand and scrubby cove beach. Just north begins narrow and scenic Rockledge Drive with its easy curves in an Old Florida setting, canopied and sun-dappled. It's immediately apparent why those nineteenth-century outdoorsmen would have struggled to reach here. This remains one of coastal Florida's most picturesque residential districts. A few low condominiums intrude, but mostly the way follows alongside old houses, grandly porched with bays among shade trees, the road nipping in and out along the lagoon shore. Here are the odd-few Mediterranean stucco and barrel tile houses, but most are clapboard, a few of stone, some sharply eaved, almost all with their docks into the lagoon, many topped by boat houses. Random and beautiful, great water oaks, massive old pines, and cabbage palms front the lagoon arching over the road. You go slowly along here, partly because you have to but surely in reverence. Even with a population of about 20,000, downtown Rockledge amounts to only a municipal building and a couple shops. Most residents of the city today live to the west. In that direction, U.S. 1, too, feels country. Stop-and-go north-south traffic largely relocated along the beach while higher speed traffic travels I-95. U.S. 1 at least for the moment remains neglected. A significant preserve of the upland vicinity is the Rockledge Scrub Site, about 130 acres. Environmental education centers are coming here, at Enchanted Forest west of Cocoa, at the Archie Carr National Wildlife Refuge, and at a site in Malabar.

Tracing this same south Brevard distance along the beach, the first A1A towns north of Sebastian Inlet, Melbourne Beach and Indialantic, have changed rapidly from open land to the clutter of highway-strip housing. How these vicinities used to be shows in the dune scrub and open beach at Sebastian Inlet State Park, with its major section here north across the inlet (see chapter 7). Open oceanfront dwindles as the road comes north out of the park. The badly fragmented Archie Carr, so important to turtle nesting, preserves only small sections because moves to conserve were put off too long. Apart from the general development pressures, a municipal policy that didn't cancel building permits long unacted on worsened the problem. Although densities have been steadily lowered through the unincorporated areas south along Melbourne Beach, these dormant permits have been transferred and revived as legal exceptions. A balance has been tipped. Housing that once would have been remote and unprofitable becomes viable as new residents gain Publix and CVS stores they can drive to nearby where development has been encroaching south.

One of the great losses was a 146-acre scrub jay site in Indialantic sought for preservation. The state joined Brevard County in the acquisition attempt. But property appraisals didn't satisfy the owner, and neither party would budge from its numbers. A developer who acquired a dormant permit came in, bulldozed the site like a moonscape, and mitigated the destruction in mainland Valkyria. What resulted, according to Dr. Duane DeFreese, "is a new housing development that provides no net value to the community and lots of service issues." For DeFreese, this was "the most heartbreaking situation" he has experienced and his only major loss in eight former years with the EELs program. "The problem," he says, "is that we argue ethical positions when the developers argue economic positions. We lose most of the arguments. People who want to preserve land aren't good enough at explaining the importance of conservation to the people who come to live in places like this. We have to be able to show the value of improved quality of life, of the whole community feeling."

Different from the routine expectations of developer-led government, DeFreese's envisions Highway A1A as an extraordinary science and high technology corridor with Kennedy Space Center as its nucleus. Other significant entities from the north include the Whitney Laboratory in Flagler County, a Hubbs–Sea World Research Institute Marine and Coastal Research Center under development in Melbourne Beach (that DeFreese serves as vice president for Florida research), the Harbor Branch Oceanographic Institution and Smithsonian Marine Station in St. Lucie County, and the Florida Oceanographic Society in Martin County. More public facilities also include the Marine Science Center at Ponce Inlet in Volusia County, a new Barrier Island Ecosystem Center that will open across the road from Hubbs, the Environmental Learning Center in Wabasso in Indian River County, and Blowing Rocks Preserve on Jupiter Island in Martin County. These are mostly new. They make significant social as well as scientific contributions to their communities. They also suggest a new way of characterizing the A1A corridor; a new calculus for combining economic as well as social and scientific arguments that can stand up to development pressures; and, maybe most important, a new way for people to see who they are in their places and to adjust their glance upward to what they might help their places become.

For an idea of what has been saved, you come north from the state park along the two-lane road atop the dune. In places, you can scan east to the sea and west to the lagoon. These sections of low coastal strand and hardwood hammock stand out among the housing as gifts to these residents and others who pass this way. A path through Coconut Point Sanctuary quickly passes gopher tortoise burrows. Mangroves have been newly planted alongside a lagoon overlook where a little beach serves for spotting dolphins or for fishing. Here are sea ox-eye daisies and a lupinelike plant with purple flower heads. Nearby, a path drops shady and cool into the Maritime Hammocks Sanctuary. Tropical hardwoods like mastic, gumbo-limbo, and fiddlewood, with its lovely orange rust-colored berries that makes a good hedge, all surround. Here are coral bean plants that have grown to full tree height, one said by county land manager Ray Mojica to be the second-largest in the state. A 2-mile loop continues along the lagoon.

As recently as the mid-forties there had been only a single lane of dirt road along the beach that would become Highway A1A. A former lifesaving station and World War II submarine watch site became the weathered Sebastian Beach Inn, one of those remote outposts for dance and romance that stick with us in innocent memory, places like the Lighthouse Restaurant, where Miamians hung out beside the sea, and Sid and Roxie's on the Overseas Highway in Islamorada, these and so many other once-popular sites up and down the coast.

Memories still settle in comfortably a mile down dirt Mullet Creek Road through a citrus grove at Honest John's Fish Camp. Roosters and peacocks, guinea fowl, and a flock of mallards supply natural noise. From the small marina you watch least terns beside mangrove islands. The camp was proved as a homestead in the 1880s. A hundred years later the site was about to look across to two golf courses and 176 condos. There was a whale of a fight, but those islets at last fell into public ownership. Now the state and county have also acquired the citrus grove, which was the last undeveloped and unprotected land on the barrier island.

Strewn around are an old barn full of dirt daubers with great gappy walls that seem held together by nets and fish buoys, the old board train station from Micco, a Cracker house put up in 1899. Barbara Arthur, who is Honest John's daughter, has pictures of her grandmother's eight children, five born in the house, three in Grant, the oldest still living and lately 102 in Palm Beach. It was Barbara's grandfather who found this place in a storm and who—with money saved from working barrier island pineapple fields—homesteaded it with his brother. Her dad made it the popular fish camp it became, though her uncle Bill was more widely known, that is, notorious. He was a bootlegger turned fishing guide in the Keys who later caught the first bonefish on an artificial fly and included Ted Williams among his pals. There's a signed picture of Williams in the old house here. Also around are displays of fishing bobs and beads, oyster knives, a handmade harpoon and a stingray barb more than a foot long. Here's the tool chest of an uncle who worked for the B&O Railroad, turtle ribs, part of a still, shells from middens, a template used for imprinting the ends of orange crates from R. T. Smith, Grant, Fla. While here, you might see an example of "Cracker air-conditioning," which is a hole in the floor with a screen across it to keep the bugs and snakes out. In winter the hole gets covered up.

There's much to love but ultimately little to celebrate. One batch of mangrove islands gets saved but back on the road on the way to Melbourne Beach a golf course development called Aquarina with seven- and eight-story apartment housing and a hotel have been tearing out the hammock between A1A and the lagoon, their combined size alone nearly equal to what's so far preserved. To the surprise of no one who's been around a year or two, Aquarina residents are up in arms about plans by the developers to keep building, threatening their views, their ambiance, *their property rights!* They collect signatures, they threaten to sue, but what has the developer done but jump through all the hoops.

As the road nears Melbourne Causeway, a rash of cheaply put-up places strings out. Everything is an exploitation, an endless row of hard-plastic signs, no sense of theming, of place. This nonplace smells of impermanence. Maybe it's the military. Maybe it's that so many are military retired. Maybe it's that by the time this section got developed nobody cared anymore. Nondescript condominiums and a Ramada Inn that looks like a penal institution are replacing the few remaining old homes. "Tootsie" cabarets hang on from the days when males worked here alone. Give thanks that Patrick Air Force Base at least keeps its shorefront open, though to the upland side the landscape erupts chockablock in institutional housing.

Among the build-up, remnants of the scene before the space program hang on. You find these in fixed-up old beach digs (Cocoa Cabanas is a favorite, though that's about to go condo) and along slow-changing country roads. Pretty Tropical Trail (C.R. 3) lollygags along Merritt Island between the Indian River and the Banana River through a landscape of palms and remnant citrus, past orchid gardens, patches of papaya, fences strewn with bougainvillea, banana groves, old barns beside old houses. The narrow road continues north, setting off again a mile north up S.R. 513 off the Eau Gallie Causeway (S.R. 518). The cutoff is not well marked.

The way runs narrow as a hummingbird beak up to Pineda Causeway (S.R. 404). Old Florida hangs on among gnarly tree trunks. Old Settlement Road cuts off only one-lane wide. Crooked Mile Road, just beyond, lives up to its name. Where the road crests just before rejoining the Trail, a vista bursts across the Banana River framed by an oaken canopy and a splash of fuchsia bougainvillea. Birds throng the flats of the Banana River. The beachside party scene exists in some unimaginable future though it's just across the Merritt Island Causeway (S.R. 520) on Cocoa Beach, a half mile north of where the causeway ends at the sea.

In that space between the easternmore of Merritt Island's two southerly prongs and the barrier island lie the Thousand Islands, a lacy scatter of partly submerged lands within Cocoa Beach limits still mostly unbridged. Developers did grab them for less than a half million back during the space boom. Now they're ready to unload them for only five times that amount. So far the city hasn't come back with an acceptable offer. Paddling guides make a living taking kayakers through the islands. Barrier island residents look out there and see what they came to Florida for. Owners of the land want fifty to eighty times the land's appraised value, which given Brevard's history seems only reasonable.

In Cocoa Beach, the town that has taken the heaviest hits from tourists, the fishing pier extends 800 feet into the sea. The pier became the icon of East Coast surfing when in 1964 notorious jewel thief Jack "Murph the Surf" Murphy from California popularized surfing here. Surfers pock the churning sea. Pubs sport surfer iconography, rock posters, Marilyn Monroe memorabilia. Midday and weekends, the outdoor bar on the pier is packed with Bud drinkers keen on the surf action and the beach bunnies. But surpassing the pier as the mark of Cocoa Beach surfing fame is the deco-style, neon-garish headquarters of Ron Jon's, the ultimate surf shop. All roads lead to this surfers' Oz, second to Kennedy Space Center among Brevard attractions and hang-10 icon of consumption as safe sex. Like the boards say, Ron Jon is one of a kind. It's McSurfboard USA, biggest b-b-b-b-b-b-b-badass of Florida roadside advertising—East Coast champ of surfer sales in the raging hormone league that leaves Macy's looking like the saggy balloon of pre-MTV retailing.

If you haven't seen the Ron Jon's billboards with yesterday's starring Surf Cruiser Shark and Korky Kangaroo or the recent versions with babes so provocative that signs tell you how many miles to the next one, you've been driving midstate Florida with your eyes closed. Odds are that like thousands of other tourists, one morning you'll drive to the Cape for a space shot and when it's postponed for bad weather or a loose bolt you'll figure, Hey! Ron Jon's! This is the place! Don't rush. Ron Jon's stays open around the clock. It's on South Banana River Boulevard, and from its premises rises the world's first neon-trimmed space rocket. It's classical in-your-face theater of commerce with its own rotating three-sided billboard—a wedding cake for Buck Rogers. Kahuna deco.

Inside this eggplant purple and green palace of postpubescent mania, there's a see-through elevator, a see-through roof with high-strung dolphins, and a rock 'n' roll beat. Its 53,000 square feet corral 75,000 must-have items from tee shirts and Frisbees to boogie boards and boomerangs—everything, like they say, for fun in the water. "We do think it's kind of deco-ish," says a spokesman for Ron—and there is a Ron even if not a Ron Jon, though Ron (who is Ron DeMenna) prefers to use only the one name—like Madonna or the artist formerly known as Prince. DeMenna was making custom surfboards in New Jersey back in the sixties when he heard that NASA was setting up shop in Florida. Good enough for Spaceport USA, good enough for Surfing USA. Cocoa Beach was bound to become, says the spokesman, "a hip, happening, hopping-around place." Especially at spring break. February 15 to May 15, Ron Jon ain't Girl Scout Troop 15. You might want a look. Then again, you might not.

Shoreside party time extends north to Port Canaveral, where on weekends a couple of thousand guzzlers at Grills get it on by the water, the dress code skimpy, sweat the great equalizer. The band covers Eagles tunes in a hot beery haze thick enough to fry grouper. Heads swivel when the cruise fleet heads out the channel. A Carnival behemoth leads the way followed by a Disney megaship pealing "When You Wish upon a Star." Like sunset at Mallory Square or deco hotels in Miami Beach, the great ships provide backdrop for the party times Floridians crave. When the charter boats tie up back from the Gulf Stream, the Eagles lose a few to Flipper—on a recent Sunday afternoon five iridescent big green and blue ones and a 27-pound red snapper off one boat alone. Fish get filleted, the party rocks.

Just before the port, the road passes through the city of Cape Canaveral. A beach trolley runs here between mid-Cocoa Beach and the port. Trailer parks remain from when they were jammed in for housing in the early days of the space program. Elsewhere, cheap fifties and sixties houses are getting redone, and even trophy houses are going in. The look is altogether unsettled, the big changes of fifty years ago still stewing. One landmark lost was the closing in 2004 of the Moon Hut Restaurant, a one-time drive-in that adapted to the space age in 1958 and became the favorite of early Cape workers. The road runs up to the port from where it used to continue straight north through today's Spaceport across the landmass behind Cape Canaveral, ending at the foot of the untrammeled beach that's the wilderness core of today's Canaveral National Seashore. A1A ended there, and drivers continued east on S.R. 402 to Titusville. Today A1A swings west at the port on a modern divided four-lane highway. At the mainland, the A1A designation vanishes for 44 miles until reappearing on the mainland in a freestanding section that proceeds east through a section of New Smyrna and then south to the northern entrance to the Canaveral National Seashore. This gap is the longest north of Miami without any A1A designation.

Historic Cocoa Village on the mainland is an attractive restoration where sidewalks have been prettied and oaks preserved, palms, bougainvilleas, and roses added. Cafes, galleries, and gift shops have moved into the old board and brick buildings that line sun-flecked sidewalks. Apartments have opened over stores. The Florida Historical Society runs a fine bookstore here at its headquarters. Thespians again tread the boards of the old Cocoa Village Playhouse. There's a visitor information center, the Central Brevard Art Association, a Christian Science Reading Room. A little sunken brick park is dedicated to Myrtice Stewart Tharpe, her memory evoked by a canopy of umbrellas shading stone benches where visitors can rest while enjoying gazebo-staged outdoor live music many weekends during winter. Thanks to John Heimberger at Natural Wood Signs, signage rises to the level of public art.

The village is a small joy corrupted to the south by the opaque Bank of America building and an execrable apartment house that replaced the gracious old Brevard Hotel, the kind of gross intrusion in a residential neighborhood that suggests developers paying off city officials. It's an in-your-face assault upon the people who live across the street in a neighborhood otherwise of Old Florida houses with yards of bougainvillea, hibiscus, and ixora. They suffer unconscionable aggression. So does the entire village on its north side. Maybe good for tax rolls and village business, but huge towers just north of the pretty district have re-created urban Newark in rude disregard of aesthetics and civility. Cocoa has fallen on hard times and in 2004 felt forced to sell off its only public-access marina, a move it chose not to submit to voter decision.

Past an impressive new library in downtown Cocoa that has little else to commend it, Rockledge Drive becomes Indian River Drive continuing along the lagoon shore. The narrow two-lane drive enchants. Hibiscus spring out, bougainvilleas bob in the breeze, poincianas arc over the road. The surrounding water moderates winter temperatures. Home dwellers risk small mango orchards. Speed bumps slow cyclists if not joggers. Citrus trees front the houses, mailboxes take the look of manatees, and docks occupy the lagoon front. Here are lovely board fences and stone planters. This too is one of the prettiest drives in Florida. One property calls itself Blissmere. Along the road just below where A1A has swung across from the port is the little Indian River

House, its handful of B&B rooms containing sepia-toned nineteenth-century photos and artifacts, its yard behind a picket fence, and with rope-trimmed steps leading through bush down to the lagoon edge.

Titusville and the Promise of Renewal

Ultimately north comes Titusville, Brevard's most underappreciated city and ironically its urban hope. In this county so disparately riven and jerry-built, Titusville, so pitifully run down, at least promises historical continuity as its restart proceeds. It's one of the region's oldest areas of settlement dating from a fort site in the late 1830s during the Second Seminole War. This was citrus country with important timbering and fisheries. County government helped sustain Titusville during the collapse of the twenties land boom and the Depression that followed. But growth was otherwise slow after the war until the space program took off at Cape Canaveral across the lagoon. Space blinded the town. NASA got going at the Cape in 1958. Five years later, the first of the county's two great coastal preserves was set aside. That was the Merritt Island National Wildlife Refuge, followed one year later by public re- opening of the first beaches taken by NASA that later became the Canaveral National Seashore. The set-asides were meant to create sweeping buffers for space program operations that were highly security sensitive. But the buffers also contained portions of the most sensitive remaining ecosystems along east coast Florida. Conservation and game hunts had long coexisted on Merritt Island. Now it became quickly apparent that the lamb and lion could continue to lie down together. Space program–generated noise would explode louder than gun pops, but the nature set-asides would be vastly greater than the game leases. The two great preserves would encompass almost 200,000 acres.

Yet when the buffers were put off limits to hunters, their backers in the local economy hardly rallied to the idea of coaxing birdwatchers down to replace them. Birdwatchers who traveled for rustic privilege were unfamiliar and perceived as likely to spend less while pursuing their passion. So Titusville, the nearest city to the island and the county seat, threw in with high tech and the future. And lost.

In 1967, the Ohio company that became Harris Corporation acquired Radiation Incorporated, a Melbourne-based manufacturer of space and military electronics. Harris relocated its headquarters, becoming a Brevard powerhouse, in time employing as many as 27,000 at various sites, today some 8,000, but in south Brevard. Other major military and space interests set up south along the coast at Patrick Air Force Base while still others set up directly at Kennedy Space Center. When government took the developer's bait and greatly expanded its compound at Viera, Titusville lost it. Of Brevard's top twenty employers, which together account for 70,000 jobs, Titusville claims only one, lately accounting for 5,000.

The collapse of its brief, rapid expansion left Titusville looking worse than its actual economic condition. The one-way north-south pairing of U.S. 1 lanes through downtown left this the sad sister of Brevard towns for racing through. Quick glances out car windows show pawnshops, martial arts studios, a pregnancy center, the Sav-A-Lot superette, Second Chapter used furniture. The FEC Titusville station shows barbed wire around its perimeter. The new courthouse is disgracefully ugly, a "modern" calamity that worsens confidence in government. So much for chrome and steel. Shopping centers stand eerily vacant except for holiness salvation storefronts. Juxtaposed but uptight about it, the section of fine homes along Riverside Drive evokes Rockledge. It's everything that downtown just a couple blocks away isn't. It's clear that those still at home here aren't yet ready to embrace downtown.

But of course, quick looks out fast-moving car windows hardly tell all. Walk the downtown and signs of life appear like grass in the cracks of broken pavement. Visionaries behind this new growth test existing limits. One is chief scientist for the contractor that provides technical services to NASA's environmental stewardship program. Another is the city's studious senior planner, another a restaurant operator whose mother did all she could to keep her away from the water but who dug in for keeps after she crewed the delivery of a shrimp boat to Trinidad. G. Ross Hinkle, the Ph.D. chief scientist with Dynamac Corporation here, says "It's like entering into a time warp in Titusville, and we love it," referring to just about everybody who does get out of the car and walk around. As if on cue, a visiting English couple in Kloiber's Cobbler and Eatery overhearing talk about Titusville as "a sleeping giant" offers, "Let it sleep."

Hinkle says, "The problem is the traffic, the one-ways." Laurilee Thompson, who runs Dixie Crossroads, her family restaurant a mile west of downtown on the way toward the interstate, wants to close down Washington Avenue and leave it only for pedestrians. "Downtown has to become a place where people want to walk and stop in shops," she says. Hinkle says that after he works with scientists at the space center, he brings them to Thompson's place to learn about the life cycle of rock shrimp, the small crustaceans she makes her restaurant's specialty. Wes Hoagland, the senior planner, "jooks" the city administrative system to make things happen faster.

Together, they see that Titusville, having fallen so low, has no place to go but up. They're guiding what happens this next time around. One of Thompson's endless contributions has been to set up her Cape Canaveral Shrimp Company in a virtually empty shopping center in a high-risk section of town. Every shrimp her restaurant serves is cleaned by hand here, and she hires in the neighborhood. A 326-foot wildlife mural her family commissioned surrounds the plant. Another surrounds her restaurant a mile west on the road toward the interstate, where she keeps adding onto a large compound of tropical gardens and newly tinkers with a butterfly house the size of a junior Astrodome that she built with her cooks at Dixie Crossroads. All this lets dinner guests enjoy themselves while waiting for tables. Her mother grew up in a house across the street.

Thompson initiated and remains guiding spirit and chief backer of the Brevard Nature Alliance–sponsored Space Coast Birding and Wildlife Festival. In 2005 in its ninth year and international in scope, it's the largest event of its kind in Florida. For her sins, Thompson, who squeezes spare time out of stone, lately served as chairperson of the county's tourist development council, at last getting fair hearing for ecotourism on a board long dominated by conventional minds. Say this for tourism, if it puts heads in beds, no matter what tourists do by day, backers will fund the activity.

Walk downtown with Hoagland and Thompson and you're in and out of a dance studio that draws customers from as far as Orlando, a sailmaker's, a custom embroidery shop. A coffee shop has restored its building's original terra cotta tile floors. The city's first bank, the Indian River State Bank, opened in 1888 and now houses a gallery. It was organized by Capt. James Pritchard, who was its president for twenty years. His daughter, Mrs. Mary Schuster, lives in downtown's reigning Queen Anne house, built in 1891 with closets in every room. Walls are hung with portraits of Pritchard ancestors going back to Revolutionary times. The initial "P" is distinctively set in the two front doors. Thompson is arranging to have the county acquire the house (scheduled for mid-2005) while Schuster continues to live here.

Sections of downtown where buildings were knocked down for the City of Chrome and Steel instead get renewed with places like Titusville Common. The Common was a street before an ornamentally enhanced pedestrian way with benches and a wrought iron arch. It flows from a parking lot turned gardenlike. Back-of-building utility meters have been framed in architectural kiosks, their covers used as notice boards for shops and downtown events. Rears of buildings are getting fixed up like their fronts because people see the backs and can enter many there. Art imaginatively sets off historical markers. One describes how the Brady Grocery Store started up the road in LaGrange, moving to Titusville in 1886. Brady rebuilt after the big fire of 1895 wiped him out, close by the new FEC station on one of the first streets paved with oyster shells. A waterfront marker for Scobie Fish and Oyster Company, recalling 1885, tells of the first town clerk who used to visit Capt. Joe Smith's fishing house on the dock where he "could buy two big mullet, scaled and cleaned for a nickel, and all the oysters I could eat for a quarter."

History is only part of what the city needs to celebrate. It's too little known as the gateway to Spaceport USA, the public attraction for Kennedy Space Center. Kennedy is well known, of course, and tells the story of the space program with both the draining emotions of calamity and the super cool of high-tech achievement. The great industrial mobilization it represents comes across with only rare belching fire and smoke. More so through simulated control rooms where countdowns mask the tensions of science and lives on the line, through views of the Vehicle Assembly Building fifty stories tall where the rockets that power space exploration vehicles get assembled for launch. Two IMAX movies tell the story as do hangar and outdoor galleries that display the generations of hardware that so far have powered the Cape's emergence as symbol of America's technology leadership. Announcements by the Bush administration for a moon base and Mars-related space endeavors excite only inured optimists. More hopeful are plans for a space shuttle "immersion experience" at the visitor complex by 2006, while everyone waits for space shuttle flights to resume in 2005.

More certain is Titusville's emergence as hub city of outdoors recreation along the A1A coast. It's already gateway through the still-rural town of Mims to an incomparable braided section of the upper St. Johns River off S.R. 46 and to Buck Lake Wildlife Management Area with its large population of scrub jays. Titusville is southern trailhead for a 49–mile recreational trail that will reach to the north side of big Lake Monroe in Volusia County and, from there, circle the lake to connect with existing Seminole and Orange County trails linked clear across Central Florida to St. Petersburg and the Gulf of Mexico. Titusville is also headquarters for the Canaveral National Seashore and sits across the Indian River from the visitor information center of the Merritt Island National Wildlife Refuge, the best-situated city for reaching both preserves.

The wildlife refuge includes spectacular birding sites along the Cruickshank Trail off Black Point Wildlife Drive and through Turnbull Bay to Mullet Head Island. Any time of year there might be 2,500 to 5,000 birds at Mullet Head—cormorants, egrets, herons, pelicans, roseate spoonbills, terns of many varieties. You can stand with a scope in six inches of water and watch cottony great blue heron chicks jumping up and down in their nests demanding to be fed, immature roseates and young nested great blue herons utterly fluff but looking like mature Einsteins. Pelicans and cormorants skim the water within feet of kayaks.

You have to wonder about the missing middle ground between Florida rushing to destruction and the vision of a DeFreese or Thompson as you walk the virtually unpeopled beaches of the national seashore. Get a sunrise start and rising color becomes the inner voice of the ocean roar. Rose that rules the sky quickly spreads across the crest of waves, on foam slathered onto the beach, on waves' sparkling retreat. From rose the sky becomes egg-yellow, gold, and silver. The beach appears hardly different from the way that shipwrecked Quaker Jonathan Dickinson would have experienced it 450 years ago. Spume blows back from waves like the silver manes of horse fury, suggesting Earth in its rotation forcing wind across its face. On a cold morning, heat from 75 million miles away warms frosty fingers. Driftwood piles against the dune, silvered by sun and wind. Sea birds cluster by the water's edge—loons, pelicans, turnstones, terns. Gulls hugger-mugger their catch of small crabs. Sanderlings and sandpipers move as if auditioning for Cirque de Soleil, their legs faster on the sand than virtuoso fingers on a keyboard. Willets poke their straw bills into receding waves for who knows what morsels. Beyond the sound of any motor in as remote a setting as east coast Florida offers, you can walk south from the last parking lot below New Smyrna along the 12-mile shore accessible only by foot while, step by step, the Vehicle Assembly Building looms steadily higher and more powerful. You realize how imperative it is that people accommodate nature more generously than so far.

7

INDIAN RIVER COUNTY

Elite Vero Beach and the Defense of Place

Figure 7.1. A bird's-eye view of the parking lot at McKee Jungle Gardens in Vero Beach, circa 1947. Courtesy of the Florida State Archives.

Figure 7.2. Sebastian Riverwalk. Courtesy of VeroBeach.com.

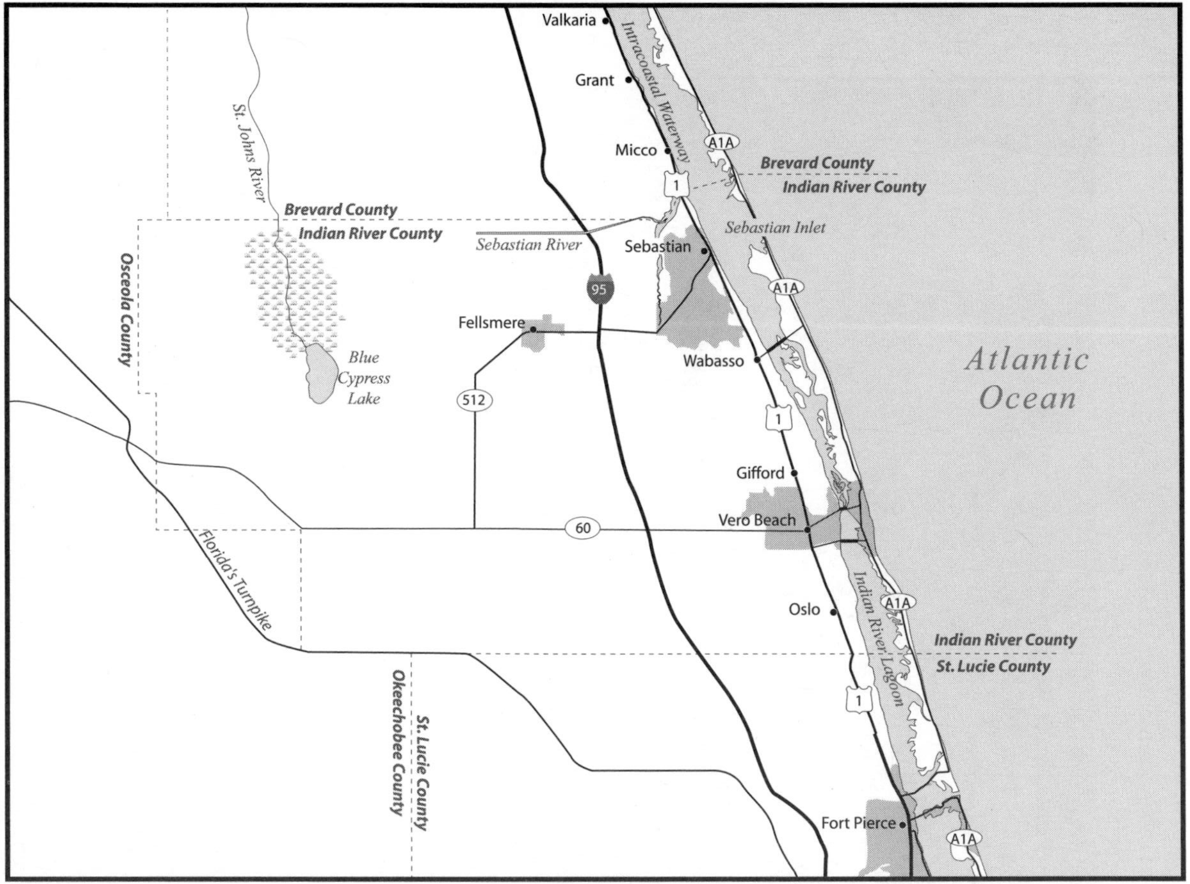

Map 7. Indian River County

Connections between nature and the arts assert themselves in Vero Beach, the seat of Indian River County, which lies midway along the A1A coast, six counties north, six counties south. Some balance prevails in this city among the seesaw uncertainties of Florida elsewhere. For Floridians seeking their bliss, this is one of Florida's most desirable places to live (in 2004, nationally ranked number seven among smaller cities by *USA Today*). The city's civic mindset repels great drifts of relocating people swept by promotional gales. Consider instead Vero's stability (the town name means "truth"). Between 1980 and forecasts for 2030, the city's numbers will barely change from 16,176 to 18,000. That's 2,000 additional people in fifty years, a timeframe when entire Florida cities have grown to 100,000 from nothing, while Indian River County itself, between 1980 and 2000, jumped from 60,000 to 113,000, and its growth further quickens today.

The nature-culture connection should not be mistaken for some developer condescension, some cultural greenwashing meant to entice concessions from dubious gifts. Instead, the connection is a gift from the people who live here to themselves and to their larger community. The arts connection is a controlling influence expressed not just in pretty objects but in institution building, in bricks and mortar, in tone and quality, in the character of the roadscape, for example, generously but not demonstratively landscaped, and in the absence of cheesy Florida iconography. Vero says yes to the beach, no to beach hangouts, yes to gated barrier island housing, no to beachfront towers. The influence is conservative in the sense of conserving rather than being driven by ayatollahs. If far from a Zen community, the place is as close to an affair of the spirit as any small residential Florida city gets.

The nature-arts connection draws attention to a regional reference. That's to the Treasure Coast, a reference that includes three counties, starting in the north with Indian River and continuing south through St. Lucie and Martin. The "treasure" refers historically to the loot of Aztec and Incan civilizations that 300 years ago washed ashore along the beach here from sunken Spanish booty fleets. Distinctly in Indian River County, the treasure might also refer to this beach community mix of impressive retirement wealth and noblesse oblige. Vero and its vicinity might better be called the Treasured Coast.

These impressions easily form as you drive along the county's Jungle Trail. The unpaved way passes through canopied coastal hammock where women in early morning walk their Irish setters and ride their saddled mares. The scene appears sprung from the pages of an old *Harper's Bazaar* or *Vogue*. In place for a century, the trail has more than once survived the schemes of developers ready to subvert its long use as a public road and capture it as a subdivision feature instead, some ornament on a Mercedes hood.

The Jungle Trail is the early road through the north portion of Orchid Island, the name given in 1887 by a Capt. Frank Forester to the barrier island that became the seaside section of Vero Beach. It was a dirt path alongside the

 Indian River Lagoon, which it rimmed to the east. At first, the path extended only 3 or 4 miles, connecting early settlers with the lagoon at a lee section where islands come close along the lagoon's eastern shore in the wind-protected Narrows. By 1920, when the Vero bridge was built from the mainland, St. Lucie County designated the trail as a public road. (Indian River County was formed from St. Lucie only in 1925.) The trail became almost 14 miles long and ran from the new bridge north to the Brevard County line.

East of the trail was the "jungle," the name given by settlers to the dense hammock that covered the island. Although today the hammock remains as thick as ever only in a few preserved sections—and more plentifully in older subdivisions than in newer ones—beautiful as the hammock was, the settlers set about cutting it down to plant citrus. They found the oak leaf compost that formed over ages yielded a soil excellent for growing fruit. Result was the premium brand known as Indian River Citrus, which gained a reputation as far away as Japan. Grapefruits of the region became prized for their thin skin and copious sweet juice.

"It's the top of the world, this Orchid Island fruit. We shipped to the White House," boasts Richard Jones, third generation and last of his family to run Jones Fruit Company. The company sign still sticks up alongside the Jones dock on the lagoon. Remnant groves still survive out back of the old slope-roof house built in 1923, when Jones was a boy of four. Awning windows front the big Florida room of the house. Jones is an exuberant octogenarian, who behaves in an altogether comfortable at-home way as if it were old-timers like himself who still occupied the shores of the lagoon.

He tells about when twenty cars at a time lined up on the dirt road to buy his citrus. Seven people worked the groves, the fruit stall, and the dock back then, picking, cleaning, squeezing, bagging and selling. Today, with citrus no longer profitably grown on the barrier island and the harvest trucks and processing plants gone, apart from the occasional passing car you hear little but the birds, the splash of waves from a passing yacht, or the creak of Jones's swing.

Jones believes he is the oldest person still living along the trail, though he's not sure about some of the newcomers in the subdivisions. They've been coming in droves for the last twenty, thirty years now that their premium houses have replaced premium fruit. Jones complains that he doesn't even find resident old-timers among the death notices of the *Vero Beach Press Journal* anymore.

"The obituaries are all about foreigners who've moved down here," he laughs, relaxed in the yard alongside a section of the trail where the subdivisions remain out of sight. He's dressed in a checked patterned shirt atop belted jeans, Sperry Topsiders without socks and a 100th Anniversary Ford cap. Still handsome in his gnarly way, he swings in front of a big oak full of philodendrons, Spanish moss, and air plants.

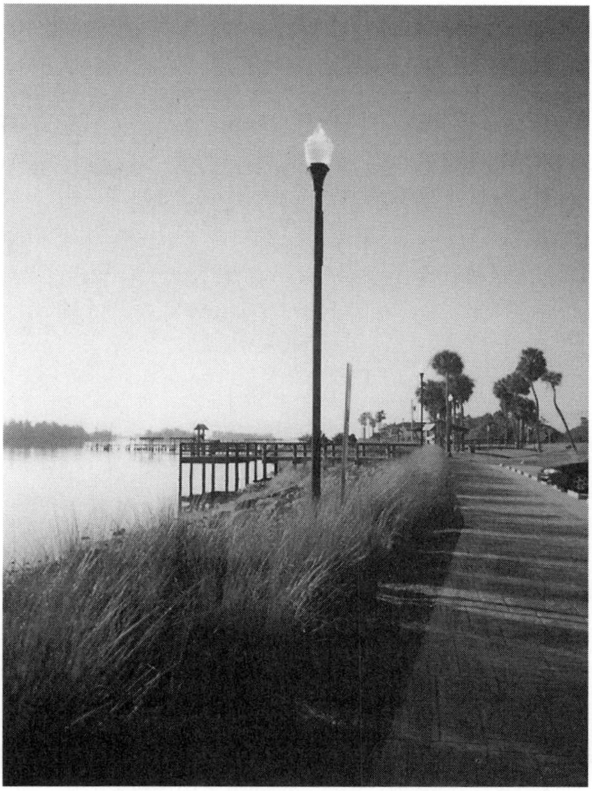

Figure 7.3. The beach walk in Vero Beach. Courtesy of VeroBeach.com.

He remembers when the trail only went up as far as today's Wabasso Road where it crosses the northernmost of the county's three bridges from the mainland. You sailed up to Sebastian Inlet at the north end of Orchid Island. "You talk about fish! I can't tell you how good it was! You could catch any kind, any size, any color. When they paved A1A through there, that was the end of all that." Crowds came and systematically began exploiting the catch.

Jones used to dive the inlet, which he fondly recalls as "a gold mine full of lost gear. We'd pull up anchors, rods, reels, bait buckets. I remember one time casting a gill net and catching 200 artificial lures. We'd pull up outboard motors and sell everything to the fellow running the beer joint. He'd put 'em up on the wall of his bar." Other times he guided big names that came to fish: U.S. Steel chairman Benjamin Fairless, J. Walter Thompson, Billy Graham. Jones's dock is listed in Walter Cronkite's *Inland Waterway Guide.* He still charges only ten dollars for boats to dock overnight.

He remembers, too, a story passed on by his father, who sold thousands of pounds of fish to Henry Flagler's people in the early 1900s. Jones repeats the tale that a prominent local historian confirms about the two Henrys, Flagler and Gifford. It was Gifford who gave Vero its name. That was soon after his family arrived in 1891. Settlement had begun in the vicinity in the 1860s.

Flagler, who was known for getting land free from the state and otherwise acquiring it cheap for his railroad, couldn't get Gifford to cooperate. After Flagler got what he wanted anyway, he put up a train station in the Negro section of town and named it "Gifford." The train station is long gone, but Gifford for more than a century has been the place that most whites avoid.

"There's conservatively speaking at least a hundred realtors around here now," says Jones. "One outfit don't list nothing 'less it's over a million dollars. Hell, Schlitt can sell you a damn place anywhere in the world," he says of the leading real estate firm in the county. "I've had all kinds of offers. I've been offered and offered and offered, but I like it here. This is my air conditioning," he says, swinging. "This is my heritage. I might sell but I won't leave this house."

Old-timers like Jones and the Jungle Trail rank among the county's prime assets. If Jones is slowing down, the trail, too, proceeds only half as far as it once did, ending in paved A1A north of Wabasso Road. It runs close by some of the most luxurious subdivisions in Florida. Yet its immunity continues robust. In 2003, the Jungle Trail became only the fourth road in America to be listed in the National Register of Historic Places. And even as elsewhere Highway A1A has been relocated away from the shore to accommodate new oceanfront mansions, the Jungle Trail, which until the mid-sixties largely constituted the north portion of A1A through Indian River County, has been relocated, too, but only to enhance its aspect. At the turn of the century, a short eastward loop was added north of S.R. 510 to accommodate a section of newly preserved hammock. The section proceeds affectionately beneath high oaks laced by Spanish moss, which is to say, through a vision of Florida remarked on by visitors for its beauty for hundreds of years.

More recently, the buffer between development and the road has been increased to 30 feet. That means that when the last subdivisions have built out along the north end of the trail, trees will once again block houses from the sight of trail users.

It was county historian Ruth Stanbridge who led the fight in the late eighties and early nineties when developers threatened the road because this dirt "intrusion" mocked their subdivisions. The developers claimed it was only a "grove road." County commissioners, not having grown up here, couldn't imagine the trail would have been the island thoroughfare. But Stanbridge's research showed that it always had been, beginning in 1920, and was never abandoned. It helped when she told how in 1961, locals drove the road to see astronaut Alan Shepard Jr. launched into suborbital flight across Sebastian Inlet. That tale wrapped the trail in the flag.

The trail—this persistent old A1A—has become even more important since 2003 because it newly supplies land access for public viewing of Pelican Island. The original Pelican Island was a 5.5-acre rookery championed by George Kroegel, the second generation of his family to homestead the west side of the lagoon. Although documents since the early nineteenth century establish the island as a significant rookery, it was Kroegel's personal conservation efforts that in 1903 won national recognition by President Theodore Roosevelt. Kroegel became the first ranger of the newly designated Pelican Island National Wildlife Refuge. That was just in time. Before designation, at a time when 5,000 pairs of brown pelicans nested on the island, an estimated 5 million birds a year were killed in the lagoon. James Hensall of Cincinnati, who cruised past Pelican Island in 1879, wrote in *Camping and Cruising in Florida*: "As we passed, we saw a party of northern tourists at the island, shooting down the harmless birds by scores through mere wantonness. As volley after volley came booming over the water, we felt quite disgusted at the useless slaughter, and bore away as soon as possible."

Pelican Island became the first in the national system of wildlife refuges that today number more than 550, and, though already part of the heritage familiar to most barrier island residents, the centennial celebration in 2003 has made the refuge more fully part of the entire county's awareness. Pelican Island is a rare distinction that affirms the county's difference. Although elsewhere in Florida private interests can threaten the existence of great natural resources—consider the threat that sugar growers continue to pose to the Everglades and how state officeholders have truckled to their interests—that kind of weak-kneed conservation is unthinkable here, where the old Kroegel homestead still stands across from Pelican Island and national honor invests residents with a passion for place. Some finger waggling of a powerful Uncle Sam seems vested in the spirit.

Today, to hold development at bay, the refuge has been expanded to 5,375 acres. You can gaze from atop the new 18-foot-high overlook to the south and see where the rooftops that replaced citrus while working their way north have been stopped by the refuge boundary, by that Sam in striped pants. The refuge expansion was part of the significant change in county affairs that followed the move to protect the Jungle Trail.

"If we hadn't pursued preservation of the old road," says Stanbridge, "so many other things would have fallen by the wayside. That was a critical point in the growth of the county. The ordinary citizen—not the politicians and not the paid lobbyists—stood up and counted. We stopped the destruction of our county in its tracks. Each person made a difference. It empowered each of us to recognize we can preserve our place."

Look to the lagoon instead of to the fringe of rooftops. Across the Narrows is the rookery itself. Birds once slaughtered at dusk now occupy every branch. At various times of year, birds of the refuge roosting and elsewhere might include not only brown and white pelicans but bald eagles, magnificent frigate birds, roseate spoonbills, wood storks, and various egrets and herons among dozens of species. Why the birds roost here and on none of the nearby islands invites speculation. Ranger Joanna Taylor thinks it's because the island is slightly higher and therefore safer for the birds than its neighbors. It's also one of the few natural islands in the lagoon. The others (typically marked by invasive casuarina pines) were created by the piling of dredge spoil. Taylor speculates that the birds may also have learned over a hundred years that on this one island alone they rest free from human predation—though in 1918, commercial fishermen, mistakenly convinced that pelicans were seriously reducing their catch, clubbed to death more than 400 defenseless pelican chicks.

While the refuge has been growing, Pelican Island itself has been shrinking, beset by tidal flow and the wake of speeding motorboats, though lately with signs of turnaround. From 5.5 acres, the island has shrunk to 2.2. Hope for its renewed enlargement rests on a helicopter-serviced fossilized oyster shell drop that in 2001 reestablished the island's original footprint. As sediment collects inside the restored barrier, the hope is that newly planted mangroves and spartina grass may take hold. Indeed, by late 2004 almost an additional half-acre had accreted.

Hope comes, too, from the Indian River Preservation League, a group formed by citrus growers and commercial fishermen when Miami interests sought to dredge and fill land close to Pelican Island. Their success in 1964 led to the successor Pelican Island Audubon Society, which plays a more embracive roll in regional conservation. Sports fishermen have long supported cleanup. They represent a $300 million recreational industry. All depend on the health of this 156-mile-long lagoon that extends almost a third the length of Florida's east coast. The lagoon's brackish waters and shore are home to almost 3,000 species of animals and almost half that number of plants, including 310 species of birds up and down its length, amounting to one of the most diverse bird populations anywhere in America. The lagoon contains 20 percent of the U.S. eastern seaboard mangrove forest. It's a north-south interstate for game fish, with bluefish, cobia, grouper, king mackerel, redfish, snapper, Spanish mackerel, tarpon—one or another species most of the year chasing baitfish through its teeming waters.

Yet the lagoon remains one of Florida's most troubled waters. If less affected today by polluted citrus runoff thanks to intense inland control efforts, a more devastating problem has become the runoff from surrounding subdivisions. Degradation has steadily worsened, afflicting marine mammals with new infections and strandings. Menacing fish kills have occurred and poisons never before reported in Florida fish have recently sickened humans after eating lagoon catch. While science seeks answers, Taylor says, "The opening of the public facilities that coincided with the Centennial has opened a lot of eyes." For one thing, better land-based management following additional barrier island acquisitions that newly connect Pelican Island National Wildlife Refuge with the Archie Carr National Wildlife Refuge, a smaller and newer bi-county conservation area to help protect nesting turtles along vicinity beaches. Property sellers have their own private interest in the lagoon's health. Reports of degrading waters harm their land values, while identification of their properties with the two refuges or along the Jungle Trail allows them to attract more dollars from potential buyers.

Yet important setbacks may or may not be overcome. In 2005, the U.S. Army Corps of Engineers was maintaining a position that would frustrate congressional intentions for early cleaning of the Indian River as part of overall Everglades restoration. The Corps would delay until 2020 spending $1.2 billion to acquire and restore 90,000 acres of natural lands that would clean runoff into the lagoon. It was a position that humiliated and angered backers of the program. They knew that by 2020 those natural lands would be sold off for development. This suggests that the entire $8.4 billion Everglades restoration plan may be tipping from its original priority of environmental protection to favor instead water supply for the additional millions of residents expected in South Florida by 2020, exactly what supporters feared. If the Corps fails to reverse itself, litigation will follow and restoration will become ruefully controversial.

Even before the storms of 2004, dolphins in the lagoon were "on the edge of a health crisis," according to studies of the Harbor Branch Oceanographic Institute just south of the county line. Weakened immune systems exposed dolphins to numerous opportunistic diseases that threatened their lagoon populations. One suspect was human contaminants, which was the subject of further study. Along east coast Florida, the storms of 2004 hit the Treasure Coast hardest, wiping out shellfish nurseries, tree nurseries, and housing. Waste materials of every sort—boat shards, roof tiles, electrical insulation, septic overflow—poured into the lagoon. It would take months if not years to assess the long-term impacts.

The Rich Quality of Life

This growing regard of wealthy landowners for the natural qualities of the barrier island affirms the difference between Indian River County and other counties nearby, for here, more than elsewhere in Florida, the rich significantly contribute to a year-round quality of life that safeguards culture and environment. They do it without parading their wealth or acting out their peccadilloes. This is no Palm Beach that can't resist making headlines. It's no nouveau Naples flaunting expensive waterfront shopping plazas or Amelia Island where chic resorts drive land sales. Nearest to Vero in character would be Jupiter Island to the south in Martin County, which, for all its wealth, sits apart as its own quasi-town, or Boca Grande on Gasparilla Island, a Gulf coast town of great wealth but large enough to support little more than the needs of its winter colonists.

Vero's wealthy islanders prefer to live behind high-walled subdivisions set off from the road by their boundary of lush native plantings. They like their privacy and seem to have impressed a like quality of life on the community in general, especially on the barrier island. Owners of patrician homes on Painted Bunting Lane and Sandfly Lane in the historic Riomar section insist on keeping their streets the way they've always been—dirt beneath canopy oaks, though philistines are trying to replace proper houses with mansions. The wealthy are so cautious about what they don't want the city to become that Vero has only the fewest hotels and motels, and these with so few rooms that sometimes the only venue that can accommodate large gatherings is the Polish American Club in mainland Wabasso. Marriott has twice tried to sidestep Vero's stiff zoning code and has twice been turned down. Few hotels? No chance of becoming another spring break town. The scariest words in the Vero vocabulary are "Daytona Beach." Even industry can't get rooms. And yes, there is an airport, but without scheduled flights. Scheduled flights might induce big-league tourism. As it is, private jets account for the bulk of point-to-point flights.

The absence of aggressive tourism with its propensity to stimulate out-of-hand development that has to be defended against lets Vero's resident-patrons shape their lifestyle in art offerings and regard for natural and historic conservation. This propensity relates broadly to "place," to the integrity of what makes places special. Even though they come only for the winter, Vero's rich significantly fund the attributes of place for the city's year-round population. A major expression occurs at Riverside Park with its three arts facilities—the Riverside Theatre, the Agnes Wahlstrom Youth Playhouse, and the Vero Beach Museum of Art. Riverside Theatre (opened in 1973) is a professional Actors' Equity house that seats more than 600. (A proposed $10 million expansion would add another 150 seats by 2007.) Broadway plays, musical groups, nationally known artists and an in-house troupe all present. The Wahlstrom Playhouse next door with 150 seats produces four shows a year and schedules additional educational programs. No surprise that during an eighties recession, at a time when the city population was its usual 17,000 and the county only about 85,000, wealthy donors raised $750,000 for the playhouse.

This same class of donors greatly benefits the Vero Beach Museum of Art, a handsome complex of Greco-modern design. During seven years at the turn of the century, donors raised the museum's endowment from $600,000 to almost $6 million. They almost tripled the museum's annual budget to $3 million while doubling the size of its physical plant by raising $6 million for new building. Museum exhibitions include national traveling shows and an emphasis on work produced by in-state artists in the Florida Gallery, one of several. The museum also presents films, humanities lectures and seminars, and musical performances and operates the largest museum art school in Florida. The museum's Ecclestone Library claims more than 3,000 holdings. Annual meetings of the museum pack its auditorium with white, pink, and tanned faces, with gray heads, gents in sockless loafers, and wives in smart frocks. All handicapped parking spaces are filled.

The Vero Beach Theatre Guild, an all-volunteer production company nearing its fifty-year mark, presents six shows each year at its mainland theater.

In their commitment to environment, the rich during that same eighties recession backed an initiative of the Pelican Island Audubon Society to develop an Indian River County Environmental Learning Center on Wabasso Island. The doors opened in 1992, an auspicious year for environmental conservation. A beautiful cypress-built facility now houses dry and wet labs and a major exhibit area and classrooms. Paddling trails lead through the adjacent marsh. At the site since 1994 is the plain board house of late Bollingen Prize–winning poet Laura Riding Jackson, relocated from near Wabasso, where Jackson lived in her late adult life without air conditioning or electricity.

In 1992, wealthy beachside precincts also helped pile up the votes for a self-taxing county measure that committed up to $26 million in bonds to acquire environmentally endangered lands. Prime lands in public hands is one way to slow development. Despite the costly hurricane damage of September 2004, county voters did it again in November, voting for another $50 million bonding program. A prime site newly available for purchase is the Jones site along the Jungle Trail. Other strategies adopted in Vero to slow development include tough tree ordinances, daunting requirements for setbacks, floor-area ratios, and building insulation, as well as high impact fees. Nothing gets built over three stories in the county, over five stories in town (a new hospital and a couple of unfortunate early buildings are exceptions, as may be an eight-story industrial building west of I-95).

"Developers would come in and say, 'You got to be kidding,'" chuckles longtime resident and retired businesswoman Alma Lee Loy. "They'd say, 'There's gotta be a way around that.' We'd say, 'Sorry, but we don't *want* a way around that.'" Nor do Veroites want their dolphins captured from the lagoon for water parks or all-terrain vehicles flattening their dunes; both activities are banned. By the late sixties, Indian River County had already banned dredge-and-fill development, becoming first or one of the first counties in the state to do so.

People who do vacation here look like people who live here: overwhelmingly white though strangely, it may seem, not wealthy. The resident rich aren't eager to attract the touring rich; it's as if, without some local residential investment that would bring them into the privileged circle, they can't be trusted. They might not understand Vero and start pushing for change. As a longtime front office worker at a beachside hotel lately said to a guest, "Vero is a CEO retreat. It's emphatically not a CEO resort."

Another difference between those who dwell here and those who vacation is that while the residential population is older, the vacationers are not. Vero's resident population is among Florida's oldest. Those sixty-five and older account for almost 30 percent of residents, those forty-five and older for half. Vacationers tend to be young families drawn by the surprisingly affordable lodgings, the parks that front the beaches, and the beach town's reputation for safety. Everyone alike dresses modestly and behaves quietly. This is a town for quiet vacationing, for casual evenings at dinner, and for early to bed.

Effect on the resident young? A young woman at work behind the counter at Chelsea's, the premier gourmet emporium on the barrier island, lately explained: "I came down after college to stay with my grandparents and get out of the cold. But it's awfully quiet here, and I'm moving to Miami."

With trees everywhere as high as buildings, what impresses about Vero is the sense of order, of amiable conformity. Vero shuns clamor. Growth is no county mantra, though it's starting to rampage along the St. Lucie County line and generally to the west. In 2004, the county commission approved an 80-foot-high building in an industrial park west of I-95 for an un-named industrial company that promised 250 "high-paying" jobs. It was exactly the kind of collapse that has convulsed St. Lucie County. The decision sent tremors through a population that thought this could never happen in Indian River. People started talking about the Fort Lauderdaling of their county.

A new visioning process is meant to regain control and industry is still only modestly courted. New Piper Aircraft with 1,100 employees remains the county's largest manufacturer. George Watson, who in behalf of the county Chamber of Commerce searches the country for suitable employers, explains that the Piper manufacturing plant is so clean that a recent banquet took place on its factory floor. (New Piper is successor to the company that pioneered the evolution of popular and personal aviation in America.) Citrus and cattle remain important agricultural activities, but residential real estate chiefly drives the economy. According to Linda Schlitt-Gonzalez, scion of Vero's foremost real estate broker, beach property now sells on average above $1.5 million. "There are five and six and sevens, some now over seven, eight, nine and ten," Gonzalez says. "The market is very good. Interest rates have helped. We have a lot of demand from retiring Baby Boomers and the fact that we're known as 'a great area' helps."

Spend some time in Indian River County and you form your own impression of the assets that set the place apart. Everyone's list of course includes the

Jungle Trail and the Pelican Island National Wildlife Refuge. Informed people would include the headwaters of the St. Johns River, recently restored to health in the most successful large-scale river restoration project in America, precursor of what's now happening with a portion of Florida's Kissimmee River and may happen with the Everglades. Best access to the headwaters is through Middleton's Fish Camp, a mom-and-pop site near Blue Cypress Lake west of S.R. 512 out newly four-laned S.R. 60. Boats for rent will get you into the marshy headwaters of the river and to extolled fishing sites like the Stick Marsh, where citrus groves acquired by the St. Johns River Water Management District were allowed to flood and help clean citrus runoff that previously poured by canal into the lagoon. Now the marsh contains the runoff, cleans it and slowly releases it without harm into the river. The headwaters constitute an inches-shallow, gorgeously clean trickle across a grassy bottom, a lustrous green shimmer across the horizon in bright sunlight. Kayaking through here connects you to Ais times. Down at kayak level, nothing intrudes above distant trees.

The assets of course include the lagoon and its northern connection to the sea at Sebastian Inlet State Park. Sebastian Inlet is one of the most popular parks in Florida, where a sometimes seething sea drives fisherfolk off the jetty while only a few hundred yards west of the bridge, waters lap gently around whale-colored shallows and families picnic. Beautiful beaches extend for miles in either direction. A new Sebastian Fishing Museum has opened at the park near where Richard Jones once sold his flotsam and jetsam. South down Orchid Island toward where the Jungle Trail meets Highway A1A is the McLarty Treasure Museum, the site of a Spanish encampment set up to salvage the 1715 Spanish treasure fleet that foundered in near offshore waters. Across the lagoon on the mainland are the San Sebastian River, a lazy paddling trail that flows beneath canopy oaks, and the San Sebastian River State Buffer Preserve, a conservation area that combines marsh and maritime hammock.

Vero's Field of Dreams

Brilliant inspiration drew Vero's field of dreams. That's Dodgertown, for more than fifty years the spring training site of the Los Angeles Dodgers and headquarters for the team's minor league system. The site is a love affair between team and town that transcends bottom lines. In the late forties, local businessman Bud Holman attracted the then-Brooklyn ball club to an abandoned World War II airfield to get ready for its major league season. During the decades that followed, the Dodgers have trained in Holman Stadium, an amphitheater wrapped around by a garden of native plants surrounded by a small inn, convention center, and a section of the old airfield that became Vero Beach Municipal Airport. Expensive houses, too, have reached to the stadium edge, but local residents, instead of complaining about the springtime bustle, worked as hard as anyone else to keep the Dodgers in Vero when team owners a while back proposed selling the site and moving their spring training west. (The Dodgers are the only West Coast team that trains in the east.) Instead, Indian River County bought the site, leased it back to the Dodgers for one dollar a year and now has the team in town for another fifty years. Walk by the jewel-like stadium and images of Jackie Robinson, Sandy Koufax, and Duke Snider form. When teams aren't playing, the imagination conjures up umpires bellowing, "Play ball!"

It's an old Florida story that if you get rid of the mosquitoes, you get developers. It's still true, but differently worked out on the south side of Vero at the Oslo Riverfront Conservation Area (ORCA). ORCA is the result of work by the University of Florida Medical Entomology Laboratory, a world-famous facility opened in 1956 to study biting insects. You can't study insects without insect habitat, so that in addition to the site's initial 38 acres of oak, palm, and pine forest, the lab has steadily sought to avoid developer encroachment. What they secured in time was an almost 300 additional acres, connecting the two parcels with a third small section acquired in 2004. The site altogether also benefits water conservation and recreation. That's the ORCA site, and it's laced with trails. These variously lead to an observation tower in a coastal wetland alongside the lagoon and past site of the "Awesome Pine," the national champion slash pine tree that boasted a 44-inch diameter before being blown down by a storm in 2004.

Nearby on the city's south side, McKee Botanical Gardens covers a much smaller but far more manicured 18 acres. It's a beautiful site that will introduce many visitors to the legendary Waldo E. Sexton. Sexton and Arthur G. McKee could never make up their minds whether they were adventurers, citrus investors, or tourist promoters. McKee wound up influencing coastal Florida more widely than Sexton, but it was Sexton whose name for years was synonymous with Vero.

The Gardens occupy the east side of U.S. 1 through a section of closed shopping plazas and other signs of hard times. Maybe like the gardens, the roadside will recover too. McKee and Sexton in the early twenties acquired 80 acres that they turned into a show garden of native and imported plants after they decided the land was too beautiful to convert to groves. They induced famed landscape architect William Lyman Phillips to design their site with the intention of attracting tourists. Though the bottom had fallen out of tourism by the time their site opened, by 1940 the gardens were drawing 100,000 visitors a year. The next blow was worse than Depression. Disney. The powerhouse attractions of Central Florida that detoured visitors away from public gardens everywhere in the state forced McKee's closure. A condominium developer soon did his work on the site. The Indian River Land Trust acquired the last 18 acres in 1994 and reestablished the remaining gardens.

Today, with its Great Hall again home to the claimant world's largest one-piece mahogany table and surrounded by ponds and palms, with its café and library, McKee figures as the perfect attraction for Vero—beautiful, quiet, best enjoyed by a slow walk.

Sexton flourished in other ways, flaunting his showmanship in a famous hotel and restaurants. Remarkably, all remain open, although rooms at the beachfront Driftwood Inn have been considerably upscaled to suit today's customer comfort. But the insides of the three restaurants remain true-to-form "Waldo," done with rough cypress walls, pressed tin ceilings, bits of gates, tile patches, ancient doors used as room dividers, pew benches, bells, cartouches. The dining rooms all resemble a tidy antique warehouse. Two are next to each other on the beach, the third in the big S-curve of downtown.

Treasured, too, despite the low-key reception the county gives tourism, is a Disney project. Wabasso Beach, north of Vero, is the site of Disney's first boutique resort separate from its theme parks. The time-share rooms sit behind the dune within the allowable 35-foot county height limit in dune colors, a muted green and brown without excessive logo displays. Disney is undoubtedly satisfied that its costly efforts to power-trip the locals failed. At first, the Mouse brought out its lobbyists big time, only to learn that Vero locals can't be power-tripped. Instead of bulldozing trees on its site, Disney had them uprooted and donated to the Environmental Learning Center. Resort managers not only keep outside lights dimmed to avoid disorienting newborn turtles seeking the sea, but they also edge doors in film so that light doesn't escape from rooms. They plant the dune to enhance habitat for the endangered southeastern beach mouse, the kind of mouse locals would rather protect. By 2001, Disney decided it wouldn't add to its resort and sold off its remaining 10 acres where low-rise condos will next challenge the beach mouse.

The Half-Truth of Vero

Yet, a downside exists to the hurrahs about Vero's affluents. They bestow largesse on their interests, which often coincide with the community's, but they also pursue some of their priorities to the greater disadvantage. In the most regrettable instance, they've not only ignored Vero's historic downtown, but they also resist its comeback. They have the downtown they want on the beach. They have their banks and boutiques, their goldsmith, their shops for "fine tailoring" and for gowns, their gourmet shops and endless real estate offices. You won't find parking meters. The News Shop tapes up pages of locals featured in the morning paper. At the corner of Beachland Boulevard at A1A they have Merrill Lynch in the First National Bank building, Northern Trust, U.S. Trust and an interiors studio that looks like it could empty anyone's bank account. Their Publix is just across the lagoon, and through the mainland downtown they have their private speedway known as the "twin pairs."

Downtown is Vero's essential legacy, the cradle of the city—what historian Don Bercaw calls "the beating heart of Vero." It's on life support. For thousands of beach residents a day, downtown is where you get up a head of steam driving west to the suburban Indian River Mall, to I-95 and back. Downtown is the blocks with those skinny sidewalks sliced back to accommodate more traffic lanes. It's the glimpse of a few restored Mediterranean-styled buildings, and, if the speedsters know their history, the place where after showing *Desperately Seeking Susan* in 1985, the movie theater went dark, and where Wodtke's Department Store said good riddance in 1995. Downtown of course was once all there was. Indian River was citrus. Citrus was king.

During the decades following World War I, you banked at the Farmers Bank, you shopped at A&P or Piggly Wiggly, at McClure's and Osceola Drug Stores, at Maher's Department Store, later at Anthony's. You saw Sam Moon for insurance. You took your kids to Alma Lee's for clothes and to Western Auto for their Western Flyer. You did gymnastics at the Community Building in Pocahontas Park, where maybe in USO times you danced with fellows from the Naval Air Station. On July Fourth, everybody came downtown for the turtle derby. Guys got their hair cut at Barrett's and ordered letterheads from Morse Printing in the Seminole Arcade. Visitors stayed at the Del Mar and the Illinois Hotels. They kept up with the *Burn-'Em-Up Barnes* serial at the air-cooled Vero Theatre and, with locals, gawked at Alice the bear at the little zoo in the park. Everything west of downtown was ranchland.

In time, downtown was left behind in the mobility that accompanied postwar prosperity. Cars carried young families to new suburbs. Old-line retailers followed their customers to suburban shopping centers, emptying downtown. Dodgertown pulled people west; shopping at Miracle Mile near the lagoon pulled people east. With business at a standstill, beach interests convinced DOT to turn Nineteenth and Twentieth Streets through downtown one-way. When you ask around Vero, what holds back the rush of renewal that has made Fort Pierce and Stuart such successful downtowns again, you hear repeatedly about the notorious "twin pairs."

Newsman Milt Thomas, who grew up in Vero and later served as director of economic development for the chamber of commerce, speaks for many when he calls the twin pairs the biggest problem facing redevelopment. "The cars speed here. They're a danger to pedestrians. They cut off one part of downtown from another. There's nothing aesthetically pleasing about those streets. It's a bypass—a city bypass right in the middle of downtown."

Scott Chisholm can point to Nineteenth Street outside his Scott's Sporting Goods where fast-laning removed 9 feet of angle parking. He points out that to get to his store, kids at Pocahontas Park have to cross nine lanes of traffic, seven of them high-speed. Property owner Roy Thompson compares Vero today with Stuart twenty years ago. "In 1980 Stuart had boarded up storefronts. People could easily have asked, 'Who needs a downtown?' Does Stuart have malls? Of course, and other shopping. But the place is thriving. It's an in-demand high-rent district, whereas we had the misfortune in 1992 of being at the end of optimizing traffic flow at the expense of livability factors."

Downtown today amounts to a block of Fourteenth Avenue—the so-called "model block"—and several institutional buildings to the side. The new Indian River County Court House, the library, and a handful of historic churches contribute to what downtown enthusiasts consider their bailiwick, but the courthouse turns its back on the historic city core and, ironically, the attractive landscaping that surrounds these institutional landmarks connects them better to neighboring residential districts than to the old commercial downtown.

The Model Block looks like a renewal primer. Through improved lighting, wide textured sidewalks, attractive pole banners, comfortable benches, better parking, and the upgrading of underground utilities, the street is a model for how to make downtown viable again. You walk on newly installed pavers, you see attractive planters, attractive globe lighting, and you feel somebody cares. But few retailers have responded. A surf shop has come and gone. Restaurants come and go. A few retailers occupy streets that provide better parking.

Downtown's one promoter willing to back his intentions with dollars is Bob Brackett, a Veroite since 1947, when his parents relocated here. He ushered in the old Vero Theatre. He bagged groceries at the old A&P. He remembers his dad as a contractor taking solar heaters off old buildings downtown. "We'd throw them off the two-story buildings and take the ceiling fans down. What are we doing now? Putting solar heaters back in, putting fans back up."

He bought the movie theater where he ushered, renovating its shops for rent, now coaxing a convincing show of interest to restore the 850-seat auditorium itself. (A new Vero Beach Merchants Association seeks to reopen the theater.) He replaced the old Seminole Building where he used to climb stairs to the second-floor dentist with a new building trimmed in architectural detailing stripped from the original. When he finished the new building in 1988, he made it headquarters of his Credit Data Services.

Altogether Brackett has bought and restored seven downtown buildings. His latest, the Courthouse Executive Center, has brought the building back to its original glory. Now used for offices, space was fully rented as soon as the building reopened. The original courtroom has been restored for meetings and functions. Typical of Brackett style, first-floor space that could command premium rents showcases Vero history. Textured glass doors open to restrooms. Matched awnings configure the facade.

But where Brackett moves, the city administration, beholden to beach interests, stalls. Says Brackett: "We're faced with people, bless their hearts, nice guys with no vision, no program. People just kind of go with the flow. They really don't know enough about where they're at. People get elected who really have no place being there. The planning department is very much in favor of doing things downtown. But engineering and the city council don't seem to be forthcoming, though some are in favor, some not. The bottom line is it's a lot of red tape, jumping through hoops, which stifles people. It discourages others who haven't done this before. It's more hassle than it's worth."

Brackett himself acknowledges that "People want a quiet town. They want to raise their kids, avoid crime. But in trying to redevelop downtown we're not trying to make it bigger and build other big buildings. We want to restore things back, fix the surroundings up around it. We want to keep what we have in good repair."

Maybe, but that's still too ambitious for beach interests that, according to one veteran observer, want no town at all. Of the beach dwellers he says: "They retire here. They follow the Bulls, the Bears. They still read the *Chicago Trib.* They worked for a big manufacturing company up there, paid taxes. Now they don't want to pay those taxes anymore. Their kids are out of school and aren't going to live here. They want their quality of life till they die. They don't want industry in here. They don't want full-time paying jobs here. They're not interested in downtown. They want this to continue a beach town." About the twin pairs, he speaks of the "political realities," a euphemism for beachside influence that won't consider compromising its quick access to the mall and the interstate.

Towns in the Pale

County towns that exist less in the squint of twin-pair drivers fare better. Fellsmere was a utopian ranch town to the northwest that flooded out in 1915, soon after its start. Today it's the heart of citrus and ranching with about 4,500 residents, mostly Hispanic, many poor among them newly assisted in education and family economy by philanthropically supported Operation Hope. Longtime rancher and former county commissioner Fran Adams has made the other big move here, acquiring the old bank building and turning it into Marsh Landing, where guests dine on tomatoes and green beans fresh from the field and catfish from Lake Okeechobee that's never been frozen. Scenes of the old town line walls beneath 15- to 18-foot ceilings. Live bands play weekends. Mexicans in town, nursing their wages from fieldwork, have opened groceries and cafes. One family manufactures tortillas sold around the state. Adams says a B&B may be coming in the old Fellsmere Inn. A combination motorsports track and entertainment venue by the interstate has closed amidst scandal. It was country but felt scammy.

East back toward the lagoon is Sebastian, sleepy when you got water from your own well, a lot busier since the new water pipe went in at the turn of the century. Sebastian, which poked along with a couple of thousand people for decades, spurted with water. Through annexation, its numbers now top 20,000, surpassing Vero and making this one of the fastest-growing cities in America. As a local resident lately complained, "It's hard to cross the street to get your mail." Yet Sebastian fancies its laidback ways, with signs entering town that still read "Welcome to Sebastian, Home of Pelican Island, Friendly People and 6 Ole Grouches. Est. 1924." Shopping plazas are going in at either end of town along U.S. 1, but the heart of town is still deciding what it wants to be when it grows up. It's mostly one- and two-story small offices and restaurants for which either new visioning or overwhelm will guide change about to happen.

Looks a lot better just a block east to the lagoon along Indian River Drive. The drive, which loops off U.S. 1 south and north again just below the big county line C-54 Canal, is green beneath coastal hammock with magnolias and oleanders among the oaks. Where the residential drive gives way to town by the water, locals stroll the newly extended wide sidewalk that now runs from U.S. 1 at the south city limits through the popular section of waterfront. In the center of the town section sits the three- quarter-size statue of Paul Kroegel alongside a new park. The Kroegel Homestead, now part of the wildlife refuge on the western shore, lies south along the drive. A few commercial fish houses remain, but they've mostly gone to seafood restaurants at the ends of docks. Arlo Guthrie did something different with an old crab plant on the water. Built himself a house. Guthrie's a local favorite. He draws big crowds whenever he plays benefits, recently at the Pelican Island Centennial event.

Earl's Hideaway, where once you didn't want to be caught looking too eagerly for anybody, has cleaned up its act. Capt. Hiram's has added Key West–cozy small rooms on the water; Davis House has built great big rooms that rent for less a block up a sloping road. A Best Western is coming, though not on the water.

Sebastian historically made its living from fishing the fecund lagoon, but even old-timers like third-generation fisherman Joe Warren offer a purely Sebastian take on bleak prospects since the net ban. "I'd like to hang on as long as possible," he said a while back. "I'd just as soon not face reality." Nobody was lately sure where to find him.

You can rent kayaks for paddling the lagoon or maybe better down the San Sebastian River in still quiet Roseland just north. Dense oaken canopies branch like organ pipes, forming tunnels above dark pools brightened by tiny purple and white flowers. On overcast days, morning glories stay open and dew makes diamonds of spider webs. Ferns ruffle overhung limbs like the sleeves of mambo musicians. Silent paddlers sometimes glimpse wild goats, bobcats, wild boars, manatees, gators, bald eagles, great blue herons. Realtors say it's not unusual for people to come off the river and go house hunting.

Between Sebastian and Vero is unincorporated Gifford, about a 2-by-2-mile district once busy with groves, now with trailer parks, poor to modest subdivisions but pockets of upscale housing among blacks who may have worked as domestic workers or hospital workers and have saved their way to prosperity. Habitat for Humanity has put up housing here. The better neighborhoods have their homeowner associations. Groceries, laundries, and other small businesses scatter through the district.

Drive around with Freddie Woolfork, director of development and marketing for the Gifford Youth Activities Center and he points out white teenage women in the neighborhood with local guys. They come for the kicks if not the dope. The police get calls and try to track them down. "The problem has mainly been apathy," Woolfork complains about county authorities. "This has been an area of low code enforcement. A lot of promises have been made over the years to improve the quality of life in Gifford." He drives past a trailer park from the seventies. "A private owner promised he would do right by the local community. He never followed through. We're still tearing down walls of mistrust and apathy, but it's getting better. A lot of people in the county think of Gifford as crime-ridden. But a lot of people are lifting themselves up."

You can see sections with water, sewers, and streetlights. Sweat equity is moving new owners into Grace Pines' forty to fifty houses. A 1908 church is becoming a museum and Gifford information center. A new $1.5 million health center is going in. The Gifford Youth Activities Center runs athletic leagues, teaches special ed classes, and has a nifty computer room that stays busy much of the day and weekends.

There's a section of Gifford east of the tracks that's fast disappearing. Locals called it Possum Top and Coon Bottom. The districts were part of people's identities. "Guys from Coon Bottom were always known as better basketball players," says Woolfork. "They were a small district and knew how to work with each other. They had unity." Now this old section has been rezoned as part of a big medical compound. Property taxes have risen so high that even older Gifford folks who lived in still-nice houses are having to move out. A "For Sale" sign on a lot says, "Zoned Medical for nursing home or medical office, retail or day care." "This is all Gifford, but now they call it Vero Beach," says Woolfork, as mainland Vero develops with mansions along the lagoon and now all the way back to where renamed Gifford has outlasted Flagler's legacy.

8

ST. LUCIE COUNTY

The Golem Within

Figure 8.1. Highway A1A in St. Lucie County. Courtesy of the St. Lucie County Tourist Development Council.

Figure 8.2. Sunrise Theatre. Courtesy of the St. Lucie County Tourist Development Council.

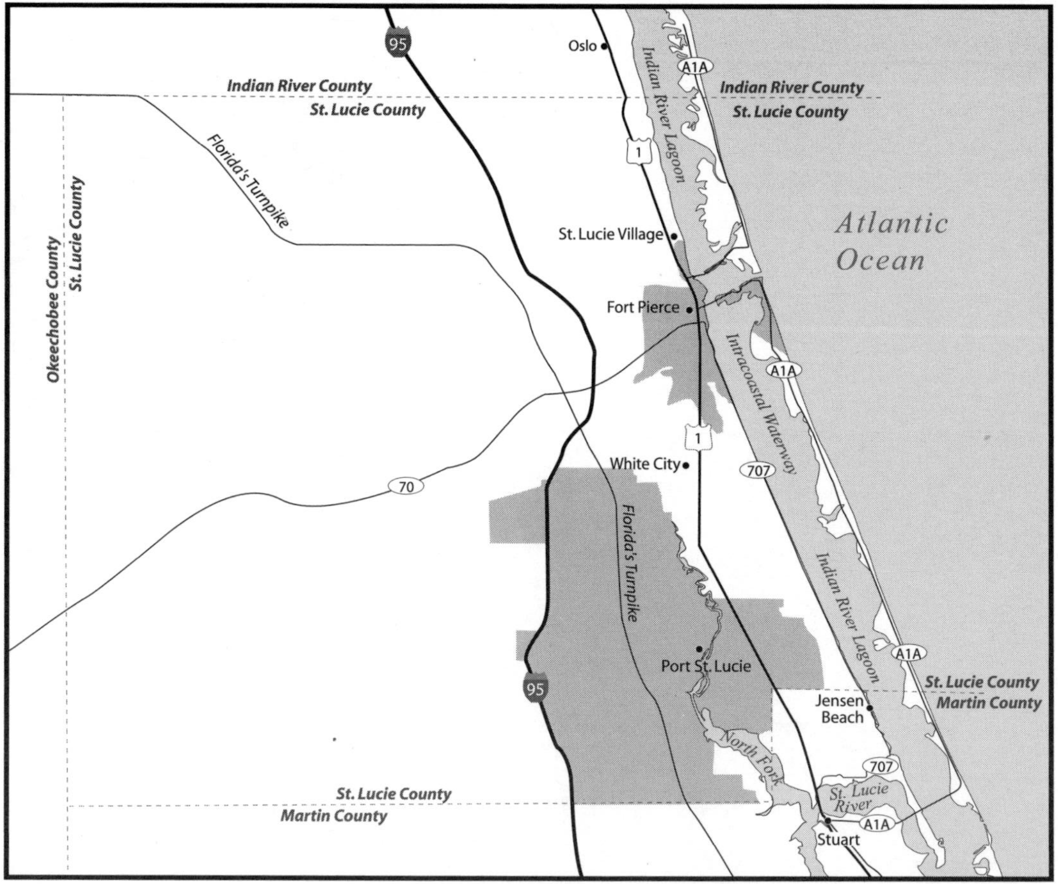

Map 8. St. Lucie County

Nowhere along Florida's lower Atlantic coast is the beach more open to the public than through St. Lucie County. Hardly anywhere is tourism less influential either in county affairs or on its own. After the 1980s, when a burst of residential towers rose along the county's barrier islands in the rush to emulate development along the Gold Coast, St. Lucie clamped down on the height of its buildings and bought up great sections of beachfront for public use. Developers largely gave up on the beach and turned west. There, St. Lucie's big resorts attach to suburban golf subdivisions, and chain motels cluster at Florida's Turnpike and I-95 exits. Nondescript motels through the county line north-south U.S. 1, and otherwise only a single hotel, a single time-share, a B&B, and a few villas, motels, and places to rent by the week along Highway A1A remind anyone that tourism is any factor at all.

The beachfront towers flank Highway A1A only along the south sides of South and North Hutchinson Islands. Otherwise, except for a nuclear power plant and a section where the road swings inland to the county seat of Fort Pierce, Highway A1A largely passes its way along maritime hammock that backs the undeveloped beaches. These extend broad and beautiful. Turtles nest here in summer, although the summer storms of 2004 here and all along the Treasure Coast destroyed about a quarter of all nests. In some sections, the road occupies a narrow land bridge between the beach and the mangrove shore along the Indian River Lagoon. Drivers pull over, set out a lawn chair, and throw a line. Although less than a quarter of St. Lucie elsewhere remains in its natural state, this long section of South Hutchinson and a lesser section of the north island remain semiwild and rarely crowded, even though beach access is user-friendly with small parking lots and in some sections bathrooms.

Mostly single-family houses and low condominiums sit back of the dune as you drive from the south toward Fort Pierce Inlet. A walkway for fishing tops the south inlet jetty; a couple of motels and restaurants front the beach. Archie's, an indoor-outdoor bar that's as relaxed as a Caribbean rum shack, sits across the shore road where, after it was battered by Hurricanes Frances and Jeanne, everybody with a hammer or paintbrush made sure the burgers-and-beer joint quickly recovered. There is no Ron Jon's surfer hangout, no shopping plaza, no day-trippers scene. The only significant change ahead will be the installation of a roundabout where A1A (here also called Seaway Drive) bends east at the inlet toward Fort Pierce.

Tourism elsewhere in Florida may serve as the handmaiden for development, but the two hardly connect in St. Lucie. Tourism underwhelms and development overreaches on its own. In St. Lucie, issues of place center on the established city of Fort Pierce and a reforming county that struggles against the hugely aggressive developer city of Port St. Lucie.

Even with tourism scarcely in the picture, St. Lucie concentrates the condition of Florida everywhere else by displaying the worst and the best of state

Figure 8.3. Downtown Second Street in Fort Pierce. Courtesy of the St. Lucie County Tourist Development Council.

land use. No one denies how bad Port St. Lucie is. Mayor Bob Minsky says, "The city was built on a swamp. The whole design is wrong." And if few observers so far recognize how good downtown Fort Pierce is, that's because few people so far know about it. The two cities snipe at each other, and Port St. Lucie feuds with the county that tries to restrain it. With its divided and fractious worldview, the county faces an uncertain future. For while downtown Fort Pierce may never influence wider county change, Port St. Lucie, Hulk-like, will menace its way ahead before it grunts to some indeterminate build-out, enormous in its appetite but still at least a generation from genuine civic realization.

Downtown Fort Pierce and the beach are where visitors want to spend their time. The two places constitute a serendipitous matched pair. Yet even visitors who come for nothing except R&R but who carry along a degree of curiosity about where they find themselves may discover that their most memorable impression will come from touring the county to view the very places they may have traveled here to avoid. In its gasp-breath, head-shaking impact, it's the only way to grasp what's going on in St. Lucie. It's surely educational.

Along a fluctuating boundary, traditional agriculture with its origins in late-nineteenth-century settlement struggles against development that mirrors the potato field–transforming impact of Long Island's post–World War II Levittown. In southwestern St. Lucie, it's citrus getting transformed. In the midst of nowhere, signs appear in the abandoned groves: "Coming soon: major gas station, convenience store, car wash, fast food." Or in the midst of nowhere becoming something really big, "Invest in the future. [Two-lane] Becker Road soon to be a major artery." Schools that teach golf create pond hazards out of wetlands. The largest Wal-Mart Distribution Center in the world is replacing pitcher plant–studded oak and pine habitat and a creek that connects to the North Fork of the St. Lucie River with a 27-acre structure, largest in America after the Vehicle Assembly Building at Kennedy Space Center. Subdivisions spread across endless acres behind entry gates florid as the facades of hotels in Aruba. If Port St. Lucie interests succeed in extending the county's urban services boundary, a historic rural world that still thrives in cattle and citrus will disappear.

Gist of the county reform effort is to keep the ag lands in production while containing Port St. Lucie growth, diversifying the economy with industry, commerce, and a science research center along the I-95 corridor, protecting rare natural assets and adding cultural and recreational qualities. It's a tall order, and not the least because until the 1990s, county policy was in almost all respects the opposite. Until even more recently, the county was an economic mess.

Fort Pierce: Up from Despair

St. Lucie had fought hard against integration with the result that a third of its population lacked high school education. Unemployment reached 12 percent (altogether 30 percent of the population may have been out of work). The poverty level reached near 20 percent. St. Lucie had become the Appalachia of east coast Florida. During Clinton prosperity, even in a tight labor market, industry wasn't rushing to St. Lucie. Florida has about a 10 to 11 percent manufacturing base. In St. Lucie, the number was half that. Instead of industry, which typically pays about 65 percent of county tax bills, residential the balance, in St. Lucie the reverse was true (and still is). But residential requires more services than industry. Reserves ran thin, and even a small disaster could have wiped out the county financially. Until 2002, there was no countywide transit and not a single bus route along U.S. Highway 1. Government served the governing.

Fort Pierce had run down so badly that denizens along Avenue D's prostitution and drug alley turned over more cash than legitimate businesses that hung on downtown. The real hub of commerce was along two-lane Highway 68, the Florida Cracker Trail, coming east from the ag lands toward town, with places like Big John's Feed and Western Wear, the big Sunbrite Citrus packinghouse, and Yavorsky's Truck Service. Cracker culture ran the town with companies renting portolets, tractors, and work clothes. Diners one after another still serve up bacon and grits and pour coffee all day. Jitneys carry workers to the fields past pawnshops and bail bondsmen. Three and four guys crowd into the cabs of pick-ups, gear flapping from open truck beds. Rows of tractors line up for roadside sale. Trailers sell fresh produce. Signs tell where you can pick Florida grapefruit.

Sears and most other retail fled south to the Jensen Beach Mall looking for the more affluent population that was moving up from Miami into Martin County. In an effort to compete, Fort Pierce tore down many of its historic buildings to supply parking that was supposed to lure shoppers back. It didn't. As Fort Pierce Main Street coordinator Doris Tillman recalls: "We tore down everything that would bring people together, that would bring people out to socialize or to entertain us. The community stopped caring." For years, only the weak anchor of city hall kept the city from drifting completely off its moorings. Even today, after 180-degree downtown turnaround, most people from elsewhere who know Fort Pierce only by its reputation still roll their eyes at mention of the place.

In large part, the turnaround has been so carefully planned to work in the real world and free of flash that it hasn't made news; everything is too deliberate and low key. When the *New York Times* discovered St. Lucie County in 2002, it wasn't for the conserving achievement of Fort Pierce but for voraciously land-consuming Port St. Lucie.

Downtown Fort Pierce is a small-bore transportation hub. FEC tracks pass through town from when, late in the nineteenth century, town became a minor rail center, a "division point" for the Florida East Coast Railway, one of the towns where trains were fueled and maintained. Rail became the preferred way for shipping citrus. The Cracker Trail, which linked Fort Pierce with Bradenton on Florida's Gulf coast, mostly saw cattle driven west for shipment to Cuba, not east for shipment to New York. Florida's scrub cattle were too scrawny and tough for New York palates. A small port sits at the end of the inlet named for the town that's channeled athwart the Indian River Lagoon and that has never been bridged where its outlet divides the Hutchinson Islands. So instead of an easy straight north-south crossing over the canal, highway A1A enters town along Seaway Drive, then heads back east again on the north side of town. During World War II, the port anchored an important navy base. Amphibious landing craft were designed, built, and launched here. You can still see one of those World War II attack boats on the grounds of the historical museum just below the south causeway bridge. The navy's underwater demolition unit that came to be known as SEALs trained in Fort Pierce. A UDT (Underwater Demolition Team) SEALs Museum on North Hutchinson Island has become one of the county's most popular attractions.

Navy notwithstanding, the port never developed significantly. Efforts to revive it late in the twentieth century were thwarted by successful competition of a half dozen larger ports south to Miami and north to Jacksonville. The private owner of the port still wants to develop its shipping capacity. People resist. They want a different kind of downtown, with a port that caters to yacht people and otherwise to recreation and leisure uses. Some talk of reviving a water taxi that temporarily moved residents when the north bridge was closed in 2003 and that would link points of interest along the lagoon from the Harbor Branch Oceanographic Institution up toward the Indian River County line past historically residential St. Lucie Village down to a pair of Smithsonian sites along Seaway Drive.

A new way of thinking began in 1995 when Fort Pierce residents in a series of workshops defined a vision for their future together. They developed a plan and began following it. They began redesigning their streets and streetscapes. They placed great value on the city's remaining look and began refurbishing its historical downtown structures while rebuilding in the Mediterranean style that stood out among the layered architectural legacy. Remarkably, design—that mix of art and architecture—began stirring capital.

The marina was rebuilt and expanded with offices, a restaurant, and additional slips. (Only Bahia Mar in Fort Lauderdale is larger.) A sumptuous traffic-calming roundabout with a planter relandscaped to bloom year-round was installed in front of the town's most important historical building, the P. P. Cobb that dates from 1882 as a general store. Its Cracker cypress architecture was restored and set off by newly widened sidewalks with paver tiles and landscaping. Parks and promenades with attractive lighting and benches went in along the shore. New public buildings went up, including a library with its reading room that overlooks the river. That library was an exercise in democracy, an abstraction that rarely achieves this specificity of significance. Although some complained about turning over a valuable site to "indigent readers" where a hotel might better be built, city planner Ramon Trias defended the location.

Says Trias, now the city's development director, "One of the most difficult challenges was to keep this reading room in front of the windows so that people, even as they sit here, can have this connection with the great beauty of the lagoon, combining in architectural aspect indoor public spaces with outdoor public spaces." The reading room windows look out onto a public plaza with fountains where, from the balustrade along the water, people can look at spiny Florida lobsters and, in winter, at manatees. "People at any income level are entitled to some of the same luxury that others would want for renting apartments downtown," says Trias. "It's the balance that a real city achieves between the public and the private."

It was Spanish-born Trias who, frustrated in his work as a Dade and Palm Beach County planner, in the mid-nineties saw opportunity in Fort Pierce and jumped at it, inspiring the city's remarkable change. Just as art historian Barbara Capitman had seen treasures when everyone else saw only dross in the dilapidated art deco buildings of Miami Beach, Trias saw glory in the architectural legacy of Fort Pierce.

The Sunrise Theatre, the old city hall, and the Raulerson Building date from the boomtime twenties, all of like character, all close together, all now restored and enjoying re-use variously for performance, offices, shops, and private and civic functions. Along these downtown blocks, new restaurants and clubs have opened in street-level spaces, taking their cue from Trias's preservation guidelines and supplying architectural character along with new uses like the popular Gately's Grill and Cafe La Ronde, though the popular restaurant-saloon Max and Meg's closed unexpectedly in 2004.

Already in use, too, and recovered from storm damage, is the new Manatee Center, a pleasant partly open-air structure with a deck at the end of a short canal for viewing manatees, which mass here in winter. The landmark Seven Gables House, built in 1905, was restored in 1998 and relocated alongside as a new city visitors center. Walking close is an amphitheater on the waterfront used for musical events, a gazebo from 1905 restored in 1997, and the Backus Gallery named for the late A. E. "Bean" Backus, dean of Florida landscape painters and a beloved Fort Pierce native. In 2004, work finished on the $1.2 million landscaped public gathering place with its benches, interactive fountain, and flags called Marina Square.

Street events—the weekly Saturday farmers' market nine months a year; the twice-monthly Marina Magic; the monthly Friday Fest and year-round festivals—help build community while showing off the unmistakable downtown renewal. The library already in place will cornerstone the city's most ambitious new project: a grand compound separated only by a park from the popular city marina with a Mediterranean-style hotel, offices, apartments, shops, and parking garage.

Plans continue moving ahead even though the storms of 2004 greatly damaged the marina, where almost 70 percent of its 240 floating and fixed dock spaces were lost. Many boats sank or were heavily damaged. The loss at Fort Pierce was typical of what happened up and down the Treasure Coast, where boating is a major contributor to the $2 billion economy of the Intracoastal Waterway.

Storms notwithstanding, success in the renewal of downtown east of U.S. 1 has led the city to extend Trias's domain west for several blocks. Spine of this east-west corridor is a section of Orange Avenue that runs from the redesigned waterfront across Highway 1 for two blocks. A federal courthouse is rising here. The city's historical museum will relocate from Seaway Drive into an old post office building alongside. At the northwest corner of U.S. 1 and Orange, Vero Beach investor Bob Brackett has acquired and renewed the landmark Arcade Building. Offices are fully occupied upstairs, but Brackett won't convert the ground floor to additional offices. He wants demand to pick up for retail on this side of the road.

Trias has beautifully redesigned the highway where it passes through the heart of downtown. He gave up 15 feet of unused city hall property to accommodate a wide landscaped median between newly curved northbound and southbound traffic lanes alongside sidewalks newly planted with foxtail palms. Few planners in small cities elsewhere could so authoritatively swap real estate from routine inutility to enhance the design quality of otherwise routine public works, but of course Trias has successfully made his case that design stimulates renewal. There is something counterintuitive to how he goes about things. Others might imagine that private demand for rentable space has to precede heightened design standards. But since Trias began his work, some fifty new businesses have opened downtown. A Community Redevelopment Area district that includes most of downtown was taking in about $60,000 in incremental taxes when Trias began. Now the annual take is up to $750,000.

Storefronts east across the highway aren't all brilliant, but that's the beauty of what Trias is accomplishing. So far, blue-collar aspects of downtown remain. Here on Orange Avenue are Babe's Billiards and St. Lucie Restaurant and Supplies. But their facades are attractive, and the sidewalks are redone in multihued brick. A few blocks south, a citrus packing plant still operates, and an old hump-backed board bridge rises sharply from the highway across the railroad tracks, at its apex throwing open a view of old houses converted to offices and, just beyond the shore drive, the lagoon. Town loves its railroad. Most striking of the murals painted on the sides of buildings is one of a Florida East Coast diesel emerging from a tunnel in trompe l'oeil fashion, bursting from its dark space onto the sidewalk. Come upon the mural unexpectedly and you jump back.

Other murals not to miss include Brackett's in the Arcade Building, which traces town history from Ais times and the days of pineapple plantations along the lagoon (pineapples were commercially grown well into the twentieth century). The mural depicts important historical figures, including Backus and Zora Neale Hurston, who lived her last years in Fort Pierce and is buried in the city's African American cemetery. A series of murals in city hall shows town from a single repeated view, again from Ais times forward, though these murals focus on architectural development. Maybe most striking is a Backus mural on the second floor of the library done for a boom-time real estate developer. A vignette shows the city imagined with skyscrapers that at the time appeared to be Fort Pierce destiny. One skyscraper resembles the pyramidal apex of the county courthouse in Miami. Miami and Fort Pierce began at the same time, both boomed by Flagler's railroad. Miami today has a population of 365,000; Fort Pierce, 38,000.

Were passenger service to resume along Flagler's Florida East Coast right of way, the Fort Pierce station would be on Orange Avenue at Depot Street, a two-minute walk from the Sunrise Theatre. Visitors would alight from their trains and have their luggage carted to the planned new downtown hotel three blocks away while themselves walking past the sidewalk cafes, shops, and park of a smart little Florida city. For those who know Winter Park just north of Orlando, it's a duplicate vision of how intimately rail can bring visitors in touch with the places they're visiting and with history that engages them enjoyably.

A few blocks north of these streets and close by the small port and a power plant along Moore's Creek is a small district of Cracker houses and older commercial buildings under renewal. The little bridge over the creek is fondly remembered as "tickle tummy" for the queasiness youngsters once reported when jostled in cars across its arch.

The first new commercial building in maybe fifty years has gone up. It's four stories on Second Street, built by the owner of a boat-financing company who moved himself and his family to Fort Pierce from Fort Lauderdale. The new building matches the Mediterranean revival look of the Raulerson Building next door. Although here and there fake parapets remain, most buildings with their mix of retail and office use pick up on the street's restored rhythm. A tenant at Second Street Station, architect Don Bergman, grew up in Fort Walton Beach in the Panhandle. He gave up West Palm Beach to locate in this small city that reminds him of where he was raised. The proprietors of Lafferandre Gallery across the street live in Port St. Lucie, but this is where they wanted their business.

Everybody comes out for lunch. Where sidewalks have been widened, bulbouts that extend at street corners accommodate café tables. You can't sit outside at Gately's without people walking by and stopping to chat. Businesspeople talk deals while others meet their spouses and children for lunch. You feel people's love affair with how the street and town have been re-imagined. Even strangers find themselves easily engaging each other. One visitor lately engaged a circuit court judge who resembled a friend. They got talking about former governor Reubin Askew, who had appointed the judge, and about the re-opening of the Sunrise Theatre.

Signage is exceptional through town. Permanent directional signs of yellow on green direct motorists and pedestrians to major public sites. The signs start at the I-95 exit to downtown (where they're hard to read and impossible in the dark) and continue all the way east along this main section of Orange Avenue. Fabric banners mounted on poles are color-coded to identify different sections of the city, such as Oakland Park and Sample Oaks. Most distinctive are the interpretive signs with locational maps. These combine lessons about architecturally significant buildings that may have been lost at the site together with a schedule of events that take place in the vicinity. These signs are mounted on attractive stanchions and include historical post cards reproduced in their yesteryear tints.

Because manatees gather in the winter through the Indian River Lagoon, these docile creatures focus a downtown public art program. Sea cows imaginatively sculpted in glass and tile, in stone and steel appear many places. Different from the cows of Chicago or lizards of Orlando, the manatees of Fort Pierce won't be auctioned off and removed. They're permanent installations, visual enhancements that further put people who walk through downtown's public spaces in touch with where they find themselves. Place, design, delight, marketing—all carom off each other. Downtown feels complete within itself. Trias keeps enchanting us, wanting us to explore and not leave. He says, "I only do the public streets and spaces between the buildings. In the ideal scenario, the private sector does the buildings, they fill in the spaces. But if it's not a nice space, the private sector is not going to come in."

Culture Further Renews the City

By 2004, it was looking as if Trias's "nice space," the return of small business, and a city decision to expand the marina were having their effect. After the first hotel deals slipped away, three developers have since come in to pitch their deals. What still remains slow is residential. Developers tell Trias that downtown is a great place but they're doing projects in Palm Beach County or Port St. Lucie and aren't ready to work with him. So far the nearest new housing has gone up on Causeway Island along Seaway Drive next to a Smithsonian Marine Station and the separate city and county co-sponsored Smithsonian Marine Ecosystems Exhibit. Some 150 low-rise condominiums replaced an old water treatment plant and trailer park. A one-day lottery sold out almost half the units to hopefuls who came from as far as California. Everything sold before completion.

There's an older residential neighborhood where the Cracker Trail nears downtown that still connects well with historic ag interests. Slip east into the city where the road widens to four lanes; setbacks measure in inches, and sidewalks are too narrow for comfortable walking. The housing stock is old, mixing every style Florida has ever seen. You can imagine the people who live in this urban section as unsung caretakers, an interim class keeping the felt but unspoken heritage alive, people more likely to vanish silently than to be overtly dispossessed as property values rise and renewal sweeps the entire town. A shadow of the industrial workforce long resident on this west side of downtown blankets these neighborhoods—neighborhoods looking drably northern, Caribbean without the jubilation. Trias lives here.

Additional new owners might be attracted to rehab the houses just north of Tickle Tummy. Others live in an old-line residential row that extends south of the city past a historic Civil War fort in a park along Indian River Drive, continuing for miles the same as those shore drives that remain from all the way up in Ormond Beach down through New Smyrna, Rockledge, and Sebastian, here too sloping above the narrow two-lane road across from the lagoon.

Trias and Tillman are both convinced that the circle will get squared when the Sunrise Theatre reopens for 2005–6. The Sunrise was a center of Fort Pierce life for sixty years beginning in 1923. It was the boom-time project of a West Virginia oilman turned Florida citrus grower. It seated 1,300 for vaudeville and movies at a time when the city population barely topped 2,100. In owner Rupert "Pop" Koblegard's memorable locution, "It is better to be ahead of the times than behind them." Maybe with better timing today, the theater will reopen with 1,180 seats and in a physical plant double the original size with an addition housing a restaurant and meeting rooms. Shops have gone in along the sidewalk. Interiors have been restored, and a historically accurate re-creation of the original lighted marquee fronts the street again. On its reopening, the theater will become the largest performing arts center between West Palm Beach and Melbourne.

Location of the Sunrise significantly differs from many theaters along the A1A coast. Here, you will come out after a performance in the heart of downtown. People who might live downtown could walk to the theater and back, stopping at restaurants or bars, strolling the waterfront. But—chicken and egg—waiting for downtown residents, who will come? Port St. Lucie residents will have to drive thirty minutes to an hour to reach the theater. Mayor Minsky wants his own performing arts center. Residents from Vero Beach face an equal drive, and they have their own Riverside Theatre, though that operates only winters. Although Stuart's Lyric Theatre is also downtown, it's less than half the size of the Sunrise.

Even while awaiting Trias's hotel compound and new housing, Fort Pierce renewal seems unstoppable. The administrator who best connects the renewing city to the reforming county is St. Lucie's director of cultural affairs Jon Ward. Ward approached his work by sucking in great gulps of air and free diving into waters of unimaginable depths. He is a lifelong artist, working in graphics, painting, and writing children's books. When he decided to make Fort Pierce home in 1990, he gave up years on the road as a traveling salesman. He had sold hip young fashion from a 40–foot mobile showroom. He lived on the bus; it was "kind of like being in space," he says.

In Fort Pierce, Ward says he has "met more people than anyplace in my adult life that either grew up and left and came back or came here to stay. Walk the street and you meet dozens of lifetime residents. It's more than just unusual. They're living in a city they're turning into a village." When he settled down, Ward launched Long Wind Publishing, which quickly gained national recognition for publishing Floridiana. He bought a derelict rooming house next to the FEC tracks in town, installed the publishing house downstairs and his wife (a fourth-generation Floridian) and himself upstairs in spaces altogether refurbished with works of art and lighting that makes everything appear in a gallery way. The space would inspire any loft dweller that new housing might attract downtown.

Ward chaired the county's cultural affairs advisory council when the director's job was created in 1999. Government was starting to pay attention to quality of life. Ward knew the county needed "serious, permanent assets, sustainable programs. You can't build cultural identity on a series of festivals." County managers call him "an aggressive meat eater, the T. Rex of culture." They support him.

Like Trias for the city, Ward moves boldly for the county. It's he who is relocating the history museum from Seaway Drive into the old post office building on Orange Avenue, at last affording easy access to people living or visiting in town. He's changing the collection. "That's been a very white institution reflecting the ethnic background of its founders," Ward says. "We're a county of great cultural diversity. We have African Americans and Mexicans. Yes, we have Beanie Backus but we also have the Highwaymen." Ward refers to the "fast-painting" school of mostly poor blacks who were trained by Backus. In mid-century, they sold works on plasterboard from the trunks of their cars for twenty-five dollars to tourists along the highway. (DeLand photographer Gary Monroe's book *The Highwaymen* became an acclaimed big seller at the turn of the century.)

Ward wants to produce a play about Zora Neale Hurston's life. He wants it from the Fort Pierce perspective. "She was past her prime here, overweight, and could no longer write," says Ward. He knows he is up against formidable counterweight from Eatonville, the Central Florida town that each January celebrates the Hurston who lived her young and spirited life there before emerging as a major figure of the Harlem Renaissance. Hurston's last home was in Fort Pierce, a simple cinderblock house where, at her death, an unknowing neighbor emptied the house and started burning its contents in the yard. A local black detective drove by, saw the fire, stopped to investigate, and realized what was going on. He took a garden hose and put out the fire. What he saved was donated to the University of Florida.

Ward wants to work with keepers of the African American oral tradition to help strengthen a community that was long held back because it was minority. He wants to collect the community's memories for a story-telling program. Early in 2004, he inaugurated a Dust Tracks Heritage Trail, named for Hurston's autobiography, that traces landmarks of her last years in Fort Pierce. Ward wants culture to bring back the neighborhood along Avenue D. It will be another test of Trias's confidence that capital follows design.

Trias has already transformed the old black neighborhood main street into something sparkling new with decorative sidewalks, decorative trash receptacles, and street lighting with yellow banners that mark the African American Lincoln Park district on their poles. On this avenue of storefront churches and vacant lots with dirt shortcuts through them, the desultory shops—Da'

Musik Den, the Fried Rice Hut, the 99-cent Store, Cee Dee's, and others—seem like beached sea creatures in alien habitat. Fixed up almost alone on the avenue, a new police substation—built Cracker-style with its second story hung over the sidewalk for shading passersby—suggests the redemptive power of architecture.

Ward is at work with a mistrustful community. Hurston's grave was left unmarked until Alice Walker found it in the Garden of Heavenly Rest, a weedy field with a single patch of bougainvillea and Hurston's grave alone tidied with its headstone installed by Walker. "Novelist, folklorist, anthropologist. Genius of the South. 1901–1960," the headstone reads. People leave stuff at the site, a cross in pennies or a note. Moore's Creek runs alongside invisible behind tangles of growth that Ward wants to clean up. Gratifying in this section of town, Lincoln Park Academy, a multiracial high school, academically ranks among the top twenty-five in America.

Ward wants a Cow Hunter Museum that celebrates St. Lucie's ranching heritage. He quickly enlisted the cooperation of Alto (Bud) Adams. Adams is the legendary second-generation rancher whose business success, environmental awareness, and photo documentation of a way of life have inspired strong county resolve to protect the county's ag traditions. (At least to the north and far west there's a chance, though the destruction of groves from the storms of '04 doesn't bode well for citrus.) Ward wants a major public arts facility, something that might play off the Smithsonian presence on Causeway Island. The county's first piece of art in public spaces will go there. He wants more art galleries, a newsstand downtown, and an important bookstore. The county has none.

Ward's patron has been Cliff Barnes, first of the reformers elected to the county commission. That was in 1992. Barnes became the lone voice for environmental awareness. For years he was on the losing side of four-to-one commission votes. But when former county land use planner Doug Coward joined the commission four years later, and the two by dint of their authority and the changing times brought the commission around, Barnes shifted his focus to issues of culture and quality of life. Barnes, a lawyer (in 2004 successful candidate for county judge), lives on North Hutchinson Island. "We want a better community, not just bigger," he said as county commissioner. "I want lots and lots and lots of parks. A huge population is coming in. We need more cultural opportunities. We don't want public buildings to look like shoeboxes, but we want to make sure that those coming in pay their fair share and even more."

So now in St. Lucie, new construction is starting to pay for what people need. The county raises money from everything except additional property taxes, though property keeps generating more as values rise and assessments keep pace. Road impact fees are up, school impact fees, fire impact fees. Next coming, an environmental impact fee. "We do this over the developers screaming that we're going to stop growth and yet growth keeps increasing more than ever," said Barnes.

Impact fees applied to development on South Hutchinson Island are paying for a bike-ped path that will run the island's length. Facilities like these are showing up throughout the county since a 1994 bond referendum that is generating $60 million over twenty years for environmental land acquisition, for recreation and culture. Barnes earlier led a referendum that generated $20 million for the purchase of lands alone.

One landmark acquired through these self-taxing issues is the Oxbow Eco-Center midway between Fort Pierce and Port St. Lucie. The facility is a natural history educational center in an area fast filling with subdivision houses. The burbs fall away behind the center where it backs to the North Fork of the St. Lucie River just downstream from White City Park. Midway Road crosses the stream here through a settlement scraped out of woods in the early 1890s. Excited by impressions of Chicago's Columbian Exposition with its White City amusement park and brightly lit midway, two immigrant Danes came south by Flagler's train, lured by news of fortunes to be made growing citrus. For a time, White City was the second-largest community in the county. Today a couple of old-time little gift shops mark the canopied road. Beyond the canoe launch in the dark-shaded park, a river road drops away with its old clapboard houses surrounded by oaks, lattice-trunk palms, and crape myrtles. Boats pull up in yards. The lane ends at an old family-run nursery.

Places like the eco-center and county policies newly favoring environmental protection and quality of life improvements have made St. Lucie more attractive for its residents and for attracting prestigious institutions. It was county money that built the new library in downtown Fort Pierce and that helped attract the Jane Goodall Institute, a retirement station for chimpanzees previously trained for U.S. scientific programs. County money too helped protect and enlarge the Savannahs, the large swath of wetlands that parallels the Indian River Lagoon and has gained protection as a state park. Improved county environmental policy helped attract an important U.S. Department of Agriculture Horticultural Laboratory that has attracted an educational corridor in the county's northwest that includes campuses of Florida Atlantic University and Indian River Community College and that interacts with the Smithsonian facility and Harbor Branch Oceanographic Institution.

In 2004, the county commission committed $10 million to add 400 acres to the park for a science research center.

"People are willing to pay higher taxes if you give them something for their money," said Barnes. "People don't want lower taxes. They want to use taxes to make them proud of their community."

Barnes's work shows best in Lakewood Park, an older suburb that made do with few amenities. A drainage canal that long divided the community has been bridged in two places and has become an amenity for an almost 4-mile long trail that runs alongside. This was one of the first trails in the county. No money had been set aside for trails when Barnes came in office. He got $200,000 a year allocated from the general fund, then rewrote an ordinance to get a portion of road impact fees for paths and trails. These fees have helped pay for 158 acres in Lakewood Park, half left as nature preserve with trails and the other half for active recreation with ball fields and a pool to come.

The county now requires 2 percent of new construction funds for art in public places. A new state-of-the-art fairground has gone in along Okeechobee Road. As DOT widens the road to the fairground, a separate bicycle trail is going along the right of way. "Ten years ago everybody knew our county was trashy. Now," said Barnes while still a county commissioner, "we're one of the fastest job-creating counties in Florida. We have the money to spend on incentives and property tax breaks to bring business in." Results show in a QVC call center, two or three others, probably a dozen boat-builders, an airplane manufacturer, a Pentagon-sized Tropicana plant expansion, the new Wal-Mart distribution center. "We have a lot of residents who don't have high technical training," Barnes said, "so these jobs are good for them.

"Oh, brother. I'm telling you. This place was in shambles. Everything good has come from a shift in focus. Instead of just telling business and developers they can do whatever they want and leave us having to put people in high-tech jails, we've demonstrated the connection between quality of life and successful governing."

Doug Coward says St. Lucie is "essentially the front line for growth management in South Florida. If there's a way to accomplish development that helps our community, I'm amenable. But I'm not for developers leaving us with the burden of paying for increased services after they're gone." Coward remains frustrated by having to cope with "a Port St. Lucie mentality that any and all growth is good." That city has reached 111,000 population and, with a landmass of 110 square miles, ranks third-largest in area of any city in Florida without any master plan and minimal coordination for how the county grows. Before Port St. Lucie shot up to its present size, business interests realized that one chamber of commerce would serve the entire county best. The chambers merged. Mayor Minsky finds the situation repressive. "I can't stand that I have a city of 100,000 and I don't have a chamber," he complains.

County efforts to maintain an urban services boundary to avoid westward sprawl are constantly frustrated by Port St. Lucie's practice of annexing adjacent land to keep growing. Developers buy land in the county, Port St. Lucie annexes, supplies water and sewers, and the urban services boundary keeps moving west until it becomes a joke. In 2004, the city annexed 15 square miles of western property where it will permit enough homes for another 50,000 people, for which developers will add two I-95 exchanges and convert a two-lane road to four lanes between I-95 and Florida's Turnpike to accommodate schools, a new university, an industrial park, and the rest of the infrastructure that will make Port St. Lucie the tenth largest city in Florida and largest between Miami and Jacksonville.

There is no stopping the city, though within days of the city's announcement, State Sen. Ken Pruitt of Port St. Lucie, chairman of the powerful Senate Rules Committee, called for a new growth-management tax on most property sales in St. Lucie County to make sure that "when you allow development to happen, the jobs go with it."

Port St. Lucie was scratched out on land maps by the Mackle Brothers and then for the most part left to the successor General Development Corporation to build. Back in midcentury, there were no growth management laws, no environmental regulations. Canals got dug to drain water from wetlands. Houses got built on small lots with wells for water and septic tanks. Runoff polluted the canals and got swept into once-clear waterways. Nobody paid property taxes because the houses qualified fully for homestead exemption. There were no jobs. People who weren't retired had to drive to work in Fort Pierce. Only a couple of roads got built to connect with the main north-south arterial through the county, which was U.S. 1. So it was, and so it still significantly remains.

Still today, 30 percent of Port St. Lucie's population commutes outside the county to work. Those commuters still mainly funnel onto U.S. 1, but now they head south instead of north, driving to Martin County. The transportation problem has become so bad that the mayor wants to build a flyover from Port St. Lucie Boulevard, one of still only two roads that connect the big city east to the highway. He refuses to consider extending Tri-Rail commuter service north from Palm Beach County. That might make still more people want to work south. He wants to build a third connector across the North Fork of the St. Lucie River, a beautiful but long-degraded stream that is the subject of three different restoration programs so far funded at some $4 million. He wants to extend that as yet unbuilt connector six lanes across the Indian River Lagoon to South Hutchinson Island beaches where, along the way, it would claim a portion of the Savannas State Park, tear out sea-grass beds, increase turbidity of the lagoon, and end up on the barrier island alongside a sea turtle nesting area earmarked for addition to the Hobe Sound National Wildlife

Refuge. West and east, the problems of the ill-born city threaten to overwhelm county resources. When he doesn't get his way, Minsky rails against "obsessive environmentalists."

"That third connector will be needed," Coward agrees, "but not across the lagoon. And where's the appropriate place for it? It isn't the widest, most sensitive swath of the North Fork, and that's where Port St. Lucie so far wants it." When the Treasure Coast Regional Planning Council did a transportation study, four governments paid for it. Port St. Lucie opted out. It doesn't want to hear about restraints, about anything that threatens what Mayor Minsky terms his city's "sovereignty." "They're doing things piecemeal depending on which developer comes in the door any day of the week," says Coward. "Why does this happen in Port St. Lucie and not in the north end of the county? To the north you have Fort Pierce, there for a hundred and more years, a community with deep roots. Port St. Lucie is thirty years old and full of people in place less than a year."

To be accurate, some have been there forty years. Nina Baranski, who works in media relations for Port St. Lucie, remembers when she showed up from Detroit in the sixties. She was pregnant. "I figured I'd get some maternity clothes when I got down. I found there weren't any stores. I had to drive to Fort Pierce. I found one rack of clothes I could wear at Sears. I asked my mother, 'Doesn't anybody get pregnant out here?' She explained that it's a retirement community, which is how it started out." Even in the seventies there was still no grocery store. You drove 10 miles one way to supermarkets in Fort Pierce or Stuart. "You learned not to forget what you needed," says Baranski. People still get in a car for a container of milk or a sack of dog food, to drive the kids to school, and of course to commute.

Mayor Minsky turns seventy-one in 2005. He was born in the Bronx and came to Florida after twenty years in the military. He got into real estate, moving to Port St. Lucie when 12,000 people lived here. He delivered mail for nine years. He had 800 stops on his route, all single-family houses. Mailmen develop a capacity for remembering names. He joined the Port St. Lucie Homeowners Association, and that kicked him into politics. The problems?

"General Development Corporation. The city was laid out with the configuration of a cemetery. They just divided it into a grid and sold off every piece they could. They ran this like a company town. When the city incorporated in 1961 with only 300 people, GDC became the first five-person city council. They promised roads; they didn't do it. They promised to expand water and sewer; they didn't do it. GDC designated parks and then sold lots for premium prices by telling buyers they'd be next to them. Then they never built the parks. GDC owned the water and sewer utility but extended sidewalks, curbs, and gutters and provided water and sewer only to those parts of the city where they themselves were building. Lawsuits started piling up against them, and they went bankrupt. By 1990, they were gone. They left 200 miles of roads unfinished. The city had to build them. People went to refinance their houses and found they owed more than the appraisals."

After years when the county ran the water and sewer utility, the city took it over at the turn of the century. Now, rapidly expanding the system, the city can get 3,500 to 4,000 new houses built a year. Although residential construction accounts for 30 percent of the city's economy, the builders, roofers, tile setters, carpet installers, and all the rest still spend their money outside the county. Apart from strip shopping centers, there are no stores in the city.

That's changing in an unsatisfactory way. A new Super Wal-Mart and a Home Depot are going up along I-95 in the section of the city called St. Lucie West. St. Lucie West is one of several big planned use developments close by the interstate. Others more high-end include The Reserve, Tradition, and Tesoro. The Reserve is actually in the unincorporated county, the other two in Port St. Lucie. In Tesoro, lots are selling for a million dollars. The selling features are golf, neighbors who all look alike, and access to I-95. The new developments are all run as Community Development Districts (CDDs). In a nutshell, a Community Development District allows developers to tax the people who buy to pay for utilities. It's a half-assed way to meet requirements of Florida's "concurrency" law, which, in an effort to avoid sprawl, requires a broad range of utilities to be in place before development begins. Somehow mesmerized by slick brochures and big-name golf course designers, high-end buyers pay. It helps that Wayne Huizenga is part of the Tesoro development team and that someone else important in the business is developing Tradition, which is modeled on Disney's Celebration. For Mayor Minsky, this high-end residential is crucial. Luxury homes pay more in taxes than the services they demand, which will help pay for the shortfall in the poorer sections of his city. High-end residential will generate demand for high-end commercial development, which will further help carry the burden of services to earlier developed sections of the city. The first Starbucks along the Treasure Coast has opened to serve Port St. Lucie's swells.

So the stores will go in to the west. They'll be high-end, though most Port St. Lucie residents will find the drive west as painful as the drive south. Yet it's east where Minsky hopes he can build some kind of downtown, partly to overcome the whole design of his city, which he acknowledges is wrong. It should have had market clusters for necessities. It should have been centralized. Now, as he says: "It's going to get bigger. We know that. We can't continue being a city where people live who can't afford to live anywhere else. We're almost completely void of any organized approach to social and cultural events. A downtown would help focus that. We need a foundation to get a performing arts center. With affluent people coming in, we have to have a certain percentage to support that kind of endeavor. It would lift the quality of life for the entire community.

"I knew that when we got more people than can fit inside Yankee Stadium that we were going to be a big city. I have a hard time distinguishing between sprawl and growth. We're a city of 100,000 without our own access to the beach. We have to go through Jensen Beach or Fort Pierce. It's hell being the newest kid on the block. Port St. Lucie has been beat up. But nobody pushes Port St. Lucie around like they used to. The county has been an obstacle to a lot of what we want to do. My city refuses to be subservient."

Instead the city accepts subservience to developers. The engineer at a development called St. Lucie Oaks was lately ready to bulldoze the oaks and leave the melaleuca, Florida's worst pest tree. He was upset because efforts to save the oaks were slowing the project. It turns out the developer didn't know the oaks were valuable. There is no "port" in Port St. Lucie. Why should oaks matter in St. Lucie Oaks?

By 2004, powerful St. Lucie County senator Ken Pruitt was calling for a growth task force to rationalize the future of the entire Treasure Coast. Pruitt, who cut his political teeth on conservation meat, couldn't any longer deny that out-of-control development forces were ravaging his county. Pressures were newly building on the rural north side in places like Lakewood Park, where residents were resisting the urbanizing of empty fields and forests. Indian River County residents were complaining about pressures spilling across the county line, while, on the south, Martin County was reacting with barely concealed hostility to new Port St. Lucie developments planned alongside. Both adjacent counties were reacting warily to Pruitt's initiative. Even Mayor Minsky perceived a new threat to Port St. Lucie's sovereignty in Pruitt's plan, while ag interests feared any moves that might keep them from cashing in when offers from developers matched their willingness to sell. Nine thousand acres were cashed in during the five years ending in 2002 alone.

By November 2004, Port St. Lucie had absorbed more than half the county population. Commissioners run from individual districts but get elected countywide. Developers, whose contributions racked up more than 70 percent of total financial support, heavily bankrolled their three favorites for the five-person commission in an election that would determine the future of county governance. All three candidates swore that developer money wouldn't influence their decisions. Apparently the voters thought otherwise. A frequent ally of Doug Coward gained reelection. So did two newcomers, one 27, the other 31. Both call for balanced growth that protects St. Lucie's environment. Apparently for now, the golem has been kept at bay.

9 MARTIN COUNTY

"A Miracle of the World."

Figure 9.1. St. Lucie Avenue in downtown Stuart, circa 1923. Courtesy of the Florida State Archives.

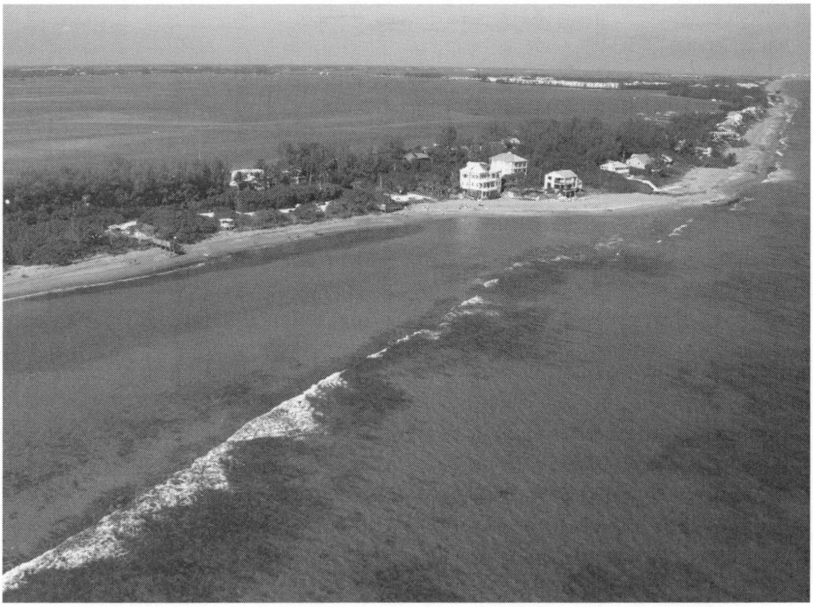

Figure 9.2. Bathtub Beach in Martin County. Courtesy of Martin County Tourism Development Board.

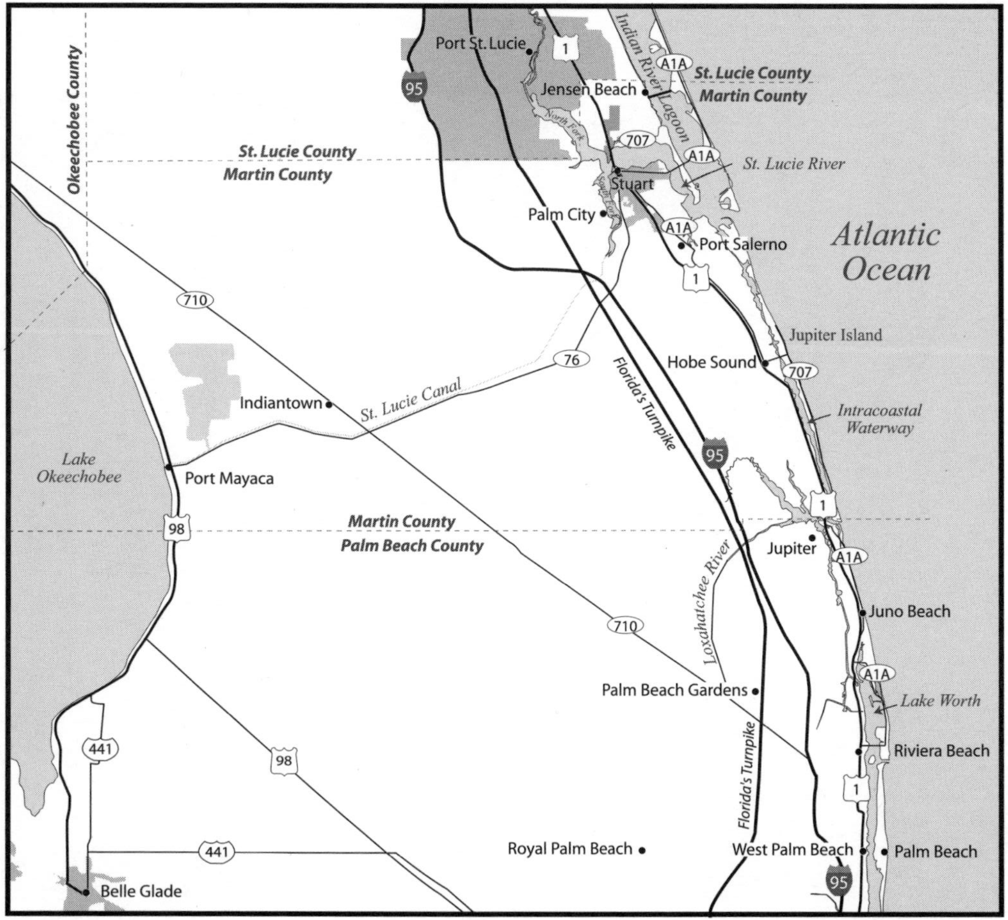

Map 9. Martin County

From atop the high bridge over the St. Lucie Canal, you gaze west across Lake Okeechobee to a shore that can't be seen. The lake at the far western rim of Martin County astounds by its size. Flat Florida tends to defy fathomable dimensions. No matter what you may have heard about it, the lake resists grasp. Its immensity can still confound small-boaters as it did boys' adventure writer Kirk Munroe in 1882, who, according to a biographer, became so lost on a paddle sailboat that after almost a week alone, with "food spoiled, his water gone, and gales whipping up alarmingly choppy waves," he could only desperately ask his diary, 'Shall I ever see home again?'"

The lake is a world-renowned recreational fishing site large enough to be seen from space. Given its size, it's no surprise that it's also the focus of endless contention. For all the best and worst reasons, people have used the lake as a dump, they've sought to install a Disney-like monorail around it, they've argued to fill it dangerously full toward its 30-foot-high brim, while others have lobbied to drop it so low that navigation through its waterway becomes hazardous. The single exorbitant change that did alter the lake was the dike that got built around its 110-mile perimeter and the extensions of that wall for additional miles alongside the river and creeks that supply it, replacing its beaches and wooded shore with the Great Unseen and limiting access to it. Catastrophic loss of life from hurricanes in 1926 and 1928 had swept away low containment berms.

Before construction of the dike, begun in 1932 and completed forty years later, the lake seasonally overflowed. Its wide spill formed and sustained the Everglades while maintaining the brackish balance of Florida Bay where the flow went to tide. The system engineered with the dike included a web of drainage canals, which overcame the same summer and fall flooding that left the coastal cities of Southeast Florida under water. Instead of a flood source, the lake behind its dike became the cities' reservoir. The system also allowed the planting of great fields of sugarcane in the drained littoral south of the lake that became the Everglades Agricultural Area and displaced an enormous swath of Glades. With the ecology of the lower peninsula staggered, the big lake has ever since centered the most contentious issues that affect South Florida environment: land use management and the limits to growth; the future of farming; Everglades restoration; Kissimmee River restoration; and water quality and quantity throughout the region where more than a third of the state's people live.

The rise of cane spread a Third World arc of have-and-have-not influence through the lake towns. Guatemalans, Haitians, and Jamaicans test their American dreams in cooped and uncivil neighborhoods under the influence of Lebanese landlords and Cuban overseers. North around the rim, cane gives way to cattle. Mobile homes make up most of the town dwellings, and over the years one economy after another—commercial fishing, dairying, and now beef cattle—have all passed or exist troubled today. Only sugar prevails, rely-

Figure 9.3. New Indian Riverside Park. Courtesy of Martin County Tourism Development Board.

ing more on the lobbied strength of its protective tariff than on any rational economics, while its continued cultivation year by year depletes the once-rich muck soil, dooming its own future. Conservationists inveigh against Big Sugar's practices but worry more that its demise might flood the region with suburban rooftops, unleashing the nightmare version of promoter dreams at least so far postponed for a hundred years.

All the lake towns lie outside of Martin County, to the south, west, and north Canal Point, South Bay, Belle Glade ("Her Soil Is Her Fortune"), Pahokee, and Okeechobee. The Martin town at the high bridge, Port Mayaca (Port "Big Water"), is no more. It was never more than a boom-time flash in the pan. All that remains are a rusting railroad bridge, abandoned sheds, and a mansion in a section of lush growth for a while run as a bed-and-breakfast, now private again. North of the bridge is the historical marker for the Conners Toll Highway that in the late twenties made the lake accessible from West Palm Beach on a three-cent-a-mile toll road. Conners, who built the road, had been a northern Democratic boss. He saw the lake of his New York past mirrored in the lake of his Florida future; it was big Lake Erie then, where his Irish mafia at the turn of the last century ruled the docks of Buffalo, and Okeechobee now. Conners's backers aimed to make the town of Okeechobee the new Chicago. Other promoters extolled mere lake settlements as future Philadelphias, and Mayaca as the new Coral Gables and Miami. But collapse of the boom banished all hope, and in 1929 Conners died (a year before the long-lived Kirk Munroe).

After years of existing for most Floridians out of sight, out of mind, the lake is now getting a 12-foot-wide trail paved atop the dike that for the moment ends its projected 110-mile loop at Port Mayaca. The trail promises to become an iconic feature of new urbanist lifestyles for which Martin County has become a state champion and which newly drive downtown renewal through Florida's lower east coast. In 2004, county plans began circulating for a Lake-to-Ocean Trail from the urban east through a series of adjacent public lands all the way to the lake. Six million Floridians live within two hours of Okeechobee. Fishing hole, reservoir, dump, Great Unseen—the lake is emerging as a multiform recreational paradise.

A Different Path

At the northern edge of conurbation and with a population of only 135,000, Martin in the late-middle of the twentieth century stepped out along a different path from where the rest of Florida was marching and now significantly leads the parade. Its leaders operate from the east side of the county, and different from Conners, having seen the past, they choose more selectively from it for driving their future.

Martin County—named for John Martin, three-time Jacksonville mayor and Florida governor from 1925 to 1929—has defied the develop-at-any-cost policies that for years have driven St. Lucie County to the north and Palm Beach County to the south. Agriculture sustained the three counties alike, but different from its neighbors, Martin never developed a commercial port and so fell back. Moreover, when the railroad came through in 1894, soon followed by the road alongside that became Highway A1A, Henry Flagler chose to promote his Palm Beach resort, not the settlements north along the St. Lucie Estuary. From 1909 to 1925, the St. Lucie River town of Stuart and its neighbors were the neglected north portion of Palm Beach County. When settlers decided to separate, they named their new county for the sitting governor whom they felt sure would refuse to veto the separation act that enshrined his name. Martin's economy over the years had largely depended on specialty crops such as pineapples, flower growing, and shark tanning that all after a time succumbed to disease, competition, and lost markets. For a time, the Seaboard Air Line Railroad made a ranch town 10 miles east of the lake its southern terminus, and notions arose about how Indiantown would capture the county seat from Stuart. But the death of Seaboard president S. Davies Warfield in 1927 and the great hurricane of 1928 that burst the boom ended those ambitions. Indiantown today farms, though newly again harboring dreams of big-time launched by a medical research institute planning a large facility nearby south across the county line.

What remained was for Martin's seasonal visitors to discover its coastal game fish abundance. These visitors came to test the great seasonally passing schools of sailfish—mythic in size, virtually winged fury when hooked—inspiring Stuart's claim to be Sailfish Capital of the World. Most who came traveled down from the North, but some later began coming, too, from western states, sailing across the Gulf of Mexico, then past Fort Myers and up the Caloosahatchee River. That river, like the St. Lucie to the east, was straightened and stitched by canal to Lake Okeechobee for flood control and navigation. Leisure boaters piloted the waterway through the big lake, then continued east to Stuart and Port Salerno, working the great game fish grounds of the St. Lucie Estuary and often sailing across the Gulf Stream to the Bahamas. Even today, with the estuary's abundance an equivocal resource, sportfishing hangouts like Pirate's Cove at Port Salerno's Manatee Pocket convey an offshore air with their tidal charts for Bahamian waters, their display of pennants for Bahamian yacht clubs, and the flow of Nassau's Kalik Beer.

The visitors were exceptional boatmen. The place they chose was exquisitely different from anywhere else along Florida's warm-weather coast, with its maze of peninsulas that shunted the water through narrows and currents that demanded sharp skills and patience. Land and water seemed at play, as if a realm that had lain waiting for discovery by those attuned to its harmonies, experienced most vibrantly winters when the sun baubled the sea in impressionist shimmers.

Then as now, giving rise to the estuary are the North and South Forks of the St. Lucie River, the South Fork attached to Okeechobee by the St. Lucie Canal. The forks broaden where they converge, then squeeze through narrows before again broadening almost 2 miles wide between the north and south shores of Stuart. Downstream beyond the town the river narrows again, veering south because hemmed in by the long, narrow barrier islandlike peninsula of Sewall's Point. At the bottom of the peninsula, the river again escapes east, passing across the mouth of Manatee Pocket (the region's ideal hurricane hole), which drops away south in protected appendage. Finally one last time before reaching the sea, tributary waters enter from the Indian River Lagoon, which bottoms into it. The lagoon itself lies separate from the sea by far South Hutchinson Island. This entire topography leaves the St. Lucie unusually complex and sensitive to scourge. As we will see, many situations trouble the system. From the north, two of the most troubling have been improved management of the Upper St. Johns River, where canals remove pesticide-charged runoff that no longer troubles the St. Johns but continues flowing through drainage canals into the Indian River Lagoon—this, and how every additional suburb along the shores of the lagoon causes noxious suspension discharged from their streets and driven south by winds that trouble the St. Lucie Estuary's attempts to sustain its own brackish hygiene.

Along these peninsulas and barrier islands and along the banks of the myriad creeks and inlets, the rich built their homes and installed their golfing greens. Where the tapering slivers of land attached back to their mainlands, businessmen not yet retired built their popular boatyards and hangouts with their worker chic sustained by their enviable patronage. Ralph Evinrude built his boat engines here in Jensen Beach, where he brought a wife, the singer Frances Langford, after the war. Langford's Outrigger Club became world famous, and the peacocks she collected continue to roam free through Jensen and neighboring Rio (pronounced *Rye*-oh), still with its twenties-era promotional stone arch. A rare mix of people who enlivened the towns perceived themselves all together engaged in a seamless mix of leisure and work dependent on the great pleasuring estuary.

Repulsing Greed

By the fifties, others besides recreationally indulgent sports fishermen had eyes for Martin. Developers from the south were ready to test the county's waters. Camp Murphy Air Base at the south end of the county was declared surplus after World War II, promising fat pickings along the scenically beautiful Loxahatchee River. Soon after, Florida's Turnpike opened the county to high-speed traffic. Locals could now reach the lower coast in less than half the time it once took. But early developers met strong opposition from Martin residents, and, with more readily salable tracts lower down the coast where their rule prevailed, their initial efforts weren't yet urgent enough to succeed. Martin's people began reacting in savvy ways. They were already a community of youthfully vigorous retirees, politically smart and with peak energy, willing to put time and dollars into keeping their new place the way they wanted for the long years they expected to stick around. Those less affluent had their own year-round stakes. Together, they got involved.

They found their model for how to proceed in the Reeds, who in the early thirties had acquired much of Jupiter Island from a bankrupt company. That barrier island extends 17 miles south from St. Lucie Inlet to Jupiter Inlet, roughly from just below Stuart toward the Palm Beach County line. The Reeds had made their fortune in Remington Arms. They were outdoors people. Jupiter Island, with its face to the sea and its back to the Intracoastal Waterway, became a Shangri-La they shared with others patrician like themselves. They were pro-active about ensuring their future. At a time when Martin, like so many rural counties, was led by humble folk no match for the dealmakers, the Reeds in 1953 chartered Jupiter Island as its own town. Soon after, when a lawsuit challenged the town's tight zoning, they drew the extraordinary conclusion that their best protection would result from putting most of their land in public trust. Their lives were already as good as lives get. They could benefit the public while remaining apart and free from pressures to develop that misfortune might force. To the north, they created the Hobe Sound National Wildlife Refuge and St. Lucie Inlet State Park. Threatened by developers to the south, they won a second suit that pledged the winner to buy out the loser. That newly acquired land—more than a mile—was turned over to the Nature Conservancy and is now the Blowing Rocks Preserve, where the sea pours through limestone outcroppings in geyserlike eruptions. The family next acquired 3½ miles across the Intracoastal and made this a second section of the national wildlife refuge. In a related move, the family convinced then Governor Spessard Holland to acquire Camp Murphy for conservation. The base became Jonathan Dickinson State Park, one of the most popular in the state system. Nearby to the north, across Bridge Street—a memorable allée of oaks leading to Jupiter Island—a smaller oceanfront parcel was donated as a park to the town of Hobe Sound.

"Oh boy! Oh boy! The developers were turning up the pressure," says Nathaniel P. Reed, patriarch of the family in the twenty-first century, who was born in 1933, the year the family came to the island. "It was a miracle of the world that we could pull all this off. But we learned that that's one of the ways you control growth. You put the land in public trust. My grandfather Joseph Reed had enough money that when he was offered vast sums, he could just laugh and say, 'No, it's mine.' We were willing to fight like holy hell to keep the county as a jewel." With Reed writ and gumption maintaining its character inviolate, Jupiter Island at the turn of the century had become America's wealthiest enclave. It hasn't hurt Florida that Nat Reed served as the powerful environmental influence in two otherwise reproachful administrations, first the epoch-ending 1960s Republican administration of Florida governor Claude Kirk, then as a powerful national influence when assistant secretary of the interior for Richard Nixon. Reed's forceful character helped lead Florida into its first significant national leadership roles, first in the eighties enacting landmark growth management laws and then adopting the Reed family strategy when Florida began acquiring conservation lands from willing sellers, a program that by 2004 had been supported by five successive state administrations and by innumerable state and county ballots that have made land acquisition the cornerstone for protecting Florida's natural legacy.

It wasn't just the pro-active vision of the Reeds that turned Martin into east coast Florida's hub of environmental enlightenment. Other threats forced the winter anglers to consider events affecting the highly engineered lake system to the west because of its impacts on coastal fishing grounds. In that inescapable but underappreciated way that everything in Florida sensitively interconnects, the U.S. Army Corps of Engineers, in one of its most egregious blunders, straightened the long meandering Kissimmee River. The move was meant to benefit farmers in the Kissimmee Valley, whose pastures were swamped when seasonal rains overflowed the river's banks for miles across low floodplain. By turning the Kissimmee into a canal, the meanders that distributed floodwaters across a wide, absorbing plain and protected Okeechobee from nutrient overload instead rifled the river's waters straight into the lake. Water levels sharply rose and fell as they never had before. When the levels were high, the littoral marsh that was the nursery for life in the lake drowned.

Robbed of its natural capacity to overflow south by the perimeter dike and by the system's drainage ditches, the lake, when tempestuously full, could be relieved only by drastic outflows. Floodgates were opened, and great tides surged down the straightened Caloosahatchee and St. Lucie Rivers. Floodgates designed to open from the bottom swept huge quantities of coarse sediments down the St. Lucie, which, along its floodway, compounded with soils scoured from the canal banks that the corps had foolishly dug vertically instead of sloped or otherwise held in place. The coarse materials began settling to the bottom and shoaling where the natural river reappeared below its upstream canal and broadened at Palm City and Stuart. Finer sediments were swept into the estuary where they smothered bottom life, while the slugs of Okeechobee's fresh (but not clean) water upset the brackish domain of the fisheries, causing an exodus of marine life able to escape from harm but leaving a great intermediate range of fish to develop foul lesions and turn belly up while straightaway killing everything else unable to swim to safety.

No small agenda began forming for the interesting people now living along Martin's barrier islands who found themselves threatened by the explosive build-up down the coast and from the west in that out-of-sight out-of-mind Strangelovian Kissimmee-Okeechobee laboratory of misguided intention. An Anglers Club and a Conservation Alliance began testing the power of the forces against them. They gained their first victories in beachfront affairs. The first took place in 1972 when the Florida Cabinet authorized new protection for Martin's oceanfront dunes by approving Florida's first beach setback line for new construction that helped prevent erosion. In a companion move, the Conservation Alliance generated $800,000 in private and government funds for the purchase of beach corridors across private property at roughly half-mile intervals that ensured public access to the sea from the St. Lucie County line down South Hutchinson Island. Dune buggies and motorcycles were quickly banned from beaches. Martin began to attract the attention of South Florida conservationists who, tired of fighting their own losing battles, were ready to move where the line might still be drawn.

Political Redeemers

Among those who early came north from Miami were Maggy Hurchalla and Joan and Peter Jefferson. They came on a political tide that was ready to sustain itself. Hurchalla, late during her twenty years as a Martin county commissioner, looked back at the South Florida she fled and recalled why the line had to be drawn where it was. "I still love Dade County," she said. "There's no place else where you can go stomping in the Everglades, sailing across a beautiful bay, diving on the reef, all within an hour of each other. But Dade's screwed-up, Broward's screwed-up, Palm Beach is screwed-up but doesn't know it yet, and if you get any farther north of here, it's cold. This is really it. This is the end of the gumbo-limbos. This is the end of the subtropics right here."

Hurchalla and the Jeffersons quickly became conservation leaders. Hurchalla was elected to the county commission in 1974—ironically, defeating Joan Jefferson. She led the county commission to legislate impact fees for recreation, roads, and schools, for downzoning, for wetlands protection, for preserving hardwood hammocks. She led the commission's opposition to spending tax dollars to keep the Houston Astros training in Stuart each spring. (The Astros relocated to Kissimmee.) Commissioners required that new golf courses keep their landscaping at least 30 percent natural. They have consistently voted against developing Witham Field into a major airport. (West Palm Beach has the nearest, 45 miles south.)

Under Hurchalla's leadership, the conservation community achieved voter approval for a $5 million beach bond issue in 1980 that generated 75 percent in state matching funds and so enabled the purchase of a mile of oceanfront. The commission followed up by leading voter approval for a $20 million Lands-For-You bond issue. Other land acquisitions have included 1,000 midcounty acres, which extend from Highway A1A to the sea and connect with St. Lucie Inlet Preserve State Park already in public hands.

While Hurchalla championed conservation at the county level, Jefferson found her electoral voice as mayor of Stuart when she was elected for the first of three nonconsecutive terms in 1979. She also proved effective in calling for development controls. In this affluent, thoughtful community, she, Peter Jefferson, and Hurchalla proved convincing. They achieved density controls at a time when no one elsewhere in Florida had done it. Limits to growth were called communistic.

Jefferson challenged the then Department of Natural Resources to shut off waste pouring into the river. Stuart, following Martin County's lead, became the first city in Florida to establish impact fees to cushion growth. The county and city both established density and height restrictions, both today, almost thirty years later, still holy writ. Stuart city commissioner and former Martin county commissioner Jeff Krauskopf calls the restrictions "axioms carved in granite, come down from the mountain."

Jefferson found the impetus for her major reforms in the debate over a developer's city of 60,000 proposed for the south end of the county. The new city would have required moats in wetlands, canals, diked containments—no recognition of the existing topography. Everything about the project was wrong. Jefferson objected successfully, pointing out how Stuart, already in place, was struggling to survive. The regional planning council, which at first supported the new development, backed down and funded the city's hiring of regional planners Andres Duany and Elizabeth Plater-Zyberk (DPZ). Coming on the heels of their acclaimed work at Seaside in the Panhandle, Stuart was DPZ's first involvement with an existing city. Duany was outspoken. He told the county they were tearing down the wrong courthouse even as they were putting up a new one to replace the little art deco building that had been so misshapenly added onto. Government had been eager to tear it down. It got saved at the eleventh hour with a state grant, stripped of its nonconforming attachments, and converted to a cultural arts center widely used today.

"Duany was really back to the future," Peter Jefferson recalls. "He was calling for granny flats, for reduced parking. He refused to force us to fill the streets with paving. Most of the time they stay vacant anyway and, paved, would create drainage problems. There was instant acceptance of his plan."

The idea was to stabilize downtown by infill, to adapt a version of an ancient Mediterranean village with dwelling units above stores and the so-called granny flats (secondary dwelling units) behind main residences. Setbacks and parking requirements were reduced. Restraints were placed on development. Design standards were set up with a palate of acceptable architectural materials. Everything new had to fit in with colors, balconies, roofs. There would be no radical transformation by glass, mirrored walls, and stainless steel. No materials were to be used that weren't in use at the time of World War II. Some sites were required to have picket fences. Jefferson rammed through the plan. She pursued infrastructure grants. A million-plus dollars came in for reorganizing the city's water, paving, and lighting. Private investment followed. The town saved the Stuart Feed Store with a $129,000 grant. It's now an expanded Stuart Heritage Museum recently upgraded with hundreds of exhibits but, to the regret of many, accomplished with the removal of Mrs. Peters Smoked Fish House, which had redolently long occupied a portion of the historic site and now relocated to Rio across the river.

Two wins involved traffic. The city prevailed over the state Department of Transportation by keeping Confusion Corner from getting signaled with traffic lights. Charles Kuralt later made the little downtown jumble of intersecting streets, roundabout, railroad tracks, and stop signs nationally famous. The town also prevailed in keeping one of the two spans of the old Roosevelt Bridge north across the St. Lucie River when a mile-long pair of new soaring spans opened in 1997. The little bridge-that-could continues to link the revived downtown directly to its marina district north across the river. Drive it and the sections of the city it connects and you escape into decades-old quiet.

Another important if incomplete win followed the ruinous flooding of the estuary again in 1998. In a quickly organized vote that fall, citizens opted to tax themselves for three years to raise $50 million in a Lands For Healthy Rivers initiative aimed at acquiring sites to protect the St. Lucie and the Indian rivers. Combined with available matching funds, the sum has amounted to more than $100 million, used equally to acquire lands for conservation and for conversion to marsh for filtering overflow waters before they reenter the

St. Lucie. The latter scheme has been accepted as part of the Comprehensive Everglades Restoration Plan and promises to be one of the earliest implemented projects of that vast public restoration project. Yet only five years after begun, after promises of "never again" by the South Florida Water Management District and long before any implementation of the cleansing marsh project, down came the waters once more, in 2003 again destroying the estuarine balance that was finally nearing recovery from its devastation of 1998.

The district's perfidy gave rise to a corrective swing of the political pendulum that had occurred in 1994. In that year, a chamber-backed campaign successfully impugned the long powerful Hurchalla Commission as economically obstructionist and overbearing. The chamber, like most real estate interests in the county, professes support for conservation as much as anyone. Sweet talk and big bucks installed a prodevelopment majority on the commission—a kind of "compassionate conservationism." Quickly, new subdivisions were permitted west of Stuart between Palm City and the I-95 delimited urban services boundary, which chamber interests were also eager to test. For most of the way west of I-95 across Martin's vast agricultural domain, limits on new housing allow only one unit per 20 acres. A lot of ranchland stretches between the boundary and the big lake. But the notorious water management district decision of 1998 reminded the electorate that it could never relax its vigil.

One leader who emerged from that episode was a Brooklyn transplant who came down on a dive trip in the seventies, fell in love with the region, and never went back. Now in real estate, Leon Abood formed a Rivers Coalition, ostensibly an umbrella group to "balance growth and environment as the primary source of our economic sustainability," but specifically driven to clean up the river once and for all. Even the development community had become outraged. For the first time, an alliance of builders, realtors, and chambers of commerce did take up the conservation cause, joining the Conservation Alliance and formulating the filter marsh alternative to the lake control system that not only decimates the estuary but wastes more freshwater in a year than the water management district supplies to all of thirsty South Florida. That became the Lands for Healthy Rivers Initiative. Who knows who votes for whom, but at the next general election, conservationists replaced two of the chamber-backed commission members, although in 2004 they failed to regain their majority.

Even so, one clash after another continues to confirm popular support for the county's commitment to slow and sustainable growth. In 1999, Martin led a consortium of public funding interests in acquiring two big tracts slated for development, one of 15,000 environmentally sensitive acres that straddle the Martin and Palm Beach County line, the other of 2,500 acres in the Atlantic Ridge ecosystem west of Hobe Sound. Of greater symbolic impact was the punitive undoing of a decision by the county commission soon after ousting of the Hurchalla majority.

The new commission in 1995 had stubbornly approved 136 apartments for unincorporated Jensen Beach in violation of the county comp plan. The developer began construction even though nearby homeowners sued, and the case made its way through the courts. Four years later, the district court ruled against the developer. A legal appeal also went against the project. A national homebuilders' lawyer incredulously pondered the consequences. "[I]f those buildings have to be torn down," he said, "[t]he precedent of this case could be detrimental to the industry. I have never heard of this happening in Florida." Residents of the units were moved out, and in 2002 the buildings came down. Nothing could more significantly have set Martin apart.

"Developers—the chamber—will admit that this is the toughest county for them to do business in," says Nat Reed. "Big-time developers who kept thinking that changed commissions would move the urban services boundary west are now selling." On point in an early 2003 decision, the commission, with its mix of progrowth and conservation members, unanimously denied a developer's request to build 886 homes on 4,579 acres of pasture along the Palm Beach line. The project was later approved when the developer came back proposing only 212 homes. That nicely works out to one in twenty. Said Martin County director of growth management Nikki Van Vonno in a recent review of that episode: "Martin County government and the citizens take their comprehensive plan very seriously. We are very different from most other places."

The county will have to increase its vigilance following a 2003 decision by the state and Palm Beach County to sponsor a jobs-producing development that its backers compare in its scope to Disney World. This is the proposed Scripps Research Institute's biomedical facility, which during a time of record budgetary shortfall in Florida was promised more than $500 million in incentives to locate in northwestern Palm Beach County. The site is only 7 miles from the Martin line and runs alongside S.R. 710, where, halfway the 15 miles to Indiantown, Scripps will likely set up its organizing site. The deal right away frenzied monied interests into calculating the ripple effects across Florida's never-ebbing tidal avarice. The Palm Beach county commissioner who represents the district of the Scripps site—who had just gotten his district's growth plan significantly scaled back—likened the Scripps frenzy to "a nuclear bomb going off and destroying everything." Martin worried the same way. Infuriating the chamber, the Martin commission, still with its malleable majority, unanimously took a wait-and-see position. Before anything gets done, said one of the commission's lately progrowth members, "Let's talk about our concerns for housing, infrastructure, and the environment." "Obviously we need to plan," said another. "We are experiencing incredible pressure from the north and south." Unspoken was the no longer preposterous notion that by demanding higher standards for development and conservation, Martin, beaconlike, would attract its share of the most affluent newcomers drawn to Scripps without giving away the bank. For these newcomers and others inching their way south from Port St. Lucie and west into the proliferating ranchettes, big Okeechobee with its recreational offers looms almost as compelling as the coast.

The Last Plans

The Scripps deal has lent urgency to a new debate about Martin's still-great expanse of undeveloped western land. The future of that agricultural realm leading to the big lake stands out as the last major land use decision that Martin will make in our time. The debate isn't about whether to develop or not. It's about the best way to avoid development at any ruinous scale. Recently enacted state legislation seeks to protect ag lands by requiring that for every acre that gets developed, an acre must be permanently preserved. W. Greg Braun, who serves on a steering committee to build consensus, talks of Martin doing better. "We're talking about higher levels of compensation for higher levels of conservation. If ag owners only transfer development rights, they get less money, but if they add hiking trails where the land contains endangered species, we'll give top dollar." Hope is high for the initiative because as Braun points out: "Even the development commissioners are much more conservation-minded in Martin County than elsewhere. There isn't one that wouldn't say that he or she doesn't want Martin to be like either St. Lucie or Palm Beach County."

Mike Busha has a far-reaching plan. Busha heads the Stuart-based Treasure Coast Regional Planning Council, which includes Palm Beach County. His idea is to give up 20 to 30 percent of the land for clustering development in rigorously controlled new urbanism projects in return for buying up development rights on everything else or acquiring the rest for conservation. Developers given the rights to build would pay for the public acquisitions. Some perceive that the new towns would be so expensive to build that Martin would become more elite than it already is. That issue hovers around every land use discussion. So far, Palm City and to a larger extent Port St. Lucie supply affordable housing for Martin's workers. Busha argues: "Nobody is coming up with a game plan about how we are going to accommodate the next 70,000 people in Martin County. I don't see anybody throwing their hands up that we can't develop at all. Yes, we may grow slower than elsewhere. We may not be the train wreck of Port St. Lucie." But Busha recognizes that Martin's comp plan is subject to amendment the same as anywhere else and that the 1-in-20 low-density regime that prevails could be upset by the return of a prodevelopment commission that would only have to follow authorized procedures to have its way. Just as bad, the 1-in-20 could spread "ranchettes" all across the west. Once in place, why couldn't financial backers of a prodevelopment commission effectively lobby them to start approving 1-in-10 and then 1-in-5?

With that thought in mind, Martin's conservationists acting as Guardians of the Martin County Comprehensive Plan proposed an amendment to the county commission. The proposal would require a supermajority of four out of five of the commission and also a voter referendum to change the urban services boundary, the four-story height limit, and other elements of the plan. The battle lines for the fall 2004 election intensified when the sitting commission voted three-to-two against putting the issue on the ballot. Even in this county where one of the nay-saying incumbents acknowledged that the boundary and the height limit were sacred, the vote would be closely watched by developers looking to get their snouts further under the tent.

Says Busha: "There's too much pressure to resist. Whatever happens [out west], there are going to be winners and losers resulting in a patchwork mess. A big regional plan would give up 20 to 30 percent and take the rest out of play. We could accommodate growth for 100 years and stay the way we want." Reed supports Busha's position cautiously. "Any commission can never lock things in," he says. He has no problem with combining 1-in-20 ranchettes, permanent ag, and the possibility of new towns. "There are no guarantees," he says, "but before even opening the door a crack, we want to think long and hard. We have seen Palm Beach, Broward, and Dade Counties crack open the door, allow development west of I-95 in the middle of some of the most productive agricultural lands, and then jump west of the Turnpike to the boundary of the Everglades. Within 90 minutes we have all the evidence in the world that the nose of the camel under the tent is one of the most dangerous decisions that can be made in Florida."

Not only in policy but also on the ground. The difference between adjacent Palm Beach County and Martin is plain to see. Drive up U.S. 1 north of the county line and the build-up fades. Signs announce wildlife crossing for the next 6 miles and habitat restoration in progress on both sides of the road. A designated bike lane appears and the entrances to Jonathan Dickinson State Park and the Hobe Sound National Wildlife Refuge Wildlife Nature Center. Buildings that run close alongside the road are low-rise even through Hobe Sound's burgeoning highway strip. To the east, old Hobe Sound is freshening with paint along Highway A1A. That road, after squeezed into U.S. 1 coming north toward the county line, separates to the east again just below Hobe Sound. But oddly, A1A runs inland here while the beach road through Jupiter Island carries a different designation. Reed doings.

The Jupiter Island road today is S.R. 707. Originally it was A1A, the same A1A that 18 miles north runs along the Hutchinson Islands in which vicinity it's S.R. 707 on the mainland, rimming the Indian River Lagoon from Jensen

Beach north to Fort Pierce. Yet that situation reverses in south Martin County because, as Reed tells the story, referring to commercialization of the coastal road already years ago happening to the south: "Mother saw that A1A would be a real problem. She met with Governor Holland. Bernie Papy, kingmaker of the Keys, chaired Department of Transportation affairs in the legislature. Mother persuaded him with brilliant foresight and intense political pressure, plus a fair amount of cash [for the relocation], to bring 707 onto the island and A1A onto the mainland," says Reed chuckling.

Today, two-lane A1A after scooting off on its own again below Hobe Sound parallels the railroad track, road and rail alike yesterday's main routes to South Florida. Decorative old light posts stand from early days. Reed influence has kept the little hub quiet, close as it is to Jupiter Island, with more practical than fashionable enterprise—a lumber company, auto care, a few professional offices and simple places to eat.

Hobe Sound is home of Florida Classics Library, a reprint publisher run by longtime county critic Val Martin. He specializes in history and conservation books, notably including *Jonathan Dickinson's Journal,* the firsthand account of the shipwrecked seventeenth-century Quaker group's difficult journey through Indian territory in the quest for salvation in St. Augustine. Martin is one of those who grew up in South Florida but came north to Stuart in 1958 because it reminded him of Hollywood before the war. Martin's environmentalism is of a purer sort than most. He repudiates the system of drainage fields meant to filter Okeechobee outflow as a way to protect the estuary, calling it "artificial environmentalism." Instead he calls for converting the St. Lucie Canal itself into a 25–mile filter marsh and public park. The solution is comparable to restoration of a large portion of the Kissimmee River now underway. In a recent letter to the *Stuart News,* he called for the powers that be "to *honestly* explain to the American taxpayer exactly how far into the unforeseeable future they propose that 220,000 acres of huge, above-ground deepwater (12 feet) reservoirs planted across Southern Florida—where none has ever existed naturally—are intended to operate using huge, air-polluting, diesel-driven pumps running constantly at extraordinary taxpayer expense, and for how long?" A spokesman for the water management district says "forever." Publisher Martin is not likely to have his way any time soon.

One of Martin's few originally published books is *Florida's Ashley Gang,* which tells the story of Florida's notorious homegrown bank robbers who, during their twenties heyday, lived 5 miles north of Hobe Sound in a wetlands that is now a housing development. Nearby north between the road and the Intracoastal Waterway is Seabranch Preserve State Park, 920 acres that show how the coast looked during Dickinson's time. Preserved here is one of the few remaining sections of globally imperiled sand pine scrub along the southeastern coast with dunes that reach to 30 feet.

Ten years ago Port Salerno nearby north lost its commercial fishing trade following passage of Florida's constitutional net ban. Sportfishing still thrives. Locals lately showed their civic pride by facing down Florida's Department of Transportation, which wanted to four-lane A1A through town. The road remains half that with new roundabouts, new curbs, and sidewalks. The town is enjoying a spirited comeback. It arcs around Manatee Pocket, where the problem of declining water quality has been arrested with an ongoing storm-water retrofit project. At one time, some 300 to 400 fishermen fished out of Salerno in winter. Only about 50 remain, operating from protected docks while the economy has shifted to yuppie waterfront business, resort trade at Pirate's Cove, and restaurants, all surrounding a newly installed waterfront boardwalk.

A1A keeps its back-roads character before reaching Stuart past Witham Field and a large light industry section. Jobs here pull morning traffic down six-lane U.S. 1 and across the high bridge over the river from Port St. Lucie. The road enters downtown Stuart on Joan Jefferson Way circling a new roundabout centered with a fighting bronze sailfish. Then Confusion Corner. Traffic creeps. It's enough to make you scream. In Stuart, folks purr. Locals love their preserved landmark. Other towns have their *castillo,* their cars on the beach, their railroad station in the park. Confusion Corner is Stuart's favorite old three-legged cat, its tipsy raconteur uncle, its security blanket.

Stuart has a quirky streak. It also has a downtown that works. Only 12,500 live here, yet it's a high-concept city where, different from much of the rest of South Florida, life feels in control. Stuart stirs a life-as-art mix that visitors eagerly come to sample. New restaurants occupy old buildings. A riverwalk, damaged by the storms of 2004 but getting rebuilt, edges the water. Idiosyncratically, the Fellowship Hall alcohol rehab center sits next door to the Lyric Theatre, first built in 1925 at a nearby site, this version saved by the Jeffersons and today busy most of the year. Postmen say they'd rather work this downtown route than any other in the 34994 zip code—which is half the city.

Downtowners extol not only Confusion Corner but Lady Abundance. Lady Abundance is the semi-draped wench with literal jugs who centers a fountain at a third downtown roundabout. She stands for something—well, ample, a kind of full-bodied satisfaction locals feel about their town. Her pedestal stands across from a popular sports bar that replaced the beloved Jolly Sailor Pub when the former Cunard Line hands who ran the place retired after twelve years. Out back in the parking lot sits their English Austin cab that they called "Fergie," now for sale.

Popular as the sports bar is, it's a small chain operation, which right away worried devotees of downtown that chains were going to replace everything mom-and-pop. To allay their anxieties, Stuart commissioners in 2005 agreed to limit "formula business" operating within 300 feet of another in the old commercial district and with additional restrictions about look and size. Extending restrictions to other sections of downtown was a possibility.

Hub of downtown is Osceola Street, and the heart of that, the 1925 post office arcade. For a while the spirit of renewal literally resided here with the Jeffersons. They bought the abandoned arcade, poked a hole in the roof, planted a tropical garden for the falling rain to water and made this the living room of their new inner-city abode. Peter Jefferson's office fronted the street, while the rest of the arcade filled with tenants. These and the dozens of other boutiques, galleries, and more practical stores, strung along three or four blocks, entice visitors with attractive wares and with service only grandmothers can remember. Yeasty smells pour from the Osceola Bakery, which delivers lunches up and down the street and encourages sampling of everything from the garlic baguettes to the "cool-as-cucumber" soup. Don Henley tapes play, and the espresso tastes rich as brewed earth. Downtown Optical posts a sign in the window: "Wanted artist for winter season. Prefer large modern works." Caramba splashes colorful South American clothing and crafts in its windows, and Nature's Way Cafe sets tables inside and out alongside the cork board that carries notices for coffeehouses, reggae, and art shows.

Among popular restaurants there's Ashley's, named for the gang that three times robbed the bank that the restaurant moved into. Guests dine bistro style in what's as much art gallery outside as in. Outside, local artists have painted a landmark impressionist mural of the town.

Vintage board houses stand nearby on side streets, some fixed up, some with tin roofs, latticed porches, and shingled dormers awaiting restoration or, regrettably, replacement by sanctioned low-rise condos. Enough of these have lately been built here and in the old Potsdam section west across U.S. 1 (where the Jeffersons' riverfront house, later a bed-and-breakfast, was torn down for one) that the city commission finally legislated a three-story height limit. A pair of shingled riverfront houses on Colorado Avenue stands sheltering vigil over a minipark with a couple of benches memorializing a fallen motorcyclist. In front of the brutal new concrete Martin County Court House stands its beautiful old art-deco predecessor, saved as a cultural center.

East of downtown, an old Florida landscape lines unpaved Hibiscus Avenue, thick with crape myrtles, jacarandas, oaks, tree ferns, and great arbors of false bananas and yellow poinciana. Here you find Possum Long House, the Garden Club of Stuart, and the Martin County Audubon Society. There's a nature center with a walk of cycads and gopher tortoise holes called Memory Lane. The path is brown with pine needles, everything overgrown around bottlebrush trees, gumbo-limbos, and buttonwood. The place is surreal in its unadvertised temptation, and you feel invited to lose yourself.

On a beautiful crisp winter morning, drive east away from downtown along Highway A1A on new bridges through Sewall's Point across the St.

Lucie and the Indian rivers onto Hutchinson Island and the words form in your mouth, "This is what Florida was meant to be!" Fisherfolk shoot the breeze while waiting for a strike. Pelicans skim low across sunlight glistening on water. Sandy bluffs rise behind waterfront docks; morning cyclists churn their miles. If the beauty masks out-of-sight troubles in that witch's brew of pollutants drained from sugar lands, these fisherfolk at leisure hardly mask popular resolve to undo the worst of the river's remaining troubles.

Just as Stuart differs from other coastal towns, Stuart's beaches differ from other beaches. No high-rises along the Martin section of Hutchinson Island, nothing over four stories, no tee shirt-and-burger strips. You cheer at the thought of throngs that undoubtedly find this beach hopelessly lacking and who stay away. Instead you get sane attractions that warm the coals of yesteryear: Gilbert's Bar House of Refuge, Bathtub Beach, the Elliott Museum (all troubled by 2004 storms, all nearly recovered). The House of Refuge dates from 1875, when these coastal beaches were the last—not the first—place you wanted to find yourself, a time when finding yourself on the beach meant you had been shipwrecked and were lucky to be alive. Nine houses were put up along Florida's desolate coast to shelter survivors. This one alone remains, a museum of relic clapboard with the dignity of its simple architecture and generous purpose. Nearby along the narrow two-lane side road before public access ends at gated cul-de-sac mansions is Bathtub Beach, so named because it's bathtub safe. A nearshore reef keeps the shallow waters calm enough for tots. The north edge collects abundant shells that, when washed by waves, click like a thousand castanets.

The same narrow road passes along the former Indian River Plantation, now a Marriott resort, a highly rated, logo-perfect golf and condo place to play. Its deli on the upland side of A1A is complete from the *New York Times* to home-baked breads. Just up A1A, the Elliott Museum celebrates the inventive genius of Sterling Elliott, whose dozens of patents included the first addressing machine, the first stamp machine, a knot-tying machine, and a four-wheeled bicycle that inspired the Stanley Steamer automobile. Vignettes include a barbershop, ice cream parlor, and a dress salon, with wonderful collections of toy soldiers, shoes, rods and reels, needlepoint, and vintage cars. Across the road is the Florida Oceanographic Society. Open to the public are its research spaces, a bookstore, boat tours of the lagoon, hands-on learning programs, and guided tours with a well-interpreted mangrove trail, though mangroves that lately grew to 50 feet high were badly damaged during the storms of 2004. Yet it's still a wizard's domain of arthritic-looking bent elbows pushing new green tops for the sun and with prop roots seeming to levitate the mangrove trunks. Nowhere along the A1A coast do mangroves grow this high, this red, this prepossessing.

Between beach and mainland along the Indian River Lagoon abides the tiny trailer park municipality of Ocean Breeze Park and Jensen Beach. The county's big Indian Riverside Park has newly gone in here along the lagoon. Nearby is the county school system's Environmental Studies Center, full of tanks and labs open to the public. Change is quickening in waterfront Jensen, but you can still explore its back streets with their old cottages, log fences, and lanes edged by flowering yards and overgrown hedges. Settlement slips away as you continue north on the mainland into St. Lucie County on county road 707 along the Indian River. A1A is back where it belongs.

10

PALM BEACH COUNTY

The Fight to Get Florida Right

Figure 10.1. The Elliot family touring A1A in Palm Beach County in 1960. Charles Barron, photographer. Courtesy of the Florida State Archives.

Figure 10.2. CityPlace. Photographer, C. J. Walker. Courtesy of Palm Beach County Convention and Visitors Bureau.

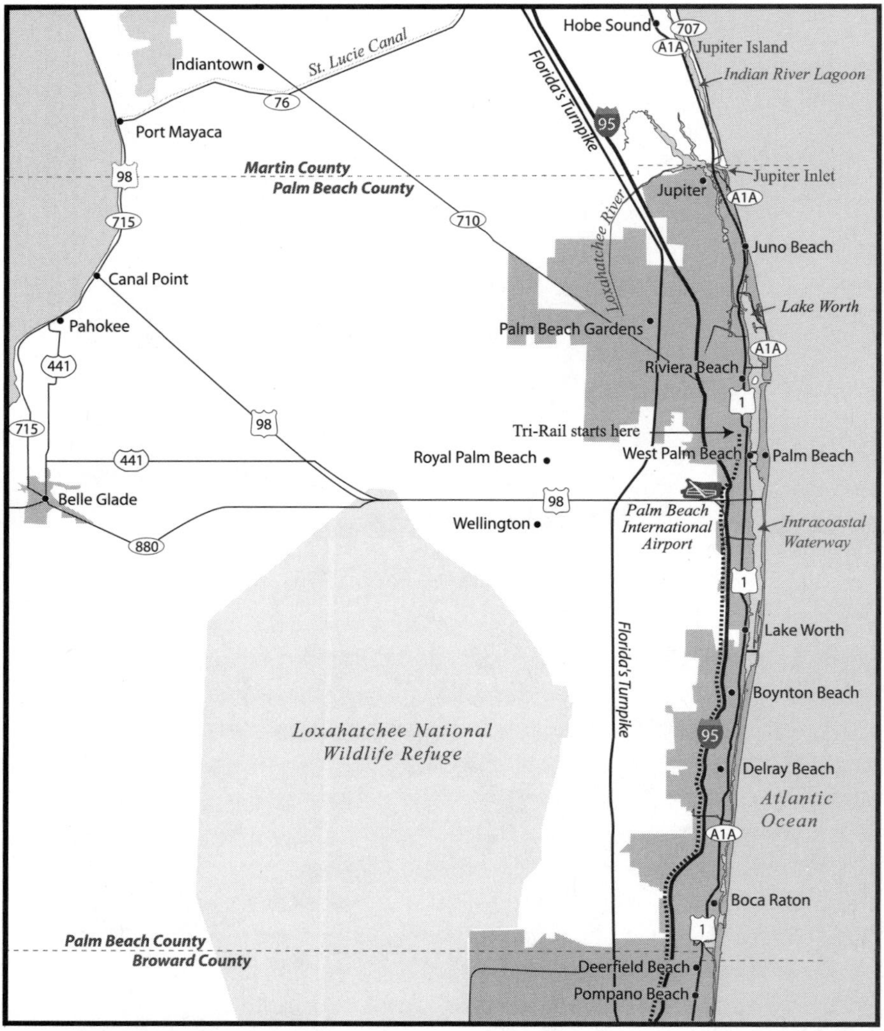

Map 10. Palm Beach County

Palm Beach County claims two cities that get Florida right. In West Palm Beach and Delray Beach, regard for the character of place significantly challenges development as usual. By their quality of downtown renewal, the two cities have led in trying to tame Florida's aggressive policy of limitless inmigration with its suburbanizing threat to natural resources and its costly impacts on quality of life. But Palm Beach County, which has pushed redevelopment of the two coastal cities through incentives known as Eastward Ho! now threatens the undoing of its policy by a joint county and state decision in 2003 to build a 1,920-acre biomedical research center in a region until now planted in citrus. Some call the new Florida home of California's Scripps Research Institute the second coming of Disney for its assured high-sprawl impact. If plans continue for Scripps to locate 10 to 12 miles northwest of downtown West Palm Beach, the research center promises not only to attract additional research companies to its new site but to intensify building pressures through regional farmlands and among the suburban towns that from their outset have been driven by lot sales.

Nobody had ever heard of Orlando before Disney. Nobody yet knows what the explosive new Scripps campus will be called, but it looms as one of Florida's next defining icons.

Before Scripps, the county commission had been struggling to reverse fifty years of bad planning with one move after another to contain growth. Citizens were ready to back reform. In 1991, they voted $100 million to acquire conservation lands, and in 1999 they did it again by voting $150 million to defend remaining farmlands from suburban encroachment. For years, one plan after another tried to keep an Agricultural Reserve viable. Palm Beach became the first county in Florida to deny development before schools were already in place that new homeowners would require. Led by county commission chairwoman Karen Marcus, staunch supporter of sane growth, the county also became the first to challenge University of Florida population forecasts that effectively require the development of additional land in fast-growing counties to accommodate forecast growth. Marcus convinced her board to develop its own forecasts that were expected to be lower than the state's, a challenge that quickly fell under attack by every interest that prefers to keep building for the newcomers that it insists have to keep coming.

But even the Marcus-led insurgency gets tossed rump-over-teakettle with the advent of Scripps, which has frenzied neighboring grove owners to cash in on booming land sales. The owners of a grove twice the size of the Scripps site want to turn their acreage into 10,000 houses—20,000 newcomers at the one site alone—plus a big-box retail center. Florida's biggest developers jumped at a county proposal to develop 2,000 acres east of the Scripps research site into "Scripps Village." Each claimed a go at the sweepstakes by putting up a $100 million line of credit or its equivalent. Current two- and four-lane roads will widen to six and eight lanes. Scrutiny of developments of high regional im-

Figure 10.3. The Henry Morrison Flagler Museum. Courtesy of Palm Beach County Convention and Visitors Bureau.

pact that normally might take a year to complete was getting pushed for completion in months. Area congressmen were pushing federal agencies to gloss over environmental impact reviews.

At the same time in 2004 that rejuvenated phosphorous-absorbing marshes were alive again with waterbirds as an early success of Everglades restoration, county commissioners under the assured development impact of Scripps gave up hopes for a growth control plan that had already cost them almost $700,000 to figure out and instead chose to allow more density than the plan permitted. "I don't know what I want to do," said Commissioner Jeff Koons. "Scripps knocked up things sideways." Which makes existing residents shudder. Given the looming development storm, one lately told the *Palm Beach Post* that she moved to the area from booming western Broward County because, "I wanted peace. I came here for peace and this is war."

The intensity of development sure to follow was marked by the willingness of the state and county to fork over more than $500 million in cash, land, and other incentives just to have Scripps set up shop in the county, a figure that soon rose another $200 million with no end in sight. Scripps has promised 585 high-salary jobs in eight years. That's more than $1 million per job. Nobody knows how the next economic downturn will affect these plans. Yet the size of the giveaway has no precedent in this state that promotes itself as the best and the most of everything yet more quietly seems forever defensive about a future still based on low-paying tourism jobs and the mixed blessing of retirement. Only outsiders seem capable of overcoming some ever-eddying drift toward stagnation. Governor Jeb Bush pushed Scripps into Florida in secret negotiations worked out with legislative cohorts. They announced their decision in a way intended to leave no doubt that any critical questioning of the project would go beyond bad judgment and would verge on the unpatriotic in Florida's wars to capture the sweetest rewards of institutional expansion and relocation.

Barely heard among the hosannas for 50,000 or 100,000 new regional residents and the multilaning of "access" has been talk about rail, even though the Scripps site is close by that track laid by Warfield's Seaboard Air Line Railroad from Indiantown to West Palm and that connects today all the way through the Tri-Rail commuter system to Miami. How easy to set the juggernaut of development rolling with a half billion in giveaways while copping annoyance when the question of rail comes up. When the South Florida Regional Transit Authority announced that the cost of extending Tri-Rail to the Scripps site would cost $150 million, nobody threw money at the idea. Different from Scripps giveaways, this case would be argued through deliberative public process. The consensus was, Let's first see what happens once people start moving in.

More certain than any commuter rail future for Scripps is the county's ultimate western sprawl in the pattern set to the south by Broward County, today built out to the already far receded Everglades. As Palm Beach County suburbanizes west into grove lands, the impacts promise to reach to big Lake Okeechobee and south to the Everglades. At a time when sugar consumption is dropping, when county cane growers face potentially rising quotas for offshore growers, and as soil conditions worsen toward their ultimate degradation, talk now surfaces about the highest and best use of far western ag lands. In a show of their hard-nosed refusal to accept limits on their free rein, growers early in 2004 threatened court action to upset an agreement with the state that allowed them continued but temporary use of lands that the state had already purchased for Everglades restoration. Growers claimed faulty process by the state that they argued should allow them to farm in perpetuity if they wanted, upsetting a critical piece of the puzzle to achieve Everglades restoration and, by delays, liable to foreclose further congressional contributions to the process. Growers began deriding restoration of what they called "a failed Everglades system," as if national and state commitments to Everglades restoration were a vast boondoggle the public had to be made aware of. In defense of highest and best use, what would be left for growers but to convert their tens of thousands of acres to rooftops, a dream of promoters for a hundred years?

That quickly surfaced as Big Sugar's opportunistic tack when it joined the contest to land Scripps, offering 1,000 free acres in the Everglades Agricultural Area (EAA) that would have begun transforming steadily soil-depleting sugar fields into lucrative rooftops. At least in the short term overplaying its hand, Big Sugar precipitated its own defeat by ensuring voter support for a fall 2004 referendum that strengthened county commission oversight of decisions that could convert agricultural and environmentally sensitive lands to housing in the EAA.

At the same time that agents of development were muzzling the complaints of public agencies analyzing Scripps land use implications, others less vulnerable to their pressures finally went to court against the county-supported plan. Acting together, 1,000 Friends of Florida and the Florida Wildlife Federation cited violations of the county comp plan, bias in support of project-favoring zoning changes, and an original report of the Treasure Coast Regional Planning Council staff (muted by the council's board) that also complained about the project's devastating impacts if sited at Mecca Farms. Litigation could embroil the project in months or years of delay, upsetting mutual commitments between the state and the San Diego-based research institute and allowing Scripps to relocate either elsewhere in Florida—Tampa and Orlando were both renewing earlier failed efforts to land the project—or abandon Florida plans altogether.

A County of Superlatives

Palm Beach is a county of superlatives and contrasts. Its 2,578 square miles reach from the Atlantic to halfway around big Lake Okeechobee—almost halfway across Florida—making it Florida's largest county along the A1A coast. Its east side is urban, while its western districts remain rural, together with adjacent counties supplying the largest native-grown portion of America's winter vegetables and much of its sugar. The county's 1.3 million people are notably bracketed by one of the wealthiest towns in America and towns on the big lake populated by former migrant workers who have been replaced by new cane harvest technology and who suffer the highest rate of AIDS in America. Between affluent suburbs and the urban coast lie enclaves beleaguered by crime.

The county fast-forwards ahead. Of 260,000 people added since 1990 alone—one-quarter of the county's entire population—95 percent chose to chew additional suburbs out of previously undeveloped land. No surprise that at the turn of the century, the Sierra Club ranked the county as the most sprawl-threatened medium-sized metropolitan area in America, and the American Farmland Trust identified the county's western farmlands among the sixth most threatened agricultural region in the nation. Agriculture in Palm Beach County? Who knew, in this place where hundreds, if not thousands, of million-dollar houses sell as fast they go up—one lately for $30 million—and new homes sell for more than they do in Broward and Miami-Dade.

"We need to figure out what we want to look like when we grow up," said Joann Davis, who works in Palm Beach County for 1000 Friends of Florida, the nonprofit watchdog of state land use planning, before the Scripps announcement. At that time she could still say: "Today, county decision-making is a real interplay between doing the right thing and being influenced by big money. But we're so addicted to the growth and development economy, we're going to have to find a more sustainable economic base." If that's Scripps and biomedical technology, a field ripely suited to coastal Florida with its immense aging population, only dreamers can imagine that the trade-off for a new research suburb might be akin to the disposition of Treasure Coast regional planners to trade a little more sprawl for a lot more conservation. As groves become subdivisions-in-waiting, Davis can only lament: "This is the thing we feared about putting Scripps in an isolated spot miles from anywhere. If you get this domino effect, there won't be anything left out there."

That search for policy balance proceeds by regional cooperation but not in the way that state planners intended. Palm Beach had been linked for economic and land use planning with the Treasure Coast from which it has effectively broken away. Adjacent Martin County has few towns and remains low-rise and rural instead of suburban to the west, intent on conserving land and favoring retirement and leisure pursuits along the coast. But south out of Martin, I-95 swings sharply to the east. Important north-south roads compress to absorb the business-driven 24-hour traffic rush. The world turns suddenly urban. The future of Florida looms. Towers rise and highway flyovers attempt to ease congestion. Blight captures old neighborhoods that defy order along U.S. 1. Martin County insists it doesn't want to become like Palm Beach County—the same as Martin's object of disdain insists it doesn't want to become like Broward, sprawled and everywhere paved over, and Broward insists it doesn't want to become like Miami-Dade, seen as chaotic and hopelessly corrupt.

One County in Three

Yet some regional planners look at the four counties plus St. Lucie, Indian River, and southernmost Monroe as a single region, stretching from Key West to Vero Beach in what the *Miami Herald* has called "one long metropolitan headache." Although political buy-in for any seven-county notion is unlikely in the near future, despite its Treasure Coast connection and the counties' domino disavowals, Palm Beach regionally does connect its future to the south. Palm Beach, Broward, and Miami-Dade inevitably form Florida's Gold Coast—Gold because that's where the money is. The three connect less by fiat, more by fact. They're where tourism flowered most exuberantly beginning 110 years ago, where Henry Flagler in Palm Beach made his grandest home, and where winter society never had it so good on mainland America, railroad cars carrying visitors directly to their quarters, and, once disembarked, with servants to pedal them around like potentates in wicker carriages. Tri-county tourism has lived off Palm Beach cachet ever since.

Gold Coast counties together contain more than one in four Floridians. They operate three of Florida's busiest airports. They're linked by a tri-county commuter rail system, the only system of its kind in Florida, newly double-tracked. Like Broward and Miami-Dade, Palm Beach will spend more than half its transportation budget for the next 25 years on mass transit, roughly $3 billion already planned for public systems. At least nominally, the three counties work together to attract business relocations (although they solicit among themselves). Fostering Gold Coast regionalism, the U.S. Office of Management and Budget in 2002 repositioned Palm Beach County from its own Metropolitan Statistical Area to another that encompasses Broward and Miami-Dade, creating a statistical entity of 5.2 million people.

These are urban people in West Palm Beach, Fort Lauderdale, and Miami. They come from the North and from Latin America. They develop urban culture, but each city has its own cultural arts council and its own major performing arts center (Palm Beach County will soon have two, the same as Broward, and Miami will have four). Local and outside performing groups popularly play venues in all counties, but filling them has become more important than direct support for performing groups based in one county or another. Although people routinely travel among the three counties for commerce and spectator sports, they move around less for culture.

If the three counties focus on the future with like minds, Palm Beach uniquely among all Florida counties educates about the past. In 2004, through a consortium steered by the Historical Society of Palm Beach County, backed by the *Palm Beach Post* and partnered with the Palm Beach County School District, all fourth-grade children began studying Florida history.

But even that history links Palm Beach with Broward and Miami-Dade. The Everglades borders all three to the west. From the east, all suffer saltwater intrusion because of their limitless demands on the freshwater aquifer. The Gulf Stream flows close to each county and nearest of all to Palm Beach, keeping its beach towns as warm and alluring in winter as beach towns in Broward and Miami-Dade. Even after years of overfishing, anglers year-round churn the waters with yachts that tie up at newly repaired marinas and occupy storage facilities more plentiful only in Broward. Here, below Jupiter Inlet, where the estuarine complexity of the Indian River Lagoon yields to more routine urban water concerns, the Intracoastal Waterway narrows most of the way to canal width. It takes on the name Lake Worth and becomes lined with mansions, condominiums, and hotels. Tourism meshes with seasonal and year-round living in sweet intensity.

In all three counties, tourism grows in importance by how it interacts with the residential growth of once-neglected coastal towns. For even as newcomers settle in suburbs, suburbanites, albeit in fewer numbers, are moving back to the coasts and downtown. Despite Scripps, planners find this new urban appeal crucial in curbing sprawl. For a long time it was the images of tourism—of the never-ending vacation—that pulled people to suburban subdivisions. Now West Palm and Delray, the same as Fort Lauderdale and Miami, turn the resident-satisfying qualities of the urban tropics into images and diversions that satisfy visitors too. Instead of tourism driving residential choice, it's now residential choice driving tourism, and not just following hotels and attractions. The hotels were always there. Now it's relocating residents livening up the shore towns and drawing visitors to their places.

The coast isn't standing Florida on its head. After decades of misplaced priorities, the coast is standing Florida back on its feet. Scripps notwithstanding, residential living, tourism, and the economies that support both in their new urban forms will accelerate in shaping Florida's future and will determine what the state looks like.

Embellishments of Everyday Life

The Palm Beach County shore that not long ago was wilderness beach today flowers in cultivated beauty. Highway A1A borders the county with residential good taste, conspicuous in landscapes and architecture and in their aesthetic interplay with typically blue seas and sunshine. The homes are more luxurious than garish, the gardens sublime. Oaken canopies shade the road in many sections and surprisingly, given the region's wealth, in many sections the road lies open to the Atlantic. Especially far north and south along the sea, big beach parks afford public leisure. In turn, the style-setting shore inspires towns west across the waterway that serve as markets for barrier island residents to adapt in resourceful and popular ways.

Towns like Delray Beach and Lake Worth show their good taste in their storefronts, their street furniture and signage, inviting browsers and shoppers along their refashioned main streets. Especially in West Palm, early close-in suburbs that fell on hard times have come back. In Old Northwood, for example, first of these renewed residential districts, house restorers who pioneered the city's bed-and-breakfast sector led the renewal, so that tourists and locals directly mix in the neighborhood. In fact, recent tourists have become the largest source of buyers of the old houses, moving in and quickly accounting for the largest numbers in residence. Different from newcomers in subdivisions, they have become active players in shaping the urban scene. Much the same has happened in Delray, where a self-guiding "cultural loop" leads visitors through historic residential and downtown entertainment districts.

Everywhere, the mainland downtowns and the beaches locate within a mile or so of each other. Galleries and shops line connecting roads and bridges across the waterway are getting brightly repainted and potted with flowers. Walkways conveniently edge the water beneath the spans. Yachts glide by pocket parks where average families launch their motorboats for outings along this waterway where it's always cool, even in summer. The towns, their connecting roads to the beach, the waterway, and the shore drive attractively play off each other. Visitors enjoy themselves moving easily back and forth. That elusive feeling of Florida, so privatized behind suburban walls, admission gates, and hotel lobbies, emerges palpably here in the embellishments of everyday life. It inspirits a state of mind that yields to the tropics as much as it seeks to capture them. The woodlands once slashed for home sites are largely gone everywhere. Long ago the images turned golden. Natural Florida became golden Florida. Both still today impel the slogans that drive the suburbs, but one glimpse of the shore style leaves the inland version like fruit trees shorn of their mangoes and citrus. The mind leaps for Florida in its full fruiting, in the way it was and how in places along the shore favored by wealth or otherwise by care its glow continues. If no longer the natural paradise that so excited Flagler, instead there have emerged the cultivated waterfronts that frame his urban promise. Even Florida can't have it all, but where it's best cared for, it can inspire the look of cities not seen since Jacksonville's flowering more than a century ago.

This atmosphere of *dolce far niente* gives rise to sophisticated leisure, connecting today's worldliness with the times of Flagler and the twenties of architect–confidant-to-the-wealthy Addison Mizner. That historic sense of place significantly accounted for the majority that in 2004 voted to have the county borrow $50 million to keep marinas and waterfront property from conversion to condominiums. Pleasures remain influenced by the style of old money; by conserving, pre-Enron corporate ways; by a time when Palm Beach charity balls still influenced the social season; and by at-home parties that invite chatter about hair appointments and private schools, about the passing of style with the passing of C. Z. Guest, and about clients worth $100 million who insist on still driving their stodgy Buick Centurys.

West Palm Beach: Not Meant for Quality

Even as similar policies drive the three cities today, West Palm looks different from Fort Lauderdale and Miami when seen from its bridges across the waterway from Palm Beach. West Palm appears as much town as city. The entire waterfront south of downtown remains low-rise residential. Even with center city towers rising, downtown feels more at home with Old Florida than its counterpart cities south. Albeit diverse, West Palm is less polyglot and anonymous, less sleek than Fort Lauderdale, less cold and incomplete than Miami. Walk its streets lined with shops and café tables; ride its open-air, rubber-wheeled trolleys; watch joggers along the trail rimming Lake Worth; and the character feels agreeably unpressured. Only Sarasota on Florida's west coast compares with West Palm, each with its waterway road that curves along rising towers and its streets off their waterfronts narrowing to form passageways into their urban core, cities in fact but with their waterfronts and open-air aspects intimating leisure.

Flagler Drive sweeps broadly along Lake Worth and affords views of mansions and hotels to the east. Here is Currie Park with its Cracker house that serves as the Palm Beach Maritime Museum, the handsome lake trail with its royal palms and now-and-again pergolas, the Palm Beach Yacht Club. Shoreview residential and office towers span a century of undistinguished architecture, among the oldest buildings the forlorn Helen Wilkes Residential Hotel still in place though scheduled for removal as part of the city's ongoing retrieval from its poorly imagined recent past. Likely replacement are midrise garden townhouses and apartments characterized by recently retired development director Nancy Graham as distinct in "scale and symmetry, proportion and public space. It's all about long-term architectural character." The reach for the sky of downtown towers only contrasts with the open waterfront more highly valued than ever and its openness protected.

West Palm today has become the most closely watched center of new urbanism strategy in Florida. Yet until yesterday, downtown was a billion-dollar dream with a panhandler's odds. Call it the Flagler curse.

Flagler, who changed everything everywhere his rails reached, chose the site west across the waterway from Palm Beach for his society's servants. Hotel workers, butchers, mechanics—*over there.* Flagler arranged this soon after laborers at his Royal Poinciana Hotel in 1894 began bivouacking in an island encampment called the Styx. The story goes that one afternoon while workers and their families attended a circus performance that he sponsored on the mainland, Flagler burned their encampment down. He had new housing ready where, as it happens, they were already having such a good time. Even if the story is mere Flagler lore, the man did get his workers off the barrier island and over to town before his hotel opened. Palm Beach was reserved for resort ambitions.

Flagler did not plan for West Palm to become a quality place. One remaining early neighborhood is Pleasant City, on the wrong side of the tracks. A local resident lately reflected that, "If you were going to open a slave quarters across from Palm Beach, wouldn't you call it Pleasant City, too?" From that stigmatic start, downtown grew slowly before the booming twenties saw a few multistory buildings rise. A canal, a road west, and a second rail line through town—together, these helped open the county's western farm districts to coastal commerce and helped boost a port north of town in today's Riviera Beach, once prime, recently downtrodden, but attempting a comeback. West Palm Beach was becoming the hub of Palm Beach County.

Bust and boom followed. Then bust again as new roads and housing relocated retailing and chased younger populations to the suburbs in search of better lives. Pratt and Whitney and RCA offered high-paying postwar jobs at plants west of town. Land developers built subdivisions in drained swamp. As the city sprawled, downtown stood around with its hand out waiting for Palm Beach tips, a seasonal activity at best, nothing you needed a thriving downtown for. Downtown died. When a team of developers in the late eighties razed 77 acres of the center city for a massive rebuilding called Downtown/Uptown, West Palm's turnaround seemed assured again. Then litigation and the economy snarled the project. Much of downtown lay naked to the sun. And yet change happened.

Downtown today is sandwiched between more fat than the pickle on a Whopper. Fat City to the west has the economic clout of close-in Palm Beach International Airport and headquarters of the mammoth South Florida Water Management District. East across Lake Worth sits Palm Beach. Cultural and governmental institutions have added downtown appeal. The $60 million Raymond F. Kravis Center for the Performing Arts went up in 1992, followed soon after by the $124 million *nomenklatura*-style Palm Beach County Courthouse. The Norton Museum, the finest collecting art museum in the Southeast outside of Atlanta, carried out an almost $100 million dollar series of expansions that by 2003 made it the foremost museum in Florida. Downtown came new headquarters for Ballet Florida, the Palm Beach Horticultural Society, the Palm Beach Opera, the Historical Society of Palm Beach County; lately, for the Children's Theatre Co. and School, and for Voices of Pride, the Gay Men's Chorus of the Palm Beaches. The Alexander W. Dreyfoos School for the Arts opened for 1,100 students at the historic Twin Lakes School. Palm Beach Atlantic College on Lake Worth began expanding a 25-acre campus at the turn of the new century, educating more than 2,500 students a year. The historic Seaboard Air Line Railroad Station re-opened with its rococo facade restored and a wall of Flagler memorabilia. Tri-Rail began carrying commuters and sightseers from down the coast to town seven days a week. The new marina opened on Lake Worth and, with Currie Park to the north, became quickly popular with outdoors recreationists of all ages.

Downtown became easy to get in and out of and to get through. Lanes were added to I-95, which runs along the western edge of the core city less than 2 miles from Lake Worth. Okeechobee Boulevard, which rims downtown to the south (some ten lanes wide and desperately needing a monumental arch to announce its civic purpose) together with Quadrille Avenue, which rims it to the north, connect each with its own bridge across the waterway to Palm Beach. Only these same two streets cross Flagler Drive, which leaves the shore even easier to navigate by car and its shore trail safer to enjoy. Through the heart of town, Dixie and Olive Avenues move traffic one-way north and south. Okeechobee Boulevard and Clematis, downtown's main street, have been relandscaped and beautified. Palm Beach, which supplies all the vacation-style hotel rooms for the city except for the B&Bs, is a 5- to 15-minute drive away.

The Flowering of West Palm

In the 1990s, then-Mayor Nancy Graham strong-willed three huge confidence builders. She moved to make downtown more friendly to the city's diverse population by installing a free playground for kids. No one in Florida had dreamed of anything like this before. Her playground was a live water sculpture that randomly bubbles up behind the old library. She added free live music Thursday nights. For many families, the water playground became like a day at the beach, packed with kids laughing like gulls. Others came for the sheer animation and, while there, discovered downtown's attractions. Where locals gathered, tourists followed.

On New Year's Eve 1993 with thousands watching, Graham pressed the button that blew up a long vacant Holiday Inn. In its place, she built the Arthur Meyer Amphitheatre for waterfront concerts and dance performances.

And she hired Andres Duany and Elizabeth Plater-Zyberk to replan the West Palm core while browbeating doubters to see the transformation through. Radically for a Florida downtown (though predictably for Duany and Plater-Zyberk), DPZ favored human-scaled moves, enticing people downtown to live instead of pouring millions into incentives for business. DPZ had achieved enough credibility by the mid-nineties that word of their hiring solidified confidence for in-town developers and building rehabbers. Alert investors could anticipate that downtown, which seemed hopeless in the early nineties, would become a turnaround success.

Their confidence has been rewarded. "Downtown is the silver lining of what's happening in the county," says West Palm lawyer and historian Harvey Oyer, in his thirties and a leader in community affairs. "Turnaround has resulted from a lot of policy moves. Part of it is just the human nature convenience factor. People moved out of downtown when it was only a 10- to 15-minute drive back. Now that it's 45 minutes and you have large-scale redevelopment projects, blighted neighborhoods have been turned into fantasy land. There's a lot to bring people back downtown."

Since turnaround began, downtown vacancies dropped from 60 percent to 5 percent, momentarily having risen again as the newer downtown began competing with the older. Yet property values continue to rise more than 10 percent a year. Walk Clematis Street around the library from Flagler Drive and you find the charm and scale of a turn-of-the-last-century American main street, still low- to mid-scale with a mix of art deco and neoclassical buildings—the beaux arts standout, the ten-story Comeau Building. The look has been freshened with new awnings and with signs and fresh paint purchased at low-interest rates and from grants and loans by West Palm's Downtown Development Authority. The first 14 artist-painted benches have added color to the street. Jupiter native Burt Reynolds tried to make a go of the old movie theater near the library, but when he failed, a local car dealer stepped in to keep the professional stage working. Clematis became a restaurant row with places like Café Mazzarello's, E. R. Bradley's Saloon, My Martini, Pescatore Seafood and Oyster Bar, and the Underground Coffee Works. Here, too, among door fronts of long-standing, are Pioneer Linen and J. C. Harris Menswear, the thirties Club 35 Sunset, and, among the newer, the boutiques Chico's and Elite's and Clematis Street Books with its Internet Cafe catering to downtown's newcomers. These newcomers are moving into apartments and lofts that rent over the stores, although the future promises more of the towers rising on Datura and Evernia and other streets back off Flagler Drive. Three hundred units get snapped up in three days even before a sales center is complete. Another 3,000 highrise units are in construction. Promising, too, are places like The Flats on a block toward the old Pleasant City section where O'Shea's Pub and Sewall Hardware remain and where the interiors of old buildings are getting redone and their façades getting Palm Beach makeovers.

Already resurgent by the late nineties, downtown at the turn of the century attempted its most radical move and challenged every other renewing Florida city by developing its DPZ-favored new low-rise residential, retail, and arts district in a European-resort style (reminiscent of how Flagler worked; he disdained Europe but everywhere adapted its architectural styles). However, approval in 2005 for a 20-story condo in the district thwarted low-rise continuity. This part of the revived downtown forms on the 77-acre Downtown/Uptown wasteland that in the mid-eighties uprooted much of the Pleasant City community. The development is called CityPlace, and, different from suburban malls, it attaches to and supplies additional residential neighbors and their purchasing power to landmark buildings kept in place when everything else got torn down. Residents occupy two stories of townhouses and condominiums above the street-level shops. They were eager to move in. Here, all 88 units sold out within ten days after announced. Residents live in a virtual town of wide landscaped sidewalks with their attractive benches and low walls. Performance takes place at the easily walked-to Kravis Center and in an old church building saved after its congregation moved out that has become the architectural heart of the development. Townhouse and condo residents and others at the fully rented 502-unit skyscraper built as part of CityPlace next to the Kravis can ride the trolley to downtown jobs. They're five minutes by car from I-95. Across Okeechobee Road is the county's new convention center (still without a hotel in 2005, which has depressed early convention bookings).

CityPlace is handsomely designed in a Tuscan style and, as such, adapts the look of Palm Beach. In the same way that Palm Beachites prefer to invest in cultural facilities on the mainland rather than build on the island and have mainlanders flock there, they welcome the CityPlace shops that add to Worth Avenue offerings. They find Armani, Barnes and Noble, FAO Schwarz (a transplant from Worth Avenue), Macy's, Restoration Hardware, Williams Sonoma, exclusive shops plus movie theaters, a new gym, and highly favored South Florida restaurants. They stroll the beautiful walks, where shops stay open late—most conveniently after an evening of performance at the Kravis.

Today the space between CityPlace and the historic downtown along Clematis, which inevitably will become one downtown, hasn't filled yet. Vacant lots remain. FEC tracks run through with locomotives that whistle more at night than anyone trying to sleep nearby might wish. The tracks impose an aesthetic divide between downtown and CityPlace. Hastening change is the new ten-story 610 Clematis Building with flats and lofts newly at the corner of Rosemary. The building gentrifies the foot of the hill that leads to what remains of Pleasant City. Cyclists already take the curve in their morning Spandex. The old Hotel Alva that's across from 610 for now houses low-income folks, some with physical and mental infirmities, but who make their way unassisted around their neighborhood.

You have to like how Publix has moved to this neighborhood where no big parking lot surrounds its doors. It's a scaled-down Publix at the north side of CityPlace. It knows where it is. It puts produce up front, much of it organic, and carries better wines and beers. It hires in the neighborhood. Many of its staff walk to work. That makes the store doubly important to what's happening locally. For people newly drawn to the vicinity, the store feeds the exuberant state of mind that moving downtown promises. Nobody moves downtown without a sense of liberation from their cars and commutes. Without the store, you would still have to get back in the car almost day in, day out, for groceries. Publix locks the door on the car. You can walk, or you can pedal a bike and fill saddlebags. You can ride the trolley. The same trolley that carries sightseers through downtown also supplies practical transportation. It gives new meaning to the Publix slogan, "Where shopping is a pleasure." New impacts of meaning correspond with this new place to live.

On the same block as 610 Clematis is the downtown version of Hibiscus House Bed-and-Breakfast, the first of so far two downtown B&Bs and the only downtown places to stay. The B&B occupies a restored turn-of-the-last-century compound in a couple of blocks of historically conforming houses on the west side of Rosemary. Owners Raleigh Hill and Colin Rayner led the renewal of Old Northwood with their B&B of the same name there. Their addition here sits almost equidistant between CityPlace and the Clematis shops and restaurants—which is to say, almost equidistant between the downtown Starbucks and the one at CityPlace.

Between Clematis and CityPlace, downtown is becoming a seven-day-a-week, night-and-day place. Both districts stay open late weekends, and crowds can become disorderly. Underage teens hang around the movie theaters at CityPlace as if at a suburban mall. Different theories about what to do have seen the kids variously driven off and virtually escorted home. There was a late-night killing along Clematis a few years ago. "Nothing good happens after 2:00 in the morning," says Hill. But more important for the long haul, West Palm mayor Lois Frankel is committed to the urban mix without the mayhem. She is clear about developing "the dynamic of an urban city. It's part of this incredible and exciting mix. It's a diverse population and we have to figure out how we all live well together. This is not a dead area. We all feel this incredible potential. We're not yet nearly as urban as we're going to be."

A new city hall will open by mid-decade, and the view-blocking, inefficient library behind the water-fountain playground will be relocated to a long-closed big-box designer showcase. Relocation of the library to the heart of Clematis will complete its latest rebound while also opening views of Lake Worth to the street.

Palm Beach

Across Lake Worth, Palm Beach has long been associated to the outside world with celebrity and scandal, while to its residents it's the best place in the world to live. That anomaly dates from early on. The Flagler era was bathed in Victorian propriety. Flagler set a prudish standard, yet long before he arrived in Florida, Flagler wrote the book as the suborner of state legislatures during his years as partner with Standard Oil. Scandal in Palm Beach has been unceasing from the moment Flagler paid off Florida lawmakers to procure a divorce from his mentally ill wife so that at seventy-one he could make his paramour, a woman half his age, his third wife. Following Flagler came Paris Singer linked with Isadora Duncan, then Joe Kennedy and Gloria Swanson, JFK and Marilyn Monroe, Roxanne and Peter Pulitzer, then William Kennedy Smith, whose dalliances kept up with those of the senior Kennedys. Only in Palm Beach, where everything is for sale, could you find on the cover of *Palm Beach Society, The Social Pictorial,* the photo of a couple captioned, "The toast of the town. Internationally acclaimed romantic artist Shari Hatchette and her marketing attorney, Dan Bohlmann."

Yet Palm Beach is essentially a new urbanist town, a place where you can walk or bicycle to work, to shop, to restaurants, to galleries, bank or beach. Even if not many do, the town is easy to get around, and Townies are altogether at home. Women will shop without makeup at the Publix just over the Royal Palm Bridge from West Palm, a place where in winter servants of the rich mingle. Everyone shows up at Greene's Pharmacy, the breakfast hangout. It's not unusual for a garbage man to buy the car of a homeowner or the police to escort an inebriated socialite home without fuss. The population has stayed at around 9,000 for decades.

Attorney Gary Woodfield says the only thing that could get him to leave would be to become third-base coach of the Yankees. Banker David Scaff says he would accept a transfer "only before a great retirement and coming right back here. This is a very, very, very easy place to live and work. I never have to get up in the morning on the way to an early meeting and have to worry about traffic." He tells the story about how not long ago a young fellow doing summer work at the bank put himself in a large crate and shipped himself to the bank's warehouse—"The Trojan Horse caper, you know? He wasn't sure what he wanted to do but he made so much noise looking around that the police arrested him. He was from a pretty good family. The bank didn't want to make a fuss. He wasn't locked up."

Palm Beach is about architecture and its influence on a heavenly townscape. Facades are mainly Mediterranean, prominently the grand Breakers Hotel with its lyrical fountains and belvedere towers, and the lovely Brazilian Court. Whitehall, the Flagler mansion, a newly designated National Historic Landmark, dignifies the monumental beaux arts style. Bermuda-Georgian appears with its lovely pastel walls and the softly terraced white tiled roofs in many homes and at the Colony Hotel. Along A1A through town—perfectly scaled South County Road—city hall and its compound of municipal buildings occupy an island of yellow stucco facades with red barrel-tile roofs, complementing shops along the way, all aligned in operetta echelon. Lawns are manicured, and arbors shade leafy side streets. Grassy swards separate pedestrians from motorists. Fountains burble. Grilled gates ornament the way. Mailboxes efface their utility, hidden in shapely shrubs that embower sidewalks with flowers. Ornamental lampposts illuminate the pretty streets. No trashy lots disfigure the public way.

Canopied and sunny paths extend north along the island, a section where visitors rarely come because the road ends at Lake Worth Inlet and parking without a town tag is illegal. Cycling along the Lake Trail affords a better look. Side streets offer the more modest houses of Townies with their attractive gardens behind walls of high hedge. Houses here are more New England clapboard than high-minded Mizner copies.

But designs for living naturally in the tropics have largely vanished. Gone are new houses with porches and wide overhangs to catch and swirl breeze through rooms where as it cools it sweeps up heat whisked out ceiling vents, or friendly verandas for sitting outdoors and rocking away balmy winter evenings. Instead, money has weakened the town's resolve to preserve its heritage look. Razing and rebuilding have taken over. A developer builds a showplace home on a waterfront lot, lives in it a year, and sells it for $4.5 million. Along comes a trust company lawyer who buys the house and lot next door. He tears down the house and builds something double the size for double the money.

"Everybody's getting a little nervous," says social observer James Jennings Sheeran. "We have architectural commissions, but there are loopholes and money talks. The town is starting to change in imagery. A nice artistic home is just going to become another palace sooner or later." Hard for the town to resist. Real estate taxes provide the revenues this town runs on. Real estate is one of the few viable industries. There were lately 600 people selling land in Palm Beach. A million is now about the entry level for a new house. A Palm Beach house might easily yield $40,000 to $80,000 in taxes. The former home of Lois Pope, widow of the deceased publisher of the *National Enquirer,* was lately on the market after two expensive face lifts for $25 million.

Earthly Trace of the Empyrean

To the outsider intent on exploring along Highway A1A, these are all small discontents. South from Palm Beach, the road marks Florida's halcyon trace, Florida's necklace of pearls, Florida's route of dreams. From Palm Beach to Boca Raton, the 30 miles of shore road link the island resorts that, like the wrecks of treasure fleets and the booty of pirates buried only bare centuries before, burnish again the coast's legend of unimaginable wealth. If the glory years of the coastal highway were few, the towns have aged gracefully, and their legacy prevails. Location of A1A through Palm Beach County in the boom that swept Florida after the First World War set the look for what Florida vacationing became all about. To this day, condos seaward of the beach road remain the ultimate retirement. This road, so beautifully landscaped even after the storms of 2004 and poised along so much of its privileged passage beside the sparkling sea, proceeds as earthly trace of the empyrean.

The road traces the route, six score years ago, of the Barefoot Mailman, a mere letter carrier who became a cultural icon by walking the beach between the vicinity of Palm Beach, where rail and water transportation ended, and Miami. These beaches, today crowded with high-rises, paved and urbanized, were a frontier teeming with bear, panther, and gators, where Seminoles paddled their dugout canoes and vagabond beachcombers lurked. Institutional authority remained governed by tides and seasons, by storm and stars, not yet by the laws of men. Three Houses of Refuge along the way gave the mailman succor and the comfort of fellow humans. The journey was three days each way. Rowboats were secured to trees where inlets had to be crossed. The mailman collected food along his route: coconuts, turtle eggs, berries. He lit a fire at night and slept on the beach. He soaped down with an insect repellent that was barely effective and otherwise endured the sand fleas and mosquitoes, counting on sea breezes at least to keep the mosquitoes at bay.

The mailman accepted "passengers," folks who for one reason or another were traveling between Palm Beach and Miami but impatient about unscheduled schooners. Passengers were instructed in how to walk on the sand but often carried more gear than they could manage. To keep his schedule, the mailman frequently found himself taking up the extra load. Sometimes the excess gear was strung from a tree and left for the return trip. Sometimes it was abandoned. Passengers who began the trip fully clothed soon encountered temperatures that reached into the nineties under full sun, other times gale winds, other times tropical downpours. They rarely arrived as duded up as they set out. One mailman lost his life in service and is commemorated with a plaque along Highway A1A at Spanish River Park in Boca Raton.

Today on an early morning along the mailman's route, the pastel stucco facades of South County Road glow egg-yellow. Across Worth Avenue and past the Colony (one-time hangout of the Kennedys' Irish Mafia and of Roxanne Pulitzer), the road passes along a mansion row with its low canyons of high hedges and palms thickly grown together, the scape sculpted in gardeners' art, green privacy walls scaled yacht-wheelhouse high. Houses divide their entries between Main and Service. All, by the Palm Beach code, uniformly display barrel tile roofs. Side streets turn to the ocean road. Unexpectedly, telephone poles run along this ritzy row. The lines remain strung above ground.

The road swings sharply to the sea atop the dune that once nourished the now-eroded beach. Beyond the low wall shows only the Atlantic, where, dunked 80 feet deep, a 1965 Rolls Royce Silver Shadow rusts as an artificial reef. Upland rise the seafront mansions, their sentinel mirrors aligning protectively for Jaguars and still unbarnacled Silver Shadows entering onto the singular drive from garages larger than houses elsewhere. Grandest along this mansion row stands Mar-a-Lago, Spanish for sea-to-lake. Mar-a-Lago occupies both sides of a sweeping curve and with its 75-foot minaret tower high above the privacy wall evokes movie palace excess. Marjorie Merriweather Post built the property for $8 million just ahead of the 1927 real estate bust (it took five years to complete). Donald Trump owns it today (the quintessential deal-maker bought it six decades later for only $7 million), turning the estate into a private club. Meanwhile, along the flank of the great house, Highway 98 begins its cross-Florida meander (longest federal road in the state), while A1A resumes its southerly wend past the Bath and Tennis Club.

Where the seaside again for a mile captures the roadway, mansions announce their sites with names like Deux Horizons and Four Winds. Whereupon the road once more breaks from the shore around Sloan's Curve, the end of the remarkable stretch of single-family zoning. There follows a succession of mere yacht clubs, golf courses, private schools, mellow roadways beneath canopied casuarinas, a parade of royal palms and tunneling arbors of sea grapes. On Sunday mornings, the soft air stirs in the whirr of racing cyclists, swift in their pelotons. Coiffed joggers and power walkers parade along the sidewalk by pretty parks. Condos, still low and without flash through this southern section of Palm Beach, rise up their sloping lawns to the sea. Yachts tied to fluted bollards bob along the Intracoastal Waterway. Mansions line the canals. On the left in Phipps Ocean Park remains the Little Red Schoolhouse from 1886, the first schoolhouse in Dade County (from when Dade extended this far north), still with its pine floor, pine desks, little iron-based chairs, and row of sand buckets in case of fire. Palm Beach Golf Club extends its course to either side of the road.

Lake Worth (the town, not the waterway) surprises. It always was a more common place. It was formed a century ago with a large Finnish population that came to farm the western region. Farming was so promising at the time that as an inducement to settle, lots in town were given as premiums to buyers of Everglades land. Today Lake Worth chiefly attracts retirees. No surprise that everything is cheaper here than elsewhere around: gas, photocopies, sundries, overnights, restaurants. You could lately play a round of high-season golf at the Lake Worth municipal course for greens fees, including cart, under fifty dollars. Winter rooms along the Federal Highway motel row can be had for sixty dollars a night. Once a year you can do even better. The locally popular Farmer Girl Restaurant feeds the world free on Thanksgiving Day.

North-south Federal Highway has been landscaped through downtown, while east-west Lake Avenue, which connects to the beach, boasts its own new sidewalk and landscape treatments. Downtown feels small town, still with utilitarian stores but newly with trendy shops, galleries, and restaurants. Downtown claims two noteworthy arts institutions: the Palm Beach Institute of Contemporary Art and the Lake Worth Playhouse with its series of dance, music, stage presentations, and, newly, a gourmet seafood market. Nearest structure to a high-rise is the six-story Gulfstream, one of Florida's last pink stucco hotels. It's listed in the National Register of Historic Places and remains a favorite with vacationing Finns.

Over the bridge to the beach is the Lake Worth Casino. No gambling palace this—only a pavilion for waterfront sport. Surfers, beachgoers, and the merely indolent affordably hang out. Especially Sunday mornings, a patient line forms outside John G.'s, surely the most popular beach restaurant in Florida.

Regrettably, Lake Worth, the water body, is nowhere more polluted than in passing through Lake Worth, the town. A few years ago Mayor Tom Ramiccio (now head of the local chamber) took the "plunge against the grunge"—a swim to get the county to fight pollution in the waterway. When he came out of the water, Ramiccio reported earaches, headaches, and 103-degree fevers. He underwent CAT scans, an MRI, and a spinal tap. According to the Associated Press, Ramiccio's doctors told him his illnesses could only have resulted from "swimming in a toilet, being around rats or in a Third World country." For the last dozen years the Plunge Against the Grunge has become an annual event, most recently attracting 12 hardy swimmers who, after their bravado, are quickly hosed down. One month after the event in 2004, a city water system problem dumped 35,000 gallons of raw sewage into the ocean.

Below Lake Worth, A1A enters Manalapan. The hulk that overcrowds the road to seaside is the Ritz-Carlton, shamefully overbuilt on its site. Walled estates follow with yacht docks behind hedges along the waterway. Mansions and merely splendid houses parade across Lake Worth. Chateau Mer au Lac stands significantly lesser (though itself hardly unsplendid) than Mar-a-Lago up the road. Where the road swings invitingly back atop the dune one more time, high drifts of coppery sea grapes shape a sloping rise windward from the beach. Across Boynton Inlet, the road enters Ocean Ridge and again swings back from shore. The Ocean Club golf course extends west, villas and Beach Club east. The rich through these precincts of privilege lately scandalized the county by their fight against installing bike lanes during a slight widening of A1A while refusing even to discuss their own long encroachment upon the right of way. Averse to installing bike lanes, Manalapan residents (321) have installed pole-mounted cameras that snap pictures of motorists, their cars, and license plates for computer checks on criminality, which, if verified, alert police. Welcome just anybody on a bike? I should say not!

A1A continues along the waterway while Old A1A takes to the dune. The absence of traffic appeals to joggers along Old Ocean Boulevard. And then Briny Breezes. You won't fail to notice the difference. After the fleets of mansions, this wonderful old cheek-by-jowl mobile-home-park-of-a-town rests directly by the sea, a mere 0.4 square miles and noticeably left off the official map of the county's *Visitors Guide.* Today's town was still a dairy with milk cows and vegetables growing by the sea into the 1950s when the Miller family began accommodating trailers. The trailer people were looking for places to park, and the Millers typically said, "Sure, if you buy some strawberries and vegetables." That's how it began, with the trailers assigned 25-foot sites that eventually became permanent assignments when the newcomers in 1958 bought the dairy from the Millers and five years later incorporated their town.

The late Hugh David for more than thirty years was the only mayor Briny Breezes had had. Of the little town, he said: "It's great to walk your dog at night along the beach. Real friendly community. We formed the town to go ahead with our lifestyle. We'd had a lot of problems with the county about zoning in 1958. Over the years some people had the idea that maybe we weren't good enough. But we have our own sewerage system. We worked out a complete electrical distribution system with Florida Power and Light. We have town codes that fit our way of life the way we were, and we wanted to keep it that way."

If some still look down their noses at Briny Breezes, Briny Breezes is quick to disassociate itself from the adjacent oceanfront enclave of unincorporated county a few odd acres south with its row of what look like retired sailor shacks and their ramshackle yards full of gear and rusting vehicles, overgrown and unkempt. Definitely none of it on the *qui vive*. Instead, it has the mood of an old hippie haunt. West across the waterway from Briny Breezes is Boynton Beach, which years ago sold off its beachfront to Ocean Ridge, another posh A1A community. Ambitious revival of Boynton's long forlorn downtown comes along slowly.

Along the beach below Ocean Ridge, appearance of the St. Andrews Golf Club and the town of Gulf Stream heralds one more enclave of manicured privilege. The road passes beneath a canopy of palms and pines that filters afternoons gray-green. A grove of royal palms struts past, grenadiers in defense of Crown. Mizner's Gulfstream Club defines the seaside Mediterranean, whereupon a policeman in white gloves appears from a phalanx of lacy palms to halt traffic in both directions for the moment it takes a golfer to cross in her cart. In late afternoon light, the intensity of Florida's grip relaxed, one envisions golfers imagining fairways behind the bougainvillea-twined fencing as gentle hills and, beyond the hills, mountains peopled by kilted and burred Highlanders.

Delray Beach, Boca Raton, Jupiter

Entering Delray, a pedestrian way fronts the accessible beach that extends north and south of Atlantic Avenue, the town's main street. Where the commercial district gives way, the two lanes of narrow curving road feel surprisingly country. The road continues south through Highlands Beach and shorefront Boca Raton, crossing the inlet on a lovely angular bridge, and soon enters into Broward County.

Delray deserves time. Matched with West Palm in the county's new urban importance, Delray burst into public awareness in the early nineties after young blacks, frustrated by a lack of recreational opportunities, had marched onto the town beach long culturally off limits. Different from the reactions of a hundred towns elsewhere, the city didn't power-trip the insurgents. It seized the opportunity to breach the racial barrier and began asking how bad the situation was and what could improve it.

Better than any town elsewhere in Florida, Delray simply works. Its impulse to improve things rather than fight old battles has let it race ahead with innovation. Unusual cooperation across racial and monied lines has allowed the city to renew its downtown less by new buildings and more by renewing the sites cherished by longtime neighborhood residents. An overall vision coupled with neighborhood empowerment has let people work at projects they can handle with volunteer organizations and a next layer up of helpfully funded community redevelopment associations, Main Street programs, and chamber of commerce backing. All together have formed the Downtown Joint Venture, which has kept government sensitive to its base of strategic support. Twice in the decade since renewal began, Delray has been named an All-American City. That kind of recognition captures investment interest and keeps everyone on track.

A key move occurred in 1993 when the Downtown Joint Venture hired Marjorie Ferrer as its marketing director. With a background in department store merchandising and an unusual gift for making whole cloth out of scraps, Ferrer has not only steered the course to bring downtown back but has done so in a way that makes visitors, both well-off and aspiring, buy into the adjacent residential districts and feel good about living near each other. In all directions, people have relocated here from up and down the coast fixing up houses and entire neighborhoods to make Delray home. In one exhilarant move, immigrant field hands have moved east from the farms to buy homes in dilapidated sections, discovering the path of upward mobility.

Everywhere around South Florida and beyond, towns in doubt about whether their renewal is on track look to Delray for answers. Delray radiates with confidence that its town is exceptional. Of all the barriers the place has broken through, maybe most important has been the wall of doubt that engenders distrust of efforts at civic improvement and creates self-animating citizens.

When the town was called Linton (for a Detroit suburb) late in the nineteenth century, Delray was pineapple-growing country, though with prospects hard because of poor transportation. When Flagler opened up the south county with his railroad in 1895, he gave the farmers a future with more assured northern markets.

Prosperity early in the twentieth century swelled as Delray along with all of South Florida got caught up in the boom. The little farm town charmed celebrities. Silent movie star Marie Dressler was a favorite visitor during the time she was known as the "Queen of Boca." Cartoonists discovered Delray. Artists and feature writers from New York came. Pineapple Grove was winter home to many, including *Terry and the Pirates* originator Milton Caniff. Work of those artists is preserved in the restored Cason Cottage downtown.

Delray was as seasonal as Palm Beach. The place shut down after its brief winter fling. And when the suburbs pulled people west and the beaches pulled tourists east, downtown about died. Yet turnaround came quickly after the African American challenge. Atlantic Avenue, the main shopping street that connects the black and white neighborhoods, was refashioned with shade trees, brickwork, and bulbouts. Awnings went up on the fronts of most buildings. Tasteful roof lines were renewed. Attractive new government buildings and the Delray Beach Tennis Center were built in the overlap between the traditionally white and black sections as the way to begin renewal of the west side. In the past ten years, store vacancies have dropped from more than 30 percent to zero. Artistically painted Adirondack chairs dress up the street (inspiring West Palm's benches). Horses and buggies animate evenings. Now retailing has spread north up historic Pineapple Grove—entered through a festive 25-foot-high aluminum arch—and west where African Americans are opening shops.

Atlantic Avenue has become the city's social center. Smart restaurants with outside tables on widened, tree-trimmed sidewalks generate a party mood as tourists mix easily with locals. Blues and jazz clubs have opened. A pair of abandoned schools bustles again as the Old School Square cultural arts center. The Ocean City Lumber Company newly thrives as a compound of retail and arts shops. "Livable city?" says Fatimah NeJane, co-owner of Palm Beach Photographic, the site of an annual winter teach-in that pulls the biggest names in photography here. "I'd say lovable city."

This town of 50,000 that used to close for the long summer and where downtown emptied daily at 5:00 p.m. now draws suburbanites from up and down the coast all year and nightly stays open till 2:00 a.m. if not later. The place is small town with terrific urban energy.

In a sure sign of municipal self-confidence, officials negotiated an unprecedented commitment from state road authorities. The city allowed routing one-way traffic along a pair of streets to either side of Atlantic Avenue in return for keeping the avenue east of I-95 free from widening. The remarkable thing is how many drivers still choose to come through the shopping district even since it has been reduced to one lane each way. They love the look. And they don't bother anybody because they move so slowly. The old Colony Hotel, which hung in from the twenties in part by opening a beach club by the sea, still captains downtown with its rocking-chair porch at the corner of U.S. 1 and Atlantic Avenue. Retro chic has brought it new life. Before the end of 2005, city planners hope to have the first rubber-wheeled trolleys running loops that connect the Tri-Rail commuter rail station with all downtown places of interest.

Those farmhands upscaling their way east to downtown Delray also invoke the town's past. One relic of ag times endures in the remarkable Morikami Museum and Japanese Gardens. In 1904, a Japanese educated in New York returned to Japan to organize a model farming community in Florida. Abetted by Flagler's Model Land Company, a subsidiary of his railroad, this became the Yamato Colony. Though in time its families all left for opportunities elsewhere, one colonist remained. This was George Sukeji Morikami, who amassed 200 acres, which, on his death in the mid-seventies, he willed to the county and state. In 1977, the site was opened as a museum. Since then—considerably expanded with a park and trails and with programs, galleries, a theater, library, cafe and store—the site has become the most important center of Japanese culture in the eastern United States.

As if an echo of Morikami beauty, gardens have been graciously restored and expanded as part of the 2000 re-opening of Sundy House, almost 100 years after it was built by a Flagler railroad foreman. Sundy House is the finest Queen Anne gingerbread house in town; it is listed in the National Register and newly provides bed-and-breakfast suites, a restaurant, and meeting rooms.

Delray, incidentally, is the first place, as far as anyone knows, where McDonald's has given up its kids' playground and replaced it with a shuffleboard court. And it was a laughable no-brainer that punctuated the end of its bumpkin era when Delray just said no to a move by the Boca Raton Junior League to establish a homeless shelter—in Delray!

Boca Raton, far south in the county, and Jupiter, far north, both reward and disappoint in the same way, but Jupiter otherwise has a lot going for it. Boca has its ultra-chic Mizner Park, where, a year after the International Museum of Cartoon Art vacated in 2003, a deal was cut to bring in the Rouse Co. to install a museum of natural history and new bookstore. Mizner Park had modeled West Palm's CityPlace, but it has no downtown to connect to. The town has a honeyed attraction to the operators of glabrous sleaze. Boca's binge for bucks late in 2004 brought word of the most expensive oceanfront condos anywhere in the county with penthouses the size of mansions—21,000 square feet for $21 million. More down to earth, the city also announced a new 30-acre botanical gardens and conservatory in partnership with the county, a project inspired by the high visitor appeal of the Morikami in Delray and somewhat comparable sites in West Palm and Coral Gables. Jupiter, also without a downtown, has become the latest section of the big county to burst the gates of rational growth and rampantly chew up land to the west to satisfy developers with easy pickings. Both Jupiter and Boca have exceptional park systems. Addison Mizner's Boca Raton Hotel, which supplied the raison d'être for the town, still welcomes clients to its greatly expanded five-star domain, while Jupiter claims the New Town of Abacoa that could lose out to what next happens around the Scripps site, too far for Jupiter opportunity—unless of course Scripps chooses a site alongside Abacoa.

Early in the new century, after years of lusting for development, Jupiter under Mayor Karen Golonka newly seeks to "keep Jupiter green." Even though hurricanes Frances and Jeanne delivered big hits—especially along the city's beaches—citizens later the same year voted to tax themselves $17 million for land conservation. The city acquired 17-acre Lighthouse Park from the Federal Bureau of Land Management and right away approved spending $600,000 to start renovating the site's WWII barracks. A new 678-acre regional park will cost another $5 to $8 million for its first phase alone (though shared with the county, which owns a portion of the land for inclusion). This will be a rare new "back-to-nature" park without ballfields or other built recreational features. Despite intense pressure to rezone a 12-acre island for development, the city stuck to its green position and kept Fullerton Island in the Intracoastal Waterway strictly for the birds (and boaters who make their way over).

A Riverwalk on the south shore of the Loxahatchee River will collect the businesses and attractions that will at last create a downtown for Jupiter and a place other than the Loxahatchee River Historical Museum to celebrate the small city. It's a distinct history that includes the hub of Jeaga culture (whose name, corrupted, became Jupiter), the 1696 shipwreck of the Quaker Jonathan Dickinson five miles north of the river mouth, the building of Jupiter Light in 1860, the Civil War Battle of the Loxahatchee at the site of today's Riverbend Park, of the briefly operating "Celestial Railroad" that connected Jupiter, Juno, Venus, and Mars before being superseded by Flagler's modern line in the 1880s, and of notoriety as a "speed trap" in the 1920s.

The river itself—a nationally designated "wild and scenic river"—newly has the attention of a "friends" organization. None too soon. Drainage for development of the upper reaches of the 6.2-mile river have reduced water flow and allowed a wedge of saltwater to move upstream, altering the Loxahatchee's ecology. Development of the Scripps site at Mecca Farms would further drain the river's headwaters slough and otherwise pollute it. Entering 2005, the Loxahatchee River Preservation Initiative had $5 million on hand and was looking for more to remove sediment and exotic vegetation and for hydrological restoration.

Just south of Jupiter on Highway A1A is little Juno Beach, a half-century-old town of fewer than 3,000 (triple that number in winter) that becomes a center of turtle watching at its Marinelife Center each year between May and September. Further south nearing West Palm again come Singer Island and Riviera Beach. Singer Island, named for the sewing machine magnate and lover, today faces massive high-rise development along its beaches. Riviera Beach, a mostly mainland town on the Intracoastal long black and poor, is desperate for outside capital and willing to become whatever money will make it.

You travel the county ultimately left wondering whether getting it right remains any less of a dream today than ever.

11 BROWARD COUNTY

The Braking of Spring Break

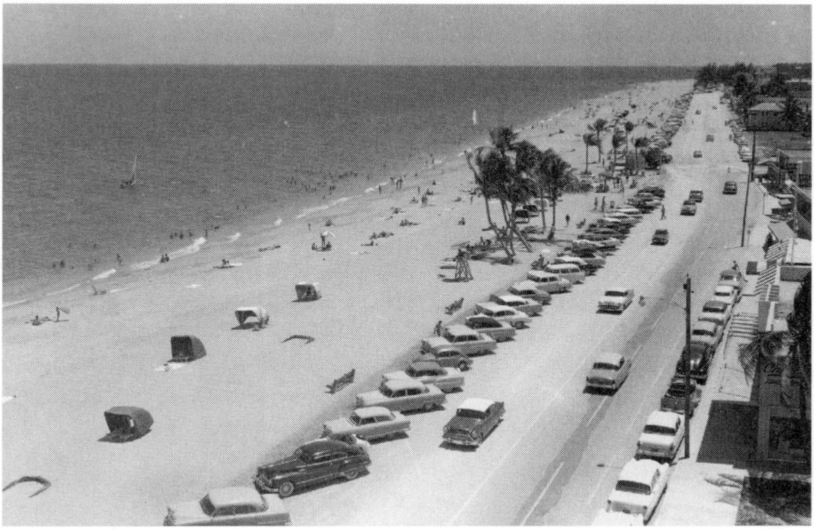

Figure 11.1. Highway A1A and 1955 Fort Lauderdale Beach. Courtesy of the Florida State Archives.

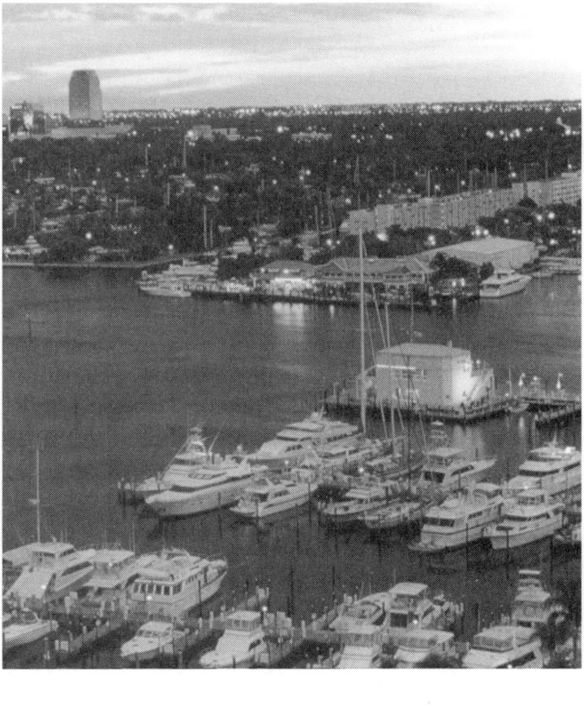

Figure 11.2. Ft. Lauderdale Harbor. Courtesy of the Greater Fort Lauderdale Convention & Visitors Bureau.

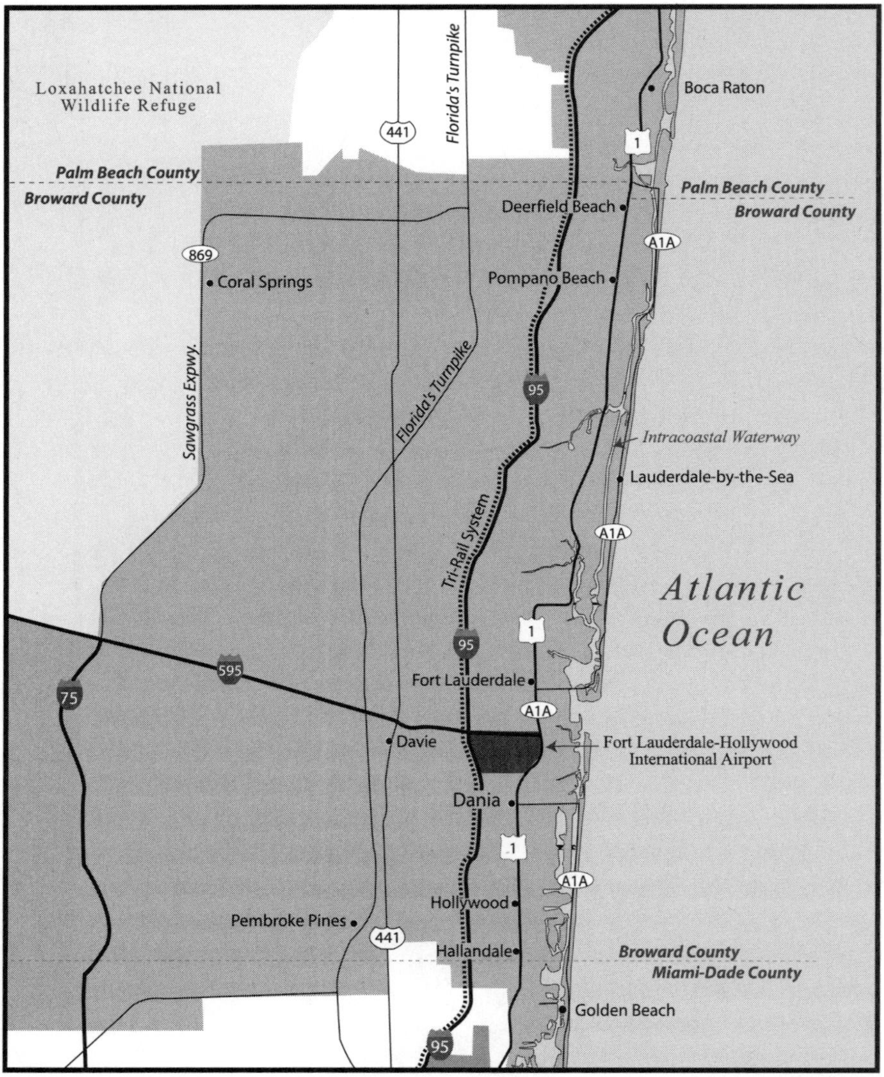

Map 11. Broward County

Like the backwash of the big wave that rolled west across Broward County in the late twentieth century, draining wetlands and paving the Everglades, Broward's frontier has newly shifted back east to the beach towns and the corridor between Highway A1A and Florida East Coast tracks where Broward began more than a century ago. Differently this time, activists from Pompano Beach to Hollywood challenge developers who—once in the name of "highest and best use" and today by wrapping themselves in the cloak of "smart growth"—seek to keep control of Broward politics. City and county commissioners who long kept developers in the driver's seat in return for favors are getting replaced by leaders from activist ranks who view citizens, instead of real estate interests, as their rightful constituents. This time the issues center less around sprawl—conservation at last is winning Broward's hearts and minds—but instead around how the rapid redevelopment of downtown and the beachfront is affecting residents already in place.

While the resurgence of Broward's urban east is refocusing investment away from the suburbs, the rapid turnaround has left residents already in downtown neighborhoods challenged by the new towers and traffic, their shadows and noise, and the rush to further quick change. It's a new field of gripes nobody expected.

Realignment in the triangular tension among developers, elected officials, and citizens has been a long time coming along Gold Coast counties, which wrote Florida's book on sprawl. But at last realignment is affecting the look and dynamic of the A1A coast in ways that suburbanites and visitors can easily grasp. The change is dazzling and the future hopeful even if the steak of renewal might ultimately not match its sizzle. No place poses these questions more sharply than Fort Lauderdale. Broward's premier city has become the most dynamic and, in many ways, the most desirable big city in Florida.

The Stand-Apart City

Though the city feels bigger and more inclusive, with 160,000 residents, it ranks not only behind the state's big five—Jacksonville, Miami, Tampa, St. Petersburg, and Orlando—but behind fast-growing, suburban Hialeah too. In Broward County itself, west-side developer towns, most of them with coming Latin majorities, are all growing faster. By 2010, Pembroke Pines, incorporated only in 1960, today with 150,000 residents and still a spatial blob, will have surpassed Fort Lauderdale, settled seventy-five years earlier. Southwest in the county, Miramar, with 100,000 people, is the third fastest growing in America with populations over 50,000.

Nonplaces notwithstanding, especially downtown, Fort Lauderdale's numbers swell with tourists and on-the-town suburbanites who—together with new downtown residents and neighborhood homeowners long in place—nightly turn the corridor along Las Olas Boulevard into the most sophisticated downtown in Florida. Ocean Drive in Miami Beach may draw more tourists and celebrity chasers, but South Beach lacks big-city feel, while everyplace else lacks Fort Lauderdale's downtown residential density. Nor does Fort Lauderdale close down at the end of the workday like other big Florida cities. Although government and office workers continue to commute between suburbs and downtown jobs, at least the well-off among them newly live where they work. Downtown isn't cheap, with rentals starting at $1,200 and few condos under $300,000. Cost notwithstanding, residential towers rise side by side with office towers faster than anywhere else in Florida. By 2005, new condo and rental units added more than 10,000 residents since the turn of the century. A new development in the approval process by itself would add between another 20,000 and 25,000 on 750 acres already assembled. It's a phenomenon no longer unique to Fort Lauderdale but most advanced here. Business and some city leaders want to double even these numbers.

Downtown claims aesthetic and leisure aspects unmatched by any big Florida city. It reaches for the sky, but it's compact. Views from the sleek towers throw open an urban aesthetic of a twinkling beachfront drive, yacht-lined canals, and the awesome tree cover. You can flaunt your Dolce & Gabbana or halter and shorts and, night by night, feel excited by how your own mood seems to reinvent this city. Mornings, you can quick-walk or jog to the beach in minutes or push open the back lobby door to the traffic-free trail alongside one of the most beautiful urban streams in America. By car, it's a straight drive west to the Everglades. The world flocks in from an airport that's virtually downtown. The big luxury cruise port is minutes away. Cosmopolitan cultural facilities are as much tied to downtown as the towers. So are chic shopping, restaurants, and watering holes. The Water Taxi gets around to most of it, with its promise that the end of a romantic ride isn't necessarily the end of a night.

Northwest of downtown lies a historic African American neighborhood in 2003 newly knit together by the opening of an art-full research library that supplies exceptional ethnic resources. A multiyear infusion of $250 million into the area has begun to groom a larger resident middle class. Beyond lies the edge city of Cypress Creek where, before the revival of downtown that began in the eighties, companies fled decay to form a suburb of office buildings and business hotels. Still today, the 14-square-mile district that was a cow pasture less than forty years ago supplies 1.5 million square feet more office space than downtown. But streets of the district empty into a techno-wasteland at night in the way that downtowns no longer do.

West extends one of the most massive suburban development incentives in America, elevated I-595 with its corridor wide enough to land jumbo jets. Only 15 miles end to end, this traffic speedway includes 310 miles of driving lanes, ninety-three bridges, three four-level interchanges, and eleven two- or three-level interchanges. By itself, the system of connectors between I-595 and I-95 encompasses an extraordinary 3 miles. At $119 million, this section alone was the biggest road-building project ever completed in Florida. In the first years after its mid-nineties completion, the highway was estimated to have generated more than 2,000 acres of commercial development, nine major business parks, 12 million square feet of office space, 160,000 new jobs, and an overall financial stimulus of more than $3.7 billion. When opened, I-595 reduced the drive between western suburbs and downtown from an hour to twenty minutes. With the new housing and development spurred by the highway, drive time predictably has reached an hour again.

By contrast, downtown seems sprung loose outside the box, a different idea of what good living is about, driven not by cheap land but by aesthetics and regard for place. It's too simple to conclude that, for Florida, downtown validates the mantra of "build it and they will come," or that when "they come" they will find a fully thought-out alternative to suburbia. But other Florida cities have faced much the same challenge and opportunity and, except for Delray Beach and West Palm Beach, no other big city learned its lesson faster and planned better. Even though Broward County government remained committed to filling every last green space with housing, and even while Fort Lauderdale city officeholders dragged their feet, aroused business leaders took charge. They not only dimmed the lodestar of suburbia. They also pried loose the chokehold that hoteliers had over tourism. In a sweep of vision unmatched anywhere in Florida, Fort Lauderdale took hold of its downtown and, even if imperfectly, changed the course not only of the city but also of the entire county and all east coast Florida.

Fort Lauderdale's twenty-first-century reemergence represents a profound change in county culture. An 1880 census revealed that what constitutes Broward today was altogether empty of people. That emptiness carried over from a notorious incident almost fifty years before.

How It Happened

In 1836, Seminoles killed a settler family in reprisal for a judicial act against them. The army weighed in, led by a Major William Lauderdale, whose legacy was the name given to the first of three successive forts at the site of what became the city. For a long time after, settlers who might have come to the New River instead settled south along the Miami River and north along Lake Worth.

Change came quickly when a road was hacked through the bush in 1892 between Lantana (in today's Palm Beach County) and Lemon City, 5 miles north of today's downtown Miami. That road ended the service of the Barefoot Mailman, who had carried the mail from one end of what was then big Dade County to the other, walking his way along the beach and into Florida legend. Henry Flagler brought his railroad through Fort Lauderdale four years later on the way to Miami.

In the biggest east coast city where someone figured larger than Flagler, Frank Stranahan came to the New River in 1893 to take charge of a frontier compound. For three years the New River Camp served as an exotic outpost in barely cleared Florida wilderness. Seminoles who canoed downstream to trade their egret plumes and gator hides for cloth and gunshot found Stranahan a sympathetic frontiersman. From his first night by the river, Seminoles camped on the grounds with him. His wife, Ivy, for most of her long life instructed Seminole children and parents in the culture of the whites. Famous adventurers came to hunt and fish at the camp, including President Grover Cleveland, Admiral George Dewey, and actor Joseph Jefferson.

Exoticism gave way to civilization when Flagler's railroad arrived in 1896. For two months before completion of the railroad bridge across the river, the tiny settlement became the train's southern terminus. This would have been the place for a hotel except that Flagler figured Fort Lauderdale as a place for growing crops instead of hosting his society guests.

In 1901, Stranahan built his new store and house where he and his wife lived out their lives. What began as a simple rectangular structure with narrow windows over the years became a handsome tropical house, where Seminoles now slept off the ground. Stranahan became postmaster, banker, and civic leader. Yet, if forever identified with the early years of Fort Lauderdale, Stranahan also stands for the tragic fall of his city and of Florida from innocence.

As the city grew and for many newcomers became merely a frontier for getting rich quick, Stranahan rued the progress he could not control. The Florida bust after the boom, worsened by hurricanes and national economic depression, caused the failure of Stranahan's Fort Lauderdale Bank and Trust Company. He became depressed as much by the tragic fate of Florida as by the loss of the savings of friends who had trusted him and for which he felt personally responsible. In 1929, he anchored himself to weights, jumped into the river, and drowned. His widow lived on another forty-two years.

For all his influence, Stranahan couldn't make Fort Lauderdale get up and even slowly go. Even by 1910, fourteen years after the railroad arrived, only 143 people lived in the city. After boom, bust, two wars, and recovery, in 1950 the county population was only 36,000. A half century later, the county topped 1.6 million. Fort Lauderdale never had Palm Beach swank. It never had that lock on the New York winter market that filled Miami Beach. Promoters today like to say that ever since they overcame spring break, the city has regained international stature.

Fort Lauderdale never had international stature. Broward was pasty and bland. It was racist and anti-Semitic. It indulged gambling and official head cracking covered up by a corrupt sheriff's department. The city was narrowly turned in on its own Midwest-spawned political isolationism and its don't-

Figure 11.3. Hollywood Beach. Courtesy of the Greater Fort Lauderdale Convention & Visitors Bureau.

lower-the-moat-plank resort style. The city never participated in forties urban renewal programs. "The rest of the world was tearing down slums, even if they were putting up godawful places," says former Downtown Development Authority director and urban advocate Frank Schnidman. "Fort Lauderdale thought urban renewal was a Communist plot."

Broward's suburban sprawl beginning in the fifties was heavily supported by escapists from integration, later by escapists from the Latinizing of Miami, then from the aftermath of Hurricane Andrew. Families not privileged to live on the ocean began exiling themselves west, taking with them their political demand for services and their taxable incomes that got them most of what they wanted. The lush lawns that flaunted their lifestyles required fertilizers and pesticides that polluted the sources of water they relied on, and they used more water than people anywhere else in Florida, a record 800 gallons per person per day, mostly for growing grass. At public expense, the South Florida Water Management District bailed out the developers who built their subdivisions in wetlands, installing massive pumps to remove floodwaters before neighborhoods drowned and spilling the "excess" into the Everglades, which the same water managers were charged with protecting and restoring. Sprawl raged and only now slows because the county has run out of land to pave over.

Sucked into the vacuum of white flight from the coast, snowbirds swarmed in retirement plumage. They wanted to know from nothing. They saw palm trees and water everywhere and figured this was paradise. Like suburbanites to the west, they couldn't imagine limits to the water they used nor limits to anything else. They became the largest population in Florida that had never driven cars up North, and as a gift to the developers who kept them coming, the city abandoned parking requirements. Of course, even nondrivers quickly find they can't live without cars in spread-out Florida cities. The retirees who flocked in to the wall of high-rises that shot up along the Galt Ocean Mile just north of Fort Lauderdale's central beach district could stack themselves high and comfortable in their air conditioning, but in their cars at ground level they hugely complicated traffic. They were numerous and they were tax-resistant, unwilling to help pay for the problems they created. Old neighborhoods and downtown declined. And more was at work ruffling Fort Lauderdale's calm.

Spring Break

Beginning in 1960 after the Connie Francis movie version of *Where The Boys Are* (the movie premiered at Fort Lauderdale's Gateway Theater, which still shows flicks), vacationing here became increasingly marked by the ritualistic acting out of college kids. A weak downtown business community bought the pitch of beachfront hoteliers that a highly dependable eight weeks of peak-dollar business each spring was better than most resort economies could hope for. It was a time when most adults traveled to warm weather destinations to give their brains a rest. Hoteliers and airline marketing people were supposed to know more about what tourists wanted than anyone. They controlled Florida destiny. In Fort Lauderdale, the hoteliers were mostly mom and pops who had invested their life savings in looking after tourists. Hundreds of them had gone into the business.

Because of Flagler, Fort Lauderdale never had grand hotels. The city had a mid-America reputation as the most white-bread of all Florida's resorts. (For years it was derided as Fort Liquordale.) Spring break was the antithesis of the city's lifestyle, but the mom and pops that made money from it were politically influential. The rest of town tolerated spring break as long as confined to the beach. Then in 1985, almost 400,000 kids came. They overflowed the beach hotels and acted up along the I-95 business corridor and downtown. Spring break, which had already become a substantial image problem, left the city reeling out of control. The beach row itself had gone terribly stale. It hadn't changed for twenty years. As its hotels and motels turned increasingly shabby, the city began losing affluent winter trade. Visitors stopped coming even during the many months that the kids were gone because headlines about teen drunks swan-diving off motel balconies and pervasive debauchery stuck in their minds.

Well before media were headlining Fort Lauderdale as an uninhibited playground, the city's conservative residents had grown disenchanted by high crime rates and the low quality of schools, conditions they largely blamed on racial integration. The old business district along Brickell Avenue was dying. Skin flicks moved into the empty storefronts. Immediately west of downtown, historic Himmarshee (today an arts and entertainment district) became a drug zone. Vagrants holed up in empty buildings risked all of downtown by setting fires to keep warm on cold nights. City dwellers that remained pulled their kids out of public schools. Others left Broward altogether, heading north to Vero Beach and across the state to Naples.

By the time the townspeople began asking what to do about spring break, they were already questioning the entire purpose of their city. They resolved to make theirs the best of its size by 1994. They chose to redevelop it in the first instance for themselves rather than for tourists or retirees. The city had an airport, a seaport, a diversified economy with agricultural lands to the west, clean industry, tourism, construction, some knowledge-based companies. The visionaries moved in two directions.

One, because the city was well situated between Palm Beach and Miami with three major airports within forty minutes, they saw they could attract CEOs of small high-tech companies who could relocate anywhere—and who increasingly brought their companies to where they themselves wanted to live. Two, they saw that different from Miami and Miami Beach (and different from West Palm Beach and Palm Beach), Fort Lauderdale and its beach were one and the same municipality. The same group of people could make things happen in both places. Downtown also had a different base from neighboring big cities.

Visions of the City

Fort Lauderdale didn't have a surplus of old buildings that had to be rehabbed, like West Palm. A few were knocked down. In their place, civic-minded developer Terry Stiles built the New River Center with its prime tenant the city's daily newspaper, the *Sun-Sentinel.* Stiles and Blockbuster founder Wayne Huizenga led the way to renewal. Huizenga rehabbed an entire block for his corporate headquarters while Stiles kept building. Sun Bank (now SunTrust) built a quality tower. Government made its own moves. In 1984, the county had already passed a bond issue to relocate government services downtown. That brought the lawyers downtown and grants for upgrading utilities.

Bill Farkas, for thirteen years the visionary director of the Downtown Development Authority, instructed business leaders that downtown renewal needed more than just office buildings and, incidentally, stores. Farkas, who went on to launch the Broward Center for the Performing Arts, recalls how his "bosses were really hot on office buildings." He had to convince them that office buildings wouldn't generate downtown excitement. People were more important, and people needed museums, a performing arts center, libraries, and public spaces. And they didn't need tourism, certainly not to begin with. "If we did it right," Farkas remembers telling them, "the tourists would find it. Indeed, it had to be a downtown for all the people, not just for the property owners."

Downtown came back to life with its cultural institutions intact, renewed and added to. Art, dance, theater, science, and learning became the elements of a virtual cultural theme park. With its capacity to attract people at leisure and enhance the setting for people at work, downtown became livable. That's when the new moves would be made to bring people back downtown to live. Downtown already had three neighborhoods that were walking close—Rio Vista, Colee Hammock, and Victoria Park. Posh canal districts extended east off Las Olas Boulevard toward the beach, while Sailboat Bend just west and Progresso just north were both renewable. By getting everything else in place, residential would become that much more desirable when the demand seemed ready for downtown towers.

In 1986, by two-to-one vote, the city approved a $42 million bond issue. The county came up with an additional $52 million for the Broward Center for the Performing Arts. That bulked up more than $90 million to make things happen. Buoyed by take-charge momentum, the city decided it would no longer tolerate spring break. Former city manager Laura Ward recalls a group of "true believers" who made the connection between the city the year-round residents wanted for themselves and the decision to get rid of the debauching kids. "We saw that government had to become pro-active and visionary. We knew what we had to do would be very controversial. People said we could never turn the beach around."

The right moves were ultimately simple, even if controversial and resisted by some hoteliers. The city stopped advertising in college papers to attract the kids. Law enforcement tightened on those who came anyway. The city laid out its plan for revitalizing the beach and timed its renewal to downtown changes. It set out to attract new, more affluent, more international markets, their visits more spread throughout the year, visitors who would want what the city was putting in place for itself and who would motivate beach property owners to upgrade hotels and stores. The wholesale change that was set in motion was far more risky than government, working with business, typically takes on all at once. It was one of those moments that happen when, frustrated and angry, people of conviction do something different.

Today, Riverwalk and the beach promenade have become the two great complementing public works achievements of the city, the signature traces of its civic inspiration. The performing arts center anchors Riverwalk to the west, followed to the east by the revitalized Himmarshee Riverwalk Arts and Entertainment District with its hip saloons and coffee shops, the Museum of Discovery and Science, and adjacent Old Fort Lauderdale, a historic compound behind a glorious arch of museums, a research center, and a fine waterfront restaurant. Adjacent is the Esplanade, an outdoor educational and freeform grassy space with exhibits that position Fort Lauderdale in terms of climate, global navigation, and the heavens. Plaques around the Esplanade honor centuries of scientists.

Riverwalk climbs over Flagler's tracks in a newly landscaped crossing. When freight trains approach the river and the rail bridge comes down, the motion suggests kinetic art because the arts sensibility is so well established through this part of town. East along the river comes Las Olas Riverfront, a recent entertainment quarter of Hollywood-shtick design that was both ahead of its time and misfigured in a city striving for some less hokey look, in 2002 losing its cinema complex that will become new riverfront condominiums. Across Andrews Avenue is the Fort Lauderdale Museum of Art and, at the northeast edge of downtown, the Marcel Breuer–designed public library, the most culturally comprehensive and user-friendly library in Florida.

Next to the east rise are the new towers, modern in their curvy facades yet light on glitz. This is Fort Lauderdale, not Miami Beach. The look is evolved, reflecting an aesthetic catch-up that adds to the city's cosmopolitan feel, linked to world capitals instead of connected with the second-rate aesthetic earlier imported from the North with its big-city tenement look and façade features that never escaped the vapid boxiness that long had marked Florida downtowns. These new towers rise up to forty-two stories on their way to fifty and more and reflect rare cooperation among developers to maximize views for residents in adjoining buildings. Nightly, new downtowners fill the al fresco wine bars and restaurants along the towers' street levels.

All through downtown, the tropically landscaped, brick-lined Riverwalk wraps around the shore of the New River. Charter boats dock at marinas among fleets of white-hulled yachts, while the walk itself winds beneath a canopy of coconut palms. Water Taxi shelters supply attractive seating under pyramidal roofs. Office workers come on breaks and for lunch. Squirrels spring their nervous energy everywhere. Huizenga Plaza, formerly Bubier Park, a long open space, is a popular site of street festivals. Come when a gaggle of schoolchildren with their lunch bags scampers past the Heritage Oak and you feel swept away by the contribution of this revived riverfront for renewing its city. Children come from the new elementary school in Victoria Park just east of downtown, the first elementary school opened in downtown since anyone can remember. The park will soon boast an amphitheater and new lighting. Meanwhile Florida Atlantic University is expanding its downtown campus. Students already mingle year-round with residents. It's a far cry from the uncivil regime of spring break.

The Andrews Avenue Bridge has been fitted on both sides with architecturally attractive stair towers so that crossing the river from one side to the other has become convenient. The tender's house of the Third Avenue Bridge is embedded with miniature paintings of the city's history. On the south side, the Riverwalk is less developed, so far an informal walkway with more parking and convenience for cars than for people. Government offices cluster one block south in a hodgepodge district. A new public sculpture park adds character. Major change will occur when residential towers rise here, too. A third major river crossing is by tunnel—the only one in Florida—that carries the Federal Highway under the New River beneath Stranahan House.

East beyond Stranahan come the upscale shops and the restaurant row of Las Olas. This is one of Florida's most beautiful shopping streets, attractive for its facades and for its landscaped median of tall trees that reach the same height as the mainly two-story buildings to either side. In recent years, the boulevard has blossomed with the sidewalk tables of popular restaurants—among these Mark's Las Olas, Le Cafe de Paris, Japanese Village, Mangos, Jacksons 450, and on the east side of Himmarshee Canal, the hoi polloi Floridian. The whole city seems to hang out at "The Flo" with the morning paper over deli-style breakfasts. Evenings, the two lanes of traffic in either direction get reduced to one, the curb lanes reserved for parking. The street feels like Christmas every night of the year. It's a civic gift.

Shops include chic men's and women's boutiques, antique stores with investment-quality work. Galleries showcase contemporary and traditional art from native America, Africa, the Caribbean and antique maps, wood engravings, and eighteenth- and nineteenth-century prints, china, crystal, jewelry, and heirloom baby wear.

Some of what goes up is less than ideal. Ironic that the expanded Riverside Hotel shows the worst aesthetic, a stack of clumsy boxes added atop the hotel that dates from the thirties and has long held on as action moved to the beach and the interstate. The Wells family, which owns the hotel and most of the property along both sides of downtown Las Olas, has been one of downtown's champions, getting merchants to stay open evenings and making the street part of the neighborhood by sidewalk widening and the traffic narrowing that allowed the installation of outdoor restaurant tables.

For newly elected city commissioners in Fort Lauderdale's political revolt of 2003, the rapid appearance of towers everywhere became the dominant issue. In one egregious in-town case, at the Waverly all setbacks were waived and the building throws shadows on homes in Victoria Park. Voters were worried, too, about the transportation impacts of all the new downtown dwellers. Many voters felt that downtown was turning too fast toward an overly dense, unvaried, paved-over district, and that control once more was in the hands of developers. Residents have repeatedly condemned plans for a monumental tower that would replace a now-closed supermarket in the heart of downtown directly behind Stranahan House. The house in 1984 had been acquired jointly by the Fort Lauderdale Board of Realtors and the Fort Lauderdale Historical Society and restored to its 1913–15 look. As if inspired by this protection of the city's numinous landmark, Fort Lauderdale in 2000 voted to tax itself to acquire the supermarket site and turn it into a park. All to no avail. The developer would not back down. Forty-two stories will rise.

Commitment to the park got Cindy Hutchinson elected to the city commission as part of a livability campaign in the voter revolt of 2003. "We've gotta have a more viable life force downtown," Hutchinson says. "I'm not crazy about the height of the new buildings, but it's a fact. We're getting better sidewalks. Now we need more pedestrian-friendly intersections. We need to build for people, not for cars. We need to force the issue and move people out of their cars. We need pocket parks, movies. The thought of density brings hair up on people's necks, but people are going to keep moving to Broward. Transit has to be part of our planning and connect with the single-family neighborhoods too."

Chris Wren, director of the city's Downtown Development Authority, agrees. He looks for more of a "live, work, and play downtown. We need additional lighting and have to find the open space." He looks for more niche uses that he says will develop when new downtown residents start looking for ways to spend the $12 million a month in disposable income they're expected to bring. "Who knows what will come out of retailer imagination? We want shoe stores, dry cleaners, more delis. We need to enhance the walkable environment of the community."

For Wren and Hutchinson, transit can't come too soon. Wren's DDA is working on a transit master plan that by 2008 would install the first of twin loops of ground-level light rail, the second by 2010. Another idea calls for a connection with Tri-Rail, the Gold Coast commuter system that links northern Palm Beach County with Miami International Airport. Another looks to renew passenger service along the FEC tracks that run closer to downtown through the Arts and Entertainment District. An existing but sporadically operating trolley hasn't helped much.

The Renewed Beach

Where Las Olas ends at the beach, the wonder is how beautifully the change has worked out—even that it was attempted. Even the crummiest beach strips in Florida attract throngs. What so sets Fort Lauderdale apart is that the people in charge reimagined their beach so well. Nature provided the beach and sea that everybody comes for. Landscape architects provided a new sculptural expression of the childlike happiness we all feel approaching any vacation shore.

The new look was created by EDSA (they pronounce each letter separately: E-D-S-A), the firm of Edward Durrell Stone Jr., internationally known for its landscape architecture. The same firm was responsible for the downtown Riverwalk. These are Fort Lauderdale people. They understood the challenge of satisfying a new civic regime while bringing business back for hoteliers who feared themselves ruined by the demise of spring break.

The most visible part of EDSA's work is the wave wall, an undulant border between a brick promenade and the beach itself. The two-foot height of the wall invites sitting and swinging your feet if you're a child or watching the world parade by in its endless next-to-nothing fashions. The wall is sculptural, flowing. Where each side street reaches the beach road, the wall yields to scrolled portals with a look that suggests the twirled tops of soft-serve frozen yogurt. At night, a tube of fiber-optic light sizzles in fuchsia, orange, and turquoise. Paired lamps top ornamental stanchions. Widened sidewalks on the upland side of the beach road accommodate sidewalk cafes. Their umbrellas with adverts for the new crop of Beaujolais suggest a Mediterranean *corniche.*

Colonies of cowled beach chairs cluster the beach, as they have forever. The beach is broad, the sea edge beautifully uninterrupted for miles. Typically on the horizon stand three or four large ships waiting to enter Port Everglades. The channel enters the port just below the posh resorts and the high-rise condos that fill in where the beach road turns inland at Seventeenth Street, just below Las Olas Boulevard and the big Bahia Mar Yacht Basin. The basin, which the city acquired from the Coast Guard after World War II, hosts the city's biggest economic event, the annual Fort Lauderdale International Boat Show, largest in the world. Boating has become the city's biggest industry, surpassing tourism in wages, employing 110,000 people with an economic impact nearing $9 billion.

If EDSA's wave wall establishes the new aesthetic, their handling of traffic along this road, which is Highway A1A, locally called Beach Boulevard, equally shapes the character of this beachfront today. Hotels never closed off the central beach. They were always on the upland side and the beach was open. But traffic overwhelmed the scene. Cars passed in both directions, two lanes each way and sometimes with a turn lane. The scene verged on a dodge-'em course. Though everybody actually using the beach was on foot—there might be thousands within any two-block area—everybody had to be ready to jump out of the way. Cars were angle-parked beside the beach and you had to cross six and seven lanes of moving traffic and parked cars from the other side to get to it. The road is now three lanes, one for parallel parking, but parking displaced by the new arrangement is harder to find than ever, spilling into the residential districts between the beach and the Intracoastal.

Both traffic lanes today flow northbound. For a mile and a half, EDSA rerouted southbound traffic a block to the west. They gently curved the two northbound lanes, complementing the wave wall for motorists, who now feel like they're moving on automatic. Unfortunately, the look isn't matched by hotels on the west side. A pair of big new residential-resort properties may challenge the torpid aesthetic. (A half dozen are going up altogether.) But the biggest recent addition, Beach Place, bulked up an unimaginative pink stucco, deco-influenced entertainment and retail hub with a Marriott hugely rising behind it. The site is architecturally pinched, boxy, and unresponsive to the wave wall that its leisure spaces look onto. North where the beach road swings inland, the look is worse. Regrettably, it's hardly better anywhere along the shore from Pompano Beach south to Hallandale. The high-rises are mean-spirited. They cast shadows across the beach and violate a sense of belonging that longtime residents have felt about their places. One immense pair of towers called the Palms, finished in 2000 between the open beach and Galt Ocean Mile, rises 450 feet in a garish, bulky pink affront. Artist Miranda Lopez, who has lived for thirty years on the west side in a two-story residential neighborhood, calls it "Gestapo architecture, the future of totalitarianism, of alien domination. The feeling you get swimming along that section of beach is that the buildings are falling over you. They overwhelm. People have stopped using that section as if in psychic protest against the abomination. The condo owners use their pool."

The casual resort scene and the aftermath of spring break seem to have influenced a casual social standard because the city's leisure style is anything but conventional. The city likes its leisure drugs. One measure: three-quarters of all arrested males test positive for marijuana, cocaine, or whatever else is on the market. It's a swingers' town, too, a place the *Miami Herald* called "Broward Gomorrah," where at some clubs, couples looking for new partners for the evening find condoms served with martinis. Broward was the only county to support casino gambling when Florida voters last retested the issue. The city has also become one of the most gay- and lesbian-friendly in Florida and one of the most diverse. Gay communities flourish in the tony Victoria Park district and in adjacent Wilton Manors, which a gay mayor has led for years.

Despite the lackluster architecture, drive along the beach, have in mind the reemergence of downtown, and this beachfront suddenly stands out not just as the resort world but as part of the everyday city of real people. What we tend to think of as two very different parts of a city—the business areas and the recreational places—in Fort Lauderdale come across as all part of one city meant for daily living. From chic lodgings along the Intracoastal, the tall buildings downtown and beyond to the west evoke a youthful downtown, cleanly erect on some adolescent morning, a workaday world the beachfront seems perpetually on vacation from. Palm groves and yacht masts surround barely visible mansions. Winters, at sunset, orange glow shimmers the water. Often as not, visitors delight in unexpected mild shivers. At night, yachts purring along waterways suggest the stealthy moves of wealth playing its unseen hand.

Pompano Beach Rebels

Pompano Beach and Hollywood, by contrast, live in an era of old-style aesthetics, though they are marked by new activism. Both are more mom-and-pop than Fort Lauderdale; both offer more humble appeals. If Fort Lauderdale is topsider casual, Pompano and Hollywood are flip-flop casual. They put on the dog less. If Fort Lauderdale still has its Elbo Room where spring breakers once rock-and-rolled and where Beethoven-by-the-Beach rocks the summer event scene, Pompano is happy with an Italian guitarist crooning to prerecorded band audio for dinner guests at a sidewalk café in a homey neighborhood. An Elvis impersonator works crowds along the Hollywood beach to push pizza.

Though with high-rises already towering along the sea, beachfront Pompano on the west side of A1A remains a town of otherwise pleasant low-rise neighborhoods. You come out of a little resort like Cottages by the Ocean onto A1A, and the road in this section below east-west Atlantic Avenue feels like a neighborhood road. The high-rises are monstrous, yet the neighborhood feels together. Every return home or to where you're staying feels comfortable. But there's no question that real estate still drives these places. Developers score big with their towers that lack the look of downtown Fort Lauderdale. They're the equivalent of garden apartments bolted thirty stories high that leave ground level still humdrum. In Pompano like Daytona, mom-and-pops hang onto old motels till they can cash out by getting a variance that allows something big to go up. Hurting for revenues, the city has been willing to do anything to attract developers, whose projects return big taxes.

That ongoing contention spares neither Pompano nor Hollywood. In Pompano, a developer scored a deal with the city that would have put a pair of forty-story towers on two sites along A1A long earmarked for parks. Both are parking lots today but at least still offer hope for better. The move was tied to redevelopment along Atlantic Avenue, the city's main street between I-95 and the beach that would have turned the Italian crooner scene into something slick and likely bound for a developer free-for-all. In the notorious Florida way of doing things, plans for redevelopment got made in summer when snowbird property owners were up north. A decision made by the city on a Friday got mysteriously changed by Monday. A mayor who closed his small construction company one day got hired by a big construction company the next. Though the town charter calls for a ten-story height limit, towers already reach forty stories, done by variances. Deals were cut without requests for proposals, and when RFPs were demanded they got written so narrowly that only one favored developer or another qualified.

It was all too much for voters, who rebelled and in 2003 decisively ousted the developer-friendly city commission majority. One developer has sued the city under its new administration for $60 million, indicating what he expected to make for deals that now might not go through. People of Pompano (POP), the citizens group that successfully challenged the old guard, now gets charged with favoring "slum and blight," the condition, which if determined to exist, allows formation of a community redevelopment agency with its tax-increment supporting renewal projects. According to POP vice president John Peppe, who has been coming to Florida since the 1940s, the problem isn't that people don't want their beach area improved. "If the corridor were just cleaned up, that would do a lot for us," he says. "That goes back to what the original CRA was to be about." Contrary groups, named to confuse the citizenry (older and contemptuously exploited as likely to be confused) call themselves People For Pompano and Pompano's People United to push developer agendas.

No question that parts of the beach area have fallen on hard times. Though the beach end of Atlantic Avenue with the Italian crooner at Caffe La Dolce Vita, the *Cheers*-like Briny Irish Pub, Frank's Ristorante, and a few apparel shops do well enough, plazas where the avenue crosses A1A suffer with tired and unappealing shops, hanging on or closed. "The proponents of megadevelopment claim that the blight is because there aren't enough people on the beach to support the shops in trouble," says Peppe. "But is it that or is it because the facilities just aren't good? When shops are good, they last and they're successful." Convinced that improved commercial districts don't require new megadevelopments, POP now plans to form a barrier-island alliance from Deerfield at the north end of the county to Hollywood. "Everyone has pretty much the same concerns," Peppe says. The developer who saw his megamillion project stalled is now peddling it in Daytona Beach.

By contrast with developer shenanigans, Pompano is home of one of Broward's most impressive public figures, county mayor Kristin Jacobs. Jacobs ran on livability issues when first elected in 1998. Today her NatureScape Broward program conducts water conservation and pollution-control courses around the county. In 2002, she led the fight for a $46-million commitment to five major greenways and trails that as a start will span almost 200 miles in this county long demeaned as the least safe for cycling in America. Initial funding will come from road impact fees that would otherwise have gone to routine highway improvements in this county that's only four years from build-out but still calculated to double in size by 2030.

Hollywood Finally Gets Un-Stuck

Hollywood developed later but faster than Pompano. In Pompano, settlement began just before the railroad arrived in 1896. The town incorporated in 1908. By contrast, Hollywood was a developer's town only begun in the twenties. Its Hoosier founder and California gold prospector Joseph Wesley Young knew no more than most developers of the time about land conservation. He scraped his mainland site bare before proceeding in like manner on the beach. But he had a vision that involved caring for the people he sold to and early on built qualities for them that remain almost seventy-five years later. Hollywood became a city marked east-west by great circular plazas that captured the eye of motorists along broad boulevards. Young dug lakes and built a golf course with a lavish clubhouse. He promised a great industrial and commercial future for his town through a seaport that he began before his untimely death at fifty-four and that, completed, became Port Everglades.

One of Young's charming legacies for his town is its French-Canadian influence. Young hired Quebec laborers, so that to this day, Quebecois visitors still return every winter. They feel at home among shop signs that say *Nous parlons français* and others that hawk Montreal's *La Presse.*

Another legacy was the city's remaining Moorish and Mediterranean style. Young's Broadwalk was meant to reflect that style. He created hotel floors with terrazzo tiles and installed sunscreens so people could dine comfortably outdoors. His buildings looked like sandcastles with gorgeous arches and keyhole elements. If that ambitious look has been largely lost over the years, the Broadwalk is still the beach area's favorite place. Residents and vacationers at the mom-and-pop motels head there daily, some just to hang out at the affordable casual restaurants, for coffee or a twirled-top ice cream, others for the beach and a swim. The Broadwalk is flush with the beach itself. It's no barrier. Gen X–ers whap volleyballs at nets that stretch along a half-mile of beach. In-line skaters sweep by with half-exposed boobs and butts. Guys walk in one direction, their glances pointing their heads sideward. The beach is Woody Allen's turn-of-the-last-century Brooklyn in *Radio Days.* If you loved the movie, you'll love the action.

One of Young's landmarks, his Hollywood Beach Hotel, still stands and—today as a Ramada Inn—still takes guests, but its future is uncertain and its past a regret. Its front faces the end of Hollywood Boulevard. Instead of enjoying a landmark approach to the hotel, motorists climb ramps that reach nose-close to the entrance, leaving a beauty disfigured by state road builders. Seen from the water, the hotel is one of Florida's great remaining examples of heyday tourist architecture.

Hollywood-born Richard Sala headed the beach-area community redevelopment agency until becoming a Palm Beach County city manager in 2004. His offices were in the old hotel surrounded by photos and images of Hollywood's heyday. The area he looked after became a more appealing beach town than Pompano. It remains more low-rise, more mixed residential and tourist. It's an affordable place for visitors, where you can sit all morning at a place like Angelo's on the Broadwalk noshing for a couple of bucks. While politicians eager to deal land to developers decry the place as "slum and blight," it's wholesomely funky, hoi polloi, more "fading Florida" worth fix-up and preserving than merely faded. Yet Sala called for residential towers.

Before leaving he worked through focus groups to re-create the original theme of Hollywood-By-the-Sea (as Young named the town). He provided low-interest loans to help mom-and-pops make improvements. He sought to improve the look of the myriad low-rise boxy buildings with architectural elements—low, pretty tower effects and other Mediterranean detail. He worked for a bond referendum to raise $20 million for infrastructure improvements that would put utilities underground, improve streetscapes, and introduce decorative elements like pavers and period lighting onto the Broadwalk. He wanted a new architectural feel for the entire beach area.

But city residents see something ulterior at work. High-rises are starting to march up from the south end of the beach. Civic activists claim that more will come as the CRA gets fat with tax increment funds. Retired Krispy Kreme manager Pete Brewer points out that when the beachside CRA district was formed, its limits stopped south after including the recently rebuilt Diplomat Hotel, itself an immense if architecturally distinctive convention hotel on the beach. That put the property taxes from the big new resort into the CRA, which Brewer charges will be used as incentives for more high-rise construction. As if to bear him out, the controversial Ocean Palms tower now rises just north. But just south of the Diplomat is an abandoned Holiday Inn. That, which would have required funds for renewal, was left out of the CRA district. "They're out of control," says Brewer of the CRA. "The sky's the limit."

Lawyer Brenda Chalifour, who lives in a beachfront apartment, calls Hollywood Beach "the best place in America to live. You look out your window. There's the beach, the ocean. What could be better?" Yet Chalifour herself acknowledges that streets flood in rain and that the CRA keeps giving breaks to developers instead of protecting the town's water—its residential lakes, the Intracoastal Waterway, the ocean itself—all troubled by polluted runoff.

Downtown Hollywood has been feeling its way forward after years of stagnation. False starts have frustrated the city from the opening of the port and the airport (both of which chiefly benefited Fort Lauderdale) to the long gap between the first and second iterations of the Diplomat Resort and some early arts initiatives on the beach and downtown. Between Fort Lauderdale and Miami, who cared about in-between? Certainly south Broward movers and shakers were more interested in all those developer towns to the west where land was cheaper than below the county line and permitting rooftops was never a problem. Even today as urban chic finally arrives downtown, the burbs are going green, high-rise, or whatever it takes to stand out among the sameness.

Sunrise, at the edge of the Glades and home of the huge Sawgrass Mills Mall, has opted for two 26-story condo towers. Pembroke Pines has organized itself a boast-worthy parks system. Coconut Creek is building a new town center devotedly following Main Street guidelines, solar powered and built of recycled materials. Hardly any of Broward's western towns isn't building an arts center (though only Pembroke Pines, built on a dairy that built on the Everglades, had the chutzpah to name its own theater the River of Grass). It's all not yet settled out in those western districts either. Some naysayers are holding onto small farms, nurseries, and stables. Little Southwest Ranches, which fought off annexation by the Pines, insists on its rural image (its motto is Preserving Our Rural Identity) though roads are getting four-laned to its edge, while Davie, long the real McCoy with its town hall a gallery of rodeo art and a McDonald's with a corral where folks in the saddle ride up for Big Macs, just saw the Armadillo Café close—gone, an authentic Southwestern pit stop with Anchor Steam on draft.

For Hollywood the retrofit seems more authentic than grasping at straws or making statements. The town has waited so long that urban enthusiasts who want to help shape their own place—who want a smaller place, more of a family atmosphere—are flocking downtown. A first stage of renewal previewed a decade ago when Hollywood Boulevard between Young Circle west to the tracks got traffic calmed and completely relandscaped. A block south, Harrison Avenue became a restaurant row. Things looked up but nobody moved in. There was no place to move to. Shops opened and closed. Preservationists who wanted to save the Great Southern Hotel on the circle frustrated a 24-story development (the hotel was four stories and built by Young).

"You have to prime the pump," said downtown CRA director Jim Edwards, who previously directed downtown affairs for the inland city of Lakeland, turning a phosphate-grimy place into one of the genuine arts hubs of Florida. "Sometimes you have to deliver straight subsidies to developers' bottom lines. If these areas could be supported without public money, they would be. You have to overcome the inability of the private sector. Just look out west. Everything was subsidized by roads, schools, utilities—look at 595!" Edwards made himself heard but too well. The city frenzied itself with handouts rained in by developers' lawyers.

To the surprise of no one watching the comeback of Florida downtowns, the first of the new projects lined up, a 12-story condominium called Radius on Young Circle sold out in one day. People camped out to get one of the 285 units even though they won't be ready till the summer of 2006. The city paid out $11 million in incentives. That should have eased the anxiety of risk-averse investors. But even after that demonstration of downtown appeal, the city committed more than twice that sum to the developer who got the green light to build 200 units above the Great Southern by agreeing to preserve it. Like Liberace laughing all the way to the bank, the same developer stands to rake in another $14 million for 400 additional apartments and retail in the northeast quadrant of the circle.

More than the promise of some two thousand new residents will keep downtown hopping. Even though overruns have doubled the cost for the big people attractor in Young Circle and postponed its completion till early 2008, the new ArtsPark with its amphitheater, its visual arts building, and recreational and landscaping features will pull people from all over the area. So will the wi-fi installation for laptops accomplished at the end of 2004.

Like never before, residential downtowns and beachfronts are driving Broward. Fort Lauderdale seems to have gotten it right. But there and elsewhere, developers are still trying to get what they want whether or not residents get what they want, and no matter the cost.

12

MIAMI-DADE COUNTY

Nothing Remotely Like It in Florida

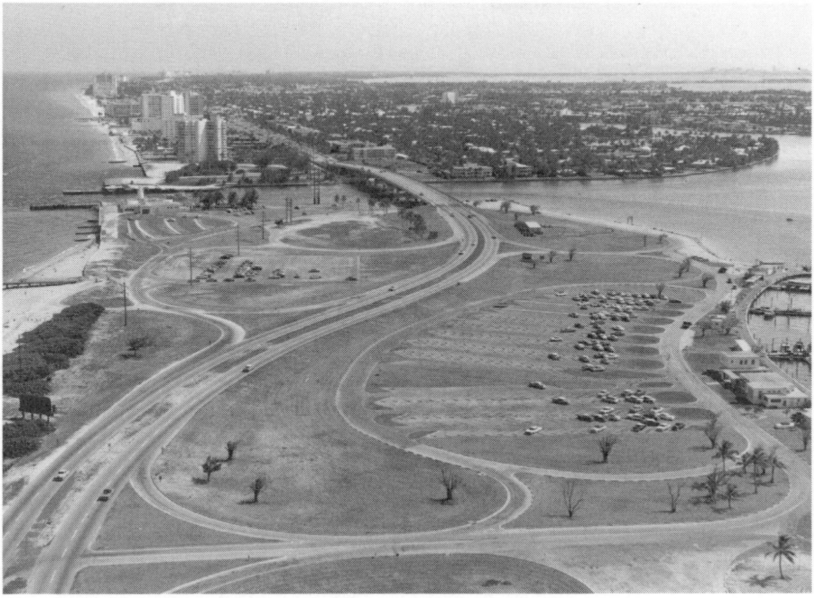

Figure 12.1. Aerial view of Highway A1A and the Miami-Dade County Haulover Bridge in 1962. Courtesy of the Florida State Archives.

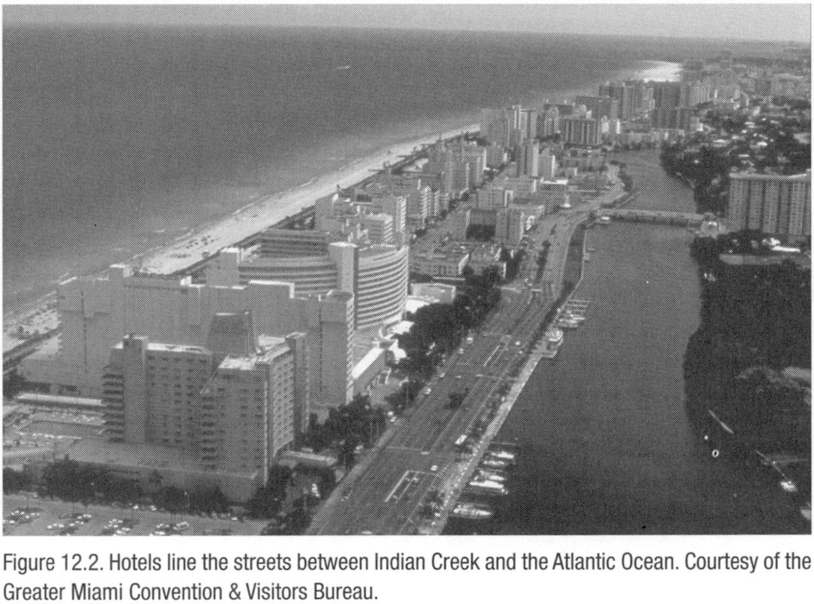

Figure 12.2. Hotels line the streets between Indian Creek and the Atlantic Ocean. Courtesy of the Greater Miami Convention & Visitors Bureau.

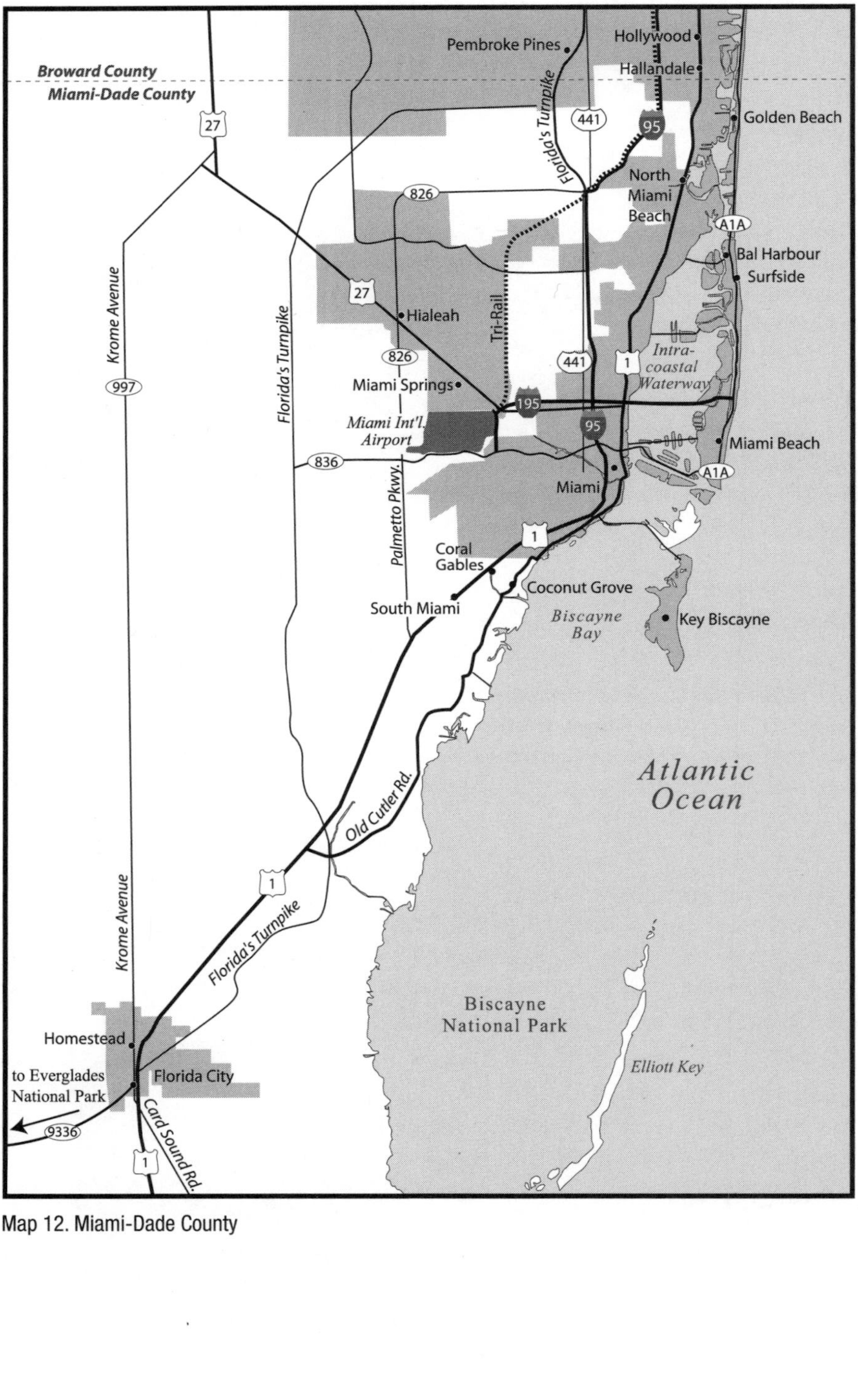

Map 12. Miami-Dade County

After its long, often interrupted but tropistic push for the Tropics, Highway A1A ends in a fanfare of resort island glory. It skirts the gaudy hotel row of Miami Beach and channels the city's Art Deco District before opening onto the last of its causeways. Across Biscayne Bay, the road serves up island mansions, yachts, and the homeport of the world's most glamorous cruise fleet. Finally, it spans the island home of a legendary seaplane company and near its end throws open a superb view of the tallest, most polyglot, and most exasperating city in Florida. Highway A1A will reappear one more time as a short section of shorefront 150 miles down the coast where the Florida Keys fritter away into the Gulf of Mexico. But here it gives way to a towering city of blue-green glass and concrete the color of sandy shore, a city altogether different by size, scale, and location on its broad bay from anywhere else in Florida. Where Highway A1A gives way at the base of MacArthur Causeway, an expressway vaults up and around the proliferating maze of towers like a Disney ride while a ramp descends to ground. The expressway conjures unstoppable growth with the power potential to solve the city's problems that persist where the causeway sinks funneling down to the ground. Not everyone will feel so optimistic. It helps to understand changes collecting along the A1A coast, the handicaps that for so long have beleaguered Florida's cities and the expectations that Floridians newly have for their downtowns and that they seem willing to bet on.

Despite endless ballyhoo, only now, for the first time in three-quarters of a century, does Miami appear ready to fill the hope long promised for it. If hope lives, that's big change for this place long hyped as the Magic City while its dark side dimmed its native luster. Less than twenty years ago a prominent writer called Miami "the place where the American dream had turned into a nightmare." Race riots, exile Cuban hit squads, cocaine wars, and corruption ravaged civic life. For its entire history, Miami spread west into the Everglades hell-bent on displacing everybody and everything that didn't conform to a developer's dream of paradise. If ethnicity and corruption still remain Miami's wild cards, the city has at least slowed its manifest destiny of paving its way clear across the River of Grass.

The mainland and Miami Beach are at last starting to link the city of international trade and the city of international leisure in an aware metropolis, functionally cooperative even while its two chief cities remain separately governed. Work and urban leisure are fusing with tourist leisure in an inevitable if not always comfortable Latinizing of these American tropics. Vacationers in search of urban character already show up in West Palm Beach and Fort Lauderdale, the way they long have in northern cities. But different from the North and except for the boom-time twenties, vacationers have never taken Florida's cities seriously, bedding down in luxury while here for land pickings and otherwise enjoying the beach.

Subtropical Florida has had to stumble its way forward. As a region discovered not by hewers of timber and drillers for oil but by consumers of leisure, Florida has ultimately formed as a place with California as its only precedent, the two together bookending America. Relentless numbers of those that first came to vacation or otherwise spend time in Florida's sunshine have come back to live. This influx, powerfully driven by GIs who trained in Miami and returned to make new lives here after World War II, created a fifty-year economy based on piling up endless subdivisions. A political culture developed indifferent to the coastal towns and urban life, pitching the future endlessly west and suburban while leaving barrier-island tourism a seasonal enclave activity and an additional anti-urban force in regional life. Bracketed west and east by economies antipathetic toward its existence, Miami was left to bake in the sun and, behind its image, beat up on blacks.

The City's Irresistible Pull

Miami's newly evolving metropolitan vision is motivating change clear up and down the coast. For as controversial as Miami and the Beach are—worldly and fast-changing for a state still set in its groove of developer patronage and dumb-and-dumber politics—the two are nonetheless prepossessing and signal where the state is heading everywhere. Upstate, you can love Miami or hate it, but you can't deny the gifts of its salience. Everywhere that Miami's immigrants relocate north, their ambition recharges local economies. Miami's world trade sends opportunists looking for competitive deals at airports and seaports all up the coast. The chance to be near Miami even if outside its grip pulls relocations everywhere down to the Treasure Coast and Gold Coast. Miami counts. It's big league. Its newspaper at least recently kicked ass with its endless exposés of crime, corruption, and incompetence, and the city launches as many celebrities as it attracts.

Even along the short coastal distance south of Miami, Homestead, long agricultural and gateway together with adjacent Florida City to Everglades National Park, has welcomed artists and gays escaping the urban clamor up the road. They're fashioning their own scaled-down sophistications in the town's appealing comeback from Hurricane Andrew.

Nor in the quickening vision does the coast throw tourism out with the sprawl so long cradled by it. Instead, tourism gains in urban character, influenced by the transition already turning the coastal resort burgs into the real cities that new eastward flows of capital are affecting. This is big change, same as in Palm Beach and Broward counties, real places influencing tourism more than, for so long in Florida, tourism influencing real places. Affected by what these new cities want for themselves—the achievement of "place" distinct in space and time—tourism is retreating from the mantras of heads in beds and pushing turnstiles. In a more complex equation, trade creates worldliness that pulls suburbanites back to the city, creating a new sophisticated downtown where artists colonize the urban edge and the vigor pulls a new type of exploring visitor. Visitor-driven leisure adds downtown color and flash, spinning off new business that gratifies new urban consumers and civic dynamics. Tourism weaves itself into the complexities of place and becomes less about attractions, more about the ungated city flow. Thirty-five years after Disney ran off with the Beach family trade, tourism in Orlando demands endless road building while still burdening the city with a one-act economy and lumpen demographics. Exigency rescued Miami and the Beach from what they would never otherwise have given up.

Nobody ever expected Florida to be where you vacationed for city life. But vacationers want to be where the locals are, and throughout the Gold Coast that's increasingly downtown. The vast populations that migrated from the North and plopped themselves in the burbs have rediscovered that Florida has always been about the beach and that they ought to get themselves closer. This evolution has occurred most forcefully in Miami Beach, where seashore frolics gave rise to year-round communities and where the demise of tourism caused by Orlando and the depression of rents that followed spurred an inflow of artists and gays, which in turn brought back a new style of urban tourism that has reenergized the residential town.

Miami is also at work at something larger. Since the city's future got swept up in the Americas forty-five years ago, the abrupt changes in countries to the south have surged Miami with economic and cultural resources never felt before. For centuries, but most notably since 1959 when Fidel Castro came to power and attempted revolution throughout Latin America, extraterritorial capital, commerce, and culture have flooded Miami. Everyone who arrives in Miami regardless of status—refugee, exile, or permitted immigrant; penniless or flush with dollars—arrives with images and expectations of America at the height of its power and Miami as its beacon landfall. Of all Florida cities, Miami alone gets endlessly renewed by the conviction that it's some enormous engine to which anything can attach and successfully get in motion. Miami is the immigrant capital of America that New York was a century ago. The city that was the model of rapacious development in Florida, dependent for every dollar on the North (the dollars gushed in as if succoring some immense remittance economy) has passed beyond the receiving end of North-South dependency and has become crucial to a new North-South dynamic that it manages better than anyplace else across the Sunbelt. Capital is a given. The trade links are in place.

Now an unprecedented migration of people is moving into 60,000 residential units newly rising downtown and along its edges. Nothing like this has ever before happened in Florida, some 100,000 new residents showing up in ten years where only a few thousand lived at the turn of the twentieth century. The numbers are moving onto the banks of the Miami River, the shore of Biscayne

Bay, into the new performing arts district and among the business towers. They occupy rentals and condos, market rate and subsidized; fueled by Latins, by the young and ambitious, by families and retireds. Frequently visiting Latins and Europeans occupy pied-a-terres. Artists and writers tend toward lofts, their forming districts of art and culture as important as the systems of commerce and communications already in place. Miami is still warm in winter. Now it's Latin and cosmopolitan too, arty and vital, and in that Latinizing significantly ahead of where America is heading. For the big cities of the North, Miami used to be the end of the line. Now it's in the middle where it wants to be, the hub city of North and South America.

When chamber of commerce types a half century ago extolled Miami destiny—a city measurable by only its own standards—they sounded like blathering boosters. Yet either they did effect a vision, or events have simply transpired the way they imagined. Unstoppable energy hangs in the air. If every other city along the A1A coast is experiencing incremental change, in Miami the change is exponential. Today the upheavals of the past half century appear as a sometimes painful, inescapable transition, and there's light, together with something terrifically live-and-let-live, in sight at the end of the tunnel.

Henry Flagler and Ralph Munroe

Henry Flagler at first had little interest in Miami. The resort town he created in Palm Beach greatly occupied him. Yet traders were long drawn to this place at the mouth of the Miami River. Tequestas flourished in the vicinity before Spanish contact, trading far north in America, as revealed by recent archaeological digs at the mouth of the Miami River. Round-the-world adventurer William Brickell set up a trading post at the ancient Tequesta site where he traded with Seminoles who canoed downstream. One remarkable Florida pioneer, the Yankee sailor Ralph Munroe, settled the community of Coconut Grove five miles south of the river. He organized the Grove on the premise that northerners would choose to vacation along Biscayne Bay precisely to experience the good life his community created out of its own renewable resources. Munroe had taken to heart Emerson's caution that humans had to start over again in wilderness to get civilization right. The motto at his cottage colony for visitors was "Insofar as possible, the hotel atmosphere is eliminated." Short-lived, that sentiment. If Spain cut off Tequesta life, Flagler unalterably changed Munroe's community once he realized that Miami was as close as you could get to Florida's offshore islands and to Panama, where markets for trade awaited.

Flagler brought his railroad in 1896. His new hotel, the Royal Palm, was inferior to anything he had already built on his way south from Jacksonville. Flagler didn't expect much from Miami. While Palm Beach would be for his leisure pals and West Palm on the mainland for workers, Miami would be the

Figure 12.3. The famous art deco hotels of South Beach. Courtesy of the Greater Miami Convention & Visitors Bureau.

equivalent of West Palm for islands that gleamed in the great railroader's eye. Precursor Miami Beach in Flagler's time was a coconut plantation. Flagler built a port and began operating ships across the Straits of Florida. Yet even as the city began to develop, he lost interest and soon began extending his railroad to Key West, the last great project of his life, completed just before his death in 1912. Miami soon settled back. The biggest spur to city fortunes in the following decade was the decision by James Dearing to build Vizcaya, his retirement palazzo, on the bay. During the two years of its construction, the project employed almost a quarter of the city's labor force. But for the land boom, the city would have grown slowly until after the Second World War. Everywhere below Jacksonville, Flagler had left coastal cities dependent on seasonal tourism. There was no other kind in Florida. People came by train to escape the cold; they left before the heat.

But the boom set Miami and all Florida into a pandemonium of development that has rarely faltered along the Gold Coast. What drove the boom was post–World War I prosperity. Henry Ford was turning out affordable cars. Carl Fisher's Dixie Highway newly linked Chicago and Miami. Flagler's trains were packing people and freight down; big ships were sailing up the deep-water channel dredged by Flagler to offload construction materials for the boom at the port he built. After the constraints of the war years, the urge to escape billowed up. Women escaped from corsets, bobbing their hair and shortening their dresses. Jazz swept the waltz out of ballrooms. Art turned avant garde, and pink palaces went up by the shore. Even Prohibition did Miami well. The city was so far off the beaten path that people imagined they could outdistance both the Feds and their own morals. Law enforcers were no match for smugglers who found limitless coves where they could land their contraband undetected.

Everyone was either building, selling, or buying land. Surprisingly, they built for posterity. A Presbyterian minister's son from Coconut Grove built the city out of tomato fields that became Coral Gables, after eighty years still one of the most cosmopolitan suburbs in America. Aviation pioneer Glenn Curtis developed Hialeah and Miami Springs in a swamp; Hialeah today is the fifth-largest city in Florida, and Miami Springs the suburb at the edge of Miami International Airport. The Grove stayed sane for a long time. Biggest change came at the Beach, where Fisher, who operated the Indianapolis Speedway and impelled cars down the Dixie Highway, transformed that coconut plantation into the resort city it became.

The Sandbar That Became Miami Beach

Early on, folks had rowed over from the mainland by boat. Blacks picnicked among them. But after Fisher acquired his beach land, blacks were welcomed only as laborers, Jews not even for toil. Emulating Flagler the railroader at Palm Beach, Fisher the auto parts magnate cleared his land of bush and on the shell, rock, and sand laid out his streets, built his houses and hotels, and planted the fast-growing shrubs, vines, and palms that almost overnight turned Miami Beach into a tropical-style resort. The Beach was about fun. No railroad station, no cemetery. The place became irresistible not just because it reached as close as possible to winter sun but because Miami Beach learned the techniques and value of press agentry ahead of anyplace else. What Miami Beach learned the rest of Florida copied.

Once the hotels started going up, promotion had to fill rooms by the thousands. A former reporter for the *Indianapolis Star,* Steve Hannegan, was hired. He became legendary for hyping the press. As the late Polly Redford recalled in her wry history, *Billion-Dollar Sandbar,* Hannegan was never off the job. When Julius Fleischmann, the baking yeast king, climbed off his polo pony at the end of a match and dropped dead, Hannegan flashed the news to editors around America with the reminder to dateline the story Miami Beach. Miami Beach *became* Florida. When Miami Beach bared leg, all Florida bared leg. When Miami Beach said, "tits and ass," all Florida said, "Amen, Brother!" The best of yesterday came to rate only a two to three against whatever today brought—six to eight if the morning paper spelled your name right, ten for a photo of a beachfront model in bikini, two fists walloping a volleyball, the impact—*Ka-boom!*—largely revealing splendors beneath the palms. Before Miami Beach, all Florida knew about was draining swamps and raising cattle and crops. Miami Beach taught Florida how to raise hell.

Although hurricanes and Depression shut down the boom, all-out development had fixed the culture that would affect Florida for the rest of the century. T. H. Weigall described how the stage was set in his 1932 book, *Boom in Paradise*:

> And so, at a time when Americans in general possessed more money to burn than even they had ever possessed before, the drift southwards began. . . . The great land corporations, sensing the possibilities of the situation, launched enormous nation-wide advertising campaigns hailing the discovery of a new earthly paradise. The boom was under way. And then the state legislature, in abolishing with one superb gesture the income and inheritance taxes and in abandoning any attempt whatever to enforce the prohibition and anti-gambling laws, joined in the chorus and definitely adopted the policy of making the wealthy and pleasure-seeking visitor its primary consideration, and practically its only one.

Crime was intimate with the good times. At the Royal Palm downtown, Flagler had carved more than an exception to the local prohibition against booze. From the start, he allowed his guests to gamble. By the time Fisher had the Beach up and running, exception became the rule. The Beach was wide open to booze and gambling. Al Capone made the Beach home. Meyer Lansky ran Murder, Incorporated, just over the county line in Hallandale. For a time the Beach was the mob's Riviera. When crime commissions in the fifties finally shut down the craps tables and roulette, dope and coke soon got the Beach inhaling and snorting. Unchanged in its ways as the twenty-first century rolled in, a former U.S. attorney called the metropolis "a smuggler's supermarket."

If crime brought notorious headlines, Hannegan's successor brought the sunshine kind. Hank Meyer brought Arthur Godfrey's radio show to the Beach. Next came Godfrey on TV, then Ed Sullivan, then Jackie Gleason. Meyer didn't bring Miss Universe but worked with the show. Those were briefly the days of good government on the Beach, a breather for building civic institutions and public trust. Families discovered the Beach, and they came from all over America. For an Ozzie-and-Harriet moment between the booze, the back-room games and the drugs still to come, Miami Beach became America's favorite vacationland.

Frumpy Dame Beats off Casinos and Mouse

After Disney, Beach tourism tanked. Hoteliers pushed casino gambling as the only comeback. First there was Vegas, then Atlantic City. Miami Beach next. What beat the gamblers' bet and brought the Beach back to its natural-born flamboyance was the remarkable art historian Barbara Baer Capitman. Hannegan and Meyer together could hardly have dreamed up a less likely redeemer of good times.

Capitman was a frumpy lady with an annoying high-pitched voice. She visited the Beach in the seventies, looked around, and discovered art deco hotels. South Beach, as the turnaround district came to be known, had turned shamelessly shabby. The hotels had never known air conditioning. They had Depression-era small rooms and tiny bathrooms. They looked across Ocean Drive to a beautiful palm-lined beach, but occupants of these superannuated properties were hardly candidates for beach-ball publicity shots. They were mostly retired New Yorkers, a Jewish caricature of what Miami Beach had become. The only people under fifty who came to visit were the oldsters' kids and their kids. Yet Capitman, attuned to a growing worldliness that followed the sixties, saw in a flash that by restoring these Depression-era hotels she could bring all of Miami Beach back to life. The Beach city council ignored her. Bankers ignored her. Miami's blue-haired preservationists detested her. Capitman—God forbid—was going to involve them in saving the Jewish *shtetl*!

A klatch of preservationists who felt excluded from the elite bunch that ran things on the mainland together with disenfranchised gays dreamed of an architectural revival that would recapture the glory days of the Beach and provide them a district for their hip lifestyles. The gays and their architect collaborators started painting hotel portholes and their ziggurat trim like pastel greeting cards. They turned Ocean Drive into a wedding cake world. While the city, mired in inanition, issued demolition permits, Capitman writhed in front of bulldozers. She did an end run around the local boobeaucracy and in Washington scored a square mile of the buildings on the National Register of Historic Places. Capitman's greatest offense may have been how eagerly the media covered her, this lady utterly sans allure, the antithesis of Beach bathing beauties.

Miami Vice helped. A sense of intrigue and danger cloaked the Beach. *Vice* in the eighties told the world Miami had become big time. Big cities had crime. They also had cachet and everything that makes life exciting. Miami Beach didn't have to compete with Disney any more. Didn't *want* to compete with Disney any more. Christo helped by wrapping the islands of Biscayne Bay pink. Suddenly fashion magazines began showing up for shoots. Modeling agencies opened. The media kept the district high profile enough that savvy rehabbers with bank connections started buying up properties. The rush was on again. City Hall awoke and jazzed up Ocean Drive with cafe-accommodating wide sidewalks, with jogging paths and greenery by the beach, the same beach the Army Corps had just renourished. Suddenly the look came together. South Beach was the tropics, America chic as St. Tropez, more affordable, warmer, cleaner, softer sand, safer than Manhattan, no passports, no customs hassles.

The Deco District took on the glamour of a big city packed into a couple of square miles. Gone the baggy-pants immigrants. In place of the Bronx and

Bialystok, Manhattan and Havana. Where the old folks in flip-flops schlepped canvas chairs to the beach, Madonna and Gloria Estefan came to cavort. Fright wigs topped drag queens; guys gyrated on bar tops in jock straps; Euro-nymphs tanned bare-breasted on the beach. Although the oldsters were largely displaced, enough hung on to give South Beach wacky juxtaposed character. Elderly Yiddish speakers mixed with transvestites, Rollerbladers and Spandex-sleek cyclists mixed with antique cars and muscular tank-topped dudes who strutted the pink sidewalks with boa constrictors instead of mere twenties-style boas wrapped around their clavicles. The Beach was back living in the flash of the act. Thirteen-year-olds routinely began flying with planeloads of relatives for bar mitzvahs at the Wailing Wall in Jerusalem. AIDS victims began flying down for one last fling at the Beach. Gianni Versace got slain at the gates of his Ocean Drive villa, and while the metropolis was still numb, the demand to view the site sent tour companies scrambling to find more buses.

South Beach became unbelievably free-form. Gay bars opened, nightclubs, funky to chic restaurants. The News Café became the hangout for espresso breakfasts at any hour, and any vacant site good for a free-floating bash announced itself by word of mouth that drew sybaritic crowds. The night scene became changeable as desire. The heavily hyped Hell—featuring a nude with a lasciviously navel-plopped dollop of chocolate—was gone before you could say, "Oh my goodness!" More provocative were the gay clubs where heteros showed up in search of a kinky charge. Here and all gone like last night's make-up were Bang, Barrio, Bash, Hombre, Les Bains, Paragon, ReBar, Van Dome, Warsaw Ballroom. Lately gone, Crobar—"A venue evocative of the unrestrained imagination of a Dali, a Cocteau, a Fellini—heaven on earth as we never envisioned it, the Venusburg of Tannheuser, Orpheus in the Underworld, La Dolce Vita and 2001."

Weekends, the bridge-and-causeway crowd showed up in this place that couldn't make up its mind whether it was Sodom and Gomorrah or Eden. But no streets were made one-way, no lanes added for cars. Bicyclists and lunatic skaters got wherever they were going faster. An urban arts sensibility took hold. The Wolfsonian-FIU Museum transformed a storage company warehouse into a showplace of propagandistic art from the industrial age. The Bass Museum housed its old masters in a museum with a new wing designed by Arata Isozaki. Robert A. M. Stern designed a new library. Across the street, Arquitectonica designed the school and studios of Miami City Ballet. In 1985, the visionary Ellie Schneiderman created ArtCenter/South Florida on Lincoln Road at a time when bag ladies and homeless had taken over that one-time Fifth Avenue of the South. The artists acquired building after building for studios where they continue to produce their cutting-edge work while rents have gone through the roof all around them.

Miami native Craig Robins, who cut his teeth on Ocean Drive development while in his early twenties, formed the redevelopment company Dacra that began moving west on the Beach. Dacra signs soon appeared everywhere along Eighth Street, Twelfth Street, Espanola Way along Washington Avenue. Each new block of redevelopment made South Beach a bigger, bolder place. Robins grooved on the combination of businesspeople in sync with preservation activists. He moved up to Lincoln Road, buying up buildings. "People never thought South Beach would go up to Lincoln Road," he remembers. "They said I was crazy." Then philanthropist Ted Arison set up the New World Symphony, America's premier training orchestra, acquired the Lincoln Theatre for its performances, and hired Starbucks-generation symphonist Michael Tilson Thomas as conductor. Thanks to Arison's lavish endowment, Frank Gehry is now designing SoundStage for the New World, a $40 million digitized production facility that will simulcast performances globally.

Strangely the music scene that flourished in the early nineties disappeared. Five or six clubs that featured singer-songwriters and touring acts all closed. The change was part of upscaling. Off-the-wall innovation gave way to the return of monied investors. They began throwing up routine high-rises below the Deco District. A citizens' revolt in 1997 installed a city council with a mandate to restrict additional beachfront towers without popular consent. But developers rushed through their plans for permits and began ringing the Beach along Flagler's ship channel like a mini-Manhattan.

The orgiastic transformation slowed, the *hipoisie* began decamping across the bay, and the Beach settled and became more organized about its future. Preservationists created one after another Beach district with newly protective historic status. In 2004, voters by a two-to-one margin extended the citizen mandate to restrict additional projects that would break height limits anywhere on the island. Further typical of change, even below the officially designated Deco District to the island rim of towering condos, the oldest hotel on the Beach, the tiny Brown's at 112 Ocean Drive, has been saved and reopened. The little Sea Crest Apartments has been incorporated into a 400-unit condo. A classic 1939 deco hotel, the Century, designed by one of the masters, Henry Hohauser, still operates, more chic than ever. The hotel's beach club across the street has been incorporated into a prize-worthy sensitive Marriott. Farther up the Beach, where an Auschwitz of destruction defied Capitman's best efforts, Hyatt now operates the deep-landmark Victor Hotel seventy years ago managed by legendary Beach hotelier Art Adler, and the lush thirties-style St. Moritz has been incorporated into the sensitive-deco Loews. New protection has been given to the Miami Modern (MiMo) hotels —notably the extravagant MiMo creations of the late Morris Lapidus: the Seville, the Fontainebleau, the Eden Roc. The North Beach Historic District is coming back now with its neighborhood mix of mom-and-pop shops, restaurants, and mostly modest hotels along Ocean Terrace.

Miami Beach population is still only 80,000, but that population is year-round now, the age demographic sharply reduced as families have moved in, many newly working on the Beach or commuting the few minutes to town. Soon transit will connect the two. If less chic, tourism has become year-round. On a Friday night in September, locals and out-of-towners pack the wide sidewalks.

Miami Beach gives way to one small A1A municipality after another up to Hallandale. Surfside stands apart for civic-minded government. It's a city of 5,000 in a square mile, about half Hispanic, the rest Anglos, African Americans, orthodox Jews, Arabs, and other Middle Easterners. It lacks flash along the beach where the hotels are nondescript, up to a middling twelve stories. To control density, the city newly limits buildings across Collins Avenue to three stories. New ordinances require more parking and increase setbacks. Early in 2004, six-term mayor Paul Novack had his way when the city passed a charter amendment that permanently limits zoning districts to their current status. "We don't believe that bigger is better," said the mayor. "When Publix wanted to double the size of its store, we said no. Our community didn't need it. We don't allow hotels to usurp Collins Avenue for valet parking. We have no debt, no bonds, no blight, no decay. Trash gets picked up six days a week. Taxes don't go up. The two biggest problems in South Florida are 'the cousins' of waste and corruption. Keep them out of the equation and you can achieve all the community's goals and objectives without selling out the community's future."

After six terms, Novack didn't seek a seventh, but his acolytes swept into office on his retirement. As for Novack, he's lately been consulting with insurgents against grabby development pressures in beachfront cities all the way up to Cocoa Beach.

Bal Harbour is patrician residential with well-spaced, attractively landscaped towers along the beach and tastefully designed garden apartments to the west. The town's landmark commercial center is the Bal Harbour Shops, the *ne plus ultra* of conspicuous consumption in Florida. Across Indian Creek to the west is Bay Harbor Islands, another residential community with its Kane Concourse strip of shops once fashionably filled with art galleries. North of Bal Harbour, big Haulover Beach Park occupies the sea to the Intracoastal Waterway. Developers newly command Sunny Isles Beach, once Miami's post–World War II motel row—the Strip—and today the worst of the A1A coast's concrete wastelands. The gaudy motels, with their frontal icons of Aztecan pyramids, Sudanese camels, Hawaiian maidens, and Venetian gondolas are all gone. Yet even as the splashy towers rise, city hall insurgents are working to protect the west side of the Strip from completing the canyon that left Miami Beach in shadows north of hotel row. Russians have become important investors. Between Sunny Isles and Hallandale sits Golden Beach, a wholly residential town where young families have lately moved in.

The Export of Miami Beach

Of all the figures that followed Capitman in advancing South Beach—Tony Goldman, who made hotel renovations a bankable investment; Neisen Kasdin and Nancy Liebman, who honored public office with their preservation commitments—Craig Robins has become the most influential. Still in his early forties, Robins now works with important culture figures in transforming South Florida. At a time when politics has polarized the country and in Florida extended the primacy of development as usual, Robins has taken the hubristic impulse in American life and applied it at the local level, where it best seems to work. He has successfully explored where the turnaround of South Beach and Lincoln Road might next prefigure his community approach to redevelopment. As the Beach became sedately more like the mainland, Robins felt challenged to go the other way. He exported the Beach style of arts-influenced community redevelopment to revive a section of Miami across the bay. His new field of dreams became the Design District centered along Fortieth Street, where interiors showrooms that flourished in the fifties and sixties had fallen on hard times after crime disrupted the nearby residential neighborhood and Miami's Haitian exiles settled in just to the north. Most of the showrooms relocated to a new district in a warehouse setting up I-95 in Broward.

"When we went across the bridge into the Design District, everybody said we'd been lucky in South Beach," recalls Robins. "No way could the soul be breathed back into Miami. But you see, South Beach isn't just a place, it's a movement. South Beach was seen as part of the real estate bubble, irrelevant, impractical and unnecessary. Yet South Beach shifted peoples' thought. It made us human again. We learned that massive buildings couldn't replace a beautiful neighborhood. So while the sky began falling on real estate values, South Beach was compounding in value at 30 percent a year. Still it's a struggle. It's an extreme amount of work to gather community activists and businesspeople together. But there was no more challenge on the Beach. It was time to conquer the division between the two sides of the bay." For Robins, South Beach and now Fortieth Street are the proving grounds for statements about the times. It's an urban design approach to development, a move consonant with bringing Miamians back east, with renewing downtown. "Culture shouldn't follow business," says Robins. "Let business exploit profound culture. If we connect the movement with the mainland, Greater Miami can become an important city."

Dacra has now acquired most of the properties in the Design District and has leased them to a global roster of designer showrooms. Like the deco hotels along Ocean Drive that became public art, so too the showrooms along Fortieth Street. They're no longer "to the trade," limiting admission to decorators and their clients, but open to everyone. From the sleek chrome, nickel, and porcelain bath designs at Waterworks to the four-story atrium in the old T. V. Moore building that shows off mansion-sized antiques, the street has acquired cachet. Weekend nights, the street sizzles with artsy crowds in new restaurants and clubs, though like on South Beach, many will hear their sizzle sputter. First and biggest, Power Studios, behind a pair of immense folk medallions, installed a hip restaurant, club recording studio, outdoor cinema, and art gallery, then watched fire chiefs shut it down for overcrowding. Comeback was bruited in late 2004. Robins has installed oversized art in the atriums of his buildings and at focal street corners. Inside at NE Second Avenue and Fortieth Street, a full-sized gondola appears raised in the form of a high-heeled shoe. Outside at North Miami Avenue and Fortieth Street, he had artists install a steroidal showroom vignette two stories high of a beach house with an Escher-like window that shows the changing sky.

Robins worked with master planners Andres Duany and Elizabeth Plater-Zyberk to plan the neighborhood. He brought in architect Terence Riley, the curator of modern design at New York's Museum of Modern Art, to design a pair of prototype Miesian courtyard houses. Knoll, designers Holly Hunt and Alison Spear, among other stylists have moved their studios into the district. The American Institute of Architects holds award presentations here. The Latin Grammys has established its headquarters here. Art Basel held its inaugural Miami opening event in the district.

Excited forecasts call for the condo frenzy affecting downtown to march straight up to the Design District. One thirty-six-story glass-walled tower between the district and the old Florida East Coast Railway yards sold out before building began. What's driving the forecast is redevelopment of the rail yard. Where elephants lately began their linked trunk-to-tail town-to-Beach parade promoting annual arrival of the Ringling Bros. Barnum and Bailey Circus, a 56-acre, $800 million city-backed project will create its own in-town neighborhood of 2,000 condos, some 350 apartments, a mega-retail center, hotel, and health club. This is in the Wynwood District, once the city's garment center, now an arts center and targeted to help generate a larger middle class for this city lately cited by the Brookings Institution for its shrinking middle class and for its rank as the poorest of the country's 100 largest cities, its median income $23,483, or barely half the American median. It helps that the neighborhood will be halfway between the airport and the Beach.

Robins speaks to this city need when he says, "Our business focuses on community building. We advocate, support, and administer neighborhoods. There's a business model in that. What we do makes an area worth more; each thing we do adds value. It's an approach much more harmonious with community goals. Rather than exploiting beauty for short-term profits, we see ourselves profiting only if the whole community is worth more. We believe it's sound business, and, in a way, it tends to be a more spiritual kind of approach. We're trying to profit by doing good."

Despite his confidence in downtown revival, Robins feels a tension between the new urbanism principles that drive him and high-rise cities. He is "tortured" by what he calls "very tall, architecturally unremarkable vertical suburbs, selling people their shoebox in the sky." Continuing his moves against the grain, he has responded to overtures from West Palm leaders. They're negotiating with him to revive a section of the Flagler Drive waterfront with residential, retail, and recreational uses. DPZ, which had earlier master-planned downtown West Palm, is working with Robins on the project. "There's an opportunity to make it the best downtown in South Florida," says Robins. "It's a place where we could make a long-term commitment." Robins has created a model for West Palm in a new low- to mid-rise residential community on a Miami Beach island that he wholly controls where the abandoned hospital where he was born was torn down for his project. Miami, he finds on the other hand, is driven by out-of-control energy. Too many players, too much the melee.

It's that Latin-driven melee that either turns visitors on or puts them off. Visitors who fly or drive to Miami and spend any time downtown right away find this the most Latin metropolis in America. Spanish is the conversational language of choice at the airport, downtown, and in close-in neighborhoods. Turn the car radio on within 40 or 50 miles of the city and rapid-fire commercials for Goya foods and Bustelo coffee attach to Latin hits like autograph hounds waiting outside stage doors for Gloria Éstefan or Julio Iglesias.

Little Havana and Overtown

As recently as twenty-five years ago, the remaking of downtown ranked high on the civic agenda. The last mayor with downtown ambitions was Puerto Rican–born Maurice Ferré. Ferré was a worldly figure. His late uncle was governor of Puerto Rico. For about a decade beginning in the late 1960s, Ferré, who held a series of elective offices, worked with the southern elites that ran the city and promised a revived cosmopolis. Greek city planner Constantinos Doxiadis was hired on. Doxiadis envisioned Biscayne Bay extending into downtown by a series of deepwater channels. Ships would tie up alongside new skyscrapers. The world would literally flow into downtown and turn this southern city into an international capital. Attention got diverted instead by the massive in-migration of Cubans. A trickle begun in 1960 became a flood in response to political repression and economic failure throughout the

Americas. During the next forty years, the city willy-nilly became an international hub without a world-class core. The urban prospect stalled.

While downtown became a processing center for refugees, the bayfront south across the Brickell Avenue Bridge became the city's financial center. Down went gracious old homes. Up went a high-rise office row and residential towers. A block west still remains one of the most attractive tree-canopied streets of the city, South Miami Avenue. Date palms and royal poinciana trees set off colorful restaurants and sidewalk cafes. Just south between the commercial and residential districts is Simpson Park, a remnant of the hammock that once covered this entire upland by the bay. Entry is free. You're walking in hammock that Ponce de Leon would have seen through his spyglass while cruising Biscayne Bay in 1513.

The round-the-clock street life that animates big-city capitals elsewhere still takes place in Miami a mile to the west along Southwest Eighth Street, Miami's Calle Ocho, the heart of Little Havana. Early Cuban refugees settled here among fading car dealerships and seedy retailing that remained as second- and third-generation descendants of early Miamians moved to sprawling subdivisions. Land was cheap. Like the gays and artists who made the depressed oceanfront of South Beach their own, here the Cubans took over. Men walk these neighborhoods in their guayaberas, women beneath their parasols. They stop for the thumb-sized paper cups of ink-black coffee called *tinto* at walk-up windows. They schmooze; they invoke Elian as they revile Fidel; they complain about *Comunistas* at the *Miami Herald.* They lament the long exile years, swear their return when the dictator falls, and pass life in a haze of lingering memory.

The public way is richly urban. On Calle Ocho, the facade of Casablanca Restaurant displays a trompe l'oeil mural that depicts a crowd all standing at the *tinto* window: Batman reading the magazine *Zig-Zag,* former Miami mayor Xavier Suarez, Lucy and Charlie Brown, Alfred E. Newman playing guitar with a Latin bongo player, the late sainted Celia Cruz, Humphrey Bogart, Michael Jackson, Superman, and Wonder Woman. At Olga Guillot Way (SW Fourteenth Avenue) at one of the still-popular open-air fruit and vegetable markets once a staple of Miami shopping, a *coco frio* (chilled coconut) stand has been converted into a vending cart for plants. You can poke your head through a life-sized cutout of ruffle-sleeved rumba musicians and have a souvenir picture snapped. One block west behind a black ornamental grill fence is Máximo Gomez Park—"Domino Park" with its open-air domino tables. A mural here depicts the leaders who attended the hemispheric Summit of the Americas in Miami in 1994, each with national flag. In stormy weather, canvas curtains drop from the barrel-tile roofs to protect players at their tables. Travertine inlays on the sidewalk honor famous Latin performers. Latin theater and nightclubs flourish, along with events like the annual International Hispanic Theatre Festival and one of the great street parties of the Americas, called simply "Calle Ocho," that follows the ten days of the annual Carnaval Miami each February.

To the near northwest is Overtown, once known as Colored Town. For most of the last century, Miami's blacks were welcomed outside these precincts only as domestic workers, as hotel workers, and as laborers. And so Overtown thrived. It became Miami's most vibrant entertainment district, a place where Billie Holiday, Ella Fitzgerald, Cab Calloway, Count Basie, and Duke Ellington performed. Whites flocked in for the name acts at the Sir John Club. Once segregation ended and blacks found they could live outside the ghetto, prosperous residents left. A second dispersion followed when Florida completed I-95 through Miami, carving up the heart of Overtown with its elevated roadway. Business moved out. Some of what remained was destroyed during the rage over the unpunished killings of blacks by white and Hispanic police during the 1980s. By the turn of the century, things were looking up. The Lyric, opened in 1913 and the last remaining of Overtown's heyday theaters, was restored and reopened as the anchor of a Historic Folklife Village. A two-block area had received the Main Street designation, and five buildings were listed in the National Register. The first new owner-occupied housing went up, its sixty-four condominiums quickly sold. The Miami Black Archives next looks to turn Overtown into a reborn shopping, residential, and tourist village. But the going will still be slow. Poverty and neglect in Overtown—that, and Miami's position as the only city in America where more than half the population has been born overseas—leave Miami with that now next-to-bottom ranking among America's poorest cities. More elsewhere grabs attention.

Downtown, Corruption, and Urban Tourists

In downtown itself, four pieces remain from earlier attempts to focus the city. On the east side, the Rouse Company developed Bayside Marketplace, cut off from the rest by the multilane motorway of Biscayne Boulevard. Also cut off is the American Airlines Arena, which replaced an arena built only a few years before and today largely abandoned at the edge of Overtown. Unconnected to the east sits the cultural plaza designed by the late Philip Johnson after his career ran out of steam, a tired re-working of Miami's pseudo-Mediterranean style on a block-filling podium 20 feet above the surrounding streetscape surrounded by walls as inviting as a stockade.

The fourth piece is the wonderful Metromover, a system of elevated trams ridden by everyone from power suit–trippers to ethnic students and down-and-outers, a mix that puts you in mind of San Francisco, there Asian, here Latin. The cars trundle about three stories high, providing a peep show into office windows and a constantly changing glimpse of the best and worst of downtown. Some mornings the cruise ships are in. Lovers hug in Bayfront Park. The Challenger Memorial sits across from the InterContinental hotel. Tall palms rise to eyesight level along lower Biscayne Boulevard. Beyond on Biscayne Bay is densely urban and residential Claughton Island and the promise of a shoreline trail to match the extending Riverwalk, also with a blueway canoe-kayak route in planning led by the Trust for Public Land. Everywhere rise the towers of the core city. For the Metromover glimpse of downtown you pay nothing. The ride is free. Its companion Metrorail—a subway in the sky built chiefly for downtown office workers—costs a buck. Transfers are free.

It's ironic that Miami has achieved one of its close connections with Latin America in how corruption has echoed a way of Latin life. Not that Miami historically hasn't bred a homegrown style of vice, as already noted. But by the mid-nineties city leaders were overwhelmed by a typhoon of graft, allegations of widespread fraud in the conduct of government contracts, dead men voting, stolen elections, virtual bankruptcy of the city, two mayors duking it out for office widely known as "Crazy Joe" and "Mayor Loco," and the anxiety that every next morning the *Herald* would report some new metaphor of ruin. That was before the descent of Republican intimidators on the city in the aftermath of the 2000 national election but already after the killing escapades of the cocaine cowboys that made every-week episodes of *Miami Vice* a national event. Anglos and blacks were deep into the corruption, but the Latin tinge clearly suggested the civic immune system was under unmanageable attack.

The reach of the plague became apparent in 1998 when the city's proudest source of civic leadership pulled up stakes for California. It wasn't the number of jobs lost—maybe 150. It was that the Knight Ridder Company, parent of the *Miami Herald* and thirty other newspapers around America, had led the city to recovery from every storm, every immigration and civic disaster for decades. The company led the fight against casino gambling through three separate ballots, which may explain why in 2004 Florida voters agreed to let Miami-Dade and Broward counties vote on installing slot machines as a local option. (Miami-Dade voted no, Broward yes.) It created an effective shadow government at a time when the county was led by one self-serving commission after another. Knight Ridder claimed it was leaving for the more assured electronic future of Silicon Valley. Nobody believed that. The company, long run by a Miami family, had been taken over by Californians. They gave Miami a fair shot. Then, like any number of other companies, Knight Ridder figured that if it didn't have to be in Miami for the city's international connections, it didn't have to put up with a city hostage to crime that lived behind walls and came out only to promote chamber of commerce slogans about what a great place this was to live. (An investigation was underway late in mid-2004 into what happened to more than $1 million in missing Chamber funds. The county commission fired the only airport director in recent times who defied crony control.) The late *George* magazine in 1998 named Miami one of the ten most corrupt cities in America. Longtime downtown chronicler Michael Lewis, editor-publisher of the authoritative business weekly *Miami Today,* could only exhort readers to "cheer when the lid comes off the sewer of corruption." A quarter of Miami-Dade residents responding to a survey about local government cited corruption as the number-one problem.

But it's more than the corruption. Miami and its various organs of government have for so long tolerated low educational standards, widespread poverty persisting alongside golden ghettos, and endless sacrifice of the public domain to palsy-walsy politics—zoning misdeeds in particular—that the loss of Knight Ridder leadership raised a question whether Miami might be permanently lamed. Miami nonetheless can claim a Florida distinction: a downtown that has kept its central retail district alive even after the decades-long rush to the suburbs. Miami never lost its century-old Burdines (now Macy's) department store. When mom-and-pop retailers moved to the malls and others closed, some stayed. More opened.

Tourists ironically kept downtown alive. Not the Europeans and Americans down from the North who throng the beach resorts to play nor the wives of South American bankers and businessmen who once or twice a year accompany their husbands here, who lounge at hotel pools and shop at malls spread through suburbia. Downtown's tourists are more colorful: the shoppers from around the Caribbean, Central and South America as well as the underclass of Overtown, drawn here by bargains. Together they became the life of downtown, the reason downtown exists. The bankers and the courthouse crowd are in and out of air-conditioned offices. Shoppers rule the streets. Downtown has sashayed to the rhythms of its own maracas.

The Rebirth of Downtown

Into the late thirties, Seminoles still walked downtown in their colorful garb. Today it's swarthy Latinas who finger bolts of fabrics, ninety-eight cents a yard; guys with their fanny packs who cut deals on cell phones, a couple of ladies in shocking green mini-swimsuits pawing over boxes of soft sole shoes. Rock 'n' roll, salsa, and merengue pour out of Flagler Street shops. In summer, cold blasts of air conditioning nip the attention of passersby as effectively as the sidewalk hawkers who pass out discount coupons to get window shoppers into the stores. Windows are filled with computers, cameras, boom boxes. Here are Toy Liquidator, *El Palacio de los Juegos,* Everything $1 Super Store, *Sonrisas* Electronics, the Dollar Store—all either still here or replaced like everything else by more of the same. TVs to tee shirts, everything is sold by price. For every Alfred I. duPont Building there's a *La Época, Équipos Médicos, Casa del Marinero.* Shop signs align in rows beneath the overhangs that protect shoppers from rain. The overhangs are a trace of a pre-air-conditioned tropical world. The shops are barely one or two generations removed from the stalls of outdoor markets in San Jose or Santo Domingo. Here among the purple and green news racks for *Éxito!* a hot dog loses its sauerkraut and mustard down a tourist's dress, the moment videotaped for the family back home in Rio. A shopkeeper beneath a shag-orange wig shaped like a mop cleans a gazpacho spill. A moving van rolls down the street with its sign: *Lo qué cuenta es el cash $*—"What counts is the money." Even an English speaker hearing English spoken downtown experiences a twinge of the foreign, of the exotic.

The whole of downtown has cast off from the rest of America, let alone from Miami. It's one huge duty-free zone accompanied by the smells of frying plantains and Clorox, the sounds of Marc Anthony and Ricky Martin. Arcades draw people off the street, whole mini-malls of shops you can browse while keeping cool. The Seybold Arcade dazzles with golden glow. The Yellow Pages lists 133 jewelers in the downtown core that claims to be, after New York City, the second-largest retail jewelry district in America. Malls are stuffed with prepared food shops. Flagler Station, for example, features (or lately featured) *El Nica Churrascos* selling a sizzling *pollo a la plancha.* Here is the Brazilian *Sol e Mar,* a credible fish house with an all-you-can-eat luncheon buffet for five dollars. Crowded together in a charming brick patio off South First Street with a florist and Brazilian music playing are Lunch Paradise "20 exquisite luncheon entrees daily," *Brasileirissimo* Coffee & Bakery, *Pastel Brasileiro, La Tasa de Oro.* An outdoors crepe maker works from a movable stand at Columbus Bazaar, once site of the Columbus Hotel, once downtown's best. Dozens of tables sit outside beneath umbrellas. A fruit vendor sells his apples and his papayas and mangoes while the Metromover rumbles above.

Two blocks north, the Wolfson Campus of Miami-Dade Community College occupies an entire block. The student body comes from around the Americas—more foreign students than any other college in America. The campus houses two art galleries and each fall hosts the largest book fair in America. Miamians commute to the campus. Students from overseas rent in neighboring districts close by Metrorail stations. So far the numbers of downtowners are too few to revive nightlife. Students don't flock to neighborhood bars as they do elsewhere in Florida's college towns. Miami's universities are all in the suburbs. This student body has no wealth to spread around. Talk has it that a branch of four-year Florida International University, already with campuses to the west and north, will expand its presence downtown. That might make a difference.

And now the new residential towers that promise to spill their thousands onto the streets at night and by their sure demands will make the streets as compelling as Ocean Drive, Lincoln Road, and Calle Ocho, and as safe. Rising to meet the towers will be the new Science Center of the Americas and Space

 Planetarium, the relocated Miami Art Museum and Historical Museum of Southern Florida in Bicentennial Park (newly Museum Park), blocks from the new performing arts center. Transit will connect downtown and the Beach, if not by trains, then by rubber-wheeled trolleys. Back-and-forth movement will become easy and fun. Voters in 2004 approved a new $1.6 billion general obligation county bond that will generate additional funds for downtown culture and renewal. Trade, culture, people living downtown, tourists—the elements are more fully in place than anywhere in Florida and more assuredly than anywhere in America. Barring some national calamity, the action is unstoppable. Three towers—two of 50-plus stories, the third 72—are rising on a long-vacant three-acre downtown parcel. Three more—one 50 stories, two 60 stories—are underway on the long neglected west side of Biscayne Boulevard across from Bayside. A group of Israeli developers has floated plans for a billion dollars of investments downtown and on the Beach. Asian companies from Korea, Japan, and Singapore looking to connect to Latin America have announced expanded Miami operations. Uber-developer Jorge Perez has just paid an unheard-of $94 million for a 5.1-acre property on the south shore of the river where he will tear down a 598-room Sheraton hotel for who knows what monument will have to bear the investment load. New ultra-posh J. W. Marriott and Conrad hotels have opened; one or two W hotels are next. The first new downtown supermarket in memory north of the river will be a Whole Foods. Shaquille O'Neal is driving a new city identity as much as his skills drive a resurgent Miami Heat, and the filming of *Miami Vice*—the movie—in 2005 will rehype every sexy image of Miami stirred year after year by episodes of the crime series *CSI: Miami,* by rap music's Source Awards, *Billboard* magazine's R&B and hip-hop awards, Latin America MTV Grammy Awards, and MTV Video Music Awards.

Discussing downtown and the Beach, Bill Farkas, executive director of ArtCenter/South Florida, says, "Our two cities aren't in competition any more in the arts." Farkas, former head of the Fort Lauderdale Downtown Development Authority and its performing arts center, says: "Half our artists are from Latin and South America. They cross back and forth between Lincoln Road and the Design District." Many have studios there and in the growing Wynwood arts district where manufacturing and warehouse sites are becoming art studios and galleries. "The two sides of the bay are integrating without anybody making an issue. It's more than economics that's influencing downtown. It's the explosion of the arts and the cultural community. It's civics, business and culture."

When the Miami Children's Museum and the venerable Parrot Jungle chose new locations in the late nineties, both chose Watson Island, site of the seaplane base where Highway A1A crosses the bay. "Before that," says Michael Spring, executive director of the Miami-Dade Cultural Council, "the safe bet would have been Kendall. It doesn't seem absurd today that families would follow. New families are moving downtown." Kendall is one of the immense Miami suburbs that sprawled the city population into the paved-over Everglades. "It's a new way of thinking," says Spring. "Just when you think the city isn't capable of changing, in rolls the next sea. You look at an international city. What do people look for when they relocate? Inevitably it's great cultural life, a level of sophistication that a cultural life plays an important role in for business. You distinguish the city by its cultural life, its buildings, its traditions. Spain promotes Spain all the time, and it's always with business, traditions and culture, all as one. Law firm recruiters say they have to be able to speak to cultural life when they try to attract the best lawyers from overseas."

Taking up Farkas's vision, Miami Downtown Development director Dana Nottingham sees downtown becoming part of the Beach experience, the nexus for commerce and culture where the residential, business, and visitor markets come together. "Downtown has suddenly become relevant to peoples' lives," says Nottingham. "It's the new Miami frontier. We don't know where it will go but it's just scratching the surface. You come downtown and you're part of an expanding universe."

Miami Today's Lewis says: "This time the turnaround is real. When people discovered downtown for residential, it happened. You're seeing mixed-use hotel, office, condo and commercial on the same blocks. Every second or third building has places to dine and some kind of entertainment offering. Developers can afford to include all this. The Four Seasons has gone up. It's sixty-six stories. Everything's at outrageous prices but the low interest rates have kept everything selling. Ten Museum Park sold out 180 of 200 units before opening its sales office. A year or two ago, there were some forty locations on the river. That's dropped to five. A lot has been speculation, but even if the market stops rising like crazy or drops, you move in.

"At Twenty-fifth and Biscayne, a developer on the water tore down a one-story apartment or motel and put up forty stories with condos starting at $400,000. Just a year ago there were drug rehab houses in the neighborhood and nobody really cared. You're eleven blocks from the Performing Arts Center, a few more from the Miami Arena, twenty-two from the heart of downtown—nothing but a bus ride or even a good walk in winter." Redevelopment north from the Performing Arts Center and the new rail yard project will renew mid-Biscayne Boulevard, which still remains what the Miami Herald calls the "boulevard of debauchery."

Ruth and Richard Shack remember fifty years ago when Miami was a city where you relocated to make it and if you didn't, you went someplace else. "It looked like a frontier. It felt like you could make a million. That point of view still exists, the psychology still prevails." Ruth Shack, a former county commissioner and longtime executive of the Dade Community Foundation, and Richard, an established arts figure, tell the story of how Hank Meyer would meet hot-shot business prospects at the airport and ask whether they wanted to become president of the chamber of commerce and tell them which boards to go for and at which restaurants to eat. The story is apocryphal but makes the point that nobody had to pay dues. "We were so hungry for leadership and still are," says Ruth Shack.

Says Richard Shack: "There's no question that downtown residential is critical. As downtown becomes a living area, an arts and entertainment district is going to spread from the performing arts center. It's going to draw people 365 days a year. Look at Lincoln Center. As soon as that started there was a tremendous rush of buildings and condominiums built around that."

"This is a place rich with diversity, conflicting ideas, and potential," says Ruth Shack. "People really say, 'It's so wonderful to come to Miami. It's so close to the United States.' This community bubbles up vitality. It's no longer just the old elite making decisions. Everybody makes decisions. We're a community on the cusp," she says. "We're either the brink of democracy, the post-future society, or on the brink of chaos."

13 MONROE COUNTY

Ultimate Love-Hate at the End of the Road

Figure 13.1. Captain Nemo's souvenir stand along the Overseas Highway in 1956 Key Largo. Charles Barron, photographer. Courtesy of the Florida State Archives.

Figure 13.2. Duval Street on Key West. Courtesy of Fla-Keys.org.

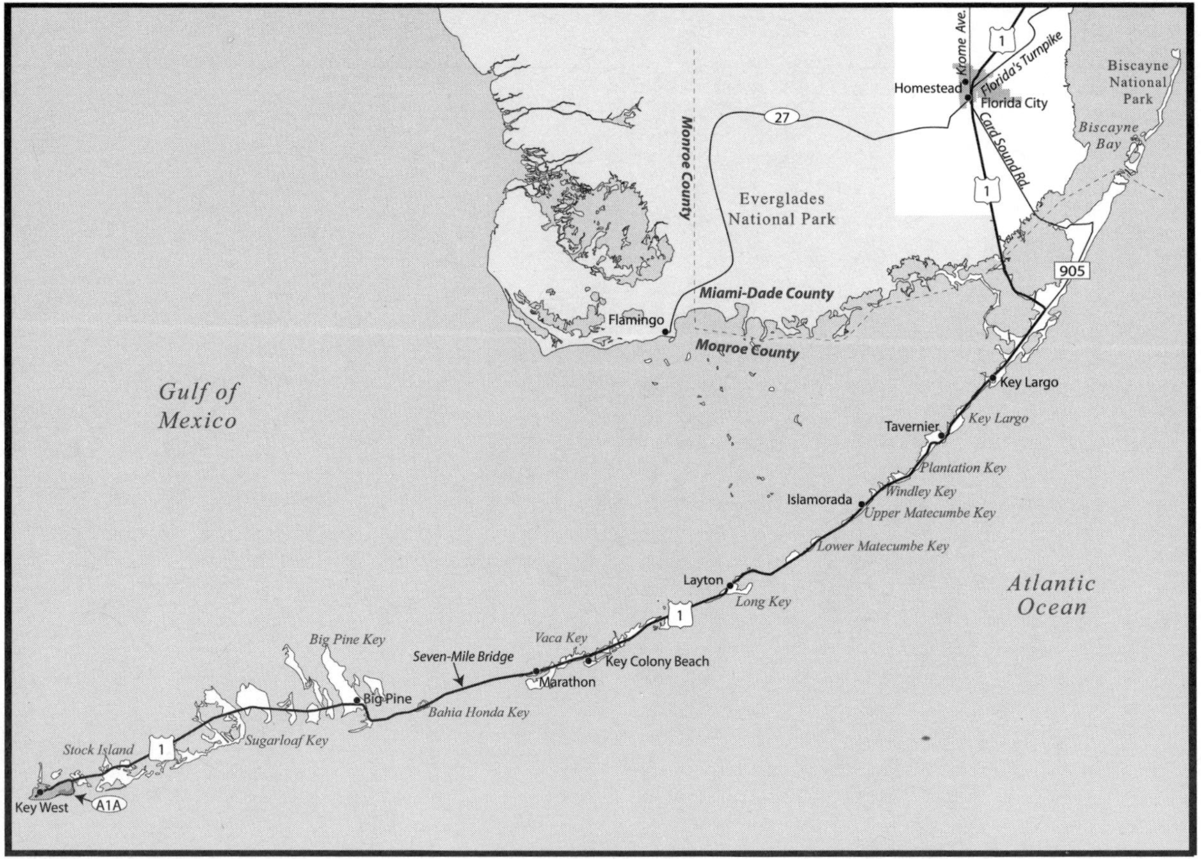

Map 13. Monroe County

People in the Keys used to say that the only thing their place had in common with the rest of Florida was a zip code prefix and a Miami area code. The Keys were too far out to be Florida. Florida was overbuilt and controlled by developers, redneck where it wasn't Disney and where it wasn't cozying up to Palm Beach. RV parks, polluted lakes and rivers, immigrant politics, race riots, land scams: Florida was Paradise Lost, while the Keys remained Eden, flipped free from the grip of Florida like a rack of foldout postcards, protected because they were hard to get to, extended off the mainland 110 miles out to sea, beyond reach of suburbia. People who lived strung out along the way were precisely turning away from everything Florida had become. The place was the claim of drifters, outcasts, change-of-lifers as well as the escapist rich—a place where you got by with shallow roots in sandy soil. History prepared their maverick way of doing things. They were preceded in these islands by pirates and by wreckers. Keys people have always been crabby, scuttling to pinch off a piece of what fell their way. Theirs was no continental economy. They wanted to be left alone.

The Keys playfully dipped its toes in the virtual Caribbean. At the foot of Florida, the archipelago arced a coral and limestone ridge southwest from the mainland, compressing the eastern Gulf of Mexico into a trough so deep and swift around the state's bare bottom that it shot a current of water clear up the coast of North America, tickling the winter shores of Western Europe with teasing warmth. By contrast, the lee basin that collected between Florida's Gulf coast and the Keys formed from lakes and rivers flowing south in their languid, almost gravity-defying Everglades cant, washing islets that bob blue-green rimmed by sandy white beaches. Where these backcountry waters escaped between the Keys eastward into the Atlantic, they bathed the only living barrier coral reef of North America. These living underwater gardens at the edge of the sea combined spectacular color with surreal fans in a matrix of species more diverse than any rain forest.

But over time, prank ways got co-opted by hucksters. The Keys became paradise with a capital P, as in Paradise Café, Paradise Dental Care, Paradise Glass & Mirror, Paradise Grooming, Paradise Guns & Ammo, Paradise Health & Fitness, Paradise Internet Services, Paradise Liquors, Paradise Movers, Paradise Optical, Paradise Petroleum Deli, Paradise Plumbing, Paradise Pool Service, Paradise Recycling, Paradise Tattoo, Paradise Transmission Service. Controlled by real estate and tourist promoters, the Keys became tarnished by schlock. Big-box retail became a feature of the Overseas Highway. The coral reef turned sickly, beaches began closing, scary viruses showed up in home- side canals. Today, Keys officials work to undo years of ruinous environmental policy while America confronts the aging of its escapist dream. For much of the twentieth century the allure hung fresh.

Until 1906, you couldn't get from any one of these hundreds of islands to the next except by boat. The first who came island-hopping were Caribs. They came from the south, followed by Calusas from the north, fighting Tequestas along the way. When the Spanish briefly thought about occupying these islands and found the bones of the battle-fallen on the southernmost large key, they called it *Cayo Hueso.* "Hueso" in Spanish means bone, which the Anglophones who later came this way heard as "west," and so what might have become Bone Key instead became Key West. The Keys never supplied the gold that obsessed Spain's New World avarice, so the Spanish never settled.

Key West, because of its natural deep harbor, never needed any landward connection. Through the nineteenth century the town prospered by sea. When the United States acquired Florida from Spain in 1821, Bahamians still pursued Britain's centuries-old parasitic dependence on ships sailing the Straits of Florida. Islanders once privateers in Her Majesty's Service attacking Spanish treasure ships became remorseless wreckers luring ships onto the reefs, or still more commonplace salvagers, scouring the Keys for whatever treasures remained afloat from unlucky mariners gone aground on their own, then dashing with their prizes back east to their islands in the stream. When the new territorial government ended Bahamian freeloading by demanding that salvage claims be registered in Key West, not only did three centuries of lawlessness ebb. Key West also peeled off to make its own history, largely separate from Keys to the north. Bahamians moved in.

They called themselves Conchs, named for the tough briny muscles screwed into their big pink shells that they pulled loose and cooked up in stews and battered. Key West grew fat on commerce, while Keys to the north—without ports, churches, or medical practitioners—attracted only those most zealous about husbanding their new dominion. The Bahamians fished or raised bananas, limes, pineapples, and tomatoes, sponging, timbering and turtling. The few did a total job. Today little native to the area remains. Forests were cut down, the soil wasted, and the sea catch, after a much longer period of uncontrolled taking, has dwindled to scant former abundance. These strippers of the resource are recalled on Upper Matecumbe Key, where gravestones that honor once-Bahamian Pinders and Russells today subside along a precarious beachfront surrounding an old cemetery on the frolic grounds of Cheeca Lodge.

Captivated by tales of hoop-earringed mariners in northern harbors, the few Americans who ventured into the Keys explored their dream by sailing first to Key West before transferring to the occasional inter-Keys trader. By 1895, the *Island Home* of Johnny Pinder introduced regular sea service into commercial life along the Upper Keys. Then Henry Flagler, whose manifest destiny was to whistle his trains through the quiet of every thatched-roof settlement along the Florida east coast, leapfrogged his railroad from the mainland, in 1912, whistling, rumbling, and parading into Key West. In 1823, President James Monroe had dispatched Commodore David Porter with a navy squadron to subdue the pirates of the Indies and so prepare Florida for statehood. Ninety years later, throughout this archipelago of indifference to civil order, Flagler secured the American imperium.

Yet the Railroad That Went to Sea managed to stay in business only twenty-three years. Flagler died within a year after his triumphal entry into Key West. His overseas extension may have been honored as one of the modern engineering wonders of the world, but it never made money.

Prohibition made the sievelike Keys a natural gateway for rumrunner operations from the Bahamas. With Repeal in 1933, fishermen skilled in navigating the mangrove channels of the Keys turned to running illegal aliens. Perhaps alone, these practitioners of legendary Keys huggermugger found the silver lining in the destruction of Flagler's railroad. A massive hurricane blew across the Middle Keys on Labor Day 1935, sweeping the track off its foundations and with it hundreds of veterans at work on the highway that soon would replace it. The overseas rail link ended. For the next three years, travelers to Key West had to ferry along much of their journey.

The railroad had presaged good times in the Keys. Flagler's Long Key Fishing Club was built directly on the Atlantic beach. Guests fished from yachts by day, dressed for dinner, and luxuriated behind screened verandas, with meals served on linen to a tycoon's order. Writer Zane Grey served as club president for three years, initiating game fish conservation, a practice since evolved into the sport of catch-and-release. Although the club blew away with the 1935 hurricane, its style of easy living dropped off the mainland grew popular with completion of the Overseas Highway and the prosperity that followed World War II. William J. Matheson had colonized Lignumvitae Key just after the Great War in 1919. The Key Largo Anglers Club north in the Keys, the Matecumbe Club in the Middle Keys, and Pirates Cove south on Sugarloaf Key were already catering to the ultrarich.

A Remnant Florida Style

The merely well-off looking for someplace new were rediscovering a remnant Florida style in the stone-faced stores and big-porched restaurants that were opening along the road. Places like the Rustic Inn, which became Sid & Roxie's (still roadside in Islamorada), drew guests to fox-trot to the hits of Tommy Dorsey and Harry James and get tipsy between courses of fresh conch and grouper. In Key Largo, the Caribbean Club—later ballyhooed for its moment of fame in the enduring Bogart-Bacall flick *Key Largo*—got its start in the forties when Carl Fisher, who had developed Miami Beach, sought to

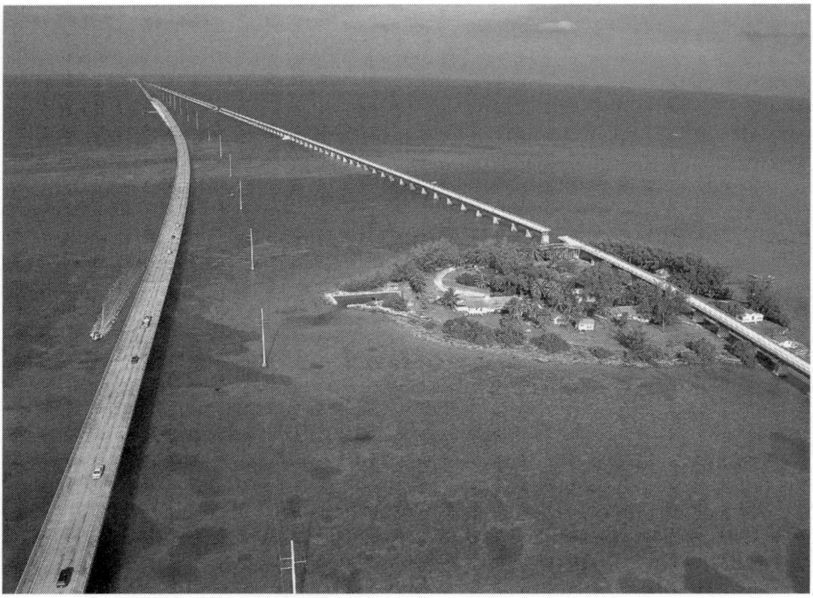

Figure 13.3. The Pigeon Key Bridge. Courtesy of Fla-Keys.org.

crank it all up again in the Keys. But Fisher died after he completed only the little hotel and restaurant.

Miami grocer Del Layton, who first saw the Keys on Flagler's train only months before the enterprise washed away, revived a version of the Long Key Fishing Club in 1968. Layton's Zane Grey would be retired Boston Red Sox slugger Ted Williams, who became the Keys' most publicized bone fisherman. Layton eventually incorporated his patch of beach and coral as one of only two municipalities along the entire stretch of road north of Key West. Key Colony Beach, Islamorada, and Marathon have since followed.

Promoters who were already banking the take from quickening tourism got a break when, in April 1982, U.S. Customs and Immigration authorities in a crackdown on drugs and illegal aliens blockaded everything moving north out of the Keys. Muscling people around like the *campesinos* of some banana republic, the police held up traffic for days, a massive inconvenience duly recorded by the nation's papers and TV. Miami PR man Stuart Newman made limeade out of that key lime when he promoted the "secession" of the Florida Keys from the U.S.A. and had the archipelago declared the Conch Republic. The laid-back, hammock style of the Keys beckoned exotic escape without need for passports or risk of crazies armed with anything more scary than a joint. "Just Do It" became the Conch Republic's advertising slogan. (Almost 25 years later, Newman's firm still has the account.)

"Just doing it" got a lot easier in the early eighties when the U.S. Navy expanded its aqueduct to Key West, for the first time supplying all the Keys linked by highway with a reliable source of freshwater for an expanding economy. Florida's Department of Transportation began rebuilding bridges, four-laning many and miles of highway. A county tax on overnight rooms funded annual advertising campaigns. Now the Keys would cash in. America couldn't help but get to work "improving" Toon Town.

With the people came the dredges and the draglines. Beachcombers who lived alone and imperceptibly added their waste to the droppings of wildlife became subdivision and trailer park dwellers behind bulkheads that tore out the mangroves. The few who at first cast lines from their yards into still near pristine canals became the many who watched the once-clear water turn pea-soup green and the snapper replaced by inedible trash fish.

In a Florida Keys too poor and too long set in antigovernment attitudes, the easy permitting of septic tanks turned the shallow limestone substrate into a filter for leeching heavy nutrient loads into nearshore waters. Westerly currents from Florida Bay and the easterly push of the Atlantic trapped a hovering pall of nitrogen and phosphorous that began overloading the natural system that protected the coral reef. To protect coastal cities, freshwater that once percolated through the Everglades into Florida Bay and maintained its brackish balance was cut off by a flood control system. Flood flows were diverted into canals, wastefully rushing water to the sea. While salinity increased in Florida Bay, the diverted freshwater shocked salt-dependent shrimp and fish. Sea grass died and algal blooms spread across hundreds of square miles, depriving bottom sponges of light for survival and juvenile lobster and shellfish of safe habitat. Unable to mature, shellfish have declined by half. Corals died away.

Keys native and commercial fisherman Karl Lessard in the 1990s recalled how 20 years before he could look to the bottom and count how many lobsters he'd caught in his traps. "It's been a long time since I could see my rope below two or three feet," he said. Commercial spear fisherman Don DeMaria at the same time told of a wall of dirty water coming out of Florida Bay and chasing fish off the reef. "It was just filthy," he said. "I couldn't even see the end of my spear gun." Islands cottony white with flocks of seabirds today sit bare green. Flocks have been reduced by more than 90 percent. Visitors who never knew the Keys before find the birdlife wondrous and the sometimes dirty green water, once everywhere tropical blue, to-die-for gorgeous.

On top of the systemic battering came piecemeal damage by short-term promoters in the name of tourism. No place in grossly mismanaged Florida has been worse served than the Florida Keys by these Flagler princelings. One developer scraped bare an entire island, filled in a lagoon, dug canals, and installed the city of Key Colony Beach. On Windley Key, the blacktopped Holiday Isle Resort promoted jet skis as an essential part of the rock 'n' roll lifestyle, threatening entire colonies of backcountry birdlife with devastating noise intrusion.

"The big hurdle," says Monroe county commissioner George Neugent, "is stopping the continued chipping away of our community character." Neugent recalls that when, as president of the Marathon Chamber of Commerce, he fought big-box retailers from building along the highway, "they wanted to hang me by my toes." Home Depot and Office Depot forwent the hanging and built their boxes anyway.

Everything afloat from cruise ships to supertankers jettisoned their trash overboard and cleaned bilges in these waters. The least careful among them ran their vessels directly into the reefs—three, one after another, at the turn of the century alone. Others jury-rig their logs, disable their pollution-preventing devices, and stir turbidity in Key West harbor where sea grasses try to take hold again. In the spirit of "Just Let Go," divers drop their anchors on the reef. Inexperienced snorkelers everywhere gasp for breath while keeping their heads above water by standing on corals. Live-aboard boaters keep the costs down on their screw-you lifestyles by dumping directly into their anchorages. Fish traps, once used widely by commercial fishermen, have everywhere been abandoned since nets were found to be more efficient harvesters. Tens of thousands of "ghost" traps left littering the sea floor continue to kill indiscriminately after their marking buoys have disappeared. Treasure hunters learned to point their boat engines down and blow canyons in the sea bottom to clear away everything that might get in the way of their hunt. Even rock on the sea floor—dead coral or limestone bits with living matter attached to it—has become stuff for plunder, literally hundreds of tons a year taken from waters of the Keys to enhance aquarium ambiance in seafood restaurants and in people's home living rooms.

It Might Have Been Different

Some saw it all coming a long time ago. When talk began toward conserving a portion of the historic Everglades in a national park, conservationists sought to have the entire Florida Keys included. Landowners shot that audacity down. A glimmer of the idea was revived almost a half century later when Florida's environmental managers in 1990 proposed making all of the Keys a state marine reserve and charging fees for driving onto the islands. Tourism operators killed this idea.

But protection couldn't be denied, and in 1990, a 3,500-square-mile Florida Keys National Marine Sanctuary was established that includes the entire reef and surrounding waters to a depth of 300 feet extending offshore roughly 2 miles in the Upper Keys and 3 miles in the Lower Keys. The enabling legislation, though fought by fish collectors and treasure hunters, hotel owners and real estate agents, was championed by two conservation heroes of Florida, the late U.S. representative Dante B. Fascell and former governor Bob Graham. At the same time that he signed the sanctuary into law, President

George Bush (devotee of bonefishing in the waters off Islamorada) also signed off on the Coastal Barriers Improvement Act, barring federal flood insurance, road aid, sewer loans, and other assistance for new development throughout the sanctuary (which includes some 8,500 acres of uplands otherwise dry enough to build on).

The sanctuary barred oil and gas drilling outright and mandated the relocation of commercial shipping to protect the islands from the kind of groundings on the reef that the year before had inspired the new sanctuary designation. A management plan set up twenty-four no-take areas and wildlife management areas. A water quality protection program called for land-based agencies to address wastewater and storm-water issues. Mooring buoys have been installed and maintained, channels and reefs more clearly marked. Education programs began for adults, school kids, and tourists. Volunteers were enlisted and research programs and enforcement programs begun in no-take areas; limits imposed on personal watercraft and powerboat racing; zones established to protect corals, reef fish, and bottom rock; and special protection provided for birds and endangered terrestrial species.

Yet the reef keeps declining. One recent study based on years of time-lapse photography found the reef decaying at the rate of 10 percent a year, which means that only patches might soon remain. Though sanctuary management has authority to act on water quality, the problem demands greater funding and local accountability. Monroe County, with the least desirable substrate for septic tanks, has the largest number of septic tanks and cesspits per capita of any Florida county and alone allows shallow injection wells for sewage. Reef Relief, the coral reef watchdog organization, jawbones government and residents directly that they can't go on living as they have in the Keys; that Monroe County will have to install nutrient-stripping tertiary treatment of sewage. Key West has done that with a $53 million new sewer system. County voters followed in 2000 by overwhelmingly authorizing $23 million in bonds for advanced wastewater treatment facilities, existing sewer line replacement, and deep-well injection of nutrient-stripped water.

Although improved sewerage elsewhere in Florida has led to explosive development, development has actually slowed in the Keys because of a state requirement that calls for twenty-four-hour Keys-wide evacuation in the case of emergencies—an approaching hurricane, for example. The early warning requirement results from limited capacity of the Overseas Highway. Based on peak numbers of residents and tourists, full evacuation could take days. Compromise effected with real estate interests now limits new residential construction to about 255 building permits a year, with additional limits on commercial building. But this hasn't slowed demand; it has intensified demand. Houses once bought for $80,000 and $90,000 are now selling for $400,000 and $500,000, getting torn down and replaced by multimillion-dollar mansions. Forget affordable housing. In Marathon, a newly appointed high school principal found out he couldn't afford his dream of living in the Keys and gave up the job. An assistant principal from an already understaffed elementary school had to move up.

The situation is even worse in Key West, which faces a total crisis in housing. Says the city's leading businessman and its chief advocate for affordable housing, Ed Swift: "People with $60,000 or even $70,000 cannot find adequate housing today. Teachers, nurses, service workers, the whole fabric of our communities is imploding while the out-of-town wealthy are buying middle-income homes, fixing them up, living in them a month or two a year and displacing the workforce.

"Walk the halls of government in Tallahassee, tell someone you're from the Keys, and the first thing they say is, 'Oh my God, I love the Keys, I hope you don't let that place change.' It's everyone's idea of a place to get away from the rest of the madness in Florida. Environmentalists or not, people in Tallahassee don't want to see any growth. 'Let's save the Keys!' But just for the rich? Or a real mixed society of people that allows the artists to survive, children to grow up and be taught? Even the wealthy won't like it if there's no services."

Key West environmentalist and restaurant operator Elliot Baron talks about workers "hot bedding, where people on sequential work shifts have to share the same bed."

Development will further slow following a recent Keys-wide study by the Army Corps of Engineers that concluded that the upland environment carrying capacity has been exceeded. County government now proposes public acquisition of all significant remaining habitat, though it could cost up to $125 million. "One side wants you to enforce regulations strictly," says county growth management director Tim McGarry; "the other side calls you a Nazi." Most developers have quit working the Keys.

The fight over development has switched to the access road in and out of the Keys, an 18-mile two-lane section, which, if four-laned for evacuation, would loose a flood of commuters and day-trippers the other way. Keys residents don't want their lifestyles further debased by crowds; business interests generally favor the mob. About the core issue of evacuation, one compromise calls for one lane in, two lanes out. The state Department of Transportation says okay to the three-laning, but only if it gets to lay a roadbed for the fourth lane. Nobody seriously takes that as compromise. Calls are increasingly heard for diverting tourist tax dollars away from advertising for more tourists to repairing the damage tourists cause. Nothing will likely happen with the road until at least 2005. Most likely to occur is the paving of a third lane meant only for emergency use north but that pressure by tourism interests will convert to regular use.

Impressions today, on arriving from the mainland onto Key Largo, suggest the Keys settling into amiable imperfection. This is mainland America's sun parlor, the shape of our four-day holiday weekend. You don't want to believe that when you get here it's the workaday world all over again. Yet, with its Winn-Dixie, Standard Oil, and numbing real estate signs, Key Largo has become the extension of Miami's Kendall. Key Largo revisits what you've left home for.

Some changes for the better aren't apparent. Crocodiles have made a comeback in the watery habitat along Card Sound Road, the long way around from Homestead onto Key Largo. A chain link fence hides the Crocodile Lake National Wildlife Refuge, putting it off-limits to visitors. Throughout North Key Largo, the state has been buying up environmentally sensitive land, altogether some 3,000 acres, much of this once planned for the failed Port Bougainville development that only twenty years ago was slated to become more populated than Key West. And the popular dive zones off Key Largo certainly have their appeal.

A kind of badass style hangs on. Drunks drive the roads like nowhere else, in the last few years running up twice the number of convictions for DUI than the state average. (In 2000, Keys businesses on average held one license to serve alcohol for every 121 residents; the comparable number for Miami-Dade, reported by the *Key West Citizen,* was one for every 450.) Guys sport beards, long hair, and hound-dog moustaches. They quit bitching when their women come back from up North. You see kids with unsure glances holding onto moms on their cell phones, moms with the hardscrabble look of single parents stranded in the Keys or drawn here because they weren't the straightest of the straight where they hailed from. They talk about their love life, their kids, the cost of living. If kids get strung out on dope in these "just-do-it" Keys latitudes, kids also run free here in the way you don't see anymore on the mainland. Running free isn't necessarily troublesome. Back behind the highway all up and down the Keys, there's still this small-town neighborhood feeling of what it was like growing up in the suburbs through prewar years.

Key Largo in the canal behind the Holiday Inn presents the kitschy juxtaposition of a gambling ship side by side with the *African Queen,* that legendary stovepipe of a boat jury-rigged for salvation by Bogart in the flick with Hepburn. Down the road is the Caribbean Club with its Pow! Zowee! sunsets out back. Otherwise, Key Largo introduces you to a view-blocking, slab style of condo-hotel, though as if to compensate, down side roads a collection of low-intensity cottage-style places to stay—places like Largo Lodge and Popp's Place—that define "Keys-easy" better than any guesthouse in Key West. You find roadside stands that sell hubcaps and tomatoes, mailboxes shaped like dolphins, and, because these Keys get surprisingly little rainfall, outrageously colorful bougainvilleas.

You have to believe that people who live here all the time wonder how come they're at work in paradise looking after others who are vacationing. The Key Largo Chamber of Commerce likes to call itself a leader in ecotourism. We all of us like to think of ourselves as better than we are.

Whatever Key Largo is becoming slips away as the highway rolls south. First impressions give way like the landscape into an absence of landmarks. The way becomes greener, less busy—almost country, a landscape of desultory shrubs where once the tropical forest stood tall. Comfortable houses hide back by the water. A bike path shows up, in time meant to run the length of the Keys.

The road swings across Tavernier Creek onto Plantation Key, which once centered an agricultural district where Bahamians to the north raised pineapples in a community called Planter and to the south raised citrus and fished. Some dozen or so frame houses built by these farmers between the time the train came through and the 1935 hurricane remain along the northbound stretch of road through Tavernier. A colony of their descendants and others drawn in the mid-twentieth century to the modest life of this town quietly keep the faith.

Down the road stands the Tavernier Hotel, oldest north of Key West, that began life as a movie theater in the twenties. The town name in French means tavern keeper, though nobody can figure how come there's this French name alone along the highway. Plantation Yacht Harbor is the site of a one-time pineapple plantation developed as a resort by R. J. Reynolds Tobacco Company. Now it's a big Islamorada city park.

Cross Snake Creek onto Windley Key and you get your first drop-dead look at the panoramic blue-green that often surrounds these islands. A lifetime of stored-up tropical images rushes in from the horizons as bay and ocean come together beneath the bridge. The magic of the Keys whistles in, the difference, the excitement. You grasp how the mood can take hold of anybody prone to stimulants to begin with.

After the Theater of the Sea dolphin attraction comes the Holiday Isle Resort and another of these stunning channels you bridge bedazzled. At the top of Upper Matecumbe Key, the Whale Harbor Resort remains popular for its seafood buffet, even if media personality Arthur Godfrey, who fished here, is forgotten. From here south, marinas and fishing fleets cluster around the ramps of channel bridges.

The highway enters "downtown" Islamorada, prettiest section in the Keys and a municipal leader in aesthetic planning, legislating against chain stores and the most responsible about waste treatment. The purple popular here is because Islamorada in Spanish means "purple place" (apparently a reference to the abundant morning glories popped out of the bush when Spanish mariners first sailed by). Parallel to the highway runs Old Highway, a scant 3 miles of road in place before new road replaced the railroad tracks. Old Highway is a pleasant, curving alternative of board fences and modest houses where locals walk and bike. It runs past the entrance to Cheeca Lodge, one of the standout resorts of the Keys.

State ferry can get you to Lignumvitae Key, one of a pair of historically important islands. The key was getaway home of Key Biscayne chemical magnate William J. Matheson. In 1919, he bought the entire 280-acre island and built a family lodge of coral rock. The state, which acquired the house in 1970 from only the second owners, has reestablished it as in Matheson times. Tongue and groove wainscoting, floors of Dade County pine, wicker furniture, and crank-up phonograph all immediately put you in touch with the early twentieth century.

A Lattice of Steel

East less than a mile from the highway and also served by ferry is Indian Key. It's only 10 acres but boasts three centuries of significant Florida history ending in the mid-1800s. The island was once home to Calusas who enslaved crewmembers of Spanish treasure fleets wrecked on the reef. Pirates organized their own wrecking parties until ousted by the navy.

A Key West wrecker who ran afoul of authorities built an entire port town here and in 1836 got the territorial council in Tallahassee to designate the key seat of a new county called Dade, named to honor the hero American major of a Seminole massacre a year before, and independent from Monroe and Key West. The end came in 1840 when an Indian attack wiped out the town, killing many, including M.D. and botanist Henry Perrine. Two years later, the Dade County seat was relocated to a hardly larger Miami. Indian Key has since remained uninhabited. Perrine's plants have grown over the ruins. A reenactment of the 1840 raid takes place each October. This is the best time to ferry over and walk the ruins.

The bridge south from Lower Matecumbe shoots itself a spectacular angle from little Craig Key across Channel Five. When Layton shows up on Long Key, you're in it and out fast as a holler on a passing train. Evenings, the road cuts through the starry twinkle in isolation. Imagination fills, but everything else thins. The soil is thin, the highway is thin, the build-up is thin, wages are thin. Commitment to a conventional moral code is thin.

Marathon takes its name from Flagler's workers' conjecture about how bridging the 7 miles of open water below Vaca Key would call for marathon exertion. The town formed during the four years the bridge took for completion. Train passengers who came this far could board Flagler's Peninsular and Occidental ships to complete the journey to Key West and Havana. Many afterward remembered the excellent tarpon fishing. Swirling waters around the abutments of the new Seven Mile Bridge proved hospitable to game fish. The rich were already ensconced 20 miles up the line at the Long Key Fishing

Club. Marathon developed as a fishing resort. It became important by default. Flagler was nearing the end of his life. His engineers were determined to reach Key West while the old man could still step down from his private car to lead the celebration. Between Marathon and Key West there would be no more hotels, no fishing camps. Marathon became the last town-sized provisioning point. So it has stayed almost to the present, though lately an orgy of commercial development has rimmed the highway, much of it to support real estate promotion in the Lower Keys. Efforts by town promoters to represent their place beautifully will never succeed until the power company replaces its massive power pylons that overpower any compensating aesthetic. If Marathon lost its port, the town gained a modest airport. In Boot Key Harbor, with a new dump station, the town gained a sizeable leisure fishing fleet. Since the fifties, a shrimp fleet also calls Marathon home, though from the highway the town lacks charm.

The Seven Mile Bridge humps 65 feet above open channel before the highway touches down, slicing across islets and fill. Fish camps, dive camps, trailer camps scatter to the water's edge. The beach at Bahia Honda was the most bewitching the railroad would pass. From out of its palm groves Flagler's engineers instead lifted their most beautiful bridge across the channel to Spanish Harbor, a lattice of steel that thirty years later the highway would piggyback on a roadbed superimposed atop.

Big Pine had 50 residents before World War II and until the eighties grew slowly. Then the new wider bridges improved access for Winnebagos. The new aqueduct reawakened developer dreams. Big Pine stretched. Population jumped from 800 in 1980 to 4,000 only ten years later. The Lower Keys Chamber trumpeted that newcomers came for a lifestyle on islands "as pristine, beautiful and wondrous as the day they were first fashioned." What newcomers found were two wildlife refuges—the Great White Heron National Refuge, created in 1938, and the National Key Deer Refuge, created in 1957 after herd numbers had declined from predation and traffic accidents to fewer than eighty.

The freshwater on Big Pine sustained the deer, which were trapped on these lower keys after floods at the end of the Ice Age. Adapted over centuries to forage what the islands sustained, they grow no larger than dogs. Even more than the Florida panther and black bear, these key deer became the symbol of colliding interests between those who insist on putting humans first and others who regard humans as part of complex natural systems. The problem is that today houses occupy grounds long used by the herd for getting around. Deer show up in backyards. Developers of posh Little Palm Island not long ago found deer swimming over to breakfast on the chef's herb garden. An electrical perimeter went up, and then, when discovered, quickly came down. Well-meaning residents feed the deer and so neutralize their natural fear of humans, leading them nearer to roadways where accidents with cars prove the greatest menace to their survival.

The Big Pine–based Conch Coalition that for years fought government over deer protection has mellowed. Few residents remain as mean-spirited as those who vented their hostility by destroying animals and depositing their carcasses at signs that limit roadway speed, instead accepting the benefits of more assured quiet lifestyles that result from government acquisition of critical deer habitat. And the deer have come back, by 2004 numbering about 600.

Fat Albert and Ample Lifestyles

At the end of the line, you reach Key West by passing quickly through the last of the Lower Keys. Cudjoe Key might yield a glimpse of Fat Albert, the U.S. Navy's balloon (actually two balloons) that flies surveillance for drugs and illegal immigrants. You skim across the Saddlebunch Keys, tufted mangrove islets, then past Boca Chica, the naval aviation base once popular with Key Westers for its palmy beach, long off-limits to civilians; past Stock Island, named for the cattle once penned here, today industrial, commercial, residential, but also site of shrimp boat docks and working marinas. Commerce will increasingly yield to dwelling units because next to no affordable housing exists anywhere nearer Key West. Property values have lately doubled. Singlewides rent for $1,000, doublewides for $1,500 and more. Florida Keys Community College is here with its Tennessee Williams Performing Theatre. So are the Florida Keys Memorial Hospital, the botanical gardens, the dump, the local Mt. Trashmore, the shuttered dog track, unrepaired side streets rutted and ponding in rain in a forlorn suburbia.

Onto Key West, the road crosses Cow Key Channel, where the bridge provides rude shelter for homeless beneath. The four-lane road divides. South Roosevelt Boulevard becomes Highway A1A again for three last miles, skirting Key West International Airport and the East Martello Museum. The boulevard rims open Atlantic and the longest beach on the key, coarse sand but popular because big and free, though you have to feed meters to park. Joggers love this stretch. Colorfully painted meals-on-wheels vans park by the sidewalk dispensing tacos and burgers. Too many new condos and hotels have gone up along the section known as the Bridle Path and behind, where housing has filled much of the remaining salt ponds that a century ago were an economic mainstay. Even the remaining few acres have recently been threatened by plans to extend airport runways east and west into the wetlands. Nearby lies an older modest suburbia bisected east-west by Flagler Avenue where once the trolley ran.

Just back of Higgs Beach, with a new jogging and rollerblading path, is McCoy Indigenous Park, named for a town mayor who, in 1978, water-skied the 122 miles to Havana, almost 50 miles nearer than Miami. An animal rescue group occupies a portion of the park along with bocce courts. Otherwise, paths wind beneath a canopy of native trees near remaining salt ponds that form a protected waterway good for paddling.

A gauntlet of exploitation runs along North Roosevelt Boulevard. Motels, fooderies, gas stations, and shopping centers pave the place over, lining the road with their grabby signs. It's the equivalent of Highway 192 outside Disney. New Town rarely shows up in brochures. Even the motels here show pictures of Old Town. Affordable housing has newly gone up across the road at Roosevelt Gardens. Will it end up like the last effort? That was at the Truman Annex, where a developer was required to build a few affordable units to get his development deal when the navy moved out. "Affordable" houses there have wound up selling for upward of $200,000. People who make the beds and wash the dishes in Old Town now mostly live on Stock Island. New Town is their service center on their way to and from work.

Two main streets enter the historic district. Truman Avenue carries Highway 1 to its end. Palm Avenue swings north along Garrison Bight, the marina with tidy new docks, edging through the navy installation at Trumbo Point. On the left is Peary Court, a housing project protested for its encroachment on popular ball fields by a former city commissioner who, Hamas-like, strapped on armaments and threatened to blow the place up. For his bravado he did time. The road takes a sharp bend and enters Old Town.

Of all Florida's places, Old Town stays most lively in the mind. From largely nondescript, the look becomes handcrafted, a carpentered town that's a cross between late Victorian and seafaring New England. Roofs slope beneath tin, bargeboards trimmed in lacy fretwork, balustrades formed of planks patterned in hearts or dolphins or bottle shapes or pineapples. Lyric style hangs in the air like jasmine while your imagination munches on gingerbread. The scale becomes residential, the pace domestic. The place is tropical, sweet-smelling, lavish with color. Flowers flutter in breeze beside pastel-painted houses and tumble over white picket fences. Words like allamanda, bougainvillea, and frangipani dissolve sweetly in the mind like caramels in the mouth. Along the lanes of Bahama Village the sounds of reggae pour out of radios beside fellows playing checkers or limning at neighborhood storefronts. White frame West Indian houses sit in yards planted with stands of cane, bamboo, bananas. The parade marches to a different drummer, yields to breezes that don't blow elsewhere. Roosters crow at noon, awakening no few musicians who gig through the night.

Small as Old Town is—a legacy thirty-eight blocks of houses mostly designed and influenced by nineteenth-century shipbuilders who knew how to make small spaces practical and beautiful—it survives largely thanks to two unsung heroes.

The first was Julius F. Stone Jr., who headed the Federal Emergency Relief Administration in Florida after the 1935 hurricane. Stone had a keen grasp of how, with nothing to lose, Key West could invent an entirely new identity for itself fashioned in terms America would adore. Stone brought artists and writers to Key West to live. He subsidized them at their craft. Visitors came to share their presence. Stone made Key West an expatriate Paris in the tropics. He turned the need for a feel-good escape from reality into an economy. His star attraction became Ernest Hemingway, who first visited Key West in 1928. Hemingway fell in love with the island, a place hard to get to, down on its luck with wonderful weather and great fishing. Hemingway already had *The Sun Also Rises* behind him. In Key West he soon produced *A Farewell to Arms, The Green Hills of Africa,* and a growing volume of stories in *Esquire* that connected him with Key West and established literary cachet for the island that continues to this day.

Twenty years later, when the historic Lowe House burned and plans were underway to raze another for a gas station, a descendant of Commodore Porter acted. Jesse Porter Newton, a fifth-generation "Conch," got the effort going with what her coterie cleverly began referring to as the Audubon House because the famous painter of birds was reputed to have once stayed overnight. Ms. Newton's drive gained momentum and led to preservation of what came to be called Old Town. Key West became a cause you could feel good about your visits supporting.

Less hero than Pied Piper, Jimmy Buffett labeled the place Margaritaville and renewed Key West's appeal for a beer-sloshing crowd after the navy largely moved out and then so did Buffett, to Palm Beach.

In the daily fantasy fest of Duval Street, pedi-cab drivers once destined for marketing careers prance by in full-body tattoos topped by seasonal Santa caps. Accountants turned fire-eaters celebrate sunset at Mallory Square while pharmacists prescribe their own health as keepers of bed-and-breakfasts. Whether at Schooner Wharf Bar over one too many Key West Pale Ales, buzzed up the road on Baby's Coffee, or strung out on dope, everyone edges a step or two over the line, self witnessing this town's incubator for incessant acting out. Even the homeless amuse by how they splice their color to the town story line. Some weave palm fronds into sun-shielding hats for sale. Others wheel by on their trashmo bikes, fore and aft sections hinged together, parading every last possession, including, rear-most, a pooch on a leash, mocking our own dreams of casting loose from tethered lives. The trashmo cycling master pedals a dog in a basket and a tray with two cups of take-out coffee in his right hand while chatting up a lady friend riding alongside.

Many of Key West's first citizens have been hardly less quirky. After the war, Harry Truman kept things going by making the place his Little White House. The press loved his colorful shirts that added to the town's raffish identity. There was Mayor McCoy water-skiing to Havana. A more recent mayor was rumrunner and later saloon keeper Tony Tarracino, who years ago fled Jersey City for as far as the train would take him when he learned the mob was setting him up for a pair of concrete boots, and whose philosophical quip is worth the fifteen dollars to wear home on a tee shirt: "If you have a tremendous sex drive and a great ego, brains don't mean shit."

If all vacations are meant to indulge us, Key West does so in spades—and in clubs, diamonds, and hearts, too. Key West is full-deck Florida, with its easy living framed by its authentic look.

"We were always laid back," recalls Marcia Anderson, a Conch who manages one of the boutique Old Town places to stay called the Paradise Inn. "We grew up riding our bicycles barefoot, hopping off to swim in every pool we knew about, and we knew them all." Marcia's boss, like many who first came on vacation, never forgot the place. "We came as hippies," recalls Shel Segal, who played keyboard at Sloppy Joe's before returning to set up his Simonton Street compound. "Louie's Backyard [the town's top-rated restaurant] was closed at the time because of a divorce between the owners. Friends and I used to take over that yard for ourselves. We just hung out. That was rich living."

The best of Old Town lies out in the open. The worst does too. All around Old Town a perimeter of hotels has been shoehorned into tight spaces in a series of buddy-buddy deals. Permits for hotels have been issued for buildings meant for apartments. It's nothing for a lawyer–city commissioner representing a transportation operator who holds a virtual city monopoly to hold himself out as representing the city when defending his client's exclusive arrangement before the state legislature. The window for folly stays open at the board of adjustments, which approves dozens of requests for converting residential space into transient accommodations, allowing densities up to eighty units an acre without providing the extra parking, security, and sewer capacity that larger numbers of transients require. After years of flaunting deception, the city attorney admitted under heavy questioning that the city was acting illegally.

It was only in the mid-eighties that Richard Heyman—America's first openly gay mayor—finally got the city to stop dumping raw sewage into nearshore waters. Around that time, conservation activists Craig and Deevon Quirolo formed Reef Relief. Having all the Keys declared a "no-discharge zone" for boat sewage has followed their successful call for the city to strip sewage of all nutrients. They have led fights against Big Sugar and the South Florida Water Management District to curb nutrient discharge into Florida Bay and to eliminate cruise ship dumping of wastes in international waters after achieving success in local waters. At the turn of the century, they led the city to install a new storm-water treatment plant. Beachgoers can enjoy another success. In 2001, Reef Relief got the city to dedicate a nearshore marine park, which, by eliminating pleasure boats from all but essential channels, is allowing a natural shore reef to develop that even waders can reach.

Duval Street near the cruise piers has become grossly commercial under the impact of thousands of day visitors from cruise ships, who descend en masse for a few quick hours of binge shopping and rote-led touring. Elliot Baron and Ed Swift, who agree on the need for affordable housing, square off on the cruise ships. Some days the behemoths rim the island's western docks five at a time, disgorging as many as 10,000 passengers—an additional two-fifths of the city's population—onto Duval Street. Swift dominates the tourist scene with his near monopoly on tourist transportation. The cruise ships alone bring him a million customers a year virtually marketing-cost free. The driver-guides who operate his trams and trolleys that briefly carry ship passengers off Duval sound their amplified spiel through the town's neighborhoods seven days a week. Noise has become a major issue for residents, who have lately gotten the mayor's ear.

By 2003, the assault led Baron and Livable Old Town, a political action committee he co-chairs, to launch a new challenge to tourism's overwhelming impacts. After years of more subdued petitioning, this time he organized a mass protest that shocked the city administration by gaining international media notoriety. Even though Key West derives close to $10 million a year in fees and taxes from cruise ships and their passengers, city officials had to pay attention. In 2004, *National Geographic Traveler* listed Key West third-ugliest among 115 of the world's great destinations, citing "crowding, poor planning and greed." CNN broadcast a Reuters report quoting Baron's comment that, "Cruise ships have changed our island into a tacky debasement from what used to be a unique island." The mayor appointed a committee whose chances of getting something done were only enhanced when the chamber of commerce boycotted the move.

What saves Duval Street is its two-lane scale, its wide sidewalks, and the palms in front of the ubiquitous tee shirt shops. (Recent favorite: "Beer: Helping white guys dance since 1846.") Early mornings on a cool day, half the crowd passes bleary-eyed, sucking hot coffee. Later they pass licking ice cream cones while toting bags from Fast Buck Freddie's, the department store as performance art (don't miss it). A peloton of cyclists rides by in colorful spandex. A guy on the sidewalk with a dog wearing shades and a macaw on the shoulder hypes tourists for three to five dollars to shoot the menagerie.

Past Key West Aloe and Lilly Pulitzer's, Key West Bight Harborwalk starts at A&B Lobster House. It's no less touristy here than on Duval but less frenzied. The walk zigzags around the waterfront, boats docked everywhere, masts, halyards, pennants filling vertical space. Harborfront Market is here, one of two family markets, this more the natural foods choice. (Fausto's, the other and older, is run by the current mayor's family.) Offshore, folks "live off the hook," anchored out, shuttling to docks and back on johnboats often as not with dogs. Little remains of the colorful shops once along Lazy Way Lane. A couple of live-aboards still sell shell art, original postcards, hammocks, and arty coconuts. From Greene Street to Waterfront Market, this was Lazy Jake's Way when Lazy Jake was here, but Jake didn't pay the rent. Of course there was a time when nobody paid the rent. Owners asked Jake to stay anyway, but he left.

Arts and culture exceed expectations. Old Town numbers maybe 100 galleries and many museums (including innumerable house museums), three live theaters, a 100-member chorale, and a 75-member symphony orchestra. If you can't ever get enough of the town, drop by Key West Island Bookstore. Hemingway wasn't alone writing here. Others included Elizabeth Bishop, Annie Dillard, John Hersey, Alison Lurie, Thomas McGuane, Richard Wilbur, Tennessee Williams and Herman Wouk. Most of them acted out in Key West, too, but at least they left the rest of us memories beyond self-indulgence.

NASSAU COUNTY

Information Sources

Amelia Island–Fernandina Beach–Yulee Chamber of Commerce 102 Centre St., Fernandina Beach 32034, 904/261-3248.

Amelia Island Museum of History 233 S. 3rd St., Fernandina Beach 32034, 904/261-7378, www.ameliaisland.com, at the Old Nassau County Jail. Archives, exhibits, and source of tours.

Amelia Island Tourist Development Council 961687 Gateway Blvd., Fernandina Beach 32034, 800/2AMELIA (226-3542), 904/277-0717, www.ameliaisland.org.

Attractions and Recreation

Amelia Island Chamber Music Festival P.O. Box 15886, Fernandina Beach 32035, 904/261-1779, www.ameliaislandchambermusic.org. Florida's incomparable annual classical music program, performances at intimate venues around town, many free. Hardly anything like it anywhere.

American Beach For information, contact the A. L. Lewis Historical Society, P.O. Box 15563, Amelia Island 32034, 904/261-3088. Historic 12-block African American beachfront community crowded by Amelia Island Plantation and Summer Beach, its 60-foot sand dune newly incorporated into the Timucuan Ecological and Historic Preserve; presided over by the legendary MaVynee Betsch—the Beach Lady—who provides tours.

Bird Emergency Aid and Kare Sanctuary (BEAKS)--West down the dirt road off Heckscher Drive, 12084 Houston Ave., Big Talbot Id. 32226, 904/251-2473, beaks@leading.net; www.beaks.org. Injured bird sanctuary open to visitors. Free admission.

Cumberland Island, Georgia (National Park Service) P.O. Box 806, Saint Marys, Ga. 31558, 912/882-4335. 17.5-mile-long barrier island with unspoiled beaches, wild horses, ruins, and the great house of Thomas Carnegie descendant Margaret Ricketson, built in 1901 and operated as an inn on the American Plan (Greyfield Inn, reservations office, 8 N. 2nd St., Chandlery Bldg., Fernandina Beach 32034, Box 900, Fernandina Beach 32035-0900, 888/817-3421, 904/261-6408; in Ga. 912/882-

 4335; www.greyfieldinn.com). Ferry operated by the National Park Service from St. Marys, Ga., and by the inn from Fernandina Beach.

Fort Clinch State Park 2601 Atlantic Ave., Fernandina Beach 32034, 904/277-7274. 1,121-acre park occupies the far peninsular corner of Northeast Florida. Recreation area surrounding historic Second Seminole War fort. 5-mile off-road cycling trail, 4,000 feet of Atlantic coast for swimming. Daily reenactment of the 1864 Union garrison.

Historic Buccaneer Trail and the St. Johns River Ferry Hornblower Marine Services, 904/241-9969, www.hornblowermarine.com/sjrf_pr.htm (information also from Amelia Island Tourist Development Council; see above). Major remaining public car ferry in Florida links Highway A1A across the mouth of the St. Johns River, crossing from Mayport to the north shore mostly on the hour and half hour, and from Fort George to the south shore mostly on the quarter and three-quarter hours.

Kayak Amelia 13030 Heckscher Dr., Jacksonville 32226, 888/30-KAYAK (305-2925), 904/251-0016, www.KayakAmelia.com. Paddle and houseboat trips through Northeast Florida's waterways and marshes.

Sea Horse Stables Concession in Amelia Island State Park, Hwy. A1A at the south end of Amelia Island, 904/261-4878. One of the few places along coastal Florida offering horseback riding on the beach.

Tours by airplane, horse and buggy, and schooner Contact Amelia Island Tourist Development Council (see above).

Dining

Beech Street Grill 801 Beech St., Fernandina Beach, 904/277-3662. Best world-ranging cuisine in this town of stellar restaurants. Sit downstairs or up in a converted house full of local artifacts.

Café Karibo 17 N. 3rd St., Fernandina Beach, 904/277-5269. Eclectic, expertly prepared food inspired by what's fresh and herbed, in a small room and garden patio that captures the owner's whimsical imagination. Everything, including desserts, homemade.

Down Under Restaurant North side of Hwy. A1A on the west bank of the Intracoastal Waterway, 904/261-1001. Family-built-and-run rustic water's-edge dining room with deck service, redolent with history at the site of an old fish camp. Seafood.

Fernandina Seafood Market 315 N. Front St., Fernandina Beach, 904/491-0765. Waterfront at the shrimp docks on the patio outside the market, mostly fresh fried shrimp and fish. Local, informal, and good.

Florida House Inn 22 S. 3rd St., Fernandina Beach, 904/261-3300. Boardinghouse-style meals feature all-you-can-eat southern cooking and more than 100 different beers. Local favorite, newly with upscale evening and patio dining.

The Grill Room In the Ritz-Carlton, Amelia Island, 4750 Amelia Id. Pkwy., 904/277-1100. Oceanside, the most upscale room on the island (jackets for men), emphasis on local gourmet food preparations, good vegetarian (including macrobiotic) options.

Le Clos 20 S. 2nd St., Fernandina Beach, 904/261-8100. Provencal cooking in a woody old downtown house.

The Marina Seafood Restaurant 101 Centre St., Fernandina, 904/261-5310. Here forever at the foot of town serving old-fashioned American food to locals (and anybody else who comes by).

Lodging

Amelia Island Plantation P.O. Box 3000, Amelia Island 32035-3000, 888/261-6161, 904/261-6161. Golf and beach resort sprawling from sea to marsh; hundreds of hotel rooms and villas. Complete in all respects.

The Amelia Island Williams House 103 S. 9th St., Fernandina Beach 32034, 800/414-9258, 904/277-2328, www.williamshouse.com. Oldest antebellum house on the island, with rare gingerbread festooning. Unmatched interior opulence, set off by 500 years of heirloom antiques. A museum for bedding down in. Full gourmet breakfast.

Bailey House 28 S. 7th St., P.O. Box 805, Fernandina Beach 32034, 904/261-5390, www.bailey-house.com. National Register–listed Queen Anne from 1895, first of the town's B&Bs and a Fernandina landmark.

Elizabeth Pointe Lodge 98 S. Fletcher Ave., Amelia Id. 32034, 800/772-3359, 904/277-4851, www.elizabethpointelodge.com. Nantucket-style big house up on stilts beside the beach, impeccably run by one of Florida's premier lodging families—and ideal for families. Buffet breakfast.

The Fairbanks House 227 S. 7th St., Fernandina Beach 32034, 800/261-4838, 904/277-0500, www.fairbankshouse.com. Italianate mansion in the "silk stocking district" with exquisite detailing, built by a leading son of Fernandina and listed in the National Register. Rare B&B with swimming pool. Full gourmet breakfast.

Florida House Inn 20 & 22 S. 3rd St., P.O. Box 688, Fernandina Beach 32034, 800/258-3301, 904/261-3300, www.floridahouse.com. Oldest extant inn in Florida—a coaching house before the Civil War—with creaks and groans in all the right places. Not to be missed. Full breakfast, free motorbikes.

Hoyt House Bed and Breakfast 804 Atlantic Ave., Fernandina Beach 32034, 800/432-2085, 904/277-4300, www.hoythouse.com. Attractive yellow and blue Victorian from 1905, replica of the Rockefeller Cottage on Jekyll Island. For quiet, request rooms away from 8th St. Full breakfast.

The Ritz-Carlton 4750 Amelia Id. Pkwy., Amelia Id. 32034, 800/241-3333, 904/277-1100. Epitome of service and style, on the water.

1735 House 584 S. Fletcher Ave., Amelia Id. 32034, 800/872-8531, 904/261-4148, www.1735house-bb.com. Boxy and beachfront, 5 large suites detailed like Clipper-day captains' quarters, including bunk beds for kids. In-suite continental breakfast.

Shopping

Centre Street Heart of a diverse shopping row largely free of the kitsch that marks Florida's historic east coast cities elsewhere. Includes 3 bookstores. Request brochures from the chamber of commerce (above).

Health Foods: Fran's Nutrition Shoppe 1881 S. 14th St., Fernandina Beach, 904/277-0030; **Nassau Health Foods** 1722 S. 8th St., Fernandina Beach, 904/277-3158.

Island Art Assn. 11 N. 2nd St., Fernandina Beach, 904/261-7020. Local artists' work.

DUVAL COUNTY

Information Sources

Cultural Events Florida Community College Jacksonville Artist Series (904/632-3373); Jacksonville Ballet Theatre (904/727-7515); Jacksonville Symphony Orchestra (904/354-5547). For other sources, contact the Jacksonville and the Beaches Convention and Visitors Bureau (below), or other listings in this section.

Jacksonville and the Beaches Convention and Visitors Bureau 550 Water St., Jacksonville 32202, 800/733-2668, 904/798-9111, www.visitjacksonville.com. Chief source of tourist information. Among other brochures, request *Experience Jacksonville's Black Heritage,* which identifies sites throughout Northeast Florida; and *Walk around Downtown Jacksonville,* which identifies and describes a dozen or so landmark buildings.

Riverside Avondale Preservation, Inc. 2623 Herschel St., Jacksonville 32204, 904/389-2449. Represents side-by-side residential districts formed early in the twentieth century, now jointly listed in the National Register. Request the leaflet *Walk around Riverside-Avondale.*

St. Johns Riverkeeper 2880 University Blvd., Jacksonville 32211, 904/256-7591, www.stjohnsriverkeeper.org. Watchdog of the river.

San Marco Preservation Society 1652 Atlantic Blvd., Jacksonville 32207, 904/396-4734. Request the leaflet *Walk around San Marco* for self-guided tour of this handsome residential and commercial district on the south side of the river.

Sports Events National Football League Jacksonville Jaguars, 1 Alltel Stadium Pl., Jacksonville 32202, 904/633-2000. For minor league information, contact Jacksonville and the Beaches Convention and Visitors Bureau (above).

Attractions and Recreation

Alexander Brest Museum 2800 University Blvd. N., Jacksonville 32211, 904/744-3950, www.themosh.org/planetarium/index.asp. On the campus of Jacksonville University, specializing in Steuben glass, porcelains, cloisonné, ivory. Free admission.

American Lighthouse and Maritime Museum 1011 N. 3rd St., Jacksonville Beach 32250, 904/241-8845. Showcases history of lighthouses in art, scale models, photos, artifacts. Free admission.

The Beaches Art Center 228 Third Ave., Jacksonville Beach 32250. Showcase for local artists relocated here in mid-2004.

Big Talbot Island State Park 20 miles east of downtown Jacksonville on Hwy. A1A, c/o Little Talbot Island State Park, 12157 Heckscher Dr., Jacksonville 32226, 904/251-2320. Salt-marsh canoe routes, beaches. Excellent for nature study, birding, photography.

Cummer Museum of Arts and Gardens 829 Riverside Ave., Jacksonville 32205, 904/356-6857, www.cummer.org. Sensitively displayed collections of European and American art with formal gardens along the river. Excellent lecture series.

Edward Waters College 1658 Kings Rd., Jacksonville 32209, 904/366-2510, www.ewc.edu. Florida's oldest independent institution of higher learning, a traditional African American school with an enrollment of 1,282 students. Site of Obi-Scott-Umunna Collection of African Art.

Florida Theatre Performing Arts Center 128 E. Forsyth St., Jacksonville 32202, 904/355-2787, www.floridatheatre.com. Splendidly atmospheric, old-line movie palace restored as a downtown performing arts hall and a preferred venue for touring acts, together with the new **Times-Union Center For the Performing Arts** 1 Riverside Ave., Jacksonville 32202, 904/633-6110, www.jacksonville.com/community/tu-center, home of the Jacksonville Symphony Orchestra.

Fort George Island State Cultural Site 16 miles east of downtown Jacksonville on Hwy. A1A; for information, Little Talbot Island State Park (see below). Historic Timucuan site with relict dunes to 55 feet, among the highest coastal points south of New Jersey. Dense jungle hammock embraces cyclists and hikers on the island's roads and trails. Ribault Clubhouse, from the twenties, newly restored and reopened as an interpretive museum with bookstore.

Jacksonville Historical Center 100 B Wharfside Way, Southbank Riverwalk at Main St. Bridge, Jacksonville 32207, 904/396-6307. From Timucuan times to the era of Cowford to the present, Jax history fully laid out with entertaining and interactive exhibits. Free admission.

Jacksonville Historical Society 317 A. Philip Randolph Blvd., Jacksonville 32202, 904/665-0064, http://jaxhistory.com. Central source for Jacksonville history; provides guided tours to historic sites. Located in the 1887 Old St. Andrew's Episcopal Church.

Jacksonville Landing 2 E. Independent Dr., Jacksonville 32202, 904/353-1423, www.jacksonvillelanding.com. "Festival marketplace" with shops, restaurants, and a site of the Jacksonville Maritime Museum (904/355-9011). A second museum site on the Southbank Riverwalk (1015 Museum Circle, Unit 2, 904/398-9011).

Jacksonville Museum of Modern Art (JMOMA) 333 N. Laura St., Jacksonville 32202, 904/366-6911, www.jmoma.org. Permanent and traveling exhibitions at this expanding museum in the heart of reburgeoning downtown.

Jacksonville University 2800 University Blvd. N., Jacksonville 32211, 904/744-3950, www.ju.edu. Private, 2,200-student, 4-year college with graduate programs, laid out along bluffs of the St. Johns River. Site of an annual festival that commemorates composer Frederick Delius's sojourn along the St. Johns, and of the Alexander Brest Museum (see above).

Jacksonville Zoo and Gardens 8605 Zoo Parkway, Jacksonville 32218, 904/757-4462, www.jaxzoo.org. Ride the train or stroll the boardwalk through this nature park and zoo with some 800 animals including an animal nursery.

J. Johnson Gallery 177 4th Ave. N., Jacksonville Beach 32250, 904/435-3200, www.jjohnsongallery.com. Finest gallery in Northeast Florida, housed in a new Mizner-like structure with strikingly modern interiors, specializes in contemporary work.

Karpeles Manuscript Museum 101 W. 1st St., Jacksonville 33206, 904/356-2992, www.rain.org/~karpeles/jax.html. Important original manuscripts and documents from world history. One of eight such museums in America. Free.

Kathryn Abbey Hanna Park 500 Wonderwood Dr., Jacksonville 32233, 904/249-4700. 450-acre oceanfront park with miles of off-road cycling, hiking, and jogging paths, freshwater lakes for picnicking and RV facility.

Kingsley Plantation Fort George Island north of the Mayport Ferry landing off Rte. A1A; for information, 11676 Palmetto Ave., Jacksonville 32226, 904/251-3537. Site of a legendary North Florida plantation and home to its owner; richly complex in the annals of slavery. Site is part of the National Park Service Timucuan Ecological and Historic Preserve on Fort George Island at the mouth of the St. Johns River. Plantation house is the oldest extant in Florida. Grounds also include more than 20 of the tabby slave houses and gardens, all open to visitors.

Little Talbot Island State Park 12157 Heckscher Dr., Fort George 32226, 904/251-2320. Beautiful shore park of shifting waterways, dunes along 5 miles of the beach, altogether covering 2,500 acres from sea to marsh. Excellent birding, fishing, with a family campground.

Mandarin Community Club 1.8 miles west from the northernmost intersection of San Jose Blvd. and Mandarin Rd., 12447 Mandarin Rd., Jacksonville 32223, 904/268-1622, www.nvo.com/mandarincomclub/door/. Heart of historic antebellum community and after the Civil War home for 17 winters of Harriet Beecher Stowe. The Club was originally the 1872 Mandarin Schoolhouse and was built at the urging of Mrs. Stowe. Also includes historic post office and general store.

Marine Science Education Center 1347 Palmer St., Mayport 32227, 904/247-5973. Information source for the marine environment at the mouth of the St. Johns River.

Mayport Naval Station At the northwest corner of historic Mayport off Highway A1A, Jacksonville 32227, 904/270-5011, www.navysite.de/homeports/mayport.htm. Third-largest naval installation in the continental United States, home to more than 20 big ships and the Mayport Lighthouse. Call to learn if open to the public on any given day.

Museum of Science and History 1025 Museum Circle, Jacksonville 32207, 904/396-

7062, www.themosh.org. Grandly scaled riverfront glimpse of the region's natural foundation. Alexander Brest Planetarium provides multimedia shows.

Museum of Southern History 4304 Herschel St., Jacksonville 32210, 904/388-3574. Displays and a library focused on the antebellum South.

Outdoor Adventures and Balloon Adventures 1625 Emerson St., Jacksonville 32207, 904/393-9030. Northeast Florida's premier source for touring the natural realm. Conducted by an outspoken advocate for regional conservation.

Pablo Historical Park 425 Pablo Ave., Jacksonville Beach 32250, 904/246-0093. Exhibits in historic buildings re-create an impression of beachside Jacksonville's early years. Restored steam engine on the grounds.

Ritz Theatre and LaVilla Museum 829 N. David St., Jacksonville 32202, 904/632-5555. Hub of renewed downtown black arts and entertainment district. First-rate historical museum and restaurant.

Skyway 904/630-3100 for information. See the city on both sides of the river from a 2½-mile elevated people mover. One of the best rides in Florida.

Southbank and Northbank Riverwalk Pride of downtown opens the riverfront to pedestrians across a mile on either side of the St. Johns with dramatic skyline views. Treaty Oak Park at Prudential Drive and at Main Street on the Southbank is site of a giant oak with a 160-foot canopy. Popular local meeting place. Water taxi service connects the two shores.

Timucuan Ecological and Historic Preserve 12713 Fort Caroline Rd., Jacksonville 32225, 904/641-7155. 46,000-acre grandly historical conservation site between the lower St. Johns and the Nassau rivers preserving wetlands and prehistoric and historic sites. Focal attraction Fort Caroline, re-created landmark for the first planned French settlement in today's America. Interpretive site, hiking and paddling trails.

Tree Hill Nature Center 7152 Lone Star Rd., Jacksonville 32211, 904/724-4646. Nature preserve encompasses 42 acres east of downtown.

University of North Florida 4567 St. Johns Bluff Rd., Jacksonville 32224, 904/620-1000, www.unf.edu. State university campus with some 15,000 students in the center of the city's sprawling southeast. Wildlife preserve with trails covers 750 acres.

Dining

Biscottis 3556 St. Johns Ave., Jacksonville, 904/387-2060. Brick walls, original art, bustling—favorite Avondale spot for sophisticated Italian food on the posh neighborhood's main street. Big wine list.

Cafe Carmon 1986 San Marco Blvd., San Marco, 904/399-4488. Best for catching the mood of the neighborhood; bilevel, arty big rooms for dining on imaginatively prepared American food with sumptuous desserts. Sidewalk tables.

Clark's Fish Camp 12903 Hood Landing Rd., Mandarin, 904/268-3474. People drive from all around the city for fresh seafood at this once-rustic, today polished and rambling woody big scene on Julington Creek. All-you-can-eat catfish.

European Street Café 1704 San Marco Blvd., San Marco, 904/398-9500. Like a TV sitcom, filled with good-looking young people keeping trim on the big choice of sandwiches and salads. Beers from around the world; desserts in taste-whetting counter displays. (Also in Riverside and toward the Beaches.)

First Street Grille 807 N. 1st St., Jacksonville Beach, 904/246-6555. Best seafood on the beach. But big and busy, so bet on a wait—especially for seats at beachfront windows. In good weather, dine on the beach deck.

Fuel Coffeehouse 1037 Park St., Riverside, 904/425-3835. After the morning buzz, stick around for soup, salad, sandwich lunches, then come back for the nightly changing acts, most live but also including anime Japanese animation and movies.

Heartworks Gallery and Cafe 820 Lomax St., Riverside, 904/355-6210. Chat up the counter help while eyeing the salads and falafel or sit back and be served in the alcoves of this Five Points art and lunch scene. Professional but relaxed; gourmet dinners Fridays.

Juliette's 245 W. Water St., in the Omni Hotel, Jacksonville, 904/355-6554. Best of downtown for American-Continental food elegantly prepared, displayed, and served. Big Sunday brunch.

La Cena Ristorante 211 N. Laura St., Jacksonville, 904/633-9255. Exquisitely prepared northern Italian food with big choice of wines from glass-enclosed wine cellar.

Matthew's Restaurant 2107 Hendricks Ave., San Marco, 904/396-9922. Newest and best of Jax upscale eating places, features 5-course tasting menu.

The Mossfire Grill 1537 Margaret St., Riverside, 904/355-4434. Anything goes in arty Riverside, so why not tacos, burritos, and the whole hoss of Southwest cookery? Chips are homemade, and you can also rope in a fine piece of fish that ain't out of the Rio Grande. Inside and outside dining.

Ragtime Tavern and Seafood Grill 207 Atlantic Blvd., Atlantic Beach, 904/241-7877. Biggest beach scene in this multilevel, woody, ferny, noisy hangout featuring live music. Specializes in Cajun and Creole seafood, with best handcrafted brew in town.

Singleton's Seafood Shack 4728 Ocean St., Mayport, 904/246-4442. A "must" for fresh seafood you can see at the house market, and for the rustic old Mayport atmosphere beside the shrimp fleet and the Mayport Ferry dock.

Sterling's of Avondale 3551 St. Johns Ave., Avondale, 904/387-0700. Warm, arty glow indoors, burbling fountains in the patio, excelling in worldly seafood and grills.

Sun Dog Steak and Seafood 207 Atlantic Blvd., Neptune Beach, 904/241-8221. Classy chrome and neon deco styling at this friendly, near-the-beach diner serving its namesake food.

Wilfried's 24 Miramar 4446 Hendricks Ave., Lakewood district, 904/448-2424. Don't be put off by the strip shopping center. Intimate-style large and elegant space with an adventuresome American menu. One of the city's best.

The Wine Cellar 1314 Prudential Dr., Jacksonville, 904/398-8989. Romantic, established continental dining room attractively casting lantern-lit shadows on paneled walls and white table covers. Just off the Southbank Riverwalk. Big wine list.

Worman's Bakery and Deli 204 N. Broad St., Jacksonville. 904/354-5702. Downtown in metro Jax since 1924, still family-run, with legendary bagels, lox, matzo ball soup. The big schmooze. Lunch only.

Lodging

Dickert House 1804 Copeland St., Riverside, Jacksonville 32204, 904/387-4762, www.dickert-house.com. Garden-style house with innkeepers who combine southern and English backgrounds. Full breakfast.

Downing Street Bed and Breakfast 2759 Downing St., Riverside 32205, 904/388-1704. 2-story, wood-frame expanded bungalow built in 1923 with hardwood floors and sash windows is a rare home-stay B&B, not an inn, with only 2 guest rooms. Full breakfast.

Fig Tree Inn Bed and Breakfast 185 4th Ave., Jacksonville Beach 33050, 877/217-9830, 904/246-8855, www.figtreeinn.com. Big-porched, 1915 shingle-style house with 6 guest rooms a block from the beach.

House on Cherry Street 1844 Cherry St., Riverside, Jacksonville 32205, 904/384-1999, www.1bbweb.com/cherry/. Croquet lawn on the river backs this solidly built, quiet, colonial-style house at the end of its Riverside side street. Four-poster beds, expanded continental breakfast.

Inn at Oak Street 2124 Oak St., Jacksonville 32204, 904/379-5525, www.innatoakstreet.com. Ornate 1902 mansion freed of historic clutter and, especially mornings, filled with light through its museum-quality spaces. 5 exceptional guest rooms, several public spaces, all with heart pine floors. Full breakfast.

Pelican Path Bed and Breakfast by the Sea 11 N. 19th Ave., Jacksonville Beach 32250, 888/749-1177, 904/249-1177, www.pelicanpath.com. Beachy guest rooms upstairs in their own wing all have views of the sea. Downstairs, a big breakfast room (serving full breakfast) sits directly alongside the beach dune.

Plantation Manor Inn 1630 Copeland St., Riverside, Jacksonville 32204, 904/384-4630, www.plantationmanorinn.com. Showy, big-pillared southern mansion with interior statuary and gracious garden. Lavish breakfast.

Riverdale Inn 1521 Riverside Ave., Jacksonville 32205, 904/354-5080. New, different, and irresistible, this 3-story Queen Anne with its 8 guest rooms is mansion-fine again the way it was in 1901, when the house became home to a pine plantation magnate's family. Rarity for Florida B&Bs is a 72-seat restaurant and bar—the Gum Bunch Pub—that plays on the original owner's turpentine wealth.

St. Johns House 1718 Osceola St., Riverside, Jacksonville 32204, 904/384-3724, www.stjohnshouse.com. Woody, Prairie-style house with a touch of formality and beautiful wall-hung quilts. Innkeepers thoroughly familiar with Jacksonville goings-on. Expanded continental breakfast. Closed July, August.

Chamblin Book Mine 4551 Roosevelt Blvd., Jacksonville, 904/384-1685. Call it a gold mine, this Fort Knox–sized warehouse of bargain books is on the west side of Jax.

Five Points Downtown Riverside is the counterculture hangout for Jax, with the city's best vegetarian restaurant (Heartworks Café, see above), best newsstand (Five Points News), best music store (Blue Moon Music), and more, all within a couple of blocks; shops for the spiked-hair set, antique collectors, and those desperately needing a custom-designed or retro frock for high visibility at the Times-Union Center for the Performing Arts, just minutes away.

Good Earth Market 10950 San Jose Blvd., San Jose, 904/260-9547. Best of the area health food stores, just south of I-295.

Penzeys 1515 San Marco Blvd., Jacksonville, 904/399-4477. Spices from around the world, some you can sample, in an open, airy—and aromatic—shop. Catalog sales.

Peterbrooke Chocolatier 2024 San Marco Blvd., Jacksonville, 800/771-0019, 904/398-2488. Since 1983, with locations in 7 neighborhoods.

Shops of Historic Avondale Charming, un-malled street of some 60 to 70 boutiques and restaurants in the "downtown" of one of the city's beautiful residential districts.

Jacksonville's south side is awash in malls.

ST. JOHNS COUNTY

Information Sources

Historic St. Augustine Preservation Board 48 King St., St. Augustine 32084, 904/825-5033.

St. Augustine Historical Society 271 Charlotte St., St. Augustine 32084, 904/824-2872, www.oldcity.com.

St. Augustine, Ponte Vedra, and The Beaches Visitors and Convention Bureau 88 Riberia St., Ste. 400, St. Augustine 32086, 800/OLD-CITY (653-2489), 904/829-1711, www.visitoldcity.com. Request the excellent yearly updated *Travel Planner,* which includes, along with other useful information, a complete list of B&Bs in addition to those listed below under Lodging.

Attractions and Recreation

Anastasia State Park S.R. A1A at S.R. 3, 1340-A A1A South, St. Augustine 32084, 904/461-2033. Broad dune-backed beaches; concession-outfitted paddling in a tidal marsh lagoon set in a hardwood forest.

Castillo de San Marcos 1 Castillo Dr., St. Augustine 32084, 904/829-6506. Great Spanish fortification on the Matanzas River, completed in 1695 after 23 years of construction, later used as a military prison, retired after use during the Spanish-American War. Today a national monument and greatest landmark of the Ancient City.

Cult of the Old Some 30 St. Augustine visitor sites proclaim themselves Old, Olde, or Oldest. Most are genuinely historic and worth a visit. Best source for information is the annual *Travel Planner* published by the St. Augustine, Ponte Vedra, and The Beaches Visitors and Convention Bureau (see above).

Faver-Dykes State Park 1000 Faver-Dykes Rd., St. Augustine 32086, 904/794-0997. Small but beautiful and biologically rich park bordering the north bank tidal marshes along Pellicer Creek. Short hiking trails, picnic areas.

Flagler College 74 King St., St. Augustine 32084, 904/829-6481, ext. 220, www.flagler.edu/. Liberal arts college ensconced in Henry Flagler's Ponce de Leon Hotel.

Fort Matanzas 8635 A1A South, St. Augustine 32086, 904/471-0116; for information, see above under Castillo de San Marcos. Fort of coquina rock erected to guard southern approaches to St. Augustine. Today approachable by Park Service ferry.

Fort Mose 2 miles north of St. Augustine east off U.S. Highway 1. National Historic Landmark site commemorates the oldest free African settlement in today's United States. For information: Fort Mose Historical Society, P.O. Box 4230, St. Augustine 32085-4230, www.oldcity.com/mose/.

Government House Museum 48 King St., St. Augustine 32084, 904/825-5033. Comprehensive look at the city's rich heritage from treasures of ongoing archaeological digs and other displays.

Guana Tolomato Matanzas National Estuarine Research Reserve GTM Reserve, 9741 Ocean Shore Blvd., St. Augustine 32080, 904/461-4054, www.nerrs.noaa.gov/GTM. This 55,000-acre federal and state research unit incorporates the former Guana River State Park and includes several sections of the Intracoastal Waterway. The Guana section occupies 2,200 acres from the Atlantic across to the Guana River, encompassing salt marshes, hardwood hammocks, coastal strand, and beach dunes that rise to 40 feet. Dirt roads for cycling and hiking.

Harbor Shuttle of St. Augustine 716 Ocean Parkway, Ocean Pines, MD 2180, 904/501-4249 (cell), 410/208-1482 (o). www.harborshuttletours.com. Ride the catamaran just for the scenery and narrated, up-close waterfront touring or to avoid the often traffic-bedeviled roads to get to waterfront restaurants and attractions. On/off options at 5 landings or stay on board for the round trip.

Limelight Theatre 11 Old Mission Ave., St. Augustine 32085, 866/682-6400, www.limelight-theatre.org. Live theater at the edge of the historic downtown at the Joukowsky Family Foundation Center for the Arts.

Old St. Augustine Village 250 St. George St., St. Augustine 32084, 904/823-9722, www.old-staug-village.com. Nine restored homes and a country store located on one block within the historic district. Each structure has a distinct theme based on a historical occupant. Guided tours.

Ponce de Leon's Fountain of Youth 11 Magnolia Ave., St. Augustine 32084, 800/356-8222, 904/829-3168, www.fountainofyouthflorida.com. National Archaeological Park, ostensive site of Ponce de Leon's 1513 landing at the ancient Timucuan town of Seloy. Tacky, in light of its significance.

Potter's Wax Museum 17 King St., St. Augustine 32084, 904/829-9056, www.potterswax.com. Pirates to Ponce to princes, their likenesses all captured.

Ripley's Believe It or Not Museum 19 San Marco Ave., St. Augustine 32084, 904/824-1606, www.staugustine-ripleys.com/. This is the original Ripley's museum, in the historic Castle Warden Hotel.

San Sebastian Winery 157 King St., St. Augustine 32084, 888/352-9463, 904/826-1594, www.sansebastianwinery.com. Sample popular Florida hybrid and muscadine grape wines after a free tour and explanation of the winemaking process in this faux historic structure downtown. November through February, live weekend jazz at the Wine and Jazz Bar in The Cellar Upstairs.

Scenic Cruise St. Augustine Municipal Marina, St. Augustine 32084, 904/824-1806. Narrated cruise through Matanzas Bay aboard the *Victory III.* Operated by the same family for more than 75 years.

St. Augustine Alligator Farm Zoological Park Hwy. A1A 1.5 miles east of the Bridge of Lions, P.O. Drawer E, St. Augustine 32085-1320, 904/824-3337, www.alligatorfarm.com. In the vicinity for more than 100 years, shows off lots of gators as well as other fauna. Creekside boardwalk for good views of the wading-bird rookery. Not as tacky as you might think.

St. Augustine Lighthouse and Museum Anastasia Island across from the Alligator Farm; 81 Lighthouse Avenue, St. Augustine 32084, 904/829-0745, www.staugustinelighthouse.com. Opened in 1874 to replace America's first lighthouse, features a 165-foot-tall tower, restored keeper's home, museum with interactive exhibits, nature trail, and art gallery.

St. Augustine's Oldest House 14 St. Francis St., St. Augustine 32084, 904/824-2872, www.oldcity.com/oldhouse. The Gonzalez-Alvarez House dates from the early eighteenth century, in its tabby, board, brick, and shingle materials that reflect the chief styles of construction through the early years of the city. Museum and ornamental gardens.

St. Augustine's Restored Spanish Quarter St. George St., St. Augustine 32084, 904/825-6380, www.oldcity.com/sites/spanishquarter/. Early sites and times of the Ancient City with reenactors in an original compound of 8 buildings.

Coastal Outdoor Center 291 Cubbedge Rd., Crescent Beach 32080, 904/471-4144, www.coastaloutdoorcentere.com. Kayak rentals, tours, lessons at the area's oldest fish camp. For tram and trolley tours of the historic district, ghost tours, harbor tours, and custom tours, get a copy of the *Travel Planner* from the St. Augustine, Ponte Vedra, and The Beaches Visitors and Convention Bureau (see above).

Whetstone Chocolates Factory Tour 2 Coke Rd., St. Augustine 32086, 800/849-7933, 904/325-1700. Free 15-minute tours include watching chocolates made followed by sampling. Gift shop.

World Golf Hall of Fame 21 World Golf Place, St. Augustine 32092, 800/948-4746, www.wgv.com. As they say, "The closest you can get to the legends of golf without carrying their clubs." Includes history of the game, IMAX film, "swing analyzer," and beyond the exhibition area, 18-hole championship course, hotel, shops, etc.

Dining

A1A Ale Works 1 King St., St. Augustine, 904/829-2977. Views tasty as the Caribbean-inspired cuisine in this woody reworking of an old dry goods and clothing store downtown by the Bridge of Lions and Matanzas Bay waterfront. Award-winning microbrewery. Family-run, not a chain.

Beech Street Coffee Co. 4285 A1A S., St. Augustine Beach, 904/461-0500. Locals' breakfast place of choice: lots of coffees, bagels, soups, sandwiches. Nothing special but the friendliness.

Café Alcazar 23 Granada St., St. Augustine, 904/824-7813. Healthy, often guitarist-accompanied lunches with homemade soups and Mediterranean specialties, inside the Lightner Antique Mall where the Alcazar Hotel guests once swam in the jumbo pool.

Cap's On the Water 4325 Myrtle St., on A1A 2.5 miles north of Vilano Beach at the landmark Castle onto 3rd St. to the water, 904/824-8794. Locals come by boat or drive over to this hangout on the Intracoastal. Think loose, think Margaritaville. Seafood and suds, though no more entertainment after neighbor complaints.

Cortesses Bistro and Flamingo Room 172 San Marco Ave., St. Augustine, 904/825-6775. Popular for its brick patio dining and art-filled indoors, no less for its affordable American and European cuisine: plenty pastas but one or two fish, chicken, veal, pork, and beef choices.

Creekside Dinery 160 Nix Boat Yard Rd., St. Augustine, 904/829-6113. Fresh fish and seafoods best enjoyed on the ample wood decks alongside the San Sebastian River marsh. Woody as well inside for when the torches don't quite discourage the no-see-ums.

Denoel French Pastry 212 Charlotte St., St. Augustine, 904/829-3974, in the Old Spanish Quarter. For when your sweet tooth bites. Here since 1966.

Eddie's Palm Valley Crossing 3020 Palm Valley Rd., Ponte Vedra Beach, 904/285-5028. Cracker food in a handsome board building that used to sit beside a wooden bridge across the Intracoastal, lately replaced by an uninspired new one.

Fiddler's Green 2750 Anahma Dr., Vilano Beach, 904/824-8897. Seafood and more served seaside in a coquina and pecky cypress, fireplace-equipped dining room at the site of the old (1926) Vilano Beach Casino.

Gypsy Cab Company 828 Anastasia Blvd., St. Augustine, 904/824-8244. Informal for food inspired without borders. Local favorite.

La Parisienne 60 Hypolita St., St. Augustine, 904/829-0055. French provincial food with all its nuances in a French Country setting.

The Manatee Cafe 525 S.R. 16, St. Augustine, 904/826-0210. Best omelets and pancakes in town plus veggie fare, often organic.

Mill Top Tavern and Listening Room 19½ St. George St., St. Augustine, 904/829-2329. Homemade soups, salads, sandwiches, munchies. Best live music venue.

A New Dawn Natural Foods 110 Anastasia Blvd., St. Augustine, 904/824-1337. At lunchtime, salads, sandwiches, sides at the food bar in this small natural foods store.

Old City House Inn and Restaurant 115 Cordova St., St. Augustine, 904/826-0184. Expertly prepared continental and world foods in a softly lit, Mediterranean-suggestive but unluxurious setting. Spanish Colonial Revival house with guest rooms dating from 1873.

Opus 39 Restaurant and Food Gallery 19 Cordova St., St. Augustine, 904/824-0402. City's best for fresh, often organic foods featuring two prix fixe dinners but—setting the tone for the stylish, arty three rooms and casually disciplined service—custom pick-and-choose dishes from whatever's in the house. Lunch and dinner, indoors and out.

O'Steen's 205 Anastasia Blvd., St. Augustine, 904/829-6974. Some people's entire social lives occur in the line outside this plain Jane of the roadside just east across the Bridge of Lions. Worth the wait for affordable shrimp, seafoods, Minorcan specialties. No drinks, no credit cards.

Raintree 102 San Marco Ave., St. Augustine, 904/824-7211. Southern meets the tropics in this gorgeous rainforest setting, famed for traditional Old South dining.

95 Cordova In the Casa Monica Hotel, 95 Cordova St., St. Augustine, 904/810-6810. Exquisitely prepared and served gourmet American foods plus items from the world's cuisines. The Ancient City's best.

Lodging

A note about B&Bs in St. Augustine. Buildings are typically old and compact with as many guest rooms as possible worked in. Ask for a room where you positively won't hear neighbors.

Casa de la Paz 22 Avenida Menendez, St. Augustine 32084, 800/929-2915, 904/829-2915, www.casadelapaz.com. Built between 1910 and 1917, this Mediterranean revival house sits along the Avenida Menendez across from the seawall. 7 guest rooms with period furnishings variously look to the water or the courtyard gardens out back.

Casa de Solana 21 Aviles St., St. Augustine 32084, 888/796-0980, 904/824-3555, www.casadesolana.com. Fourteenth-oldest house in St. Augustine and a residence since 1763, situated alongside an unusually large grassy compound behind high walls. Rooms all different, all styled early St. Augustine Spanish. Avoid thin-walled rooms. Full breakfast.

Casa Monica Hotel 95 Cordova St., St. Augustine 32084 904/827-1888, www.casamonica.com. One-time Flagler property returned to elegance with 138 rooms and suites in the historic district. The city's best.

Centennial House Bed and Breakfast 26 Cordova St., St. Augustine 32084, 800/611-2880, 904/810-2218, www.centennialhouse.com. City offical's house built at the turn of the twentieth century, renovated for B&B use almost a century later. Substantial, quiet, clapboard house with eight un-precious themed rooms and cottage, all with hardwood floors and comfortably luxurious style, some with fireplaces, whirlpools. Tops for sleeping. Full breakfast.

Coquina Gables Oceanfront Bed and Breakfast 1 F St., St. Augustine Beach 32080, 904/461-8727, www.coquinagables.com. 1926 oceanfront home nicely adapted for an up-style B&B with more than an acre of lawn. Plush white-upholstered easy chairs fill the great room between burnished hardwood floors and hand-hewn Honduran heart of pine beams of the cathedral ceiling. 3 king-bedded rooms in the main house have ocean views; 3 queen-bedded rooms in the Garden House, each with its own entrance. Gourmet breakfast, pool, and solarium.

House of Sea and Sun 2 B St., St. Augustine Beach 32090, 904/461-1716, www.houseofseaandsun.com. Built by a Flagler heir in the early 1920s, the house rambles across 3 floors of finery-rich rooms with a path onto the beach. Full breakfast.

The Hut Summer Haven. Contact Susan and Tom Schmidt, 1060 Highmont Rd., Pittsburgh, Pa., 15232, 412/441-7409. Paradise on the Summer Haven River 100 steps from the beach. Dates from 1888 with 3 bedrooms, second-story viewing deck, riverfront porch with rocking chairs and coquina rock fireplace. Sleeps up to 6 with 1 bath. No AC.

Kenwood Inn 38 Marine St., St. Augustine 32084, 800/824-8151, 904/824-2116, www.kenwoodinn.com. Built in 1865 as a private home, a guest house since 1886, today a small hotel of some 15 rooms with B&B style including rocking chair porches and a rare pool. Rooms delightfully nautical and well detailed.

The Lodge Summer Haven, 888/963-8272, www.beachcottagerent.com (click on Vacation Properties, then The Lodge); available only by the week. Side by side with The Hut (see above), dates from 1895, retrofitted with modern comforts, with 5 bedrooms, 2 baths, kitchen, coquina rock fireplace and wraparound porch, furnished with art, photos, and antiques of the Mellon family, descendants of whom still own it.

The Lodge and Bath Club at Ponte Vedra Beach 607 Ponte Vedra Blvd., Ponte Vedra Beach 32082, 904/273-9500, www.pvresorts.com. Most intimate of the posh PVB resorts, this with only 66 rooms; impeccably laid-out and serviced. Oceanfront.

Marriott at Sawgrass Resort 1000 TPC Blvd., Ponte Vedra Beach 32082, 800/457-4653, 904/285-7777, www.sawgrassmarriott.com. Where you want to be to be seen in the right places. Big and golfy.

Ponte Vedra Inn and Club Ponte Vedra Beach 32082, 800/234-7842, 904/285-1111, www.pvresorts.com. Charming for years after their debut in 1928, the wonderfully old-fashioned beachfront cottages have been replaced by condo units, golf villas, an entire residential/retirement scene upscaled and trendy. No less beautiful for all that.

St. Augustine AYH Hostel 32 Treasury St., St. Augustine 32084, 904/829-6163 (answered 8–10 a.m., 5–10 p.m.). Open year-round; all ages welcome.

St. Francis Inn 279 St. George St., St. Augustine 32085, 800/824-6062, 904/824-6068, www.stfrancisinn.com. Creaky, sloping, catawampus-angled, antique-filled, more dowdy than sprightly—for all that beloved by generations of Florida travelers. This is the oldest lodging in Florida, from 1837 (original house from 1791). Full hot-cooked buffet breakfast.

The Antique Dealers Association of St. Augustine The Antique Market, 325 S.R. 16, St. Augustine 32084, 904/824-9394, www.antique-mkt.com. Some 15 dealers in a one-time food and general store.

Belz Factory Outlet World I-95 at S.R. 16, Exit 95, 904/826-1311. The big Orlando-area outlet mall here takes over the east side of I-95.

Dat'l Do-It World Headquarters 3255 Parker Dr., St. Augustine, 800/468-3285. Locally grown hot—HOT—peppers in sauces, relish, wine, mustard, jelly, vinegar. Available all around the historic quarter; no need to try to find this way out of the way place.

St. Augustine Historical Society Museum Store 22 St. Francis St., St. Augustine 32084, 904/824-2872. Carefully researched reproductions of historical area artifacts.

St. Augustine Historic District Distinctive shops everywhere. Especially don't miss the handful along Aviles Street.

St. Augustine Outlet Center I-95 at S.R. 16, Exit 95, 904/825-1555. 95 outlet stores on the west side of I-95.

Wolf's Head Books 48 San Marco Ave., St. Augustine, 800/521-5061, 904824-9357. Antiquarian books looked after by a dedicated booklover. Just north of the historic district.

Whetstone Chocolates 2 Coke Rd., St. Augustine, 904/825-1700. Family-run for nearly 40 years.

FLAGLER COUNTY

Information Sources

African American Cultural Society P.O. Box 350607, Palm Coast 32135-0607, 386/437-1011.

Flagler Beach Chamber of Commerce 313 Moody Blvd., Flagler Beach 32136-0005, 800/298-0995, 386/439-0995, www.flaglercounty.com/fbcc.

Flagler County Chamber of Commerce; Flagler County Tourist Development Council 2 Airport Rd. off S.R. 100, Star Rte. Box 18-N, Bunnell 32110, 386/437-0106, 800/881-1022, 904/237-0106, www.flaglerpcchamber.org.

Attractions and Recreation

A1A River and Sea Trail Scenic Highway (see Flagler County Chamber of Commerce, above). Marineland to Beverly Beach trace with 11.3-mile bike path in portions along the sea.

Bulow Plantation Ruins State Park Off Old Dixie Highway, 12.5 miles north of Ormond Beach; P.O. Box 655, Bunnell 32110, 386/517-2084, www.myflorida.com. Coquina ruins and northern trailhead for 6.8-mile Bulow Creek Hiking Trail that connects south to Bulow Creek State Park.

Flagler Auditorium 3265 E. Hwy. 100, Bunnell 32110, 386/437-7547. Venue for touring performers, orchestras, and stage plays.

Flagler Beach Historical Museum 207 S. Central Ave., Flagler Beach 32136, 386/517-2025. Built in the old city fire station, new museum tells the town history through exhibits. Books for sale.

Florida Agricultural Museum 1850 Princess Pl. Rd., Palm Coast 32137, 386/446-6799. Work in progress on a 370-acre site on the road to Princess Place Preserve (see below).

Gamble Rogers Memorial State Recreation Area 3100 S. A1A, Flagler Beach, 386/517-2086. Broad beach backed by dunes along the Atlantic flyway. Passive recreation includes short nature trail, saltwater swimming with 34-site camping area.

Guana Tolomato Matanzas National Estuarine Research Reserve 9741 Ocean Shore Blvd., St. Augustine 32080 (for mail); off A1A near the north county line, 904/461-4054, www.dep.state.fl.us/coast/sites/northeast/gtmnerr/info.htm. Exhibits and information about the estuary that forms around Florida's last naturally occurring inlet.

Holden House Museum 204 E. Moody Blvd., Bunnell 32110, 386/437-0600, 386/439-3093. In a 1918 house built by a pharmacist, tells the county history in exhibits with pharmacy paraphernalia. Open only 10 a.m. to 1 p.m. Wednesdays.

Marineland 9610 Oceanshore Blvd., Marineland 32080, 904/471-1111, www.marineland.net. Attraction hub of tiny town that was the first exhibition area for dolphins and other sea creatures. Limited hours.

Parks Many county and city recreational parks run off Highway A1A and otherwise edge the sea and rim the Intracoastal Waterway through the county. **Malacompra** near Bings Landing is an important Seminole-era archaeological site. For information about the parks: 386/437-7490, www.flaglerparks.com. **Graham Swamp** is a large hardwood swamp with trails that connect with Bulow Creek. Information about Graham Swamp: 386/329-4404, www.sjr.state.fl.us. **Haw Creek Preserve** at Russell Landing, which is listed in the Great Florida Birding Trail, is located west in the county where the settlement of St. Johns Park once flourished. It's west off C.R. 305 with a casual waterfront restaurant at the end. Contact county parks.

Pellicer Creek Aquatic Preserve Corridor 20-mile brackish tidal creek, part of a large marsh system that drains into the Matanzas River. Offers enjoyable paddling between saw-grass banks.

Princess Place Preserve 386/437-7490. Requires 1½ miles of dirt-road driving. Hauntingly beautiful 1,435-acre natural resource conservation area where Pellicer Creek empties into the Matanzas River, with a hunting lodge that became a turn-of-the-last-century social milieu for the northern rich. Open to the public on weekends.

Washington Oaks State Gardens State Park 6400 N. Oceanshore Blvd., Palm Coast 32137, 386/446-6780. Site covers almost 400 acres from the sea edge to the Matanzas River. Unusual features include the coquina rock beach and the ornamental gardens from when the site was owned by General Electric's chairman Owen D. Young and his wife. Their home serves as an interpretive center.

The Whitney Laboratory 9505 Ocean Shore Blvd., St. Augustine 32086-8623, 904/461-4000, www.whitney.ufl.edu. Marine research facility of the University of Florida with occasional free public lectures and monthly presentations on marine science. Between the shore road back of the beach and the Intracoastal Waterway.

Dining

Blue 1224 S. A1A, Flagler Beach, 386/439-3275. New and justly famed through the region for fresh seafood and made-from-scratch chef specialties served indoors or on the ocean-view porch. Off the lobby of the Topaz Hotel.

Cannatella's Café 1005 N. A1A, Flagler Beach, 386/439-2888. Cajun with atmosphere across from the beach.

The Golden Lion Café 500 N. A1A, Flagler Beach, 386/439-3004. Seafood, steaks—the usuals in a family-run indoor-out shack with sand floors outside. Across from the beach.

JT's Seafood Shack 242 Oceanshore Dr., Hammock, 386/446-4337. Popular seafood restaurant in the old biker bar that once was Peggy's Place, the funk cleaned up but not yet polished.

Lulu's Landing 3861 C.R. 2006, Bunnell, 386/437-4288. Less redolent of Old Florida since it got spiffed up but still at the end of the road at Bull Creek on Dead Lake and worth the trip for country cooking.

Old Germany Restaurant 2251 S. Old Dixie Hwy., Bunnell, 386/437-0111. German, Bavarian, European food.

StarFire Café and Market 3590 S. A1A, Flagler Beach, 386/439-7827. Gourmet catering perfect for the beach (across the road) or come in comfort for casual fine dining (including notable vegetarian fare) among the racks of wines and delicacies. Run by folks who brought first-class dining to Flagler.

Tropical Breeze Café 2316 S. Oceanshore Blvd., Flagler Beach, 386/439-2020 (at the Island Cottage Resort). Cuisine of the Mediterranean and Caribbean served inside or on the patio. Elegant and sparkling, white cloth and candlelight dining.

Lodgings

The Club at Hammock Beach 200 Ocean Crest Dr., Palm Coast 32137, 888/696-6730, 386/246-5500, www.hammockbeach.com. Palm Coast's most luxurious 3- and 4-bedroom condominiums often available for overnight bookings. Complete with spa and restaurant and on the sea.

Harborside Inn at Palm Coast Resort 300 Clubhouse Dr., Palm Coast 32137, 800/654-6538, 386/445-3000, www.palmcoastresort.com. Upscale motel-style lodgings at a posh golf resort with a restaurant, bar, pool.

Island Cottage by the Sea 2316 S. Oceanshore Blvd., Flagler Beach 32136, 800/845-5275, 386/439-0092, www.islandcottagevillas.com. Large, ribbony suites, downstairs and up in an art-filled, island-style compound with swimming pool and restaurant fashioned by an artist and her yacht-builder husband, across from the beach.

Palm Coast Villas Motel 5454 N. Oceanshore Blvd., Palm Coast 32137, 386/445-3525, www.palmcoastvillas.com. Coquina-rock kitchen-equipped cottages with multipaneled windows on beautiful grounds. No commercial clutter around. Choice.

The Shire House Bed and Breakfast Inn 3398 N. Oceanshore Blvd., Palm Coast (mail to Flagler Beach 32136), 800/345-4394, 386/445-8877, www.theshirehouse.com. Large and luxurious new house 4 1/2 miles north of

Flagler Beach across from the sea, combines English styling with modern comforts including screened pool. Full breakfast.

Topaz Hotel/Motel 1224 S. Oceanshore Blvd., Flagler Beach 32136, 800/555-4735, 386/439-3301. Homage to eccentricity with a lobby full of railroading paraphernalia below Victorian rooms—all well suited to this large house built in 1923 by a prominent Florida architect as his beach home (across the 2-lane beach road today). Swimming pool out front and separate wings of motel rooms.

Whale Watch Motel 2448 S. Oceanshore Blvd., Flagler Beach 32136, 877/635-5535, 386/439-2545, www.whalewatchmotel.com. Comfy, quiet mom-and-pop place with fridge and coffeemaker in rooms on the shore road directly across from the beach.

White Orchid Inn and Spa 1104 S. Oceanshore Blvd., Flagler Beach 32136, 800/423-1477, 386/439-4944, www.whiteorchidinn.com. Sophisticated deco digs with a Japanese trace styled by restaurateurs from the Hamptons. Days begin with gourmet breakfasts, end with wine and cheese. Pool and spa across from the beach.

Shopping

Pegasus By the Sea Books 216 S. 3rd St., Flagler Beach, 386/439-1535. Thousands of used books in the gi-normous garage of the owner's house. Big choice of Floridiana.

StarFire Café and Market (see above under Dining).

VOLUSIA COUNTY

DAYTONA BEACHES

Information Sources

Daytona Beach Area Convention and Visitors Bureau 126 E. Orange Ave., Daytona Beach 32114, 800/854-1234, 386/255-0415, www.daytonabeach.com; off-site information center at Daytona USA, 1801 W. International Speedway Blvd., Daytona Beach, 386/253-8669.

Cultural Council of Volusia County 386/756-5953, www.celebratingculture.com. Complete listings of cultural sites and arts events in the county.

Florida International Festival P.O. Box 1310, Daytona Beach 32115-1310, 386/257-7790 (box office), www.fif-lso.org. Odd-year, biannual summer music and theater festival featuring the London Symphony Orchestra. Daytona Beach's hallmark cultural event.

Attractions and Recreation

Bethune-Cookman College 640 Mary McLeod Bethune Blvd., Daytona Beach 32114-3099, 386/481-2000, www.bethune-cookman.edu. Rich collection of architectural and museum sites honoring the African American contribution to American education and history, housing memorabilia of college founder Mary McLeod Bethune.

Boardwalk Amusement Area, Oceanfront Bandshell, and Main Street Pier Landmark cluster of facilities and attractions, site of oceanfront action. Includes *Salute to Speed* historic exhibit, gondola skyride, and revolving "Space Needle" for exceptional views. Call for concert schedule in the Bandshell, 386/255-6996, www.bandshell.org.

The Casements 25 Riverside Dr., Ormond Beach 32176, 386/676-3216, www.ormondbeach.com/thecasements. Former winter home of John D. Rockefeller, now a city-run cultural center with a mishmash of things to look at.

Cinematique of Daytona N&S Cinema 6, 331 Bill France Blvd., Daytona Beach 32114 (no patron phone), www.cinematique.org. The region's premier art cinema.

Daytona Flea and Farmers Market 2987 Bellevue Ave., Daytona Beach, 386/253-3330, www.daytonafleamarket.net. One of Florida's largest flea markets, open Friday-Sunday, year-round. Free admission.

Daytona USA 1801 W. International Speedway Blvd., Daytona Beach 32114, 386/947-6800, www.daytonausa.com. Exhibitions range from historical and hands-on to video and IMAX film capturing the history of motor racing that changed the course of this king city of speed. Gift shop.

Halifax Historical Museum 252 S. Beach St., Daytona Beach 32114, 386/255-6976, www.halifaxhistorical.org. Cherished exhibits of early and heyday Daytona Beach. Wonderful miniature replica of boardwalk area from 1938.

Haunts of the World's Most Famous Beach Daytona Beach, 386/253-6034, www.hauntsofdaytona.com. Tours that blend history, science, and haunting tales. Reservations required.

Jackie Robinson Ballpark 105 E. Orange Ave., Daytona Beach 32116, 386/257-3172, www.daytonacubs.com. Historic site where the legendary all-star began his professional career.

Living Legends of Auto Racing Museum 253 Riverside Drive, Holly Hill 32117, 386/257-2828, www.livinglegendsofautoracing.com. Early racing memorabilia, antique cars, photos. Free admission.

Main Street Pier 1200 Main St., Daytona Beach 32116, 386/253-1212. 700-foot-long fishing pier with attractions.

Marine Science Center 100 Lighthouse Drive, Ponce Inlet 32127, 386/304-5545, www.marinesciencenter.com. Multipurpose installation combines sea turtle research and rehab center with artificial reef aquarium, habitat dioramas, interactive displays, library, wet/dry lab, and new Mary Keller Seabird Rehabilitation Sanctuary. Boardwalk and trails allow for wildlife and habitat observation.

Mary McLeod Bethune Performing Arts Center, 640 Mary McLeod Bethune Blvd., Daytona Beach 32114, 386/481-2778, www.mmbcenter.com. New $23 million stage hosts cultural events, including internationally acclaimed performers.

Museum of Arts and Sciences (MOAS) 1040 Museum Blvd., Daytona Beach 32116, 386/255-0285, www.moas.org. Heart of Daytona Beach's cultural life set in the 60-acre Tuscawilla Preserve. Combines interpretive nature sites with permanent galleries of three centuries of American, African, and modern Cuban art plus traveling exhibits, a gallery of prehistory, and a planetarium. MOAS originates many of the state's important traveling exhibits.

North Peninsula State Recreation Area Hwy. A1A, 5 miles north of Ormond Beach, 386/517-2086. 2 miles of oceanfront beach hardly busy during the week.

Ormond Memorial Art Museum and Gardens 78 E. Granada Blvd., Ormond Beach 32176, 386/676-3347, www.ormondartmuseum.org. Attractive small set of galleries in a garden space.

Ponce de Leon Inlet Lighthouse 4931 Peninsula Dr., Ponce Inlet 32127, 386/761-1821, www.ponceinlet.org. National Historic Landmark, completed in 1887 with paths and support structures intact. Historical maritime exhibits, tours, and a 203-step climb to the top for panoramic views. Surrounding area in Lighthouse Point

Park (south end of Peninsula Drive, 386/756-7488) offers swimming and nature trails.

Riverfront Marketplace. Decoratively restored historic commercial street along the Halifax River features the Halifax Historical Museum, shops, restaurants, taverns. Notable sites along a 10-block area extending up North Beach Street include everything from Brownie the Town Dog's grave marker to Seaside Music Theater (see below) and more.

Seaside Music Theater 176 N. Beach St., Daytona Beach 32116, box office 800/854-5592; otherwise 386/252-6200; www.seasidemusictheater.org. Full pit orchestra–supported, year-round Broadway-caliber productions, at the Theater Center of Daytona Beach Community College (1200 International Speedway Blvd.).

Southeast Museum of Photography 1200 International Speedway Blvd., on the grounds of Daytona Beach Community College, Daytona Beach 32116, 386/254-4475, www.smponline.org. Brilliant exhibitions from around the world and permanent collection. Florida's only museum exclusively dedicated to photography.

Sugar Mill Botanical Gardens 950 Old Sugar Mill Road, Port Orange 32129, 386/767-1735, www.dunlawtonsugarmillgardens.org. Botanical gardens and English sugar mill ruins at the site of a one-time amusement park, Bongoland, with concrete dinosaurs. Also here, a human sundial.

Sunny Daze and Starry Nites Cruises Docked at Aunt Catfish's Restaurant, Port Orange, 386/253-1796, www.sunnydazerivercruises.com. Drift through creeks and tributaries along the Halifax River; see pelicans, herons, egrets, manatees, and/or dolphins. Capt. Mark Sheets explains historical and ecological points of interest.

A Tiny Cruise Line Halifax Harbor Marina, "E" Dock, 425 S. Beach St., Daytona Beach 32116, 386/226-2343, www.visitdaytona.com/tinycruise. Wild dolphins, jumping fish, and graceful wading birds are often close by as this small 1890s-style launch glides past islands and estates along the Halifax River.

Tomoka State Park 3 miles north of town, 2099 N. Beach St., Ormond Beach 32174, 386/676-4050. Unbusy gem of the state system with paddling and nature trails and the bijou museum of deco-era artworks by Fred Dana Marsh.

Trolley Boats Shoppes at Ocean Walk Village, Kiosk #2, 250 N. Atlantic Ave., Daytona Beach 32116, 386/238-3738, www.trolleyboattours.com. Amphibious adventure that includes land drives through historical Daytona Beach and a float along the Halifax River without leaving your seat.

Tuscawilla Preserve Discovery Center At the Museum of Arts and Sciences (see above). Opened in 2004, outdoor environmental learning center. Follow a network of boardwalk trails leading to interactive exhibits. Learn about local flora and fauna, environmental protection, wetlands, and non-native plants. Free admission.

Wilbur Boathouse 4200 S. Peninsula Drive, Wilbur-By-The-Sea 32127, 386/761-4446. Historic site under restoration, potentially for a canoe/kayak launch on the Halifax River.

Anna's Trattoria 304 Seabreeze Blvd., 386/239-9624. Popular for pastas in a stylish little family-run, deco-style restaurant close by the beach.

Aunt Catfish's On the River 4009 Halifax Dr., Port Orange, 386/767-4768. They call it "Down South river cookin'"—Cajun, low country, local. Mostly fish, seafood served in a big shed on the Halifax River.

Billy's Tap Room and Grill 58 E. Granada Blvd., Ormond Beach, 386/672-1910. Ormond's oldest, evokes the era of racing cars on the beach. Hearty American basics—beef, chicken, pork, seafood.

Crabby Joe's 3701 S. Atlantic Ave., Daytona Beach Shores, 386/788-3364. Site makes it: deck and grill on the Sunglow Fishing Pier over the water.

Down The Hatch Seafood Restaurant 4894 Front St., Ponce Inlet, 386/761-4831. Nautical art and artifacts on rough-milled cypress walls around big picture windows recall this site of an old fish camp on the Halifax River.

European Cafe 210 S. Atlantic Ave., Ormond Beach, 386/672-8834. Outstanding homemade German and Czech cuisine served in a setting of red-and-white-czeched (ahem!) table covers surrounded by beer steins, travel posters, and a lifetime's collection of Old World souvenirs.

Frappes North 123 W. Granada Blvd., Ormond Beach, 386/615-4888. Successfully introduced lighter, eclectic cuisine to the beaches. Three intimate rooms with an old woody look.

Julian's 88 S. Atlantic Ave., Ormond Beach, 386/677-6767. Long-established, family-run, serving grills and seafood in the big, dark, dining room behind the high tiki facade. Tux-attired waitresses belie the restaurant's affordability.

La Crepe en Haut In the Fountain Square shops, 142 E. Granada Ave., Ormond Beach, 386/673-1999. Nouvelle-inspired French cuisine served in a setting of elegant pink napery and fresh flowers, intimate and dimly lit. Best (and priciest) in the area, here since 1979.

Old Spanish Sugar Mill Restaurant 30 minutes west of Daytona, a landmark Florida restaurant where you prepare your own pancakes on griddles built into each guest table. One of a kind. Come midweek and avoid the line. Historic and located in a state park with a popular spring-fed swimming hole (DeLeon Springs State Park, DeLeon Springs, 386/985-5644).

Parks Seafood Restaurant 951 N Beach Street, Daytona Beach, 386/258-7272. Family-run since 1976 and a local favorite, on the Intracoastal Waterway with inside and out dining. Shuns the nautically cute for expertly substantial seafood preparations of every kind. Popular early-bird menu.

Racing's North Turn Beach Bar and Grille 4511 S. Atlantic Ave., Ponce Inlet, 386/322-3258. At the site of the first Grand National Race in 1949, for oceanfront dining and live entertainment.

Rosario Ristorante at the Live Oak Inn 448 S. Beach St., Daytona Beach, 386/258-6066. Varied Italian by Chef Rosario Vinci served in a beautifully restored historic home, now a B&B (see below).

The Vin'Yard 140 W. Granada Blvd., Ormond Beach, 386/672-5223. Premier deli sandwiches and more to go.

Lodgings

Bahama House 2001 S. Atlantic Ave., Daytona Beach Shores 32118, 800/571-2001, 386/248-2001, www.daytonabahamahouse.com. Family-run, small beachfront high-rise with clean, motel-style rooms. Continental breakfast, cocktail reception daily included. Pool.

Cabana Colony Cottages 2501 S. Atlantic Ave., Daytona Beach 32118, 386/767-8939, www.daytonashoreline.com. A top buy on the beach. Spacious, better-than-beachy self-catering cottages feel like home, all steps from the beach, some with sea views. Adjacent Shoreline Motel under same ownership, also several cuts above average.

Casa del Mar Beach Resort 621 S. Atlantic Ave., Ormond Beach 32176, 800/245-1590, 386/672-4550, www.Vac-club.com. Pick of Ormond beachfront resorts, a touch of swank. Pool. Time-share; rooms not always available.

Coquina Inn Bed and Breakfast 544 S. Palmetto Ave., Daytona Beach 32116, 800/805-7533; 386/254-4969, www.coquinainndaytonabeach.com. Elegant, antique-filled conversion of a parsonage into one of Florida's finest B&Bs. Listed in the National Register, a block from the town marina.

Coral Sands Inn and Seaside Cottages 1009 Ocean Shore Blvd., Ormond Beach 32176, 800/441-1831, 386/441-1831. 18 attractive cottages and 68 ocean-view rooms in a 5-story hotel, many with kitchens. Furnished a tad better than motel units.

Lilian Place Bed and Breakfast 111 Silver Beach Ave., Daytona Beach 32118, 877/873-7579, 386/323-9913, http://www.lilianplace.com. Built in 1884 and one of the city's oldest homes, listed in the National Register of Historic Places, the house overlooks the Halifax River 2 blocks from the beach. Classic Queen Anne splendid in period furnishings. Wraparound porch.

Live Oak Inn 444–448 S. Beach St., Daytona Beach 32114, 800/881-4667, 386/252-4667. Oldest buildings in Daytona Beach, quaint, nicely old, and full of antiques with its own restaurant. Overlooks the Halifax River from across the street.

Miss Pat's Inn—A Bed and Breakfast 1209 S. Peninsula Dr., Daytona Beach 32118, 866/464-7772, http://www.misspatsinn.com. Beautifully appointed, doll house–like yellow 1898 house with rocking chair wraparound porch. Most of the 7 rooms equipped with whirlpool tubs and hardwood floors. Full breakfast, complimentary soft drinks, coffee, and snacks all day.

Old Salty's Inn 1921 S. Atlantic Ave., Daytona Beach Shores 32118, 800/417-1466, 386/252-8090, www.oldsaltys.com. Full of nautical gear, one of the better oceanfront motels with a big mix of rooms on 2 floors.

Tropical Manor Motel/Audrey's Beach House 2237 S. Atlantic Ave, Daytona Beach Shores, 800/253-4920, 386/252-4920, www.tropicalmanor.com. Beach House ranks as one of the nicest oceanfront cottages with 2 bedrooms, 2 baths, sleeps 7, dining room, living room, full kitchen, large patios, heated pool.

The Villa Bed and Breakfast 801 N. Peninsula Dr., Daytona Beach 32118, 386/248-2020, www.thevillabb.com. Gorgeous pink Mediterranean revival mansion from Daytona's second heyday of the twenties. Occupies more than an acre behind gates. Detailed with antiques and listed in the National Register. Pool. Full breakfast. 10-minute walk to the beach.

Shopping

Angell and Phelps Chocolate Factory 154 S. Beach St., Daytona Beach, 800/969-2634; 386/252-6531, www.angellandphelps.com. Known for high-quality, handmade chocolates made fresh in small batches daily. Free, guided 30-minute tour through the chocolate-making process.

Health Foods: Harvest House Natural Foods Market 4032 S. Ridgewood Ave., Port Orange, 386/756-3800; 124 S. Nova Rd., Ormond Beach, 386/677-7723; **Love Whole Foods** 275 Williamson Blvd., Ormond Beach, 386/677-5236

Shoppes at Ocean Walk Village 250 N. Atlantic Ave., Daytona Beach, 877/845-WALK (9255), www.oceanwalkvillage.com. Oceanfront shopping, dining, and entertainment complex notable chiefly for its 10-screen cinema, Starbucks, and Harley-Davidson apparel.

NEW SMYRNA BEACH

Information Sources, Attractions, Recreation

New Smyrna Beach Visitor Center 2238 S.R. 44, New Smyrna Beach 32168, 800/541-9621, 386/428-1600, www.nsbfla.com.

Southeast Volusia Chamber of Commerce 115 Canal St., New Smyrna Beach 32168, 877/460-8410, 386/428-2449, www.sevchamber.com.

Southeast Volusia Historical Society 120 Sams Ave., New Smyrna Beach 32168, 386/478-0052. Located in the 1901 Connor Free Library, renovated as a historical museum. Source of authoritative historical guided tour, brochure, displays.

— — —

Arts on Douglas 123 Douglas St., New Smyrna Beach 32168, 904/428-1133. Best of contemporary works by regional artists.

Atlantic Center for the Arts 1414 Art Center Ave., New Smyrna Beach 32168, 386/427-6975, www.atlanticcenterforthearts.org. Florida's premier source of master instruction for mid-career artists. Exhibitions, performances, tours, open to the public.

Black Heritage Museum 314 N. Duss St., New Smyrna Beach 32168, 386/424-2266. A near century-old collection of memorabilia and artifacts mostly about the history of local race relations in a former black parish church from 1899. Also included are replicas of African American inventions and authentic African masks.

Canaveral National Seashore Entry gate 9 miles south of New Smyrna Beach at the end of Highway A1A (headquarters, 308 Julia St., Titusville 32796, 321/267-1110); for more information, see chap. 6, Brevard County. The park lies mainly in Brevard, but its most convenient access to the ghost town of Eldora and to the Timucuan shell midden Turtle Mound is through New Smyrna.

Downtown New Smyrna Beach Historic Walking Tour Brochures from the Community Redevelopment Agency, 210 Sams Ave., New Smyrna Beach 32168, 386/424-2266, or from the chamber of commerce (see above). Essential guide to interpreting downtown New Smyrna, includes sites from Turnbull times and along Canal Street, many restored for different uses. More than 50 historic sites in the area, many worth a drive.

Harris House 214 S. Riverside Dr., New Smyrna Beach 32168, 386/423-1753. Gallery and teaching facility affiliated with Atlantic Center for the Arts. Features Florida works. Gift shop.

Little Theatre of New Smyrna Beach 726 3rd Ave., New Smyrna Beach 32168, 386/423-1246. Winter community theater.

New Smyrna Speedway 3939 SR 44, New Smyrna Beach 32764, 328/427-4129. Year-round stock car racing.

Sugar Mill Ruins 600 Mission Rd., New Smyrna Beach 32168, 386/736-5953. Landmark site from the mid-nineteenth century.

Dining

The Breakers 518 Flagler Ave., New Smyrna Beach, 386/428-2019. Like eating at a sock hop. Surfer dudes and dudettes pile in and outside at the big beachfront deck for best burgers, fried seafood, sandwiches. The beach scene.

Goodrich's 263 River Dr., Oak Hill, 386/345-3397. Open October-April. Old, wooden place to eat, its rear up on pilings in the Mosquito Lagoon. Ordinary fried seafood; go for the atmosphere.

JB's Fish Camp and Seafood Restaurant 859 Pompano Ave., New Smyrna Beach, 386/427-5747. Waterside on the Indian River just before the gate to the Canaveral National Seashore. Seating for some 200 spreads around the shacklike interior and waterside on the plank deck. Immense sizzling platters of sometimes formerly frozen seafood, fresh-cut veggies, big yellow ears of corn. Informal and big favorite with locals.

Kelsey's Riverview Restaurant 101 Flagler Ave., New Smyrna Beach, 386/428-1865. Between the Riverview Hotel and the Intracoastal Waterway, surf and turf in an atmospheric red-brick-interior big room with upstairs (inside) dining and tables by the water.

Victor's Backstreet Café 103 S. Pine, New Smyrna Beach, 386/426-5000. The house specialty—swamp cabbage soup—was recently named Official Soup of the State of Florida. A heritage place, Victor's also serves famous barbecue.

Coastal Waters Inn 3509 S. Atlantic Ave., New Smyrna Beach 32169, 386/428-3800. One of the more attractive among the beachfront lodgings marked by its pillared facade. Resort-style motel rooms including some with kitchens. Pool.

Longboard Inn Bed and Breakfast 312 Washington St., New Smyrna Beach 32168, 386/428-3499, 888/655-2025, 386/428-3499, www.longboardinn.com. Cute, arty, and beautifully remodeled 6-room Cracker house with polished plank floors, wood decks—a renovator's dream job.

Night Swan Intracoastal Bed and Breakfast 512 S. Riverside Dr., New Smyrna Beach 32168, 800/465-4261, 386/423-4940, www.nightswan.com. Beautifully composed 3-story house from 1906 with 15 rooms across the street from the Indian River. Full breakfast.

Riverview Hotel 103 Flagler Ave., New Smyrna Beach 32169, 800/945-7416, 386/428-5858. Classic 1885 bridgetender's house turned B&B behind lobster-red, picket-balconied, tin-roofed, jigsaw-trimmed exterior. Key West–style rooms. Pool and continental breakfast.

Shopping

Flagler Avenue Lattice-faced old buildings along 4 blocks from Halifax River to the sea, the street supplies delights for window shoppers with its artwork, benches, brick sidewalks, decorative streetlights, and Old Florida landscaping. Lots of beachwear apparel shops, antiques, books, arts and crafts, places to eat.

West Volusia

Disclaimer: Although it is twenty to twenty-five miles west of Highway A1A, I do properly refer to the following section of Volusia County in the text because of its easy accessibility to Daytona Beach and New Smyrna Beach. I have counseled the region's River of Lakes Heritage Corridor for several years. The region is known as St. Johns River Country and its source for travel information is the West Volusia Tourism Advertising Authority, 300 S. Volusia Ave., Orange City 32763, 800/749-4350, 386/775-2006, www.stjohnsrivercountry.com. Among the region's notable attractions are the Pioneer Center for the Creative Arts in Barberville; the Southern Cassadaga Spiritualist Camp Meeting Assn. in Cassadaga; DeBary Mansion in DeBary; Stetson University, houseboating centers across from Hontoon Island, the Gillespie Museum of Minerals and Main Street DeLand; equestrian friendly Lake Helen; the important winter manatee refuge at Blue Spring State Park in Orange City; DeLeon Springs State Park, the Old Spanish Sugar Mill Restaurant, Lake Woodruff National Wildlife Refuge and the Spring Garden Ranch Training Center in DeLeon Springs; Lyonia Preserve in Deltona; and the important centers of fern cultivation in Pierson and Seville.

BREVARD COUNTY

SOUTH BREVARD

Information Sources

Brevard County Parks and Recreation Department 2725 Judge Fran Jamieson Way, Viera 32940, 321/633-2046, www.brevardparks.com. Request a guide to parks and nature centers.

Brevard Cultural Alliance 2725 Judge Fran Jamieson Way, Bldg. B, 1st Floor, Viera 32940, 321/690-6817, www.artsbrevard.org. 24-hour cultural tourism events information available at 321/690-6819, www.brevard.cc.fl.us/BCA. Also detailed information on theater, museums and galleries, major public attractions, with performance and events schedules.

Brevard Tomorrow P.O. Box 2276, Cocoa 32923-2276, 321/632-8222, www.brevardtomorrow.com. Broad-based consensus-building not-for-profit concerned with governance, civic infrastructure, education and workforce, economy and land use, and growth.

Florida Space Coast Office of Tourism 2725 Judge Fran Jamieson Way, B-105, Viera 32940, 321/637-5483, www.space-coast.com.

Historical Resources Request the *Guide to Historical Landmarks in Brevard County* from Liberty Bell Memorial Museum (1601 Oak St., Melbourne 32901, 321/727-1776); **The Florida Historical Society and Alma Clyde Field Library of Florida History** (435 Brevard Ave., Cocoa 32922, 321/690-1971, www.florida-historical-soc.org), provides a professional research facility as well as lectures, exhibits, and books for sale; **The Brevard Museum of History and Natural Science** (2201 Michigan Ave., Cocoa 32926, 321/632-1830, w); **U.S. Air Force Space Museum** (Cape Canaveral Air Force Stn., 191 Museum Circle, Cape Canaveral Air Station, 321/853-3245); **North Brevard Historical Museum** (320 S. Washington Ave., Titusville 32796, 321/269-3658).

Melbourne–Palm Bay Area Chamber of Commerce 1005 E. Strawbridge Ave., Melbourne 32901-4782, 800/771-9922, 321/724-5400, www.melpb-chamber.org. Request copies of their brochures on historic downtown Melbourne and a walking tour of the district.

Archie Carr National Wildlife Refuge 1339 20th St., Vero Beach 32960-3559, 772/562-3909. Fragmented 9.5 miles of beachfront turtle nesting grounds highly impacted by development.

Brevard Museum of Art and Science 1463 Highland Ave., Melbourne 32936-0835, 321/242-0737, www.artandscience.org. Combines former Space Coast Science Center with its exploration exhibits from nature to space, plus arts teaching and exhibition facility with local art and museum shops. Lectures, concerts, workshops, summer camps, and more.

Brevard Zoo 8225 Wickham Rd., Melbourne 32940, 321/254-WILD (9453), www.brevardzoo.org. Some 400 animals with a 22-acre wetlands for paddling.

Florida Institute of Technology 150 W. University Blvd., Melbourne 32901, 321/674-8000, www.fit.edu. Botanical gardens open to the public. Brochure for walking tours turns up surprising historic sites at this campus not yet 50 years old.

The Henegar Center 625 E. New Haven Ave., Melbourne 32901, 321/723-8698, www.henegar.org/center. Old downtown school recycled as a performing arts center.

Maxwell C. King Center for the Performing Arts 3865 N. Wickham Rd., Melbourne 32904, 321/242-2219, www.kingcenter.com. Showcase for touring name acts.

Melbourne Village Town Hall, 535 Hammock Road, Melbourne Village 32904, 321/723-8300, www.angelfire.com/fl/tmv (3 miles west of downtown Melbourne north of U.S. 192). Pick up brochure of historic sites and tour this mellowed-out intentional community, so far sheltered from the highway hodgepodge.

1916 House 5795 U.S. 1, Grant. To visit, contact Grant Historical Society, P.O. Box 44, Grant 32949, 321/723-8543. This little yellow pine 1916 house on the Indian River Lagoon now serves as society headquarters.

Sea Turtle Preservation Society P.O. Box 510988, Melbourne Beach 32951, 321/6761701, www.seaturtlespacecoast.org. Protection advocates in a region of globally important nesting beaches. The main organization conducts turtle walks during nesting season.

Sebastian Inlet State Park 9700 S. A1A, Melbourne Beach 32951, 321/984-4852 (15 miles south of Melbourne Beach). Premier saltwater fishing location along Highway A1A. Also beach swimming; surfing; boating with canoe, kayak, and power boat rentals; and camping. Site of Sebastian Fishing Museum.

Dining

The Blueberry Muffin 1130 A1A, Indialantic, 321/725-7117. Homey beside the road, serves breakfast through the day and sandwiches.

Bonefish Willy's 2459-B Pineapple Ave., Melbourne, 321/253-8888. Laid-back with lounging chairs beside the lagoon, 40 tightly packed seats outside and in the old shack with open beams. Crab cakes and otherwise mostly seafood. If it's raining and people can't sit on the deck, the wait can get up to 2 hours. People come back or hang out in their cars.

Café Stella Blue 3625 N. Harbor City Blvd., Melbourne, 321/259-4000. 7-tables small on the big highway, affordable international food with owner-chefs in the kitchen and on the floor, no surprise that you need reservations.

The Cove Restaurant 1462 A1A, Satellite Beach 32937, 321/777-2683. Low, shedlike, here for 45 years across from the sea, a family favorite for steaks, seafood, and nightlife at the club next door. Famous for early birds.

Dorado Grill 1220 N. Hwy. A1A, Indialantic, 321/984-9309. Cold-looking little place serves the freshest fish in big portions.

Gizmo's Reef 4263 N. Harbor City Blvd., Melbourne, 321/253-1369. Old-style raw bar and saloon on the mainland between Pineda and Eau Gallie. Plank deck and dock landing on the Indian River Lagoon. Pastas, soups, salads, broiler food, wings, and such. Pool tables, juke box, slamming screen door.

Sebastian Beach Inn 7035 S. Hwy. A1A, Melbourne Beach, 321/728-4311. Winning location directly on the beach. Former lifesaving station and World War II submarine watch station (the tower's still there), now big weekend party scene with live music. Seafood, beef, poultry, pasta.

The Strawberry Mansion and **Mister Beaujeans Bar Grille and Breakfast** 1218 E. New Haven Ave., Melbourne, 321/723-1900. Companion restaurants in side-by-side historic homes on the east side of downtown Melbourne. The early-twentieth-century mansion was home to famed hostess Nannie Lee. Now serves pasta, seafood, chicken, beef—some southern style—in the mansion's dimly lit, intimately elegant rooms. Informal Mister Beaujeans serves breakfast, then burgers and mostly grazing food.

Lodgings

Crane Creek Inn Waterfront B&B 907 E. Melbourne Ave., Melbourne 32901, 321/768-6416, www.cranecreekinn.com. Extended 1925 house on a tributary of the Indian River Lagoon with 5 guest rooms, variously rustic and tropical, public rooms with an overall polished Old Florida style. Manatees and many bird species seasonally watchable from the dock, where there's a whirlpool. Expanded continental breakfast.

Melbourne Harbor Suites 1207 E. New Haven Ave., Melbourne 32901, 800/242-4251, 800/226-4251 in Fla., 321/723-4251. Low-rise waterside motel-style units all with kitchens across U.S. 1 from historic downtown Melbourne. Pool.

Oceanfront Cottages 612 Wavecrest Ave., Indialantic 32903, 800/785-8080, 321/725-8474, www.oceanfrontcottages.com. 4 luxurious suites with kitchens on an oceanfront side street. Outstanding buy.

Tuckaway Shores Resort (formerly Sharrock Shores Resort) 1441 S. A1A, Indialantic 32903, 800/820-1441, 407/723-3355, www.tuckawayshores.com. Quiet, 3-story, 31-

unit motel directly on the beach south of the more built-up area and on the way to Sebastian Inlet, popular fishing spot. Large units with and without kitchens. Pool.

Windemere Inn by the Sea 815 S. Miramar Ave., Indialantic 32903, 800/224-6853, 321/728-9334, www.windemereinn.com. Sumptuously styled like a classical French townhouse, accommodates guests in pampering suites plus cottages on the water.

Shopping

Health Foods: Community Harvest 1405 Highland Ave., Melbourne, 321/254-4966; **Natureworks Natural Food Supermarket** 1135 W. New Haven Ave., in the Office Depot Plaza, 321/674-5002, the big one with café; **Organic Food Centre** 862 N. Miramar Ave., in the Indialantic Shopping Center, 321/724-2383, with a juice and sandwich bar; **Wild Oats Community Market** 1135 W. New Haven Ave., Melbourne, 321/674-5002.

CENTRAL BREVARD

Information Sources

Cocoa Beach Area Chamber of Commerce 400 Fortenberry Rd., Merritt Id. 32952, 321/459-2200, www.cocoabeachchamber.com. (Information centers at Ron Jon Surf Shop; Astronaut Hall of Fame; Best Western Cocoa Inn (exit 201 off I-95); Sterling Casino Lines Terminal 2 at Port Canaveral (exit 205 off I-95).

Cocoa Main Street 430 Delannoy Ave., Cocoa 32922, 321/633-0806.

Florida Space Coast Office of Tourism (see above under South Brevard).

Attractions and Recreation

Ace of Hearts Ranch and Equestrian Center 7400 Bridal Path Lane, Cocoa 32927, 321/638-0104, www.aceofheartsranch.com. Riding classes, trails, horse boarding, beach rides November through April at Canaveral National Seashore.

Brevard Museum of History and Science 2201 Michigan Ave., Cocoa 32926, 321/632-1830.

Cocoa Beach Kayaking 321/784-4545, www.cocoabeachkayaking.com. Experienced waterway tour operator.

Cocoa Beach Pier Half-mile north of S.R. 520 off Hwy. A1A, 321/783-7549. 840-foot pier into the Atlantic includes restaurants and places to rent fishing gear.

Florida Solar Energy Center 1679 Clearlake Rd., Cocoa 32922, 321/638-1000. Displays about how to live energy efficiently in Florida.

Walking Tour of Historic Cocoa Village. More than a dozen sites within a 6-block area including the Cocoa Village Playhouse, 113-year-old Travis Hardware, and guided tours of citrus pioneer Edward P. Porcher's grandly pillared 1918 mansion. Request brochure from Brevard Museum of History and Natural Science (above).

Bernard's Surf 2 S. Atlantic Ave., Cocoa Beach, 321/783-2401. Here a block from the beach since 1948, woody rooms lined with booths backed by celebrity photos. Lusty American food. Includes Rusty's Raw Bar. More hooked on seafood? Bernard's also shines at Rusty's Seafood and Oyster Bar (628 Glen Cheek Dr., Port Canaveral, 321/ 783-2033).

Cafe Margaux 220 Brevard Ave., Cocoa Village, 321/639- 8343. Sophisticated bijou dining spot off a chic shopping plaza, the style belle époque behind brocade drapes and lacquer screens, the food French and northern Italian with special attention to game birds.

Daniel's Motorcycles and Café 8660 N. A1A #108, Cape Canaveral, 321/868-5225, www.danielscafe.com. California-style café, gourmet pizzas, seafood, steak. Large selection of microbrews. Two classic 1940s Indian motorcycles.

Flaminia's Famous Italian Kitchen 3210 S. Atlantic Ave., Cocoa Beach, 321/783-9908. Hole-in-the-wall family-run Italian. Eat here and save. Art, Chianti bottles, ferns, and paddle fans.

Grills Seafood Deck and Tiki Bar Sunrise Marina in the Cove at Port Canaveral, 505 Glen Cheek Dr., 321/868-2226. Casual, open-air place on the water at the port next to where the fishing fleet lands. Best fresh fish sandwiches, salads, bacon-wrapped scallops.

The Mango Tree Restaurant and Gardens 118 N. Atlantic Ave., Cocoa Beach, 321/ 799-0513. Exquisite continental fare for big occasions in a one-of-a-kind tropical hothouse setting with chandeliers and Persian rugs on paver tiles and floor-to-ceiling etched glass doors that look onto topiary gardens.

Lodgings

Cocoa Beach Oceanside Inn 1 Hendry Ave., Cocoa Beach 32931, 800/874-7958, 321/ 784-3126, www.cocoabeachoceansideinn.com. Attractively landscaped 6-story oceanfront resort, all units with balconies, better-styled rooms than most. Pool.

Crawford's Cocoa Cabanas 1901 S. Atlantic Ave., Cocoa Beach 32931, 321/799-0307, www.cocoacabanas.com. Handful of exceptionally clean, fully equipped beachfront units on the south side of Cocoa Beach. Leisurely, unpretentious, walking close to restaurants. Always in demand. Try anyway. (Site will convert to condos by 2006 or 2007.)

The Inn at Cocoa Beach 4300 Ocean Beach Blvd., Cocoa Beach 32931, 800/343-5307, 321/799-3460, www.theinnatcocoabeach.com. Motel risen to B&B style, directly on the beach (behind Ron Jon Surf Shop) with continental breakfast and evening wine and cheese. French provincial reproductions, large rooms and suites, most overlooking the sea. Pool.

Pelican Landing Oceanfront Motel 1201 S. Atlantic Ave., Cocoa Beach 32931, 321/783-7197, www.pelicanlandingresortcb.com. 11 kitchen-equipped apartments all on the beach, each accommodating 4. Top value.

Surf Studio Beach Resort 1801 S. Atlantic Ave., Cocoa Beach 32931, 321/783-7100, www.surf-studio.com. 2-story little garden resort on the beach, all units kitchen-equipped. Pool.

Shopping

Cocoa Village Information at historic Porcher House, 321/639-3500. Dozens of shops, restaurants, theater in the old lagoonside town.

Ron Jon Surf Shop 4151 N. Atlantic Ave., Cocoa Beach 32931, 321/799-8888, www.ronjons.com. Open 24 hours, 7 days a week. Top dude of Florida surf shops, shrine to what's happenin'. Also houses Cocoa Beach Surf Museum.

Sunseed Food Co-op 6615 N. Atlantic Ave., Cape Canaveral 321/784-0930. Eclectic, Haitian art to yo-yos, Meher Baba wall art, books to pick up and read, magazines galore. Old porcelain-topped kitchen tables. Fresh vegetarian soups, sandwiches including fresh fish of the day. Also in the co-op, **The Grateful Day Cafe** (321/783-7330), more varied vegetarian with organic wines by the glass, plus microbrewery beers and ciders.

NORTH BREVARD

Information Sources

Florida Space Coast Office of Tourism (see above under South Brevard). Request the magazine *It's More Than Just Birding . . . Florida's Space Coast, A Complete Guide to Nature and Outdoor Resources in the County.* Also a source for information about the **Space Coast Birding and Wildlife Festival** (321/268-5224, www.spacecoast-birding.com). The annual November event is the largest festival of its kind in Florida. Its celebration of natural Brevard draws visitors from overseas.

Space Coast Audubon Society 321/504-3064, www.indianriveraudubon.org.

Space Coast Paddlers Club 321/636-0701, www.spacecoastpaddlers.org. For paddling, also visit www.kayakguide.com.

Surfing www.surfline.com.

Titusville Area Chamber of Commerce 2000 Washington Ave., Titusville 32780, 321/267-3036, www.titusville.org. Request historic tour brochure.

Canaveral National Seashore 308 Julia St., Titusville 32796, 321/267-1110, www.nbbd.com/godo/cns/. Headquarters office in downtown Titusville. Only wilderness seashore remaining in Florida.

A Day Away Kayak Tours 321/268-2655, adayaway@aol.com. Trips through Merritt Island National Wildlife Refuge, Indian River, Mosquito Lagoon, and Pelican Island.

Enchanted Forest Sanctuary South of Titusville on S.R. 405; for information, contact Friends of the Enchanted Forest, P.O. Box 10128, Titusville 32783-0128, 321/267-7367, www.nbbd.com/godo/ef/. First of the conservation areas acquired under Brevard's 1990 Environmentally Endangered Lands program. Nature trails climb onto the desertlike scrub, drop to the long-abandoned Addison Canal. Gopher tortoise and eastern indigo snake habitat.

Horseback Riding: Flying D Ranch Titusville, 321/268-5955.

Kennedy Space Center Visitor Complex Delaware North Park Services of Spaceport, Inc., Kennedy Space Center 32899, 321/449-4254, www.KennedySpaceCenter.com. The gateway to space with all its expanded visitor attractions, including the U.S. Astronaut Hall of Fame with the largest collection of astronaut personal memorabilia displayed.

Merritt Island National Wildlife Refuge P.O. Box 6504, Titusville 32782-6504, 321/861-0667, www.nbbd.com/godo/minwr/. 220-square-mile area encompassing the Kennedy Space Center. Home to more threatened and endangered species than all the other refuges combined. On the Atlantic Flyway, an excellent birding venue. Also home to gators, deer, and, reportedly, Florida panthers.

North Brevard Historical Museum 301 S. Washington Ave., P.O. Box 6199, Titusville 32782, 321/269-3658. Traces regional history from the early nineteenth century forward with displays of cultural artifacts.

Valiant Air Command Warbird Museum 6600 Tico Rd., Titusville, 321/268-1941, www.vacwarbirds.org. Historic warplanes from World War I through Vietnam with military flying gear, uniforms, and artwork. Gift shop.

Dining

Dixie Crossroads 1475 Garden St., Titusville, 321/268-5000. Pioneer family restaurateur and award-winning conservationist Laurilee Thompson runs what may be the most popular restaurant in Florida. Freshest, least expensive local seafood packs the no-frills landmark daily for lunch and dinner. Long waits some nights.

Kloiber's Cobbler and Eatery 337 S. Washington Ave., Titusville, 321/383-0689. Red-bricked, open-beamed, old-fashioned main street storefront full of midcentury movie star photos; serves soups, salads, sandwiches, quiche—and homemade fresh fruit cobblers with ice cream.

The Dickens' Inn Bed and Breakfast 2398 N. Singleton Ave., Mims 32754, 877/847-2067, 321/269-4595, www.dickens-inn.com. Plain but graciously looked after 2-story pre–Civil War board house utterly evokes pioneer citrus times. Groves outside the windows. Full breakfast.

Indian River House Bed and Breakfast 3113 Indian River Dr., Cocoa 32922, 321/631-5660, www.indianriverhouse.com. Pioneer house across the narrow street from the Indian River, fixed up full of historical artifacts. Unpretentious, and guests lovingly looked after.

INDIAN RIVER COUNTY

Information Sources

Cultural Council of Indian River County 2145 14th Ave., Ste. 11, Vero Beach 32960, 772/770-4857, www.cultural-council.org. First and last word on everything cultural.

Environmental Learning Center 255 Live Oak Dr., Vero Beach 32963, 772/589-5050. Contact for dolphin watching, tours to Pelican Island National Wildlife Refuge, visits to poet Laura Riding Jackson's historic home, paddling, wading, walking tours. Interpretive exhibits.

Indian River County Historical Society 2336 14th Ave., Vero Beach 32961, 772/778-3435. Limited hours in the 1903 Florida East Coast Railway station on 14th Avenue just north of 22nd Street.

Indian River County Tourist Council 1216 21st St., P.O. Box 2947, Vero Beach 32961, 772/567-3491. Ask about charter fishing, pontoon boat rentals, canoeing, and more.

Main Street Vero Beach 2145 14th Ave., Suite 14, Vero Beach 32961, 772/770-0101. What's happening in the old downtown under restoration.

Pelican Island Audubon Society P.O. Box 1833, Vero Beach 32961, 772/567-3520.

Attractions and Recreation

Heritage Center 2140 14th Ave., Vero Beach 32960, 772/770-2263. Indian River Citrus Museum displays history of this world-famous citrus region with photos, old packing labels that have become collectors' items, farm tools, archives, harvesting equipment, a video, and gift shop.

McKee Botanical Garden 350 U.S. 1, Vero Beach 32962, 772/794-0601, www.mckeegarden.org. Restored (if scaled-down) tourist site of the 1930s renowned for its tropical specimens, ponds, landmark celebration hall. Ask about tours.

McLarty Treasure Museum 11 miles north of Beachland Blvd., beachside Vero, north along Hwy. A1A, 772/589-2147. Part of the Sebastian Inlet State Park, houses exhibits and treasure from the 1715 Spanish treasure fleet that was wrecked offshore by hurricane. Slide program presents the story. Site occupies a Spanish salvor camp.

Mel Fisher's Treasure Museum 1322 Hwy. 1, Sebastian 32958, 772/589-9874. Houses prizes from the wreck of the *Atocha,* which sank off the Florida Keys in 1622, and from ships in the hurricane-wrecked Spanish treasure fleet of 1715.

Oslo Riverfront Conservation Area (ORCA) North side of Oslo Rd./9th St. SE, just east of U.S. 1 on the Indian River Lagoon, 772/567-8000, ext. 237, www.ifas/ufl.edu/veroweb/ORCA/. Almost 300 acres with 22 miles of diversified forest and wetlands trails.

Pelican Island National Wildlife Refuge (Office) U.S. Fish and Wildlife Service, 1339 20th Street, Vero Beach 32960, 772/562-3909, ext. 258, www.pelicanisland.fws.gov. Located in the Indian River Lagoon offshore Sebastian; for tours, contact the Environmental Learning Center (above). Bird sanctuary—first in the national refuge system—since 1903.

Riverside Theatre/Riverside Children's Theatre 3250 Riverside Park Dr., Vero Beach 32963, 772/231-6990, www.riversidetheatre.com. Best seasonal professional theater for miles around. Ditto for kids.

Sebastian Inlet State Park 9700 S. A1A, Melbourne Beach 32951, 772/904-4852. Glorious vistas from the high bridge that divides the park's 587 acres north and south of the inlet. Outstanding fishing, shrimping, clamming; clean, open beaches without commercial build-up, excellent surfing—one of the best sites on Florida's Atlantic coast. Campsites, seasonal ranger-led turtle nesting tours. Park open around-the-clock.

St. Sebastian River State Buffer Preserve Off Fellsmere Rd. east of I-95, 561/984-4940 (to the St. Johns River Water Management District office). Big, almost 17,000-acre conservation set-aside for wildlife viewing, paddling, cycling, hiking. Straddles the Sebastian River between Indian River and Brevard counties. Free.

Vero Beach Museum of Art 3001 Riverside Park Dr., Vero Beach 32963-1807, 772/231-0707, www.verovbmuseum.org. Exceptionally good small city facility features traveling exhibitions, works of regional artists, arts education programs, special events, excellent arts library.

Dining

Black Pearl Brasserie and Grill 2855 Ocean Dr., Vero Beach, 772/234-7426. Moody and romantic (though sometimes crowded) in a woody residential zone just south of the city. Affordable gourmet menu with Caribbean influence among fish, fowl, veal, more. Choice.

Capt. Hiram's 1606 N. Indian River Dr., Sebastian, 772/589-1345. Over the water, splashy (like the motel it's attached to, mate to the one in Vero). Popular with locals. Seating inside and out. Seafood plus the other usuals.

Chelsea's on Cardinal 3201 Cardinal Dr., Vero Beach, 772/234-8300. Best deli anywhere on A1A (okay, 2 blocks off). In a town of good eating, the best reason to picnic. Prepared entrees, salads, divine pastries, wines. In the heart of the beachfront downtown.

Chez Yannick 1601 S. Ocean Dr., Vero Beach, 772/234-4115. Sleek, romantic with 2 fireplaces in winter and poolside dining summer. Best continental cuisine.

Hibiscus Coffee and Tea 2205 14th Ave., Vero Beach, 772/778-4138. Everybody's favorite downtown short-order breakfast and lunch take-out place. Inside or at sidewalk tables.

Hurricane Harbor 1540 Indian River Dr., Sebastian, 772/589-1773. The original—on the water, funky, weather-beaten, divine when a wind's up. Seafood, surf-and-turf items, big servings, frequent entertainment. Convivial.

Marsh Landing 44 N. Broadway, Fellsmere, 772/571-8622. Authentic out-in-the-boonies setting for fresh country food. Breakfast, lunch, and dinner plus weekend entertainment. Don't miss it!

Mrs. B's Family Inn 8245 20th St., Vero Beach, 772/569-1989. Out west of town on Highway 60. Where the road-trekkers park for home cooking.

The Ocean Grill 1050 Sexton Plaza, Vero Beach, 772/231-5409. Spacious pecky cypress rooms, romantically lit, best seating by the beachfront windows. A Waldo Sexton original impressively full of artifacts. Here since 1941. Fish, seafood, grills, homemade bread.

The Patio 1103 U.S. 1, Vero Beach, 772/567-7215. A Waldo Sexton original on the mainland, more artifacts and with an impressive early-bird menu. Hugely popular. Not to be missed.

The Quilted Giraffe 500 S. U.S. 1, Vero Beach, 772/978-4242. Irresistibly creative cuisine started in downtown Vero, now on the highway toward McKee Tropical Garden.

Lodging

Capt. Hiram's Islander Resort 3101 Ocean Dr., Vero Beach 32963, 800/952-5886, 772/231-4431. Little 2-story motel dressed up Key West–colorful. Best units are those upstairs with open-beamed cathedral ceilings. Lots of wicker and pickled finishes, florals, louvers—wonderful texturing. Pool.

Davis House Inn 607 Davis St., Sebastian 32958, 772/589-4114. 3-story B&B; rustic furniture in immense rooms with much open space. Fridge and microwave. Just up from the shore road. Continental breakfast included.

Disney's Vero Beach Resort 8250 Island Grove Terr., Vero Beach 32963, 800/359-8000, 772/234-2000, www.dvcresorts.com. First-rate compound of beautifully detailed Cape Cod–style peaked-roof structures. On the beach with restaurants, fun and games.

Ferndale Lodge 11450 Indian River Dr., Sebastian 32958, 772/589-5247. Big lawn slopes to the Indian River Lagoon. Old-timey, family-run efficiencies, wonderful and affordable. Book far ahead.

Middleton's Fish Camp Blue Cypress Lake, 22 miles west of Vero off S.R. 60, 800/258-5002, 772/778-0150, www.middletonfishcamp.com. Run family-friendly by the Middletons for fisherfolk and others canoeing the lake or St. Johns River marsh. Fully equipped canalside cabins.

Pennwood Motor Lodge 9295 N. U.S. 1, Sebastian 32958, 866/742-9240, 772/589-3855, www.pennwoodmotorlodge.com. Large single-story mom-and-pop highway motel with big grounds. Rooms and efficiencies. 10 minutes to the beach. Pool. Affordable.

Riviera Inn 1605 S. Ocean Dr., Vero Beach 32963, 772/234-4112. Boutique compound around a jewel-like pool behind colonnades of Mediterranean-style arches with attractive landscaping. Motel-sized rooms but with smartly coordinated fabrics, colors. Popular Chez Yannick restaurant (above).

Sea Turtle Inn 835 Azalea Lane, Vero Beach 32963, 772/234-0788. Spacious, stylish units 2 blocks from the beach include microwave, fridge, coffeemaker, toaster. Pool.

Shopping

Healthway of Vero 646 Miracle Mile Plaza, Vero Beach, 772/569-5663.

Ocean Drive Distinctive shops north and south of Beachland Boulevard and nearby on the boulevard itself.

ST. LUCIE COUNTY

Information Sources

Main Street Fort Pierce 131 N. 2nd St., Ste. 211, Fort Pierce 34950, 772/466-3880, www.cityoffortpierce.com. Hosts "Friday Fest" downtown Fort Pierce on the first Friday of each month with live music, street dancing, vendors. Also hosts "Ghost Walks of Fort Pierce Past" on second Wednesdays, as well as the new "Bike Fest" Thursday nights.

Seven Gables House Visitor Center 490 Indian River Drive, Fort Pierce 34950, 772/468-9152. Operated by the St. Lucie Chamber of Commerce, this historic home located on the Indian River between the Backus Gallery and the Manatee Center provides visitor information, including maps and brochures for St. Lucie County.

St. Lucie County Chamber of Commerce 2200 Virginia Ave., Fort Pierce 34982, 1626 SE Port St. Lucie Blvd., Port St. Lucie 34952, 772/595-9999, www.stluciechamber.org.

St. Lucie County Tourist Development Council 2300 Virginia Ave., Fort Pierce 34982, 800/344-8443, www.visitstluciefla.com. Request a *Guide to Vacationing in St. Lucie County.*

Attractions and Recreation

A. E. "Bean" Backus Gallery and Museum 500 N. Indian River Dr., Fort Pierce 34950 772/465-0630, www.backusgallery.com. Permanent collection of Florida's foremost landscape artist displayed in a 4,000-square-foot downtown gallery. Museum also features works by members of the Florida Highwaymen, who originated in Fort Pierce. Gift shop.

Bear Point Sanctuary 772/462-1504. Hiking, fishing, birding beside a salt-marsh mangrove forest south of Seaway Drive on A1A on S. Hutchinson Island.

Fort Pierce Farmer's Market Fort Pierce City Marina, Saturday mornings in winter, featuring fresh produce, baked goods, and crafts. Summer market on Avenue D, Fort Pierce.

Fort Pierce Inlet State Park 905 Shorewinds Dr., Fort Pierce 34949, 772/468-3985. On North Hutchinson Island, the larger of two sections, walkway-connected Jack Island, covers 631 acres rimmed by mangrove swamp and a 4.3-mile trail. Free admission. At the foot of North Hutchinson, the park borders Fort Pierce Inlet and the ocean. Swimming and surfing are popular here, and a short self-guiding trail leads through a maritime hammock. Red mangroves along the western shore are best explored by paddle. Central Florida Surfing School operates from the park; information: www.surfschoolcamp.com.

Fort Pierce Jai Alai 1750 S. Kings Hwy., Fort Pierce 34945, 800/JAI-ALAI (524-2524), 772/464-7500, www.jaialai.net. The fast-paced Basque sport played with *cesta* and *pelota* (basket and ball); wagering allowed. Live Jai-Alai action January through April; fronton itself open year-round for simul-cast wagering.

FP&L Energy Encounter/Turtle Walks 6501 South Ocean Drive, Jensen Beach 34949, 800/334-5483, 772/467-7746, www.fpl.com/encounter. Located next to FP&L Power Plant, Energy Encounter features interactive games for children and also hosts monthly programs for adults about energy conservation and environmental protection. Turtle Walks Friday and Saturday nights in June and July, groups led by area biologists on beaches of Hutchinson Island to find endangered sea turtles nesting. Reservation start in April; the programs always fill.

Harbor Branch Oceanographic Institution 5600 Old Dixie Hwy., Fort Pierce 34946, 772/465-2400, www.hboi.edu. Nonprofit research and educational center, here since 1971, operates with a staff of 185 and nearly 200 volunteers from its canalfront setting close to the Indian River on 480 acres between Fort Pierce and Vero Beach. Research vessels and submersibles have successfully completed many at-sea missions funded by the National Oceanic and Atmospheric Administration, the National Science Foundation, NASA, the Department of Defense, and numerous other government and university auspices. Campus also encompasses some of the last pristine coastal hammocks on the east coast of Florida, extending from mangroves on the lagoon through a red maple–sweet bay–magnolia swamp and scrub ridge on old dunes. Visitors center, gift shop, and tours. Campus tours and boat tours of the Indian River Lagoon daily.

Heathcote Botanical Gardens 210 Savannah Rd., Fort Pierce 34982, 772/464-4672. Former 3½-acre nursery acquired for public gardens now with its exotics largely gone—but also many native shade trees—since the storms of '04. Japanese gardens and a horticultural library.

Historic St. Lucie Village 4 miles north of downtown Fort Pierce on the west shore of the Indian River Lagoon. Listed in the National Register of Historic Places.

Hutchinson Island by Horseback Reservations: 772/489-4FUN (4386). Three Sundays a month, riders can rent a horse at Frederick Douglass Memorial Park to ride along the South Hutchinson Island beach and through undeveloped pinewoods.

Manatee Observation and Education Center 480 N. Indian River Dr., Fort Pierce 34950, 772/466-1600, ext. 3333, www.manateecenter.com. Downtown at the edge of the Indian River Lagoon, favorite wintering site of manatees, best viewed from the second story of the observation tower beside the environmental ed center. Staff runs a number of educational programs such as moonlight kayak trips on the Indian River. Gift shop.

The Navy UDT-SEAL Museum 3300 N. A1A, N. Hutchinson Id., Fort Pierce 34949, 772/595-5845, www.navySEALmuseum.com. Museum and grounds commemorate the U.S. Navy underwater demolition teams known as Frogmen and SEALs. Gear includes midget submarines and a chair from the conference room of deposed Panamanian strongman Gen. Manuel Noriega.

North Fork of the St. Lucie River (touring): Canoe and kayak rentals at River Park Marina (Prima Vista Blvd., Port St. Lucie, 5 miles east of I-95 Exit 63C, or 1 mile west of U.S. 1 on Prima Vista, 772/340-3993). Or **tour onboard** the 19-passenger pontoon boat *River Lilly.* Details at 772/489-8344. Reservations required.

Oxbow Eco-Center 5400 NE St. James Dr., Port St. Lucie 34982, 772/785-5833, www.stlucieco.gov/erd/oxbow. Environmental education center on 220 acres along the North Fork of the St. Lucie River. Naturalist-led interpretive tours, exhibits, programming includes nighttime hikes and "owl prowls," as well as canoe tours of the St. Lucie River.

Savannas Recreation Area 1400 E. Midway Rd., Fort Pierce 34982, 772/464-7855, http://www.stlucieco.gov/leisure/savanna.htm. 550-acre freshwater lagoon wilderness, 7 miles south of downtown, once used as a city reservoir and almost drained for development, now a popular wildlife-viewing site.

Smithsonian Marine Station 701 Seaway Dr., Fort Pierce 34949, 772/465-6630, www.sms.si.edu. Aquariums and exhibits in a stylized Cracker house show ecosystems of the Indian River Lagoon and offshore waters as well as reef systems of the Caribbean.

St. Lucie County Historical Museum 414 Seaway Dr., Fort Pierce 34949, 772/468-1795. http://www.st-lucie.lib.fl.us/museum/index.htm. Modest, unpromotional site fits low-key Fort Pierce, which it commemorates best in an ever-expanding table model of downtown a century ago. Much more of the times. Relocation plans in the works.

Sunrise Theatre for the Performing Arts 117 S. 2nd St., Fort Pierce 34950, 772/461-4884, www.sunrisetheatre.com. Currently under renovation. When the Sunrise opens in 2005, it will seat more than 1,000 people for community events and touring Broadway shows. Originally built 1923 as a movie house, it operated until the mid-eighties.

Urca de Lima Underwater Archaeological Preserve. NN. Hutchinson Island. Site consists mainly of hull fragments and lies about a quarter mile north of the Navy SEAL Museum and 200 yards from shore on the first offshore reef in 10–15 feet of water. The *Urca de Lima* was part of a 1715 fleet of 11 ships returning to Spain from Cuba wrecked by hurricane.

Archie's Seabreeze 401 S. A1A, Fort Pierce, 772/460-8888. Convivial, open-air, Caribbean-style bar on the shore road. It's the suds, not the food.

The Beer Garden 101 N. 2nd St., Fort Pierce, 772/460-7700. German brew in the downtown historic district. Big selection of draft and bottled beers plus dinner entrees—schnitzels, sauerbraten, wursts.

Cafe La Ronde 221 Orange Ave., Fort Pierce 772/595-1928. Best crabmeat and portabello mushroom dish in town. Affordable gourmet lunch.

Captain's Galley 825 N. Indian River Dr., Fort Pierce, 772/466-8495. Locally popular off-the-water old house turned into seafood restaurant. Breakfast and lunch.

Dino's Family Restaurant 2001 N. U.S. 1, Fort Pierce, 772/465-5217. Big variety of homemade Italian and American entrees, all affordable in a plain roadside place 10 minutes north of downtown.

Gately's Grill 101 N. 2nd St., Fort Pierce, 772/468-7071. Lunch baskets and burgers, complete dinners. Best sidewalk dining in town.

Ian's Tropical Grill 927 North U.S. 1, Ft. Pierce, 772/785-9169. Chef-prepared Caribbean-style seafood in an island setting just west of the historic downtown. A second Ian's has opened in Rio (1250 NE Dixie Hwy., 772/334-4563).

Johnny's Corner Family Restaurant 7180 S. U.S. 1, Port St. Lucie, 772/878-2686. Long-established local favorite with dozens of affordable dinners.

Kristi's on the Ocean 2400 S. A1A, S. Hutchinson Island, 772/465-4200. At Ocean Village (below), seafood overlooking the sea.

Mangrove Mattie's 1640 Seaway Dr., Fort Pierce, 722/466-1044. Upscale American food under the slowly rotating fans and hanging baskets beside Fort Pierce Inlet.

Theo Thudpucker's Raw Bar and Seafood Restaurant 2025 Seaway Dr., Fort Pierce, 772/465-1078. Locally popular beachside saloon with separate dining room close by the fishing jetty.

Tiki Restaurant and Raw Bar 1 Ave. A, 772/467-1188. At the Fort Pierce City Marina, with an open, high tiki roof, serving sandwiches, burgers, salads, fish, and seafood baskets. Happy hour. Downtown happening place.

Lodgings

Club Med "The Sandpiper" 3500 SE Morningside Blvd., Port St. Lucie 34952-6199, 772/398-5100, www.clubmed.com. International clientele at this 500-acre St. Lucie River–side family-style club carpeted with 45 holes of golf, 19 tennis courts, 5 pools, 3 restaurants. Guest rooms brightly tropical in three 3-story lodges. Best food in the county.

Dockside-Harborlight Inn Resort 1160 Seaway Dr., Fort Pierce 34949, 800/286-1745, 772/468-3555, www.docksideinn.com. Long-popular inlet-facing motel keeps buying up adjacent properties, now with at least 2 pools and fishing docks. Complex includes standard motel rooms and kitchen-equipped apartments.

Ocean Village 2400 S. A1A, Fort Pierce 34949, 772/489-6100, www.oceanvillage.com. Oceanfront golf resort with fully equipped condos for rent.

Villa Nina Island Resort Bed and Breakfast 3851 North A1A, N. Hutchinson Island, Fort Pierce 34949, 772/467-8969, www.villanina.com. 5-room riverfront home with pool overlooking the Indian River Lagoon. Bright high-ceilinged rooms and private entrances as well as access to both the river and ocean. Continental breakfast.

Shopping

Health Foods: Nature's Den 8759 S. U.S. 1, Village Sq., Port St. Lucie, 772/878-9704; **Nutrition World** 2501 S. U.S. 1, Fort Pierce, 772/464-3598.

MARTIN COUNTY

Information Sources

Historical Society of Martin County 825 NE Ocean Blvd., Stuart 34996, 772/225-1961 (in the Elliott Museum, see below).

Hobe Sound Chamber of Commerce 8994 SE Bride Rd., Hobe Sound 33455, 772/546-4724, www.hobesound.org.

Jensen Beach Chamber of Commerce 1910 NE Jensen Beach Blvd., Jensen Beach 34957, 772/334-3444, www.jensenbeachchamber.org. Good source of information for seasonal turtle watching.

Martin County Conservation Alliance P.O. Box 1923, Stuart 34995, 772/283-2325.

Stuart-Martin County Chamber of Commerce 1650 S. Kanner Hwy., Stuart 34994, 772/287-1088, www.goodnature.org. Request the brochure *Historic Walking Tour of Downtown Stuart.* Locates and describes some 3 dozen sites through this historic Main Street district. Includes buildings from wood-frame vernacular through deco and various revival styles.

Attractions and Recreation

Bathtub Beach Park For information: Martin County Parks and Recreation, 2401 SE Monterey Rd., Stuart 34996, 772/221-1418. At the southern tip of Hutchinson Island. Especially at low tide, the nearshore worm reefs (see Reefs, below) create a great shallow pool (hence the name) ideal for children. Lifeguards, rest rooms, and showers.

Bicycle Rentals: The Bike Shop 119 SW Monterey Rd., Stuart 33455, 772/283-6186; **Mac's Bike Shop** 3472 NE Savanna Rd., Jensen Beach 33455, 772/334-4343; **Village Bike Shop** 8937 SE Bridge Rd., Hobe Sound 33455, 772/546-7751, www.villagebike.com.

Blowing Rocks Preserve 574 S. Beach Rd., Hobe Sound 33455, 561/744-6668, http://nature.org/wherewework/northamerica/states/florida/preserves/art5522.htm. More than a mile of limestone sea frontage with explosive wave-driven blowholes. Preserve of 73 acres includes trail and important sea turtle nesting beach.

Canoe, Kayak Tours: Jupiter Outdoor Center 18095 Coastal Hwy. A1A, Jupiter 33477, 877/748-6686, 561/747-9666, www.jupiteroutdoorcenter.com.

Coastal Science Center of the Florida Oceanographic Society 890 NE Ocean Blvd., Stuart 34957, www.floridaoceanographic.org. Expanding teaching, research, and exhibit facility focused on the ecology of coastal hardwood hammocks, marsh and mangrove forest communities. On the Intracoastal Waterway. Gift shop.

Courthouse Cultural Center 80 E. Ocean Blvd., Stuart 34994, 772/287-6676. Changing year-round exhibitions in the little art deco courthouse saved from destruction during the renewal of downtown.

Elliott Museum 825 NE Ocean Blvd., Hutchinson Id. 34957, 772/225-1961. Crackerjack exhibits that showcase the achievements of a far-reaching inventive genius. Includes knot-tying, addressing and stamp machines, vintage cars, antique bric-a-brac, lots of Americana.

Gilbert's Bar House of Refuge 301 SE MacArthur Blvd., Hutchinson Id. 34957, 772/225-1875. Restored 1875 oceanfront lifesaving station rich with early furnishings (managed by the Elliott Museum, see above).

Historic Lyric Theatre 59 SW Flagler Ave., Stuart 34994, 772/286-7827, www.lyrictheatre.com. 1926 movie house restored with 500 seats for stage plays and musical events.

Jensen Beach Historical Museum 1899 Jensen Beach Blvd., Jensen Beach 34957, 772/334-3444. Across from the Indian River Lagoon in downtown Jensen, thorough review of the town's early plantation days.

Jonathan Dickinson State Park 16450 SE Federal Hwy., Hobe Sound 33455, 772/546-2771; concession 772/746-1466; www.floridastateparks.org. Mammoth east coast park of almost 11,500 acres includes the lower stream of the federally designated wild and scenic Loxahatchee River. Concession arranges ranger-led boat tours to an upstream pioneer homestead. Popular for paddling, birding, hiking, horseback riding. Rental cabins and campgrounds available.

Reefs A limestone reef from 5 to 35 feet deep covers some 6 square miles of submerged lands offshore from St. Lucie Inlet State Preserve Park (see below), though newly subject to exotic, smothering algae. Closer to shore and prominent in Martin and St. Lucie Counties, a band of worm-formed reefs occurs in shallow water. Martin County also promotes a system of artificial reefs. All reefs attract a great variety of fish species and related marine life. For information: Martin County Office of Coastal Management, 2401 SE Monterey Rd., Stuart 34996, 772/288-5927. For dive information, contact the Coastal Science Center (above).

Savannas Preserve State Park 9551 Gumbo Limbo Lane, Jensen Beach 35957, 772/340-7530, www.floridastateparks.org. More than 5,000 acres across 10 miles from Jensen Beach to Fort Pierce, encompassing parts of the Atlantic Coastal Ridge, wetlands, and pine flatwoods, and constituting the largest freshwater marsh system along Florida's southeast coast.

South Fork St. Lucie River Management Area Access east of I-95 on S.R. 76, right on Cove Rd., again on Gaines Ave. into the county park. Information: South Florida Water Management District, P.O. Box 24680, West Palm Beach 33416; or 3301 Gun Club Rd., West Palm Beach 33416, 800/432-2045, 561/686-8800, www.sfwmd.gov. For an exceptional glimpse of wild Florida on water and ashore, enjoy an easy upstream paddle of less than 3 miles to a landing and, from there, a linear mile-long hiking trail through canopied forest.

St. Lucie Inlet Preserve State Park c/o Jonathan Dickinson State Park (see above). Estuarine peninsula extends some 6 miles north of the last automobile access into coastal wilderness jurisdictionally divided by the Hobe Sound National Wildlife Refuge (see under Palm Beach County, chap. 10) and the state preserve. Miles of beach provide important turtle nesting area. Atlantic surf, exceptional birding, ¾-mile boardwalk, dock near the inlet for boating over from mainland Port Salerno.

Treasure Coast Wildlife Hospital 2800 SE Bridge Rd., Hobe Sound 33455, 772/546-8281. Tours of the hospital. Picnic lawn and gift shop.

Dining

The Ashley Restaurant 200 W. Osceola St., Stuart, 772/221-9476. Art-filled and convivial in an old bank building named for the gang that repeatedly robbed it. Pasta, chicken, veal, beef, fish. Soup and sandwich free for starving artists.

The Black Marlin 53 W. Osceola St., Stuart, 772/286-3126. Dark, intimate room on the main street, staff knowledgeable about fish (and more). Affordable.

Casa Bella Ristorante 512 W. 3rd St., Stuart, 772/223-0077. Lovely and affordable in a restored Old Florida house a minute's walk from Inn Shepard's Park.

Catfish House 11500 SE Federal Hwy., Hobe Sound, 772/54507733. All-you-can-eat specials in a CBS-plain spot, way popular with locals.

Conchy Joe's 3945 NE Indian River Dr., Jensen Beach, 772/334-1130. Relentlessly island style with its palm out the peaked roof, hides, skins, trophy mounts, raw bar, typically reggae playing. Seafood, overlooking the lagoon.

The Deck Restaurant (see below, under Lodgings, at Harbor Inn and Marina, Stuart, 772/692-1200). Grill your own custom-cut fish and steaks at this friendly over-the-water spot.

Flagler Grill 47 SW Flagler Ave., Stuart, 772/221-9517. Chic, arty storefront as "haute" as cuisine gets downtown, and plenty satisfying for that. Long and narrow like an old railroad station grill. Round-the-world fare.

Harry and the Natives 11910 SE Federal Hwy. (at Bridge Rd.), Hobe Sound, 772/546-3061. Landmark pecky cypress, authentic old Hobe Sound hangout here since 1940. Breakfast and lunch.

Light fare in downtown Stuart: Osceola Street Herbs and Juice Bar 26 Osceola St., 772/221-1679. Salads, sandwiches, veggie and fruit juices. **Osceola Bakery** 38 W. Osceola St., 772/287-BAKE (2253). Daily lunch specials, soups, salads, sandwiches, coffees, pastries. **Nature's Way** 25 Osceola St., in the Post Office Arcade, 772/220-7306. Salads, sandwiches, soups, coffees, juices, frozen yogurt.

Luna Italian Restaurant 49 Flagler Ave., Stuart, 772/288-0550. Tables and booths inside, tables out, for down-home Italian. The affordable choice.

Rotties 10900 S. Ocean Dr., Jensen Beach, 772/229-7575l. Burnished wood, sophisticated terrace dining on South Hutchinson Island overlooking the sea. Beachside tiki bar.

11 Maple Street 11 Maple St., Jensen Beach, 772/334-7714. Upscale, in the gourmet latitudes in a picket-fenced, shingled, garden-set old house. Worldly cuisine influenced by an owner-chef's Cajun memories.

Lodgings

Caribbean Shores 2625 NE Indian River Dr., Jensen Beach 34957, 772/334-4759, www.caribbeanshores.com. Splashy colorful efficiency cottages (a few motel rooms) on the Indian River Lagoon. Pool.

Casa d'Este Bed and Breakfast Inn 4030 NE Indian River Dr., Jensen Beach 34957, 772/225-2729. Beautifully maintained, lawn-surrounded, European-run house on the north side of Jensen overlooking the Indian River Lagoon. Top buy.

Driftwood Resort 4150 NE Indian River Dr., Jensen Beach 34957, 772/334-2237. Kept-up, grassy Old Florida motel across the road from the lagoon. All units with cooking. Less than 10 minutes to the beach.

Harbor Inn and Marina 307 N. River Dr., Stuart 34994, 772/692-1200, www.harborinnandmarina.com. Tiny rooms and baths plus larger efficiencies in an enclave on the north side of the St. Lucie. Affordability and restaurant on the water make the place.

Hutchinson Island Marriott Resort 555 NE Ocean Blvd., Stuart 34996, 800/775-5936, 888/236-2427, 772/225-3700, www.floridatreasures.com/marriott.html. Renowned, 200-acre recreational oceanfront golf resort. Units of every kind, pastel, tropical. Eroded beach; fuller beach 5 cycling minutes nearby. Restaurants, pool—the works.

Inn Shepard's Park 601 W. Ocean Blvd., Stuart 34994, 772/781-4244, www.innshepard.com. Only B&B in Stuart recycles a 2-story, roughly 100-year-old house in the historic Potsdam District across the street from its large namesake waterfront park, a 10-minute walk from downtown. Modest furnishings, floors of heart pine, and windows of a wonderful crank-out sort.

Shopping

A few interesting shops along Osceola Street, the walking-friendly main street of historic downtown Stuart.

PALM BEACH COUNTY

LAKE WORTH, PALM BEACH, WEST PALM BEACH, AND NORTH IN THE COUNTY

Information Sources

Chamber of Commerce of the Palm Beaches 401 N. Flagler Dr., West Palm Beach 33401, 561/833-3711, www.palmbeaches.org.

Downtown Development Authority 400 Clematis St., Ste. 202, West Palm Beach 33401, 561/833-8873, www.westpalmbeachdda.com. Source for updates on downtown.

Greater Lake Worth Chamber of Commerce 811 Lucerne Ave., Lake Worth 33460, 561/582-4401, www.glwcoc.org/g/wcoc.

Historical Society of Palm Beach County 139 N. County Rd., Ste. 25, Palm Beach 33480, 561/832-4164, www.historicalsocietypbc.org.

Northern Palm Beaches Chamber of Commerce 1983 PGA Blvd., Palm Beach Gardens 33408, 561/694-2300, www.npbchamber.com.

Palm Beach Chamber of Commerce 45 Cocoanut Row, Palm Beach 33480, 561/655-3282, www.palmbeachchamber.com.

Palm Beach County Convention and Visitors Bureau 1555 Palm Beach Lakes Blvd., Ste. 204, West Palm Beach 33401, 800/554-PALM (7256), 561/471-3995, www.palmbeachfl.com.

Palm Beach County Cultural Council 1555 Palm Beach Lakes Boulevard, #300, West Palm Beach, Florida 33401, 561/471-2901, ArtsLine 800/882-2787, www.pbccc.org. Comprehensive listings for art, history, theater, etc.; only a sampling follows below.

Attractions and Recreation

Ann Norton Sculpture Gardens 253 Barcelona Rd., West Palm Beach 33401, 561/832-5328, www.realpages.com/annnorton. Towers of brick and arches of granite in a 2½-acre pantheist shrine, including some 300 varieties of palms. Outside of nature, one of the most impressive sites in Florida.

Armory Art Center 1703 S. Lake Ave., West Palm Beach 33401, 561/832-1776. 1939, WPA-sponsored, deco-style National Guard Armory, since 1986 a nonprofit community visual art center. Youth programs, art education, and exhibitions chiefly feature Florida artists. Free admission.

Distinct participant sports: Diving reefs from 25 to 100 feet with corals, ledges, and sponges a mile offshore. Popular wreck dives include the 1965 Rolls Royce sunk in 80 feet of water 100 yards off the beach. Dozens of dive shops service the sport with gear and boats up and down the coast (inquire at the CVB, above). For **paddling: Canoe Outfitters of Florida** 8900 W. Indiantown Rd., on the Loxahatchee, Jupiter, 888/272-1257, 561/746-7053, www.canoes-kayaks-florida.com. Self-guiding and guided trips.

Flagler Museum 1 Whitehall Way, Palm Beach 33480, 561/655-2833, www.flagler.org. Gilded mansion of Henry and Mary Lily Flagler, his private rail car, the *Ferdinand Magellan,* inside the new Flagler Pavilion. Gift shop. Gilded-age high tea served in the Whitehall Café.

Hallpatee Seminole Village at Knollwood Groves 8053 Lawrence Road, Boynton Beach 33436, 800/222-9696, 561/734-4800. Take a tram ride through Palm Beach County's oldest working orange grove and tropical flowering jungle. Also visit a Native American village and alligator pit featuring Saturday gator-handling shows.

John D. MacArthur Beach State Park 10900 S.R. A1A, North Palm Beach 33408, 561/624-6950; nature center 561/624-6952. Subtropical coastal habitat with nearly 2 miles of barrier island beach. Turtle nesting ground and site of rare lower east coast Indian middens. Fishing, picnicking, shell collecting, snorkeling, and swimming.

Jupiter Inlet Lighthouse 500 S.R. 707, Jupiter Lighthouse Park, Jupiter 33477, 561/747-8380. Oldest structure in the county (from 1860), guided tours courtesy of the Loxahatchee River Historical Museum (see below).

Lion Country Safari 18 miles west of West Palm Beach on U.S. 98/441, 561/793-1084, www.lioncountrysafari.com. 500-acre drive-through wildlife preserve has more than 1,300 animals from around the world, plus nature trails, boat rides, small amusement park, petting zoo, and reptile exhibit with a KOA campground.

Loxahatchee River Historical Museum 805 N. U.S. 1, Jupiter 33477, 561/747-6639, www.lrhs.org. Shows and tells the history of this one-time county seat and rail terminus from where the Barefoot Mailman carried the mail to Miami. Tours of the DuBois pioneer home and the Jupiter Inlet Lighthouse (see above). Gift shop.

Marinelife Center of Juno Beach 14200 U.S. Hwy. 1, Loggerhead Park, Juno Beach 33408, 561/627-8280, www.marinelife.org. Aquariums and marine life exhibits foster understanding of the fragile ocean environment. The rehabilitation facility supplies a closer look at endangered sea turtles. The center sits within a park with short dune trails and an observation tower.

Mounts Botanical Garden 561/233-1749, 531 N. Military Trail—between Belvedere Rd. and Southern Blvd., at the west end of PBIA—West Palm Beach 33415, www.mounts.org. Palm Beach County's oldest and largest public garden. 3 planted acres of tropical and subtropical fruit trees, rainforest, rose garden, herb garden, palm collection, xeriscape area, tropical vegetable garden. Free admission.

Norton Museum of Art 1451 S. Olive Ave., West Palm Beach 33401, 561/832-5196, www.norton.org. Florida's premier museum with more than 5,000 objects concentrated in American, Chinese, contemporary, and European work. Museum store, cafe, gardens; Sunday programs of music, education, and meetings with artists.

Okeeheelee Nature Center 7715 Forest Hill Blvd., about 1 mile west of Jog Road, West Palm Beach 33413, 561/233-1400. Inside 1,000-acre Okeeheelee Park, 2½ miles of trails through 100 acres of native pine flatwoods and wetlands. Interpretive center of local flora and fauna. Gift shop, nature courses. Free admission.

Palm Beach Zoo at Dreher Park 1301 Summit Blvd., West Palm Beach 33405, 561/533-0887, www.palmbeachzoo.org. More than 500 animals in a 23-acre zoological garden. Kids especially enjoy the ARK (Animals Reaching Kids) petting zoo. Boat rides on Baker Lake.

Pine Jog Environmental Education Center 6391 Summit Blvd., West Palm Beach 33415, 561/686-6600. Exhibits on regional ecosystems and recycling as well as almost a mile of trails with a self-guiding brochure. Free admission.

Raymond F. Kravis Center for the Performing Arts 701 Okeechobee Blvd., West Palm Beach, 800/KRAVIS-1 (572-8471), 561/833-8300, www.kravis.org. Leading downtown performing arts venue midway between I-95 Okeechobee Road interchange and the beach.

Roger Dean Stadium 4751 Main St., Abacoa 33458, 561/775-1818, www.rogerdeanstadium.com. Florida's only dual-team spring training facility playing host to the St. Louis Cardinals and the Florida Marlins. Roger Dean Stadium was recently recognized as the fifth-best spring training facility in the nation by *Baseball America.*

Society of the Four Arts 2 Four Arts Plaza, Palm Beach 33480, 561/655-7227, www.fourarts.org. Intimate collection of arts venues includes music and cinema productions, museum, sculpture gardens and library.

South Florida Science Museum 4801 Dreher Trail N., just north of Summit Blvd., east of I-95 underpass, West Palm Beach, 561/832-1988, www.sfsm.org. Aquarium, public telescope in the Aldrin Planetarium; Gibson Observatory, native plant center, science theater, and changing exhibits year-round in the main hall.

Tours/Cruises: Diva Duck Amphibious Tours 561/844-4188, www.divaduck.com. 75-minute, narrated, musical land and sea tours. Tour begins at CityPlace in Downtown West Palm through historic neighborhoods, then splashes into the Intracoastal Waterway for a cruise past the spectacular mansions of Palm Beach. **Empress of Palm Beach Dining Cruises** 900 East Blue Heron Blvd., Singer Island, Florida, 561/842-0882. **Palm Beach Water Taxi** 98 Lake Dr., Palm Beach Shores, 561/683-8294, www.palmbeachwatertaxi.com. Daily narrated sightseeing, nature, sunset and moonlight cruises. Shuttle service to and from downtown West Palm Beach's Clematis Street District, Singer Island, Palm Beach Gardens, Peanut and Munyon Islands as well as waterfront restaurants and attractions. **The Manatee Queen** 1065 N. Ocean Blvd (A1A), Jupiter, at The Crab House Restaurant, 561/744-2191. Intracoastal Waterway sightseeing excursions and Loxahatchee River, Jupiter Island, and sunset tours. **Water Taxi of the Palm Beaches** 11511 Ellison Wilson Rd. (at Panama Hattie's), North Palm Beach 33408, 561/775-2628, www.water-taxi.com. Locations on the Intracoastal Waterway at Panama Hattie's Restaurant and Jupiter Seasport Marina. Narrated 90-minute, scenic tour from Palm Beach to Jupiter Island as well as the Loxahatchee River. See mansions, wildlife, and seasonal manatees. Dine-and-cruise specials.

Dining

Arezzo PGA National Resort and Spa, 400 Avenue of Champions, Palm Beach Gardens, 561/627-2000, half-hour drive west from downtown. Excellent Italian with half-portion pastas available in a room light, woody with warm fabrics, Italian posters, and music from Vivaldi to Sinatra.

Bice 313½ Worth Ave. (entry on Peruvian), Palm Beach, 561/835-1600. Milanese restaurant expanded around the States, settled here at the site of the legendary Petite Marmite. Richly brass and dazzling in its floral arrangements. Exquisite northern Italian food with crackling glazes on dessert pastries.

Bizaare Avenue Café 921 Lake Ave., Lake Worth, 561/588-4488. Living room–like with stuffed chairs, sofas, ferns, antiques and art, all tables different. The food, too, in its variety: tapas, crepes, pastas, gourmet pizzas, salads, desserts.

Cafe L'Europe 331 S. County Rd. in the Esplanade on Worth Avenue, Palm Beach, 561/855-4020. Where Palm Beachites host their intimate parties when too busy to fuss at home. English country house setting for traditional and spa-version continental cuisine, everything to-the-touch perfect. Dressy. Reservations a must.

Cafe Protegé 2400 Metrocentre Blvd., West Palm Beach, 561/687-2433. Named for its connection with the Florida Culinary Institute on the north side of town, the talent is obvious from the classy Med-style room to artisan breads, knowledgeable American-continental entrees and dessert pastries like Ph.D. productions for the course on sin.

Chuck and Harold's 207 Royal Poinciana Way, Palm Beach, 561/659-1440. After 30 years, sooner or later everybody shows up at this deli-style choice for soups, roasts, posh desserts. Less expensive "twilight dining" and late-night menu. Popular Sunday brunch.

Ciao Ristorante 3416 S. Dixie Hwy., West Palm Beach, 561/659-2426. Classical northern Italian, removed here more than 20 years ago from the high-rent districts. Outstanding arborio risottos, pasta primavera with jumbo shrimp, calamari, shrimp and vegetable souffle.

Couco Pazza 915 Lake Ave., Lake Worth, 561/585-0320. Plain but intimate downtown storefront features Tuscan cuisine that draws beach crowds for its affordability. Expect weekend lines.

E. R. Bradley's Saloon 104 Clematis St., West Palm Beach, 561/833 3520. Crowd-pleaser bang on the waterfront, serving three meals and, after 10 p.m., haven for sun-drenched regulars dancing in the aisles and even the parking lot. Mostly surfer-Dan bartenders double as DJs spinning everything from Beach Boys to Blur, though with occasional live bands.

Farmer Girl Restaurant 1732 N. Dixie Hwy., Lake Worth, 561/581-0317. Down home, locally popular, where for more than 15 years they've fed the world free on Thanksgiving Day. Big salad bar and daily specials that include meat loaf, liver and onions, and the like.

Green's Pharmacy 151 N. County Road, Palm Beach, 561/832-0304. Lunch counter and dinerlike seating that still draws a power-breakfast scene, everybody from wistful one-time Kennedy watchers to short-order cooks off the boat from St. Lucia. Burgers, sandwiches, homemade soups, daily entrée specials, frothy milkshakes.

Howley's 4700 S. Dixie Hwy., West Palm Beach, 561/833-5691. Music, a bar, and outdoor seating newly added, this is still the last of the popular south-side family places, where the motto "Cooked in sight—must be right" fits with the big variety of home-style meals (baked ham, meat loaf, London broil, grilled chicken)—complete dinners around $10.

John G's Lake Worth Casino Beachfront Lake Worth, 561/585-9860. Favorite breakfast place for miles around up on the beach dune in a row of small shops beside the town-operated swimming pool across from the fishing pier. Big portions at low prices, always with a line Sunday mornings. Best buys on the blackboards.

North in the county: Harpoon Louie's 1065 N. A1A, Jupiter, 561/744-1300, directly across the river from Jupiter Light. Just north across the bridge is the **Lighthouse** (1510 U.S. Hwy. 1, Jupiter, 561/746-4811), here since the thirties serving breakfast around-the-clock and featuring classic American meat loaf and roast chicken but also surprise gourmet things, always given prosaic names so not to scare away the regulars. More fish houses opposite each other with indoor-out seating on the Intracoastal Waterway in North Palm Beach/Palm Beach Gardens: **Panama Hattie's** (11511 Ellison Wilson Rd., 561/627-1545) and the larger **Waterway Cafe** (2300 PGA Blvd., Palm Beach Gardens, 561/694-1700), each with early-bird menus. For more popular-priced seafood, the **Crab Pot** (386 E. Blue Heron Blvd., Riviera Beach on the Intracoastal, 561/844-2722). Many early-bird patrons. Run here!

Spoto's Oyster Bar 125 Datura St., West Palm Beach, 561/835-1828. Who's Who mixes with average Joes, Janes, and Jimmy Buffett spotters. Eating? It's seafood, steaks, pasta, and high-rated key lime pie.

Ta-Boó 221 Worth Ave., Palm Beach, 561/835-3500. Great style from the burnished bar to the foliage-rich fireplace room. Only outsiders don't seem to know everybody. Here except for three seasons since 1941. Dinner salads, grills, fish, lobster, ribs, steaks—same menu all day and less costly than many Palm Beach choices.

The River House 2373 PGA Blvd., Palm Beach Gardens, 561/694-1188. Waterfront for fresh seafood, steaks, chops, chicken, and duck. *Wine Spectator* award winner for the last 5 years.

Blossom's Otahiti 3169 Horseshoe Circle W., West Palm Beach 33417, 561/640-9295, www.blossoms-otahiti.com. Jamaica-born Blossom runs an international B&B but will serve guests traditional Jamaica food on request—"let's say right after regular breakfast is done," she says. Ask for codfish and ackee, curried goat, oxtail, fried plantain. Don't ask? You'll simply enjoy the high-standard hospitality in the 5 suites of a suburban ranch house surrounded by bougainvillea just west of West Palm.

The Brazilian Court 301 Australian Ave., Palm Beach 33480, 561/655-7740, www.braziliancourt.com. Charm of the BC is its lyrical, low-rise garden behind French doors, a setting for languorous sighs. Sunshine-yellow cosseting rooms with a hint of theater set the mood for romance. Chef Daniel Boulud's New World cuisine for dining.

The Breakers South County Rd., Palm Beach 33480, 800/833-3141, 561/655-6611, www.thebreakers.com. Flagler's towering legacy, between its golf course and the sea, the essential tradition of Palm Beach. Classical from its Parrot Walk to its frescoed Florentine dining room, meant for at least once in every lifetime.

The Chesterfield Hotel 363 Cocoanut Row, Palm Beach 34480, 800/CHESTR-1 (243-7871), 561/659-5800, www.chesterfieldpb.com/. Clubby, intimate, Mizneresque public spaces; smartly porcelain, chintz and cushiony in thick-carpeted guest rooms where, at the desk, you might want to compose a letter to the queen.

The Colony 155 Hammon Ave., Palm Beach 33480, 800/521-5525, 561/655-5430, www.thecolonypalmbeach.com. Beloved for the bar and gardens of this yellow, Georgian-style stack, guests enjoy pampering among rooms of Persian rugs and potted palms; Maisonette across the street for longer stays. Poolside Bimini Bar and Royal Room Cabaret.

Grandview Gardens Bed and Breakfast 1608 Lake Ave., West Palm Beach 33401, 561/833-9023, www.grandview-gardens.net Garden-set, Mediterranean-styled 1923 house with terra cotta floors. Five guest rooms with French doors, public rooms with 2-story ceilings and bits of original pecky cypress. Swimming pool. Across the street from Howard Park in the historic Grandview District, walking close to Kravis Performing Arts Center and CityPlace, ten minutes from the airport. Breakfast buffet.

The GulfStream Hotel 1 Lake Avenue, Lake Worth 33460, 561/540-6000, www.thegulfstreamhotel.com. National Register–listed 6-story pink stucco main street landmark across from a park and the Intracoastal Waterway. Many times refurbished, most recently for the best, tastefully uncluttered. Pool; walking close to downtown theaters, restaurants, and galleries; walking close to the beach, though trackless trolley also makes rounds.

Heron Cay Bed and Breakfast 15106 Palmwood Rd., Palm Beach Gardens 33410, 561/744-6315, www.heroncay.com. Estatelike but informal island-style home on 2 landscaped acres with pool and Intracoastal Waterway dock. 6 rooms from small to rambling with antique and contemporary furnishings. Unlike anything else.

Hibiscus House 501 30th St., West Palm Beach 33407, 800/203-4927, 561/863-5633, www.hibiscushouse.com. West Palm's most knowledgeable innkeepers restored their former mayor's house, then its twenties neighborhood to acclaim while presiding over a glory of decorative arts, bijou gardens, pool, and eclectic, comfortable guest rooms.

Hippocrates Health Institute 1443 Palmdale Ct., West Palm Beach 33411, 800/842-2125, 561/471-8876, www.hippocratesinstitute.org. Alternative health center founded by Ann Wigmore occupies 20 mostly wooded acres with pool west of the airport. Lodgings from cottages to entire houses. Various residential programs offered.

Jupiter Beach Resort 5 N. A1A, Jupiter 33477, 800/228-8810, 561/745-7152, www.jupiterbeachresort.com. Complete upscale, Caribbean-style oceanfront retreat in an otherwise residential area. Only about 150 rooms, cool-looking in tropical motifs. Long ample beach and Sinclairs for oceanfront dining. Sea turtle walks June and July.

Mango Inn Bed and Breakfast 128 North Lakeside Drive, Lake Worth 33460, 561/533-6900, www.mangoinn.com. Iron beds, catchy colors, eclectic spaces, a private cottage, and waterfall garden pool. Stylish and ritzy for Lake Worth.

Palm Beach Historic Inn 365 S. County Rd., Palm Beach 33480, 561/832-4009, www.palmbeachhistoricinn.com. Across South County Road from city hall in an arcade of refurbished shops entered through a courtyard. Guest rooms up steep carpeted stairs favor frills and pillows among their surfeit of Victorian decor. Breakfast in rooms.

Parador of the Palm Beaches 1000 S. Federal Hwy., Lake Worth 33460, 561/876-6000, www.theparadorinn.com. Former big- league hotelier falls in love with the B&Bs of Puerto Rico and re-creates his own in a compound of 1930–54 houses with beamed cedar ceilings, hardwood and terrazzo floors, and a courtyard, fern gardens, and Caribbean styling throughout. Imaginative colors.

PGA National Resort and Spa 400 Avenue of the Champions (just west off Florida's Turnpike), Palm Beach Gardens 33418, 800/633-9150, 561/622-7599, www.pga-resorts.com. Best of the west on 2,340 acres with 90 holes of golf, spa, restaurants (see Arezzo, above), shops and everything else deluxe you can think of.

The Plaza Inn Palm Beach 215 Brazilian Ave., Palm Beach 33480, 800/233-2632, 561/832-8666, www.plazainnpalmbeach.com. Small hotel idiosyncratically fun; deco exterior, cupid rosette lobby ceiling, cameo pool gardens, and rooms romantic in filmy fabrics. Free parking and breakfast.

Royal Palm House 3215 Spruce Ave., West Palm Beach 33407, 800/655-3196, 561/863-9836, www.royalpalmhouse.com. Airy curtains set off 4 boldly painted rooms. Common areas are bright or meditative at this 1925 Mediterranean-style, 2-story Old Northwood house. Tropical gardens surround a cottage and pool.

Sabal Palm House Bed and Breakfast Inn 109 N. Golfview Road, Lake Worth 33460, 561/582-1090, www.sabalpalmhouse.com. In residential downtown Lake Worth, sumptuous breakfast piles satisfaction on top of 7 handsome guest suites and rooms that combine Old World character with polished pine floors. Chagall and Dali rooms, Renoir suite exceptional. French doors onto the balcony of this tropically designed house. Nice arrangement for free use of the GulfStream Hotel pool with a free drink chit. Savvy goings on here.

Tropical Gardens Bed and Breakfast 419 32nd St., West Palm Beach 33407, 800/736-4064, 561/848-4064, www.tropicalgardensbandb.com. Key West–style pool and patio, tropical colors splashed around this tropical house from the 1930s. 2 poolside cottages, one with kitchenette; other rooms small but comfortable.

Shopping

CityPlace In-town residential village north of Okeechobee Road and connected to downtown West Palm—top new urbanism site in the state—has become prime venue for specialty chain stores and indie retailers in a highly walkable setting.

Downtown West Palm Beach: Give thanks, mostly mom-and-pops, few chains, fill storefronts along Clematis and nearby streets.

Health Foods: Mother Nature's Pantry Health Food Stores and Restaurants 4513 PGA Blvd., Palm Beach Gardens, 561/626-4461; 2411 N. Ocean Blvd., Singer Island, 561/845-0533. **Nutrition World** 1937 N. Military Trail, West Palm Beach, 561/684-0777; 2568 PGA Blvd., Palm Beach Gardens, 561/626-4377. **Wild Oats Natural Marketplace** 7735 S. Dixie Hwy., Lantana, 561/585-8800.

Hoffman's Chocolate Shoppe and Gardens 5190 Lake Worth Rd., Greenacres, 888/281-8800, 561/967-2213, www.hoffmans.com. Long-established chocolate factory and gift shop in tropical gardens with model train village.

Worth Avenue For the latest, the greatest, best or most in Palm Beach.

BOCA RATON, BOYNTON BEACH, DELRAY BEACH, AND SOUTH IN THE COUNTY

Information Sources

Greater Boynton Beach Chamber of Commerce 639 E. Ocean Ave., Ste. 108, Boynton Beach 33435, 561/732-9501.

Greater Delray Beach Chamber of Commerce 64 SE 5th Ave., Delray Beach 33483, 561/278-0424, www.delraybeach.com.

Palm Beach County Convention and Visitors Bureau (see above).

Attractions and Recreation

Arthur R. Marshall Loxahatchee National Wildlife Refuge Rte., 1, Box 278, Boynton Beach 33437, 561/734-8303, visitor center; 561/732-3684, headquarters. Canoeing, fishing, hunting along a 5½-mile trail allowed in various sections. A short boardwalk trail extends from the visitor center, where exhibits, information, and interpretive programs are available. Abundant wildlife viewing: deer, egrets, gators, herons, ibis, occasionally raccoons and snail kites, and migratory ducks in winter. Less often seen: bobcats and river otters. A refuge bird list that includes some 250 species available at the visitor center.

Boca Raton Historical Society 71 N. Federal Hwy., Boca Raton 33487, 561/395-6766. Highly regarded for its stewardship of two landmark buildings: Town Hall and the FEC Railway Station (the Count deHoernle Pavilion), both listed in the National Register of Historic Places. The society sets the admirable architectural tone for the city, assisting downtown redevelopment.

Boca Raton Museum of Art 501 Plaza Real, Boca Raton 33432, 561/392-2500. The city's premier cultural institution dates from 1950 and recently relocated to Mizner Park. Nineteenth- and twentieth-century modern masters plus photography from 1840 onward. Museum sponsors a lecture series, an art school, and museum shop.

Children's centers Boca has two good places for kids. **Children's Museum of Boca Raton** (498 Crawford Blvd., Boca Raton 33432, 561/368-6875) offers year-round series of story telling, sing-alongs and other musical events, and exhibitions in the pioneer Myrick home. Exhibits and tours for schools are available at this nonprofit community project housed in the city's second-oldest wooden building. Special events include Kids Fest in April, Cracker House Crazy Days in August, and Breakfast with Santa in December. Gift shop. **Children's Science Explorium** (300 S. Military Trail, Boca Raton 33486, 561/347-3913) is a hands-on activities center that features computer learning and exhibits on a range of scientific phenomena. Gift shop.

Delray Beach Tennis Center 30 NW 1st Ave., Delray Beach 33444, 561/243-7360, www.delraytennis.com. As good as it gets for this sport, a $2.5 million state-of-the-art facility with 19 clay and cushion courts open to the public and a stadium that seats 8,200 for national tournaments.

Florida Atlantic University 777 Glades Rd., P.O. Box 3091, Boca Raton 33431, 561/297-3000, www.fau.edu. Architecturally undistinguished 850-acre campus (formerly a U.S. Air Force base) with satellites in 3 counties accommodates 25,000 students. Student-faculty ratio lately a favorable 20:1 with the highest proportion of "eminent scholars" to total faculty in the 11-campus Florida State University system. Excellent performance hall and TV production center. Academic strengths in ocean engineering and marine biology. Downtown Fort Lauderdale campus houses the College of Urban and Public Affairs, in the forefront of issues concerning sprawl. FAU also administers Pine Jog Environmental Sciences Center in West Palm Beach (see above).

Morikami Museum and Japanese Gardens 4000 Morikami Park Rd., Delray Beach 33446, 561/495-0233. Since 1977, leading east coast interpretive center of Japanese culture on a gift of land from George Sukeji Morikami, who emigrated from Japan in the early 1900s as a member of the Yamato Colony farming community. Performance center, rare-plant exhibits, art events throughout the year. Restaurant, gift shop. *Ryokan* (inn) and Zen temple in prospect.

Old School Square 51 N. Swinton Ave., Delray Beach 33444, 561/243-7922. Once abandoned, 2 schools from 1913 and 1925 make up the 4-acre Old School Square Historic District (listed in the National Register), now a performing arts center and galleries that include a collection of military miniatures. The complex includes Cason Cottage (5 NE 1st St., Delray Beach 33444, 561/243-0223), which houses the Delray Beach Historical Society.

Parks Boca Raton's pride is its beach parks, largest of which is **Red Reef Park** (1400 North S.R. A1A, 561/393-7815 [for all parks]), which covers 67 acres along the beach and Intracoastal Waterway, including the Gumbo Limbo Environmental Education Center. **Spanish River Park** (3001 N. S.R. A1A) and **South Beach Park** (400 N. SR A1A) also front the beach, Spanish River extending from beach to Intracoastal Waterway with picnic sites and nature trails.

Tours: Loxahatchee Everglades Tours 14900 W. Lox Rd., Boca Raton, 800/683-5873, 561/482-0880. Operates airboat tours in the north Everglades. **Ramblin' Rose Riverboat** 801 E. Atlantic Ave., Delray Beach, 561/243-0686. Operates lunch, brunch, and dinner cruises past the mansions of Boca Raton and Manalapan.

Dining

Bistro Zenith 3011 Yamato Rd., Boca Raton, 561/997-2570. Arty, avant garde, neon-highlighted with an open kitchen that turns out everything from western-style wraps to sherry ginger-glazed oven-roasted filet touched with dry mustard and brown sugar.

Boca Diner 2801 N. Federal Hwy., Boca Raton, 561/750-6744. Upscale Boca loves this 24-hour diner just north of town that specializes in Greek foods (spanakopita, stuffed grape leaves) plus standard American fare for breakfast, lunch, dinner. Big portions, big winner.

Boston's on the Beach 40 S. Ocean Blvd., Delray Beach, 561/278-3364. Big on Bean Town. Splashy images show off Ted Williams, Rocky Marciano, and Bob Cousey. Menu features Sam Adams, New England clam chowder, and a Maine lobster sandwich. Across the road from the beach with sidewalk seating.

Dakotah 624 270 E. Atlantic Ave., Delray Beach, 561/274-6244. Hip, contemporary décor pulls the crowds almost as much as the first-rate Caribbean and South Florida cuisine. One of the downtown leaders.

De La Tierra In historic Sundy House (see below), 106 S. Swinton Ave., Delray Beach 33444, 561/272-5678. Exceptional 4-corners-of-the-earth cuisine served in dazzling gardens and inside in 3 rooms variously decorated with original Warhols, lattice-framed ceiling vines, garage door walls, cut-coral, and hardwood floors. Imaginative.

Gazebo Cafe 4199 N. Federal Hwy., Boca Raton, 561/395-6033. In a modest shopping center but serving consistently fine food. Counter seats at the big open kitchen and tables in dining rooms with inside trees. Classic continental cuisine with a fresh seafood pasta daily and a classic bouillabaisse.

Station House Restaurant 233 Lantana Road, Lantana, 561/547-9487. Superb seafood in a replica of the old Lantana train depot (c. 1920). Comfortable, relaxed amidst saltwater fish tanks and hanging plants. Maine lobsters in their own separate tanks.

Tom's Place 7251 N. Federal Hwy., Boca Raton, 561/997-0920. The original of many restaurants of the same name run by the same family. Endless soul food good as it gets served among endless images of sports all-star patrons. Look for lines winter weekends.

Zemi 5050 Town Center Circle, Boca Raton, 561/391-7177. Indoor/outdoor eyecatcher with its see-and-be-seen clean geometric sight lines. Open kitchen turns out wide range of big fresh salads to quail and house-made duck sausage and lots more worth sinking your teeth into.

Lodging

Boca Casa by the Ocean 365 N. Ocean Blvd., Boca Raton 33432, 561/392-0885. Few but spacious, upscale apartments in a private tropical garden with swimming pool across the shore road from the beach. Full kitchens, completely equipped. Book far ahead to get in.

The Boca Raton Resort and Club 501 E. Camino Real, P.O. Box 5025, Boca Raton 33431, 800/327-0101, 561/395-3000, www.bocaresort.com. Ever re-imagining itself for its wealthy clientele, Addison Mizner's original Cloister in its Cote d'Azur pink remains Boca's heart of it all, today with tower and beachfront lodgings, second tower coming.

The Colony Hotel and Cabana Club 525 E. Atlantic Ave., Delray Beach 33447-0970, 800/552-2363, 561/276-4123, www.thecolonyhotel.com. Like the Boca, built in 1926 and Mediterranean style, the Colony is far less formal, smaller, and downtown, not set apart. Favored by older, less ritzy clients. Free shuttle to the Cabana Club at the beach.

Crane's BeachHouse 82 Gleason St., Delray Beach 33483, 866/372-7263, 561/278-1700, www.cranesbeachhouse.com. Three-story old motel completely transformed as a tropical lodge with gardens full of hot colors and cool breezes between the Intracoastal Waterway and the beach—easy walking to either. Rooms are arty fun, suites arty in a less whimsical, more refined way with high-quality rattan, paver tiles, and matched accessory pieces. Pool, fountains, tiki bar.

Riviera Palms Motel 3960 N. Ocean Blvd., Delray Beach 33483, 561/276-3032. From the fifties, good buy across from the beach, 17 ordinary 2-story units with Danish modern furnishings. Best are the suites, lately only $10 more than rooms. All with kitchens plus pool. Inquire whether there are phones in units.

Sea Breeze of Delray 820 N. Ocean Blvd., Delray Beach 33483, 561/276-7496. Also from the fifties but more upscale and residential-style, 23 units, two stories and one, the latter more spread out, more luxurious. Beautifully maintained with complete kitchens. Heated pool, little clubhouse, grassy lawns.

The Seagate Hotel and Beach Club 400 S. Ocean Blvd., Delray Beach 33483, 800/233-3581, 561/276-2421, www.seagatehotelbeachclub.com. Spacious Bermuda-style compound across from the beach with two pools, beach sports gear, and smart restaurant. Quality cane and rattan furnishings in complete and romantic rooms.

Sundy House 106 S. Swinton Ave., Delray Beach 33444, 561/272-5678, www.sundyhouse.com. Finest Queen Anne house in town (from 1902; listed in the National Register), the acre site turned into curator-perfect tropical gardens and pool with 11 equally evocative, equatorial world–inspired, romance-inducing guest rooms and suites.

Shopping

Atlantic Avenue in downtown Delray is full of mom-and-pop shops, while Mizner Park shops in Boca exude chic in the setting of an outdoor residential mall and cultural showplace.

Health Foods: Whole Foods Market 1400 Glades Rd., Boca Raton, 954/447-0000.

BROWARD COUNTY

Information Sources

Broward County Chamber of Commerce 3045 N. Federal Hwy., Fort Lauderdale 33306, 954/630-0070.

Broward County Governmental Center 115 S. Andrews Ave., Fort Lauderdale 33301, 954/831-4000, www.broward.org.

Broward Cultural Affairs Council 100 S. Andrews Ave., Fort Lauderdale 33301, 800/249-ARTS (2787), 954/357-7457; hotline in Broward 954/357-5700; www.browardarts.net.

Greater Fort Lauderdale Chamber of Commerce 512 NE 3rd Ave., Fort Lauderdale, 954/462-6000, www.ftlchamber.com.

Greater Fort Lauderdale Convention and Visitors Bureau 100 E. Broward Blvd., Ste. 200, Fort Lauderdale 33301, 800/22-SUNNY (227-8669) or 954/765-4466, www.sunny.org.

Greater Fort Lauderdale Lodging and Hospitality Association 1628 N. Federal Hwy., Ste. 200, Fort Lauderdale 33305, 954/567-0766, www.ftllodging.com.

Greater Hollywood Chamber of Commerce 330 N. Federal Hwy., Hollywood 33020, 800/231-5562, 954/923-4000, www.hollywoodchamber.org.

Tri-Rail Commuter Rail Authority 305 S. Andrews Ave., Ste. 200, Fort Lauderdale 33301, 800/874-7245, 954/357-8400.

Arts and Performance

Art and Culture Center of Hollywood 1650 Harrison St., Hollywood 33020, 954/921-3274, www.artandculturecenter.org. In a 1924 house, offers exhibitions throughout the year, as well as concerts, lectures, workshops, and performing events.

ArtServe Holiday Park Library, 1350 E. Sunrise Blvd., Fort Lauderdale 33304, 954/462-9191, www.artserve.org. Provides half-price tickets to events in a tri-county area on show day.

Broward Center for the Performing Arts 201 SW 5th Ave., Fort Lauderdale 33301, 954-462-0222, www.browardcenter.org. Broadway musical or serious drama, modern dance or ballet, classical music or Grammy-winning pop concerts performed in either the 2,700-seat Au-Rene Theater or the 590-seat Amaturo Theater.

Cinema Paradiso 503 SE 6th St., Fort Lauderdale 33301, 954/462-2424, www.fliff.com. Home base for the Fort Lauderdale International Film Festival and for a multi-ethnic theater company housed in a renovated church.

Fort Lauderdale Children's Theater 640 N. Andrews Ave., Fort Lauderdale 33304, 954/763-6882, www.flct.org. Productions featuring local kids.

Museum of Art 1 E. Las Olas Blvd., Fort Lauderdale 33301, 954/525-5500, www.moafl.org. Houses one of the largest collections of CoBrA (Copenhagen, Brussels, Amsterdam [1935–45]) art in the world and an equally distinguished collection of works from the American Ashcan School.

Young At Art Children's Museum 1584 S.R. 84, Davie 33317, 954/424-0085, www.youngatartmuseum.org. Displays art especially for children.

Historical Museums

Bonnet House 900 N. Birch Rd., Fort Lauderdale 33304, 954/563-5393, www.bonnethouse.org. Across from the beach romantic home of a prominent twentieth-century art couple now open to year-round visits. Swans and monkeys, orchids, and indigenous flora inhabit the grounds; art fills the house.

Fort Lauderdale Antique Car Museum 1527 SW 1st Ave., Fort Lauderdale 33315, 954-779-7300, www.antiquecarmuseum.org. Permanent display of 27 prewar Packard Motorcars and memorabilia, featuring Calvin Coolidge's car and the Franklin D. Roosevelt Library and Gallery.

Old Dillard Museum 1009 NW 4th St., Fort Lauderdale 33311, 954/765-6952. Occupies a National Register landmark school showcasing African art and jewelry among a variety of hands-on exhibits and cultural artifacts.

Old Fort Lauderdale Village and Museum, 231 SW 2nd Ave., Fort Lauderdale 33311, 954-462-4431, www.oldfortlauderdale.org. The historical 1905 New River Inn is home to the old Fort Lauderdale Museum of History. Visit the Pioneer Lifestyle Museum housed in the historic 1907 King-Cromartie House.

Stranahan House 335 E. Las Olas Blvd., Fort Lauderdale 33301, 954/524-4736, www.stranahanhouse.com. Treasury of earliest Fort Lauderdale recollections in this pioneer house on the New River.

Parks

Hugh Taylor Birch State Recreation Area 3109 E. Sunrise Blvd., Fort Lauderdale 33304, 954/564-4521, www.floridastateparks.org. Birch Park consists of 180 acres donated by pioneer settler Hugh Taylor Birch. Birch's park legacy since 1949 has provided canoe and hiking trails, picnic areas, gift shop and visitor center incorporated in Birch's final home, which he called Terramar (land to sea) and built in 1940 at age 90. An underground passageway leads from the park beneath Highway A1A to the beach. Ranger-led walks are conducted at various times of year through the maritime hammock.

John U. Lloyd Beach State Recreation Area 6503 N. Ocean Dr., Dania 33004, 954/923-2833, www.floridastateparks.org. Encompasses 251 acres of barrier island between the ocean and the Intracoastal Waterway. Its north end abuts Port Everglades. The division is striking between the natural park area and the industrial port and is marked by a paved, lighted fishing jetty at the edge of the port channel. The park provides passive recreation with a short hammock walking trail, picnic areas, and a gift shop. Park beaches are an extension of beaches uninterrupted all the way from north Miami-Dade County through Hallandale and Hollywood to Dania.

Regional Parks Broward County's regional parks (www.broward.org/parks) include several with special features. **Tradewinds Park,** for example, with 540 acres in the municipality of Coconut Creek, includes **Butterfly World** and a riding stable. **Quiet Waters Park** with 427 acres in Deerfield Beach offers cable waterskiing (as distinct from boat-towed waterskiing). **Brian Piccolo Park,** far to the west of the county in Cooper City, offers Florida's only velodrome. **Markham Park,** to the west in Sunrise, with 665 acres, offers an outdoor target range. A water playground is the special attraction of **C. B. Smith Park** in Pembroke Pines and at **Topekeegee Yugnee (T.Y.) Park** in Hollywood. Largest of the county parks is **West Lake Park** (751 Sheridan St., Hollywood 33019, 954/357-8118) with 1,400 acres. The **Anne Kolb Nature Center** provides exhibits on wetlands and tidal action in this mangrove environment. Canoe rentals, extensive trails, and new narrated boat tours. For information on all county parks: 954/357-8100.

Participant Sports

Calm Water Electric Boat Rentals and Water Limo Service Marina Bay Resort, 2525 Marina Bay Drive W., Fort Lauderdale 33312, 954/791-8600. 18- and 21-foot electric boats for rent and captained limousine service.

Golf and Tennis Fort Lauderdale offers more than 50 golf courses, most open to the public, and some 550 tennis courts in the beach communities alone. The most central tennis center (where Chris Evert learned the game from her teacher-pro dad Jimmy) is at **Holiday Park** (701 NE 12th Ave., Fort Lauderdale 33304, 954/761-5378), with 18 clay and 3 hard-surface courts (14 of the clay courts lighted).

Water Sports Full Moon Kayak Co. P.O. Box 22003, Fort Lauderdale 33335, 954/328-5231, www.fullmoonkayak.com. Urban and natural settings alike offer options for vacationing paddlers: mild beach surf, still lakes, tidal mangrove-lined creeks, and the Intracoastal Waterway. View historic sites, wildlife, architecture, cruise ships, and super yachts. Water sports also include offshore, waterway, and marsh fishing, canoeing and kayaking, waterskiing and kite surfing plus exploring the Florida Everglades.

African-American Research Library and Cultural Center 2650 Sistrunk Blvd, Fort Lauderdale 33311, 954/625-2800, www.broward.org/library/aarlcc. Exhibition hall, theater, and more than 75,000 books, documents, artifacts that focus on the experience of people of African descent.

Ah-Tha-Thi-Ki Museum Big Cypress Reservation off-I-75, 23 miles to Exit 14, then 17 miles north, 863/902-1113, www.seminoletribe.com/museum. The "unconquered" Seminoles present their history and culture through films and exhibits, rare artifacts, nature trails, and living village. **Billie Swamp Safari** here (800/949-6101, www.seminoletribe.com/safari) offers a gloss on an Indian village as well as swamp tours, a restaurant, and overnight barebones cabins.

Broward County Historical Commission 151 SW 2nd St., Fort Lauderdale 33311, 954/765-4670, www.broward.org/history. Houses archives of Broward County history and displays of photos and artifacts of the county's past.

Broward County Main Library 100 S. Andrews Ave., Fort Lauderdale 33361, 954/357-7397, www.browardlibrary.org. One of the county's important multipurpose resources. Located in an 8-story structure designed by Marcel Breuer Associates; in addition to books, it houses the Bienes Center for the Literary Arts, the Broward Cultural Affairs Division, an art gallery, a 300-seat theater that schedules readings and performances, and a gift shop.

Buehler Planetarium and Observatory Broward Community College Central Campus, 3501 SW Davie Rd., Fort Lauderdale 33314, 954/201-6681. Provides an observatory and guided explorations of the night sky.

Butterfly World Tradewinds Park, 36700 S. Sample Rd., Coconut Creek 33063, 954/977-4400, www.butterflyworld.com. Beautiful attraction where you can stroll among thousands of live butterflies in their natural habitat.

Everglades Holiday Park-Sightseeing Tours, 21940 Griffen Rd., Fort Lauderdale 33332, 954/434-8111, www.evergladesholidaypark.com. Airboat journeys through the River of Grass. Fishing guide tours, boat rentals, and 24-hour general store.

Flamingo Gardens and Wray Botanical Collections 3750 S. Flamingo Rd., Fort Lauderdale 33330, 954/473-2955, www.flamingogardens.org. Connect with nature at 6-acre botanical gardens and wildlife sanctuary. Exotic and native plants, citrus groves, and champion Florida trees. Bird of Prey Center and free-flight walk-through aviary, alligators, flamingos, and bobcats.

Fort Lauderdale Historical Museum 219 SW 2nd Ave., Fort Lauderdale 33311, 954/463-4431. Features permanent collections and changing exhibits as well as performances and docents in period costumes.

Graves Museum of Archaeology and Natural History 481 S. Federal Hwy., Dania 33004. Closed in 2005.

IGFA Fishing Hall of Fame and Museum 300 Gulfstream Way, Dania Beach 33004, 954/922-4212, www.igfa.org. Part museum, part hall of fame—all promotional on behalf of angling. It's hard to circle around to, so call for directions. World-class state-of-the-art facility includes 7 galleries, outdoor marina, living wetlands with live alligators and virtual fishing.

Museum of Discovery and Science and **Blockbuster IMAX Theater** 401 SW 2nd St., Fort Lauderdale 33311, 954/467-6637, www.mods.org. Offers a hands-on explorium that specializes in children's exhibits of art, science, and natural history plus the immense IMAX theater.

Sawgrass Recreation Park Highway 27, 2 miles north of I-75 North, 800/457-0788, 954/389-0202, www.evergladetours.com. Narrated Everglades airboat tours, eighteenth-century Indian village, live alligators, reptile show, wildlife exhibit, Florida panther, camping boat rentals, and fishing.

Spectator Sports

Baseball Broward offers National League baseball with the **Florida Marlins** (www.floridamarlins.com) at Pro Player Stadium (which though in Miami-Dade County is closer to downtown Fort Lauderdale and the beach than it is to downtown Miami and Miami Beach). Also **Baltimore Orioles Spring Training** Fort Lauderdale Stadium, I-95 and Commercial Blvd., 954/776-1921, www.theorioles.com. Watch team practice at no charge beginning in mid-February. Exhibition games in March.

Dania Jai-Alai 301 E. Dania Beach Blvd., Dania 33004, 954/428-7766, www.betdania.com. Pioneer fronton in Florida, with pari-mutuel betting.

Five Star "Championship" Rodeo Bergeron Rodeo Grounds, Davie, 954/384-7075, www.fivestarrodeo.com. Professional rodeo cowboys compete in 7 major rodeo events including bareback and saddle bronco riding, steer wrestling, and bull riding.

Florida Panthers Hockey Office Depot Center, 1 Panther Pkwy., Sunrise 33051, 954/835-TEAM (8326), www.floridapanthers.com. Also offered at the Office Depot Center is a wide variety of family shows and concerts (954/835-8000, www.officedepotcenter.com).

Gulfstream Park 901 S. Federal Hwy., Hallandale 33009, 954/454-7700, www.gulfstream.com. Florida's premier thoroughbred track, with pari-mutuel betting, home of the Florida Derby.

Hollywood Greyhound Track 831 N. Federal Hwy., Hallandale 33009, 954/454-9400, www.hollywoodgreyhound.com. Offers pari-mutuel betting.

International Swimming Hall of Fame 1 Hall of Fame Dr., Fort Lauderdale 33316 (just below Las Olas Blvd. at the beach), 954/462-6536, www.ishof.org. Outstanding facility with two Olympic-size pools and a museum with Olympics memorabilia from more than 100 countries. International and collegiate swimming and diving competitions take place here much of the year. Also here: **Fort Lauderdale Aquatic Complex** 501 Seabreeze Blvd, Fort Lauderdale, 954/828-4580, www.fortlauderdale.gov. Swimming exhibitions and competitions.

Miami Dolphins Football Pro Player Stadium, 2269 Dan Marino Blvd., 305/623-6100. Mail: 7500 SW 30th St., Davie 33314. Ticket info: 888/FINS TIX (346-7849), www.miamidolphins.com. NFL Dolphins training camp begins third week of July at the Nova Southeastern University Campus, 7500 SW 30th St., Davie 33314, 954/452-7000.

Pompano Park Racing 1800 SW 3rd St., Pompano Beach 33069, 954/972-2000, www.pompanopark.com. Live harness racing and poker from October through May. Simulcasting day/night year-round. Free admission and parking.

Seminole Casino Hollywood 4150 N. S.R. 7, Hollywood 33024, 954/961-3220, www.semtribe.com.

Seminole Coconut Creek Casino 5550 NW 40th St. (NW 54th St. off of Sample Rd.), Coconut Creek 33063, 866/2-CASINO (222-7466), www.seminoletribe.com. Open 24 hours, 7 days a week. Offers high-stakes bingo with prizes up to $100,000.

(Brian Piccolo) Velodrome and Skate Park 9501 Sheridan St., Cooper City 33024, 954/437-2626, www.broward.org/parks. Velodrome, skate park, track bikes available for rent, and various classes, including in-line skating plus Brian Piccolo Racquet Center, 12 clay tennis courts and 6 for racquetball.

Tours/Cruises

Carrie B. Harbor Tours Riverwalk, Las Olas Blvd. and SE 5th Ave., Fort Lauderdale, 954/768-9920, www.carriebcruises.com. Offers 90-minute cruises of the New River, Intracoastal Waterway, and Port Everglades.

Everglades Holiday Park Sightseeing Tours See above under Science and Education Attractions.

Flamingo Gardens and Wray Botanical Collections See above under Science and Education Attractions.

Goodyear Blimp 1500 NE 5th Ave., Pompano Beach 33060, 954/946-8300. Offers lighter-than-air rides aloft.

Jungle Queen Riverboat Cruises Bahia Mar Yacht Basin, Fort Lauderdale 33316, 954/462-5596, www.junglequeen.com. Offers daytime and dinner cruises.

Lauderducks BeachPlace, 17 S. Ft. Lauderdale Beach Blvd., Fort Lauderdale 33316, 954/GO-QUACK (467-8225), www.lauderducks.com. Cruise the streets of Fort Lauderdale's shopping, entertainment, and beach districts aboard a World War II DUKW and the waterways for close-up looks at mansions, marinas, and yachts.

Pro Dive Glass Bottom Boat Tours and Snorkeling Bahia Mar Yacht Basin on A1A, Fort Lauderdale 33316, 954/467-6030, www.prodiveusa.com. Operates a 60-foot glass-bottom tour to the coral reefs, while from the same yacht harbor, the venerable *Jungle Queen* sails on its New River cruises.

Riverfront Cruises and Anticipation Yachts Las Olas Riverfront, Fort Lauderdale 33316, 954/463-3440 or 954/527-0075, www.anticipation.com. Cruise the calm waters of Fort Lauderdale's inland canals in safe and comfortable luxury yachts. Groups welcomed. Private parties available on Anticipation Yachts.

Rockmore Cruises 1755 SE 3rd Ct., Deerfield Beach 33441, 954/426-4006, www.rockmoreus.com. Daily lunch, dinner, and sightseeing cruises along the Intracoastal Waterway.

Sawgrass Recreation Park See above under Science and Education Attractions.

Tropical Sailing 801 Seabreeze Blvd., Fort Lauderdale 33316, 954/579-8181, www.tropicalsailing.com. Catamaran sailing, 2½-hour ocean sightseeing cruise, champagne sunset trips, dinner cruise, half-day and full-day private charters.

Water Bus 651 Seabreeze Blvd., Fort Lauderdale 33316, 954/467-6677, www.watertaxi.com. The pick of ways to get around the Venice of America and to and from many popular hotels and restaurants.

Dining

Fort Lauderdale shines with good places to eat, many affordably. Check the Friday **South Florida Sun-Sentinel** for a wide range of restaurant reviews. The **Miami Herald** and **Palm Beach Post** also review Broward restaurants.

Affordable choices include **Cafe Europa** 726 E. Las Olas Blvd., Fort Lauderdale, 954/763-6600. Pizzas, focaccia, calzones, sandwiches, salads. Sidewalk tables on the lovely shopping street. **Ernie's Bar-B-Q** 1843 S. Federal Hwy., Fort Lauderdale, 954/523-8636. A local favorite for barbecue. Outrageous libertarian political cartoons on the walls and an upstairs open-air porch. **The Floridian** 1410 E. Las Olas Blvd., 954/463-4041, beats anyplace for reading the morning paper over a plate of everything you've ever imagined for breakfast—including a bottle of Mumm's. Counter, table, or sidewalk service. **O'Hara's Hollywood Jazz Cafe** 1903 Hollywood Blvd., Hollywood, 954/925-2555. Serves up the best jazz in town and sidewalk eats at the heart of the landscaped boulevard.

Aruba Beach Cafe 1 Commercial Blvd., Lauderdale-By-the-Sea, 954/776-0001. Big meals and fun times here at A1A on the ocean. Watch the beach action at the closest spot to Anglin's Pier. Big bar, a sea of tables, fresh seafood, pastas, stir-fries, grazing food. Young crowd loves it, international tourists, too. California in Florida with a Caribbean name.

Bimini Boatyard 1555 SE 17th Street, Fort Lauderdale, 954/525-7400. More Caribbean and California in a lighthouselike setting. Inside and deck seating. Big fish menu, pizzas, salads, pastas. Casual. Affordable daily specials.

Brooks 500 S. Federal Hwy., Deerfield Beach, 954/427-9302. Large family-run restaurant balances volume and people-pleasing virtues of fresh, imaginatively prepared food, attractive settings, and above all value—265 seats and still a line forms. Service crisply French, menu French-American. Table d'hote dinners include appetizer, salad, entrée, and dessert averaging around $30 per person. Big wine list with affordable selections.

Café Claude 1544 SE 3rd Ct., Deerfield Beach, 954/421-7337. Intimate, authentically Gallic and greatly admired French restaurant in the Cove shopping plaza.

Cafe Maxx 2601 E. Atlantic Blvd., Pompano Beach, 954/782-0606. One of the first and consistently among the best featuring fresh Caribbean-Florida fusion cuisine. Artful, sophisticated cafe setting crowded nightly with locals—which of course attracts tourists.

Cap's Place 2765 NE 28th Court, Lighthouse Point, 954/941-0418. You get here by launch that recalls rum-running from Bimini. The place appears dim like bare succor in gloom. The castaway mood rates an Oscar for staging—except that it's been here since long before the manicured mansions beside their finger canals. Cap's Place in the Intracoastal Waterway dates from the twenties, when Captain Theodore Knight capped three generations of Knight sheriffs and lighthouse keepers by taking up bootlegging and running games of chance. His food was a good enough front to draw Dempsey, Roosevelt and Churchill, DiMaggio, JFK, and every Palm Beach ingénue who'd ever scandalized her trust officer by falling for a con job in pants. That was Cap, and he kept his clientele boating over for almost 40 years until he died in 1964 at 93. Al Hasis, taken in by Cap as a 16-year-old runaway, took over. Al's kids still run the place. Same fish nets, shark jaws, snake skins, high uncushioned booths, same resinous bar where Capone grubbed the gambling take.

Chima 2400 E. Las Olas Blvd, Fort Lauderdale, 954/712-0580. Brazilian steakhouse with gaucholike staff serving traditional Brazilian barbeque specialties, notably *rodizio* with filet mignon, lamb chops, and sirloin.

The Deck Restaurant 401 N. Fort Lauderdale Beach Blvd. (Hwy. A1A), 954/463-7423. In the Bahama Hotel across from the beach, often overlooked 30-year-old, 3-meal-a-day affordable dining served with a casual, ocean-view atmosphere. Lots of unusual fare, from a breakfast veggie frittata to dinner calamari. Poolside bar.

Don Arturo 1198 SW 27th Ave., Fort Lauderdale, 954/584-7966. Pick of the Cuban, dark, oaken, garlicky, with all the roast pork, green sauce, and black-beaned items that make this cuisine a favorite for non–lite eaters.

Fifteenth Street Fisheries 1900 SE 15th St., Fort Lauderdale, 954/763-2777. Popular, long-established seafood restaurant on the Intracoastal Waterway also serves exotics like gator and 'roo. Upstairs is formal (and higher priced), downstairs casual with seating inside and out. Nautically adapted Old Florida style with a fish-friendly staff.

Giorgio's Grill 606 N. Ocean Dr., Hollywood, 954/929-7030. Big room on the Intracoastal centers a Mediterranean village that includes Taverna Opa plus a bakery and market. Popular from the open kitchen: pan-seared crusted salmon with stewed leeks, shrimp in garlic butter.

Johnny V 625 East Las Olas Blvd., Fort Lauderdale, 954/761-7920. One of South Florida's acclaimed chefs, Johnny Vinczencz, has opened his own first restaurant, featuring a bold Caribbean-inspired New American menu. Tapas menu available in the lounge and bar. Sleek, urban decor contrasts with Vinczencz's robust cuisine.

Las Olas Cafe 922 E. Las Olas Blvd., Fort Lauderdale, 954/524-4300. Charming, intimate in a lovely brick courtyard with an oak trimmed in twinkling lights and set between the boulevard and the river road. Good selection of pastas, seafood/fish, vegetable plate.

Le Tub 1100 N. Ocean Dr., Hollywood, 954/921-9425. The name hardly suggests the million-dollar view of this laid-back hangout on the Intracoastal Waterway. Once a Sunoco station, it's now a beer, burger, and seafood place redolent of the old Everglades, from its dim and woody hand-built insides to its old bathtubs that look like the landscape's taking 'em all over. Hard not to like.

Fancy roadside markets? Find your way to half-century-old **Ludwig's Market,** 4191 N SR 7, Hollywood, 954/987-4560, just south of Stirling Road, open from October to March. It's pumpkin heaven from when the family-run market opens in fall through Thanksgiving, 100 tons worth on hand with some jack-o-lanterns-in-waiting weighing in at 500 lbs.

Mangos Restaurant and Lounge 904 E. Las Olas Blvd., Fort Lauderdale, 954/523-5001. Lively indoor/outdoor atmosphere on the main stem, serving American food. Entertainment nightly, reservations.

Mark's Las Olas 1032 E. Las Olas Blvd., Fort Lauderdale, 954/463-1000. Metallic hard-surface interiors carom the buzz around this home base of an acclaimed innovator of new American cuisine. Menu roams the world with Caribbean spiny lobster, saffron seafood linguine, and an oak-grilled pork chop with Scotch bonnet barbecue sauce and mango chutney.

Primavera Restaurant 830 E. Oakland Park Blvd., Oakland Park, 954/564-6363. Pilasters and figureheads elegantly set off large tables comfortably apart at this restaurant that operates smooth as mascarpone. Favorite for deeply satisfying northern Italian food—far better than suggested by its shopping center setting.

Rino's Tuscan Grill 1105 E. Las Olas Blvd., Fort Lauderdale, 954/766-8700. Big return to Las Olas for long-time Broward favorite owner-chef Rino Balzano who in his new three-section, quickly acclaimed restaurant offers formal dining inside, a small café-style porch, and a waterfront garden patio. Handmade pastas include pumpkin-filled tortellini and black lobster ravioli; second courses, baby quails in Chianti over polenta and an aromatic mix of fish and seafood in marinara sauce.

Sage French Cafe 2378 N. Federal Hwy., Fort Lauderdale, 954/565-2299. Fresh foods, fresh herbs, mostly light cuisine of salads, French country fare, chicken, quiche. Large portions, top service, country setting in a little shopping center.

Sea Watch 6002 N. Ocean Blvd., Fort Lauderdale, 954/781-2200. Upscale fish house on the ocean dune. Rich paneling, upholstered chairs, sumptuous views of the beach and sea through picture windows. Many lounges, many floors. Big choice, big portions.

Shirttail Charlie's 403 SW 3rd Ave., Fort Lauderdale, 954/463-3474. Directly on the New River across from the performing arts center. Open decks, umbrellas, gazebo bar. Altogether informal, wonderful for lunch, romantic for dinner. Seafood mostly, a few grills.

Sublime 1431 N. Federal Hwy., Fort Lauderdale, 954/615-1431. Breakthrough in vegan cuisine. The best food of its kind in Florida. The restaurant is large yet intimately spaced, its lighting and waterfall designer chic, and offers as swell an evening out as anyplace else first-class. Beautifully prepared and served lasagnas, loaves, steamed dishes plus full bar and retail store with animal-friendly crafts. Expensive and busy.

Sugar Reef 600 N. Surf Rd., Hollywood Beach, 954/922-1119. Crayolas in tumblers let guests add their own color to the splashy Caribbean style of this little open-air cafe where reggae accompanies adaptive Creole food—tropical fish stew, seafood pasta, baby back ribs with fresh mango and cilantro. Opens onto the Broadwalk overlooking the beach.

Try My Thai 2003 Harrison St., Hollywood, 954/926-5585. Big dining room full of wall-hung ties, which guests frequently leave for the Thai/tie connection. What you might expect from Thai food—and what you might not: tender gator served with chili paste. **Try My Thai . . . too** 1507 N. Federal Hwy., Fort Lauderdale, 954/630-0030.

Victoria Park 900 NE 20th Ave., Fort Lauderdale, 954/764-6868. At the edge of a residential neighborhood just off Sunrise Boulevard, delightful, tiny French-Caribbean cafe with island art, splashy fabrics, trompe l'oeil windows and mirrors that make the room look bigger. Features Jamaican style pork loin, smoked salmon with potato pancake, pastas, chicken with a honey glaze.

Lodging

Broward beach towns all boast inexpensive places a few blocks from the beach, most with pools, gardens, and clean (if small) rooms. In Hollywood and north in the county, some of these lodgings can be found affordably on the beach. The better of these places are included among Superior Small Lodgings, a program begun in Broward County that now extends through perhaps a dozen more Florida counties. All Superior Small Lodgings—there are more than 100—are evaluated yearly. From year to year some properties are dropped, others added. They have in common that all are meant to be clean, safe, no more than 50 rooms and personally run. A single free brochure lists all these properties in Broward County. Inquire from Greater Fort Lauderdale Convention and Visitors Bureau (see head of Broward County listings).

Least expensive units typically are smallest with the least desirable views, maybe with only a single window. Off-season rates (typically after Easter and until mid-December) are often half or less than half what they are on season. Discounts always extend to bookings by the week.

More affordable properties include **Winterset Apartment/Motel** 2801 Terramar St., Fort Lauderdale 33304, 954/564-5614, www.thewinterset.com. A modest 29-unit property for many years run by Arlyne and Robert Poirier (who speak French). It's pieced together from 3 once separately owned buildings so that it now has 2 swimming pools. The little, minimally embellished **Nina Lee Imperial House** (3048 Harbor Drive, Fort Lauderdale 33316, 954/524-1568) contains 14 units at the south end of the beach area with its swimming pool set in a lawn between the motel wings. **A Little Inn By The Sea** 4546 El Mar Dr., Lauderdale-By-The-Sea 33308, 954/772-2450, www.alittleinn.com. Tropical theming, lots of public space for breakfasts (included in the rate), for lounging, socializing, indoors and out. All 29 units have an ocean view or private balcony.

The Atlantic 601 N. Beach Blvd., Fort Lauderdale 33304, 954-567-8020. www.luxurycollections.com/atlantic. Potential 5-star. 123-suite hotel and condominium resort on the beach road opened 2004. On site, a gourmet restaurant, pool, private cabanas, and European-style spa.

Banyan Marina Apartments 111 Isle of Venice, Fort Lauderdale 33301, 954/524-4430, www.banyanmarina.com. Vacationers who value both privacy and style will find they've discovered Fort Lauderdale as good as it gets here. German-born Dagmar and Peter Neufeldt look after 10 spacious units on a finger canal island off Las Olas with consummate care. Units feature quality rattan, glass tables, thoughtfully chosen art, collections of crafts. All units with kitchens. Pool beside a big banyan with woody walkway through its upper story. A privileged arrangement.

Blue Seas Courtyard 4525 El Mar Dr., Lauderdale-By-The-Sea 33308, 954/772-3336. Provides 13 clean, tropically furnished rooms, efficiencies, and bedroom apartments on a quiet street a block from the beach with a heated pool.

Carriage House Resort Motel 250 S. Ocean Blvd., Deerfield Beach 33441, 954/427-7670, www.carriagehouseresort.com. Cleanest of the clean, a block from the beach. Georgette and Carl Bondel speak French and German as well as English. Heated pool, 30 units.

Cottages by the Ocean (3309 SE 3rd Street) and **Pineapple Place** (3217 NE 7th Place), both in Pompano Beach, 954-956-8999, www.4rentbythebeach.com. Two comfy-cozy properties owned by hotelier Elaine Fitzgerald. Cottages by the Ocean is a restored forties miniresort that's altogether homelike, 2 blocks to the beach and hardly farther to shops, restaurants, and fishing/diving activities. Pineapple Place, a 4-unit property, has fully outfitted 1- and 2-bedroom apartments across Ocean Boulevard.

Driftwood on the Ocean 2101 S. Surf Rd., Hollywood 33019, 954/923-9528. Best choice in south Broward. 49 units from hotel rooms to 2-bedroom apartments, on the beach at the (quiet) end of Surf Road with pool. English and French spoken. Clean and almost stylish.

Eighteenth Street Inn 712 18th St., Fort Lauderdale 33316, 954/4678-7841. On unusually spacious in-town landscaped grounds, this 6-suite/room compound sits tropically behind a garden gate with fountains, pool, and walkways that lead to a French-doored recreation and breakfast room and imaginatively themed guest rooms to either side. Savvy longtime innkeepers know the town. They're a block off a waterfront restaurant row, a less-than-10-minute drive to the beach.

Green Island Inn 3300 NE 27th St., Fort Lauderdale 33308, 954/568-5093. In every way, the best value in the city: location, setting, hospitality, price. The same family has looked after this serene walled acre with its tropical gardens and 2-story inn for more than 30 years. Its merely comfortable to exceptional Caribbean-style rooms stay affordable because the site was long ago paid off. A block from the beach with pool.

The Hillsboro Club 901 Hillsboro Mile, Hillsboro Beach 33062-2801, 954/941-2220. Rare clubby Old Florida resort started as a boys' school in the 1920s, later became a private club-based resort. Remains open only to club members late November through April. At other times, outsiders welcomed (reservations required) in bright wicker and lattice rooms, suites, and cottages. Pool, gardens, tennis courts, boardwalks and directly on the beach close by Hillsboro Light. Inquire whether dining room open summers.

Hollywood-By-the-Sea Bed and Breakfast 301 Jackson St., Hollywood 33019, 866/927-5301, 954/927-5301, www.hollywoodbytheseabandb.com. Large house from the founding heyday of Hollywood-By-the-Sea (as the town was once called) a block from the beach, transformed into an exuberantly artful B&B. Enticements include the sink that makes washing up a gallery experience, the works of James Jones (who once lived here), and more. Chummy Dean Liotta looks after you. What do you want for breakfast? Eat by the pool.

Hyatt Regency Pier 66 and **Spa LXVI** 2301 SE 17th St. Causeway, Fort Lauderdale 33316, 954/525-6666, www.pier66.com. As central as it gets for boating types. Where the 17th Street Causeway crosses the Intracoastal Waterway in Fort Lauderdale is where you find the signature feature—the spiky Statue of Liberty–like crown atop its 17-floor tower, home of the revolving Pier Top Lounge that takes 66 minutes to rotate through its cycle, offering panoramic views of the city and sea. Also, 142-slip marina, aquatics center for scuba diving, snorkeling, and fishing arrangements, the Spa LXVI (66), and overall the 22 garden-and-waterfront acres of this resort with its 388 rooms and suites, 6 restaurants and lounges, tennis courts, 3 pools, and complimentary water shuttle to the beach. Commendable recycling program on an average week in the height of the season salvages 6,000 aluminum beverage cans and 4,000 lbs. of newsprint. **Grille 66** overlooks the waterway for imaginative American food and live music.

La Casa del Mar 3003 Granada St., Fort Lauderdale 33304, 800/739-0009, 954/467-2037. 300 feet off the beach, a private home added onto now a 2-story, gay-friendly B&B with pool and patio bar.

Lago Mar Resort and Club 1700 S. Ocean Lane, Fort Lauderdale 33316, 800/524-6627, 954/523-6511, www.lagomar.com. Mom-and-pop of all mom-and-pops, begun (and still owned) by the Banks family in 1948—long ago enough that this resort today rambles through generations of lodgings sprung from the original hotel by the beach at a time when far South Beach wasn't really where it was at. Today Lago Mar (the name means lake to sea) sprawls indulgently over 10 acres from the ocean to Mayan Lake, and it's very much where you want to be: 475 feet of ocean frontage behind a wide beach. The swimming lagoon alone covers 9,000 square feet with a palm-studded island. Newer units and public spaces are European in their muted style yet tropical in colors. Large aquarium backs the check-in desk. Altogether low-rise, apart, and privileged.

Lauderdale Colonial 3049 Harbor Drive, Fort Lauderdale 33316-2491, 954/525-3676. Presents the style of a small resort with tiki huts in the pool/garden area and large frontage for parking yachts on the Intracoastal at the mouth of the New River. Views upstream across the palm-lined waterfront homes to downtown are stunning. 14 spacious lodgings furnished in rattan.

Marriott's Harbor Beach Resort and Spa 3030 Holiday Dr., Fort Lauderdale 33316-2498, 800/525-4000, 954/525-4000, www.marriottharborbeach.com. Broward's flagship resort since 1984. Its 16 acres reach across a broad beach with 1,100 feet of seafront. Its public style is crystal chandeliers, recessed lighting, sumptuous chintz-covered rattan, and matched mahogany veneers; its room look is corporate clean in tans and beige with thick carpets and deeply tufted upholstery. Broad decks and lush gardens surround the pool fed by a dramatic waterfall, one of the best features. 5 tennis courts.

Martindale Apartment/Motel 3016 Bayshore Drive, Fort Lauderdale 33304, 800/666-1841, 954/467-1841, www.martindaleatthebeach.com. Shows deco styling and neon flash, a sidewalk canopy, and a garden and pool area recessed from the street. A little less sun, a little more privacy, 19 units on 3 stories.

Pillars at New River Sound 111 N. Birch Rd., Fort Lauderdale 33304, 800/800-7666, 954/467-9639, www.pillarshotel.com. Newly redone 21 units arrange U-shape directly on the Intracoastal with a yacht dock and a swimming pool in the gardens between the wings of rooms. Pale colors, pastels, and chintz set a mood of the Mediterranean tropics. Exceptionally well done.

Riverside Hotel 620 E. Las Olas Blvd., Fort Lauderdale 33301, 800/325-3280, 954/467-0871, www.riversidehotel.com. Here since 1936, ever upgraded, a full-service hotel of 217 rooms and suites with distinct Mediterranean look, its lobby and restaurants opening directly onto the heart of downtown Las Olas.

Royal Palms Resort 2901 Terramar St., Fort Lauderdale 33304, 800/237-PALM (7256), 954/564-6444 (SSL), www.royalplams.com. Beautiful, gay-friendly, B&B-style miniresort on 2 stories and only 2 blocks from the beach, its pool in a tropical garden.

Spa Atlantis Health and Fitness Resort 1350 N. Ocean Blvd., Pompano Beach 33062, 800/583-3500, 954/590-1000, www.spaatlantisresort.com. Oceanfront health and fitness spa redone in 2002 features 89 rooms and suites, all nonsmoking. No alcohol, caffeinated beverages, refined sugar, or dairy. Impressive array of treatment rooms, plus 2 outdoor heated pools and juice bar. Fitness programs include aerobics, spinning, kickboxing, body sculpting, yoga, tai chi, meditation, plus Pilates and the new Gyrotonicâ.

Westin Diplomat Resort and Spa 3555 S. Ocean Dr., Hollywood 33019, 888/627-9057, 954/602-6000, www.diplomatresort.com. Hollywood's outstanding, eye-catching, 39-story new resort. A South Florida landmark utterly made over, it re-opened in 2002 with 996 rooms and suites. Also includes The Country Club at The Diplomat, 60 balconied suites that lavish mansionlike comforts on guests with tapestry-like area rugs on plank floors. 18-hole golf course and 30,000-square-foot European-style spa.

Wyndham Resort and Spa 250 Racquet Club Rd., Fort Lauderdale 33326, 954/389-3300, www.wyndham.com. Classy, big resort either just refurbished or almost so with golf, tennis, gourmet restaurants, complete spa far west in the county just off I-75 at the start of its Everglades crossing. (Name could be changed.)

Shopping

Clark's Out of Town News 303 S. Andrews Ave., Fort Lauderdale, 954/467-1543. Has it all in great stacks and bins of papers, magazines, paperbacks. At the foot of the Andrews Avenue Bridge, close by everything downtown you'll want to visit, parking out back.

Dania Beach Historic Antique District Antique fanciers will want to visit the city of Dania, antique hub of Florida, with more than 100 shops and stalls, which extend for several blocks on both side of Federal Highway just south of Fort Lauderdale/Hollywood International Airport (which is actually in Dania Beach).

The Galleria E. Sunrise Blvd., Fort Lauderdale, 954/564-1015, www.galleria.com. Newly renovated mall featuring Neiman Marcus, Saks Fifth Avenue, Coach, Sharper Image, Macy's, Dillard's, and Capital Grille.

Health Foods: Health Depot 1515 N. Federal Hwy., Fort Lauderdale, 954/568-2248. **Naturally Yours Holistic Health Market** 107 N. Powerline Rd., Deerfield Beach, 954/426-6488. **Nutrition Depot** 1764 E. Oakland Park Blvd., Fort Lauderdale, 954/565-3624; 35 S. Federal Hwy., Deerfield Beach, 954/420-5587; 413 N. Federal Hwy., Pompano Beach 954/786-9323. **Whole Foods Market** 2000 N. Federal Hwy., Fort Lauderdale, 954/565-5655. **Wild Oats Natural Marketplace** 2501 E. Sunrise Blvd., Fort Lauderdale, 954/566-9333.

Las Olas Shops www.lasolasboulevard.com. Along Las Olas Boulevard, downtown, a multiblock outdoor promenade of upscale fashion, antique, and home furnishings shops that line either side with outdoor cafes, restaurants, and pubs interspersed.

Sawgrass Mills 12801 W. Sunrise Blvd., Sunrise, 954/846-2300, www.sawgrassmills.com. At the far opposite end of the county, geographically and culturally is Broward's mammoth contribution to the world of shopping, Florida's largest retail and entertainment center, featuring 400 name-brand stores, outlets, restaurants and entertainment venues. Save up to 70 percent at stores like OFF 5th Saks Fifth Avenue Outlet, Last Call from Neiman Marcus, Calvin Klein Outlet Stores, Guess Outlet, Ralph Lauren, and more. New since summer of 2004 is **Wannado City** (www.wannadocity.com), a family theme park where kids play in realistic and imaginative settings. Includes 60 kids' role-playing venues with more than 250 careers.

MIAMI-DADE COUNTY

Information Sources

Artificial Reef Dive Program 33 SW 2nd Ave., Ste. 300, Miami 33130-1540, 305/372-6881.

Bicycling Miami-Dade Bicycle/Pedestrian Program 111 NW 1st St., Ste. 910, Miami 33128, 305/375-4507. For Bike-Miami Suitability Map, bikes on Metrorail, and other cycling information.

Black Archives, History, and Research Foundation of South Florida 5400 NW 22nd Ave., Miami 33142, 305/636-2390. Preserves African American history and features Miami's Overtown Folklife Village and area landmarks in exhibits, manuscripts, and photos. Tours.

Coconut Grove Chamber of Commerce 2820 McFarlane Rd., Coconut Grove 33133, 305/444-7270, www.coconutgrove.com.

Coral Gables Chamber of Commerce 360 Greco Ave., Coral Gables 33146, 305/446-1657, www.gableschamber.org.

Dade Heritage Trust 190 SE 12th Terr., Miami 33131, 305/358-9572, www.dadeheritageturst.org. Premier preservation group.

Greater Miami Chamber of Commerce 1601 Biscayne Blvd., Miami 33132, 305/350-7700, www.greatermiami.com.

Greater Miami Convention and Visitors Bureau 701 Brickell Ave., Ste. 2700, Miami 33131, 800/240-4292, 305/539-3000, www.miamiandbeaches.com. Ask for the *Greater Miami and The Beaches Vacation Planner,* the most complete for any county, and myriad special-interest brochures; especially good are those for distinct neighborhoods. Nonetheless, note that this is a membership organization. Sights, sites, restaurants, lodgings, and so on aren't described unless they're members. For additional information, inquire at any of the other sources listed in this section as well as in the *Miami Herald* (especially its Weekend section) and the weekly *Miami New Times.* Check these same sources about nightlife, something otherwise not covered here because the scene changes too fast.

Historical Association of Southern Florida 101 W. Flagler St., Miami 33130, 305/375-1492, www.historical-museum.org. Keeper of the southern Florida legacy (especially for Miami-Dade County).

Key Biscayne Chamber of Commerce 88 W. McIntire St., Key Biscayne, 305/361-5207, www.keybiscaynechamber.org.

Miami Beach Cultural Park 12-acre arts and culture site just off Collins Avenue at 22nd St. Home to the newly expanded Bass Museum, Miami City Ballet, and a newly expanded regional library.

Miami-Dade County Cultural Affairs Council 111 NW 1st St., Ste. 625, Miami 33128-1964, 305/375-4634, hotline 305/557-5600, www.tropiculturemiami.com. Complete source for county arts information, including performing arts groups at the lesser stages: Actor's Playhouse, Area Performance Gallery, Bakehouse Art Complex, Edge Theater, El Carousel, Joseph Caleb Auditorium, Minorca Playhouse, Power Studios in the Miami Design District (may be temporarily closed), Ring Theater, and about America's pioneer Art in Public Places program.

Miami-Dade Transit Agency 305/638-6700, www.co.miami-dade.fl.us/transit. Metrorail, Metromover, buses.

Miami Design Preservation League 1001 Ocean Drive, Miami Beach 33119, 305/672-2014, www.mdpl.org. Operates Art Deco Welcome Center at this address.

South Dade Visitors Information Center 160 U.S. 1, Florida City 33034, 800/388-9669, 305/245-9180, www.tropicaleverglades.com.

Surfside Tourist Board 9301 Collins Ave., Surfside 33154, 800/327-4557, 305/864-0722, www.town.surfside.fl.us/tour.html.

Attractions and Recreation

Actors' Playhouse at the Miracle Theater 280 Miracle Mile, Coral Gables 33134, 305/444-9293, www.actorsplayhouse.org. Professional Equity theater in a restored landmark movie house. Presents the National Children's Festival each October.

The Alliance 927 Lincoln Rd., Miami Beach 33139, 305/531-8504, shows off-Hollywood, foreign, and experimental films.

Ancient Spanish Monastery 16711 W. Dixie Hwy., N. Miami Beach 33160, 305/945-1461, www.floridagoldcoast.com. Brought to America by William Randolph Hearst and relocated to Miami, this structure from 1141 originally stood in Segovia, Spain.

Art Deco Historic District See Miami Design Preservation League, above. Youngest National Register Historic District includes more than 800 historic buildings from the 1920s and 1930s in lower Miami Beach. Good free beaches, intense people-watching and nightlife.

Art Museum at Florida International University 110 SW 8th St., Miami, 305/348-2890, http://fiu.edu/~museum. At the SW 107th Avenue main campus, features faculty and traveling exhibitions with an outdoor sculpture garden.

Barnacle State Historic Site 3485 Main Hwy., Coconut Grove 33133, 305/448-9445. Classical Florida house and grounds of revered settler Ralph M. Munroe, whose Emersonian vision has kept the Grove at least somewhat special for a century and a quarter. Original furnishings.

Bass Museum of Art 2121 Park Ave., Miami Beach 33139, 305/673-7530, www.bassmuseum.org. $8.1 million Arata Isozaki–expanded facilities include a sculpture terrace, café, and museum shop while tripling exhibition space at this established center of old masters. Serves as hub of a new Miami Beach Cultural Park, which includes an expanded public library and new home for the Miami City Ballet.

Bill Baggs Cape Florida State Park 1200 S. Crandon Blvd., Key Biscayne 33149, 305/361-5811. Hugely popular mile and a quarter of palm-lined beach with an 1846 lighthouse open to the public. Fishing, water-sports rentals, food concessions. West of the town on the Key is Crandon Park with additional miles of beach (4000 Crandon Blvd., Key Biscayne 33149, 305/361-5421). At Crandon, visit the Marjory Stoneman Douglas Biscayne Nature Center, 305/642-9600. Named for the late conservationist, this complex of airy structures with nature trails provides collections and interpretive materials about shore life. Guided tours.

Biscayne National Park 9700 SW 328th St., Homestead 33033, 305/230-7275, www.nps.gov/bisc. Underwater park plus islands with trails, all offshore.

Charles Deering Estate 16701 SW 72nd Ave., Miami 33157, 305/235-1668, www.metro-dade.com/parks. Side-by-side, old Richmond Cottage and Stone House architecturally span the pioneer and boom eras of South Florida. Once the residential estate of a farm equipment magnate, today an important county park with only lightly disturbed native ecology.

Colleges and Universities Of most interest to the traveling public among several higher learning institutions are: **Florida International University** For campus locations and all other information, 305/348-2000, www.fiu.edu. Founded in 1972, today with 34,000 students (from 130 countries), 1,000 faculty, and 2 campuses, FIU ranks high for its School of Hospitality, creative writing program, tropical biology programs, and management information systems. **Miami-Dade College** Wolfson Campus, 300 NE 2nd Ave., Miami 33132, 305/237-3000, www.mdc.edu. Established in 1959, MDC awards more associate degrees than any other school in America; in the recent school year, 83,000 students were enrolled in credit courses. The Wolfson Campus downtown is site of the Miami Book Fair each November, largest event of its kind in America. **University of Miami** P.O. Box 248106, Coral Gables, 33124, 305/284-2211, www.miami.edu. Chartered in 1925, UM is one of the largest private research universities in the Southeast, with a student body of more than 15,000; it excels in the fields of marine biology and architecture and in competitive athletics.

Coral Castle 28655 S. Dixie Hwy., Homestead 33033, 305/248-6345, www.coralcastle.com. Roadside attraction that persists from the early forties, its architectural art in coral rock created by a lovesick Latvian.

Coral Gables House 907 Coral Way, Coral Gables 33145, 305/442-6593. Limestone-built family home of the founder of Coral Gables dates from 1899. Operates as a house museum with limited visitor hours.

Coral Gables Venetian Pool 2701 DeSoto Blvd., Coral Gables 33134, 305/460-5356, www.venetianpool.com. Boom-time stone quarry converted to a lyrically beautiful public pool of Mediterranean- style pavilions, palm trees, Venetian-style lampposts. Snack bar.

Crandon Park 4000 Crandon Park Blvd., Key Biscayne, 305/361-5421, www.miamidade.gov/parks. Miles of broad popular beach with typically gentle sea 25 to 30 minutes across a scenic causeway from downtown Miami.

Domino Park 1444 SW 8th St., Miami 33135, 305/285-1684. Properly known as Máximo Gómez Park, named for an important figure in the Cuban wars of liberation. Mainly popular with elderly Cuban men who play dominoes and chess there.

Douglas Entrance 800 Douglas Rd., Coral Gables. Graceful 40-foot entry arch to the city off Calle Ocho, lyrical reminder of the boom-era city today housing offices in bustling Little Havana.

Edge Theatre 35 NE 40th St., Miami, 305/531-6083. New works in an intimate Design District setting.

Everglades National Park Visitor Center at 40001 S.R. 9336, Homestead 33034, 305/242-7700, http://www.nps.gov/ever/. The only subtropical preserve in North America, a designated World Heritage Site, International Biosphere Reserve, and Wetland of International Importance—impressive titles, but apparently the preserve is not important enough to ensure even its partial restoration.

Fairchild Tropical Gardens 10901 Old Cutler Rd., Coral Gables 33156, 305/667-1651, www.ftg.org. Legacy of botanist David Fairchild, a treasury of palms, cycads, rare tropical plants that includes ponds, arboretum. Tram and walking tours including 2-acre rainforest with waterfalls.

Florida Grand Opera 1200 Coral Way, Miami, 800/741-1010, 305/854-1643, www.fgo.org. In Miami and Fort Lauderdale, 5 full productions each season from November to May.

Freedom Tower 600 N. Biscayne Blvd., Miami 33132. Former *Miami News* building modeled on the Giralda Tower in Seville, significant as government processing center for tens of thousands of Cuban refugees beginning in 1962. Once again planned for renewal.

Fruit and Spice Park 24801 SW 187th Ave., Homestead 33031, 305/247-5727, www.miamidade.gov/parks/fruit_spice. Fascinating guided (or self-guiding) introduction to the fruits and spices of tropical Florida, all grown here, selections available from the gift shop.

Gablestage 1200 Anastasia Ave., Coral Gables 33134, 305/4455-1119. Ambitious and innovative works, mainly drama.

Gusman Theater for the Performing Arts 174 E. Flagler St., Miami 33132, 305/372-0925, www.gusmancenter.org. Ornate twenties theater turned into major downtown performing arts center.

Historical Museum of Southern Florida 101 W. Flagler St., Miami, 305/375-1492, www.historical-museum.org. Dugout canoe, vintage trolley, space capsule all form part of the permanent collection that traces South Florida from prehistory to the present. Special exhibits throughout the year plus excellent book and gift store.

Holocaust Memorial 1933–1945 Meridian Ave., Miami Beach 33139, 305/538-1663. Emotionally draining, sculpturally triumphant installations suggest the horror of the Holocaust.

Jewish Museum of Florida 301 Washington Ave., Miami Beach 33139, 305/672-5044, www.jewishmuseum.com. A former Orthodox synagogue from 1936 and listed in the National Register of Historic Places commemorates the Jewish Diaspora while focusing on Jewish life in Florida in the permanent exhibition called *Mosaic.* Changing exhibits as well.

Lowe Art Museum 1301 Stanford Dr., Coral Gables 33146, on the campus of the University of Miami, 305/284-3535, www.lowemuseum.org. First of the campus museums in Miami, houses the Kress Collection of Italian Renaissance and Baroque Art, as well as collections of Native American and twentieth-century work.

Matheson Hammock Park 9610 Old Cutler Rd., Coral Gables 33156, 305/665-5475. Favorite mangrove-bordered swimming hole off one of the city's most picturesque drives. On Biscayne Bay with large picnic areas and hammock trails. Water not as clear as it once was but acceptable. Restaurant, water sports. Next to Fairchild Tropical Gardens (see above).

Miami Art Museum 101 W. Flagler St., Miami 33130, 305/375-3000, www.miamiartmuseum.org. In the downtown cultural plaza, founded as an exhibition hall, MAM is now assembling a permanent collection. Imaginative exhibitions focus on Western art from World War II to the present.

Miami Beach Botanical Garden 2000 Convention Center Dr., Miami Beach 33139, 305/673-7256, www.miamibeachbotanicalgarden.org. Limited hours but worth a visit for the range of flora found in tropical South Florida.

Miami Children's Museum 980 MacArthur Causeway, Miami 33132, 305/663-8800, www.miamichildrensmuseum.org. One of the best in the Southeast, in its new Arquitectonica-designed site beside Biscayne Bay.

Miami Circle Brickell Point, south shore at the mouth of the Miami River, www.nps.gov/bisc/miamicircle.htm. Believed to be 2,000-year-old trace of the Tequesta tribe; stone relic 38 feet in diameter, likely once a ceremonial platform, astrological calendar or merely the footing for a structure. Recently under cover awaiting decision about site use.

Miami City Ballet 2200 Liberty Ave., Miami Beach 33139, 305/929-7010, www.miamicityballet.org. Premier performing arts institution of the city. Performs throughout Florida.

Miami City Hall 3500 Pan American Dr., Coconut Grove 33133, 305/579-6093. Beautiful murals in this original Pan American seaplane base that early during the Great Depression linked Miami with Central and South America.

Miami Jai-Alai 3500 NW 37th Ave., Miami 33142, 305/633-6400. Close-to-the-airport jai-alai fronton offers pari-mutuel betting at the high-speed Basque sport (dining room).

Miami MetroZoo 12400 SW 152nd St., Miami 33177, 305/251-0400, www.miamimetrozoo.com. Cageless zoo including the free-flight Wings of Asia Aviary with more than 400 birds. Restaurant, gift shop. About 45 minutes from town.

Miami Museum of Science and Space Transit Planetarium 3290 S. Miami Ave., Miami 33129, 305/854-4247; planetarium 305/854/4242; www.miamisci.org. Part natural history museum, part explorium, reveals everything from extinction of the dinosaurs to virtual reality. Teamed with Smithsonian Institution for traveling exhibitions.

Miami Seaquarium Rickenbacker Causeway, Virginia Key 33149, 305/361-5705, www.miamiseaquarium.com. Oldest of South Florida's operating marine parks features tank fish to killer whales. Easy access off the popular causeway.

Monkey Jungle 14805 SW 216th St., Miami 33187, 305/235-1611. Monkeys from around the world in cultivated habitats. Guided presentations throughout the day. Also rare parrots and a gift shop.

Museum of Contemporary Art (MOCA) 770 NE 125th St., N. Miami 33161, 305/863-6211, www.mocanomi.org. Suburban site for this important showcase of avant garde exhibitions.

Oleta River State Park 3400 NE 163rd St., North Miami 33160, 305/919-1846. Mangrove forest surrounds scenic waterway that empties into Biscayne Bay. Beach, paddling, fishing, off-road cycling trails. Rental cabins by reservation.

Opa-locka City Hall 727 Sharazad Blvd., Opa-locka 33054, 305/688-4611. Hub of Arabian Nights–themed architecture of this one-time developer town now a far suburb working its way back as a viable community.

Parrot Jungle Island 1111 Parrot Jungle Trail, Miami 33132, on Watson Island, MacArthur Causeway, across from the Miami Children's Museum, 305/2-JUNGLE (258-6453), www.parrotjungle.com. New $46 million, 18.6-acre home with Everglades exhibit, petting zoo, picnic pavilions, food court, theater.

Rubell Family Collection 95 NW 29th St., Miami 33137, 305/573-6090, www.southbeach-usa.com/art/rubell/. Virtual museum representing late-twentieth-century art.

Sanford L. Ziff Jewish Museum of Florida 301 Washington Ave., Miami Beach 33139, 305/672-5044, www.jewishmuseum.com. In far South Beach, installed in a 1930 restored synagogue. Tells the story of almost 250 years of Jewish settlement in Florida.

Teatro Avante 235 Alcazar Ave., Coral Gables 33134, 305/445-8877, www.teatroavante.com. Site of the annual summer International Hispanic Theatre Festival and Spanish-language stage productions the rest of the year.

Tigertail Productions 842 NW 9th Ct., Miami 33136, 305/324-4337. The city's first and best source of contemporary, innovative stage works from around the world. Chiefly focused on dance and performance art.

Tours Almost no limit to the operators that will take you by bus, Tri-Rail, walking, or other ways around the metro area. A few programs stand out. David Brown's **Miami's Cultural Community Tours** (305/663-4455, www.miamiculturaltours.com) supplies close looks and meetings with the people of Little Haiti and Little Havana. Brown has been doing these and other tours for more than a dozen years. **Everglades Hostel and Tours** (20 SW 2nd Ave., Florida City 33034, 800/372-3874, 305/248-1122, www.evergladeshostel.com) leads equally informed tours into the national park. Dr. Paul George leads tours just about everywhere history abides for the **Historical Museum of Southern Florida** (see above) (305/375-1621, historictours@historical-museum.org). The **Miami Design Preservation District** (see above) operates tours of the Art Deco District. **Miccosukee Indian Village and Airboat Tours** MM 70 (U.S. 41, 18 m. west of Krome Ave., Miami 33144, 305/223-8380, www.miccosukee.com) offers airboat tours into the heart of the Everglades past islands where elders lived without electricity in a world largely dependent on nature.

Venetian Pool 2701 DeSoto Blvd., Coral Gables 33134, 305/460-5356, www.venetianpool.com. Beautiful freshwater coral rock pool created as a promotional lure to sell Coral Gables land in the 1920s. Enhanced with bridges and grottos, always popular. Food service.

Vizcaya Museum and Gardens 3251 S. Miami Ave., Miami 32139, 305/250-9133, www.vizcayamuseum.org. One of America's grandest house museums on the shores of Biscayne Bay, an ornate Renaissance-style villa. Shop, food service. Tours and site of an annual Renaissance fair.

Wolfsonian/Florida International University 1001 Washington Ave., Miami Beach 32139, 305/535-2602, www.fiu.edu.wolfsonian. Superbly curated collection of propagandistic and nationalistic art from the second Napoleonic period through World War II. A glory of the city in brilliantly redone interiors of a Mediterranean-style warehouse.

World Chess Hall of Fame and Sidney Samole Chess Museum 13755 SW 119th Ave., South Miami 33186, 786/242-4255, www.uschesshalloffame.com. $2.3 million headquarters for the Cooperstown of chess, a 37,000-square-foot museum of artifacts relocated from Washington, D.C., including a Walk of Fame and computerized stations for teaching the game and a theater.

Dining

Anokha 3195 Commodore Plaza, Coconut Grove, 786/552-1030. Adding spice to a routine restaurant row whose chief appeal is the outdoor tables for watching the passing parade, Anokha serves family-style Indian food, including *roti,* curries, basmati rice dishes, and sharply seasoned biryanis.

Azul 500 Brickell Key Dr., Miami, 305/913-8358. Miami's first AAA five-diamond restaurant soon after opening in 2003 shows no signs of slipping. This handsome contemporary room with floor-to-ceiling windows in the Mandarin Oriental Hotel hints at yacht-like pleasures overlooking Biscayne Bay and downtown. Dishes feature prawns, oysters, mussels, sea urchins, lobsters, and ceviches along with classic fowl, lamb, and beef preparations.

Baleen 4 Grove Isle, Coconut Grove (in the Grove Isle Hotel), 305/857-5007. Evenings of music and dim lights from the whimsical monkey-detailed chandeliers indoors, the twinkling lights and breezes off Biscayne Bay on the terrace. Imaginatively done seafoods.

Bice 2669 S. Bayshore Dr., Coconut Grove (in the Grand Bay Hotel), 305/860-0960. Family-run small but global chain of native Italian restaurants that entered Florida in Palm Beach later in the Grove. Inspired homemade pastas, classic Italian lamb, veal, and seafood dishes in a large room gracious with wood surrounds and art.

Café Tu Tu Tango 3015 Grand Ave., Coconut Grove, 305/529-2222. Original of this arty, high-concept group for grazers looking to sample the world—tuna sashimi, Cajun chicken egg rolls, chicken pizza with poblano peppers, picadillo empanadas. At CocoWalk in the heart of the Grove.

Casa Panza 1620 SW 8th St., Miami, 305/643-5343. Small, cellarlike Calle Ocho storefront devoted to *patria* with hanging hams, chorizos, chilies, and garlic—and cheek kisses for regulars. Traditional fare from white bean soup to skewered shrimp, garlic snapper, and osso bucco in mushroom sauce.

Casa Tua 1700 James Ave., Miami Beach, 305/673-1010. Gorgeous al fresco white-cloth dining under lamp glow or inside at tables with daily fresh flowers and olive oils to match your entrée choice, this 85-seat restaurant specializes in gourmet Italian, including fresh pastas, a Merlot-marinated tenderloin *carpaccio,* and garlic-redolent lamb chops.

Chef Allen's 19088 NE 29th Ave., Aventura, 305/935-2900. Almost 20 years after having created New World Cuisine, master chef Allen Susser still turns out his Caribbean/Latin/European fusion foods in a living room–like shopping center space: antipasto of charred rare tuna, rock shrimp with salsa verde, goat cheese–crusted lamb chops.

China Grill 404 Washington Ave., Miami Beach, 305/534-2211. Sybarites' favorite for the great show of glass, onyx, and space-saucer chandeliers, the din of music and gibber. Worldly, wok-prepared ginger-curry lobster, grilled garlic shrimp with black fettuccini, sautéed calf's liver with roasted garlic. Expensive but big servings.

Crystal Cafe 726 Arthur Godfrey Rd., Miami Beach, 305/673-8266. This is hometown Miami Beach, 41st Street, where people shop for hardware and groceries, so though "Crystal" sounds uppish, it's the antithesis of flash. In its non-SoBe black-and-white gallery styling, the Cafe concentrates on food, served in unusually large portions. It's Mittel European soul food, dishes like osso bucco and chicken paprikash, but also sea bass, seafood risotto, and pastas.

Da Leo Trattoria 819 Lincoln Rd., Miami Beach, 305/674-0350. Family from Lucca, the city of olive oil, lays its glistening touch on the Road. Art up and down the walls above fan-caressed banquettes inside, many more tables outside. House salad fills big bowls, the minestrone keeps the tomato in check, big choice of pastas, homemade focaccia. Lovely and affordable.

Delicias del Mar Peruano 2937 Biscayne Blvd., Miami, 305/571-1888. Peruvian style stands out in the fast-food darkness along this nondescript boulevard. Behind the plain-Jane front, Peruvian *auténticos,* eager to please, present outstanding seafood soups and stews, further rewarding with low prices.

Donut Gallery 83 Harbor Dr., Key Biscayne, 305/361-9985. Golfers up for early tee times, insomniacs, parks people—later, bankers—hug the counter and the hi-tops for big breakfasts. A more hurried set than frequents the beachside resorts comes midday for short-order lunches. Some of the soul of old Key Biscayne hangs in here.

Doraku 11104 Lincoln Road, Miami Beach, 305/695-8383. Two culinary inspirations—the refined Kansai (including Buddhist vegetarian dishes) and the more contemporary Tokyo (sushi, sashimi and tasty rolls)—combine in a peaceful un-Beach-like setting with Japanese art and music that celebrates Pan-Asian cuisine. Some 25 varieties of fish and seafood are served by the piece, while exquisite rolls might combine steamed lobster, asparagus, and crab stick among other select ingredients.

Eleventh Street Diner 11th St. & Washington Ave., Miami Beach, 305/534-6373. Best 24-hour restaurant (you can avoid the crowd around 5 a.m.) with the most original scene in South Beach, a 1948 Wilkes Barre, Pa., diner relocated here a decade ago. You may not see Julio Iglesias but count on models on their way home from a shoot, backpackers from the Clay Hotel, and everybody else up for a $10 pitcher of Bass Ale to go with the London broil, the pot roast, the quesadillas, or grilled pork chops.

Escopazzo 1311 Washington Ave., Miami Beach, 305/674-9450. One of the two great Italian restaurants of the District that make you forget where you are. Utterly kitsch-free, the place for a pampering good meal. Only about a dozen tables in a high-ceilinged room made more lofty by its large Roman mural, its trompe l'oeil big picture window. Ornate draperies and the elaborate cornice add to the ensconcing. Exquisite risotto, the fat grains full of flavor; pastafazool earthy, thick; linguine barely pliable exudes peak flavor in a tomato and arugula sauce. Exceptional seafoods. Not to be missed.

Giacosa 394 Giralda Ave., Coral Gables, 305/445-5858. Wonderfully informed Italian ambiance with tapestry-inspired upholstery, Venetian drawings, fresh flowers, wait staff watchful as *carabinieri* at an open bank vault. To rave for, the risotto with salmon and beluga caviar, snapper in a rock-salt crust, veal medallions with wild Italian mushrooms.

Granny Feelgood Restaurant and Market Place 25 W. Flagler St., Miami, 305/377-9600. Thirty or more years have caught up with this one-time hippie delight. Bankers now come for the healthy vittles—salads, tofu, and pasta dishes, fresh fish and chicken. Finish off with the moist carrot cake.

Islas Canarias 285 NW 27th Ave., Miami, 305/649-0440. In a plain-Jane little shopping center, beloved for down-home Cuban food served at the counter or the 20 or so tables filled with the faithful. Typical: corn meal casserole with crab and plantains, whole fried red snapper, shrimp Creole.

Le Bouchon du Grove 3430 Main Hwy., Coconut Grove, 305/448-6060. French brique-a-braque sets the tone for everything from breakfast cafe au lait and croissants to dinners of pot-au-feu, bouillabaisse, and tarte tatin.

Le Provencal 382 Miracle Mile, Coral Gables, 305/448-8984. Unforgettably colorful with art and furnishings evoking the south of France, long-established Le Provencal excels with its bouillabaisse, filet mignon with bernaise, veal scallops in a Calvados and mushroom sauce.

Los Ranchos of Coral Gables 2728 Ponce de Leon Blvd., Coral Gables, 305/446-0050. Don't think heart-healthy in this pit of Nicaraguan gluttony where the regulars overload on fresh fried pork rinds, deep-fried cheese-filled tortillas, ceviche, grilled jumbo shrimp, and mainly steaks: charbroiled sliced tenderloin, tenderloin with fresh garlic, mushrooms and parsley, filet with mushroom sauce. Flan three ways (burp!) for dessert. Also at Cocowalk in the Grove, at The Falls (see below under Shopping), and in the heart of Little Nicaragua in Sweetwater.

Mark's South Beach 1120 Collins Ave., Miami Beach, 305/604-9050. Patron saint of Miami's ascent to food fame two decades ago, chef Mark Militello (after giving up North Miami for Fort Lauderdale and lately adding Boca Raton) newly ranks as top toque on the Beach from the restored Nash Hotel on lower Collins. As on Las Olas, again the open kitchen, but here, instead of the high decibel metals of Las Olas, a radiant, cultured look of the Beach in its fifties heyday with French doors onto the hotel pools. Freshest fish (combined with seafood, wine sauces, even, brilliantly, collards and ham hocks), pricey ingredients (foie gras, saffron, shiitakes, wild rice), consummate compositions.

New Chinatown 5958 S. Dixie Hwy., S. Miami, 305/662-5649. Creatively changing menu keeps this large and unclichéd neighborhood choice popular year-round. Specialties might include a spicy shrimp extravagance with bamboo shoots and wood ear mushrooms, fillets of grouper, big variety of tofu entrées.

The News Café 800 Ocean Drive (at the Cardozo Hotel), 305/538-6397. Landmark Ocean Drive eatery with what seem hundreds of tables inside and outside one of SoBe's famed hotels. Guests come for the bagels, bowls of fruit, for the classy cards, out-of-town papers and magazines, but mainly for the 24-hour round-the-clock schmooze and people sightings. Also on Lincoln Road.

Norman's 21 Almeria Ave., Coral Gables, 305/446-6767. Warm woods, brilliant bouquets, and crystal glow set off the polished cuisine of super chef Norman Van Aken. Relish the inspired blending of ingredients rarely matched—passion fruit, rum, basil oil, calabaza seeds—subtly worked into salads, seafoods, meats. Recently introduced, a menu of raw food gourmet dishes. Highly recommended: the midweek sampling menu, which changes nightly.

North 110 11052 Biscayne Blvd., Miami, 305/893-4211. Burnished tin ceiling, warmly lit woodwork, and stained glass wall features cloister this intimate 96-seat dining room in the county's wealthy northeast where there's an edge to everything but price—grilled filet mignon served in "onion soup" topped with Swiss cheese toast accented with a drizzle of chili oil or yucca-crusted snapper with a black bean and shrimp broth with dried yellow tomatoes, for example.

Ortanique on the Mile 278 Miracle Mile, Coral Gables, 305/446-7710. Pastel-bright interiors and tropically fresh presentations draw the adventurous to this intimate, 40-table Caribbean outpost on the main stem of only recently meat-and-potatoes Coral Gables. Bahamian black grouper with a marinade that includes the juice of Jamaica's hybrid ortanique citrus stands out among piquant fish presentations.

Osteria del Teatro 1443 Washington Ave., Miami Beach 305/538-7850. While the flash burns itself out all up and down the Beach, Osteria glows steady (since 1988) across from the Italian-like colorful arcade onto Espanola Way. Low, laced-canvas ceilings, intimate and marked by a refined clink and clatter, the room accommodates only 20 tables with orchids on white covers that stand out against walls of gray, gray, and gray. Always many daily specials that might include pappardelle sautéed with imported porcini mushrooms, sautéed mixed seafood and herbs with linguine wrapped in parchment, poached snapper and fresh scallops, grilled marinated rack of lamb.

Pacific Time 915 Lincoln Rd., Miami Beach, 305/534-5979. Asia landed on South Beach when master chef Jonathan Eismann opened this 100-seater that from its opening a decade ago has seen the curious become the faithful. It's not the decor, which is plain, almost art-less in a storefront off the road. Nor is it the portions. You will loosen no belt here. It's the food from scratch that typically features 8 different fish entrées variously done with roasted sesame rice and oysters, with shallots, mirin and ginger, with napa, bean sprouts, and green onions. A few land animal choices, some exceptional vegetarian dishes, a fine beer list (Sierra Nevada, Anchor Porter, a couple of Sam Smiths) and wines of course including sake.

Palme D'Or 1200 Anastasia Ave., Coral Gables, 305/445-1926 (in the Biltmore Hotel). Among the most expensive meals this side of the bay, you'll need a golden palm to pay the check. You've virtually paid for a room upstairs in the city's most luxurious hotel (see Biltmore Hotel, below). But assuming you win the Lotto, you'll come to celebrate and won't be disappointed, neither by the ping of the crystal decor nor by the food. Chef Philippe Ruiz is a young master whose classical French training embraces the nouvelle and curiosity about Miami's New World ingredients. Foie gras and truffles here come with a dried fruit compote; lobster bisque with crab ravioli. Mainly the menu features fish and seafoods.

Pascal's on Ponce 2611 Ponce de Leon Blvd., Coral Gables, 305/444-2024. Always room for one more inspired haven of Gallic sensibility in this town of worldly beguilements. French favorites here benefit from chef Pascal Oudin's finesse, a ragout of wild mushroom with porcini, rack of lamb with herb and grain mustard crust. Full service bar including champagnes by the glass.

Perricone's Marketplace and Café 15 SE 10th St., Miami, 305/374-9449. Capture a new Miami downtown in the making here in the Brickell District where the suits unwind nightly. Trendy gourmet market fronts a softly lit, sophisticated northern Italian restaurant built into a relocated old barn where the affordable menu features lobster ravioli, seafood pastas, rosemary chicken. Linger for the gelatto, homemade cakes, mousse. Also affordable and Italian in the neighborhood: **Rosinella's** 1040 S. Miami Ave., 305/372-5756.

Provence Grill 1001 S. Miami Ave., Miami, 305/373-1940. In the yuppie corridor just off Brickell Avenue, fast complementing the office towers with after-hour lifestyles, the Grill serves traditional French cuisine in a laid-back setting with porch tables that add to the neighborhood ambiance. Affordable fare includes chicken, duck, veal, snapper, delicious but none of it heart-healthy.

Red Fish Grill 9610 Old Cutler Rd., Coral Gables, 305/668-8788. Come for the Old Gables setting, beside the beach lagoon in Matheson Hammock Park. Tables inside and beneath the palms outside the old stone pavilion (but the sand fleas can be excruciating outside at dusk). Fish and seafood the specialties from a limited menu.

Restaurant St. Michel Alcazar Ave., Coral Gables, 305/444-1666. Delightful bistro off the lobby of the city's finest small hotel (see Hotel Place St. Michel, below) ranks as one of the Gables' longest established, lately with sidewalk tables for cool weather dining. The look is arty with French posters, a rough plaster ceiling that hints at a grotto, lovely mosaic work at the entry off the lobby, while the menu is Floribbean, specialties including snapper with a tropical fruit salsa, breast of chicken with cumin and cilantro, Jamaican jerk marinated double pork chop with caramelized red onion marmalade.

Roger's Restaurant and Bar 1601 79th St. Causeway, North Bay Village, 305/866-7111. Outdoor dining gets a boost at this unpretentious, big, brick-paved waterside deck with protected banquettes and tiki bar. Informal, inexpensive American favorites include roast chicken, fried catfish, a few pasta, pork, and beef items—all also served in the dark wood and brick room that looks onto an open kitchen.

S&S Restaurant 1757 NE 2nd Ave., Miami, 305/373-4291. Here since the Depression with prices that take you half-way back. Homemade stuffed cabbage, meat loaf, chopped steak all under $10, served by waitresses who greet regulars at the chrome counter by name.

Seafood downtown on the Miami River Two choices close by each other on the north side (fish markets as well as restaurants) include **Garcia's Seafood Grille** (398 NW N. River Dr., Miami, 305/375-0765), across from the river, more homey, more Latin, most friendly, least expensive, with excellent grouper chowder, ceviche, calamari, conch, seafood Caesar; and **Joe's Seafood** (400 NW River Dr., Miami, 305/374-5637), best dockside ambiance, always a couple of boats tied up, whole snapper the house specialty. On the south side, **Bigfish 2000 Restaurant** (55 SW Miami Ave. Rd., Miami, 305/373-1770) shows a touch of elegance surreally (and successfully) juxtaposed beside Miami's scuttlebutt stream where the paella, seafood mixed grill, and platters of whole fish all tempt. Linger long over the wine while the glow of a place like no other in Miami settles in.

Shorty's Bar-B-Q 9200 S. Dixie Hwy., Miami, 350/670-7732. Here just below South Miami since before Miami had any reputation for food other than 'cue and it's still the best. Wood tables, beneath ceiling fans, where everybody sits together. Don't even think of coming at lunch hour unless you get off on the spice-smoky redolence.

Siam Lotus Room 6388 S. Dixie Hwy., S. Miami, 305/666-8134. Affordable, exceptional Thai in a plain room popular with area families. Look for squid salad and the usual Thai dishes prepared here with remarkable freshness and flavor regardless of the spicy heat.

Soyka's Restaurant, Café, and Bar 5556 NE 4th Ct., Miami, 305/759-3117. Catalyst of change in the lately run-down west edge of Morningside, this outpost of South Beach entrepreneur Mark Soyka behind curved deco facade packs a high-ceilinged warehouselike space with intentional industrial styling. Look for comfort food—pizzas, grilled shrimp, meatloaf.

Suzanne's Vegetarian Bistro 7251 Biscayne Blvd., Miami, 305/758-5859. Three miles north of downtown, in the renovating but still posh-impaired Lemon City–Little River District (north of Soyka's in Morningside), Miami gets a vegan restaurant of distinction. From soups and salads to pastas, veggie loaves and homemade desserts (heck, everything's homemade), it all rates as "cuisine."

Talula 210 23rd St., Miami Beach, 305/672-0778. In the Beach arts district, the 75-seat main room shows warm brick and wood surrounding rustically uncovered wood tables. Eclectic cuisine features lovely enhancements—yellowtail snapper with wild mushroom risotto, arugula, lime butter; black angus rib eye priced by the ounce with pancetta and aged cheddar smashed potatoes, ale-battered onion rings, and Cabernet demi glace.

Tantra 1445 Pennsylvania Ave., Miami Beach, 305/672-4765. Over-the-edge sensual trip from the fresh grass to tickle your toes and the waterfall to tickle your ears to the aphrodisiacal ingredients combined in Asian-inspired exotic cuisine meant to tickle your other parts. Divine saffron-scented bouillabaisse, Vietnamese tofu stew (for tickling vegetarian palates), filet mignon with gorgonzola ravioli. Nobody said seduction comes cheap.

Tap Tap 819 5th St., Miami Beach, 305/672-2898. Floors, ceilings, chairs, tables, bar stools, fire extinguisher box, pay phone, bathroom doors—everything splashed with Haitian art indulging icons of voudoun. What you don't sit on you can buy in the gallery upstairs, everything accompanied by live music. Not to say the food isn't remarkable. That, too, is authentically Haitian, including *cabrit* (goat), *griyo* (pork), superb whole fish plus fruit desserts. A best buy.

Timo 17624 Collins Ave., Sunny Isles, 305/936-1008. Anyplace decent would have succeeded in Sunny Isles, bereft of class from its start. Instead Timo brings exceptional bistro-style fare to the hood, serving corn soup with seared scallops and chorizo, warm mozzarella wrapped in eggplant with clay-baked Roma tomatoes, homemade pastas, various fish, lamb, and beef items. Locals fill the unfussy, white-tabled room, so that weekend seating often comes with a wait.

Tony Chan's Water Club 1717 N. Bayshore Dr., Miami, 305/374-8888. Consistently rewarding in a bayside hotel (that keeps changing names) at the foot of the Venetian Causeway, Tony Chan's flames innovative Chinese cuisine from its open kitchen. They serve delicate fish soups, one with roasted pine nuts, another of spinach and seafood. And following, dishes of shark fin, tableside wok-prepared seafoods, and tofu braised with conch, shrimp, squid, chicken, roast pork, and more.

Tropical Chinese Restaurant 7991 SW 40th St., Miami 33155, 305/262-7576. Authentic as the racked copies of the *Chinese World Journal* and busy with the city's sizeable Chinese population. Instead of high-gloss lacquer, high food concepts from the big open kitchen. Dim sum popular for weekend brunch. Otherwise, try conch sautéed with honey soy bean and Chinese broccoli; sizzling black bean chicken; hot clay pot of wine-marinated roast pork and lobster. Veggie choices galore.

Versailles 3555 SW 8th St., Miami, 305/444-0240. House of glitter and babble operates at jackhammer roar—so naturally everybody talks even louder. Brashly affirming Cuban lust for life, a daily must in Little Havana either for the beef, pork, chicken, and fish dishes routinely served with rice, beans, and plantains in the green-marbled, sculptured and mirrored interior or the *tinto* counter for a shot of high-octane Cuban coffee.

Lodging

Beach House 9449 Collins Ave., Surfside 33154, 305/535-8600. The name says it all: a tired near-half-century-old beachfront hotel redone as the first in memory that's casual in wickery comfort, unpretentious with plank floors, that shuns every architectural style from deco to glitz. Not without its Ralph Lauren high-end styling and the latest in-room gadgetry for business travelers. 170 rooms with topiary garden, state-of-the-art gym, and bar aquarium with 200 seahorses. Atlantic restaurant features seafood.

The Biltmore Hotel 1200 Anastasia Ave., Coral Gables 33134, 800/727-1926, 305/445-1926, www.biltmorehotel.com. Splendor in the boonies when it opened in 1926, the Biltmore was reborn a decade and a half ago once more as Coral Gables' hospitality landmark. Its 300-foot copper-clad tower, derived from Seville, tops 300 rooms and suites in French elegance, grand ballrooms, the outstanding Palme d'Or dining room for modern French cuisine (see above), a lobby of high-pillared elegance, shops, a fitness suite, the more-than-Olympic-sized pool, and fronts an 18-hole golf course and tennis center.

Casa Grande Suite Hotel 834 Ocean Dr., Miami Beach 33139, 800/688-7678, 305/672-7003, www.casagrandesuitehotel.com. Can't find the way in? From its baffled entry to its calming suites (only 29, earthy in dhurrie rugs, Indonesian teak, and mahogany), this 5-story inn supplies Zen quiet in the midst of SoBe tumult. Luxuriously large baths plus the rewards of 'tude-lacking professional staff, fresh flowers, morning paper. Where did this place come from? The best.

Century Hotel 140 Ocean Dr., Miami Beach 33139, 305/674-8855, www.centurysouthbeach.com. Less is more, a mere 2 stories and located well out of "the scene," where minimalist Mediterranean decor juxtaposes with classical built-in deco details—decorative tiles, friezes, arches—by past master deco architect Henry Hohauser. Rooms in the Beach Club section are directly on the beach. Patio restaurant.

Cherokee Rose Lodge 3734 Main Hwy., Coconut Grove 33133, 305/461-2878. Two exceptional units in the home of the late, venerated Judge Anderson, an Old Florida house with tiled and grandly sloped roof behind a high coral stone wall. The Casita with its own kitchen is an airy pavilion topped by a trayed ceiling and filled with world-begotten ornaments at the end of a jewel-like pool. The suite, upstairs in the house itself, is high-ceilinged, again with terra-cotta tile floor and a comfortable bath all hospital white. Full breakfast in the Florida room behind French doors.

The Clay Hotel/Miami Beach International AYH-Hostel 1438 Washington Ave., Miami Beach 33139, 800/379-CLAY (2529), 305/534-2988, www.clayhotel.com. Hippest place on the Beach, the hangout for international backpackers who capture what's really fab about the scene (which is the beach and SoBe action as backdrop for a cheap good time). Basic hotel rooms, youth hostel bunk beds in the restored heart of N.B.T. Roney's 1920s "Spanish Village." Round-the-clock food service; delightful shops alongside on Espanola Way. Rooms with and without baths, all have phone, fridge, ceiling fan. AC optional.

Conrad Miami 1395 Brickell Ave., Miami 33131, 800/CONRADS (266-7237), 305/503-6500, www.conradhotels.com. Ensconced in a 36-story silver tower of embracing design, guests register on the 25th floor for rooms that offer striking views of the bay and equally striking amenities: all lights on dimmers, shower doors on universal hinges, towels the size of full body wraps, Spanish marble baths, a soothing consistency between the tower's exterior and interiors of neutral beige and gray. Services include the excellent Atrio Ristorante with its attractive water features and the intimate bar, Noir.

The Delano 1685 Collins Ave., Miami Beach 33139, 800/555-5001, 305/672-2000, www.delanohotel.com. The Big Z, as in buzz, gauze, pizzazz, sizzle when it reopened in 1995 (built in 1947), the 14-story Delano, now with Versace gone and Madonna decamped from Miami back to the West Coast, has become, like the Fontainebleau, the doyen of its time. The first high-design concept of the Deco District, it's for imagining yourself bathed in celebrity glow. Not for lobby lizards, the crowds (when not dispersed into their 208 sanitarium-white guest rooms) instead gather beside the shallow 150-foot-long pool and at the bar and Blue Door restaurant—exceptional for fusion cuisine (French, tropical, Asian, imaginative and beautiful) served beneath high ceilings or on the terrace overlooking the lawn and palm tree–lined pool.

Four Seasons Hotel and Tower 1001 Brickell Bay Dr., Miami 33131, 800/819-5053, 305/358-3535, www.fourseasons.com. Striking luxurious 70-story tower—tallest building south of Atlanta—with 221 guest rooms and suites in the mid-stratospheric range sumptuously understated, wood-stroked, burnished in glow-bathing light and with dramatic panoramic windows. 3 pools, superior spa, restaurants, many bayfront enhancements.

Grove Isle Club and Resort 4 Grove Isle Dr., Coconut Grove 33133, 800/88GROVE (884-7683), 305/858-8300, www.groveisle.com. Unmatched waterfront inn of 49 spacious, tile-floored, lanailike rooms, each with its own view-filled terrace on Biscayne Bay. At the low-rise end of an islet of residential towers.

Hotel Astor 956 Washington Ave., Miami Beach 33139, 305/672-7217, www.hotelastor.com. Makes the case for lodging off the beach by its sheer cool and completeness in so small a space. Count on the Astor to stay fashionable for the long haul because, though ordinary when built in 1936, it's been transformed with timeless good taste. The 4 stories mass around a jewel-like pool with the dignity of a tropical embassy. French doors open on original terrazzo floors with striking sail patterns. Lighting everywhere is on dimmers, typically subdued and highlighting colorful art. Guest rooms (originally 69, now 42) are softly beige, blonde with burnished woods and baths in marble. Cushions are plump, beds firm, towels deeply absorbent, windows double glazed. Downstairs, the Astor Bar and Grille.

Hotel Impala 1228 Collins Ave., Miami Beach 33139, 800/646-7252, 305/673-2021. Exquisite detailing behind a Mediterranean revival thirties-ish facade a block off the beach. Everything matches or contrasts in this completely redone boutique hotel with marble floors, ornate wrought-iron furniture, surreal Spanish art, modified sleigh beds. In the adequate-sized bath, towels thick for pampering and Italianate fixtures, while other nice touches include a vase of orchids and galvanized buckets as wastebaskets.

Hotel Inter-Continental Miami 100 Chopin Plaza, Miami 33131, 305/577-1000, www.interconti.com. Ornate, Latin, worldly, sits at the mouth of the Miami River on Biscayne Bay, 34 stories with 644 rooms and suites. Dramatic lobby atrium features a massive 18-foot sculpture by Sir Henry Moore. Guest rooms sleek with tropical woods, brushed fabrics, metal accents. Pool, fitness center, quarter-mile jogging track. Gourmet Le Pavilion restaurant off the lobby.

Hotel Ocean 1230 Ocean Drive, Miami Beach 33139, 800/783-1725, 305/672-2579, www.hotelocean.com. Outstanding SoBe remodeling, the 1936 Mediterranean-style shell worked into 31 large spaces (27 ocean-view) mainly furnished with deco pieces. Soundproofed windows (but earplugs never a bad idea in rooms along the Drive). Delightful indoor-out Les Deux Fontaines restaurant specializes in seafood and serves outdoors on the fountain terrace or in the brasserie behind French doors.

Hotel Place St. Michel 162 Alcazar Ave., Coral Gables 33134, 305/444-1666, www.hotelplacestmichel.com. Lovely vine-covered, 3-story European-style inn with a pair of observation towers plus canopied ground-level windows. Dates from 1926 and captures the early look of the city, now largely shadowed by high-rise offices. Floors creak, there's an old gated elevator, newspapers get racked in the little lobby. Rooms take the triangulated shape of the building, furnished with European antiques, teak parquet floors. A pair of corner rooms with balconies onto the city. A charming (and romantic) anachronism much loved by a nonshowy celebrity clientele. Restaurant St. Michel off the lobby (see above).

Hyatt Regency Miami 400 SE 2nd Ave., Miami 33131-2197, 800/233-1234, 305/358-

1234, www.hyatt.com. 615 subtly furnished rooms and suites in a 24-story tower on the downtown side of the Brickell Bridge over the Miami River. Colorful Agam lobby sculpture. Fitness center, pool, riverfront promenade, shops, Asian-themed dining, and incorporates the James L. Knight International Convention Center.

J.W. Marriott 1109 Brickell Ave., Miami 33131, 800/228-9890, 305/329-3500, www.marriott.com. The colors are deep, the style corporate: reds, greens, and orange more muted than tropical, their arrangements in lobby and rooms controlled. Attention to details includes feather pillows, marble bathrooms, and ergonomic work areas, here consistently spread over 22 floors in 300 rooms and suites. Also here, three restaurants and lounges and spa.

Loews Miami Beach 1601 Collins Ave., Miami Beach 33139, 800/23-LOEWS (235-6397), 305/604-1601, www.loewshotels.com/hotels/miamibeach. Eye-stopping capture of deco style in a modern grand 18-story hotel on the avenue, with 690 rooms in the new tower, another 100 in the restored St. Moritz that connects next door, altogether with 6 restaurants, pools, fitness center, mesmerizingly symmetrical palm court.

Mandarin Oriental Miami 500 Brickell Key Dr., Miami 33131, 305/913-8270, www.mandarin-oriental.com/miami/. Dramatically modern $85 million bayside hotel aimed at the intercontinental business trade with 327 rooms and suites in serenely residential Asian modern style, from shoji doors to understated sculptural wood and upholstered guestroom pieces, all with a feng shui sensibility. Dining, pool, fitness center, island jogging path.

Marlin 1200 Collins Ave., Miami Beach 33139, 800/OUTPOST (688-7678), 305/531-8880, www.islandoutpost.com. Thoroughly satisfying in its Jamaican and African styling, a virtual showplace of Jamaica's competence in furniture, art, and wit worked into 12 suites unequaled for panache. Entertainment centers, superior bath amenities. Complimentary continental breakfast at the Leslie Cafe, a block away on the Drive. Shabeen Cookshack and Bar in the lobby serves island dishes (oxtail, curried goat, steamed fish with root vegetables) and a lovely warm mango crisp with Dragon Stout ice cream. Mmmmm, good, Mon! Also fruit juices and island drinks.

Mayfair House 3000 Florida Ave., Coconut Grove 33133, 800/433-4555, 305/441-0000, www.preferredhotels.com. Swank, incomparably detailed boutique hotel pincushion quiet in the tumult of downtown Coconut Grove. Superior blend of deco, Victorian, belle époque styles. Concierge service. Restaurant, lounge, rooftop pool, shops of the Streets of Mayfair.

Mermaid Guest House 909 Collins Ave., Miami Beach 33139, 305/538-5324. Hand-painted dressers, gaily colored walls, communal kitchen that guests use for frequent house parties on the tropical patio. Captures posthippie exuberance that makes the Mermaid an oasis of laid-back frolic in a scene elsewhere earnest about its good times. Only 10 units, a block from the beach.

Miami River Inn 118 SW S. River Dr., Miami 33130, 305/325-0045, www.miamiriverinn.com. The hub of renewal in East Little Havana on a site that occupies the last remaining garden compound of the early twentieth century—terrifically evocative of its time. The 40 rooms all different and filled with period antiques collected by owner and leading Miami preservationist Sallye Jude. A 10- to 15-minute walk over the bridge to downtown. Pool, outdoor spa, on-site parking. Continental breakfast.

The National Hotel 1677 Collins Ave., Miami Beach 33139, 305/532-2311, www.nationalhotel.com. Rated by preservationists as the peerless restoration among deco hotels, the 154-room National recaptures its 1940 moment in large spaces, high ceilings, and period detailing in ornamental iron, neon, antique mirrors, and hatbox chandeliers. Rooms are pastel (with balconies in the Palm Garden wing), public rooms lavish in oak and terrazzo. The 12-story-high domed cupola is a Deco District landmark; the 205-foot-long, palm-lined pool ends at the beach, a glamorous signature. Restaurants, bars.

Omni Colonnade Hotel 180 Aragon Ave., Coral Gables 33134, 800/533-1337, 305/441-2600, www.omnihotels.com. Worked into a landmark Coral Gables site, takes its name from the pillared walkway along Miracle Mile adapted in the upper-level outdoor pool overlooking downtown. Conservatively styled luxurious rooms. Restaurants, lounges, rooftop pool.

Ritz-Carlton Hotels Suddenly from none, 3 in the resort areas: **Ritz-Carlton Coconut Grove** 330 SW 27th Ave., Coconut Grove 33133, 786/470-1111, www.ritzcarlton.com for all. **Ritz-Carlton Miami Beach** 1 Lincoln Rd., Miami Beach 33139, 786/276-4006. **Ritz-Carlton Key Biscayne** 455 Grand Bay Dr., Key Biscayne 33149, 305/365-4183. Elegant in the more traditional Ritz style (not like the more exotically themed homage to Cesar Ritz in Orlando), everywhere with pools, in-house dining, and true to the staff conviction that "We are ladies and gentlemen serving ladies and gentlemen."

Silver Sands Beach Resort 301 Ocean Dr., Key Biscayne 33149, 305/361-5441, www.key-biscayne.com/accom/silversands. Motel-style miniresort directly on the beach. All units with kitchenettes. No elevators, no hoopla. What the Key was once all about.

Sonesta Beach Resort 350 Ocean Dr., Key Biscayne 33149, 305/365-2340, www.sonesta.com/keybiscayne. Aztecan, arty, breezy, beachfront, tropical, architecturally unflamboyant—the only traditional seaside resort without SoBe pretense and with the spaciousness of Caribbean resorts. Once here on the Key, you'll never have to cross the bridge to town again. Notably Sonesta, too, no exception to unvarying good management. Dining rooms include the gourmet Purple Dolphin with Sonesta's usual brilliant art, and Two Dragons Chinese/Japanese cuisine. Pool, golf, tennis, water sports, shops, and more.

Trump International Sonesta Beach Resort 18001 Collins Avenue, Sunny Isles Beach 33160, 305/692-5600, www.sonesta.com/sunnyisles. It's Sonesta management that carries this property more than the Donald's name. A slender tower by the beach with 390 rooms and suites, elaborate pool area, in-hotel dining, spa, and the rest of the usuals, the hotel far outshines anything else in this resort area fast becoming towered but once nothing but family motels; the area still hasn't caught up with the sophistications that guests in places like this look for. Don't bother unparking the car.

Shopping

Art galleries Chief venues include Bay Harbor Islands, Lincoln Road, Miami's 40th Street Design District, and Coral Gables with its Gables Gallery Night open house the first Friday of every month.

Aventura Mall 19501 Biscayne Blvd., Aventura, 305/935-1110. Major regional mall with Bloomingdale's, Macy's, Lord and Taylor. Big new Kid's Adventure Club indoor playground.

Bal Harbour Shops 9700 Collins Ave., Bal Harbour, 305/866-0311, www.balharbourshops.com. Neiman Marcus and Saks 5th Avenue anchor this tropical-bowered and priciest of Miami-area malls where novelty is never out of fashion—newly with Celine, Dahlia, and Zegna.

Bayside Marketplace 401 Biscayne Blvd., Miami, 305/577-3344, www.baysidemarketplace.com. Marina-facing waterfront mall pulls the usual national chains plus pushcart-based start-up vendors, the scene livened with buskers. Popular with the out-of- town cruise crowd before ship departures.

Books & Books 265 Aragon Ave., Coral Gables, 305/442-4408; 933 Lincoln Rd., Miami Beach 305/532-3222. Fountainhead of everything between covers. Best source for books, antique books, informed book talk, author signings.

Brickell District Centered around SW 8th St. and South Miami Avenue, Miami. Ready-to-boom residential, retail, and nightlife district just west of Brickell Avenue office towers. Attractive street landscaping, restaurants, core Publix and Blockbuster stores already in place; nearby, the long-standing Tobacco Road nightspot. Look for independent shops and chain boutiques.

Calle Ocho SW 8th St. from about LeJeune Rd. east to SW 12th Ave., Miami. Heart of Little Havana with its fruit stands, window openings for a *cafecito, botánicas,* shops of all kinds.

Cocowalk 3015 Grand Ave., Coconut Grove, 305/444-0777. Chain stores shoehorned in among cinemas, restaurants, and night spots.

Dadeland Mall 7535 N. Kendall Dr., Miami, 305/665-6226. First of the big Miami malls features Macy's, Saks Fifth Avenue, Lord and Taylor, Abercrombie and Fitch.

Downtown Miami Flagler St. west from Biscayne Blvd. and surrounding streets. Potpourri of enticingly Latin-staffed and Latin-marketed stores featuring electronics for export, fashion, restaurants, and the original Burdines, leading Florida department store that debuted in Miami in 1898, but is now Macy's.

The Falls 8888 SW 136th St., in the county below South Miami, 305/255-4570. Sumptuously beautiful unenclosed mall anchored by Bloomingdale's and Macy's.

Health Foods: Whole Foods Market 21105 Biscayne Blvd., Aventura, 305/933-1543. The national chain's estimably complete source on Miami's north side. Big deli. **Wild Oats Community Market** 11701 S. Dixie Hwy., 305/971-0900. The other national chain, on Miami's south side, and also on Alton Road (1020), Miami Beach.

Little Havana To Go 1442 SW 8th St., Miami, 888/642-8262, 305/857-9720. Crafts, souvenirs, clothing that evoke pre-Castro Havana and Cuban culture in Miami today. Touring information.

Loehmann's Fashion Island 18703 NE Biscayne Blvd., Aventura, 305/932-4207. Non-mall stores, Loehmann's the bargain draw.

Miami Design District Either side of NW 40th Street between N. Miami Ave. and NW 2nd Ave., 305/573-8116, www.designmiami.com. Longtime district of interiors showrooms fast-changing into a splashy public art gallery, restaurant, and retail-as-lifestyle district led by DACRA development firm's South Beach mover-shaker Craig Robins.

Miracle Mile Heart of downtown Coral Gables: Douglas Rd. to LeJeune Rd. Roughly 5 blocks of streetfront shopping along one of the city's historic main stems. On-street angle parking.

The Streets of Mayfair 2911 Grand Ave., Coconut Grove, 305/448-1700. Once ritzy mall built to lure wealthy South American shoppers trying to figure how its attractive but street-shunning architecture can lure everyday folks. Worth a look for its vine-laden over-design.

Village of Merrick Park 358 Avenue San Lorenzo, Coral Gables, 305/524-0200. Babylonian in its excess and its hanging gardens, Coral Gables' entry in the precincts of high-end consumption boasts the first Nordstrom's in Florida plus a second Neiman-Marcus in metro Miami, Elemis Spa, Jimmy Choo and Sonia Rykiel among dining spots, and a picture-perfect setting that attracts photo shoots and those outfitted as if they're ever ready.

MONROE COUNTY

Listings for the Keys are arranged differently from those in the other travel guide sections. Since there is only one road down and back, information for the most part is laid out northeast to southwest (the Middle and Lower Keys actually run east to west). In some instances, dining and lodging information is grouped together for comparisons among places close to each other or otherwise of like character. Abbreviations: MM = Mile Marker; BS = Bayside; OS = Oceanside

THE FLORIDA KEYS

Florida Keys and Key West Tourism Council P.O. Box 1147, Key West 33041, 800/FLA-KEYS (352-5397) www.fla-keys.com. Inquire about a new twice-daily luxury bus service that was to connect Miami International Airport with Key West and maybe intermediate stops beginning in 2005.

UPPER KEYS: KEY LARGO

Information Sources

Legendary Key Largo Chamber of Commerce MM 106, BS, 10600 Overseas Hwy., Key Largo 33037, 800/822-1088, 305/451-1414, www.keylargo.org.

Florida Keys Paddlers' Atlas Bill and Mary Burnham's new four-color guide due late 2005 from Globe Pequot Press.

Attractions and Recreation

Dagny Johnson Key Largo Hammock Botanical State Park C.R. 905, ¼-mile north of its intersection with the Overseas Highway. Information c/o John Pennekamp Coral Reef State Park (see below, under Diving). Harboring 84 protected plant and animal species, one of the largest contiguous tracts of tropical West Indian hardwood hammock found in the United States and named for a recently deceased champion of Keys conservation.

Diving Ocean waters jurisdictionally divide into the nearside **John Pennekamp Coral Reef State Park** MM 102.5, OS, P.O. Box 487, Key Largo 33037, 305/451-1202; concessioner: Coral Reef Park Co., P.O. Box 1560, Key Largo 33037, 305/451-1621, fax 305/451-1427; and the farther-out **Key Largo National Marine Sanctuary** MM

102, Ocean Drive, Key Largo 33037, 305/451-1644, www.florida-keys.fl.us/ntmarine.htm. (Both adjoin **Biscayne National Park** in Miami-Dade County to the north.) Together, the two comprise 178 nautical square miles of coral reefs, sea-grass beds, and mangrove swamps. Divers and snorkelers proclaim these some of the best reef waters of the world. Best conditions are at the farther-out barrier reef nearer the Gulf Stream. Dive shops nearby along the highway provide full services, the park concessioner included. Make reservations winters and all weekends. Concession includes a gift shop and snacks. Beach swimming; canoes, sailboats, and motorboats for rent; glass-bottom boat tours. In your own boat or with a rental, use the mooring buoys when in the vicinity of the reef. The wonderful and sad story about Pennekamp and the sanctuary is that they're close enough to the mainland that throngs can easily get here. Some 75,000 boats a year come on down. No matter that there's a minimum fine of $100 for even minor anchor damage to the corals, more than a few among the million and more divers and snorkelers for the entire Keys chain a year—many neophytes, many simply uncaring—do serious damage. **Key Largo Undersea Park** (MM 103.2, OS, 51 Shoreland Drive, Key Largo 33037, 305/451-2353) provides its Jules' Undersea Lodge, an undersea guest house (see below, under *Lodgings*).

Dining

Lots of wonderful little places to eat in Key Largo. You get the feeling that the soul of the place resides in these roadside shacks as well as in the cottage-type places to stay. These places are run by the people who want to stay come hell or high water (developers or hurricanes) as if they might outlast both afflictions and see their place redeemed.

Crack'd Conch MM 105, OS, 10545 Overseas Hwy., 305/451-0732. Family-run, dollar bills stuck to the walls, an astonishing variety of well more than 100 beers.

The Fish House MM 102.4, OS, 305/451-HOOK (4665). A seafood market up front, a dining room of captain's chairs beneath a ceiling of fish nets out back. Big portions, always a party mood.

The Hideout Restaurant MM 103.5, OS, Transylvania Avenue to the end, 305/451-0128. Best Friday-night buy, serving an all-you-can-eat fish fry for $8.95. Otherwise, breakfast and lunch near Largo Sound.

Mrs. Mac's Kitchen and **Harriette's Restaurant** are the 2 classic joints for a schmooze with coffee and grits. **Mrs. Mac's Kitchen** (MM 99.3, BS, 305/451-3722) offers nightly specials like meatloaf with mashed potatoes and gravy. Two can get out of here with 3-course dinners around $35. Down the road is **Harriette's Restaurant** (MM 95.7, BS, 305/852-8689), serving breakfast and lunch only. Reasonable. Counter service both here and at Mrs. Mac's.

Caribbean Club MM 104, BS, 305/451-9970. Do stop at this waterfront bar equally dedicated to the legend of Humphrey Bogart and convivial drinking. Pool table and wonderful sunset views.

Lodging in paradise ain't cheap, and rates vary widely depending on type of unit, time of year, whether midweek or weekend, and how much owners want your business.

A group of four little cottage resorts are run by people who have been here long enough so their places feel settled in. All are bayside, good for swimming. Best for its rainforest landscaping and comfortably cozy woody, tiled, and screened cottages is **Largo Lodge** MM 101.7, 101740 Overseas Highway, Key Largo 33037, 305/451-0424, 800/In-The-Sun, www.largolodge.com. It's got a bit of beach. **Sunset Cove Motel** MM 99.5, P.O. Box 99, Key Largo 33037, 305/451-0705, www.sunsetcovebeachresort.com. Rates for its facilities-equipped waterfront and a high-spirited style, though the cottages don't have the hideaway character of Largo Lodge. A concrete menagerie pops out like a Jurassic Park among the bougainvilleas and hibiscus. **Bay Harbor Lodge** MM97.5, 97702 Overseas Highway, Key Largo 33037, 305/852-5695. Units are concrete block stucco motel rooms and efficiencies on grounds well set apart from neighbors, with much tropical planting and good waterfront facilities. **Popp's Motel** MM 95.5, Route 1, 95500 Overseas Highway, Key Largo 33037, 305/852-5201, fax 305/852-5200. Here on Florida Bay for 45 years. Though called "motel," all units have kitchens. The feel is more commercial than magical, but the waterfront is wonderful.

Bayside resort properties include **Marriott's Key Largo Bay Beach Resort** (MM 103.8, 103800 Overseas Highway, Key Largo 33037, 305/453-0000, 800/932-9332, www.marriottkeylargo.com), and the **Sheraton Beach Key Largo Resort** (MM 97, 97000 Overseas Highway, Key Largo 33037, 800/539-5274, 305/852-5553).

Kona Kai Resort MM 97.8 BS, 305/852-7500, 800/365-7829, www.konakairesort.com. Small, medium-upscale resort with art gallery.

UPPER KEYS: ISLAMORADA

Information Sources

Islamorada Chamber of Commerce 82216 Overseas Hwy., Islamorada 33036, 800/322-5397, 305/664-4503, www.islamoradachamber.com.

Attractions and Recreation

Florida Keys Wild Bird Rehabilitation Center MM 93.6, BS, 93600 Overseas Hwy., Tavernier 33070, 305/ 852-4486, www.fkwbc.com. Laura Quinn's center provides the closest most visitors will get to a large variety of wildlife. Even uninjured wildlife shows up.

Windley Key Quarry Fossil Reef Geological State Park MM 84.9, BS, P.O. Box 1052, Islamorada 33036, 305/664-2540. Visitors can view the inside of a fossilized coral reef first quarried for building the Overseas Extension of the Florida East Coast Railroad at this 32-acre park.

Theater of the Sea MM 84.5, Islamorada, 305/664-2431. Has occupied a quarry used for building Flagler's railroad since 1946. Marine life includes performing dolphins, sea lions, aquariums, touch tanks. Swim-with-the-dolphins, sea lions, and sting rays programs available. A lot of stray cats around you can adopt.

The Florida Keys Memorial (Hurricane Monument) MM 81.5, OS, between the new and old highways. Commemorates the Labor Day Hurricane of 1935, which roared across Islamorada, destroying the railroad and construction camp with hundreds of workers on the Overseas Highway.

Houseboats A couple of outfits rent houseboats, a wonderful way to explore the backcountry. **Florida Keys Sailing School, Inc.** (MM 85.9, BS, P.O. Box 1525, Islamorada 33036, 305/664-8718), and **Coral Bay Marina** (MM 81.2, BS, P.O. Box 1414, Islamorada 33036, 305/664-3111). Rough average is about $150 a day, depending on size of boat and number of rental days.

Indian Key Historic State Park Oceanside off MM 78.5, P.O. Box 1052, Islamorada 33036, 305/664-2540. Site of pre–Civil War hugger-mugger by a wrecker who made the islet the seat of early Dade County. Burned to the ground in 1840 during the Second Seminole War. Accessible by park service boat, ranger-guided tours twice daily, Thursday-Monday.

The **San Pedro Underwater Archaeological Preserve State Park** marks a ship lost in 1733 with Mexican and Chinese treasures. The wreck sits in 18 feet of water about 1.25 nautical miles south of Indian Key. Contact Long Key State Recreation Area (305/664-4815).

Dining

For breakfast and lunch, try tearoom-cozy **Copper Kettle Restaurant** (MM 91.8, OS, Tavernier, 305/852-4113), everything around $5–$6.

Top local spot: **Craig's** (MM 90.5, BS, Plantation Key, 305/852-9424) for rave-worthy fresh grouper sandwich, Saturday all-you-can-eat fish fry and other specials. The counter's best for an earful of what's going on.

Three restaurants operate at **Whale Harbor** (MM 83.5, OS, Islamorada, 305/664-4959), a popular marina with a fishing fleet and water toys for rent. **Whale Harbor Inn,** famed for its immense all-you-can-eat buffet for around $25, less for the early-bird version 4–5:30 weekdays and noon-4 Sundays. Across the parking lot, the **Dockside Restaurant and Lounge** serves a waterside breakfast, while upstairs in the **Harbor Bar and Grill** you can get lunch or dinner to midnight in a dark, resinous combo bar/nightclub/restaurant where the crowd starts hopping with happy hour about the time the fishing fleet's in.

Squid Row MM 81.9, OS, 81901 Overseas Hwy., Islamorada, 305/664-9865. One step up from a fishing shack, one giant leap up for seafood lovers is this woody, nautical restaurant run by Plantation Key seafood wholesalers.

Lorelei MM 82, BS, Islamorada, 305/664-4656. Combines bar/restaurants/nightclub on the water. Sunset's big here, always with a boater crowd and live act. Dining inside dressier than the deck bar.

Marker 88 MM 88, BS, Plantation Key, 305/852-9315, 305/852-5503. Poly-polished hatch covers, Tiffany-style lamps, and candles set this restaurant apart. So does the gourmet cuisine. Dining room not directly on the bay. Seafood mainly, perfectly prepared. Big wine list for the Keys.

Pierre's MM 81.5, BS, 81590 Overseas Hwy., Islamorada, 305/664-3225. Sparkling white plantation house with blue shutters on Florida Bay. Mahogany and teak, leather, rattan, kilim rugs, and terrazzo floors set off 20 tables in the upstairs dining room, a tour de force of worldly good taste matched by an international menu drawn from the Caribbean, Europe, and the East. Additional 50 seats on the veranda for breathtaking sunsets. Next door, the laid-back **Morada Bay Beach Cafe** offers a more affordable bistro-style menu.

Lodging

Key Lantern Motel MM 82.1, BS, P.O. Box 484, Islamorada 33036, 305/664-4572, www.keylantern.com. Basic and cheap fifties style. No waterfront, no pool.
Bed & Breakfast of Islamorada MM 81.1, OS, 81175 Old Highway, Islamorada 33036-9761, 305/664-9321. Friendly, casual style in a couple of ungussied, knick-knacky rooms. Full breakfast. Stay here.

The Islander Resort MM 82.1, P.O. Box 766, Islamorada 33036, 305/664-2031, www.islanderfloridakeys.com. Lots of rooms and top value on 20 family-run, family-friendly oceanfront acres. Here since 1951 and recently remodeled, all 114 rooms now with kitchenettes plus beachside dining and bar. A best bet.

Ragged Edge Resort MM 86.5, OS, 243 Treasure Harbor Rd., Islamorada 33036, 305/852-5389, www.ragged-edge.com. Affordable and comfortable, provides a hideaway oceanfront setting for individually styled rooms, efficiencies, apartments. No beach but a pool and sea swimming.

Casa Morada MM 83, BS, 136 Madeira Rd., Islamorada 33036, 888/881-3030, 305/664-0044, www.casamorada.com. Three women, while diving the Keys, bought this bayside motel they converted into a chic resort. White walls of 16 suites show off tropical color in orchids and art. Screened balconies enclose Jacuzzis for two while affording views across gardens to a pool by the bay that a bar manager—Jamaican, no less, who ought to know—says "feeds the soul."

Cheeca Lodge MM 82, OS, P.O. Box 527, Islamorada 33036, 800/327-2888, 305/664-4651, www.cheeca.com. One of the two most upscale resorts of the Keys (for the other, see The Moorings Village, below), does everything superbly from food to room decor to facilities. Seasoned, caring, competent people in charge with unmatched dedication to conservation.

The Moorings Village MM 81.6, OS, 123 Beach Rd., Islamorada 33036, 305/664-4708, www.themooringsvillage.com. As upscale as the Cheeca Lodge (see above) but lower-key, with fewer staff, more beachy, French-run, designer perfect with brilliant island-style cottages complete for housekeeping. One of the best anywhere in Florida.

Across the highway from each other on Plantation Key are the **Rain Barrel Arts and Craft Gallery** (MM 86.7, BS, 86700 Overseas Hwy., Islamorada, 305/852-3084), where some 400 artists and craftspeople show, some from their own studios in a tree-filled browsing area; and **Treasure Village** (MM 86.7, OS, 86729 Old Highway, Islamorada, 305/852-0511), in Art McKee's old treasure museum. More upscale and less rustic; studios too.

MIDDLE KEYS: MARATHON

Information Sources

Marathon Chamber of Commerce 12222 Overseas Hwy., Marathon 33050, 800/262-7284, 305/743-5417, www.floridakeysmarathon.com.

Attractions and Recreation

Dolphin Research Center MM 59.5, BS, Grassy Key, P.O. Box 522875, Marathon Shores 33052-2875, 305/289-1121. Combines research, rescue, and swim-with-dolphin programs (which require reservations more than a month ahead).

Long Key State Park MM 67.5, OS, P.O. Box 776, Long Key 33001, 305/664-4815. Provides a so-so beach and short hiking and canoe trails. 60 camping sites.

Museum of Natural History of the Florida Keys MM 50, BS, P.O. Box 500536, Marathon 33050, 305/743-9100 www.flmnh.ufl.edu. Pride of the Middle Keys encompasses a hands-on children's museum, a historical village under restoration, the 63-acre Crane Point Hammock, and the natural history museum with gift shop, which centers activities here.

Pigeon Key MM 45, BS, Marathon 33050, 305/289-0025, www.fla-keys.com/marathon. 2.2 miles west of Marathon in Florida Bay, a 4-acre island that makes you hopeful about the Keys. Former construction camp for the original Seven Mile Bridge still with seven original structures. Operated by an environmental education group for research and education with a museum commemorating history of the bridge.

Sombrero Beach Just before MM 50, OS, lies east of town about 2 miles along Sombrero Beach Road. It's a pleasant, typically uncrowded sandy county beach with safe swimming and good play facilities for children. One of the best coral reefs of the Middle Keys lies close offshore, but not swimming close. Free.

Dining

Gallagher's Little Gourmet Restaurant MM 57.5, OS, Grassy Key, 305/289-0454. Tops for food, atmosphere, and big-portion value. Unhaughty roadside look belies gourmet fare and party mood among guests, who keep coming back.

Herbie's MM 50.5, BS, 6350 Overseas Hwy., Marathon, 305/743-6373. Screened porch makes a picniclike setting at one-time beer joint and raw bar now popular for fried-fish baskets and combo seafood platters.

Village Cafe MM 50.5, BS, Gulfside Village Shopping Center, Marathon, 305/743-9090. Family-run, serves three meals a day with southern Italian specials.

Seven Mile Grill MM 47, BS, 1240 Overseas Hwy., Marathon, 305/743-4481. From the road, shows off everybody's rear end at the open counter, chowing down on food top-ranked for All-American taste. Key lime and peanut butter pies outstanding.

Lodging

Eclectic mom-and-pop places edge the highway between Long Key and Marathon. In terms of price, lowest to highest (rather than by descending mile markers), these start with stay-put houseboat lodgings at **Sea Cove Motel** (MM 54, OS, 12685 Overseas Hwy., Marathon 33050, 305/289-0800). Small, sparse at the end of a workaday-looking motel compound. Curiously satisfying.

Bonefish Resort MM 58, Rte. 1, Box 343, Grassy Key 33050, 305/743-7107. Cottages to either side of a sandy lane between highway and sea. A kicked-back but cared-for place.

Price commends three motels between Grassy Key and Marathon. North to south, consider: **Gulf View Motel** (MM 58.5, BS, Marathon 33050, 305/289-1414), well-maintained, sharper-than-standard, 2-story units (avoid those close to the highway). Pool, no beach, though a dock with lawn furniture, free canoes, and pedal boats. **Bonefish Bay Motel** (12565 Overseas Hwy., OS, Marathon Shores 33050, 800/336-0565, 305/289-0565), an older, family-run attractively landscaped compound. Pool, dock, boat ramp. Conservationist Richie Moretti's **Hidden Harbor Motel** (MM 48.5, BS, 2396 Overseas Hwy., Marathon 33050, 800/362-3495, 305/743-5376, www.hiddenharbormotel.com) is standard motel with a video store up front and turtle hospital. Pool, boat dock, ramp.

Lime Tree Bay Resort Motel MM 68.5, BS, P.O. Box 839, Layton, Long Key 33001, 305/664-4740, 800/723-4519, fax 305/664-0750. Occupies a waterfront bulge in the road and a niche for a lot of comfort in imaginative spaces. Top local choice.

Conch Key Cottages MM 62.5, OS, Marathon 33050, 800/330-1577, 305/289-1377, www.conchkeycottages.com. Settles a peace-and-quiet castaway mood on its own little causeway-linked island. Keys-rustic with beautiful cove beach.

Hawk's Cay Resort and Marina MM 61, OS, Duck Key, Marathon 33050, 305/743-7000, 800/432-2242, www.hawkscay.com. Biggest resort and best buffet breakfast in the Keys with everything, including spa, except golf for 400 units. Luxurious.

Shopping

Food for Thought 5800 Overseas Hwy., Marathon, in the Gulfside Village, MM 51, 305/743-3297. Best general bookstore and health foods store outside of Key West.

Information Sources

Lower Keys Chamber of Commerce MM 31, OS, Overseas Hwy., Big Pine Key 33043, 800/872-3722, 305/872-2411, www.lowerkeyschamber.com.

Attractions and Recreation

National Key Deer Refuge Office at Winn-Dixie Shopping Center, 701 Key Deer Blvd., 305/872-0774. Once beleaguered by hostile property owners but now recovering in numbers thanks to an unexpected change in heart and rigorous protective policies, key deer are most often sighted out Key Deer Boulevard and across the bridge on **No Name Key.** Best time for sighting is early morning and early evening. Feeding or harassing deer is against the law.

Blue Hole Down Key Deer Boulevard. A freshwater borrow pit from railroading days with a short walking trail and observation deck. Adjacent is **Watson's Hammock,** a rare hardwood forest on this otherwise predominantly pine island.

Big Pine Kayak Adventures MM 30, BS, P.O. Box 431311, Big Pine Key 33043, 305/872-7474, www.keyskayaktours. Operates kayak trips into the backcountry with its myriad waterfowl and mangrove channels.

Looe Key Florida Keys National Marine Sanctuary, 305/292-0311, http://floridakeys.noaa.gov. Divers and snorkelers find stressed yet still-colorful coral reefs in a 5.3-square-nautical-mile offshore area from Big Pine, Ramrod, and Summerland Keys.

Bahia Honda State Park MM 37, Big Pine Key 33043, 305/872-3210. Best public beach in the Keys. Dunes, mangrove, and hardwood forests. Bayside cabins and rental boats available. Gift shop.

Perky Bat Tower Stands at the intersection of whim and history back behind the Sugar Loaf Lodge (see below). In 1929, it was meant to house bats to be used as natural mosquito control. Didn't work. No admission (and no bats).

Fantasy Dan's Airplane Rides Sugarloaf Key Airport, MM 17, BS, 305/745-2217. Offers sightseeing rides in a single-engine plane over the Lower Keys and Key West. Sunset and champagne flights by reservation only.

Dining

Big Pine Coffee Shop MM 30, BS, 305/872-2790 Serves fried fish, steaks, sandwiches on red-checked covers beneath fish mounts and ceiling fans. Sun room is a pleasant choice. Three meals daily since 1958, 365 days a year.

Mangrove Mama's MM 20, BS, 305/745-3030. Pick of the Lower Keys. In a latticed, slanty roofed art-filled Conch house from 1919 that oozes authenticity. Outstanding Keys food, including steamed brown rice. Sunday evening reggae.

Baby's Place Coffee Bar 3178 U.S. Highway 1, MM 15, 305/744-9866. The best coffee. They call themselves the southernmost coffee roasters in America, but what they offer are the best aromas in paradise. They serve fresh oversized pastries to go with your high-caffeine Cafe Perfecto, your Peruvian Chanchamayo, your Ethiopian Yergachefe—or, if you're craving the hair of the dog, an Anchor Steam. They ship beans around the world.

Lodging

Fewer choices in this stretch of the Keys because anybody who gets this far is likely to go all the way to Key West. Yet stopping short pampers a different and maybe a better state of mind.

Big Pine Key Fishing Lodge MM 33, OS, P.O. Box 430513, Big Pine Key 33043-0513, 305/872-2351. Family-run, with efficiencies and mobile homes at the head of Big Pine Key; rec room and bait and tackle shop.

Three good places are all near each other out Long Beach Road on Big Pine Key. These are three bed-and-breakfasts, each 2 stories on the ocean with views of the sea that go on forever and get you yearning that your vacation might go on the same. The three (in order of how you reach them heading off the highway) are **The Barnacle Bed and Breakfast** 1557 Long Beach Dr., Big Pine Key 33043, 305/872-3298, www.thebarnacle.net; **Casa Grande** 1619 Long Beach Dr., Big Pine Key 33043, 305/872-2878, http://floridakeys.net/casagrande/; and **Deer Run Guest House on the Atlantic** P.O. Box 431, Big Pine Key 33043, 305/872-2015, http://www.floridakeys.net/deer/. All are wonderful Keys hideaways, each distinctive, yet each with big screened upstairs sitting areas, each with a palm tree beach. The water is shallow, and if you want to swim you have to get yourself a quarter mile out or so. Each will give you a boat to paddle or old sneakers you can wear walking across the bottom.

Sugar Loaf Lodge MM 17, 17001 Overseas Hwy., Sugarloaf Key 33042, 800/553-6097, 305/745-3211, http://www.sugarloaflodge.com/. Satisfies equally for a marina resort or motel. Marine store, tennis, pool, dolphin show, waterfront restaurant and bar, plus air strip. Informal.

Little Palm Island 28500 Overseas Hwy., OS, Little Torch Key 33042, 800/3GETLOST (343-8567), 305/872-2524. On its own unbridged islet, distant at the Atlantic edge, flings castaway beachfront pampering with gourmet attention from meals to all details. Outstanding staff, management; sky-high prices.

KEY WEST

Information Sources

Key West Chamber of Commerce 402 Wall St., Key West 33040, 800/527-8539, 305/294-2587, www.keywestchamber.com.

Key West International Airport 3491 S. Roosevelt Blvd., 305/296-5439. Flights to and from Miami, Fort Lauderdale, Orlando, Naples, Tampa, Fort Myers, St. Petersburg, Atlanta, and Nassau.

Old Island Restoration Foundation Hospitality House, Mallory Square, 305/294-9501, www.oirf.org. Created in 1960 by citizens seeking to preserve historic architecture. Works to preserve historically significant buildings.

House Museums

Most of the attractions described below charge for admission or request a donation. Many are listed in the National Register of Historic Places.

Audubon House 205 Whitehead St., 305/294-2116, www.audubonhouse.com. A 3-story vernacular house built in the early nineteenth century by Key West's first harbor pilot, Capt. John Geiger. Audubon visited, which was reason enough to attach his name to the house when it was restored, today with Audubon engravings as well as antiques and, downstairs, a fine gift shop and tropical gardens.

Casa Antigua 314 Simonton St., 305/292-9955, www.pelicanpoop.com. Site of an early-nineteenth-century house where Jefferson Davis visited after the Civil War. Present coral rock house dates from 1919 as one of Key West's first important, albeit small, hotels. Hemingway and his second wife, Pauline, stayed here in 1928. Later a bordello, nightclub, haven for beats and dopers. Stunning atrium pool and garden occupy the rear today, while up front is the Pelican Poop Shoppe for gifts. Buy something and you generally get to visit out back.

Curry Mansion 511 Caroline St., 305/294-5349, www.currymansion.com. Home of millionaire Milton Curry. It's a Victorian landmark with antique furnishings and Tiffany appointments that serves today as the front of a guest house by the same name. Stay overnight and you tour free.

Ernest Hemingway Home and Museum 907 Whitehead St., 305/294-1136, www.hemingway.com. Rare stone, New Orleans–style house where Hemingway and Pauline lived together from 1931 to 1940. While resident here, Hemingway wrote the nonfiction *Death in the Afternoon* and *Green Hills of Africa,* the novel *To Have and Have Not,* and the beginning of *For Whom the Bell Tolls.* When they split up in 1940, Hemingway moved to his Finca Vigia outside Havana, while Pauline remained at the house until her death in 1951. The house has pieces of original Hemingway furnishings and a large collection of the Nobel Prize winner's works for sale.

Heritage House Museum 410 Caroline St., 305/296-3573, www.heritagehousemuseum.org. Dates from 1834 as a ship captain's house and site of the first freshwater well on the island. The house most recently belonged to Jessie Porter, who with the Mitchell Wolfsons led preservation efforts in the city. To the rear is a cottage once occupied by poet Robert Frost. Recordings of his poetry are played, while the main house features original furnishings, antiques, and seafaring artifacts collected by seven generations of Jessie Porter Newton's family.

Harry S Truman Little White House 111 Front St. 305/294-9911, www.trumanlittlewhitehouse.com. Sits in the precincts of the Truman Annex, a gated Key West period development. The house dates from the 1890s and was adapted for Truman's use during 175 vacation days of his presidency. In 1990, the house was restored to the 1946–52 Truman era. A gift shop features Truman memorabilia.

Wreckers' Museum—The Oldest House 322 Duval St., 305/294-9502. Classic Conch house dates from about 1829. The home of Capt. Francis Watlington, who is believed to have lived from 1804 to 1887. Presumably the oldest house in Key West. Interiors display a history of the wrecking life as well as an antique doll house.

Tennessee Williams House 1431 Duncan St. Not a house museum but notable in any case, this modest, Bahamian-style house is privately owned and is not open to the public. Under the terms of the purchase, the house cannot be used to exploit the name of the famed playwright. (This is the only house of the group located outside of Old Town.)

Other Attractions

Beaches Most accessible and free is **Smathers Beach** along South Roosevelt Boulevard. For information about the beach at **Fort Zachary Taylor State Historic Site,** see below. Various lesser beaches, none with sand comparable to mainland beaches, can be found at the ends of many north-south streets.

East Martello Museum and Gallery 3501 S. Roosevelt Blvd., 305/296-3913, www.kwahs.com/martello.htm. One of two towers under design and construction for the defense of Key West for more than 20 years, finally abandoned in 1873. The east tower was acquired in 1950 by the Key West Art and Historical Society, improved over the years, and today through its art exhibits traces the history of the city. Noteworthy are the permanent collections of woodcarvings by Key West native Mario Sanchez and "junk artist" Stanley Papio.

Fort Jefferson National Park Dry Tortugas, P.O. Box 6208, Key West 33041, 305/242-7700, www.nps. Sits almost 70 miles west of Key West on the largest of a cluster of coral islands called the Dry Tortugas. Major use of the fort dates from between 1849 and 1874 when the site was considered the "Gibraltar of the Gulf." The site became a national monument in 1935 and a national park in 1992. Access is only by boat or seaplane. Sizeable populations of turtles and seabirds nest on these islands. Diving, snorkeling, and swimming are popular.

Fort Zachary Taylor State Historic Site P.O. Box 6560, Key West 33041, 305/292-6713. Provides the best beach in Key West. Built between 1845 and 1866 surrounded by water, the fort is today landlocked. It contains the largest collection of Civil War armament in the United States and a museum. Guided ranger tours take place daily at noon and 2.

Key West Aquarium 1 Whitehead St., 305/296-2051, www.keywestacquarium.com. Built during the Julius Stone administration of the city as its first visitor attraction. Houses sea life as well as a touch tidal pool and a 50,000-gallon Atlantic shore exhibit.

Key West Museum of Art and History 281 Front Street, 305/295-6616, www.kwahs.com/customhouse.htm. Great architectural treasure of Old Town that, since 1999, occupies the landmark old Key West Custom House with its Mediterranean arches and a tropical gallery in the gaudy Richardsonian Romanesque style. Built in 1891, the 4-story structure also served as a post office and federal courthouse. It was abandoned in 1974 before acquisition by the Key West Art and Historical Society. The museum houses traveling exhibitions and a permanent display that recalls the sinking of the *USS Maine* in Havana Harbor. That act in 1898, which triggered start of the Spanish-American War, was investigated in the old custom house. Also noted for changing Hemingway exhibitions from an impressive archive.

Key West Lighthouse Museum 938 Whitehead St., 305/294-0012, www.kwahs.com/lighthouse.htm. Surrounds the final version of the principal Key West signal for mariners as well as the keeper's quarters as these appeared in the late nineteenth century. The first lighthouse was built in 1825 to warn ships of the reef. Destroyed by hurricane in 1846, it was replaced by the current lighthouse in 1848, to which 20 feet were added in 1894 so the light would continue its signal above the height of new buildings. The lighthouse was decommissioned in 1969, the tower restored and re-opened to the public in 1989. Visitors can enjoy a panoramic view of the city and surrounding waters from 88 spiral stairs up, and peruse a history of lighthouse keeping in the Keys in the keeper's quarters.

Library 700 Fleming St., 305/292-3595. Maintains outstanding archives of the city in a beautiful pink stucco building.

Mallory Square www.sunsetcelebration.org. Outdoor site of a sundown celebration that symbolizes the wacky, contrived, and political aspects of contemporary Key West life. Crowds begin gathering about two hours before sundown where buskers begin entertaining and vendors set up tables to hawk what keeps them free of having to work 9–5 jobs, so long as it's handmade or otherwise acceptable to the Key West Cultural Preservation Society. (Can you believe that "sunset" has become juried?!) No matter how over-reported the occasion has become, young adults especially find the sunset ritual one of the safer occasions for meeting up. Some tourism promoters would rather have cruise ships at the dock, but the ships would block the sunset. Others think the ritual is good for business because of the free publicity it generates. "I think they would love to put out little plastic tables with umbrellas and sell piña coladas," said former mayor Tony Tarracino of promoter plans to improve the scene. So far it remains largely spontaneous.

Sonny McCoy Indigenous Park White Street off Atlantic Boulevard. Features the largest public collection of tropical native plants in the Keys—more than 125 species. It's also the site of an animal rehabilitation clinic formerly located at the Turtle Kraals at Land's End Marina. McCoy was the mayor who water-skied to Havana.

Mel Fisher Maritime Heritage Museum 200 Greene St., 305/294-2633, www.melfisher.org. Connects the Keys to the region's early European history along a route for treasure ships that plundered the Americas. Galleries display the underwater finds retrieved by the noted late treasure hunter and tell the story of his epic quest. Noted for exhibition of the *Henrietta Marie,* the only excavated and identified slave ship, and other changing maritime heritage exhibitions.

Old City Hall 510 Greene St., 305/292-6718, phone for the Historic Florida Keys Foundation, located here. Brick Italianate building that dates from 1892 and was restored and re-opened to the public 99 years later. The Preservation Board office is a good source of local touring information.

Reef Relief Environmental Education Center 201 William St., 305/294-3100, www.reefrelief.org. Introduces visitors to the ecology of the Keys through videos, publications, and programs. Reef Relief is the leading volunteer advocacy group for sound environmental practices in the Keys. A visit to their offices at Key West Bight makes sense for anyone planning to dive the reef or who otherwise wants to find out more about the workings of natural Keys systems.

Ripley's Believe It or Not! Odditorium 108 Duval St., 305/293-9694. Shows kitsch-and-kaboodle of oddities that Robert Ripley made a career of collecting from around the world. Collection is especially organized for children, and the first display on entering asserts—Believe It or Not—that Duval Street runs from the Atlantic Ocean to the Gulf of Mexico.

San Carlos Institute 516 Duval St., 305/294-3887. Key West's shrine to Cuban independence. Opened in 1871 by Cuban exiles in Key West to organize for the overthrow of Spanish rule. The institute has twice relocated, and in the late eighties its original and present site had deteriorated to the point that it was in danger of demolition. Since restoration of the Spanish colonial-style building and its re-opening in 1992 as a Cuban cultural center, the institute has run afoul of the poisoned politics between Cuba and Cubans living in Florida. Hugger-mugger between contending groups has kept management in flux. Have a look anyway.

Saint Paul's Episcopal Church 401 Duval St., 305/296-5142. Dates from 1831, the edifice was twice destroyed by hurricane, once by the great fire of 1886. The present church was built in 1914–19 and features a striking collection of stained glass windows depicting the life of Jesus.

West Martello Tower Atlantic Blvd. at White St., 305/294-3210. Dates from 1861 and houses the Key West Garden Club, with periodic floral exhibitions.

Tours

For **backcountry boat tours,** use **Dancing Water Spirit Charters** with Capt. Victoria Impallomeni (Murray's Marine, 5710 U.S. 1, MM 5, Key West 33040, 305/294-9731, www.captainvictoria.com). Capt. Victoria is a Conch, operating for more than 20 years, lately with the 6-passenger, 22-foot bimini-topped open fisherman, *The Imp II.* She's terrific with kids, flexible about departing when you want, and devoted to preserving the environment as best anyone can. Rates for her tours have lately been running about $300 for a half day, $400 for full day. Book at least a month ahead winters.

Conch Tour Train 201 Front St., Key West 33040, 305/294-5161, www.conchtourtrain.com. Offers Key West's most popular tour on 64-passenger, gas-powered trams. Narrated tours last 90 minutes, cover about 14 miles, and you can get on and off just about anyplace along the way. Each of four connected trams has its own loudspeaker so you can hear the narration wherever you sit.

Cuban Heritage Trail Pick up a free map from the Historic Key West Foundation, Old City Hall, 510 Greene St., Key West 33040, 305/292-6718. Covers 36 sites mostly in and near Old Town and traces such important Cuban contributions to the city as the rise of the cigar industry, the nurturing of Jose Martí's leadership of the Cuban revolutionary movement, and the Cuban exodus during the Castro regime.

Dive trips Best bet is to contact **Reef Relief** (see above) about who's best paying attention to preserving the reef. Try to avoid operators who pack too many people on their dive boats or who issue gloves (which makes it easier for people in the water to touch the corals).

Dry Tortugas: Seaplanes of Key West 8471 S. Roosevelt Blvd., Key West 33040, 305/294-0709, www.seaplanesofkeywest.com. Trips by seaplane can be arranged half day, full day, or with overnight camping, with or without snorkeling. Flight time averages 40 minutes each way, with about 2 hours on the island for half-day trips. Reservations required. The catamarans **MV Yankee Freedom** (800/634-0939, 305/294-7009, www.yankeefreedom.com), and **Fast Cat** (800/236-7937, 305/292-6100, www.drytortugasferry.com) make the crossing in 2 hours with between 4½ and 6 hours on Garden Key for touring nineteenth-century relic Fort Jefferson and for exceptional birding.

Glass-bottom boat tours Two companies offer tours to the reef, typically a 90- to 120-minute trip offered 3 or 4 times daily, depending on season (more trips in summer). (**MV Fireball**, departs Duval Street docks, 305/296-6293; **MV Discovery**, departs Land's End Marina, 305/293-0099.)

Kayak tours These range from short 3-hour trips to overnighters, offered in nearby Gulf waters and into the backcountry by many. Oldest is **Mosquito Coast** (310 Duval St., Key West 33040, 305/294-7178, www.mosquitocoast.net), operating 6-hour tours most days, departing from their office by car before putting in.

Key West Cemetery For tour times and further information—reservations "pretty well" required—call 305-292-6718. Key West Historic Florida Keys Foundation operates twice-weekly tours of this historic, above-ground burial site that dates from 1847, now in the heart of what became an expanded Old Town. Tours take place starting at the Sexton's Office at the corner of Margaret and Angela Streets.

Key West Nature Bike Tours 305/294-1882. Depart from Moped Hospital located at the corner of Truman Avenue and Simonton Street. Clunker bikes with big baskets.

Old Town Trolley Tours 122 Simonton St., Key West 33040, 305/296-6688, www.trolleytours.com. Like the Conch Tour Train, trolleys take passengers on 90-minute narrated tours through the city, with 9 stops where you can get on and off. The trolleys are more enclosed than the tour train, but they're under the same ownership, and the experience is much the same; you only have to do one or the other.

Guide To Old Key West Island City Heritage Press, P.O. Box 56, Key West 33041, 305/294-8380. The best walking and cycling guide to historic Key West is this one by historian Sharon Wells. The guide divides the city into 8 or so tours. It's free, it's authoritative, it's widely distributed through the city, and there's nothing else like it. Also good for linking sections of Old Town is **Pelican Path,** produced by the Old Island Restoration Foundation (P.O. Box 689, Old Mallory Square, Key West 33041, 305/294-9501).

Theater For theater, three stages present productions during winter and sometimes at other times of year: **Red Barn Theatre** 319 Duval St., 305/296-9911; **Tennessee Williams Theatre** 5901 W. College Rd., Stock Island, 305/296-1520; **Waterfront Playhouse** 310 Wall Street at Mallory Square, 305/294-5015.

Dining

Following choices are listed from least expensive to most.

Sugar Apple 917 Simonton St., Key West, 305/292-0043. Sandal-sized counter in this natural foods store for restorative chow after any debauch: home-made soups (a bowl served over organic brown rice with salad $5.95), all kinds of veggie sandwiches, salads, organic tofu lasagna, juices, smoothies, and more.

Waterfront Market 201 William St., at Key West Historic Waterfront, 305/296-0778. Here they sell custom sandwiches from the deli located inside the best health/gourmet market in the Keys. Good variety of breads, veggies plus cheeses and meats sliced to order. Fresh-squeezed juices, fresh coffee. Eat at waterside tables. You could do a lot worse.

Blue Heaven 729 Thomas St., in Bahama Village, 305/296-8666. For ambiance and outstanding food, a veritable Caribbean yard under the shade trees, roosters scratching in the dirt, kids swinging from ropes. Once a bordello, dance hall, and billiard parlor. Hemingway refereed boxing matches here, and there's an old water tower out back used by Flagler's railroad workers. Upstairs, the house is now a gallery of local art, while downstairs you can eat in the brightly painted clapboard room or outside at tables beneath the trees where for Sunday brunch they feature an electric hammered dulcimer. Everybody shows up. Caribbean cooking with natural foods. Outstanding.

PT's Late Night Bar and Grill 920 Caroline St., 305/296-4245. Big sports bar with TVs and pool tables. More funky than jock in atmosphere. Homemade meatloaf, chicken breast stuffed with Monterey Jack and cheddar cheese, fresh seafood and garden burgers, fried gator tail. Gets loud when they've got two or three ballgames going.

Mangia Mangia 900 Southard St., 305/294-2469. Fresh pasta served in an old Key West house full of splashy big-canvas art, patio dining, too. Affordable with big wine list, great atmosphere, excellent food, top service, run by the island's most outspoken environmental advocate.

The Rusty Anchor Seafood Restaurant 5510 3rd Ave., Stock Island, 305/294-5369. Pulls local fishermen so you can have confidence this is fish as fresh as you get unless you catch it yourself. Warehouse-sized space, historic photos on the walls, fishing paraphernalia but no big production. Servers all savvy about the menu, no pretense.

Pepe's Cafe and Steak House 806 Caroline St., 305/294-7192. As they remind you here, the year they opened, 1909, was the year MSG was isolated from seaweed in Tokyo and they haven't used it since. This is the oldest eating house in the Keys, with high-backed booths, tables, and a bougainvillea-filled patio. Oysters, steaks, pork, chicken, a few fresh fish choices. Serves all meals starting 6:30 a.m.

Half Shell Raw Bar Land's End Village at the foot of Margaret Street, 305/294-7496. Reminds why great fish houses and great bars go together. Waterfront and sailors salt both scenes alike. Saloon mood falls from open beams like a drift net dropping over a school of tuna. They still talk about the night the zaftig chick lay down on the bar, poured tequila in her bellybutton, and insisted her guy have a drink. No posh. Instead, paper plates on picnic tables, menus on blackboards, plank floors, awning windows that open onto docks where charter and tour boats tie up. Classic blues and rock 'n' roll play. Bar staff yank the gong when the Conch Tour Train rolls by in case touring guests are ready to get back aboard. They ring it, too, for big tips—or toot "the 20 percent horn." The sounds, the pelicans over the water, the grouper, shrimp, catch of the day, the key lime pie—all fresh to sassy. Neither food nor attitude's frozen.

Café Sole 1029 Southard St., 305/294-0230. Provence-influenced seafood, meats, pastas in delightfully textured spaces. Behind the white picket gate, dine at bamboo-enclosed outdoors tables beneath the trees or in lattice-surrounded indoor tables. Intimate, unpretentious, local favorite.

Kelly's Caribbean Bar, Grill and Brewery 301 Whitehead St., 305/293-8484. Either the only or one of the few breweries in the Keys and maybe more notable because it's set up in what used to be the Pan American Airways office. Pan Am memorabilia includes airline-embossed shaving kits and flight crew logs to Sikorski S-38 seaplane props that spin now as ceiling fans in the Crash Room Bar. Also rooftop dining. Food slants toward tropical.

Antonia's 615 Duval St., 305/294-6565. Combines urban style with exceptional food. Dark. Burnished wood setting that backs away from a wine bar with banquettes and free-standing tables. Top servers, many here since opening in 1979. Pastas, grilled fish, *zuppa di pesce,* nightly specials. Popular with locals.

Mangoes Restaurant 700 Duval St., 305/292-4606. Equally well-established among townies and tourists, serves its Floribbean cuisine indoors and out in a tropical garden. Specialties include a "mushroom martini" (varieties of marinated mushrooms in a martini glass) and a snapper with mango/passion fruit sauce.

Alice's 1114 Duval St., 305/292-5733. Famed chef Alice Weingarten adds the beautiful touches to comfort food (items like Aunt Alice's Magic Meatloaf) and equally to the exotics (ostrich-Cuban style)—spanning the range; dinner only.

Bacchus 1125 Duval St., 305/296-6706, ext 39. The other Weingarten restaurant, serves 3 meals daily at three venues, all at the guest house La Te Da daily, the menu contemporary Mediterranean (whole yellowtail snapper, braised lamb shanks, daily pasta and risotto selections). Sit poolside, upstairs or street level.

Cafe Marquesa 600 Fleming St. at the Marquesa Hotel, 305/292-1244. Very stylish, very fast-forward in fashion, intimate on a small stage—this may be quintessential Key West *now*—seats maybe 50 in a beautifully lit room with flowers at the table, open kitchen. Look for pan-fried cracked conch with black bean–mango relish and vanilla bean rum sauce; a Jamaican lentil gumbo with smoked chicken and brown basmati rice, grilled black grouper with tomato-ginger broth. Desserts also out of the ordinary—for example, key lime cheesecake instead of pie.

Pisces 1007 Simonton St., 305/294-7100, www.pisceskeywest.com. Serves in intimate rooms lined with the works of Key West artists and a second-story deck under trees and stars. The house dates from 1892 as a tinware and stove store, later a cigarmaker's house. One of the best since 1983. French cuisine featuring lobster tango mango, flamed in cognac with shrimp in saffron butter, mango, and basil. One of the best wine lists.

Louie's Backyard 700 Waddell Ave., 305/294-1061. Long one of the city's top restaurants, serves indoors and out in a National Register–listed, Conch-adopted house open to beach and sea, indoors with large canvases of Keys art, outdoors with cocktail and dining decks beneath trees on the beach. Island-themed menu with superb desserts. Don't miss it.

Drinking

Three bars stand out. These include the **Schooner Wharf Bar** (202 William St., Key West Historic Waterfront, 305/292-9520), outdoors under its tiki top, where the bartenders from everyplace else in town come to hang out. Almost always live entertainment in the adjoining Singleton warehouse. **Sloppy Joe's Bar** (201 Duval St., 305/294-5717) is the quintessential Key West tourist bar, open to the street, live music starting almost as early in the morning as the boozers show up, land-office business in Hemingway tee shirts because Sloppy Joe Russell was Hemingway's drinking buddy and sometimes charter boat captain. Russell later became the fictionalized rumrunner Harry Morgan in Hemingway's *To Have and Have Not.* Part of the original manuscript among a cache of Hemingway memorabilia was found in the back of the bar in 1962. **Captain Tony's Saloon** (428 Greene St., 305/294-1838) is where Sloppy Joe's was located during most of Hemingway's years in Key West until the landlord one day suddenly raised the rent and Joe Russell overnight moved out and set up on Duval Street. The place was long owned and otherwise fronted after 1961 by the late Tony Tarracino. Capt. Tony took the place over after the bar turned gay and the navy placed it off limits. Tony was fishing in those days. He made the place hippie headquarters. Clapton came, Jerry Jeff Walker. Tony let the kids sleep all over the place. He brought them bologna sandwiches. Tony loved to chew on the stories, including his stint as mayor. Once after a winning Vegas trip, Tony told how he "brought three hookers back. Rose asked if she could leave her card at the bar for any high rollers planning to come out." Today you can see the cards strung from the rafters by the thousands. Also a couple of graves you can ask about. Back of the stage there's this fading collection of Hemingway and Capt. Tony stuff you can read during the day. Live acts sometimes.

For listings of principally or exclusively gay lodgings, contact the **Key West Business Guild** 513 Truman Ave., Key West 33040, 800/535-7797, 305/294-4603, www.gaykeywestfl.com.

Caribbean House 226 Petronia St., Key West 33040, 800/543-4518, 305/296-1600. Tiny albeit colorful rooms in a restored Conch house in the Bahama Village district of Old Town. Private bath, fridge, and cable TV come with rooms plus continental breakfast. Two minutes from **Blue Heaven** (see above under Dining). Pain about this place is that to get a room you have to show up first thing in the morning for the following night. No reservations.

Eden House 1015 Fleming St., Key West 3340, 800/533-KEYS (5397), 305/296-6868, www.edenhouse.com. 10 so-called "European rooms," which is to say, minimal rooms with baths down the hall, one for women, one for men. Place is otherwise a full-service guest house with swimming pool, Jacuzzi, attractive gardens and a beery happy hour every afternoon. Altogether 39 units in the main house (built in 1924 as a general store and residence) and the adjacent 1898 Effie Perez House. Mike Eden has more tenure at this trade than just about anybody in Key West. The place started as a hippie hangout. Mike's watched the place change and goes with the flow.

The Frances Street Bottle Inn 535 Frances St., Key West 33040, 800/294-8530, 305/294-8530, www.bottleinn.com. Rooms here are white and bright with tropical colors, minimally furnished but more as a matter of style than cost-saving. House interiors are altogether pale-toned. With only 5 rooms, it's small enough to be convivial. The bottle name comes from their bottle collection. Continental breakfast included.

Merlinn Guest House 811 Simonton St., Key West 33040, 305/296-3336, www.merlinnguesthouse.com. Classic Caribbean-Mediterranean–style Key West guest house with 18 rooms, small and minimally furnished with pool, gardens, and a convivial atmosphere with evening rum punches and full breakfast. (Lately, 2 single rooms available cheap—for Key West, that is—but without AC.) Two spacious and arty rooms up in the trees. Some with kitchens.

The Popular House, also known as **Key West Bed and Breakfast** 415 William St., Key West 33040, 800/438-6155, 305/296-7274, www.keywestbandb.com. Few people get Key West as right as innkeeper Jody Carlson, who combines rusticity and sophisticated art with big-hearted hospitality. Her Old Town house dates from Key West's heyday in 1898. It's a classic Conch house, 2 stories of spindle porches with double columns and gingerbread bracketing, peaked roof with fretwork and louvered dormer. Behind the picket fence and up the 5 steps she keeps the door open. Typically narrow Key West lot bursts with tropical plants that surround a large Jacuzzi and sauna set in a plank deck. Jody's been in Key West for 20 years now. Benefit from her savvy.

Duval House 815 Duval St., Key West 33040, 800/223-8825, 305/294-1666, www.duvalhousekeywest.com. No longer the price leader it was in the early eighties when a couple of Californians restored the 2 side-by-side 100-year-old cigarmaker tenements. Units styled in pastels with shelves of books, quality crafts, stenciling, armoires, wicker, and antiques. Larger units may include private balconies or porches, but all guests share the big gardens, pool, luxurious pool house with its library and games, its comfy rattan, and upholstered pieces where mornings bring continental breakfast. Duval Street location, yet rooms stand back from the street for good sleep.

The Artist House 534 Eaton St., Key West 33040, 800/582-7882, 305/296-3977, www.artisthousekeywest.com. Most architecturally intriguing of Key West guest houses, located in the heart of Old Town. It's a 2½-story Conch Victorian with 6-sided turret and 2-story bay-windowed tower. Gingerbread, jigsaw-cut balustrades, pedimented transoms atop etched glass windows, high ceilings, tall louvered shutters, wraparound porches, spire-topped iron fencing, pillared entry account for some of the charm. Interiors feature quirky Georgian styling with French-doored bathrooms, walls of pocket doors, antiques, a sinuous interior staircase in the Turret Suite that hugs a Victorian-papered wall on its way to its namesake turret bedroom. The small backyard with orchids and palms holds a Jacuzzi made over from a cistern. The house comes by its name because built at the turn of the century by Gene Otto, who became one of Key West's most prominent artists and gardeners. He lived here for 40 years—a guest house since 1979.

Simonton Court 320 Simonton St., Key West 33040, 305/294-6386, 800/944-2687, www.simontoncourt.com. Combines Bahamian and Key West style in its 4 distinct sections. The street gives hardly a clue of what lies behind the gate: a virtual 2-acre settlement, private, its lanes under tropical foliage, 3 full-sized pools. Here, too, even the least expensive rooms nonetheless admit you into the full scene. Lots of built-ins. The original house, part of an 1880 Cuban cigar factory, is built of Dade County pine. Cottages, once workers' quarters, are now beautiful cypress spaces with sleeping lofts done in chintz-covered rattan. Newer suites are softly lit with more stylized rattan, wallpapered, skylighted, more sculptural, some in the newest mansion building done in antiques and reproductions. Some units with kitchens or kitchenettes, many with decks. Continental breakfast, wine, champagne served.

The Curry Mansion Inn 511 Caroline St., Key West 33040, 800/253-3466 (in Florida), 305/294-5349, www.currymansion.com. Owner Edith Amsterdam sets a mood to suit her hospitable style. Mornings start with buffet breakfast around the pool; evenings with cocktails, accompanied by live piano. Setting is the home of Milton Curry, Florida's first home-grown millionaire. The mansion is a dazzling white heap of architectural ornament modeled on a Newport cottage open as a museum by day (see above under Attractions) and where you can bed down in upstairs rooms full of gewgaws at night. Less frilly but more in Key West revival style are rooms in 2 guest wings, each 2 stories, one surrounding the pool out back, the other directly across the street. Both are done in pastels, furnished in wicker and rattan, carpeted, paddle-fanned, with large baths. Free parking on the grounds, pool privileges at the Pier House, a 4-minute walk and only one minute from Duval Street. Take time to climb through the attic, set up as a whimsical museum from Curry's time, climb the ladder to the widow's walk for a view of the old city. Rates include breakfast and cocktails.

Island City House Hotel 411 William St, Key West 33040, 800/634-8230, 305/294-5702, www.islandcityhouse.com. Still another glorious compound. Great island presence established by 2 separate entrances from 2 streets through 2 nineteenth-century buildings beset by luxuriant gardens. The original house belonged to a Charleston merchant who added a third floor so the family could take in guests when the railroad arrived. The house on William Street is one of the most beautiful steamboat Victorian facades in Old Town. Equally striking is the gingerbread arch beset with bougainvillea that opens off Eaton Street through a bricked entry. The original carriage house surrounds the arch. Set within the gardens is the Cigar House, replica of a cigarmaker's house that once occupied the site, beautifully reconceived some 25 years ago by ardent preservationists Sallye and Jim Jude, who brought this property back after it had been condemned—a stunning achievement (though they have long since sold the property). Suites in this house open directly onto the deck that surrounds the pool and Jacuzzi. Suites only and all with kitchens. Antiques and reproductions with plank floors, handmade curtains, cushioned rattan. Continental breakfast.

The Paradise Inn 819 Simonton St., Key West, 800/888-9648, 305/293-8007, www.theparadiseinn.com. Occupies a walled and luxurious garden compound of 18 attached and free-standing suites on first or second floors with Cracker-style exteriors, urbane interiors, typically subdued, bone-colored, palms on curtains faintly patterned, plank floors ashen. But accents are sharp, like color splashed in art and crane fountains of brass that flow into an icy blue-bottomed pool. Expanded continental breakfast. Pool, off-street parking.

Dewey House 504 South St., Key West, 800/354-4455, 305/296-5611. The 1906-built, Queen Anne-style former private residence of educational philosopher John Dewey. It's directly on the beach. 8 large, sumptuous rooms with public spaces that open onto patios, pool, and the sea, wonderfully relaxing for continental buffet breakfast or afternoon tea on the house. Only B&B directly on the beach. Off-street parking.

The Banyan Resort 323 Whitehead St., Key West 33040, 800/225-0639, 305/296-7786. Virtually its own attraction on almost 2 acres with tropical gardens—65 different species, many flowering at the same time. Grounds include 6 white clapboard Victorian homes listed in the National Register and 2 more in conforming design. Guests enjoy 2 pools, whirlpools, and a tiki bar. Free off-street parking a blessing here only a block below Duval Street and a 3-minute walk from sunset carryings-on at Mallory Square. Highest-quality wicker and upholstered furnishings, some units with interior staircases, all but studios with kitchens. Property operates as a time-share.

The Marquesa Hotel 600 Fleming St., Key West 33040, 800/869-4631, 305/292-1919, www.marquesa.com. In 1988, the Marquesa introduced new standards of elegance to the intimate lodgings trade of Old Town. If anything, the standards raised further with the doubling of rooms set in luxuriantly landscaped hill gardens. Architecture marked by sentinel dormers and sharply pitched roofs stamps this 1884 structure as one of a kind. Marquesa is the antithesis of the laissez-faire debauchery going on a mere block away on Duval. Spaces are both coolly detached and warmly detailed, comfortably balancing mahogany elegance with wicker cheer. Details encompass pedestal lavatories and silencing buttons on the bottoms of chair legs, Caswell-

Massey toiletries and exquisite millwork, botanical prints and lustrous chintz. Guests enjoy 2 pools and indoor on-site parking. Excellent Marquesa Cafe adjoins (see above under Dining). Staff is in all respects equal to the site.

Wyndham Casa Marina Resort 1500 Reynolds St., Key West 33040, 800/626-0777, 305/296-3535, www.casamarina.co. The king of Key West resorts. When it opened in 1921, 9 years after Henry Flagler's triumphal entry with his train into Key West, its beach site was far to the southeast of anything so far built on the island. As events proved, the Casa was greatly ahead of its time. The hotel lasted a mere 10 years. Julius Stone's revival of the city on the strength of tourism got the hotel reopened. Then came takeover of the property by the military and eventual closure after the Peace Corps made the last mess of it. More recent revivals by Marriott in 1999 by Wyndham (incorporating a property called The Reach) have restored much glory. Two compatible wings fit the resort for corporate meetings and otherwise for a corporate style of leisure that courts vacationers for whom plenitude and the big gesture count for more than Key West's more familiar style of laid-back informality. Rooms approximate the mood of living rooms and bedrooms for the managerial class, conservative in color, furnished with reproduction antiques, humming with ACs, heat lamps, minibars. Full resort service and activities make the property appealing to families willing to pay the price. Guests enjoy 1,100 feet of beach dining in Flagler's, the pleasures of several bars, the great pool, shops.

Pier House Resort and Caribbean Spa 1 Duval St., Key West 33040, 800/327-8340, 305/296-4600, www.pierhouse.com. No question that this is one of the great resorts of the town. The place flaunts its sexy image. The imagery is good-looking youthful. The hotel sports topless beaching, a sybaritic spa, 5 bars and restaurants, cool jazz and salsa rhythms to vibrate the juices. Once site of the Havana Docks, the Gulf beachfront occupied by the villa- and villagelike little resort today sits at the foot of Duval Street. It took form in 1968 and for its first decade did much of the promoting of Key West that helped put the town back on the map. For years its Chart Room bar was where the city unofficially ran its business (Old City Hall is only a block away). Today the resort is a "must" stop for first-time visitors. Anything you're in town for happens here or just outside the perimeter. Guest rooms range from okay to top of the line, cool in stylized rattan, cane, chintz, and Key West wall art. Best rooms overlook the Gulf with private balconies.

The Gardens Hotel 526 Angela St., Key West 33040, 800/526-2664, 305/294-2661, www.gardenshotel.com. In addition to the Marquesa, the other most elegant lodging of Key West. It was purely inspired to rescue the most famous gardens of Old Town from neglect by carefully installing on its grounds a minihotel catering to guests for whom setting and amenity, rather than action and clichéd imagery, would be everything. These were the gardens of Key West's "lady of the orchids," Peggy Mills. Mills had the good fortune to start her project during the times when Key West was broke and property affordable. For 40 years she cultivated this quarter-block of Old Town, in 1968 opening her tropical forest to the public. The place stood vacant for 13 years before the first restorers, 14 months later, debuted their hotel set romantically in an arboretum. Brick paths lead to seating areas lush with orchids, bromeliads, giant crotons, balsa tree, orange jasmine, triangle and ponytail palms, and hundreds more species. Intermingled are a 3-tiered Georgian fountain and four 6-foot-tall earthenware jars that date from 1785 in Cuba, each weighing a ton and today treasured antiquities. New owners in 2004 installed a more tropical look, no less devoted to plantings and fine art than previous owners.

Shopping

For art, **Haitian Art Company** (600 Frances St., 305/296-8932) for a large variety of works a notch and two below the island's top work. **Lucky Street Gallery** (1120 White St., 305/294-3973) for exceptionally original work.

For books, best is **Key West Island Bookstore** (513 Fleming St., 305/294-2904), which offers one of the best local shelves in Florida. The store specializes in works of Hemingway, Tennessee Williams, and other authors connected with Key West. Store publishes an annual catalog, is site of local book signings, and is a prime supporter of the annual Key West Literary Seminar. **Valladares and Son** (1200 Duval St., 305/296-5032) sells thousands of magazines and a big selection of out-of-town papers. Hemingway helped put the first generation of Valladares news vendors in the business by arranging to get them their account with the *New York Times,* still delivered daily and Sunday (though you can pick it up daily as well at vending machines around town). Also widely circulated around town are the daily *Key West Citizen* and the weekly *Solares Hill* (unreliable for out-of-town subscriptions), as well as the *Miami Herald.*

For food outside of restaurants, **Fausto's Food Palace** (522 Fleming St., 305/296-5663; also at 1105 White St., 305/294-5221) has been purveyor of produce, meats, sundries, deli foods, gossip and lore since 1926. A block off Duval, newly with gourmet selections and a killer deli. **Waterfront Market** (see above). For a corner grocery experience complete with Cuban sandwiches and legal speed (*bucce,* the tiny cup you toss back and buzz all day from), don't miss **5 Brothers Grocery** (930 Southard St., 305/296-5205).

For Key West specialties, **Key West Aloe Fragrance and Cosmetics** (540 Front St., 305/294-5592) sells skin care products made of tropical plants and scents. **Key West Hand Print Fashions and Fabrics** (201 Simonton St., 800/866-0333, 305/294-9535) prints art as fashion and sells it, albeit dearly. **Lazy Way Shops** (205 Elizabeth St.) are the last of the old Key West hippie shops. Live-aboards sell shell art, original art post cards, arty coconuts. **Fast Buck Freddie's** (500 Duval St., 305/294-2007) is the department store as art, the Macy's Thanksgiving Parade brought inside off the street, a Key West institution.

INDEX

Page numbers in bold type indicate photographs.

Born in a taxicab on the 59th Street Bridge in Manhattan, Herb Hiller now lives in Florida, where he initiated the Florida bicycle movement and the bed-and-breakfast movement, and has helped develop trails, farmers' markets, and heritage corridors. As a former executive director of the Caribbean Travel Association, he initiated people-to-people programs and the Caribbean Tourism Research Center in Barbados. He is a founding director of the St. Johns River Alliance and a former board member of the Florida Humanities Council and American Youth Hostels. For five years he was founding editor of the Ecotourism Society newsletter. His writing has appeared in the *Atlantic, National Geographic Traveler,* and *Land and People,* and he is the author of *Guide to the Small and Historic Lodgings of Florida* and co-author of *Season of Innocence,* a narrative of the Ralph Munroe family in early Coconut Grove.